Practical Measurements for Evaluation in Physical Education

Third Edition

Barry L. Johnson
Corpus Christi State University
of the University of South Texas System

Jack K. Nelson
Louisiana State University

 Burgess Publishing Company
Minneapolis, Minnesota

Consultants to the Publisher:

Eloise M. Jaeger
University of Minnesota

Robert D. Clayton
Colorado State University

Editor: Wayne Schotanus
Production Manager: Morris Lundin
Art Director: Joan Gordon
Layout Artists: Barb Warrington
                  Mari Ansari
Sales/Marketing Manager: Travis Williams

Copyright © 1979, 1974, 1969 by Burgess Publishing Company
Printed in the United States of America
Library of Congress Card Number 78-69797
ISBN 0-8087-1052-4

0   9   8   7   6   5   4   3   2   1

Preface

In the third edition of *Practical Measurements for Evaluation in Physical Education,* the authors have adhered to the same purposes as were set forth in the original edition:

1. To develop within the prospective physical education teacher a greater understanding and appreciation of the need and the application of tests and measurements in the evaluation process.
2. To offer several practical and economical tests in the various performance areas which can be used by the average physical education teacher in a typical school situation.
3. To attempt to define and discuss the different abilities, to present brief summaries of pertinent research findings, and to identify problems involved in isolating and measuring the particular components of performance.

The statistics chapter has been completely revised in this edition. We realize that there are diverse opinions with regard to the scope and depth of coverage of statistics in a tests and measurements text. In this revision, we have tried to stay with the practical theme of the book by simplifying the computational procedures and, at the same time, providing for more versatile and functional application of the statistical techniques.

Some tests have been added, some deleted, and some modified as a result of further assessment and experimentation and in response to the many helpful suggestions we have received from reviewers. Some new illustrations have been added and new norms have been developed for a number of the tests. In keeping with the increasing utilization of the metric system we have included metric values along with the English measurements in some of the norms tables. We did not insert metric measurements in most of the test descriptions, since this would be too cumbersome and confusing. Moreover, when the official conversion to the metric system occurs, the tests themselves will likely be altered so that the dimensions will be in whole numbers. In other words, rather than merely converting the shuttle run from 30 feet to 9.25 meters, the distance probably will be changed to 9 (or 10) meters. A brief conversion table is provided in Appendix F for students who may wish to gain greater familiarity and competency in the use of metric units of measurements.

In this edition we have continued to emphasize practicality, as indicated in the title. Obviously there are other good tests in the different areas besides the ones we have presented. Tests requiring expensive equipment have been generally excluded. Therefore, the reader must not be lulled into complacency with the idea that the tests presented in this text or any other are the only ones available or that they are necessarily the best measures in each area.

There have been further changes in the organization of the chapters in this edition. It is hoped that the reorganization will provide a more logical and functional sequence for the reader. Part One provides an introduction into the field of measurement and evaluation and a historical overview. Basic statistical techniques, criteria for selecting and evaluating tests, steps in scientific test construction and test administration, and suggestions for grading are included in Part Two. In Part Three the components of physical fitness are discussed, and practical measurements of these components are presented. Also, the measurement of body composition is included in the physical fitness section. Part Four contains tests of other motor performance areas, including power, agility, balance, speed and reaction, sports skills, rhythm and dance, kinesthetic perception and motor performance test batteries. Part Five is devoted to cognitive and affective domains of measurement (social qualities and attitude assessment and knowledge testing).

To become effective in any endeavor, one must know where he or she is going and have some means of knowing how well his or her goals have been achieved. Therefore, it is hoped that the readers of this book, whether they are undergraduate or graduate students or teachers in the field, will develop an attitude of evaluation that transcends the mere utilization of tests and measurements. The theme of this book is that it is the person who is doing the evaluating, not the test or measuring device, that is the key to successful evaluation. A test that has high validity and reliability coefficients may be utterly worthless if it is not administered and interpreted correctly.

The authors wish to express their gratitude to the many individuals who have contributed so much in the preparation of this book. We will be forever indebted to our former teachers and advisers, Dr. Ted Powers, Baylor University, Dr. H. Harrison Clarke, University of Oregon, and Dr. Joy W. Kistler, Louisiana State University. We are grateful to the authors of the many tests that are presented in the text and to our colleagues and graduate students whom we have so relentlessly prevailed upon for testing and constructing norms.

We also wish to thank the students of the Department of Health, Physical Education, and Recreation at Corpus Christi State University for their assistance in providing illustrations for this book.

Barry L. Johnson
Jack K. Nelson

Contents

Part One
Introduction to Physical Education Measurement and Evaluation

Chapter One

Orientation toward Measurement and Evaluation in Physical Education

The physical educator must be skilled in evaluation processes. The *general objectives* that have been set forth by the physical education profession, such as development of organic efficiency and neuromuscular skills, social and emotional adjustments, and improved mental performances, are indeed worthy goals and certainly ambitious ones. The evaluation of progress in achieving these objectives requires knowledge and skills in different areas of human behavior. Because general objectives are stated in broad general terms, they are usually vague and difficult to evaluate. Thus, *behavioral objectives* are formulated to specify the behavior that reflects successful achievement of a general objective. And it is with behavioral objectives that specific measurement is used to determine to what extent the goals are achieved. Further discussion of objectives will be presented later.

Probably the most common misconception concerning evaluation in physical education is that it is employed only in the process of grading. Certainly grading is an important matter and one that has been discussed and debated copiously. Chapter 5 is devoted to this topic. Yet, despite its prominence it is by no means the only, nor the most important, reason for possessing an adequate knowledge of evaluation techniques.

Basic Terms

Before we explore more fully other purposes for evaluation, it seems appropriate to identify and discuss the following basic terms:

Test—A test is a form of questioning and/or measuring used to assess retention of knowledge and capability or to measure ability in some physical endeavor.

Measurement—Measurement is an aid to the evaluation process in that various tools and techniques are used in the collection of data.

Evaluation—Evaluation transcends mere measurement in that basically subjective judgments are based upon the data collected in the measurement process. Such judgments may aid us in determining the extent to which we are accomplishing our objectives.

Research—Research is used to designate those careful investigations conducted to extend knowledge, or to further explore and verify that which has already been explored.

From the above we can see that a test is merely one form of measurement, while measurement itself involves all the tools which

Figure 1-1. Dip Test—A Test of Muscular Endurance

may be employed in the collection of data. While testing may be thought of as being conducted in a formal manner, a measure may be made informally as well as formally. Thus, tests and measurements provide information about a specific act which has taken place at a specific time.

Evaluation is a more general concept indicating a consistent level of performance while giving meaning to the tests and measures conducted. In order to make an intelligent evaluation, one must know the desired objectives, know which tools are most effective for the collection of data, and make unbiased judgments concerning educational significance.

Research has to rely on scientifically constructed tests and measuring instruments in order to reach a satisfactory conclusion. Thus, tests and measuring instruments are basic tools of research, and the measurements course should be thought of as one of the prerequisites to research. It should also be pointed out that it is through research that the physical educator is able to determine effective means of measurement and evaluation. Consequently, each area complements the other.

The Need for Measurement in the Evaluation Process

There are many reasons for employing tests and measurements. Moreover, once the data have been collected, the interpretation and utilization of the information may have varied application. To be more specific, a test that is given for the purpose of improving the learning process may be put to further use by the teacher in grading and/or in interpreting the program to pupils, administrators, teachers, and other interested groups.

Some of the reasons for the utilization of tests and measurements in the evaluation process are to:

1. Motivate students when there appears to be a leveling off of interest in the instruction. Tests also help the teacher to end the unit of instruction with a high level of interest.
2. Help the teacher assess students' performances.
3. Help students evaluate their own knowledge and/or skills in various physical activities.
4. Enable the teacher to objectively measure improvement by testing before and after the unit of instruction.
5. Assist the teacher in pinpointing the limitations as well as the strong points in a program.
6. Aid the teacher in evaluating different methods of instruction.
7. Provide a means for determining the better performances within a group and to gain insight as to the potential ability of others.
8. Provide a basis for the classification of players and teams for practice and competition.
9. Diagnose needs in relation to body mechanics, fitness, and motor skills.
10. Help establish age, sex, and grade level norms for use within a school or school district as well as for comparison with national norms.
11. Determine status and changes in status brought about by physical education for public relations purposes.
12. Collect data for research.
13. Help determine the relative values of sports activities in terms of meeting desired objectives.
14. Determine the needs of individuals within the program and the extent to which educational objectives have been accomplished.
15. Enable the teacher to evaluate his own teaching effectiveness.

Principles of Tests and Measurements in Evaluation

Success in a program of evaluation is of a greater certainty when sound principles are understood and followed. When the following principles are adhered to, greater depth and meaning are given to the total physical education program.

Figure 1-2. Grip Dynamometer— A Measure of Grip Strength

As a Means to an End

Measurement and evaluation should be considered as means to an end and not as ends in themselves. Testing just for the sake of testing is not only a waste of time, but an actual obstruction in the total educational process. When measurements are conducted, there should be a guiding purpose for which the resulting data may be used. Therefore, measurement and evaluation are the means by which we accomplish the task of developing well-adjusted and physically educated students. Judicious use of evaluation procedures can give the direction to teaching that cannot be obtained in any other way. Evaluation can help inform teachers of beneficial changes that occur for each student and ultimately for society.

Related Objectives

Measurement should be conducted for the purpose of evaluating the outcomes of physical education in the light of educational objectives. Examples of general objectives in physical education were listed on page 2. Because general objectives are stated in broad general terms, they are usually vague and invite argument over their achievement. Thus, the trend today has been to supplement general objectives with specific objectives stated in behavioral terms. This, in effect, makes general objectives more meaningful. For example, the general objective that deals with the development of neuromuscular skill might be supplemented by the following behavioral objectives:

1. The student will be able to score at least 16 points on the side step test of agility.
2. The student will be able to balance statically for at least 20 seconds on one of three trials of the Bass Stick Test.
3. The student will be able to jump vertically 10 inches above standing-reaching height on the vertical jump test.

If we are serious about our profession, we must be aware of our general objectives and then develop specific behavioral objectives to help determine the status and needs of our students as well as the effectiveness of our program.

Determining Needs

Measurement must aid in determining the needs of the individual and the group. Measurements provide the teacher with opportunities to evaluate needs and then gear the physical education program toward the aim of satisfying the needs of each individual or group. Moreover, there are times when tests should be used to classify and place students into groups that may be taught more effectively than might otherwise be possible.

Determining Value of Equipment, Materials, and Methods

Measurement should provide a special service to the evaluation process in the physical education program that seeks aid in improving teaching methods and in determining the worth of physical education equipment and materials. Through repeated measurements, it is possible to identify and eliminate inferior equipment and materials as well as abandon certain methods which tend to make the physical education program inferior.

Measurement Is Broader than Tests Alone

The program which employs only tests is a limited program in physical education. The test

Figure 1-3. Bass Stick Test— A Measure of Static Balance

is only one form of measurement in our field; therefore, physical educators should consider many types of measurement for use in the evaluation process. Moreover, evaluation is broader than measurement in that it is a process that utilizes data collected from tests and measurements to make a comparison with concepts of value.

Objective and Subjective Measurement

There is considerable advantage to be gained in having a number of objective measures in the evaluation program, particularly in the process of awarding grades. Students, parents, and administrators understand objective measures more readily, and, consequently, they are more easily defended. However, the physical education teacher can never divorce himself from subjective evaluation, nor should he even try. It is a simple fact that certain performances require qualitative, rather than quantitative, evaluation. However, the physical education teacher should be alert to the fact that when subjective measurement is called for, every effort should be made to make his subjective evaluation as objective as possible. It is commonly accepted that no amount of objective measurement will replace sound judgment, nor is there anything wrong with subjective judgment when the tester is qualified to evaluate the quality being measured. In a sports skill such as tennis or basketball, for example, there are no objective tests which can measure all the factors involved in actual competition. Some qualities are more accurately measured than others, and, therefore, the objectivity coefficient will vary accordingly. If a test item is capable of being measured easily, such as in units of time or distance, it should have high objectivity. On the other hand, if it is hard to measure, as in the case of a stunt on a trampoline or an attitude assessment, then a lower objectivity coefficient is acceptable.

Instruction and Practice Normally Precede Testing

Unless the performance test is designed to measure educability or initial status, it should normally follow a period of instruction and practice to ensure safety and familiarity with the test items. In those cases where instruction and practice interfere with the purpose of the test, it must be made certain that the directions for each test item are quite clear and that performance hazards are eliminated. Moreover, the practice of measuring a student at the beginning of a semester with any test used for developmental purposes without identifying specific weaknesses, prescribing definite activities to overcome the deficiencies noted, and then following the prescription before retesting is a waste of time.

Standards for Evaluation and Types of Evaluation

Evaluation is the process of giving meaning to measurement by judging it against some standard. Two commonly used standards today are criterion referenced and norm referenced.

Criterion-Referenced Standard. This standard is concerned with the degree to which a student has a level of competence; it requires that the task be defined in very explicit terms. For example, a criterion-referenced standard for 6th-grade girls might be the ability to perform 35 bent-knee sit-ups in two minutes. The students who meet this standard are judged to have achieved an acceptable level for this test item.

Thus, a criterion-referenced standard is useful when it is desirable that all students achieve a given level of competence. It therefore should reflect a realistic level for all normal students.

Norm-Referenced Standard. This standard is based on statistical procedures and is used to judge an individual's performance in relation to others of the same age, sex, and particular ability level. For example, a norm-referenced standard might be that a student who performs 55 sit-ups in two minutes is at the 95th percentile. In other words, 55 sit-ups is a greater number than that performed by 95 percent of students of the same age and sex.

In using a criterion-referenced standard, the teacher would know only that a student had met an acceptable level of performance. But in using a norm-referenced standard, the teacher could employ the information to motivate the student to strive for the highest percentile before the next testing.

Concerning the types of evaluation, there are two which have been used through the years, and which have been identified specifically in recent years as *formative* and *summative*.

Formative Evaluation. A skillful teacher uses this type of evaluation throughout the instructional stages of the unit of learning. It promotes high levels of learning among all the students and pinpoints areas where further development and learning are needed. It is usually based on specific objectives (such as to hold a headstand five seconds) and utilizes criterion-referenced standards.

Summative Evaluation. Summative evaluation is used by the teacher at the end of the unit of instruction and may result in far-reaching decisions. It can be used to determine whether broad objectives have been achieved and to determine the degree of achievement. Thus, norm-referenced standards are usually used in summative evaluation.

The most effective evaluation program includes both formative and summative procedures. This insures that some measurement is utilized throughout the unit of instruction to facilitate the learning process.

Conducted in a Professional Manner

Measurements programs should be conducted in a professional and unbiased manner. Testing conditions must be exactly alike for all students within the group to ensure fairness and validity, since it is quite evident that a change in conditions produces different results. Thus, if we attempt to motivate one student during a test, we should attempt to motivate them all in order to get unbiased results. This also implies that test directions be explicit and that they be rigidly followed to ensure accurate scores. Where possible, well-trained and experienced testers should direct comprehensive measurements programs, and it is, of course, essential for research. Teachers should strive to eliminate opinion and to be as objective as possible in measurement and to maintain a professional attitude in evaluation.

Consideration of the Whole Individual and His Environment

Evaluation of measurements data should be interpreted in terms of the whole individual in relation to his environment. A student who has done exceptionally well for several months but suddenly begins to do poorly due to circumstances beyond his control should be evaluated on a different basis than students whose performance has been consistent throughout the semester. Similarly, a student who does poorly on a skill test, who is obviously a better performer than the test indicates, should not be condemned for one day's performance. The better the teacher is able to get to know his students, the more effectively he will be able to evaluate.

Functioning Soundly within School Grading Policies

The physical education evaluation program must make every attempt to function soundly within the objectives and grading policies of the school and on an equal basis with other subjects. In defending the use of physical education grades (in the four basic activity classes) toward the cumulative scholastic average at his university, a dean of education (1) stated that there is considerable agreement on the importance of health and physical fitness to success in life; and, therefore, failure to use such grades in computing academic averages would cross the institution's stated purpose of helping students in *the full development of their talents and personalities.*

Reference

1. Robert E. May, "A Dean of Education Speaks . . .," *Journal of Health, Physical Education and Recreation,* September, 1965.

Chapter Two

A Brief Historical Overview in the Areas of Physical Education Tests and Measurements

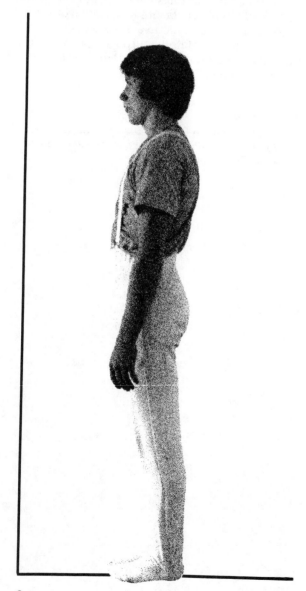

Tests in the Literature

A review of the literature that deals with tests and measurement in physical education reveals that valuable contributions have been made by numerous individuals as well as by various organizations. Many different types of tests have been developed, and a vast number of measuring instruments have been employed ranging from the simple yardstick to the complex electrical equipment used in physiological testing. The brief history presented below includes some of the important contributions in specific testing areas.

Age, Height, Weight, and Body Types

Most of our earliest research studies were concerned with measurement in this area. For example, in 1860 Cromwell completed a study on the growth of school children for ages eight to eighteen and discovered that boys were shorter and lighter than girls during the approximate ages of eleven to fourteen. He noted that after fourteen the boys became taller and heavier and continued their growth longer than girls (2). In 1861 Edward Hitchcock of Amherst began collecting data from measurements in this area, and he is generally recognized as the leading figure in anthropometric testing between the years of 1860 to 1880 (6). In 1878 D. A. Sargent began a measurements program at Harvard University and compiled considerable data on students. These data were published some fifteen years later in the form of percentile tables which indicated standards based on anthropometric and strength measures for both men and women at different years of college life (45). In 1902 D. W. Hastings undertook a study of the growth of the human body from the fifth to the twenty-first birthday and later published a manual based upon his findings (45). Other contributions made in this area include: (a) McCloy's Classification Index (31) based upon age, height, and weight; (b) Wetzel's Grid Technique (50) which used age, height, and weight measures to plot and evaluate growth and development on a grid with seven physique channels; (c) Pryor's Width-Weight Tables (39) which used the width of the pelvic crest and the width of the chest and standing height in determining normal weight; and (d) Meredith's Height-Weight Chart (36) which identifies normal and abnormal growth patterns. Concerning the establishment of body types, the following contributors should be mentioned: Kretschmer (28), one of the earliest workers in this field, classified individuals into asthenic (thin type), athletic (muscular type), and pyknic (fat type) categories and attempted to relate body type to personality; Sheldon (46), influenced by Kretschmer, refined his system of classification and began a life's work of studying the ramifications of somatotypes. His three basic components were termed ectomorphy (characterized by leanness), mesomorphy (characterized by muscular hardness), and endomorphy (characterized by heavy softness); Sills (48) introduced a fourth somatotype called omomorphy, which is characterized by a V-type build with large shoulders and chest and small hips and legs; Cureton (17) devised a simple physique rating scale that could be used by the non-expert in establishing the general physique type based on a subjective rating of external fat, muscular, and skeletal development.

Power Measurement

Although power performances have been measured in athletic events through the centuries, it was not given a great deal of attention by physical educators until after Sargent's publication in 1921 of The Physical Test of a Man (41). Then McCloy (33), working with Sargent's vertical jump test, found satisfactory correlations with the total point score of the following track and field events: 100 yard dash, running high jump, standing broad jump, and 8 pound shot put. Other noteworthy contributors to knowledge in this area were Capen (9) and Chui (11), who conducted studies revealing the importance of strength gains in increasing velocity; and Bovard and Cozens (7), who designed the leap meter for measuring vertical jump power. Recently, Glencross (21) has experimented in this area in an attempt to develop and validate tests of power. The names and contributions of other researchers in power measurement may be found in Chapter 12.

Agility Measurement

Agility measurement as a specific area does not have a long or extensive background. However, contributions made in this area include the following: (a) Royal H. Burpee's test of

Figure 2-1. Dr. David Brace (Deceased) University of Texas at Austin. Photo courtesy of Dr. Mary Lou LeCompte, University of Texas at Austin

agility (known as the Burpee Test or the squat thrust test); (b) McCloy's scholarly endeavors in the area of motor ability, which included agility measurement (34); and (c) the analysis of agility tests by Young (51), Gates and Sheffield (20), and Sierakowski (47).

General Motor Ability Measurement

Sargent pioneered testing in the area of general motor ability in the 1880s for the purpose of assessing athletic ability in men. In 1901 Sargent developed a test consisting of six simple exercises which were to be executed in a 30 minute period without rest. Several years later Meylan of Columbia University developed a comprehensive physical ability test which included running, jumping, vaulting, and climbing (6). In 1924 J. H. McCurdy served as chairman of the National Committee on Motor Ability Tests which established a number of such tests. In 1927 David K. Brace developed his famous Brace Motor Ability Test for the purposes of classification and measuring achievement. McCloy suggested that Brace's test was basically a motor educability test, and after much research McCloy in 1931 revised the

Brace test in an attempt to increase its validity as a measure of motor educability. This revision is now known as the Iowa Brace Test. In 1932 the Johnson Motor Educability Test, named after the originator of the test battery, Granville Johnson, was designed for the purpose of sectioning classes into homogeneous groups. Since the publication of his test, research has revealed that it has predictive value as a general motor educability test, particularly as far as predicting success in learning tumbling skills (27). Other contributions to this area of measurement include: (a) Kenneth Hill's motor educability test for junior high school boys; (b) Aileen Carpenter's study of motor ability and motor capacity; and (c) Arthur Adam's Sports Type Motor Educability Test. McCloy combined size, maturity, power, motor educability, and large muscle speed into a general motor capacity test which sought to assess innate potential in the area of motor ability. This was undoubtedly the most comprehensive effort to predict potential for physical achievement in a similar fashion to the way intelligence tests are used. A number of other motor ability tests have been devised, but

space does not permit adequate discussion here. This area of measurement is covered in Chapter 17.

Balance Measurement

Balance measurement is another area that does not have a long or extensive background. Ruth Bass is probably the most widely known contributor in this area with her practical tests of static and dynamic balance which were published in 1939. Other researchers who have made contributions in this area are Anna Espenschade, Thomas Cureton, Thomas P. Whelan, and Robert F. Lessl. The names and contributions of other researchers in balance measurement may be found in Chapter 13.

Kinesthetic Perception

Numerous studies have been conducted which have attempted to measure and evaluate different forms of kinesthetic perception. The study of kinesthesis has posed a special enigma to physical educators due to its acknowledged importance in physical performance and its elusiveness in resisting measurement and even definition. Special mention should be made of M. Gladys Scott for her work in this area. Other researchers who have made significant contributions are Bass, Henry, McCloy, Russell, Slater-Hammel, Wiebe, Witte, and Young. Other contributions may be noted in Chapter 19.

Flexibility Measurement

Formal tests of flexibility did not appear in the professional literature until 1941, when Dr. T. K. Cureton, Jr., published a group of practical performance-oriented tests (15) which subsequently became widely used. These tests were based on his master's thesis, which was completed at Springfield College in 1930 (16). Later, Professor C. H. McCloy changed the tests from absolute or performance-oriented tests to relative tests. All of Cureton's tests with the exception of the ankle flexibility test were linear measures. The ankle flexibility test relied on the use of a protractor to secure the measure in terms of degrees of rotation.

Jack Leighton quickly followed Cureton by reporting new measures of flexibility in 1942

Figure 2-2. Dr. C. H. McCloy (Deceased) State University of Iowa. Photo courtesy of Dr. Edward Capen, University of Tennessee

(29). Leighton's flexometer, a scientific instrument that evolved from a modification of the goniometer, made possible many new types of rotary flexibility tests.

The popularity of the hip flexion exercise, where students are advised to keep knees straight and touch fingers to toes, was evidenced by the development of several test modifications to the exercise. First, Cureton's 1930 version, which he called the Forward Bending of Trunk Test, was established (16). Then, the Scott-French Bobbing Test (44) evolved with a bench and attached scale so that students could stand and attempt to reach lower than their toes. Third, Wells and Dillon published a Sit and Reach Test (49) with a horizontal and elevated scale that provided scores in negative and positive units. And finally, in 1966, Johnson modified the Wells and Dillon test, which resulted in all positive scores by merely lining a student's heels on the 15-inch mark of a yardstick and having the student reach as far down the stick as possible (26). Specific directions and local norms were later established ranging from as low as 4 inches to as high as 32 inches.

Four sports- and dance-oriented flexibility tests were also devised in 1966 (26). These tests, which related to gymnastics, certain types of dance, and swimming, were identified as the Bridge-up Test, Side Splits Test, Front Splits Test, and Shoulder Rotation Test. In 1972, seeking to get more exact measures with these tests, Johnson developed a simple and inexpensive testing instrument which he called a Flexomeasure (27). The device was then modified for use with seven different flexibility tests in 1977 (25). Other contributions may be found in Chapter 6.

Rhythm and Dance Measurement

This area of measurement has been plagued by a lack of experimentation for the development of objective and practical tests. While the well-known Seashore tests have been extensively used in research, they have not been found to be practical for physical education measurement. Moreover, objective instruments for measuring rhythm have been devised but are not feasible for the average teacher's use. However, special mention should be made of the following test constructors for presenting tests which can be useful to teachers of rhythm and dance: (a) I. F. Waglow, (b) Eloise Lemon and Elizabeth Sherbon, and (c) Dudley Ashton. Other contributors to this area of measurements may be found in Chapter 17.

Speed and Reaction Time Measurement

Numerous studies have been conducted in physical education, psychology, and other fields which have investigated various facets of reaction time and speed of movement. Psychologists have been primarily concerned with response measurement as it relates to learning, whereas physical education researchers have been mainly concerned with methods of improving speed of movement and reaction time and how these factors influence physical performance. Although there are a number of variables that affect measurement of speed and reaction time, such as motivation, set, sensory discrimination, and practice, the measuring devices are generally quite precise. The leadership and research of Dr. F. M. Henry in this area of measurement is recognized as a prime factor in many of the studies which followed. Other contributions may be found in Chapter 15.

Strength Measurement

Sargent provided the chief impetus for strength measurement during the early years of our profession. It was during this period that the dynamometer and the spirometer were developed and utilized for testing in Sargent's Intercollegiate Strength Test (5). The Universal Dynamometer, developed in 1894 by J. H. Kellogg, was used to test the static or isometric strength of a large number of muscles. Then, in 1915 E. G. Martin developed a resistance strength test to measure the strength of muscle groups with a flat-faced type spring balance (5). In 1925 F. R. Rogers refined the Intercollegiate Strength Test and proved its validity as a measure of general athletic ability. Rogers also created the Physical Fitness Index (the PFI), including in it a new statistical technique for determining norms of physical achievement. He later showed how his PFI program could be adapted to the physical needs of the individual. McCloy developed a strength test that he felt was an improvement over the Rogers Strength Test in terms of administration, scoring, and validity. McCloy's test left out the lung capacity test which he did not consider to be a strength measure (27). It might also be noted at this time that chin-ups and dips, which were items in Sargent's, Rogers's, and McCloy's strength tests, were not exclusively strength items, but were muscular endurance items as well. Thus, only the following three items of these early strength tests were pure measures of strength: (a) back strength, (b) leg strength, and (c) grip strength. In 1928, Edwin R. Elbel, while working on his master's degree at Springfield College, found that strength could be increased by short static (isometric) contraction exercises. However, interest in isometric exercises seemed to remain dormant for the next two decades. In fact, it was not until 1953, when the startling results of Hettinger and Muller's experiments on isometric strength training were published, that a new era in strength training began. As mentioned previously, static strength testing was not new, as evidenced by the early use of the dynamometer and the comprehensive measurement of strength by H. Harrison Clarke with the tensiometer. This instrument was originally designed to measure aircraft cable tension, but was adapted by Clarke to measure strength of various muscle groups.

Figure 2-4. Dr. T. K. Cureton, Jr. (Retired) University of Illinois

Muscular Endurance Measurement

The history of muscular endurance measurement closely parallels that of muscular strength testing. Hitchcock and Sargent compiled extensive data on muscular endurance of the arms and shoulders of college men in the latter half of the nineteenth century (6). In 1884 Mosso, an Italian physiologist, invented the ergograph and helped establish the relationship between physical condition and muscular activity. Mosso also pointed out that the body's ability to do work depends upon adequate nutrition and that fatigue of one set of muscles affects others as well (9). In 1922 an adaptation of Mosso's ergograph made it possible to study successive muscular contractions on a smoke drum. H. Harrison Clarke and other researchers have conducted a number of studies on the Kelso-Hellebrandt ergograph using larger muscle groups than were used with the earlier ergograph of Mosso. Test items such as chin-ups and dips that combine both strength and endurance have been utilized as either strength measures or muscular endurance measures or both on many physical

Figure 2-3. Dr. H. Harrison Clarke (Retired) University of Oregon. Photo, Dr. Clarke pauses during phase of the Medford Growth Study

fitness tests, strength tests, and motor ability tests. The measurement of strength and muscular endurance will be covered in depth in later chapters.

Cardiovascular Endurance

In 1905 Crampton (14) developed a rating scale to obtain data on the general physical condition of a person by observing changes in the cardiac rate and arterial pressure on assuming the erect position from a lying down position. This test obviously influenced the work of other investigators to follow, including McCurdy, Meylan, Foster, Barach, and Barringer (35, 6, 9). In 1920 Schneider (43) reported findings concerning a rather comprehensive test which had been used to assess fatigue and physical condition. The test had been employed to determine the physical state of aviators in World War I by the Air Force (6).

In 1925 Campbell published a test involving breath holding and recovery after exercise. This preliminary study later developed into the Campbell Pulse Ratio Test. Tuttle, influenced by Campbell's work, developed the Tuttle Pulse Ratio Test and conducted a considerable amount of cardiovascular research during the 1930s.

In 1943 the Harvard Step Test (8) was developed by Brouha and his associates to determine the general capacity of the body to adapt and recover from work. The work consisted of stepping up and down on a bench at a prescribed cadence. The pulse rate was taken at set intervals after exercise. This test has been extensively used in testing and research programs.

In addition to McCurdy, Brouha, and Tuttle, other outstanding contributors to knowledge in cardiovascular measurements have been Cureton, Clarke, Henry, Larson, Karpovich, and McCloy to name but a few. In recent years cardiovascular research and measurement have become somewhat more sophisticated with the increased use of machines in determining the behavior of the circulatory and respiratory systems under various test conditions.

Dr. Kenneth Cooper (12), formerly of the U.S. Air Force, did extensive research in an attempt to establish a rating scale for measuring relative values of activities in terms of circulorespiratory conditioning. His research showed the importance of such activities as running, swimming, cycling, walking, handball, basketball, squash, and others in the develop-

ment of circulorespiratory endurance. Cooper provides a simple 12 minute run-walk scale for people to evaluate their own condition.

Physical Fitness Measurement

Physical fitness has always been one of the foremost goals of physical education. The measurement of physical fitness and methods of developing fitness have been topics of national concern through the years. The medical doctors who constituted the early leadership in the profession were initially attracted to physical education because of their interest in physical fitness. It was mutual interest in physical fitness and other physical measurements that prompted the meetings leading to the formation of our national organization, now known as the American Alliance for Health, Physical Education, and Recreation (AAHPER). A great deal of credit must be given to the Turner societies in the 1800s for promoting an interest in the development and maintenance of physical fitness through gymnastic exercise programs. The Turners were mainly German immigrants who had fled to the United States in the 1840s because of political pressures in Europe. Turnerveins were established throughout much of the East and the Midwest. These societies took advantage of every opportunity to sell their programs of gymnastics and physical fitness to the schools. As a result of their efforts, gymnastics and developmental exercises made up the greater part of the physical education programs around the nation until the early 1900s. Increasing popularity of team games and lighter recreational type activities then began to crowd out the more formal physical development programs. The draft statistics in World War I brought national attention to be focused on a need for increased physical fitness of the American youth. Consequently, the states passed laws making physical education mandatory in the schools. The natural play movement spearheaded by Wood and Hetherington and others brought about a decrease in emphasis on physical fitness in the 1920s and 1930s. Again, a world war generated national concern over the need for physical fitness. During World War II the Army, the Navy, and Air Force established their own physical fitness test batteries, and considerable research was done in this area. After the war the nation relaxed again only to be jarred awake by the startling results of the Kraus-

Weber test in which American children were shown to be decidedly inferior to European children in this test of minimum muscular fitness. As a result, in 1956 President Eisenhower established the President's Council on Youth Fitness, which was to focus national attention on the need for physical fitness programs in the schools. In 1958 the AAHPER Youth Fitness Test was developed for boys and girls (in grades five to twelve) with national norms. In 1965 and again in 1975 the test went through revisions, but it never escaped the criticism of many researchers who desired a separation of the motor fitness items from the test (1). More recent attempts at physical fitness test construction have drawn closer to your authors' concept that a physical fitness test should include at least one item of strength, flexibility, muscular endurance, cardiovascular endurance, and body composition or height-weight rating. The reader is referred to Chapter 11 for further discussion of physical fitness measurement.

Sports Skill Measurement

Among the earliest reported sports skills tests were the Athletic Badge Tests devised in 1913 by the Playground and Recreation Association of America. The test items pertained to the sports of volleyball, tennis, baseball, and basketball. In 1918 Hetherington developed tests for the California decathlon which made use of a graduated score plan (6). In 1924 Brace reported a six-item skill test in basketball (6), and a year later Beall (3) completed an experimental study in tennis to determine a battery of tests for that sport. Increasing interest in testing of sports skills was evident in the 1930s, and throughout the following thirty years many fine tests were proposed, developed, and utilized by physical educators. However, for many years there had been an often expressed need for nationally standardized tests. This lack of national standards had been frequently cited as one of physical education's biggest failings. In response to this need, AAHPER initiated a sports skills test project in 1959 to determine standards for at least fifteen sports activities. This project began under the direction of the Research Council of AAHPER, with David K. Brace serving as test consultant and Frank A. Sills as chairman. The tests and norms have made it possible to more effectively evaluate skill performance, bring about greater motivation, and improve

teaching. References and further contributions for this area of measurement may be found in Chapter 16.

Posture Measurement

The earliest contributions made in this area of measurement were in the form of records and anthropometric charts by Hitchcock, Sargent, J. W. Seaver, Luther H. Gulick, Thomas D. Wood, Delphine Hanna, and others. During the 1930s and 1940s a great deal of interest was shown in developing methods of measuring and evaluating posture. Studies were presented which reported the use of such instruments as the Cureton-Gunby conformateur, Korbs's comparograph, the posturemeter, the scoliometer, x-rays, pedograph, photography, and rating scales. Difficulty in devising practical, objective instruments for assessing posture, plus the lack of definite criteria as to what good posture should entail for different individuals, resulted in a drop in the number of reported studies on the topic in the 1950s. Nevertheless, articles on posture have continued to appear in the professional literature, which indicates that there has not been a lessening of concern as to the importance of good posture.

Social Qualities Measurement

McCloy focused attention on the measurement of social qualities by physical educators in an article which appeared during the first year of publication of the *Research Quarterly* (32). In 1936 O'Neel (38) and Blanchard (4) published separate behavior rating scales for use in physical education. Despite the reluctance in this area to yield to objective measurement, there has been an imposing number of studies published and new measuring instruments reported in the last thirty years. Physical educators have long recognized that continuous attempts should be made to measure social qualities if development in this area is to be one of physical education's objectives. The work of J. L. Moreno (37) and Helen Jennings (24) in sociometric measurement has been of great value to physical educators as well as to counselors and other teachers. The late Charles C. Cowell (13) made splendid contributions in this area in physical education. Considerable progress has been made in attitude assessment, and such names as Carlos Wear, Gerald Kenyon, and others have been prominent in this area.

Knowledge Measurement

Among the earliest published sports knowledge tests was a basketball knowledge test published by J. G. Bliss (5) in 1929. Since that date numerous sports knowledge tests have been constructed and published in the professional literature. Unlike other subject areas, standardized tests have not been available on a commercial basis, and, consequently, physical educators have had to prepare their own or locate tests from the literature to duplicate. Outstanding contributors to the literature in the area of sports knowledge tests have been Esther French (19), Catherine Snell, Katherine Ley (30), Gail Hennis (22), Rosemary Fisher (18), and Jack Hewitt (23). References and further contributions for this area of measurement may be found in Chapter 21.

Concluding Statement

The quantity and quality of research in physical education have continued to improve, which is to be expected. This is certainly not meant to imply any criticism of the early researchers. On the contrary, physical education has been extremely fortunate to have had such excellent and inspiring leadership in the areas of research and tests and measurements. As in any profession, students must profit from the experiences of the professors and strive to improve upon the work of those who have gone before.

It has been observed that scientific endeavors in all fields have had rather crude beginnings. To confirm this phenomenon we need only recall the primitive practices in the history of medicine, the simple, awkward designs of the early automobiles, and the hilarious first attempts of men to fly. Yet, when one considers the tremendous advances that have been made in these fields in the last quarter of a century, the prognosis for progress in evaluation in physical education should indeed be encouraging. Physical education is a relatively new field. This is attested to by the fact that many of the persons named in this chapter as being early leaders in the area of tests and measurements are still active today or only recently passed away.

We must guard against complacency and discouragement. The history of tests and measurements in physical education reveals that in some areas no further research efforts have been reported for twenty or thirty years. It is imperative that we continue to seek new and better ways of measuring those traits which we have already had some success in measuring and, at the same time, make renewed and vigorous efforts to assess those qualities which heretofore have baffled attempts at measurement.

With new and more precise measuring devices, improved methods of analyzing data, increased emphasis on research in graduate study, combined with the fact that more persons are seeking advanced degrees, the future indeed looks bright.

References and Bibliography

1. AAHPER, *AAHPER Youth Fitness Test Manual,* Washington, D.C.: American Alliance for Health, Physical Education, and Recreation, 1976.
2. Baldwin, Bird T., *Physical Growth and School Progress,* Washington, D.C.: Bureau of Education Bulletin No. 10, 1914, p. 143.
3. Beall, Elizabeth, "Essential Qualities in Certain Aspects of Physical Education with Ways of Measuring and Developing Same" (Unpublished master's thesis, University of California, 1925).
4. Blanchard, B. E., "A Behavior Frequency Rating Scale for the Measurement of Character and Personality in Physical Education Classroom Situations," *Research Quarterly,* 6:56-66, May, 1936.
5. Bliss, J. G., *Basketball,* Philadelphia: Lea and Febiger, 1929.
6. Bovard, John F., and others, *Tests and Measurements in Physical Education,* Philadelphia: W. B. Saunders Company, 1950.
7. Bovard, J. F., and F. W. Cozens, *The "Leap Meter," An Investigation into the Possibilities of the Sargent Test as a Measure of General Athletic Ability,* Eugene: University of Oregon Press, 1928.
8. Brouha, Lucien, "The Step Test: A Simple Method of Measuring Physical Fitness for Muscular Work in Young Men," *Research Quarterly,* 14:31-35, March, 1943.
9. Burton-Opitz, R., "Tests of Physical Efficiency," *American Physical Education Review,* 27: 153-159, April, 1922.
10. Capen, Edward K., "The Effect of Systematic Weight Training on Power, Strength, and Endurance," *Research Quarterly,* 21:83-93, May, 1950.
11. Chui, Edward, "The Effect of Systematic Weight Training on Athletic Power," *Research Quarterly,* 21:188-94, October, 1950.

12. Cooper, Kenneth H., *The New Aerobics,* New York: Bantam Books, Inc., 1970.

13. Cowell, Charles C., "Validating an Index of Social Adjustment for High School Use," *Research Quarterly,* 29:7-18, March, 1958.

14. Crampton, Ward C., "A Test of Condition," *Medical News,* LXXXVIII: 529, September, 1905.

15. Cureton, T. K., Jr., "Flexibility as an Aspect of Physical Fitness," *Research Quarterly Supplement,* 12:388-390, May, 1941.

16. _____, "Objective Test of Swimming" (Unpublished master's thesis, Springfield College, 1930).

17. _____, *Physical Fitness Appraisal and Guidance,* St. Louis: C. V. Mosby Company, 1947.

18. Fisher, Rosemary B., "Tests in Selected Physical Education Service Courses in a College" (Microcarded dissertation, State University of Iowa, 1950), p. 72.

19. French, Esther, "The Construction of Knowledge Tests in Selected Professional Courses in Physical Education," *Research Quarterly,* 14:406-424, 1943.

20. Gates, Donald D., and R. P. Sheffield, "Tests of Direction as Measurements of Different Kinds of Motor Ability in Boys of the Seventh, Eighth, and Ninth Grades," *Research Quarterly,* 11:136-147, October, 1940.

21. Glencross, Dennis J., "The Nature of the Vertical Jump Test and the Standing Broad Jump," *Research Quarterly,* 37:353-359, October, 1966.

22. Hennis, Gail M., "Construction of Knowledge Tests in Selected Physical Education Activities for College Women," *Research Quarterly,* 27:301-309, October, 1956.

23. Hewitt, Jack E., "Hewitt's Comprehensive Tennis Knowledge Test," *Research Quarterly,* 35:147-155, May, 1964.

24. Jennings, Helen, *Sociometry in Group Relations,* American Council on Education, 1948, 1959.

25. Johnson, Barry L., *Practical Flexibility Measurement with the Flexomeasure,* Portland: Brown and Littleman Company, 1977.

26. _____, "Practical Tests of Flexibility" (Unpublished study, 1966).

27. _____, and Jack K. Nelson, *Practical Measurements for Evaluation in Physical Education,* Minneapolis: Burgess Publishing Company, 1974, pp. 70-86.

28. Kretschmer, E., *Physique and Character,* New York: Harcourt Brace and Company, 1925.

29. Leighton, Jack, "A Simple Objective and Reliable Measure of Flexibility," *Research Quarterly,* 13:205-216, May, 1942.

30. Ley, Katherine L., "Constructing Objective Test Items to Measure High School Levels of Achievement in Selected Physical Education Activities" (Microcarded dissertation, University of Iowa, 1960), p. 25.

31. McCloy, Charles H., "Athletic Handicapping by Age, Height, and Weight, *American Physical Education Review,* 32:635-42, November, 1927.

32. _____, "Character Building through Physical Education," *Research Quarterly,* 1:41, October, 1930.

33. _____, "Recent Studies in the Sargent Jump," *Research Quarterly,* 3:235, May, 1932.

34. McCloy, Charles H., and Norma D. Young, *Tests and Measurements in Health and Physical Education,* New York: Appleton-Century-Crofts, 1954.

35. McCurdy, J. H., "Adolescent Changes in Heart Rate and Blood Pressure," *American Physical Education Review,* 15:421, June, 1910.

36. Meredith, Howard V., *Physical Growth Records for Boys and Physical Growth Records for Girls,* Washington, D.C.: National Education Association.

37. Moreno, J. L., "Who Shall Survive? A New Problem to the Problem of Human Relationships," Washington, D.C.: Nervous and Mental Disease Publishing Company, 1934.

38. O'Neel, E. W., "A Behavior Frequency Rating Scale for the Measurement of Character and Personality in High School Physical Education Classes for Boys," *Research Quarterly,* 7:67, May, 1936.

39. Pryor, Helen B., *Width-Weight Tables,* Stanford, Cal.: Stanford University Press, 1940.

40. Reilly, Frederick J., *New Rational Athletics for Boys and Girls,* Boston: D. C. Heath and Company, p. 191.

41. Sargent, D. A., "The Physical Test of a Man," *American Physical Education Review,* 26:188-94, April, 1921.

42. _____, "Twenty Years' Progress in Efficiency Tests," *American Physical Education Review,* 18:452, October, 1913.

43. Schneider, E. C., "A Cardiovascular Rating as a Measure of Physical Fatigue and Efficiency," *Journal of American Medical Association,* LXXIV:1507, May, 1920.

44. Scott, M. Gladys, and Ester French, *Evaluation in Physical Education,* St. Louis: C. V. Mosby Company, 1950.

45. Seaver, Jay W., *Anthropometry and Physical Examination,* Meriden, Conn.: Curtis-Way Company, 1909, pp. 14-15.

46. Sheldon, W. H., and others, *The Varieties of Human Physique,* New York: Harper and Brothers, 1940.

47. Sierakowski, Frances, "A Study of Change of Direction Tests for High School Girls" (Master's thesis, State University of Iowa, 1940).

48. Sills, Frank A., "A Factor Analysis of Somatotypes and Their Relationship to Achievement in Motor Skills," *Research*

Quarterly, 21:424-37, December, 1950.

49. Wells, Katherine F., and Evelyn K. Dillon, "The Sit and Reach—A Test of Back and Leg Flexibility," *Research Quarterly,* 23:118, March, 1952.

50. Wetzel, Norman C., "Physical Fitness in Terms of Physique, Development, and Basal Metabolism," *Journal of American Medical Association,* 116:1187-95, March, 1941.

51. Young, Kathryn E., "An Analytic Study of the Tests of Change of Direction" (Master's thesis, State University of Iowa, 1937).

Part Two
Statistics and
Its Application
in Test
Construction,
Evaluation, and
Grading

Chapter Three

Basic Statistical Techniques

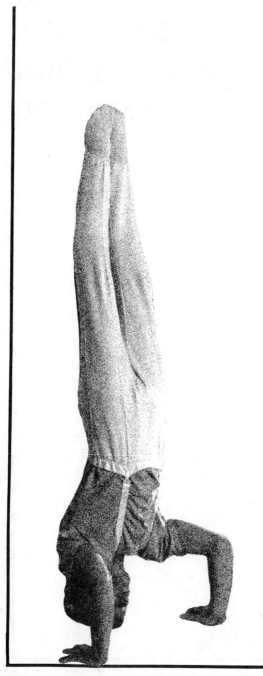

Introduction

One of the essential steps in evaluation is to be able to analyze and present the products derived from tests and measurements. The prospective teacher is continually admonished to refrain from testing merely for the sake of testing. The physical educator can spend hours carefully and skillfully measuring, but without the ability to organize and analyze the data, the information cannot be interpreted and effectively used to evaluate the program. This then brings us to the subject of statistical analysis.

Mention of the word *statistics* usually brings about a shudder of fear or revulsion on the part of the prospective teacher. There may be a number of reasons for this attitude—a poor background in mathematics, intimidation by the terminology and formulas, etc.—but whatever the reason, it is an unfortunate situation. When faced with that part of teacher preparation that includes statistics, the reluctant student grits his teeth and endures the daily assignments and struggles through the quizzes. He firmly resolves that he will never, by choice, encounter the subject again; nor will he use the wretched computations in his teaching. Thus, he enters the field minus a very valuable tool of his trade.

With the recalcitrant student in mind, we will attempt to present this portion of the evaluation process as simply and as practicably as possible. We will use what has often been called the cookbook approach, wherein the teacher need not understand the derivation of the formulas, which may be likened to the ingredients. Instead, he merely follows the steps to achieve the end product. The authors would be among the first to agree that the researcher and specialist in tests and measurements should have a rather extensive background in statistics. However, it goes without saying that the teacher in the field does not necessarily possess this background, and thus the most important thing is that he should be able to use with confidence some basic statistical tools that are required for effective evaluation. A basic understanding of statistics is of value to any teacher. Some of these values are as follows:

1. A knowledge of statistics is essential in order to conduct research and report the results.
2. The teacher is better able to understand and profit from professional literature, especially research publications.
3. A knowledge of statistics is necessary in

order to effectively evaluate available tests on a scientific basis.

4. Statistical analysis gives more meaning to test data and thus aids in the understanding and interpretation of scores for both the teacher and the students.
5. A knowledge of statistical techniques can be of considerable help in the grading process.
6. Statistical analysis is a necessary part of test construction.

Basic Terms

Before we explain the operation of statistics, it seems appropriate to identify and discuss the following terms:

Statistics—This is a means by which a set of data may be described and interpreted in a meaningful manner and also a method by which data may be analyzed and inferences and conclusions drawn.

Population—A population refers to all of the subjects within a defined group. For example, it may be all the male tenth grade boys in a particular high school (or the whole nation, for that matter).

Sample—A sample is a part of a population. In the above example, a sample could be a group of the tenth grade boys selected from that particular school.

Random sample—A randomly selected sample is one in which every member of the specified population has an equal chance of being selected.

Frequency distribution—This is a method of grouping the data. It is a table that presents the raw scores or intervals of scores and the frequencies with which the raw scores occur.

Ungrouped data—Ungrouped data are simply the raw scores presented as they were recorded. In other words, no attempt is made to arrange them into a more meaningful or convenient form.

Grouped data—Grouped data are scores that have been arranged in some manner, such as from high to low or grouped into classes or categories, in order to give more meaning to the data or to facilitate further calculations.

The Calculator versus the Frequency Distribution

In the past in most educational statistics textbooks, the major emphasis was on the use of grouped data, and certainly there are still some advantages in working with frequency distributions. Before the age of calculators grouped scores were generally faster to use even though the procedures were more indirect and complicated. Today, however, the use of pocket calculators is widespread among students from grade school through graduate study. There are a number of inexpensive calculators on the market that provide the mathematical functions required by the average physical education teacher. Consequently, the function of frequency distributions has greatly diminished in importance.

Therefore, in keeping with recent trends in statistics, practically all of the statistical techniques in this text will involve ungrouped data and the so-called computer methods of computation.

Measures of Central Tendency

One of the first questions any student asks upon seeing his own score is, "What was the average?" He asks this completely unaware that he is now dealing in statistics. He merely wants to know how he stands in relation to the rest of the group. Despite the fact that he has not had the privilege of taking a formal course in statistics, he knows from his past school experiences that there usually are a few high scores, a few low scores, and that most tend to cluster in the middle. The average tells him how most of the class did. This then is a measure of central tendency. It is a single score which best represents all the scores. The three basic measures of central tendency are the mean, the median, and the mode.

The Mean. The mean is simply the arithmetic average. It can be computed by adding all the scores and then dividing by the number of scores involved. The symbol for the mean of a population is μ, and for a sample, $\overline{X}$. The mean is by far the most commonly used measure of central tendency and, for the most part, the most reliable. The main weakness of the mean is that, with a small sample, extreme scores have a misleading effect. For example, in the following group of scores the mean is 10, and it is representative of the group.

$$\begin{array}{r} 12 \\ 11 \\ 10 \\ 9 \\ 8 \\ \hline \Sigma X^* = 50 \end{array} \qquad \text{Mean } (\overline{X}) = \frac{\Sigma X}{N} = \frac{50}{5} = 10$$

*The symbol Σ, the Greek letter *sigma*, means summation; X stands for scores; thus ΣX means the sum of scores.

However, if we add an extreme score such as 30 to the above group of scores, the mean changes considerably.

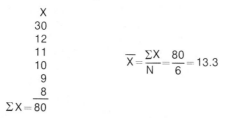

The mean of 13.3 is not representative of the group since it is higher than every score but one. Although this example may in itself be a bit extreme, it is hoped that it illustrates the point that one should always consider the number of cases and *look* at the data rather than blindly trusting statistics.

The method of computing the mean employed above will not suffice with grouped data. A technique which is appropriate, called the short method, will be described later.

The Median. The median is that point at which 50 percent of the scores lie above and below it. In other words it is the mid-point, or 50th percentile. By using the scores that were shown in the above discussion of the mean, the principal advantage of the median can be demonstrated. In the first illustration the median score is 10, which is the same as the mean.

The median is easily obtained in this case by locating the middle score. In some instances it is a point rather than an actual score, as is illustrated by the second example.

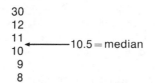

The main advantage of the median should now be evident: The addition of extreme scores has relatively little effect.

When the scores are arranged from high to low, the median is easily obtained and can be utilized as a quick and ready average. When the data are grouped, the task of locating the median is not so easy and is mostly used in that case when percentiles are wanted. This procedure will be shown later.

The Mode. This measure of central tendency is defined as the score which occurs the most frequently. It is a very rough measure and is used for description more than for any exact analysis. For example, the word mode is sometimes used in describing fashions; it simply indicates what most people are wearing. When scores are ungrouped, the teacher needs merely to locate the score (or scores, for there may be more than one mode) that appears the most number of times. Because there may be more than one mode, it is the least reliable of the three measures of central tendency that are generally used. When the data follow a typical normal curve, the mean, the median, and the mode will fall in the same place.

Measures of Variability

Variability may be defined as the scatter or spread of scores from a point of central tendency. When we measure the variability of a group of scores, we are determining the amount of scatter or spread in the scores. This information tells us how homogeneous or heterogeneous a group is. While two groups may have the same mean or median, they may differ considerably in variability. For example, if five students completed 84, 80, 78, 75, and 73 sit-ups, their mean was 78. Another group of five students completed 98, 95, 78, 65, and 54 sit-ups and their mean was also 78. However, it can be seen that there is an obvious difference between the two groups concerning the variability of their scores.

The measures of variability discussed in this text are the range, standard deviation, and variance.

Range. While the range is the simplest measure of variability, it is crude and quite limited in that it is completely dependent upon the two most extreme scores in a group of scores. Generally speaking, a large range usually indicates a large degree of variability. The range is defined as the difference between the highest and lowest score in a set of data. Technically, the formula is (High score−Low score)+1. The addition of 1 is necessary to include both the highest and lowest scores within the range.

Standard Deviation. The standard deviation is one of several measures of variability. It reflects the magnitude of the deviations of the scores from their mean.

Measures of variability augment measures of central tendency in providing more information about a group of scores. It was stated earlier that one of the first questions a student asks concerning a test is to find out the average. A second question is, "What is the highest (or lowest) score?" The student has learned in his school experience that the range tells him how the scores varied and, consequently, more about his performance in relation to the class. However, the standard deviation is a much more precise measure of variability than the range, and it is thus frequently employed in research studies.

The following set of scores will be used to demonstrate the calculation of the standard deviation: 12, 8, 7, 16, 6, 2, 20, 10, 8, 1, 4, 10, 8, 6, 2.

Note that in Table 3-1 these scores are ungrouped in that they have not been arranged in any specific order. The steps in computing the standard deviation are as follows:

Step 1. Add the scores. This is ΣX. Obviously, when there are many numbers and/or when the numbers are large, a calculator or an adding machine is of immeasurable help.

Step 2. Square each score. Most pocket calculators can cumulatively square and add the squared values. If the calculator has a memory key both the ΣX and the ΣX^2 can be obtained in one operation.

Step 3. Insert the necessary data into the formula.*

$$s = \sqrt{\frac{N\Sigma X^2 - (\Sigma X)^2}{N(N-1)}}$$

In order to calculate the standard deviation, it is necessary to compute square root. Most calculators have square root keys. A description of the steps involved in computing square root is provided in Appendix B.

*The symbol for the standard deviation of a population is the Greek small letter *sigma* (σ) and for a sample, s.

Table 3-1
Calculation of the Mean and Standard Deviation from Ungrouped Scores

X	X^2	
12	144	$\bar{X} = \dfrac{\Sigma X}{N} = \dfrac{120}{15} = 8$
8	64	
7	49	$s = \sqrt{\dfrac{N\Sigma X^2 - (\Sigma X)^2}{N(N-1)}} =$
16	256	
6	36	
2	4	$\sqrt{\dfrac{15(1338) - (120)^2}{15(15-1)}} =$
20	400	
10	100	
8	64	$\sqrt{\dfrac{20{,}070 - 14{,}400}{15(14)}} =$
1	1	
4	16	
10	100	$\sqrt{\dfrac{5{,}670}{210}} =$
8	64	
6	36	
2	4	$\sqrt{27} =$
$\Sigma X = 120$	$\Sigma X^2 = 1{,}338$	
		5.2

Variance. Another common measure of variability is variance. It is the standard deviation squared. It is computed as a part of analysis of variance procedures and is frequently referred to as mean square (MS). Actually, the definition of variance is the mean of the squared deviations from the mean. The symbol for variance of a population is σ^2 and for a sample it is s^2.

The Normal Curve. The normal curve is a theoretical distribution based upon probability. The basis for most of the statistical methods is the assumption of a normal distribution. The normal curve is bell shaped and symmetrical (Figure 3-1) and based on an infinite number of cases.

Many human qualities are distributed in this manner because they follow the laws of chance. Heredity, environment, social conditions, and other factors produce traits in a frequency of occurrence that follow the laws of chance. Actually, very few distributions are perfectly normal. However, if the numbers are sufficiently large, many of the traits we measure follow the shape of the normal curve quite closely. Our concept of what is normal or average is based on this phenomenon. For example, in a given population of ten year old boys of a particular race and location you will find some very short, some very tall, and most about the same size. The same is true for strength, speed, neuromuscular skills, mental abilities, and other traits.

In the normal distribution, one standard deviation above and below the mean encompasses the middle 68.26 percent or approximately 2/3 of the scores. Plus and minus two standard deviations include approximately 95 percent of the scores, and plus and minus three standard deviations account for over 99 percent of the distribution.

Standard Scores

Many of the measurements taken by physical educators are in different units. For example, there may be scores recorded in seconds as in the 50 yard dash, or in feet as in the softball throw, or in repetitions as in sit-ups. Moreover, the physical educator measures strength in pounds; he records the number of times a student volleys a tennis ball against a wall; he scores the vertical jump in inches; he charts the zone in which a golf ball lands; he uses written test scores, ratings, game scores, and various and sundry other units of measurement.

The combining of scores from separate tests has often posed a difficult problem for teachers who lack the knowledge, or the desire, or both to transform raw scores into some form of standard score. There are a number of scales that can be used. We will only describe two, the T-scale and percentiles.

The T-Scale. The T-scale converts raw scores into normalized standard scores with a mean of 50 and a standard deviation of 10. The T-scale can be constructed by any of several methods. The T-scale for any specific raw score can be determined by the following formula

$$\text{T-score} = 50 + \frac{10}{s}(X - \overline{X})$$

where s is the standard deviation of the raw scores, X is the specific score in question and $\overline{X}$

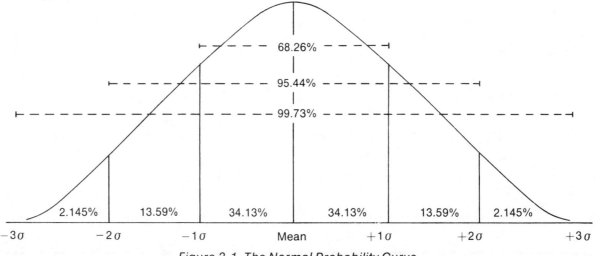

Figure 3-1. The Normal Probability Curve

is the mean of the group of scores. To illustrate, suppose a student made a score of 94 on a test in which the mean was 80 and the standard deviation 20. Substituting in the formula we have

$$T = 50 + \frac{10}{20}(94 - 80) = 50 + .5(14) = 50 + 7 = 57$$

Any T could be computed in this way.

However, another approach that we feel offers a relatively easy and expedient method of establishing a T-scale from a set of raw scores is described below. For purposes of illustration, the steps are described using the same fifteen scores that were utilized in the calculation of the mean and standard deviation from ungrouped data.

Step 1: Compute the mean and standard deviation for the data. From our calculations we found a mean of 8 and a standard deviation of 5.2.

Step 2: Multiply the standard deviation by .1. This gives us a T value of .5. Note: The T-scale encompasses five standard deviations above and below the mean. Five standard deviations below the mean is assigned 0 and each standard deviation above this is assigned ten points. Thus, four standard deviations below the mean has a T-score value of 10, three standard deviations below 20, etc., up to five standard deviations above the mean, which has a T-score value of 100. Consequently, one T is 1/10 of the standard deviation.

Step 3: Construct a table of numbers by placing 50 in the center of a page and numbering upward to 100 and downward to 1. Place the mean of the raw scores opposite the number 50 at the center of the table (see Table 3-2).

Step 4: Next, add the value obtained in Step 2 (.5) to the mean and to each subsequent number to represent T-scores 51 to 100 (i.e., $T_{51} = 8 + .5 = 8.5$; $T_{52} = 8.5 + .5 = 9$, etc.). Conversely subtract the constant from the mean and from each number thereafter to determine T-scores 49 to 0 (i.e., $T_{49} = 8 - .5 = 7.5$; $T_{48} = 7.5 - .5 = 7$, etc.).

Step 5: Round off the scores in order to correspond to the actual raw scores. We will then have a T-scale such as is shown in Table 3-2.

It should be pointed out that in the normal probability curve, plus and minus 3.5 standard deviations includes nearly all the cases. The T-scale extends plus and minus five standard deviations. Consequently, T-scores for a distribution that closely approximates the normal curve may be expected to range usually from about 85 to 15. This may give rise to some confusion on the part of the student who is conditioned to thinking that scores in the 70s and 80s are only fair. For this reason, some educators prefer the Hull scale rather than the

Table 3-2
Construction of a T-Scale

T-Score	Raw Score	T-Score	Raw Score
80	23	56	11
78	22	54	10
76	21	52	9
74	20	50	8
72	19	48	7
70	18	46	6
68	17	44	5
66	16	42	4
64	15	40	3
62	14	38	2
60	13	36	1
58	12	34	0

T-scale. The Hull scale extends 3.5 standard deviations above and below the mean. Therefore, there is more likelihood that scores will be found in the upper and lower ends of the scale. On the other hand, advocates of the T-scale maintain that one of the big advantages of the scale is that since the 0 and 100 are so distant, it would be very rare to find future scores that couldn't be placed on the T-scale. Regardless of the scale that is used, there must be proper interpretation of the scores to the students. Referring back to Figure 3-1 of the normal distribution, it can be seen, for example, that one standard deviation above the mean (a T-score of 60) is better than 84 percent (50+34.13 percent) of the scores, that two standard deviations above the mean (a T of 70) represents a score better than 98 percent of the scores, etc.

One note of caution is that the physical education teacher should periodically revise his T-scale. As more scores are accumulated, the mean and standard deviation should be computed again to verify their accuracy, and, if warranted, a new T-scale should be constructed. The T-scale should not be expected to change markedly once it has been established with a sufficient number of observations. The physical educator would be remiss, however, if he did not continue to inspect and evaluate his norms, just as he should regularly evaluate his total tests and measurements program.

Percentiles. One of the more common ways of presenting norms is the use of percentiles. The physical educator frequently has occasion to use percentiles, since many standardized tests (notably the AAHPER Youth Fitness Test and the AAHPER Sports Skills Tests) present their scores in this manner. Generally speaking, the students are fairly well oriented in the interpretation of percentiles.

A percentile score informs the student what proportion of the group scored below him. For example, a percentile rank of 80 means that 80 percent of the people taking that particular test had scores lower than that and 20 percent had higher scores. When percentiles are used, scores from different tests can be compared to show how a student scored in relation to the others on each test.

In most statistics and tests and measurements books, percentiles are calculated from a frequency distribution. This will be demonstrated later in the chapter. However, we can demonstrate one method of computing percentiles with a small number of scores that have been arranged from high to low. The same scores that were utilized in the T-scale will serve as the data.

Step 1: List the scores from high to low.

Step 2: Divide the number of cases into 100 positions so that each case takes up 100/15 or 6.666 positions (rounded to 6.7).

Step 3: Place the 100 percentile at the highest case and subtract 6.7 for each case to yield the percentiles shown in Table 3-3.

Step 4: Round off the percentiles and, in the case of tied cases, average them and then round them off.

A principal weakness of percentiles is that they assume equal distance between score units. However, in the normal curve the scores are clustered around the middle, and, consequently, a small change in scores results in a rather large change in percentile points. Likewise, a relatively large change in score is

Table 3-3
Simple Calculation of
Percentiles with Ranked Scores

Score	Percentile	Rounded Percentile
20	100	100
16	93.3	93
12	86.6	87
10	79.9	
10	73.2	77
8	66.5	
8	59.8	60
8	53.1	
7	46.4	46
6	39.7	
6	33.0	36
4	26.3	26
2	19.6	
2	12.9	16
1	6.2	6

needed to produce a change in percentile rank at the ends of the scale. To illustrate using the above scores: A change in raw scores from 7 to 8 corresponds to a percentile change of 46 to 60; on the other hand, a change from 16 to 20 in raw scores only changes the percentile 93 to 100. Since percentile scores are ranks and, as illustrated previously, they change at different rates, it is not considered mathematically sound to average percentiles. For these reasons and the fact that extreme scores may be encountered in the future that cannot be placed on the scale, the use of the T-scale or other standard scores is usually preferred over percentiles.

T-scores, percentiles, and other standard score scales represent an invaluable tool for the teacher. Their application for grading purposes will be discussed in Chapter 5. Besides grading, T-scores may be used in the construction of a test battery, in establishing a profile assessing performance in various areas, and for any of the many occasions in which one wants to compare scores from different types of tests.

Calculation of Percentiles from Grouped Scores

Percentiles can be found by grouping the data into a frequency distribution, then computing a cumulative frequency column and interpolating within the step intervals.

The Frequency Distribution

With a large number of scores and especially when the range of scores is large, the organizing of scores from high to low is best done by constructing a frequency distribution using step intervals.

A step interval is merely a small range of scores, such as scores from 96 to 100. In this case the size of the step interval is 5. In other words all students who had scores of 96, 97, 98, 99, or 100 are placed in this interval. The next step interval below this would be from 91 to 95, and the next from 86 to 90, and so on. It can be readily seen that once the scores are placed in a step interval, they lose their individual identities. Consequently, when scores are put in step intervals, they are called grouped data.

The following steps may be used in setting up a frequency distribution:

Step 1: Establish the range of the scores. The range of a set of scores is one plus the difference between the highest score and the lowest score. Example: If the high score is 80 and the low score is 40, the range would be 41. To further illustrate, the following scores represent the push-up scores of sixty college men: 30, 17, 12, 41, 36, 24, 25, 18, 26, 30, 20, 18, 47, 32, 25, 12, 9, 31, 38, 34, 22, 22, 37, 53$_h$,* 26, 20, 6, 16, 29, 42, 13, 27, 35, 5$_l$,* 31, 26, 22, 15, 29, 37, 28, 24, 17, 25, 25, 38, 32, 10, 17, 27, 27, 20, 21, 15, 34, 28, 30, 16, 23, 25. With a high score of 53 and a low score of 5, the range would be $48 + 1 = 49$.

Step 2: Determine the size and number of step intervals. A step interval is one of a number of groups in which scores are tabulated. Generally speaking, we should try to keep the number of such groups between ten and fifteen. If we were to arbitrarily select 4 as the width of our interval, we could divide 4 into the range of 49 and determine that we would have about 12 intervals. Likewise, if we were to arbitrarily decide that we wanted 12 intervals, we could divide 12 into our range of 49 and find that the width of each step interval would be approximately 4.

Step 3: Set up the step intervals. Starting at the bottom, the lowest step interval must include the lower score. Thus, our low score of 5 could be included in an interval of 2-5, 3-6, 4-7, or 5-8; any of these would do. The authors have selected 4-7 for convenience sake. In figuring 4-7 as an interval width of 4, we should keep in mind that it is 4 through 7 which is more indicative of 4 points. The next interval up would be 8-11 and so on until we have encompassed our top score. Although we usually write step intervals using whole numbers, they actually begin at .5 below and extend up to but not including .5 above. Thus our lowest step interval begins at 3.5 and ends at 7.4. Table 3-4 shows a frequency distribution set up with the sixty scores previously listed.

Step 4: Tabulate Raw Scores. After the step intervals have been completed, tally each raw score in the proper interval until all scores have been tallied, and compute the frequency column as shown.

At this point it should be noted that the scores within each interval have lost their specific identities, and therefore, if we need a number to best represent them, we use the midpoint of the interval. For example, in the interval of 24-27, the midpoint would be 25.5. To calculate the midpoint one must remember the actual limits of the interval. In this case the size of the interval is 4 and the lower limit is 23.5. So

Table 3-4
Frequency Distribution

Interval	Tallies	Frequency
52-55	I	1
48-51	0	0
44-47	I	1
40-43	II	2
36-39	THL	5
32-35	THL	5
28-31	THL IIII	9
24-27	THL THL III	13
20-23	THL III	8
16-19	THL II	7
12-15	THL	5
8-11	II	2
4-7	II	2
		N = 60

one-half of 4 is 2, which, when added to 23.5, equals 25.5.

Calculating Percentiles

Percentiles can be found in grouped data by the steps listed. We will calculate the 50th percentile (the median). The median can be found in grouped data by the use of a cumulative frequency column and interpolation within the step interval. The following steps may be used in computing the median from a frequency distribution:

Step 1: Since the median is the midpoint of the scores and we have 60 scores in the familiar push-up example, multiply $.50 \times 60 = 30$ to get the halfway point.

Step 2: Establish a cumulative frequency column by starting at the bottom interval and progressively recording the total number of scores accumulated at each interval level. This is shown in Table 3-5.

Step 3: Identify the interval that contains the thirtieth score. We can quickly see from our cumulative frequency column that the thirtieth score falls within the 24-27 interval.

Step 4: Find the median within the interval.

Table 3-5
Calculation of Percentiles from a Frequency Distribution

Score	f	Cum. f		Sample Computations		(Rounded)
52-55	1	60				
48-51	0	59				
44-47	1	59				
40-43	2	58				
36-39	5	56	P_{90}	90% of 60 = 54	$35.5 + 3/5 \times 4 = 37.90$	(38)
32-35	5	51	P_{80}	80% of 60 = 48	$31.5 + 2/5 \times 4 = 33.10$	(33)
28-31	9	46	$P_{75}(Q_3)$	75% of 60 = 45	$27.5 + 8/9 \times 4 = 31.06$	(31)
24-27	13	37	P_{50} (MDN)	50% of 60 = 30	$23.5 + 6/13 \times 4 = 25.35$	(25)
20-23	8	24	P_{30}	30% of 60 = 18	$19.5 + 2/8 \times 4 = 20.50$	(21)
16-19	7	16	$P_{25}(Q_1)$	25% of 60 = 15	$15.5 + 6/7 \times 4 = 18.93$	(19)
12-15	5	9	P_{10}	10% of 60 = 6	$11.5 + 2/5 \times 4 = 13.10$	(13)
8-11	2	4				
4-7	2	2				
	N = 60					

Since the actual lower limit of the 24-27 interval is 23.5 and only 6 scores are needed out of the 13 scores appearing in that interval, we compute the following formula:

$$\text{Median} = \text{ILL} + \frac{\text{SN}}{\text{IF}} \times i$$

Key
ILL—*Interval Lower Limit*
SN—*Scores Needed*
IF—*Interval Frequency*
i —*Interval Width*

$$\text{MDN.} = 23.5 + \frac{6}{13} \times 4$$
$$\text{MDN.} = 23.5 + 1.85$$
$$\text{MDN.} = 25.35$$

Any percentile can be calculated in the same manner. In Table 3-5 the computation of certain percentile points are shown.

One merely counts up the cumulative frequency column to find the interval which contains the desired score. Then the proportion of the scores that is needed is computed and that value is added to the lower limit of the interval.

The 25th percentile is called the first quartile (Q^1) and P^{75} is the third quartile (Q^3). Quartiles are sometimes used as cutoff points for screening purposes.

Other Standard Scores

There are several scales available for placing test scores on a common table. Appendix E contains further discussion of standard scores in regard to the Hull Scale and Z scores.

Correlation

Correlation refers to the relationship of one variable to another. Physical educators and coaches frequently would like to know the relationships between various abilities and peformances. For example, a coach may want to know if there is any relationship between increases in leg strength and speed of a lineman's charge. The physical educator may wish to know the relationship between performance in a distance run and performance on a step test. Moreover, an understanding of correlation is necessary in determining validity, reliability, and objectivity as steps in test construction and in evaluating tests already published.

The coefficient of correlation (r) is most commonly used in determining relationships numerically. This method is especially useful when the number of paired scores is large (twenty-five or more). When the number of paired scores is small (twenty-five or less), the rank-difference or *rho* (ρ) method is frequently used. In either case, the relationship may vary between $+1$ and -1, or from a perfect positive relationship to a perfect negative relationship. If we were to test a group of men on strength and power and found that the strongest men were nearly always best in power performance, we could expect a high positive correlation. However, if as strength increased, power tended to decrease, we could expect a high negative correlation. If we tried to correlate two sets of data that were totally unrelated, we would get a coefficient of 0. In actual practice, we seldom get $+1$, -1, or 0 coefficients because of the many uncontrolled variables which influence the two variables that are being correlated. The problem of interpreting coefficients of correlation, as to what is high, low, and average, is sometimes difficult. The number of subjects involved directly determines how high the coefficient must be to reach statistical significance. But this in itself is misleading because a relatively *low* correlation can be statistically significant if the number of subjects is large.

Probably one of the most important factors regarding the size of the coefficient has to do with the purpose for which the correlation is computed. For example, a coefficient of correlation of .65 may be considered quite high when a specific measurement such as leg strength is correlated with performance in a particular sport. On the other hand, a coefficient of .65 is quite low when the correlation is between the scores made on the odd and even numbered questions on a written examination. Certain arbitrary rankings as to what correlations are considered to be high, average, and low are sometimes given. The following scale is an example of interpretation of coefficients of correlation in general terms.

$r = .00$ (no relationship)
$r = \pm.01$ to $\pm.20$ (low relationship)
$r = \pm.20$ to $\pm.50$ (slight to fair relationship)
$r = \pm.50$ to $\pm.70$ (substantial relationship)
$r = \pm.70$ to $\pm.99$ (high relationship)
$r = \pm1.00$ (perfect relationship)

Such rankings are, of course, merely rough guides and, as was stated above, their worth is dependent upon the purposes for which the computation was done. For instance, for demonstrating reliability of a test, a coefficient of correlation of at least .80 is desired, and should preferably be higher. Methods of establishing test reliability will be discussed in Chapters 4 and 21.

In essence, if the purpose is to predict future performance of an individual, then the coefficient of correlation must be much higher than if the purpose is to just establish a relationship between two traits. However, this leads to another misconception concerning the characteristics of correlation. The misconception, which can be rather dangerous, is to assume that a correlation shows causation. Suppose that a rather high correlation is found between physical fitness and scholastic achievement. The conclusion might erroneously be made that academic achievement results from being physically fit. Although there may be some causation present, the correlation itself does not support this assumption. In any correlation there may be several other factors which are actually responsible for both performances. In the above example a more absurd interpretation would be that gains in scholastic achievement would result in improved physical fitness.

One of several ways of intepreting coefficients of correlation is by means of the *coefficient of determination* (4). In this method one merely squares the r and the resulting r^2 represents the proportion of variance in one variable that can be accounted for by the other variable. To illustrate, suppose that the coefficient of correlation between the X variable, speed, as measured by a sprint, and the Y variable, agility, as measured by a shuttle run, was $r = .80$. Then $r^2 = .64$. This is interpreted as indicating that 64 percent of the variance in the agility score was accounted for by the variability in the speed score. This method points out rather strongly that a high coefficient of correlation is needed to reveal a marked degree of association. An r of .30 indicates only 9 percent association, for example, and an r of .40 only 16 percent. On the other hand, when the r is very high, the degree of association is also high. To illustrate, an r of .97 indicates that 94 percent of the variability of one variable is accounted for by the variance in the other variable.

One further precaution should be mentioned regarding correlation. One should not interpret a coefficient of correlation as a percentage of perfect relationship. This is often done, probably because coefficients of correlation are usually reported in hundredths. In any event, this results in gross misunderstanding. While it is beyond the scope of this book to go into a discussion of the meaning of statistical significance, it should be emphasized that in relation to the coefficient of determination, an r of .50 is not half as large as an r of 1.00 and an r of .75 is not merely three times as large as a correlation coefficient of .25. By using the coefficient of determination (r^2), it can be seen that an r of 1.00 is four times as strong as a correlation of $r = .50$ and that an r of .75 is nine times as large as an r of .25.

Rank-Difference Method of Correlation. The rank-difference method is a convenient tool for teachers who want to obtain a quick measure of relationship between two sets of scores involving a small number of subjects. This method uses the rank that each student attains on each test; then the relationship is established in terms of the degree of difference between rankings. The symbol for this coefficient is the Greek *rho* (ρ), and the formula is

$$\rho = 1 - \frac{6 \, \Sigma \, D^2}{N(N^2 - 1)}$$

The steps involved in computing the correlation coefficient by this method will be illustrated by the data presented in Table 3-6. In this example, we have devised a skill test in badminton to establish the validity (the degree to which the test measures what it is supposed to measure) of our test. Our students have completed a round-robin tournament in badminton and have been ranked according to their order of finish in the tournament. We reason that if our test is valid, those persons who were most successful in the tournament should score the highest on the skill test, and the losers the lowest. We administer our test and rank the students from first to last. For purposes of illustration, only fifteen subjects are used.

Step 1: Rank the scores on both tests. Notice that in the rankings for the skill test there are two ranks of 3.5, and there are three persons with a rank of 10. This is due to duplicate scores. In the first instance two students scored the same on the skill test and, therefore, deserved the same rank. However, they take up two positions, which are 3 and 4. An average is computed ($3 + 4 = 7 \div 2 = 3.5$), and both students are given the rank of 3.5. Four places have been accounted for now, so the next rank is 5.

Table 3-6
Rank-Difference Method of Correlation

Subject	Skill Test Score	Tournament Games Won	Rank in Skill Test	Rank in Tournament	D	D²
1	20	14	1	1	0	0
2	16	12	2	3	1	1
3	12	13	3.5	2	1.5	2.25
4	12	10	3.5	5	1.5	2.25
5	10	11	5	4	1	1
6	9	6	6	9	3	9
7	8	9	7	6	1	1
8	7	8	8	7	1	1
9	6	5	10	10	0	0
10	6	7	10	8	2	4
11	6	4	10	11	1	1
12	5	0	12	15	3	9
13	4	2	13	13	0	0
14	3	3	14	12	2	4
15	2	1	15	14	1	1

N = 15

36.50

$$\rho = 1 - \frac{6\Sigma D^2}{N(N^2-1)}$$

$$= 1 - \frac{6\,(36.50)}{15\,(15^2-1)} = 1 - \frac{219}{(15)\,(224)} = 1 - \frac{219}{3360} =$$

$$1 - .07 =$$

$$\rho = .93$$

Similarly, three students had identical scores which took up positions 9, 10, and 11. An average is again computed (9+10+11= 30÷3=10), and the rank of 10 is assigned to each. The next rank after these three is 12. The last rank should equal N.

Step 2: Determine the differences between the rankings on the two tests and enter in column D. Since these differences are to be squared, the plus or minus is not important.

Step 3: Square each number in the difference (D) column and total these values (ΣD²).

Step 4: Find the coefficient of correlation by substituting the obtained values into the formula.

In the hypothetical example above we found a very high degree of validity for this skill test in badminton. It should be pointed out that the relationship could also have been established by use of the product-moment method. The rank-difference method is quick and simple, but it becomes impractical with a large number of scores.

Product-Moment Method of Correlation with Ungrouped Data. In Table 3-7 the push-up scores (X) and fitness index scores (Y) from the Harvard Step Test are shown for fifteen students. The following steps describe the procedures for determining the relationship between push-up performance and cardiovascular fitness by the product-moment method of correlation. The symbol for the product-moment coefficient of correlation is r.

Step 1: Compute the mean for each set of scores. The mean for push-ups $(\overline{X})$ is found to be 22 and for the step test scores $(\overline{Y})$, 73.

Step 2: Subtract each score in column X from the mean $(\overline{X})$ and enter in column x. Similarly, subtract the scores in column Y from $\overline{Y}$ to form column y.

Step 3: Square each value in column x and y and enter as x^2 and y^2 respectively. Obtain the sum for each column ($\Sigma x^2 = 734$, $\Sigma y^2 = 1714$).

Step 4: Multiply x and y values. The xy column represents the product-moment

Table 3-7
Calculation of the Coefficient of Correlation for Ungrouped Scores
by the Product-Moment Method

Student	Push-up X	Step Test Y	x	y	x^2	y^2	xy (+)	xy (-)
1	28	84	6	11	36	121	66	
2	23	74	1	1	1	1	1	
3	13	57	-9	-16	81	256	144	
4	16	63	-6	-10	36	100	60	
5	17	80	-5	7	25	49		-35
6	24	72	2	-1	4	1		-2
7	25	70	3	-3	9	9		-9
8	26	65	4	-8	16	64		-32
9	10	59	-12	-14	144	196	168	
10	33	91	11	18	121	324	198	
11	25	73	3	0	9	0		
12	20	60	-2	-13	4	169	26	
13	18	73	-4	0	16	0		
14	16	83	-6	10	36	100		-60
15	36	91	14	18	196	324	252	
N=15	ΣX=330	ΣY=1095			Σx^2=734	Σy^2=1714	915	-138
	$\overline{X}$= 22	$\overline{Y}$= 73					Σxy=777	

$$r = \frac{\Sigma xy}{\sqrt{(\Sigma x^2)(\Sigma y^2)}} = \frac{777}{\sqrt{(734)(1714)}} = \frac{777}{\sqrt{1,258,076}} = \frac{777}{1122} = .69$$

values. These indicate the distance that each student lies in relation to the mean of each set of scores. Note that there is a column for positive cross-products and a column for negative values. Find the algebraic sum of these two columns ($\Sigma xy = 777$). If the column of negative cross-products were higher, it would indicate a negative correlation.

Step 5: Substitute the obtained values into the formula, and determine the coefficient of correlation ($r = .69$).

Another method may be used with ungrouped data which is actually less laborious, but it utilizes a more imposing looking formula. This method is to assume the means to be 0 and to use the raw scores and then a correction

factor. It uses the same principle as was outlined in calculating standard deviation from ungrouped data. The formula is

$$r = \frac{N(\Sigma XY) - (\Sigma X)(\Sigma Y)}{\sqrt{N(\Sigma X^2) - (\Sigma X)^2}\sqrt{N(\Sigma Y^2) - (\Sigma Y)^2}}$$

As illustrated, Table 3-8 shows the body weights and the scores (in seconds) for the flexed-arm hang test for ten girls, twelve years of age. In calculating the coefficient of correlation by this method, each score is squared, the cross-products of the X and Y scores are computed, and the resulting totals of each column are inserted into the formula.

In this case a high negative correlation is obtained. This indicated that the heavier girls

Table 3-8
Calculation of Coefficient of Correlation for Ungrouped Scores
Using Deviations Taken from Zero (Computer Method)

Student	Weight X	F.A.H. Y	X^2	Y^2	XY
A	80	35	6400	1225	2800
B	117	10	13689	100	1170
C	96	19	9216	361	1824
D	85	22	7225	484	1870
E	92	25	8464	625	2300
F	100	15	10000	225	1500
G	130	5	16900	25	650
H	125	8	15625	64	1000
I	93	15	8649	225	1395
J	88	20	7744	400	1760

N = 10 $\Sigma X = 1006$ $\Sigma Y = 174$ $\Sigma X^2 = 103,912$ $\Sigma Y^2 = 3734$ $\Sigma XY = 16,269$

$(\Sigma X)^2 = 1,012,036$ $(\Sigma Y)^2 = 30,276$

$$r = \frac{N(\Sigma XY) - (\Sigma X)(\Sigma Y)}{\sqrt{N(\Sigma X^2) - (\Sigma X)^2}\sqrt{N(\Sigma Y^2) - (\Sigma Y)^2}} \quad r = \frac{10(16269) - (1006)(174)}{\sqrt{10(103,912) - (1006)^2}\sqrt{10(3734) - (174)^2}}$$

$$r = \frac{162,690 - 175,044}{\sqrt{27,084}\sqrt{7064}} = \frac{-12,354}{13,860} = -.89$$

were not able to hang as long on the bar as the lighter girls. In other words, the greater the body weight, the poorer the performance on this test.

Comparison of Groups by Analysis of Variance

There may be times when the physical educator or coach would like to compare methods of training or teaching, or different groups of performers, or to determine whether significant improvement resulted from a particular training program, etc. In order to do this, the significance of the observed difference must be determined. The word *significance* is of critical importance in such comparisons because it refers to the fact that we are dealing with samples rather than with the entire population. Consequently, we must determine whether an observed difference is attributed to chance error of sampling or is in fact a real (significant) difference.

It should be understood that successive samples from a population would not be expected to have identical means. In fact, if 1000 samples were drawn, for example, their means would approximate a normal curve. Differences between sample means also approximate a normal distribution, and a test of the significance of the difference between means must be applied.

The Null Hypothesis. The null hypothesis is commonly used for statistically testing the significance of the difference between means. The null hypothesis states that there is no real difference between means, that any observed difference is due to sampling error. Therefore, any difference between means must be of a certain magnitude in order to reject the null hypothesis and conclude that the difference is real. If the difference isn't large enough, the investigator fails to reject the null hypothesis and must conclude that the difference was due to sampling error.

Analysis of Variance and the F Test. In testing the null hypothesis for the difference between sample means, the F test may be used to determine the significance of the difference. It should be pointed out that a t test may also be employed for this purpose when there are just two groups to be compared. In fact, when there are just two groups, F is equal to t^2.

The authors have elected to present only the F test by analysis of variance in this section. This decision was determined in part by con-

siderations of space and time. It was also based on the fact that analysis of variance is more prevalent in the research literature, and thus it may be of more practical value to the student in reading and understanding research studies. Moreover, analysis of variance is more versatile in that it can be employed when there are more than two groups to be compared (whereas the t test cannot); it can be utilized when there is more than one variable to be analyzed; and the procedures are used in computing intraclass reliability coefficients, which will be described later in the chapter. However, for the interested student, two simple t tests have been included in Appendix D.

Analysis of Variance for Comparing Independent Samples. There are many occasions where the investigator wishes to compare two groups that represent independent samples. A physical educator may want to compare running times of two groups who had trained by different methods, or perhaps compare the physical fitness scores of students of whom one group had a required physical education program and another group had not, or possibly compare social adjustment inventory scores of boys against the scores of girls. In each comparison, the samples are drawn from independent populations; hence the means are considered to be uncorrelated means.

To illustrate the steps involved in a comparison of independent samples, let us suppose that in order to establish evidence of validity for a basketball skills test we constructed, we administered the test to two groups of players. One sample represented varsity players, the other sample intramural players. We will assume that our sampling procedures were sound.

The mean of the varsity players is 9 and the mean of the intramural players is 2.5. We wish to determine whether this difference in mean test performance is significant or whether it is attributable to sampling error.

The reader is already acquainted with the bulk of the computations since some of the procedures are identical to the computer method for correlation and standard deviation. The steps are illustrated in Table 3-9.

Step 1: Sum the raw scores for each group (ΣX). Obviously, in this example, it has already been done since we had to compute ΣX in order to calculate the means that were given above.

Step 2: Add the two sums together to get a Grand ΣX.

Table 3-9
Analysis of Variance for Independent Groups

Group I			Group II		
Varsity Basketball Players			Intramural Basketball Players		

X	X^2		X	X^2	
10	100		3	9	
16	256		6	36	
5	25		2	4	
6	36		3	9	
12	144		7	49	
8	64	$\overline{X}_1 = \dfrac{\Sigma X_1}{n_1} = \dfrac{72}{8} = 9$	6	36	$\overline{X}_2 = \dfrac{\Sigma X_2}{n_2} = \dfrac{50}{10} = 5$
9	81		10	100	
6	36		1	1	
			8	64	
			4	16	

Step 1: $\Sigma X = 72$ $\Sigma X^2 = 742$

Step 1: $\Sigma X = 50$ $\Sigma X^2 = 324$

Step 2: Grand $\Sigma X = 72 + 50 = 122$

Step 3: Grand $\Sigma X^2 = 742 + 324 = 1066$

Step 4: $SS_T = \text{Grand } \Sigma X^2 - \dfrac{(\text{Grand } \Sigma X)^2}{\text{Total N}} = 1066 = -\dfrac{(122)^2}{18} = 1066 - 826.9 = 239.1$

Step 5: $SS_B = \dfrac{(\Sigma X_1)^2}{n_1} + \dfrac{(\Sigma X_2)^2}{n_2} - C = \dfrac{(72)^2}{8} + \dfrac{(50)^2}{10} - 826.9 = 898 - 826.9 = 71.1$

Step 6: $SS_W = SS_T = SS_B = 239.1 - 71.1 = 168$

Step 7: $MS_B = \dfrac{SS_B}{k\text{-}1} = \dfrac{71.1}{2\text{-}1} = 71.1$

Step 8: MS_W $\dfrac{SS_W}{N-k} = \dfrac{168}{18-2} = 10.5$

Step 9: $F = \dfrac{MS_B}{MS_W} = \dfrac{71.1}{10.5} = 6.77$

Step 3: Square each raw score and compute a Grand ΣX^2.

Step 4: Compute the total sum of squares (SS_T) by the formula

$$SS_T = \text{Grand } \Sigma X^2 - \dfrac{(\text{Grand } \Sigma X)^2}{\text{Total N}}$$

Note: The last half of the equation represents the correction (C) factor which is necessary because we are using the raw scores themselves rather than deviations of the scores from the mean. The formula could be written:

$$SS_T = \text{Grand } \Sigma X^2 - C$$

We will now separate the total sum of squares into two parts: the between-group sum of squares and the within-group sum of squares.

Step 5: The between sum of squares is computed by the following procedure:

$$SS_B = \dfrac{(\Sigma X_1)^2}{n_1} + \dfrac{(\Sigma X_2)^2}{n_2} - C$$

Step 6: The within sum of squares is obtained by simply subtracting the between sum of squares from the total sum of squares:

$$SS_W = SS_T - SS_B$$

Step 7: The variance, or mean square (MS), for the between groups is found by dividing the SS_B by the degrees of freedom for groups, which is the number of groups minus 1. The symbol for groups is usually given as *k*, so we will express the computation as

$$MS_B = \frac{SS_B}{k-1}$$

If, for example, we have four groups, the degrees of freedom would be $k-1 = 4-1 = 3$.

Step 8: Next, the variance for the within-group component (MS_W) is determined by dividing the sum of squares for within groups by its degrees of freedom, which is the total number of subjects (N) minus the number of groups (k):

$$MS_W = \frac{SS_W}{N-k}$$

Step 9: The last computational step in analysis of variance is to compute the *F* ratio, which is the ratio between the two mean squares:

$$F = \frac{MS_B}{MS_W}$$

Step 10: In order to determine whether the *F* ratio is significant or, in other words, whether there is a real difference between the varsity and intramural players, we must consult Table C-1 in Appendix C. Let us assume that we have set the level of significance at the .05 level (this will be explained more fully later). The criterion value which is used to determine whether the *F* is significant is found by locating the *column* in the table with the degrees of freedom (*df*) of the between-groups MS. The table heading for the columns is "Numerator Degrees of Freedom." In this problem, the *df* for between

groups is k-1, i.e., 2-1=1. Next, we find the *row* that corresponds to the within-groups *df*, which is N-k (18-2). The rows are titled "Denominator Degrees of Freedom" in the table. The intersection of the appropriate column and row for 1 and 16 *df* is 4.49 for the .05 level of probability. Our *F* of 6.77 exceeds the value necessary to reject the null hypothesis at the .05 level of significance, and we can therefore conclude that there is a significant difference between the varsity players and the intramural players on the performance test.

In research publications, the summary of the analysis of variance is usually shown by a table similar to Table 3-10.

F Distribution and Tests of Significance. It is beyond the scope of this book to provide a comprehensive explanation of the *F* distribution and hypothesis testing. As a general statement it can be asserted that the probability of rejecting the null hypothesis is heavily dependent upon variability within samples and sample size.

It is self-evident from the *F* ratio that if there is a large within-groups variance (MS_W) in relation to the between-groups variance (MS_B) the size of the *F* will be decreased. This situation is much more likely to occur with small samples than with large samples since the within variance is calculated by dividing the within sum of squares by (N-k) *df*. Consequently, a larger denominator would reduce the variance, provided of course that the within sum of squares was not proportionately larger. However, the variability within groups is also influenced by sample size insofar as larger samples tend to more closely approximate the population, which in turn reduces the size of the variance. Another term often used for within variance is *error*.

Table 3-10
Summary of Analysis of Variance for Test Performance of Varsity and Intramural Basketball Players

Source of Variation	Sum of Squares	Degrees of Freedom	Mean Square	F
Between	71.1	1	71.1	6.77*
Within	168.0	16	10.5	
Total	239.1	17		

*Significant at the .05 level.

An examination of the F tables in Appendix C reveals that the values needed for significance are greater with small samples (as reflected by $N-k$) than for larger samples. The reader is referred to practically any basic statistics textbook for a discussion of the Type I and Type II errors with regard to hypothesis testing. A Type I error with the null hypothesis is when a hypothesis is rejected when it is true, in other words, when one concludes that there is a difference between two samples when actually there is none. The Type II error is when a hypothesis is accepted when it should be rejected.

A researcher can reduce the probability of committing the Type I error by establishing a lower level of significance. For example, significance at the .10 level (alpha level) means that you are willing to be wrong (i.e., conclude that there is a difference when the difference is actually due to chance or sampling error) 10 times out of 100. The researcher could reduce the probability of making a Type I error by setting the alpha level at the .05 level, which means an incorrect decision 5 times out of 100, or lower yet at the .01 level, which reduces the possibility of incorrect decision to 1 out of 100.

The alpha level should be set at the onset of a study. The .05 and .01 alpha levels are the two most frequently used in research. The Type I error is considered more serious than the Type II. The probability of making the Type II error increases of course as the probability of making the Type I error is reduced. One of the most effective ways to reduce the Type II error is to secure larger samples. As was stated earlier, a larger sample often automatically reduces the within variance because it tends to more closely approximate the population.

Perhaps the essence of the preceding discussion can be conveyed by a simple example. If a teacher were to adopt a new method of teaching, he or she would want to be reasonably sure that the method was indeed superior to the old method. Consequently, the teacher would not be nearly as willing to change methodology as the result of a study in which an observed difference favoring the new method was found on the basis of a very small number of subjects as he or she would when the same difference was evidenced by a comparison involving large samples. Obviously, the large sample would more likely represent the population from which it was drawn than the small sample.

The F tables in Appendix C are based on that premise, which is why a higher F is needed with small samples than large. The tables are so constructed in order to reduce the probability of committing the Type I error. The F values needed for significance are in turn larger for the .05 level of significance than for the .10 alpha level, and the F value needed for the .01 level is greater still.

Analysis of Variance for Comparing Correlated (Paired) Samples. For illustrative purposes, let us assume that we wish to determine whether a particular conditioning exercise program is effective in producing significant improvement in physical fitness. A fitness test was administered to a group of 10 students at the beginning of a semester and again at the end of the semester after the students had participated in the exercise program. The average improvement in the physical fitness test was 2. Note that we are using small numbers simply for ease of presentation. In actual practice, if the difference was very small, it would be most unlikely that the investigator would bother to test it for significance. Furthermore, we are only using 10 subjects; obviously, in a real situation we would want to use an adequate number of subjects for increased confidence in any inferences that might be drawn from the results.

The initial and final fitness test scores for the 10 subjects are shown in Table 3-11.

This comparison requires a slightly different procedure than the previous one, which involved two independent groups. Although this study also seeks to test the significance of the difference between two sets of scores, the major difference is that the same people are being tested twice. Therefore, the two scores are correlated because we would expect each subject's final score to be related to his or her initial score regardless of treatment. (The same relationship would be found in a study using matched groups.) This poses a problem in that a considerable amount of the within (error) sum of squares can be attributed to the pairing of scores because of the "carryover" of differences within the groups from the initial to the final test. Hence, this presents a new source of variation that has to be computed.

The steps in the analysis of variance for correlated (or repeated) measures are as follows:

Step 1: Obtain the ΣX and the ΣX^2 and compute the total sum of squares (SS_T) exactly as done in Table 3-9.

Table 3-11
Analysis of Variance for Correlated Groups (Repeated Measures)

Initial Test	Final Test	(Σ rows)	(Σ rows)^2
5	6	11	121
3	5	8	64
4	9	13	169
8	10	18	324
1	4	5	25
6	5	11	121
2 $\quad \bar{X} = 4.0$	6 $\quad \bar{X} = 6.0$	8	64
5	7	12	144
2	3	5	25
4	5	9	81
$\Sigma X = 40$	$\Sigma X = 60$	Grand $\Sigma X = 100$	(Σ rows)$^2 = 1138$

$$\Sigma X^2 = (5^2 + 3^2 + 4^2 + \ldots + 5^2) = 602$$

Step 1: $SS_T = \Sigma X^2 - C = 602 - \dfrac{(100)^2}{20} = 602 - 500 = 102$

Step 2: $SS_B = \dfrac{(\Sigma X)^2}{n_1} + \dfrac{(\Sigma X_2)^2}{n_2} - C = \dfrac{(40)^2}{10} + \dfrac{(60)^2}{10} - 500 = 520 - 500 = 20$

Step 3: $SS_R = \dfrac{(X_{11} + X_{12})^2 + (X_{21} + X_{22})^2 + \ldots + (X_{n1} + X_{n2})^2}{\text{(Number or measures)}} - C$

$$= \dfrac{(5+6)^2 + (3+5)^2 + \ldots + (4+5)^2}{2} - 500 = 569 - 500 = 69$$

Step 4: $SS_E = SS_T - SS_B - SS_R = 102 - 20 - 69 = 13$

Step 5: $MS_B = \dfrac{SS_B}{k-1} = \dfrac{20}{1} = 20$

Step 6: $MS_R = \dfrac{SS_R}{R-1} = \dfrac{69}{9} = 7.67$

Step 7: $MS_E = \dfrac{SS_E}{(k-1)(R-1)} = \dfrac{13}{(1)(9)} = 1.44$

Step 8: $F = \dfrac{MS_B}{MS_E} = \dfrac{20}{1.44} = 13.89$

Step 2: Compute between-groups sum of squares (SS_B) in the same manner as in the previous example.

Step 3: Compute the sum of squares due to the pairing effect of the test-retest. This is done by adding the initial and final test scores for each subject, squaring the sums, and then adding all the squared sums for the 10 subjects.

The sum of the rows squared is divided by 2 since there are 2 scores making up each sum. The usual correction factor (C) is then subtracted. We will label the resulting sum of squares for subjects or rows, SS_R.

$$SS_R = \frac{(X_{11}+X_{12})^2+(X_{21}+X_{22})^2+\ldots+(X_{n1}+X_{n2})^2}{\text{(Number of measures in each row)}}$$

$$-\frac{(\text{Grand } \Sigma X)^2}{N}$$

Step 4: The remaining sum of squares constitutes the error sum of squares (SS_E) which is often referred to as *residual* or *interaction*.

$$SS_E = SS_T - SS_B - SS_R$$

Step 5: Compute the variance for between groups as in Table 3-9.

$$MS_B = \frac{SS_B}{k-1}$$

Step 6: The variance, or mean square, for subjects is computed by dividing the SS_R by its degrees of freedom, which is one less than the number of subjects, or rows.

$$MS_R = \frac{SS_R}{R-1}$$

Step 7: The error (or residual or interaction) MS is obtained by dividing the SS_E by $(k-1)$ $(R-1)$ degrees of freedom.

$$MS_E = \frac{SS_E}{(k-1)(R-1)}$$

Step 8: Compute the F ratio by the formula

$$F = \frac{MS_B}{MS_E}$$

Step 9: Consult Table C-2 in Appendix C for appropriate degrees of freedom for numerator and denominator—in this case, 1 and 9 *df.* The F required at the .01 alpha level at the start of the experiment is set at 10.56. Since our F ratio surpassed this, we can reject the null hypothesis at the .01 level and conclude that significant improvement in physical fitness was attained through the conditioning exercise program.

The summary of the analysis of variance for the fitness gains is shown in Table 3-12.

Note: If the researcher had computed the analysis of variance for independent groups, the F would not have been significant. (For practice, the reader is encouraged to compute the F by the independent group method.) If this had been done, the researcher would have committed a Type II error.

Other Forms of Analysis of Variance. We have presented analysis of variance in its simplest form. There are a number of more complex designs which are used to detect different sources of variation. We have used examples with only two groups (or sets of scores). Analysis of variance can be performed with any number of groups. In fact, the main advantage of analysis of variance over the *t* test is that the *t* test can not be used when more than two means are to be compared, because the means are no longer independent and the probability of committing the Type I error is increased.

Table 3-12
Summary of Analysis of Variance for Improvements in
Physical Fitness as a Result of a Conditioning Program

Source of Variation	Sum of Squares	Degrees of Freedom	Mean Square	F
Subjects (rows)	69	9	7.67	
Between groups	20	1	20.00	13.89*
Error	13	9	1.44	
Total	102	19		

*Significant at the .01 level.

When an analysis of variance is performed with three or more groups, the significant *F* test does not indicate where the differences are but only that there are differences among the groups. Consequently, one must employ further analysis such as orthogonal comparisons or a multiple-range test such as the Scheffe, the Tukey hsd, the Duncan Multiple Range, or Newman-Keuls, etc. The reader is referred to Clarke and Clarke (2) or Morehouse and Stull (5) for discussion of the multiple-range tests. Steel and Torrie (9) cover orthogonal comparisons.

When two or more variables are to be compared, two-way analysis of variance procedures allow for comparisons of the main effects plus the interaction of variables which enable the investigator to determine the effects of one variable in the presence of another.

Covariance is an extension of analysis of variance which permits a kind of statistical matching of groups by adjusting the final means for any differences in initial means. In all of the analysis of variance designs the basic model is the same, which is the division or partitioning of the total variation in scores into different components—or sources of variation—between and within groups.

Intraclass Correlation Coefficient by Analysis of Variance

The concept of reliability is discussed in Chapter 4. It refers to the repeatability of performance. Obviously, a test that would not yield consistent results if the same individuals were to take it more than once would be of little value. Traditionally, product-moment correlation has been employed to estimate the reliability of a test by correlating the scores of a group of subjects on one day (or test administration) with the same subjects' scores on another day (or trial).

Safrit (6) provides a comprehensive discussion of the limitations of the product-moment correlation coefficient for this purpose. Baumgartner and Jackson (1) also discuss and document reasons for the impropriety of the product-moment correlation for test reliability and objectivity. Three main weaknesses are cited:
1. The product-moment correlation is a bivariate statistic, whereas reliability and objectivity estimates are univariate. In other words, product-moment correlation is designed to establish the relationship between two variables such as chinning performance and body weight. Reliability, on the other

hand, deals with only one variable, and concerns the consistency of subjects on repeated measures of the same test. Similarly, objectivity involves one test (or variable) scored by two or more testers; thus it too is a univariate statistic.
2. Product-moment correlation is limited to just two scores. Frequently, more than two trials are given, and the tester is interested in obtaining the reliability of multiple trials or the objectivity of a test with more than two judges. For example, if a test calls for three trials, the product-moment method dictates that either the tester give three more trials with the average of each set used for the correlation, or perhaps that one additional trial be given and the first two trials then correlated with the last two trials. In either case, one or more extra trials must be given just for reliability purposes.
3. The product-moment correlation does not permit as thorough an examination of the different sources of variability on multiple trials as does the intraclass correlation coefficient by analysis of variance. As an example, if you correlate the average of the first three trials with the average of the last three trials, you would not have taken into consideration the trial-to-trial variation within each set of trials.

Steps in Computing Intraclass Correlation by Analysis of Variance. The symbol *R* will be used for the intraclass correlation coefficient. The reader will quickly note that the steps in computing *R* are nearly identical to the analysis of variance calculations previously covered.

There are a number of different statistical designs that can be employed to analyze different sources of variance. As with practically all statistical techniques, there are differences of opinion as to the relative merits of each design. The reader is again referred to Safrit (6) for a more comprehensive discussion and pertinent references.

We will present only one design that we believe will suffice for the majority of test situations in which the tester wishes to estimate the reliability of a test (or objectivity of judges). We will use an example situation in which the tester seeks to determine the reliability of four trials on a vertical jump test for girls. We will only use 5 subjects for simplicity of presentation. The steps are illustrated in Table 3-13. Steps 1 through 7 are the same as analysis of variance for paired measures presented in Table 3-11.

Table 3-13
Intraclass Correlation for the Reliability
of Four Trials on the Vertical Jump

Subject	Trial 1	Trial 2	Trial 3	Trial 4		(Σ Rows)	(Σ Rows)^2
A	8	9	11	10		38	1444
B	8	7	6	5		26	676
C	12	15	17	19		63	3969
D	9	13	12	15		49	2401
E	12	10	10	8		40	1600
ΣX	49	54	56	57	(Grand ΣX)	216	10090

$$\Sigma X^2 = (8^2 + 8^2 + 12^2 + \ldots + 8^2) = 2586$$

Step 1: $SS_T = 2586 - \dfrac{(216)^2}{20} = 2586 - 2332.8 = 253.2$

Step 2: $SS_B \text{ (trials)} = \dfrac{(49)^2 + (54)^2 + (56)^2 + (57)^2}{5} - 2332.8 = 7.6$

Step 3: $SS_R \text{ (subjects)} = \dfrac{10090}{4} - 2332.8 = 2522.5 - 2332.8 = 189.7$

Step 4: $SS_E \text{ (interaction)} = 253.2 - 7.6 - 189.7 = 55.9$

Step 5: $MS_B \text{ (trials)} = \dfrac{SS_B}{k-1} = \dfrac{7.6}{4-1} = 2.53$

Step 6: $MS_R \text{ (subjects)} = \dfrac{SS_R}{R-1} = \dfrac{189.7}{5-1} = 47.43$

Step 7: $MS_E \text{ (interaction)} = \dfrac{SS_E}{(k-1)(R-1)} = \dfrac{55.9}{(3)(4)} = 4.66$

Step 8: $\text{(trials)} = \dfrac{MS_B}{MS_E} = \dfrac{2.53}{4.66} = .54$

Step 9: $R = \dfrac{MS \text{ (subjects)} - MS \text{ (error)}}{MS \text{ (subjects)}}$

$MS \text{ (subjects)} = 47.43 \quad MS \text{ (error)} = \dfrac{SS_{trials} + SS_{interaction}}{df_{trials} + df_{interaction}} = \dfrac{7.6 + 55.9}{3 + 12} = 4.23$

$R = \dfrac{47.43 - 4.23}{47.43} = .91$

Step 1: Compute the total SS.

Step 2: Compute SS for trials (columns), which we have referred to as between groups in previous examples.

Step 3: Compute sum of squares for subjects (rows).

Step 4: Compute SS for interaction (designated as SS_E in Table 3-11).

Step 5: Compute mean square for trials (MS_B).

Step 6: Compute mean square for subjects (MS_R).

Step 7: Compute mean square for interaction (MS_E).

Step 8: Compute *F* test for trials (Table 3-14). In this step we are determining whether there

Table 3-14
Summary of Analysis of Variance for Reliability Estimate

Source of Variation	Sum of Squares	Degrees of Freedom	Mean Square	F
Subjects	189.7	4	47.43	
Trials	7.6	3	2.53	
Interaction	55.9	12	4.66	.54*
Total	253.2	19		

*Not significant at the .05 level.

were significant differences among the trials. There are varying opinions as to what should be done if a significant difference is found.

On the one hand, it can be argued that the performance should be consistent from one trial to the next and, if not, any trial-to-trial variance should be attributed to measurement error.

On the other hand, it has been observed on numerous occasions that performances may improve with increased trials due to a learning effect and/or release of inhibitions. Thus, it is contended that this source of variance should be removed from the estimate of reliability.

A decision therefore must be made by the tester whether to include or remove any significant trial-to-trial variability from the error component. Since the authorities are not in agreement on the issue, we do not pretend to have the solution. However, in most instances, it would seem that common sense could dictate the decision or at least offer logical alternatives.

First, it should be of interest to the tester whether or not there are significant differences among trials. If there are not significant differences, then the variance for trials is simply included as part of measurement error.

If a difference is found, the tester should analyze the scores to detect any trend such as a learning phenomenon. If no trend is apparent, that is, if it appears to be a matter of random differences, we would advise that the trial variability not be removed but that it be considered measurement error.

Baumgartner and Jackson (1) advocate a procedure whereby if a significant F for trials is found, the tester discards the trials which are quite dissimilar from the rest of the trials. A new analysis is performed with the remaining trials and another F for trials is computed until no

significant trial differences are found. This procedure seems most appropriate when there is an apparent trend, such as when the subjects show early improvement and then level off. For example, if five trials on a shuttle run agility test yielded a significant F for trials with means of 11.6, 11.2, 10.7, 10.6, and 10.7 seconds, the tester might logically discard the first two trials and compute another analysis with the last three trials. If there were no significant trial differences with the new analysis, the tester would then include whatever variance was found for trials in the error component. Moreover, it would indicate that the subjects should be given a couple practice trials prior to their test trials.

Step 9: Compute R. The formula for R reflects a ratio of true score to observed score variance. Theoretically, any individual's observed score consists of his or her true score plus error score. The sources of error will be discussed in some detail in Chapter 4. We know from our own experiences, however, that we do not perform identically from one time to the next. The fact that we do not score the same on every trial is mostly due to measurement error. So in theory any single score can be considered as representing one's true score plus whatever measurement error exists. Furthermore, the variance of a group of observed scores equals the variance of the true scores plus the variance of the error scores.

Reliability can be defined as the true score variance divided by the observed score variance. In estimating reliability (R) from a set of scores, the formula is

$$R = \frac{MS_{(subjects)} - MS_{(error)}}{MS_{(subjects)}}$$

Note: Since we have suggested that be-tween-trial variance be included as measurement error, either with or without adjustments for trend (Step 8), the mean square for error will consist of the *combined* sum of squares for trials and interaction divided by the degrees of freedom for *both* trials and interaction, i.e.,

$$MS_E = \frac{SS_B + SS_E}{df_B + df_E}$$

In the example in Table 3-14, the *F* for trials was not significant, so the variance for trials was included with the error variance and R was computed to be .91. The same procedures could have been applied for the objectivity of different testers or judges. Instead of trials the columns would be testers or judges.

Problems (Chapter 3)

1. Find the mean, median, and mode for the following scores: 10, 17, 9, 5, 3, 15, 4, 8, 10, 20, 9, 7, 9, 3, 6.
2. Compute the mean and standard deviation for the following sets of scores:
   a. 13, 11, 6, 3, 15, 10, 5, 8, 7, 12, 1, 7, 8, 8, 11, 2, 7, 8, 8, 6, 9, 10, 8, 9, 8.
   b. 9, 12, 15, 11, 10, 7, 20, 15, 11, 12, 15, 20, 10, 8.
   c. 18, 21, 17, 18, 10, 23, 18, 25, 15, 22, 20, 18, 12, 20, 12, 21, 20, 15, 17, 18.
3. Construct T-scales for the three sets of data in problem 2.
4. Rank the following 12 students on right- and left-grip strength and compute a rank-order correlation between the two variables.

Student	Right Grip (kg)	Left Grip (kg)
A	32	30
B	42	36
C	39	33
D	35	37
E	40	37
F	31	27
G	30	35
H	38	36
I	42	38
J	34	32
K	38	39
L	43	40

5. Using the same raw scores as in problem 4, compute the product-moment correlation using the deviation method.
6. Construct a frequency distribution with a step interval of four for the following physical fitness test scores, and calculate the 10th, 30th, 50th, 70th, and 90th percentiles.

60	50	40
64	62	46
55	43	74
42	58	50
80	49	61
54	59	68
58	75	54
53	57	44
48	56	70
71	33	52
55	52	55
46	65	40

7. Determine the correlation between grip strength (X) and a tennis wall volley test (Y) using the computer method.

X	Y	X	Y	X	Y
107	25	153	19	117	15
130	30	110	10	115	23
143	44	148	24	100	26
112	34	121	38	155	31
88	6	98	22	106	16
124	14	141	18	113	19
104	12	165	29	103	38
120	28	110	21	95	13
118	20	104	25	112	28
102	9	122	24	129	22

8. Use analysis of variance to compare the mean performance on a volleyball wall volley test of Group A, which practiced 45 minutes daily, with Group B, which practiced two days per week for 1½ hours each

day. Test the mean difference for significance at the .05 level.

Group A	Group B
30	26
38	27
36	34
29	24
35	23
37	32
28	25
40	20
35	22
32	19
	23

9. Determine whether the following students in a beginning badminton class made significant improvement in a cardiovascular fitness test by analysis of variance with repeated measures.

Student	Pre-test	Post-test
A	60	65
B	43	50
C	65	65
D	64	72
E	76	80
F	81	80
G	59	63
H	69	66
I	72	74
J	58	57

10. Calculate the reliability of three trials on a volleyball skills test using the intraclass correlation technique.

Subject	Trial 1	Trial 2	Trial 3
A	3	6	4
B	6	8	2
C	5	5	3
D	10	9	12
E	4	7	6
F	18	15	16
G	1	7	3

References and Bibliography

1. Baumgartner, Ted A., and Andrew S. Jackson, *Measurement for Evaluation in Physical Education,* Boston: Houghton Mifflin Company, 1975.
2. Clarke, H. Harrison, and David H. Clarke, *Advanced Statistics with Applications to Physical Education,* Englewood Cliffs, N.J.: Prentice-Hall, 1972.
3. Freund, John E., *Modern Elementary Statistics,* 3rd ed., Englewood Cliffs, N.J.: Prentice-Hall, 1967.
4. Garrett, Henry E., *Statistics in Psychology and Education,* 5th ed., New York: Longmans, Green and Company, 1958, p. 179.
5. Morehouse, Chauncey A., and G. Alan Stull, *Statistical Principles and Procedures with Applications for Physical Education,* Philadelphia: Lea & Febiger, 1975.
6. Safrit, Margaret J. (ed.), *Reliability Theory,* Washington, D.C.: American Alliance for Health, Physical Education, and Recreation, 1976.
7. Snedecor, George W., *Statistical Methods,* 5th ed., Ames, Iowa: Iowa State University Press, 1956.
8. Spiegel, Murray R., *Outline of Theory and Problems of Statistics,* New York: Schaum Publishing Company, 1961, 1962.
9. Steel, Robert G. D., and James H. Torrie, *Principles and Procedures of Statistics,* New York: McGraw-Hill Book Company, Inc., 1960.
10. Underwood, Benton J., Carl P. Duncan, Janet T. Spence, and John W. Cotton, *Elementary Statistics,* New York: Appleton-Century-Crofts, 1954.
11. Weber, Jerome C., and David R. Lamb, *Statistics and Research in Physical Education,* St. Louis: C. V. Mosby Company, 1970.
12. Wert, James E., Charles O. Neidt, and J. Stanley Ahmann, *Statistical Methods in Education and Psychological Research,* New York: Appleton-Century-Crofts, 1954.

In order for the physical education teacher to effectively evaluate tests that are available for use in his program, he should have some knowledge concerning the construction of tests. Included in the procedures for test construction are the criteria by which a test may be judged. It is also believed that this information will enable the teacher to acquire confidence in his efforts to establish tests of his own.

Basic Concepts in Test Evaluation

As in any area of specialization, it is necessary to have a basic understanding of the terms that are used. Four of the most basic concepts involved in test construction and evaluation are *validity, reliability, objectivity,* and *norms.*

Validity refers to the degree to which a test measures what it was designed to measure. To the beginner in the field of tests and measurements this concept may seem so basic that it scarcely deserves mention. Nevertheless, many tests are found to be rather weak in this most basic consideration. Probably every student has had the unnerving experience of being given a test which seems to pertain to some course other than the one in which he is enrolled. In such cases the test fails in content validity by not being related to the material that has been covered in the course.

Another example of poor testing is in the case of the student who can beat everyone in the badminton class, but whose grade is lowered because he does poorly on one skill test (which consists of bouncing a bird off a wall). In this instance the teacher, in his zeal to employ objective measures, has overlooked their main function—which is to supplement other means of evaluation. In addition to the teacher's misuse of the test, the test itself did not represent an accurate measure of a person's ability to play badminton. We should hasten to say that, in many cases, volleying tests demonstrate high validity. The point we were attempting to make in the above example was that the test constituted a somewhat artificial setting, and it touched upon only a small facet of the game. Obviously, then, in order for a test to be valid, a critical analysis must be made as to the nature of the activity and the skills and special abilities that are involved.

Since there are different purposes for testing and since validity refers to the degree to which

Chapter Four

Test Evaluation, Construction, and Administration

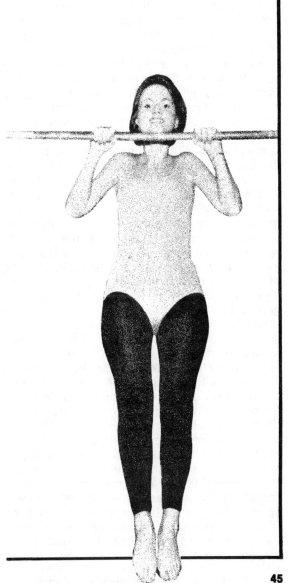

a test achieves its purpose, it follows that there are different types of validity. We will briefly describe four kinds of validity and ways by which validity may be established. The reader should keep in mind that there may be considerable overlap among the different types of validity depending upon the purpose(s) for using a test.

Face Validity. A test has face validity if it appears obvious that it is a measure of the ability in question. A test that calls for a student to walk along a narrow board or beam is obviously a test of dynamic balance. A test that requires a subject to run rapidly in and around closely spaced obstacles can be considered to have face validity as an agility test, and so on. While face validity does not lend itself to any type of statistical coefficient, it is a very important concept that unfortunately is too often overlooked by testers in search of highly objective measures.

A tester should always be cognizant of face validity since it is of paramount importance from the student's point of view. More will be said about face validity as we discuss other concepts of validity as well as the other functional criteria for judging the worth of a test.

Content Validity. An example of lack of content validity was given in the introduction of the chapter whereby students sometimes are unable to associate a final examination with what was covered in the course. Whether or not a test possesses content validity is a subjective judgment. However, it is fundamental for tests which aim to measure what students have learned in a class. If, for example, 90 percent of the instruction in beginning tennis concentrated on the forehand and backhand ground strokes and the service, the skill tests should attempt to assess these skills if they are to demonstrate content validity. It stands to reason that face validity of the test item serves to reinforce content validity in skill testing.

Criterion Validity. Sometimes a test is used to predict future performance or is used in place of another test which is perhaps longer or requires more elaborate equipment or facilities. The terms *predictive validity* and *concurrent validity* have been used to designate these concepts. Both are based on a criterion which is considered to represent the performance or characteristics in question. A college entrance examination is an example of a test that attempts to predict success in college, which is the criterion. Motor-educability tests were developed in physical education a number of

years ago. It was hoped that such tests would predict the ease with which one could learn motor skills. Obviously, the identification of the proper criterion is of critical importance. As a general rule, the use of more than one criterion is recommended.

Often it may be advantageous in terms of time, equipment, facilities, or other conditions for a physical educator to be able to use a shorter, less elaborate, or less rigorous test in place of another. For example, suppose that a teacher wishes to measure cardiorespiratory fitness. It is generally acknowledged that the most valid measure of this parameter is maximal oxygen consumption, which requires expensive equipment for the necessary gas analysis, considerable time for individual testing, and subjects who are willing to exercise maximally. Thus, it would be desirable to develop a test that did not require such expensive equipment, could employ mass testing, and was submaximal. The construction of such a test may employ maximal oxygen consumption as the criterion.

Round-robin tournaments and/or judges' ratings are sometimes used as criteria for sports skills tests. The tournament and ratings of course take time, scheduling, and special arrangements, and, therefore, it would be advantageous to utilize skill tests if it could be demonstrated that they are suitable indicators of the criteria.

The degree of association of a measure with the criterion is usually evaluated statistically by correlation. In Chapter 3 the reader was cautioned that correlation does not imply causation. Consequently, a test may correlate with the criterion, but it may not be apparent why it correlates. It could well be that another factor, or factors, is associated with both variables and is actually the cause of the relationship. A former colleague who had been a tennis coach for many years maintained that he could devise a test of throwing apples in a basket which would correlate as highly with ratings of tennis playing ability as some of the tennis skills tests. Although he never followed through with his claim, he was undoubtedly basing his assertion on the fact that there are probably some underlying motor abilities necessary for successfully throwing apples into a basket that would also contribute to success in tennis. Another example is the Knox Penny Cup Test that consists of running and dropping a penny in one of three cups which are painted different colors and placed in a row on the floor. As the student runs toward the three cups, the tester calls out a color, thereby requiring the student to make a rapid choice of action. The author of the test reported a very high correlation with a criterion of basketball playing ability. In this case, the choice-response factor which is probably being measured by the penny cup test is also a desirable quality in basketball, and this could account for the correlation. However, the test completely fails with respect to face validity and content validity and would not likely be accepted by students as a measure of basketball skill. So once again, face validity should never be ignored in test construction and the potential user of a test must not be totally concerned with (or misled by) statistical evidence of validity.

Construct Validity. The term *construct validity* refers to the degree to which performances on a test correspond to the abilities or traits that the test purports to measure. Construct validity can be established in different ways, but methodology is mostly based on testing the theory that underlies the parameter. For example, the LSU Step Test, which is presented in Chapter 9, consists of five pulse counts: before exercise, immediately after exercise, and one, two, and three minutes into recovery. The test is based on the constructs that these pulse measures do reflect differences in cardiorespiratory fitness; that is, a person with a high degree of fitness generally has a lower pulse rate at rest, his or her pulse count is lower after a standard workout, and the recovery rate is faster. Consequently, if it is a valid test, conditioned individuals should have a lower profile of pulse counts than unconditioned subjects.

An experimental study could be set up to establish construct validity based on the underlying theory as follows: all subjects are given the step test and then assigned to groups; one group serves as control and does not undergo any conditioning; another group engages in a physical conditioning program; and perhaps another group is given an exercise program of greater or lesser intensity or duration. The step test can be said to demonstrate construct validity if it reflects the expected gains in cardiovascular fitness as a result of the conditioning programs. The degree to which it can distinguish between levels of fitness may be evaluated by whether it reveals a difference between the two exercise programs.

Another method by which construct validity can be estimated is by correlating the test with another test of its kind since a cardiovas-cular test could be expected to correlate with other cardiovascular tests. However, construct validity may be very appropriate when there are no existing measures of the ability in question that are widely accepted as valid tests. An example might be perceptual motor ability, for which there is no acknowledged criterion measure such as the example of maximal oxygen consumption for cardiovascular fitness. It would be logical, then, that a tester would examine the constructs underlying perceptual motor performance and seek to evaluate his or her test in light of these constructs.

Reliability may be thought of as the repeatability of a test. A student's score should not differ markedly on repeated administrations of the same test. Some measures require exact duplication in order to be considered reliable, while other measures are allowed more leeway. For example, a scale would not be acceptable at all if it did not give the same reading each time a specified weight was placed upon it. On the other hand, one would scarcely expect a student to obtain the exact same score on a golf test in which he hits balls into numbered circles. In the latter example there are too many factors involved which would tend to reduce the probability of identical scores.

Reliability and validity are interrelated in that if you cannot achieve consistent measurements the test simply cannot be considered valid. To illustrate, suppose that a physical education teacher wishes to measure leg strength. Using a dynamometer and belt arrangement, he is able to obtain an accurate measure of force exerted by the legs. However, the angle at which the leg extension test is performed is very difficult to determine. Consequently, although the teacher obtains an accurate (and valid) measure of a particular student's leg lift at the specified angle, he may find that there is considerable variation in his scores on subsequent tests because of the difficulty in establishing the correct angle—resulting in a low reliability coefficient. Furthermore, when he tests a group of students for leg strength, his inability to establish the same angle for everyone results in an invalid measure of the group's leg strength at the desired position.

On the other hand, a test can be reliable and yet not valid. Suppose that in an attempt to isolate and measure leg strength a teacher has the students push upward on a bar that is placed on their shoulders and attached to a dynamometer. Regardless of the fact that he obtains consistent (reliable) scores on repeated tests, the amount that each student can lift is limited by the amount of weight that the back can support. Consequently, the strength of the legs, which is much greater than that of the back, is not being isolated, and this results in an invalid measure of leg strength.

In Chapter 3 the point was made that theoretically any observed score contains the subject's true score plus measurement error. Therefore, reliability is defined as the true score variance divided by the observed score variance. Measurement error encompasses many things, some of which are obvious while others may be more obscure.

Possible influences on a student's performance from one occasion to another on the same test (sources of measurement error) include: the clarity and consistency of instructions; the number of trials given; the subject's state of health; concentration and determination; whether spectators are present; any differences in the subject's conception of the importance of the test, i.e., the many factors encompassed under student motivation; length of the test; fatigue; environmental effects of temperature and humidity; the scoring procedures; whether or not knowledge of results is given; any differences in test administration procedures; and the length of time between trials. Ordinarily, the concept of reliability assumes that the time interval between a test and retest is not long enough to allow real changes in ability that might be attributed to maturation, learning, forgetting, or changes in physical condition.

There are different ways by which a tester can establish reliability. The test-retest method is often preferable in physical performance tasks. A test-retest could be given on the same day or on different days. One would expect higher reliability coefficients for the former than the latter since it is likely that the variables influencing performance would be more comparable when the test is given twice on the same day. The reader is referred to Chapter 3 for the discussion pertaining to intraclass correlation coefficients.

The reliability of written tests and tests that have a number of trials, such as reaction time tests and some accuracy tasks, is sometimes determined by what is called the split-halves technique. This method usually involves a division of the test into a set of odd-numbered trials or items and a set of even-numbered trials or items. The two sets are correlated. Then, because the test has been halved, the correlation

is stepped up by a formula $\dfrac{2r}{1.00 + r}$ in which r represents the correlation between the two halves of the test. It should be noted that this technique is not as appropriate as the intra-class correlation coefficient since it uses a bivariate statistic for a univariate situation. Moreover, a split-halves correlation and step-up procedure usually produce a spuriously high r.

In addition to the many factors associated with the test situation and the subject's physical and emotional condition, it also should be noted that reliability is affected by the spread or variance of the scores. Unless there is a reasonable distribution of performances among the subjects, the trial-to-trial reliability coefficient will be low. A teaching technique that is sometimes employed to demonstrate this point is to ask the students to guess what the correlation would be in this example:

> Five individuals were tested on two separate days on the standing broad jump. Each person jumped 6 feet the first day and 6 feet the second. What is the test-retest reliability?

Most students will guess that the R (or r) will be 1.00 or perfect. Actually, it will be 0.00 because there is no scatter or spread of scores within the sets of data. (Try it with either R or r.)

The length of a test is an important factor. Generally speaking, the more trials, the higher the reliability. Common sense indicates that we could find a more reliable estimate of a student's true ability in free throw shooting if we gave the student 30 trials rather than only 2 or 3. Another generality is that performances which call for near maximal exertion, such as strength or power measures, require fewer trials for reliability purposes than performances which demand more precise neuromuscular responses, such as accuracy tasks.

Objectivity of a test pertains primarily to the clarity of the directions for administering and scoring the test. High objectivity is when different teachers can give a test to the same individuals and obtain approximately the same results. Naturally, we are assuming that the testers are equally competent.

Objectivity and reliability are related but are, nevertheless, distinct concepts. A stop watch is a highly reliable device for measuring the time it takes for a student to run 440 yards. Yet, if the directions are not clear as to when to start the watch—at the sound of the gun or upon seeing the smoke—then there is an increased likelihood for error. Moreover, if there are no standardized procedures for scoring, some testers will record scores to the nearest half second, others to the nearest tenth of a second, and so on. Thus, a reliable measuring device does not guarantee objectivity.

Norms are values considered to be representative of a specified population. A test that has accompanying norms is definitely preferred to one that does not. They provide information for the student and the teacher to enable them to interpret the student's score in relation to the scores made by other individuals in the same population. An understanding of what constitutes the "same population" is necessary in order to intelligently use norm tables.

Norms are usually based on age, grade, height, weight, or various combinations of these characteristics. In norm tables for physical performance there are separate scales for boys and girls; in written tests this distinction is usually not made. The important factor is that the interpretation of norm tables is done in light of the specific group from which the norms were compiled. For example, a standing broad jump of 8 feet would not be impressive at all if done by a college athlete, whereas it would indeed be an outstanding achievement if performed by a ten-year-old boy.

In order to evaluate performance in relation to a set of norms, one must first evaluate the adequacy of the norms. There are several factors that should be considered.

1. The number of subjects that were used in establishing the norms should be sufficiently large. Although sheer numbers do not guarantee accuracy, generally speaking the

Figure 4-1. Shuttle Run Test—A Test of Agility

larger the sample, the more likely it will approximate the population.

2. The norms should represent the performance of the population for which the test was devised. It would not be appropriate to compile norms from a select group, such as physical education majors, to represent all college students in a physical performance test. Similarly, the user of norms should not evaluate the performance of his students on the basis of norms designed for a different population.

3. The geographical distribution that norms represent should be taken into account. Considerable variation in performance is often found among students in different geographical locations. For the most part local norms are of more value to the teacher than are national norms.

4. The clarity of the directions for test administration and scoring is definitely involved in the evaluation of the accompanying norms. Obviously, if the testing and scoring procedures utilized by the teacher are not identical to those employed by the testers who compiled the norms, then the norms themselves are worthless.

5. Norms are only temporary and must be periodically revised. Certain traits, characteristics, and abilities of children today differ from those of children a number of years ago. Consequently, the date on which the norms were established should be considered and weighed accordingly.

Additional Criteria for the Selection and Evaluation of Tests

In addition to the basic concepts of validity, reliability, objectivity, and norms, there are several other features that should be considered in selecting and evaluating tests. These will be presented in the form of questions that one might ask before selecting a particular test to use as part of his evaluation program.

1. *Is the test easy to administer?* Ease of administration involves many things including time, equipment, space, number of testers needed, etc. These will be taken up separately, but this one basic question is an example of the whole being greater than the sum of the parts. The administrative feasibility of a test extends to the attitude that the tester, and certainly the students, have toward that particular test. There are some physical fitness tests, for example, that are so rigorous that some students actually become ill and many others suffer from soreness for days afterwards. In such a case as this, the test could have high validity, reliability, and objectivity coefficients; it could possess any number of desirable test characteristics, such as economy of time, space, equipment, etc.; but it would still be unacceptable. Thus, ease of administration encompasses the entire realm of administrative considerations, including attitude in relation to the contribution that the test can make to the program.

2. *Does the test require expensive equipment?* A formidable item to consider in any school testing program is cost. There is no doubt that with unlimited resources, elaborate instruments, machines, and electronic devices could be applied to measure human performance with great precision. In reality, however, the physical education budget rarely permits the purchase of expensive equipment that is only applicable to a specific test. Some tests must be excluded for exactly this reason. One of the outstanding features of the AAHPER Youth Fitness Test is that it requires almost no equipment. Occasionally a teacher may have to compromise to some extent by selecting a test having less accuracy than another but requiring less equipment.

3. *Can the test be administered in a relatively short period of time?* A perpetual problem that confronts most physical educators is the numerous encroachments upon class time. Recognizing this, most authorities recommend that tests and measurements programs should consume no more than 10 percent of the total instructional time. Therefore, any single test battery must be evaluated in terms of economy of time as well as of money.

Economy of time can be a very important factor in test selection, and often the teacher is faced with a dilemma. In order for a test to meet the demands of validity and reliability, a sufficient number of trials must be given which may consume more time than the teacher wishes to spend. Attempts to compromise, by reducing the number of test items and/or trials, usually result in a serious loss in validity and reliability, thereby reducing the intended worth of the test. The problem is compounded in short activity units where time for instruction and practice is at a premium.

4. *Can the test be used as a drill during practice sessions?* Although this feature of a test is not always desirable, it can offer a partial solution to the problem stated above concerning economy of time as well as of other test criteria. For example, the more familiarity the students have with a test, the less time is needed to explain the administration and scoring procedures. In addition, practice of the test also serves to reduce the sometimes misleading effects of insight into the nature of the test, which may cause a rather pronounced rise in scores in the middle or latter portions of the test.

If the test is a measure of skill and represents the actual abilities that are required in the activity, then it would seem that its use as a form of practice would be logical and desirable. This line of reasoning is based on the principle of content validity—in other words, one should be tested on what is practiced. On the other hand if the test is artificial and the student practices more for the test than the total activity in question, then, of course, such a test is not suitable as a drill during practice sessions.

5. *Does the test require several trained testers?* Since some test batteries contain a number of individual test items, in the interest of time it is almost imperative that more than one person be called upon to administer the test. Furthermore, some test items require more skill and experience to administer than others. This requires training and practice. If more than one person is going to be giving the same test, objectivity coefficients should be established.

Besides the training and practice that are involved, the utilization of several testers requires considerable planning and organization. Naturally, arrangements must be made to have the testers available at the proper time; pre-test meetings are usually required; and various other details of coordination need to be accomplished.

Thus far it would appear that tests that call for several testers are undesirable. It should be quickly pointed out that there are times when tests of this nature are of immense value. One such instance is when large-scale, comprehensive evaluation is advocated, as is sometimes done for physical fitness testing at various times during the school year. Generally, placement and screening tests are most effectively administered in this way.

To summarize, whenever the abilities that are to be measured necessitate the use of several test items, or when a particular test item requires a specialist to administer it, then the utilization of trained testers is not only expedient but necessary. On the other hand, the teacher who must evaluate students in various activities ordinarily does not have other staff members or trained assistants available; thus, he or she must bear this in mind in the selection of tests. While the use of students as testers may be profitable to the student testers as well as the teacher, there are times when this is not administratively feasible or desirable.

6. *Can the test be easily and objectively scored?* Certainly this criterion has been mentioned or alluded to a number of times in the foregoing discussion. Nevertheless, there is a need for further comment regarding this feature of a test. Specifically, one should consider the following factors: (a) whether or not a test requires another person to act as an opponent, a thrower, a server, etc.; (b) whether or not the students can test and score themselves during practice sessions; and (c) whether or not the scores adequately distinguish among different levels of skill.

The first consideration, concerning the role of another individual involved in the performance of the testee, represents somewhat of a paradox in the construction of a performance test. In most sports the skill of the opponent definitely has a direct bearing on an individual's performance. In activities such as tennis, badminton, handball, volleyball, football, to name but a few, the quality of the performance of a player is relative to the skill of the opponent. In other sports such as golf, archery, bowling, and others, a person's performance can be immediately assessed by his score alone (playing conditions being equal for everyone, of course). Therefore, in many activities a performance test simply cannot take into account the influence that is rendered by the competitive situation.

Recognizing this restriction, the makers of performance tests have attempted to isolate the skills that are involved and measure them independently. However, if the isolated skills call for the services of another individual, either acting as an opponent or a teammate, then, of course, objectivity is reduced. To illustrate, in an attempt to duplicate the actual activity, it may be desirable to have someone serve the shuttlecock to the person being tested on the high *clear* stroke; or to have someone pitch to a student being tested on batting; or to have someone run a pass pattern to test an individual's skill at passing a football. In these cases it is obvious that the skill of the other individual could greatly affect the testee's score. This is not to say that tests of this type are inferior. On the contrary, if the other person is sufficiently skilled and his performance is constant for each subject, this can be a very effective and efficient method of evaluation. This individual might very well be the teacher, but of course there are some problems that arise in planning and organizing a testing arrangement such as this, and there are the factors of sufficient number of trials and fatigue on the part of the teacher.

In striving to avoid the influence of another person and preserve high objectivity, there is the danger of creating an artificial situation. Having a student hit a softball from a batting tee and bounce the ball himself before stroking in tennis are examples of situations which are not found in the actual game conditions. This, then, is the paradox inherent in performance test construction — scientific precision versus gamelike conditions.

A second consideration in scoring a test is whether or not the students can test and score themselves. Although this feature of a test is not always applicable, it is usually of considerable importance when the test is to be used as a teaching aid. For instance, a wall volley drill in tennis might be employed as a regularly scheduled exercise and rainy day activity for developing proficiency in the basic strokes. It also might be one of the measuring devices used in evaluation. In this situation the students could benefit from self-testing throughout the course in providing them with a record of progress and, at the same time, blocking the possible negative effects of confronting a unique test situation at the end of the unit.

A third aspect of scoring that should be considered relates to the precision with which test scores can differentiate among persons of different abilities. This consideration overlaps with so many other characteristics of testing that it will only be

mentioned briefly here. Tests that stress speed are sometimes prone to encourage poor form. Some wall volley tests are examples of this in that an individual may be able to achieve a higher score by standing very close and using mainly wrist action rather than the desired stroking movement.

In some tests the units of measurement are not fine enough to reflect various levels of ability. A classic example is an agility test in which the student scores a point each time he crosses a center line as he runs from one side of the court to the other. Because of the distance involved and the limited opportunity to earn points, most of the scores are identical within a range of about three points. Other examples would include test items scored on a pass-or-fail basis and tests using targets with widely spaced point values.

Related to the above are tests which are designed to measure the accuracy of the individual in hitting a ball, a shuttlecock, etc., into particular scoring zones on a court. Several tests employ a rope or string placed above the net, or at other spots on the floor, to separate the skilled player who correctly places the shot from the *sloppy* performer who might hit the same scoring zone but with a poor shot that would be unsuccessful against an actual opponent. Similarly, attention should be given to the probable action of a real opponent in marking the zones on a playing court. For instance, areas that are just barely out-of-bounds should be given some point value if it is logical that the opponent would not let a ball (or shuttlecock, etc.) land in that area for fear that it might fall good. In addition, it should be assumed that the more highly skilled players will deliberately hit shots that land close to boundary lines, as these are ordinarily the hardest to return. Therefore, it does not seem appropriate that a good player should be penalized—to the extent that he receives no points—for barely missing on what would probably be a good shot in an actual game.

7. *Is the test challenging and meaningful?* Of vital importance to the success of any testing program is the attitude with which the students approach the tests. Generally speaking, most students like to be tested. The challenge of the task, the information that is derived, and the curiosity and competitive nature of the individual are some of

the factors which operate to produce a favorable testing situation. Needless to say, students also can learn to dread tests for any number of reasons. Sometimes an individual feels unduly threatened by a test in which he is made to feel inferior and an object of ridicule. In other instances a student may feel inadequately prepared, or he may place too much importance on the results. In still other circumstances a student may regard the test as being unfair, too strenuous, too easy, or perhaps meaningless.

Therefore, the physical educator should seek to capitalize on the positive motivating properties that are generally inherent in physical performance tests. The tests and the conditions in which they are given should be carefully considered with regard to student enjoyment. This is a time when the physical education teacher has an excellent opportunity to establish a favorable teacher-student relationship through encouragement and individual attention.

The test itself must be challenging. To do this it must offer sufficient latitude in scoring to accommodate large differences in ability. A disadvantage of a test such as pull-ups is that there are almost always students in a class who cannot do a single pull-up and, therefore, receive a score of zero. Similarly, a test should allow opportunity to record improvement. Referring again to pull-ups, a student may have improved during the course to the point where he could just about pull himself up to chin level, which for that student might represent a significant gain in strength; but he still receives a zero. At the other extreme, there are some tests

Figure 4-2. Rhythm Test Construction

that have a performance ceiling and make no provision for better scores after a particular level has been attained.

Related closely to the challenging aspect of a test is the degree to which it is meaningful. Performance tests should involve the actual skills that are used in the activity; and the skills should be measured as much as possible in gamelike situations. A softball test in which the student is asked to catch a ball that is thrown out of a second-story window can hardly be considered realistic. Granted that it would have built-in validity since it does involve the catching of a softball. However, it would seem rather difficult for a teacher to convince a student that his ability to play softball was being assessed in such an *ungamelike* situation. Doubly hard might be the task of interpreting the efficacy of the physical educator's evaluative techniques to the public who observe students attempting to catch balls thrown out of a window.

Test selection, then, must couple scientific considerations with common sense. There can be no substitute for good judgment. The physical educator must be constantly alert to the needs and interests of the students as they pertain to tests and measurements as well as to the program of which they are a part.

Steps in Test Construction

When published tests are either not available or not exactly suitable for the physical educator's particular situation, it becomes necessary for him to construct his own test. Although it is not imperative that a teacher read books on tests and measurements in order to simply devise a test for one's own use, it does require skillful analysis and technical training to construct a test that is scientifically sound. Moreover, many teachers are reluctant to try their hand at formulating tests because they lack confidence in their ingenuity and in their knowledge of test construction.

The following steps are suggested to guide the physical educator in devising a physical performance test that will adhere to the criteria of validity, reliability, and other basic principles.

Step 1: Analyze the game or physical qualities in question in order to determine the skills or factors that are to be measured. This,

of course, necessitates a thorough understanding of what is involved in the physical performance that is being evaluated. A mere listing of the components of the activity is insufficient. One must be able to determine the relative importance of each component. Naturally, some abilities involving strategy and reaction to an opponent are ordinarily not considered in this analysis because of the difficulty in measuring those qualities.

Step 2: Select test items that measure the desired qualities. Unquestionably, this is one of the most crucial steps in the entire test construction procedure. The items must be chosen with regard to their importance as well as their propensity to be measured accurately.

The test items may be selected from other established tests; they may be chosen through the utilization of a jury of experts; or they may be determined arbitrarily by the physical educator after analyzing the performance in question. If the test pertains to a sport, the test item should conform as much as possible to the actual game situation and not be taken out of context. If the test is for physical fitness or motor ability, the test item should not favor persons of a particular size and penalize others unless body size is meant to be a factor in the performance, such as the fact that obesity is not compatible with physical fitness.

The test items generally should stress good form as well as the main scoring criteria. It has been observed that in some tests the student can achieve a higher score by using an unorthodox style rather than the prescribed form.

The literature contains numerous test items that have been used for measuring various components of physical fitness. In this case the test maker might choose test items in accordance with their compliance with some established criteria. These criteria might entail restrictions as to time, equipment, space, or other considerations pertinent to one's local situation.

It must be remembered that any test item is only a sample of the total performance or quality. This concept must be thoroughly understood by the teacher when formulating the test and especially when evaluating the results. In devising the test items, care must be taken to isolate as much as possible the desired ability. If the test situation is too complicated, the results may be misleading. This is particularly true when a test item is to be used for diagnostic purposes. To illustrate, if the teacher is attempting to measure arm and shoulder girdle strength, a test item such as the shot put would not be suitable because of the uncontrolled variables of past experience and technique. On the other hand, test makers sometimes make the mistake of isolating a skill or trait to such an extreme that the test item becomes meaningless.

Step 3: Establish the exact procedures for the administration and scoring of the test. In accomplishing this obvious step the physical educator must resort to a certain amount of trial and error. The best laid plans on paper may be totally inoperable in practice. Furthermore, the directions for testing and scoring may appear to be perfectly clear when the test is tried on only one or two subjects. However, marked revisions may be necessary after giving the test to a number of people, due to differences in the way the directions may be interpreted, or perhaps due to unanticipated levels of performance.

The clarity and simplicity of directions have a direct bearing on the reliability and objectivity of a test. The test maker should strive to establish procedures that facilitate the administration of the test both from the standpoint of the tester and testee. Validity is also obviously impaired if the student does not fully understand the directions.

Step 4: Determine the reliability of each test item. As described previously, a reliability coefficient can be calculated on the basis of any number of trials, by a test-retest situation, or by the split-halves method. These are some considerations involved in accomplishing this step:

a. The subjects that are selected for testing should, of course, be representative of the population for whom the test is intended.

b. In establishing the score value that is to be used to indicate the performance of each subject for each of the trials or test administrations, care should be taken to obtain an appropriate measure. In other words, a sufficient number of trials should be given, the test directions should be made perfectly clear, and ample opportunity should be afforded each person to become accustomed to the test itself. These suggestions have been mentioned before, but it is important that they be considered.

A further consideration with regard to scoring and reliability pertains to the question of whether one should use the average score or the best score. For example, should you use the best of three trials on a standing broad jump or the average of the three trials? The decision probably involves several factors including convenience of scoring on the part of the tester in that the best score is easier to extract than the average. Some argue that you ultimately want the student's best performance; others maintain that the best score may not be representative of the student's typical performance. The type of test is definitely a factor. In reaction time testing, for example, the best score may be the result of anticipation of the stimulus and thus may actually be a false score.

In regard to whether the average or best score is more reliable, most of the research findings have shown that the average score is more reliable.

c. The reader is referred to Chapter 3 for discussion of correlation and factors to consider in the interpretation of a specific coefficient of correlation. Test makers generally recommend that a test should have a reliability coefficient of at least .70 to be acceptable. Naturally, the higher the coefficient the better. Some authorities feel that a coefficient of at least .85 should be required in order to satisfy the criterion of reliability. Certainly one should not expect perfect correlation, due to the normal variations in performance noted in individuals from one time to the next.

Low reliability coefficients ordinarily call for revisions in the test item or for its elimination. Sometimes just allowing more trials will greatly improve the reliability. Some types of physical performance are much harder to measure reliably than others. Tests of kinesthesis, for example, generally are notoriously lacking in reliability due to the nature of the test items.

One final admonition for teachers who are judging tests based on coefficients of reliability, validity, and objectivity is that *these values mean nothing if the person using the test is not a competent tester. A particular test can be highly reliable when administered by one person but completely unreliable if it is given by a careless or untrained tester. It is also certainly possible for a skilled, conscientious person to obtain a higher reliability coefficient than that which is published.*

Step 5: Compute the objectivity of each test item. This step is accomplished by having two competent testers administer the test item to the same individuals. Correlation is again employed to determine the extent of agreement between the different test administrators. Most of the considerations that were discussed regarding reliability are applicable here. Needless to say, objectivity is directly related to the skill and integrity of the testers as well as to the clarity and simplicity of the instructions and scoring procedures of the test.

Step 6: Establish validity. This procedure in test construction may be approached in several ways. The test maker may wish to use more than one method or a combination of methods. The most common procedures utilized in establishing validity are enumerated as follows:

a. The students' performance on the homemade test can be correlated with their scores made on a previously validated test. If a high correlation is obtained, the test maker can claim that his test is valid. It should be obvious, however, that this procedure has certain weaknesses. In the first place the validity coefficient only demonstrates the degree to which the new test coincides with the other test; consequently, it can only be shown to be as valid as the older test, never more valid. This last point is especially noteworthy because in the majority of cases, a person is prompted to devise a new test in order to improve upon the present evaluation tools.

b. If the test in question is designed to measure performance in an activity such as tennis, badminton, handball, etc., it can be effectively validated by correlating the scores on the test with the results of a round-robin tournament. If it is valid, the persons placing highest in the tournament should score highest on the test, the poorest players should have the lowest scores, and so on through the different levels of ability.

c. In some activities, such as team sports, round-robin tournaments are not feasible. However, a comparable validating procedure can be employed by utilizing the ratings of experts as the criterion to which the performance on a test is correlated. The experts must be selected with care, but at the same time it is not necessary to obtain the services of nationally known figures for this purpose. To illustrate, if the test pertains to performance in basketball, the varsity basketball coaches could certainly be considered qualified to rate basketball skills, provided ample opportunity is allowed for observing each student. In addition, scales must be devised that are suitably graduated in order to differentiate between various levels of ability. For example, specific point values are usually given for arbitrary standards of performance, such as five for excellent; four, good; three, average; two, etc. If several judges are used, the average rating is ordinarily correlated with the score made on the performance test. Judges' ratings can also be utilized in validating individual activities as well as team sports.

d. Another approach which is quite similar to the method just described involves comparison of persons of known levels of ability on their test performance. In this method individuals are assigned to different groups which supposedly represent different degrees of proficiency. The formation of the groups may be done through ratings by competent judges, such as a coach rating his varsity players, his junior varsity players, his freshmen, etc.; or, it may be accomplished by simply selecting whole groups of performers on the basis of their status as a group. For instance, the varsity may be assumed to represent the highest level of ability, the junior varsity next, the freshmen next, intramural players next, and, finally, perhaps physical education students just beginning the activity. After the test has been administered to all the subjects, the test performances of the different groups are then compared to determine the degree to which the test differentiated among the assumed levels of ability. A variation of the same approach involves the use of a number of teams that are considered to represent different degrees of skill based on their order of finish in a tournament or conference standings. It can be readily seen that there are bound to be some erroneous assumptions as to the various levels of ability due to upsets, unusual circumstances, and the indistinguishable clustering effect that is found at the middle of any performance scale which conforms to normal distribution.

e. The last method of determining validity that will be presented here involves the use of a composite score of all the test items in the battery as the performance criterion. Fre-

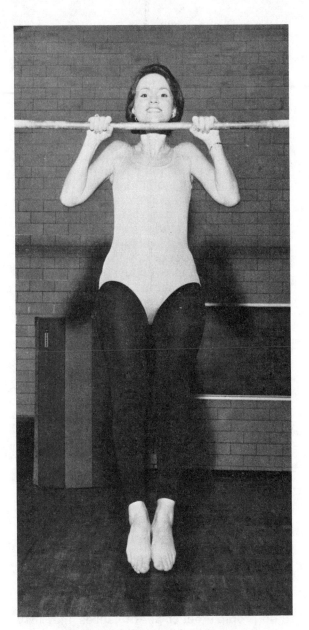

Figure 4-3. Flexed-Arm Hang—
A Test of Static Muscular Endurance

items. Multiple correlation can then be employed to select the test battery which is composed of the test items that correlate highest with the criterion and lowest with one another. The latter is necessary because a test item that correlates highly with another one is considered to be measuring the same thing and is therefore superfluous. Consequently, if two test items are found to be highly related, the one that correlates highest with the criterion would be selected.

If there are a considerable number of test items, this process can select the least number of items to comprise the test battery. Regression equations can also be used to predict what an individual would do on the total performance based on his scores on the selected items.

f. The basic procedures just described above can be used to establish the validity of each test item in any battery. In cases where the composite score is not considered appropriate, the items can be correlated with judges' ratings, tournament standings, established tests, etc., to determine the validity of each item. The items should then also be intercorrelated to eliminate duplication.

Step 7: Revise the test in light of the findings of the steps just described, and finalize the written instructions for administering and scoring the test.

Step 8: Construct norms. A large number of subjects who are representative of the population for whom the test was intended should be given the test, and their scores recorded. The scores can then be converted to percentiles or T-scores (or whatever suitable score form is wanted). Norms for each test item should be prepared, and usually norms for the composite or total score are also desirable.

Test Administration

Several recommendations pertinent to test administration, scoring procedures, and suggestions for standardization have already been covered in this chapter. Specific pointers are also given with the directions for each of the tests presented in later chapters. However, some general test administration recommendations will be given here.

The Boy Scout motto "Be Prepared" could easily pertain to test administration. Sloppy, inaccurate testing or perhaps even the lack of

quently, physical fitness tests are established in this manner. The scores for the various test items that were selected as measures of the basic components are converted to standard scores and are then added. This total is assumed to represent physical fitness, or motor ability, or sports skills, or whatever is being tested. Then each test item is correlated with the criterion (total score) and with each of the other

testing by physical education teachers may well be due to neglect of planning and organization or to ignorance of the effort needed for a good testing program.

Preparation for testing includes attention to many details such as score sheets, efficient arrangement of testing stations, collection of necessary equipment, and training of testers.

1. The preparation of score sheets or score cards may seem too trivial to mention, but it can be an important factor and it requires considerable forethought. Do you want score cards that each student can carry from station to station or score sheets at each test station?

   The score card has some advantages in that it facilitates recording of scores; the tester doesn't have to look through a list of names. It also can be helpful from the standpoint that the students are allowed more time to examine and reflect upon their performances on the different tests.

   The score sheet has the advantage of lessening the possibility of losing scores, a situation that may occur when a score card is mislaid or not turned in. The only other advantage is that a score sheet reduces the possibility of students "altering" their scores.

2. The arrangement of testing stations requires careful deliberation since there may be several factors to consider. Of primary consideration are the possible effects of fatigue. One would want to make sure that strenuous tests are not placed back to back or that a distance run is not scheduled first.

   It also may be important to arrange test stations in light of available equipment. For example, if three tests require stopwatches and only two are available, it is obvious that one of the tests needs to be scheduled on another day.

   The tester must be mindful of the time required for each test, and tests which take a particularly long time to administer may be handled best by making two test stations.

3. The training of testers is a vital step in tests that have several stations. One can never assume that a person is a competent tester just because he or she has read and understands the test instructions. It is strongly advised that practice sessions be held with a sample of subjects to help clarify directions and standardize procedures. Also, the testers should be given as much information as possible concerning measurement of the particular abilities to which they are assigned.

4. Familiarity with the test items and practice of them by the students have been stressed previously. Failure to allow for this represents a major source of measurement error. To test this assertion we suggest you give a test item to a sample of subjects—even a fairly familiar item such as a standing broad jump. Allow four trials. Almost invariably you will observe improvement with each trial. It is simply common sense that familiarity with a test will increase reliability. A distance run, for example, requires practice in order for a student to learn his or her optimal pace. An agility test yields better scores on subsequent trials because of learning and improved technique in running the pattern. The same phenomenon can be observed in most types of performances. It is also highly recommended that students be allowed to get into some degree of condition before being subjected to rigorous fitness tests. Failure to do so is not only unwise from a medical standpoint, but also is likely to promote fear, resentment, and improper attitudes toward fitness and physical education.

5. The standardization of instructions is another important and often overlooked administrative detail. Care must be taken that some students are not given additional or different information concerning what is considered to be adequate or good performance, suggested goals, etc. Sometimes a tester will attempt to motivate students by giving false norms, such as by telling them that younger students performed better or by mentioning an "average" score that is actually extremely high. Research has shown that although such tactics sometimes do promote better performances, they may also have an adverse effect, as in the case where a student stops trying in order to rationalize his or her failure as a matter of not trying rather than a lack of ability.

6. The competent tester will make a careful, detailed checklist of test equipment needed, floor-marking materials, measuring tapes, pencils, stopwatches, etc. A vast amount of time is wasted when the tester must hurry about after the start of the class period in order to locate some small but necessary item such as chalk for a vertical jump test. A mental rehearsal of each test item is advised.

Moreover, it is wise to assemble test materials that can be stored and readily set up when a test is to be given, rather than having to "start from scratch" each time. A sample materials and supplies checklist is provided in Appendix G.

7. Last, but of fundamental importance, is scoring and interpreting the test results. In some tests calculations are required, such as dividing body weight into strength scores. It saves much time and effort if someone performs the calculations as each person is tested instead of waiting to perform the calculations for perhaps hundreds of scores after the testing.

Interpretation and diagnosis are often sadly neglected. The use of up-to-date, local norms helps to a considerable extent, especially when students are knowledgeable as to what the norms mean and have ready access to them. If the testing is to have real value, however, there should be follow-up. After initial screening, further testing may be indicated to construct a more comprehensive and accurate profile of a student's status.

Finally, it is hoped that after a student's strengths and weaknesses have been identified through sound testing, a carefully planned program of activities will be prescribed in keeping with the student's needs.

Summary

Much more could be said about test construction, test selection and evaluation, and administration. In fact, an entire book could be devoted to this area. Certainly it represents the very essence of the tests and measurements program. Separate coverage could have been accorded the construction of written tests, attitude scales, social adjustment inventories, and other measuring tools. It was simply not within the scope of this chapter. The interested reader is referred to Chapters 20 and 21 and to other sources that pertain to knowledge of test construction, the devising of attitude scales, and other measuring tools. The primary consideration in evaluating any test, and the basic steps in constructing a test of any type, are the same.

The underlying message of this chapter, and in fact the theme of the entire book, pertains to the intelligent application of tests and measuring tools. An evaluating device can only be valid, reliable, and objective if it is utilized properly. Norms yield worthwhile information only when the tests are administered and scored in the same way for each individual and only when the individuals are from the same population. With these thoughts in mind we are ready to turn our attention to the discussion and presentation of some practical measurements for evaluation in specific areas in physical education.

Bibliography

1. Clarke, H. Harrison, *Application of Measurement to Health and Physical Education,* 4th ed., Englewood Cliffs, N.J.: Prentice-Hall, 1967.
2. Garrett, Henry E., *Statistics in Psychology and Education,* 5th ed., New York: Longmans, Green and Company, 1958.
3. Lien, Arnold J., *Measurement and Evaluation of Learning,* Dubuque, Iowa: Wm. C. Brown Company, Publishers, 1967.
4. Mathews, Donald K., *Measurement in Physical Education,* 3rd ed., Philadelphia: W. B. Saunders Company, 1968.
5. Safrit, Margaret J. (ed.), *Reliability Theory,* Washington, D.C.: American Alliance for Health, Physical Education, and Recreation, 1976.
6. Weiss, Raymond A., and M. Gladys Scott, "Construction of Tests," in AAHPER, *Research Methods in Health, Physical Education, and Recreation,* 2nd ed., Washington, D.C.: American Alliance for Health, Physical Education, and Recreation, 1959.

Chapter Five

Grading in Physical Education

Philosophical Concepts of Grading in Physical Education

Educators are in close agreement concerning the importance of basing measurement and evaluation upon the objectives which guide the educative process. However, they differ considerably concerning what objectives should be measured and how they should be measured. Moreover, students are becoming more vocal against the traditional grading systems used in a majority of the schools. Thus, the following pages of Part II are devoted to consideration of some of the concepts of grading.

Considering Educational Objectives

The objectives which are most commonly listed as worthy of pursuit in physical education are (a) neuromuscular skill; (b) physical fitness; (c) social development; and (d) acquisition of knowledge. While some educators in the field would measure each objective as nearly equal as possible in determining grades, others would support the use of only two or three which they considered to be unique to the field of physical education. For example, Duncan (8) supports sports and dance skills and physical development as the unique objectives in our field. From this viewpoint social and mental fitness objectives are still important; however, the physical educator's primary emphasis is not directed toward them. Unfortunately, other less informed physical educators tend to completely ignore measurement and evaluation from the standpoint of our more widely recognized objectives, but concern themselves with awarding grades based upon such administrative details as the number of absences, the number of times the student failed to dress out, the number of times he was tardy, whether he took showers after activity, uniformed properly, etc. Rather than grade on the number of absences, it might be a wiser administrative procedure to require students to repeat any course which has been missed a certain number of times. Otherwise students who are penalized for missing a few classes, as such, may be penalized twice in that they may make a poor showing on test days due to previous absences. On the other hand, students who miss a few classes, not enough to have to repeat, but who still do well on test days should not be penalized at all. This is the usual situation in other subject areas. As educators we should be primarily concerned with measuring educational objectives, not administrative objectives.

Improvement Versus Status

Some physical educators become quite concerned as to whether we should grade on improvement or on class status. While some teachers feel that improvement (the progress made between the initial and the final test) is of utmost importance in determining grades, most physical educators support the concept of grading on relative achievement commensurate with grading practices in other subject areas. Moreover, many teachers wish to avoid the following *disadvantages of grading on improvement in physical education*:

1. It is time consuming in that it requires the teacher to give approximately the same test twice (once before instruction and again after instruction).
2. In some skill and fitness activities it may be dangerous to test students without prior instruction and physical training.
3. When students know or suspect that improvement is a basis for grading, they will perform at a minimal level on the first test in order to show greater improvement on the second test.
4. When all students do their best on both tests, the weaker student may have an advantage in that it may be easier for him to improve when he is at the lower end of the scale than when he starts out already near the top.
5. Improvement based grading is not compatible with experiences apt to occur in real life situations. For example, a member of a sales organization might make the greatest improvement during a twelve month period but may still be the lowest man on the staff in total sales. Consequently, he receives less commission than the others and probably will still be the least likely to receive a promotion.
6. Similarly, improvement-based grading is not in accordance with grading in other subject areas. In subjects such as math, English, and history, the usual procedure is to merely total the points achieved on the various tests and reports and to assign grades based on those totals. Obviously, the students with the higher totals receive the higher grades and those with less points receive lower grades in this system.

However, in improvement grading, it would be possible for students with less knowledge and skills to actually receive higher grades.

Effort Versus Performance

Although most educators laud diligent effort, it is the actual performance that tends to be rewarded in life. For example, a salesman who works very hard five days a week may earn only $100 per week while one of his associates works only two days a week selling the same products and earns $300 per week. We find the same situation in sports. While one youngster may work hard seven days a week, he may still place second in a track meet to another youngster who practices less. Certainly we admire and encourage supreme effort, but actual relative performance can not be denied in assigning grades.

Many physical educators find it difficult to award higher grades to those gifted students who attend class less and work less than other students but who score exceedingly well on test days. But, if we wish to parallel the awarding of grades with real-life situations and thus prepare students to face the future realistically, we must give prime consideration to actual performance. Moreover, we must recognize that some students, no matter how much effort they exert, may never achieve above average performance.

Future Growth Versus Present Status

Another point of philosophical contemplation is whether to consider a student's future growth and development or to consider only his present status for grading purposes. It has been said that whatever exists in any amount can be measured, and by the same reasoning it must be recognized that what does not yet exist cannot be measured. However, education is fundamentally interested in the student's future growth and development, although it does not yet exist (4). Thus, this type of measurement evolves into evaluation which is not only different but more difficult than that measurement which is concerned with the student *here and now* as the finished product (5). While some educators would tend to follow the *here and now* method in a strict sense, others would place primary emphasis on the student as they see him *here and now* but make adjustments where there is no denying that future growth and development are inevitable. Such adjustments are merely qualitative judgments.

Ability to Repeat Versus Ability to Work with the Material

Still another point of interest is whether we should evaluate the student's ability to repeat that which has been presented or be concerned with what he can do with what he has learned. One of the most widely held views is that learning is the successful acquisition of material or skill which has been set out to be learned. This is sometimes called the *input* method, where the teacher is the transmitter of the information or skill and the student's mind is a sort of storage reservoir until such time as he is called upon to reproduce it on a test (4). However, there are others who support the *output* method and who strive to present students with important concepts or general ideas and then grade on how well the student can work with what he has learned insofar as showing initiative, new ideas, improved concepts, patterns, skills, or movement is concerned.

Teaching for Testing Versus Teaching for Learning

Sometimes the educator gets caught up in scientific movement to measure only those things which can be measured quantitatively (1). Moreover, he may tend to teach only those facts and skills which can be isolated for scientific measurement and grading. When this situation develops it is unfortunate, for there are many other things which need to be covered. A common pitfall for teachers is to teach only test information that will appear on a nationally standardized test in order for the class to rank high on norm comparisons. While this may boost the teacher's ego and raise his prestige in the eyes of others as an outstanding teacher, it is built on a false assumption, and the practice cannot be condoned.

Independent Class Status Grading Versus Grouped Class Status Grading

Although most educators teach different sections of the same course identically and group such sections together for assigning grades, it should be recognized that certain classes might have advantages over others. For example, in a conditioning course where cardiovascular endurance is a major objective, sections meeting three times a week may have an advantage over sections meeting twice a week, since a person can do only so much jogging per period in developing endurance. Moreover, time of day, weather conditions, and other factors may have a more advantageous influence on one course section than on another. Thus, the educator may feel it important to consider each course section as an independent unit and evaluate each student according to his ability and opportunity to achieve the objectives in that course section.

If we were to look at the towns along a highway, we would undoubtedly find in each town successful, average, and less successful people. In each town people will have achieved their status independent of the influence of other towns. The same can be true of different schools or of different course sections within a school. There is no sure way to standardize all conditions whereby an A grade in one course section would be an A in all course sections, or that an A in one school would also be an A in another school, or that an A under one teacher would be an A under a different teacher.

Since unique circumstances surround each course section, some educators feel that the best that they can do is to determine which students in a course section accumulated the most points and thereby assign them an A, and then which students accumulated enough points for a B, and then so on down to the lowest group for that course section. Each section would be treated independently. On the other hand, if class sections are grouped for grading purposes, the teacher must assume that all students have equal opportunity to achieve and that all conditions were equally favorable for each course section. While such equalization may be possible, it could prove most difficult to achieve.

Multiple Observation for Grading

A teacher should not rely solely on one method of evaluation or on a single instrument in collecting scores for determining grades. It would seem much more desirable to use a combination of many instruments and procedures that take into account course objectives, the various facets of performance, and the multiple needs of the students. It is not enough that the teacher merely test skill performance; he should also measure knowledge and physical fitness and then combine the observations to determine the overall grade.

Reporting Grades

The final grade for a course should be reported in nothing more than a matter-of-fact manner. The grade should be based on total points accumulated. For example, the instructor, upon being queried by a student, might report as follows:

> You had a total of 225 points which ranks you fifth out of the thirty students in the class. This places you within the B level.

This type of reporting is divorced from the influence of trying to use grades for discipline or in trying to justify assigning high grades to low level performers and low grades to high level performers. It is a matter-of-fact presentation of "Here are the tests, reports, and other assignments completed and these are the points you accumulated."

Principles of Grading

By way of summary, it is important that basic principles of grading be recognized and followed:

1. Measurement and evaluation for grading purposes must be based on the educational objectives of the course, not trivial or insignificant rules and procedures.
2. Grading in physical education should be commensurate with grading in other subject areas of the school.
3. The awarding of grades should be closely related to experiences occurring in real-life situations where honors, promotions, and rewards result, thereby preparing students for life after graduation.
4. Grades should be assigned on the basis of the number of points accumulated in a course, reflecting the students' relative achievement in meeting the objectives.
5. Grades should be based on a sufficient number of observations. In physical education, grades should be based on more than one objective.

Determining Grades in Physical Education

Determining grades in physical education classes is one of the most perplexing problems that physical educators face. Since grades should be the result of accurate evaluations of the student's achievement toward the major objectives, varied evidence must be collected and weighted to assure validity and fairness. The primary purpose of grading is to report to the student, the parents, and interested educational administrators an evaluation of the student's achievement. The logical steps which are necessary for effectively determining grades in physical education are discussed below.

Selecting and Loading Course Objectives

In physical education classes, the instructor must rely upon logic and philosophy to determine what objectives are most important in accordance with the nature of the activity and the needs of the student. The emphasis varies from one instructor to another and from course to course. Thus, one instructor may select and load the objectives in a particular course as follows: physical fitness, 50 percent; skill, 25 percent; and knowledge, 25 percent. In this case the area of social development was not considered in terms of making up part of the grade; instead the teacher might elect to use the results of social measurement for guidance purposes. Another instructor might feel that skills should make up 40 percent of the grade; physical fitness, 25 percent; knowledge, 25 percent; and social development, 10 percent. As can be seen from these examples, the amount of weight an objective carries in evaluation depends upon the philosophy of the teacher as well as on the particular course that is being taught.

Selecting and Administering Tests for the Instructional Unit

If an instructional unit covers a six week period, then an adequate but reasonable number of tests should be selected to assess student progress within this period. The selection of tests should be made on the basis of the weighted objectives for the course and the type of activity in which the students engaged during the instructional unit. The data in Table 5-1 represent scores of eight tests that were administered during a six week softball unit. Four tests are skill items (representing 50 percent of the unit grade), two tests are physical fitness items (representing 25 percent of the unit grade), one test is for knowledge (representing 12.5 percent of the unit grade), and one test is for social measurement (representing 12.5 percent of the unit grade). In the illustration, each test item is considered to have equal weight; therefore, each item would be worth 12.5 percent. Consequently, once raw scores have been converted to scale scores or some type of standard score, the teacher can merely total the standard scores and convert them into letter grades. Obviously, this would not always be the case. Some items may be weighted more heavily than others, so they would be multiplied by that weight before the grand total is computed.

Treating Raw Scores

Since raw scores from different tests are not directly comparable, it becomes necessary to use some type of score which will reduce such variables as time, distance, and rating scores to a common denominator. Two methods of treating raw scores are presented below as examples.

Rating Scale Scores. This method is recommended for use with small classes (thirty students or less). It is expedient and can be used by those with a limited background in statistics. The following steps may be used for this method:

1. Record raw scores from each test item in every other blank by the student's name. This leaves a space for each test item's scale score to be recorded later. Example:

Name	Pull-ups	Scale Score	12' Run-Walk	Scale Score
A.L.	17		2	
A.D.	8		2.2	
A.J.	10		2.4	
B.B.	5		1.0	
B.C.	19		1.5	
B.D.	14		2.1	
C.C.	6		1.3	
C.D.	12		1.6	
C.E.	16		1.8	
D.E.	3		2.5	

2. Rank the raw scores from high to low and assign five points to the highest 10 percent of scores; four points to the next 20 percent of scores; three points to the next 40 percent of scores; two points to the next 20 percent

of scores; and one point to the lowest 10 percent of scores. Example:

Pull-ups	Scale Score	12' Run-Walk	Scale Score
19	5 points	2.5	5 points
17	4 points	2.4	4 points
16		2.2	
14		2.1	
12	3 points	2.0	3 points
10		1.8	
8		1.6	
6		1.5	
5	2 points	1.3	2 points
3	1 point	1.0	1 point

3. If the test item is to be weighted for extra points, multiply the weight of the item times the scale score. Example: In this case the teacher decides to give the pull-up test a weight of two. Thus, A.L. would have four scale points times two for a total of eight points for pull-ups; and three scale points times three for a total of nine points for the 12 minute run test.

4. Transfer scale points or weighted scale points into the score book. Example:

Name	Pull-ups	Scale Score	12' Run-Walk	Scale Score
A.L.	17	8	2	9
A.D.	8	6	2.2	12
A.J.	10	6	2.4	12
B.B.	5	4	1.0	3
B.C.	19	10	1.5	6
B.D.	14	6	2.1	9
C.C.	6	4	1.3	6
C.D.	12	6	1.6	9
C.E.	16	8	1.8	9
D.E.	3	2	2.5	15

NAME	Accuracy Throw	T-Score	Fungo Hitting	T-Score	Speed Throw	T-Score	Fielding Ground Balls	T-Score	Softball Throw	T-Score	50-Yard Dash	T-Score	Knowledge Test	T-Score	Social Test	T-Score	Total T-Score	Average T-Score	Observation Method	Curve Method	Absolute Method
	6-Weeks Skill Test—50% (AAHPER Items)								**Phy. Fit.—25%** (AAHPER Items)				**Know. 12½%**		**So.D. 12½%**		**Computations**		**Grading Methods**		
1 A.L.	25	72	39	66	14.2	57	20	63	291	80	6.3	55	97	68	89	62	523	65	A	A	A
2 A.D.	16	54	34	60	17.6	45	18	57	176	46	6.8	49	80	53	96	68	432	54	B	B	C
3 A.J.	12	46	28	53	15.6	48	14	43	195	51	6.5	52	65	39	78	52	384	48	C–	C	D
4 B.B.	11	44	19	41	15.3	53	18	57	180	47	6.4	53	90	62	68	42	399	50	C	C	C
5 B.C.	17	56	28	53	13.9	58	17	53	190	50	6.6	51	66	40	87	60	421	53	B–	C	C
6 B.D.	14	50	21	44	18.3	43	20	63	249	64	6.9	48	72	45	77	51	408	51	C	C	C
7 C.C.	23	68	17	39	14.5	56	15	47	171	45	6.5	52	88	60	93	65	432	54	B	B	C
8 C.D.	15	52	37	63	15.6	52	18	57	185	49	6.7	50	64	38	65	40	401	50	C	C	C
9 C.E.	10	42	26	50	13.2	60	17	53	163	43	7.0	47	78	51	79	53	399	50	C	C	C
10 D.E.	13	48	15	36	14.8	45	16	50	235	63	6.0	58	96	67	72	46	413	52	C	C	C
11 D.I.	13	48	32	58	18.9	41	20	63	155	40	7.0	47	71	44	95	67	408	51	C	C	C
12 D.K.	21	64	11	31	14.8	55	12	37	190	50	6.7	50	77	50	74	48	385	48	C–	C	D
13 E.E.	14	50	26	50	14.9	54	16	50	150	39	5.6	62	87	59	71	45	409	51	C	C	C
14 E.L.	9	40	40	68	12.8	61	10	30	226	60	7.1	45	68	42	86	59	405	51	C	C	C
15 E.M.	12	46	29	54	19.9	38	20	63	195	51	6.5	52	76	49	56	32	385	48	C–	C	D
16 F.G.	8	38	14	35	16.2	50	17	53	141	36	7.7	39	95	66	76	50	367	46	D	D	D
17 F.H.	4	30	31	56	14.9	46	9	27	218	58	6.0	58	75	48	63	47	370	49	C	C	D
18 F.P.	19	60	25	49	16.7	48	19	60	198	52	6.4	53	85	57	83	56	435	54	B	B	C
19 G.G.	13	48	36	63	16.2	50	6	17	117	29	6.6	51	58	33	70	44	335	42	F	D	F
20 G.Z.	7	36	13	34	12.1	64	17	53	213	57	6.1	57	75	48	66	40	389	49	C	C	D
21 G.J.	12	46	30	55	21.2	33	17	53	185	49	10.6	7	84	56	73	47	346	43	F	D	D
22 H.I.	18	58	23	46	15.3	47	19	60	180	47	6.7	50	60	35	61	36	379	47	D	D	D
23 H.M.	6	34	35	61	26.1	17	9	27	207	55	6.2	56	73	46	85	58	354	46	D	D	D
24 H.O.	11	44	21	44	17.2	47	16	50	198	52	6.7	50	63	37	72	46	370	46	D	D	D
25 I.K.	17	56	29	54	10.0	71	19	60	203	54	6.3	55	75	48	58	34	442	54	B	B	C

*Note that the observation method rendered the nearest approximation to the normal curve with the twenty-five average T-scores.

T-Scores. A second method of treating raw scores is to convert them into T-scores. The T-score has the advantage of always being positive and in whole numbers between 0-100. The expedient method shown in Chapter 3 is recommended with large groups.

While converting raw scores into T-scores may seem like excessive work, it soon becomes as familiar as other less acceptable scoring systems. A major advantage of the T-score method is that it shows the arithmetical distance of each score from the mean of the distribution, thus avoiding a distortion of differences. See Chapter 3 for greater detail concerning T-scores.

Converting Total Points or Average Points into Letter Grades

Once all of the different test items have been numerically scored, treated, and totaled, it usually becomes necessary to convert total points or average points into letter grades of A, B, C, D, and F for the report card. Converting total or average points into letter grades may involve any one or more of several methods. The methods of curve grading, grading by absolute standards, and grading by observation of scores are discussed below with examples given for each using the average T-scores shown in Table 5-1.

Grading on an Absolute Standard

In this method, the teacher or the school sets up standards whereby each student's final score must fall into a scale such as: 95-100=A; 85-94=B; 76-84=C; 66-75=D; and below 65=F. For this system to work satisfactorily, the measuring instruments must be right, or the teacher will end up adjusting the difficulty of tests so that the majority of students will not end up with extremely high or low grades. Table 5-2 shows the computations that are necessary to convert the average T-scores into percentages for the scale. Notice that the highest average T-score of 65 must be treated as the highest possible score in order to bring the other scores up high enough to fit into the scale.

Other obvious disadvantages to absolute grading are the following: (a) that frequently additional computations must be made after final average scores have been computed in order to satisfactorily fit such scores into the absolute scale pattern, and (b) that allowances are not made when differences are slight and

Table 5-2
Converting Average T-Scores into Percentages for the Absolute Scale

$$\frac{65}{65}(100) = 100$$

$$\frac{54}{65}(100) = 83$$

$$\frac{48}{65}(100) = 74$$

$$\frac{50}{65}(100) = 77$$

$$\frac{53}{65}(100) = 82$$

$$\frac{51}{65}(100) = 78$$

$$\frac{48}{65}(100) = 74$$

$$\frac{54}{65}(100) = 83$$

$$\frac{46}{65}(100) = 71$$

$$\frac{54}{65}(100) = 83$$

Absolute Scale*	Frequency	Grade
95 − 100	1	A
85 − 94	0	B
76 − 84	13	C
66 − 75	10	D
0 − 65	1	F
	N = 25	

*Note that when all 25 percentages are computed, grading by absolute standards resulted in too many Cs and Ds and no Bs.

Interval	Tallies	f	d	fd	fd^2	Computations
64-65	1	1	8	8	64	$C = \dfrac{\Sigma fd}{N} = \dfrac{21}{25} = .84$
62-63	0	0	7	0	0	
60-61	0	0	6	0	0	$Ci = .84 \times 2 = 1.68$
58-59	0	0	5	0	0	$AM = 48.50$
56-57	0	0	4	0	0	$M = AM + Ci = 48.50 + 1.68$
54-55	||||	4	3	12	36	$M = \underline{50.18}$
52-53	||	2	2	4	8	$s = \sqrt{\dfrac{\Sigma fd^2}{N} - C^2} \; X\,i$
50-51	⫽⊔⊔⊓ ||	7	1	7	7	$s = \sqrt{\dfrac{137}{25} - .84^2} \times 2$
48-49	⫽⊔⊔⊓	5	0	0	0	$s = \sqrt{5.48 - .7056} \times 2$
46-47	||||	4	-1	-4	4	$s = \sqrt{4.7744} \times 2$
44-45	0	0	-2	0	0	$s = 2.19 \times 2$
42-43	||	2	-3	-6	18	$s = \underline{4.38}$

$$N = 25 \qquad \Sigma fd = 21 \quad \Sigma fd^2 = 137$$

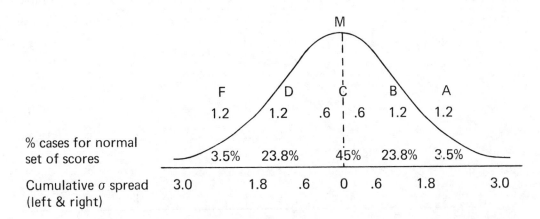

Figure 5-1. The Normal Curve Showing Letter Grade Areas with Sigma Values

one score inhibits the next higher grade from being assigned.

Curve Grading

Curve grading is based upon the mean and standard deviation found for a group of scores. Although many teachers indicate that they grade on a curve, very few actually find the mean and standard deviation which are needed for true curve grading.

The steps necessary for curve grading are presented as follows:

1. Set up a frequency distribution and compute the mean and standard deviation for a set of scores. Table 5-3 shows this step using the average T-scores from a six-week softball unit.

2. Divide the number of letter grades to be used into the *sigma* spread of six (since 3s above the mean and 3s below the mean contain practically all the scores). Example: Using the five letter grades of A, B, C, D, and F, we divide 6s by 5 and get 1.2s per letter grade (2).

3. Figure the *sigma* range per letter grade with the mean at the midpoint of the C range. Example: See Figure 5-1.

    C range=Mean $\pm$.6s (since the mean splits the 1.2s area of the C range, we have .6s above and below the mean).

    B range=.6s to 1.8s above the mean (.6s+1.2=upper limit of 1.8s).

    A range=1.8s and above.

    D range=.6s to 1.8s below the mean.

    F range=1.8s and below.

4. Figure the score range per letter grade. From our previous computations on the softball grading unit (Table 5-3), we found a true mean of 50.18 and a standard deviation

of 4.38. Thus, we have the information necessary for the computations in Table 5-4.

5. Figure the frequency of scores in each grade range as shown in the f column of Table 5-4.

6. Plot the curve for the group. See Figure 5-2.

The above application of curve grading to the final scores of twenty-five students in a six-week softball unit yielded 4 percent As, 16 percent Bs, 56 percent Cs, 24 percent Ds, and no Fs. The deviation between the percentages elicited here and those cited earlier in Figure 5-1 where scores were normally distributed is due to a lack of normality of scores for this small classroom-size group.

By comparing the sample grading curve (Figure 5-2) with the ideal grading curve (Figure 5-1), any one or more of the following implications may become evident to the teacher as he evaluates the testing situation:

1. The test factors making up the final composite score average were too hard for the group.

2. The group was a little below average in comparison with past groups who had taken the same tests.

3. The teacher failed to cover certain skills and knowledges thoroughly before testing.

4. There perhaps were not enough cases to exhibit normality.

While curve grading is a scientific approach to assigning grades and enables the teacher to evaluate the testing results in terms of what should be normal, it has the following disadvantages:

1. It is more applicable to groups larger than those found in the average classroom.

2. It requires additional computations after final average scores have been computed.

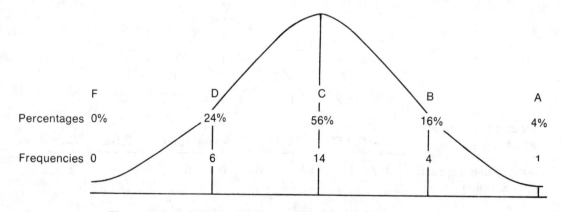

	F	D	C	B	A
Percentages	0%	24%	56%	16%	4%
Frequencies	0	6	14	4	1

Figure 5-2. Curve Grading Based on Twenty-five Final Scores

Table 5-4
*Computing the Score Range per Letter Grade**

Grade	σ Value X Standard Dev. ± Mean	Grade Scale (Rounded)	Frequency
A		59 & above	1
B	1.8 X SD of 4.38 = 7.884 + M of 50.18	54-58	4
C	0.6 X SD of 4.38 = 2.628 ± M of 50.18	48-53	14
D	1.8 X SD of 4.38 = 7.884 – M of 50.18	42-47	6
F		41 & below	0
			N = 25

*Computations for the A and F range are not necessary when the C, B, and D ranges are computed first.

3. It may distinguish between two scores when there is only as slight a difference as one point, resulting in one score getting a lower grade than the other.

4. When strictly followed, it frequently allows above-average students to *coast* and still get a high grade, while weak students may work exceedingly hard and never get higher than a D or F.

Grading by Observation of Scores

This method is quite simple in that final scores are merely listed down a page in a high-to-low order. After closely observing the scores, lines are drawn between the natural breaks in scores which frequently separate upper and lower groups from the large average group. If a break does not appear within a reasonable distance, keen judgment must be used in determining where the cut-off point is, say between a B and a C. In cases where scores run close together, some teachers find it satisfactory and fair to designate the top score of what they would normally consider to be in the C group as a B- (although it may eventually be recorded as a B), and the next lower score would be considered as a C. This procedure is shown in Table 5-5. Usually some type of a rough guide should be followed in determining how many As, Bs, Cs, etc., should be given. For example, the highest 10 percent of the scores could be assigned As; the next 20 percent Bs; the next 40 percent Cs; the next 20 percent Ds; and the lowest 10 percent Fs. It is important to note that this system imposes somewhat of a normal curve on the students and yet, with small classes, the actual performances may not approach normality. Thus, the percentages given for As, Bs, Cs, etc., need not be followed slavishly, but it should be used merely as a guide. If the teacher feels that the class was especially good, he may assign more high grades and less low grades and vice versa if he felt the class was below par.

Assigning grades by observation of scores allows the teacher to use the performance of a student in relation to that of classmates who have been through the same procedure, plus, the teacher is free to use his keenest insight in assigning grades with both individual capacity and standards in mind. Another advantage of this method is that additional computations are not necessary once the average T-scores have been computed.

Contract Grading

Bloom and others (3) suggest that the physical education teacher could preestablish what performance scores will indicate mastery of material. Then, it would be possible for all students to receive grades of A in a course, depending upon such factors as the abilities of the students and the pedagogical process of the instructor. In this method, grades are determined from pre-test criteria rather than from actual test data.

Determining the Final Letter Grade from Sub-Area Letter Grades

Up to this point our discussion has centered upon accumulating points in various testing areas (objectives) and then, as a last step, assigning the letter grade. However, some teachers prefer to establish letter grades for

Grade and Value Scale

Grade	Value
A+	12
A	11
A-	10
B+	9
B	8
B-	7
C+	6
C	5
C-	4
D+	3
D	2
D-	1
F	0

Example I. Weighting of Objectives (will vary with different units)

Skills	50%	= .50
Knowledge	25%	- .25
Fitness	15%	= .15
Social	10%	= .10

A student is graded as follows:

Objective	Grade	Points	Percent	Point Value
Skills	B+	9	.50	4.5
Knowledge	C-	4	.25	1.0
Fitness	B	8	.15	1.2
Social	C	5	.10	1.0
			Total Value =	7.2

Thus, a total value of 7.2 in the grade and value scale indicates a final grade of B-.

Example II. Different Weighting of Objectives

Skills	40%	= .40
Knowledge	20%	= .20
Fitness	30%	= .30
Social	10%	= .10

A student is graded as follows:

Objective	Grade	Points		Percent	Point Value
Skills	C-	4	X	.40	1.6
Knowledge	B+	9	X	.20	1.8
Fitness	D	2	X	.30	.6
Social	A	11	X	.10	1.1
				Total Value =	5.1

Thus, a total value of 5.1 in the grade and value scale indicates a final grade of C.

Figure 5-3. Determining the Final Letter Grade from Sub-Area Letter Grades

each major objective and then make a decision as to the final letter grade. Thus, two examples are given in Figure 5-3 whereby sub-area letter grades are converted into a total value and then compared to a grade and value scale for the final grade.

Summary

To briefly summarize the important points concerning grading in physical education classes, it must be remembered that the grade should reflect achievement toward the objectives for the unit of instruction. Administrative policies such as tardies and absences should not be scored and figured as a factor in the grade.

The steps to grading for a unit of instruction are listed as follows:
1. Establish sound objectives or goals for the unit.
2. Determine the importance or weight of each objective before instruction begins.
3. Select and administer a practical number of tests during the unit of instruction.
4. Treat raw scores and derive either grand total points or average points.
5. Convert total or average points into letter grades by one of the following methods:
   a. Absolute standards.
   b. Curve grading.
   c. Observation of scores.

Although there are many varied methods of grading, there is probably no one best method

Table 5-5
Grading by Observation of Scores

Six Weeks Average T-Scores (Softball)		
65	=	A
54		
54	=	B
54		
54		
53	=	B–
52		
51		
51		
51		
51	=	C
50		
50		
50		
49		
49		
48		
48	=	C–
48		
47		
46	=	D
46		
46		
43	=	F
42		

to fit all situations. However, the physical educator should make every effort to establish a fair and sound method of testing and grading which will fit into the evaluation policies of the school.

Bibliography

1. Barrow, Harold M., and Rosemary McGee, *A Practical Approach to Measurement in Physical Education*, Philadelphia: Lea and Febiger, 1964, pp. 436-453.
2. Bayles, Ernest E., "The Philosophical Approach to Educational Measurement," *Educational Administration and Supervision*, 26:455-461, September, 1940.
3. Bloom, Benjamin, and others, *Formative and Summative Evaluation*, New York: McGraw-Hill Book Company, 1971.
4. Bovard, John F., Frederick W. Cozens, and E. Patricia Hagman, *Tests and Measurements in Physical Education*, 3rd ed., Philadelphia: W. B. Saunders Company, 1950, pp. 3-4.
5. Brubacher, John S., *Modern Philosophies of Education*, 3rd ed., New York: McGraw-Hill Book Company, 1962, p. 253.
6. Dewey, John, "Progressive Education and the Science of Education," *Progressive Education*, 5:200, August, 1928.
7. _____, *The Sources of a Science of Education*, New York: Liveright Publishing Company, 1929, pp. 64-65.
8. Duncan, Ray O., "Fundamental Issues in Our Profession, *Journal of Health Physical Education Recreation*, May, 1964.
9. Fabricius, Helen, "Grading in Physical Education," *Journal of Health Physical Education Recreation*, May, 1967.
10. Garrett, Henry E., *Statistics in Psychology and Education*, 6th ed., New York: David McKay, 1966.
11. Hanson, Dale L., "Grading in Physical Education," *Journal of Health Physical Education Recreation*, May, 1967.
12. Kilpatrick, William H., *A Reconstructed Theory of the Educative Process*, New York: Columbia University, 1935, pp. 29-30.
13. Larson, Leonard A., and Rachael D. Yocom, *Measurement and Evaluation in Physical, Health, and Recreation Education*, St. Louis: C. V. Mosby Company, 1951.
14. Mathews, Donald K., *Measurement in Physical Education*, Philadelphia: W. B. Saunders Company, 1963, pp. 313-328.
15. Remmers, H. H., and others, *A Practical Introduction to Measurement and Evaluation*, New York: Harper and Row, Publishers, 1965, pp. 286-302.
16. Singer, Robert, "Grading in Physical Education," *Journal of Health Physical Education Recreation*, May, 1967.
17. Smith, Fred M., and Sam Adams, *Educational Measurement for the Classroom Teacher*, New York: Harper and Row, Publishers, 1966, pp. 194-199.
18. Solley, William H., "Grading in Physical Education," *Journal of Health Physical Education Recreation*, May, 1967.

Part Three
Physical
Fitness
Measurement

Distinction Between Physical Fitness and Motor Fitness

Since the days of the early Greeks, physical fitness has been an important objective of physical education. In fact, the desire to establish a scientific approach to the development of physical fitness was the primary reason for the meeting of physical educators in 1885 that resulted in the birth of our profession.* Through the years, interest in physical fitness has been somewhat cyclic in nature, being affected by draft statistics, the emphasis on fitness during time of war, and the Kraus-Weber Test in which American youth were found to be inferior when compared with children of other countries with regard to minimum muscular fitness.** The latter, of course, resulted in President Eisenhower's establishing in 1956 the President's Council of Youth Fitness which launched the recent wave of concern for physical fitness.

Yet, despite the long-standing concern for physical fitness and the vast amount of research on the subject, there is evidently considerable difference of opinion within the profession as to what elements constitute physical fitness. Perhaps this is typical of any concept within the disciplines that attempt to study human behavior. For example, members of the medical profession do not always agree on what is the definition of health. The lack of agreement regarding the concept of physical fitness basically centers around whether or not items involving skill and ability should be included in such a battery. Some authors list only the relatively basic elements, such as strength, muscular endurance and cardiovascular endurance. Others build from this base and include items of agility, flexibility, power, balance, speed, and neuromuscular coordination.

Definitions are largely matters of opinion. Consequently, we certainly cannot settle the issue. *For the record this text endorses the concept of physical fitness which includes the elements of strength, muscular endurance, circulorespiratory endurance, and flexibility, and freedom from obesity.* The other qualities, we feel, are abilities which underlie motor performance but are not essential for basic physical fitness. In other words, a person does not have to possess speed, agility, power, etc., which make for success in athletics, in order to be physically fit. If the reverse were true, then a person who is slow of foot, poorly coordinated, or crippled could never be physically fit. We might add that we include the element of flexibility in physical fitness primarily because it is important in preventing injury while carrying on one's daily activities, and it is an indicator of regularity of exercise and fitness. We do not wish to imply that everyone should be able to do the splits or be able to tie themselves into knots.

Recently, more and more physical educators are adding weight control, or freedom from obesity, as a component of physical fitness. The impetus for this no doubt came from the medical profession. The many medical problems associated with obesity call for cooperative effort between the medical fields and physical education. Although the causes of obesity are complex, lack of physical activity is a major behavior characteristic held in common by a large percentage of obese persons. Moreover, regular physical exercise has been shown to be an effective means for reducing fat and maintaining sufficient muscle mass. Physical fitness is sometimes defined in terms of the capacity to do work. In this context, obesity is definitely a negative factor and thus the avoidance of obesity qualifies as a viable component of health-related (physical) fitness.

The term *motor fitness*, while often used synonymously with physical fitness, was coined to include elements which involve more abilities than those basic physical fitness components yet was not to encom-

---

*Eugene Nixon, and Frederich W. Cozens, *An Introduction to Physical Education*, revised by John E. Nixon and Florence S. Frederickson, Philadelphia: W. B. Saunders Company, 6th ed., 1964, p. 209.

**Hans Kraus, and Ruth Hirschland, "Minimum Muscular Fitness Tests in School Children," *Research Quarterly*, 25:178-188, May, 1954.

pass the various neuromuscular coordination skills which make up general motor ability. Motor fitness takes into account efficiency of basic movements and therefore would involve such elements as power, agility, speed, and balance.

It seems important that we should not be too careless in the use of the various terms. It well may be that it is more desirable to develop (and measure) motor fitness than basic physical fitness in the schools. The objectives of physical education include the development of efficiency in the fundamental movements, as well as the development of neuromuscular skills and organic efficiency. However, the distinction between skill and organic fitness should be made clear to the student. *Two examples that represent opposite but equally unfortunate misconceptions come to mind. First, the student with poor skills should be made to realize that he still can be physically fit. Second, it is just as important that the individual who excels at throwing a softball for distance understands that this does not make up for scoring lowest in the mile run insofar as physical fitness is concerned.* As usual, proper interpretation is imperative in order for the maximum worth of a test to be realized.

Tests for measuring each of the components of physical fitness as viewed by your authors are presented in the following five chapters: Chapter 6, flexibility; Chapter 7, strength; Chapter 8, muscular endurance; Chapter 9, cardiovascular endurance; and Chapter 10, anthropometric measurements, body build, and body composition. To our knowledge, there are no standardized test batteries that are made up solely of these components, other than the Texas Governor's Physical Fitness Test and the South Carolina Fitness Test. While these tests separate fitness and motor performance items, they lack a true measure of strength, and in the case of the Texas test, there is no flexibility item or body composition item.

The available published tests of the armed services, tests of the different state departments of education, etc., actually fall under the category of motor fitness tests as we have defined them. In fact, some of the test items, such as skill in throwing a ball, would be more appropriately classed as general motor ability test items. A number of these published tests are presented in Chapter 18 under the heading Motor Performance Test Batteries.

In Chapter 11, we have suggested some physical fitness batteries for boys and girls in elementary, junior high, and high school and college that adhere to our concept of physical fitness.

Chapter Six

The Measurement of Flexibility

Flexibility, as a component of physical fitness, is the ability of an individual to move the body and its parts through as wide a range of motion as possible without undue strain to the articulations and muscle attachments. When we speak of flexibility, we inevitably hear of such terms as *flexion,* where the angle of the body and its articulations are decreased through movement; *extension,* where the angle of the body and its articulations are increased through movement; *hyperextension,* where the angle of a joint is extended beyond its normal range; *double jointedness,* a nonexistent condition, but nevertheless a term used when referring to a person with unusual flexibility in certain positions; and finally, *muscleboundness,* an unfortunate term used to describe cases of inflexibility when an individual happens to have well-developed muscles. Regardless of how you define or describe it, flexibility provides another dimension in performance that allows a higher degree of freedom and ease of movement coupled with some important implications for greater safety from injury. Moreover, flexibility measurement brings to light other concepts which must be identified in order to properly select and score available tests. For example, it appears necessary to identify two types of flexibility tests:

1. *Relative Flexibility Tests,* those designed to be relative to the length or width of a specific body part. In these tests you measure not only the movement, but also the length or width of an influencing body part.
2. *Absolute Flexibility Tests,* those where you measure only the movement in relation to an absolute performance goal. For example, on the splits you determine the distance between the floor (which is the goal) and the performer's seat (20).

Still further, flexibility scores may be reported as a result of *linear measurement,* where scores occur in inches or millimeters as determined from use of a tape measure, yardstick, or flexomeasure; and *rotary measurement,* where scores occur in degrees of rotation as determined by the use of a protractor, goniometer, or flexometer. Although flexibility correlates minimally with some motor abilities, it is usually considered to be an important factor in certain activities, as exemplified by the diver flexing and extending in the air; or by the swimmer executing the butterfly stroke with the dolphin fishtail kick. Since it is difficult to determine how much flexion-extension is good or bad for an individual, the coach and student must evaluate the degree needed in each specific joint in terms of ease of performance and safety in the activity or part of the body that is involved. Flexibility is also usually mentioned when one is describing physical fitness. A loss in flexibility is frequently noticed as being one of the first signs of getting *out of shape.*

Uses of Flexibility Tests

Several ways by which flexibility tests are utilized in physical education classes are as follows:
1. As a factor in physical fitness tests.
2. As a means to determine potential in certain sports activities.

3. As a means for determining achievement and skill grades when flexibility performance is a specific objective in the teaching unit.
4. As a means to diagnose the extent of a previous injury or the cause of poor posture.

Practical Tests of Flexibility

The Leighton Flexometer (29) and the electrogoniometer (1) are usually regarded as the most accurate instruments for the measurement of flexibility; however, the tests presented may be accurately and satisfactorily utilized with an inexpensive instrument, the aluminum flexomeasure (22), in those schools which do not have the more expensive equipment. While the tests presented in the following pages contain college-age norms, complete elementary norms (grades one through six) are available

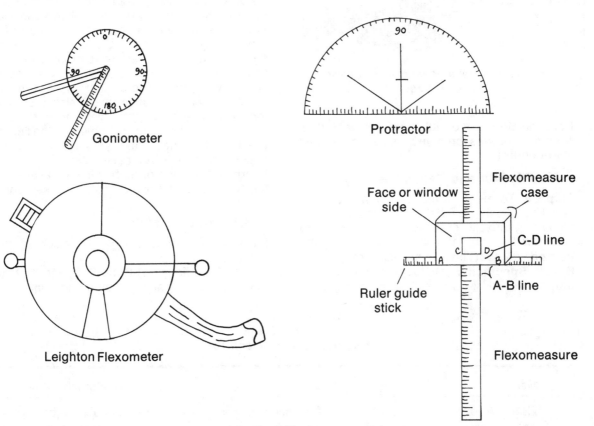

Figure 6-1. Flexibility Instruments *

*Various flexibility instruments are available for use in flexibility measurement. Information on these instruments is available from these companies:
Electrogoniometer—Electrogoniometer Manual, Springfield College (Dept. of HPER), Springfield, Mass.
Flexomeasure with instructions and performance norms—B & L Products Company, P.O. Box 473, Portland, Tex. 78374.
Goniometer—Rajowalt Company, Atwood, Ind.
Leighton Flexometer—C. H. Stoelting Company, 1350 S. Kostner Ave., Chicago, Ill. 60623.

Figure 6-2. Flexomeasure Position for Splits Test

press to handstand in floor exercise as well as in other gymnastic skills.

Age Level: Ages six through college.

Sex: Satisfactory as a test for both boys and girls.

Reliability: An *r* of .94 was found when the best score of three trials was recorded from separate testings and correlated.

Objectivity: An *r* of .99 was found when the scores from an experienced tester were correlated with scores from an inexperienced tester.

Validity: Face validity was accepted for this test.

Equipment: Flexomeasure case with yardstick and tape. See Appendix I for alternate test without flexomeasure.

Directions: (1) Line up the 15-inch mark of the yardstick with a line on the floor and tape the ends of the stick to the floor so that the flexomeasure case (window side) is face down. (2) Sit down and line up your heels with the near edge of the 15-inch mark and slide your seat back beyond the zero end of the yardstick. (3) Have a partner stand and brace his or her toes against your heels. Also, have an assistant on each side to hold your knees in a locked position as you prepare to stretch. (4) With heels not more than 5 inches apart, slowly stretch forward, while pushing the flexomeasure case as far down the stick as possible with the fingertips of both hands. Take your reading at the near edge of the flexomeasure case.

Scoring: The best of three trials measured to the nearest quarter of an inch is your test score.

from the Brown and Littleman Company (21). Norms for grades three and four are presented in Appendix H.

Modified Sit-and-Reach Test (22)

Purpose: To measure the development of hip and back flexion as well as extension of the hamstring muscles of the legs. The object is to see how far you can extend your fingertips beyond your foot line with the legs straight.

Sports Specificity: (1) Vaulting, diving, and trampoline skills; (2) straight-arm, straight-leg

Bridge-up Test (22)

Purpose: To develop hyperextension of the spine.

Sports Specificity: (1) Butterfly event; (2) high jump event; (3) balance beam and floor exer-

Table 6-1
Modified Sit-and-Reach Test

Men	Level	Women
23¾ - Above	Advanced	25¾ - Above
21¼ - 23½	Adv. Intermediate	22½ - 25½
18¾ - 21	Intermediate	20 - 22¼
17 - 18½	Adv. Beginner	18 - 19¾
Below - 16¾	Beginner	Below - 17¾

Based on the scores of 100 college men and 100 college women at Corpus Christi State University, Corpus Christi, Tx., 1977.

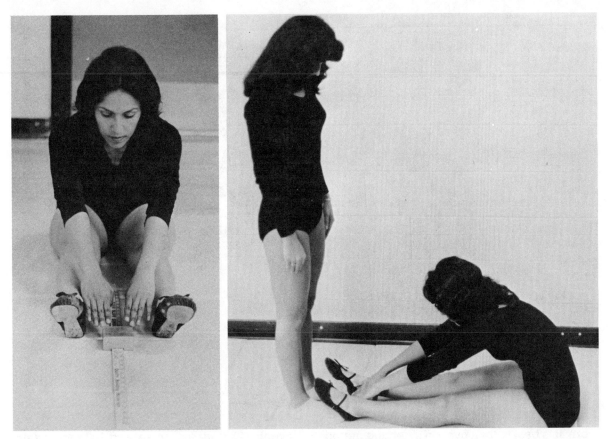

Figure 6-3. Modified Sit-and-Reach Test

cise skills in gymnastics; (4) modern dance and ballet movements.

Age Level: Ages six through college.

Sex: Satisfactory as a test for both boys and girls.

Reliability: An *r* of .97 was found when the best score of three trials was recorded from separate testings and correlated.

Objectivity: An *r* of .99 was found when the scores from an experienced tester were correlated with scores from an inexperienced tester.

Validity: Face validity is acceptable for this test when students are strong enough to extend the body from the floor.

Equipment: Flexomeasure case with yardstick and ruler guide inserted. Be sure the *A—B* line of the case is nearest the zero end of the yardstick. See Appendix I for alternate test without flexomeasure.

Directions: (1) Assume a supine (back-lying) position on the floor (or a mat) and tilt your head back as you push upward, arching your back while walking the hands and feet as close together as possible. (2) Your partner, located at one side, places the zero end of the yard-

stick on the mat or floor and slides the flexomeasure case vertically upward until the ruler guide touches the highest point of your arched spine. The reading (to the nearest quarter of an inch) is taken in the case window at the lower (*C—D*) line.

Scoring: The best score (to the nearest quarter of an inch) of three trials is recorded and then subtracted from your standing height (floor to navel).

Example:
Standing height = 46 inches (floor to navel)
Best arch = 30
       Score   16 inches

The closer your arch upward gets to your standing navel height, the better your score. Thus, the less the difference, the better the performance.

Additional Pointers: (1) Your thumbs should be next to your ears as you push your body upward from the floor. (2) If you are too weak to push upward, your head may remain on the floor as you arch your back for the measurement. (3) Do not strain unduly to arch for a good

Figure 6-4. Bridge-up Test

score. It is best to train over an extended period of time and thus avoid injury. (4) The tester should slide the case upward rapidly to get the correct reading since this exercise is difficult for some individuals to hold.

Front-to-Rear Splits Test (20)

Purpose: To develop the extension of the legs from front to rear. The object is to get the crotch as close to the floor as possible.

Sports and Dance Specificity: (1) Hurdling event; (2) floor exercise and balance beam events; (3) dance leaps (figure skating, ballet and modern dance, etc.).

Age Level: Ages six through college with extra training recommended for elementary students prior to testing.

Sex: Satisfactory as a test for both boys and girls.

Reliability: An *r* of .91 was found when the best score of three trials was recorded from separate testings and correlated.

Objectivity: An *r* of .99 was found when the

Table 6-2
Bridge-up Test

Men (Inches)	Men (Centimeters)	Level	Women (Inches)	Women (Centimeters)
12.5 - Less	31.8 - Less	Advanced	11.75 - Less	29.8 - Less
16.25 - 12.75	41.3 - 32.4	Adv. Intermediate	15.00 - 12.00	38.1 - 30.5
20.75 - 16.50	52.7 - 41.9	Intermediate	17.75 - 15.25	45.1 - 38.7
28.25 - 21.00	71.8 - 53.3	Adv. Beginner	20.75 - 18.00	52.7 - 45.7
Higher - 28.50	Higher - 72.4	Beginner	Higher - 21.50	Higher - 54.6

Based on the scores of 100 college men and 100 college women at Corpus Christi State University, Corpus Christi, Tx., 1977.

Table 6-3
Front-to-Rear Splits Test

Men		Level	Women	
(Inches)	(Centimeters)		(Inches)	(Centimeters)
2 - 0	5.1 - 0	Advanced	1½ - 0	3.8 - 0
6¼ - 2¼	15.9 - 5.7	Adv. Intermediate	4½ - 1¾	11.4 - 4.4
12¼ - 6½	31.1 - 16.5	Intermediate	8 - 4¾	20.3 - 12.1
15¾ -12½	40.0 - 31.8	Adv. Beginner	9¾ - 8¼	24.8 - 21.0
Above - 16	Above - 40.6	Beginner	Above - 10	Above - 25.4

Based on the scores of 100 college men and 100 college women at Corpus Christi State University, Corpus Christi, Tx., 1977.

Figure 6-5. Front Splits

scores from an experienced tester were correlated with scores from an inexperienced tester.
Validity: Face validity was accepted for this test.
Equipment: Flexomeasure case with yardstick and ruler guide inserted. Be sure the *A—B* line of the case is nearest the zero end of the yardstick.
Directions: (1) From a stand, extend the legs apart from the front to rear and lower the crotch as near to the floor as possible. Make it a slow steady motion without bouncing. (2) As you lower, an assistant should be positioned behind you with the zero end of the yardstick on the floor. (3) When you reach your lowest point, the case is raised upward until the ruler guide rests under your crotch. The reading to the nearest quarter of an inch is taken in the case window at the lower (*C—D*) line.
Scoring: The best score of three trials is recorded as the performance score.
Additional Pointers: (1) The knees must be locked at the moment of measurement. (2) The performer's hands may touch the floor for balance during the test.

Side Splits Test (22)

Purpose: To develop the extension in spreading the legs apart. The object is to get the crotch as close to the floor as possible.
Sports and Dance Specificity: (1) Vaulting, floor exercise, and balance beam events; (2) modern and ballet dance.
Age Level: Ages six through college.
Sex: Satisfactory as a test for both boys and girls.
Reliability: An *r* of .92 was found when the best score of three trials was recorded from separate testings and correlated.
Objectivity: An *r* of .99 was found when the scores from an experienced tester were correlated with scores from an inexperienced tester.
Validity: Face validity was accepted for this test.
Equipment: Same as for the Front-to-Rear Splits Test.
Directions: Same as for the Front-to-Rear Splits Test, except extend your legs apart (side-to-side) until your crotch is as near to the floor as possible.

Figure 6-6. Side Splits

Table 6-4
Side Splits Test

Men	Level	Women
3 - 0	Advanced	2¾ - 0
8 - 3¼	Adv. Intermediate	7½ - 3
17½ - 8¼	Intermediate	16¾ - 7¾
22½ - 17¾	Adv. Beginner	21½ - 17
Above - 22¾	Beginner	Above - 21¾

Based on the scores of 100 college men and 100 college women at Corpus Christi State University, Corpus Christi, Tx., 1977.

Scoring: Same as for the Front-to-Rear Splits Test, except use the scale presented in Table 6-4.
Additional Pointers: (1) The knees must be locked at the moment of measurement. (2) The performer's hands may touch the floor for balance during the test. (3) The performer's hips must not shift past the vertical during the measurement.

Shoulder-and-Wrist Elevation Test (22)

Purpose: To develop shoulder and wrist flexibility. *Note:* Since it is difficult to elevate the shoulders in this test without extending the wrists, the movements of these two joints are combined for the score.
Sports Specificity: (1) Gymnastics (bars and floor exercise skills); (2) butterfly stroke in swimming; (3) wrestling.
Age Level: Ages six through college.
Sex: Satisfactory as a test for both boys and girls.
Reliability: An *r* of .93 was found when the best score of three trials was recorded from separate testings and correlated.
Objectivity: An *r* of .99 was found when the

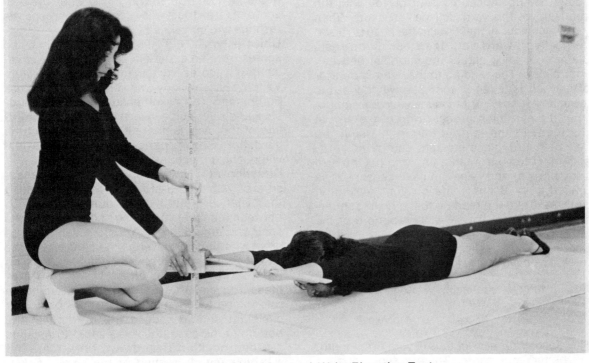

Figure 6-7. Shoulder-and-Wrist Elevation Test

Table 6-5
Shoulder-and-Wrist Elevation Test

Men	Level	Women
6 - 0	Advanced	5½ - 0
8¼ - 6¼	Adv. Intermediate	7½ - 5¾
11½ - 8½	Intermediate	10¾ - 7¾
12½ - 11¾	Adv. Beginner	11¾ - 11
Above - 12¾	Beginner	Above - 12

Based on the scores of 100 college men and 100 college women at Corpus Christi State University, Corpus Christi, Tx., 1977.

scores from an experienced tester were correlated with scores from an inexperienced tester.

Validity: Face validity was accepted for this test.

Equipment: Flexomeasure case with yardstick and ruler guide inserted, plus one extra yardstick. Be sure the A—B line of the case is nearest the zero end of the yardstick. See Appendix I for alternate text without flexomeasure.

Directions: (1) Assume a prone (facedown) position with your arms straight and grasp the extra yardstick about shoulder width apart. (2) Raise the stick upward as high as possible while keeping your chin on the floor and elbows straight. (3) As you raise the stick, an assistant should be positioned in front of you with the zero end of the yardstick on the floor. When you reach your highest point, the case is raised vertically upward until the ruler guide rests under your stick and at the midpoint between your hands. The reading to the nearest quarter of an inch is taken in the case window at the lower C—D line. (4) Measure your arm length from the acromion process (top of the arm at the joint) to the middle fingertip. Using the flexomeasure, place the zero end of the yardstick next to your middle fingertip (as the arm hangs down) and raise the flexomeasure case until the A—B line rests on your acromion process. Take the reading to the nearest quarter of an inch at the A—B line (bottom of the case).

Scoring: Your best lift of three trials is subtracted from your arm length.

Example: Arm length	=	30 inches
Best lift	=	16
Score		14 inches

The closer your arm lift gets to your arm length, the better your score. Thus, a score of zero would be perfect.

Additional Pointers: Although some individuals are so flexible that they can move the stick beyond the highest vertical point, the measurement must be taken at the highest vertical point.

Trunk-and-Neck Extension Test (20)

Purpose: To develop ability to extend the trunk and neck.

Sports Specificity: (1) Gymnastics (floor exercise, beam); (2) butterfly stroke and wrestling.

Age Level: Ages six through college.

Sex: Satisfactory as a test for both boys and girls.

Reliability: An r of .90 was found when the best score of three trials was recorded from separate testings and correlated.

Objectivity: An r of .99 was found when the scores from an experienced tester were correlated with scores from an inexperienced tester.

Validity: Face validity was accepted for this test.

Equipment: The flexomeasure case with yardstick and ruler guide inserted. Be sure the A—B line of the case is nearest the zero end of the yardstick. See Appendix I for alternate test without flexomeasure.

Directions: (1) Have your assistant get a measure of your trunk and neck length by taking the distance to the nearest quarter of an inch between the tip of your nose and the seat of the chair you are sitting in. Your position must be erect with the chin level as the zero end of the yardstick is placed between your legs and on the seat level of the chair. Next, the flexomeasure case is raised until the bottom of the ruler guide touches the tip of your nose. Your assistant should record the reading at the bottom of the case (the A—B line). (2) Assume a prone position (facedown) on a mat, and with your hands resting at the small of your back, raise your trunk upward as high as pos-

Figure 6-8. Trunk-and-Neck Extension Test

sible from the floor. A partner should hold your hips by placing his or her hands on the back of the thighs (base of the buttocks). Your assistant, located to the front, places the zero end of the yardstick on the mat and slides the flexomeasure case vertically upward until the upper edge of the ruler guide touches the tip of your nose. The reading to the nearest quarter of an inch is taken in the case window at the lower (*C—D*) line.

Scoring: Subtract your best of three lifts from your trunk and neck length score.

Example: Trunk and neck length = 32 inches
Best trunk lift = 15
Score 17 inches

The closer your trunk lift gets to your estimated trunk and neck length, the better your score. Thus, a score of zero would be perfect.

Shoulder Rotation Test (24)

Purpose: To measure the extent to which the shoulders will rotate with as narrow a grip as possible.

Table 6-6
Trunk-and-Neck Extension Test

Men	Level	Women
3 - 0	Advanced	2 - 0
6 - 3¼	Adv. Intermediate	5¾ - 2¼
8 - 6¼	Intermediate	7¾ - 6
10 - 8¼	Adv. Beginner	9¾ - 8
Above - 10¼	Beginner	Above - 10

Based on the scores of 100 college men and 100 college women at Corpus Christi State University, Corpus Christi, Tx., 1977.

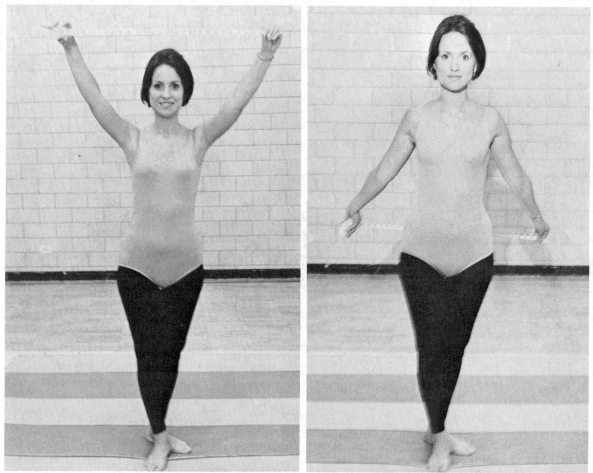

Figure 6-9. Shoulder Rotation Test

Sports Specificity: (1) Butterfly, crawl, and backcrawl strokes in swimming; (2) dislocate and inlocate on the rings, uneven bars, and horizontal bars in gymnastics.

Age Level: Ages six through college.

Sex: Satisfactory as a test for both boys and girls.

Reliability: An *r* of .97 was found when the best score of three trials was recorded from separate testings and correlated.

Objectivity: An *r* of .99 was found when the scores from an experienced tester were correlated with scores from an inexperienced tester.

Validity: Face validity was accepted for this test.

Equipment: 60 inches of rope and flexomeasure with yardstick and guide stick inserted.

Directions: (1) Grasp one end of the rope with your left hand and grasp the rope with your right hand in a like manner a few inches away. (2) Extend both arms to full length in front of your chest and rotate the rope over your head.

As you meet resistance in rotating your shoulders, you must let the rope slide within the grip of your right hand so that the arms can spread and allow you to lower the rope until it is resting across your back. (3) Keeping your arms locked, rotate to the starting position and measure the number of inches of rope between the thumbs of your hands. The least amount of distance indicates a better level of performance. (4) Secure the maximum shoulder width across the back from deltoid to deltoid with the flexomeasure.

Scoring: Your shoulder width is subtracted from the total inches of your best score of three trials.

Example: Best trial   = 30 inches
Shoulder width = 19
Score   11 inches

Thus, the lower the score, the better the performance.

Table 6-7
Shoulder Rotation Test

Men	Level	Women
7 - Less	Advanced	5 - Less
11½ - 7¼	Adv. Intermediate	9¾ - 5¼
14½ - 11¾	Intermediate	13 - 10
19¾ - 14¾	Adv. Beginner	17¾ - 13¼
Above - 20	Beginner	Above - 18

Based on the scores of 100 college men and 100 college women at Corpus Christi State University, Corpus Christi, Tx., 1977.

Ankle Extension (Plantar Flexion) Test (22)

Purpose: To develop ankle extension (plantar flexion).

Sports and Dance Specificity: Swimming, diving, gymnastics, dance and jumping events. In gymnastics, dance and diving, ankle extension adds to the beauty of movement while in swimming and jumping events its adds to mechanical efficiency.

Age Level: Ages six through college.

Sex: Satisfactory as a test for both boys and girls.

Reliability: An r of .88 was found when the best score of three trials was recorded from separate testings and correlated.

Objectivity: An r of .99 was found when the scores from an experienced tester were correlated with scores from an inexperienced tester.

Validity: Face validity was accepted for this test.

Equipment: The flexomeasure case with yardstick and ruler guide inserted. Be sure the A—B line of the case is nearest the zero end of the yardstick. See Appendix C-2 for alternate test with protractor.

Directions: (1) Remove your shoes and take a sitting position on the floor with your right leg as straight as possible. (2) Have your assistant place the zero end of the yardstick on the floor and slide the case downward until the ruler guide is resting across the lowest point of the shin bone. (3) Extend the ankle and repeat the measurement at the highest point of the foot (either the toes or instep) during maximum extension. (4) Repeat the procedure for the left foot. (5) Record the difference between the upper foot line (during extension) and the lower shin bone line to the nearest one-eighth of an inch for each foot.

Scoring: Average the right foot difference with the left foot difference score and compare your performance to the scale in Table 6-8.

Ankle Flexion (Dorsi Flexion) Test (24)

Purpose: To develop ankle flexion and stretch the gastrocnemius (calf) and heel cord.

Table 6-8
Ankle Extension (Plantar Flexion) Test

Men	Level	Women
¾ - Less	Advanced	½ - Less
1½ - 1	Adv. Intermediate	1¼ - ¾
2 - 1¾	Intermediate	1¾ - 1½
3 - 2¼	Adv. Beginner	2¼ - 2
Above - 3¼	Beginner	Above - 2½

Based on the scores of 100 college men and 100 college women at Corpus Christi State University, Corpus Christi, Tx., 1977.

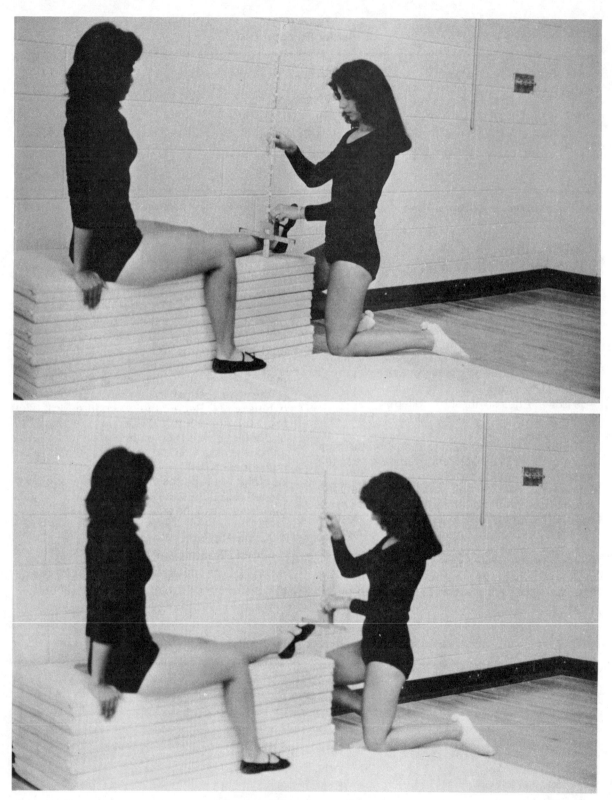

Figure 6-10. Ankle Extension
(Plantar Flexion) Test

Figure 6-11. Ankle Flexion (Dorsi Flexion) Test

Sports Specificity: (1) Forward landings from horizontal distance jumps and vaults; (2) excess lean as in wrestling; (3) flight of ski jump.

Age Level: Ages six through college.

Sex: Satisfactory as a test for both boys and girls.

Reliability: An *r* of .88 was found when the best score of three trials was recorded from separate testings and correlated.

Objectivity: An *r* of .99 was found when the scores from an experienced tester were correlated with scores from an inexperienced tester.

Validity: Face validity was accepted for this test.

Equipment: A yardstick or measuring tape is required.

Directions: Stand back from a wall, keeping heels flat on the floor, and lean into the wall touching the hands, chin, and chest. Develop as much distance between the wall and a heels-flat stance as possible. The hands may be extended against the wall as you give in and touch the chin and chest, but the body and knees must be kept straight. Have your assistant measure the distance between the toe line and the wall (after the best lean forward is made with the heels flat on floor). (2) Have your assistant measure standing body height from floor to chin.

Scoring: Subtract the distance of your best lean from your standing body height (floor to chin) and compare your performance to the scale in Table 6-9. Allow three trials on the lean to the wall and record the best one to the nearest quarter of an inch.

Example: Standing height = 53 inches (floor to chin)
Best lean = 33
Score   20 inches

The closer your lean distance gets to your standing height distance, the better your score. Thus, a score of zero would be perfect.

Table 6-9
Ankle Flexion (Dorsi Flexion) Test

Men	Level	Women
26½ - Less	Advanced	24¼ - Less
29½ - 26¾	Adv. Intermediate	26½ - 24½
32½ - 29¾	Intermediate	30¼ - 26¾
35¼ - 32¾	Adv. Beginner	31¾ - 30½
Above - 35½	Beginner	Above - 32

Based on scores obtained from Mike Morgan, Corpus Christi State University, Corpus Christi, Tx., 1976.

Problems of Measurement

Several problems are apparent in conscientiously measuring the flexibility of students. First, the teacher or coach must decide whether the test scores should be *relative* to the length or width of a body part or *absolute* in terms of what the student can do as related to a predetermined goal of performance. Generally, the absolute method is desirable when flexibility training and testing are for purposes of sports performance. Recalling our earlier example of the splits, in absolute flexibility testing you are in reality saying, "I don't care how tall or short you are, I just want to know how close you can lower your seat to the floor."

Second, we have long known that flexibility is highly specific by nature. This is to say that you might be quite flexible in one body area and only slightly flexible in another. Thus, we commonly encounter the problem of finding only one flexibility item in a physical fitness test battery. While it might be the ideal item for some students, it could be the worst possible selection for others. Therefore, we really need to present a choice of one out of three flexibility items to allow each student to perform the one that is most successful for him or her.

Third, certain practical tests, such as the front-to-rear splits and the shoulder rotation, are time consuming due to the difficulty of getting elementary students to achieve the correct position. However, this problem can be minimized by having demonstrators available or pictures posted to help prepare each student prior to testing.

And finally, there is a need for scoring scales and norms at the elementary, junior high, and senior high levels.

Findings and Conclusions from Flexibility Measurement and Research
Regarding the Nature of Flexibility

Flexibility does not exist as a single general characteristic, but rather as a highly specific ability to the individual joints of the body (9, 13, 16, 26). Thus, a person who is very flexible in one joint may be average in another, and quite inflexible in still a third.

Like other components of physical fitness, flexibility can be improved through training. Numerous independent studies reveal significant improvement as a result of regular training (3, 8, 11, 28, 35, 42).

Children, ages 6 to 12, generally become progressively more flexible each year until they reach adolescence (13, 19, 36, 37, 38). Moreover, studies of boys and girls of comparable ages agree that girls are generally more flexible (15, 18, 38, 43).

Regarding the Effects of Exercise, Sports and Preliminary Training Procedures on Flexibility

Specific flexibility training procedures involving static stretch and ballistic stretch methods have been studied with significant gains reported for each (8, 27, 30). Although no significant difference was found between the two methods, Riddle's research (40) indicated each method to be superior to a combination of the two. In recent years, however, physical educators and athletic trainers have favored the static stretch method, claiming less chance for muscle tears and strains. Much of this support for static stretch is based on the research of deVries (8).

In a study by Frey (14), the sauna was investigated for effects, if any, on hip flexion. While only one of three hip flexion tests showed any significant improvement from this type of heat application, it is a normal procedure in physical therapy to apply heat and then to allow some cooling before application of static stretch techniques. This cooling procedure was not evident in Frey's study and could possibly explain the lack of significance found on the two straight-leg hip flexion tests. In another study by Fieldman (12), greater hip flexion performance was found when the test was preceded by a pretrial of the same test and even more so when related warm-up exercises were administered prior to the test.

Concerning the effects of physical education activities and sports on flexibility, the following findings have been reported: (a) gymnastics and tumbling activities brought significant increases in flexibility for select body parts (7, 26); (b) rowing (42), exercycling (2), and modern dance (3) participation also resulted in select areas of flexibility improvement; and (c) general physical education activities were superior to weight training and isometric training for increasing flexibility (39), but weight training did not decrease flexibility performance (27, 31). Thus, it can be seen that the human body responds in terms of increasing its flexion and extension as a result of the demands that certain sports, exercises, and activities place upon it.

Regarding Flexibility Testing Procedures

Professional concern has existed for many years regarding the relationship, if any, that exists between anthropometric measures and flexibility. While studies by Mathews (32, 33), Fieldman (11), and Harvey and Scott (17) found no significant relationship, Broer (4) and Dinkheller (10) found that students with a longer trunk-plus-arm measurement have a significant advantage on the hip flexor test. Moreover, McCloy's quotient (34) was devised to take into account the lengths of influencing body parts on certain flexibility tests. Thus, controversy still exists on this question, and it is therefore important for the teacher or coach to determine whether the end results of flexibility measurement are best obtained through the use of relative or absolute flexibility tests.

References and Bibliography

1. Adrian, Marlene, Charles M. Tipton, and Peter V. Karpovich, *Electrogoniometer Manual,* Springfield, Mass.: Physiological Research Laboratory, Springfield College, 1965.
2. Angle, Nancy K., "The Effect of a Progressive Program of Exercise Using the Exercycle on the Flexibility of College Women" (Unpublished master's thesis, University of Washington at Seattle, 1963).
3. Bennett, Colleen L., "Relative Contributions of Modern Dance, Folk Dance, Basketball, and Swimming to Motor Abilities of College Women," *Research Quarterly,* 27:261, October, 1956.
4. Broer, Marion, and Naomi Galles, "Importance of Relationship Between Various Body Measurements in Performance of the Toe-Touch Test," *Research Quarterly,* 29:262, October, 1958.
5. Cureton, T. K., Jr., "Flexibility as an Aspect of Physical Fitness," *Research Quarterly Supplement,* 12:388-389, May, 1941.
6. _____, "Objective Test of Swimming" (Unpublished master's thesis, Springfield College, 1930).
7. Derk, Gerald M., "The Changes Occurring in Strength and Flexibility During Competitive Gymnastics Season Involving High School Boys" (Unpublished master's thesis, University of Kansas, 1971).
8. deVries, Herbert, "Evaluation of Static Stretching Procedures for Improvement of Flexibility," *Research Quarterly,* May, 1962.
9. Dickinson, R. V., "The Specificity of Flexibility," *Research Quarterly,* 39:792-794, October, 1968.
10. Dinkheller, Ann L., "Factors Affecting Flexibility," (Unpublished master's thesis, University of Iowa, 1960).
11. Fieldman, Harold, "Effects of Selected Extensibility Exercises on the Flexibility of the Hip Joint," *Research Quarterly,* 37:326-331, October, 1966.
12. _____, "Relative Contribution of the Back and Hamstring Muscles in the Performance of the Toe-Touch Test after Selected Extensibility Exercises," *Research Quarterly,* 39:518-523, October, 1968.
13. Forbes, Joseph, "Characteristics of Flexibility in Boys" (Microcarded doctoral dissertation, University of Oregon, 1950).
14. Frey, Harold J., "A Comparative Study of the Effects of Static Stretching Sauna, Warm-up, Cold Applications, Exercise Warm-ups on Flexibility of the Hip Joint" (Microcarded doctoral dissertation, University of Utah, 1970).
15. Hall, D. M., "Standardization of Flexibility Tests for 4-H Club Members," *Research Quarterly,* 27:296-300, October, 1956.
16. Harris, Margaret L., "A Factor Analytic Study of Flexibility," *Research Quarterly,* 40:62-67, May, 1969.
17. Harvey, Virginia P., and Gwendolyn D. Scott,

Reliability of a Measure of Forward Flexibility and Its Relation to Physical Dimensions of College Women," *Research Quarterly,* 38:28-33, March, 1967.

18. Hoffman, Virginia, "Relation of Selected Traits and Abilities to Motor Learning" (Microcarded doctoral dissertation, Indiana University, 1955).

19. Hupprich, Florence L., and Peter Sigerseth, "The Specificity of Flexibility in Girls," *Research Quarterly,* 21:32, March, 1950.

20. Johnson, Barry L., "Flexibility Assessment," *SDAAHPER Proceedings,* 1978.

21. _____, *Flexibility Tests and Scoring Scales for Elementary Schools,* Portland, Tx.: Brown and Littleman Company, 1977.

22. _____, *Practical Flexibility Measurement with the Flexomeasure,* Portland, Tx.: Brown and Littleman Company, 1977.

23. _____, "Practical Tests of Flexibility," (Unpublished study, Northeast Louisiana University, September, 1966).

24. _____, and Mary J. Garcia, *Fitness and Performance for Everyone,* Portland, Tx.: Brown and Littleman Company, 1977, pp. 56-67.

25. _____, *Gymnastics for the Beginner: A Coeducational Approach,* Manchaca, Tx.: Sterling Swift Publishing Company, 1976, pp. 6-8.

26. Kingsley, Donald B., "Flexibility Changes Resulting from Participation in Tumbling" (Microcarded master's thesis, University of Oregon, 1952).

27. Kusinitz, Ivan, and Clifford E. Keeney, "Effects of Progressive Weight Training on Health and Physical Fitness of Adolescent Boys," *Research Quarterly,* 29:294, October, 1958.

28. Lafuze, Marion, "A Study of the Learning of Fundamental Skills by College Freshmen Women of Low Motor Ability," *Research Quarterly,* 22:156, May, 1951.

29. Leighton, Jack, "A Simple Objective and Reliable Measure of Flexibility," *Research Quarterly,* 13:205-216, May, 1942.

30. Marchbank, William J., "A Study of the Johnson Shoulder Rotation Test" (Unpublished study, Northeast Louisiana University, 1970).

31. Massey, Ben H., and Norman L. Chaudet, "Effects of Systematic, Heavy Resistive Exercise on Range of Joint Movement in Young Male Adults," *Research Quarterly,* 27:50, March, 1956.

32. Mathews, Donald, and others, "Hip Flexibility of College Women as Related to Length of Body Segments," *Research Quarterly,* 28:355, December, 1957.

33. _____, "Hip Flexibility of Elementary School Boys as Related to Body Segments," *Research Quarterly,* 30:302, October, 1959.

34. McCloy, Charles Harold, and Norma D. Young, *Test and Measurements in Health and Physical Education,* New York: Appleton-Century-Crofts, 1954, p. 227.

35. McCue, Betty F., "Flexibility Measurements of College Women," *Research Quarterly,* 24: 323-324, October, 1953.

36. Miller, Charles J., "The Relationship of Flexibility in Boys to Age" (Microcarded master's thesis, University of Maryland, 1954).

37. Odgers, Thomas W., "A Study of the Relationship between Flexibility Measures, Skill Performances and Chronological Ages of Six- to Thirteen-Year-Old Boys" (Unpublished master's thesis, University of Oregon, 1969).

38. Phillips, Marjorie, and others, "Analysis of Results from the Kraus-Weber Test of Minimum Muscular Fitness in Children," *Research Quarterly,* 26:322, October, 1955.

39. Rallis, Socrates, "A Comparison of Three Training Programs and Their Effects on Five Physical Fitness Components" (Unpublished master's thesis, Wayne State University, 1965).

40. Riddle, K. S., "A Comparison of Three Methods for Increasing Flexibility of the Trunk and Hip Joints" (Microcarded doctoral dissertation, University of Oregon, 1956).

41. Scott, M. Gladys, and Ester French, *Evaluation in Physical Education,* St. Louis: C. V. Mosby Company, 1950.

42. Shaw, Terrance M., "Changes in the Flexibility of Selected Joints of Crewmen Following a Season of Rowing" (Unpublished master's thesis, University of Oregon, 1968).

43. Smith, Jean A., "Relation of Certain Physical Traits and Abilities to Motor Learning in Elementary School Children," *Research Quarterly,* 27:228, May, 1956.

44. Wells, Katherine F., and Evelyn K. Dillon, "The Sit and Reach—A Test of Back and Leg Flexibility," *Research Quarterly,* 23:118, March, 1952.

Other Studies of Interest

Burley, Lloyd R., and others, "Relation of Power, Speed, Flexibility, and Certain Anthropometric Measures of Junior High School Girls," *Research Quarterly,* 32:443, December, 1961.

Carruth, Wincie A., "An Analysis of Motor Ability and Its Relationship to Constitutional Body Patterns" (Microcarded doctoral dissertation, New York University, 1952).

Davies, Evelyn A., "Relationship Between Selected Postural Divergencies and Motor Ability," *Research Quarterly,* 28:4, March, 1957.

Dintiman, George B., "Effects of Various Training Programs on Running Speed," *Research Quarterly,* 35:462, December, 1964.

Garcia, Mary Jane, "A Study of Flexibility in Elementary School Children" (Unpublished study, Corpus Christi State University, 1974).

Hutchins, Gloria Lee, "The Relationship of Selected Strength and Flexibility Variables to the Anteroposterior Posture of College Women," *Research Quarterly,* 36:253-269, October, 1965.

Lawrence, Susan, "A Study of the Flexibility and Stability of the Feet of College Women" (Microcarded master's thesis, Smith College, 1955).

McMorris, R. O., and E. C. Elkins, "A Study of Production and Evaluation of Muscular Hypertrophy," *Archives of Physical Medicine and Rehabilitation,* 35:420-426, July, 1954.

Olsen, Barbara H., "An Investigation of the Relationship of Ankle, Knee, Trunk and Shoulder Flexibility to General Motor Ability" (Microcarded master's thesis, University of Oregon, 1956).

Sigerseth, Peter O., and Chester Haliski, "The Flexibility of Football Players," *Research Quarterly,* 21:398, December, 1950.

Tyrance, Herman J., "Relationship of Extreme Body Types to Ranges of Flexibility," *Research Quarterly,* 29:248, October, 1958.

Chapter Seven

The Measurement of Strength

Strength is frequently recognized by physical educators as the most important factor in the performance of physical skills. While strength may be generally defined as the muscular force exerted against movable and immovable objects, it is best measured by tests which require one maximum effort on a given movement or position. The two types of muscular contraction most frequently measured in physical education classes are dynamic (isotonic) contraction and static (isometric) contraction. Isotonic contraction takes place when muscular force moves the object of resistance so that contraction takes place over a range of movement. Isometric contraction takes place when muscular force is exerted over a brief period of time (usually 6 to 10 seconds) without movement of the object of resistance or the body joints involved. Both types of contraction may be easily and inexpensively measured by the physical educator in the average school situation. While a certain degree of strength is necessary in performing daily activities and sports skills, a high degree of strength is regarded by the authors as a luxury which makes for greater ease of performance and for a feeling of vitality well worth the effort necessary to acquire and maintain it.

Since strength is a physical fitness component, it must be related to each individual and it should be measured in relation to the individual's body weight. Thus, a person who weighs 150 pounds and who can pull 175 pounds to a chin-up position should be considered stronger than an individual whose weight is 225 pounds and who can pull only 230 pounds to a chin-up position. In the first example, the 150-pound man would score $\frac{175}{150} = 1.17$* while in the second example, the 225-pound man would score $\frac{230}{225} = 1.02$. What does this mean in terms of physical fitness? First, the lighter man is stronger per body pound. If his life depended on his ability to pull his own body weight up and over a bar, his chances of success would be greater than that of the other man. Second, the heavier man, in order to attain a higher state of fitness strength, must

*The Hoffman formula, which has been extensively used by competitive lifters, is less convenient since it involves a table of figures that you must constantly refer to. Also, it relates to competitive sport, not to individual health and fitness.

either lose some body weight or develop additional strength or both.

Because strength and power are terms which are often used interchangeably (this is particularly true of isotonic strength), it was felt necessary to present some observations which should help distinguish between them: (a) Strength is only a component of power. Power also includes the components of time and distance. (b) While in both power and isotonic strength tests an object of resistance is moved through a range of motion, the isotonic strength test differs in the following respects:

1. The object of resistance is always near, if not at, maximum load.
2. The object of resistance is never released with the idea of gaining height or distance.
3. The range of movement is not as exaggerated nor as complete.
4. Measurement is based on the amount of weight moved through a specified range and not upon distance or time elements.

Uses of Strength Tests

Several ways in which strength tests should be utilized in physical education classes are as follows:

1. As a factor in physical fitness tests.
2. As a means for determining potential in specific sports activities.
3. As a means for determining achievement and grades in conditioning and weight training classes.
4. As a means of evaluating the possible solutions to overcoming poor postural positions or to pinpoint areas of weakness which need strengthening for better performance.
5. As a means of motivating students toward a feeling of accomplishment and satisfaction through strength increases.

Practical Tests of Relative Strength

Only a few of the practical tests of strength in terms of time, equipment, and cost are presented here. In these tests where special testing instruments are necessary, the cost is not unreasonable for most schools. Unfortunately, it was not feasible to present all the strength exercises that are practical for measurement. The following relative strength tests are presented under the headings of Isotonic Strength Tests, Spring Scale Strength Tests, and Isometric Strength Instruments. All are scored in terms of strength relative to body weight.

Isotonic Strength Tests (27)

Objective: To measure strength during a complete range of movement in the following items: (a) pull-up test, (b) dip test, (c) bench squat test, (d) sit-up test, (e) bench press, (f) standing vertical arm press test.

Age Level: Recommended for ages twelve through college.

Sex: Refer to each individual test item.

Reliability: Refer to each individual test item.

Objectivity: Refer to each individual test item.

Validity: Refer to each individual test item.

Equipment and Materials: Refer to each individual test item.

General Directions: (a) Students should be allowed to become familiar with the isotonic strength tests through the use of similar weight training exercises at least several days prior to testing. When students are not familiar with the tests to be given, it will usually take more than two trials to determine their maximum effort for each test. This, of course, requires a greater amount of time for testing. (b) On each test item, the student should be allowed two trials (if he so desires) in which he can move the maximum amount of weight possible for that test. Each student should load his own bar or strap with weight plates, and if he successfully completes the movement on the first trial, he should be given an opportunity to add more weight and try to attain a higher score. If the student was unsuccessful in completing the first trial, he should remove some of the weight for the second trial. Should the second trial be unsuccessful also, the student should take a short rest and then be retested with a further reduced load. (c) Students should be allowed to warm up before reporting to the testing station, but they should be cautioned not to overwork. (d) Several weight bars and straps should be available so that as one student finishes, the next one will have his weights adjusted and ready for testing. All students should be required to use a shoulder-width grip in such tests as chin-ups, dips, bench press, vertical presses, etc.

Scoring: The best score of two trials is recorded over the student's body weight and then divided and recorded. If the student does not desire to take a second trial, the first score is divided by his body weight.

Isotonic Test Items

Pull-up Test (27)

Objective: To measure the strength of the arms and shoulders in the pull-up movement.

Age Level: Ages twelve through college.

Sex: Recommended for boys only.

Reliability: An *r* of .99 was found for this test when scores were recorded on separate days using students familiar with the exercise.

Objectivity: An *r* of .99 was reported by Ronald Taylor, 1972.

Validity: Face validity was accepted for this test.

Equipment and Materials: A horizontal bar raised to a height so that all subjects may hang with their feet off the floor should be used. It is also necessary to have several 2½, 5, 10, and 25 pound weight plates available for use. A rope or strap is necessary to secure the weights to the waist of the performer, and one

Figure 7-1. Pull-up Test

Table 7-1
Raw Score Norms for Pull-up Test

Raw Scores Are Figured by Dividing Body Weight into
the Additional Weight Successfully Used in the Test

	College Men	
Prior to Training Scores	Performance Level	After 9 Weeks' Training Score
.42 - Above	Advanced	.56 - Above
.31 - .41	Adv. Intermediate	.41 - .55
.16 - .30	Intermediate	.20 - .40
.06 - .15	Adv. Beginner	.09 - .19
.00 - .05	Beginner	.00 - .08

Based on the scores of 80 college men, Corpus Christi State University, Corpus Christi, Tx., 1976.

chair should be available to stand on in taking the preliminary position on the bar.

Directions: After securing the desired amount of weight to the waist, the student should step upon the chair and take a firm grasp (palms facing away from face) on the bar. As he assumes a straight arm hang, the chair is removed while the performer pulls upward until the chin is above the bar. As the performer lowers downward, the chair is replaced under his feet. If a second trial is to be taken, the student may step down and readjust the weights before he repeats the exercise. (See Figure 7-1.) Also, see general directions on page 95.

Scoring: The best score of two trials is recorded in terms of the amount of extra weight satisfactorily lifted. A student who cannot execute the exercise with more than his own body weight would, of course, receive zero. (See Table 7-1.) The best score is divided by body weight for the test score.

Safety: The performer should be assisted to and from the chair as he mounts and dismounts with the extra weight.

Additional Pointers: (a) The performer should refrain from lifting the legs or using a swing action to get upward. (b) The tester may extend his arm horizontally across the performer's thighs to prevent a lifting of the legs during the pull-up. (c) For individuals who cannot chin their own body weight, the following procedure may be used in terms of measurement and motivation: Hang a tape (cloth) measure from the bar so that it bisects the point of the performer's chin as he pulls and slides the chin upward along the tape. Score the performer in terms of the number of inches he gets his chin

from the top of the bar. For example, the best non-chinner might get his chin 1 inch from the top of the bar and consequently score a minus one, whereas a weaker performer might lack six inches and receive a minus six as his score.

Dip Strength Test (27)

Objective: To measure the strength of the arms and shoulders in the dip movement (a vertical lowering and push-up movement).

Age Level: Ages twelve through college.

Sex: Recommended for boys only.

Reliability: An r of .98 was found when scores were recorded on separate days using students familiar with the exercise.

Objectivity: An r of .99 was reported by Charles Prestidge, 1972.

Equipment and Materials: Two parallel bars raised to a height so that all subjects are supported freely above the ground (in the lowered bent arm support) are used. Weight plates, straps, and a chair are again required just as in the pull-up test.

Directions: After securing the desired amount of weight to the waist, the student should step upon the chair and take a secure grip on the bars. As he assumes a straight arm support, the chair is removed and the student proceeds to lower himself downward until the elbows form a right angle. As the student pushes up to a straight arm support, the chair is replaced under his feet. If a second trial is to be taken, the student may step down and readjust the weights before he repeats the exercise. (See Figure 7-2.) Also, see general directions on page 95.

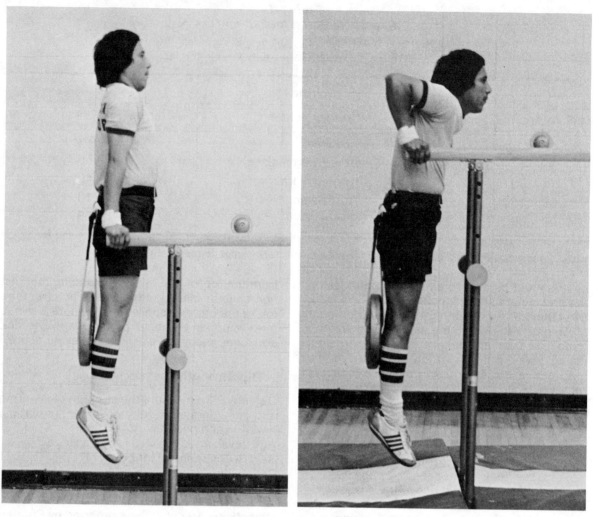

Figure 7-2. Dip Strength Test

Table 7-2
Raw Score Norms for Dip Strength Test
Raw Scores Are Figured by Dividing Body Weight into
the Additional Weight Successfully Used in the Test

College Men		
Prior to Training Scores	Performance Level	After 9 Weeks' Training Scores
.60 - Above	Advanced	.74 - Above
.46 - .59	Adv. Intermediate	.61 - .73
.23 - .45	Intermediate	.36 - .60
.10 - .22	Adv. Beginner	.21 - .35
.00 - .09	Beginner	.00 - .20

Based on the scores of 80 college men, Corpus Christi State University, Corpus Christi, Tx., 1976.

Scoring: Same as for pull-up test. (See Table 7-2.)

Safety: Same as for the pull-up test.

Additional Pointers: (a) The performer should refrain from swinging or kicking in returning to the straight arm support position. (b) The tester should extend his fist upward from the bar so that the performer's shoulder will touch it when the elbows form the right angle. (c) For students who cannot push to a straight arm support with their own body weight, the following procedure may be used in terms of measurement and motivation: Attach a scale alongside the parallel bars (marked off in one inch intervals). Mark on the scale the performer's shoulder location (point of the acromion process) while in the straight arm support. Score the performer in terms of the number of inches he gets his shoulders (point of the acromion process) from the straight arm position on the push upward.

Bench Squat Test (27)

Objective: To measure the strength of the legs and back in lowering to, and arising from, a sitting position.

Age Level: Ages twelve through college.

Sex: Recommended for both boys and girls.

Reliability: An *r* of .95 was found when scores were recorded on separate days using students familiar with the exercise.

Objectivity: An *r* of .99 was reported by Mike Recio, 1972.

Validity: Face validity was accepted for this test.

Equipment and Materials: Use an adjustable bench, fold-up mats, or wooden drink cases to get the seat level adjusted to lower patella

Figure 7-3. Bench Squat Test

(knee-cap) level. Also, secure a barbell, weight plates, and a thick towel to pad bar.

Directions: After adjusting the desired amount of weight on the bar, two assistants place the bar upon the shoulders (and behind the neck) of the student as he stands near the edge of the mats or bench. With the feet a comfortable distance apart and a firm grasp of the hands on the bar, the student lowers to an erect sitting position on the mats or bench. Then, without rocking back and forth, the student returns to the standing position. After the two assistants remove the weight, the performer may readjust the weights if a second trial is to be taken. (See Figure 7-3.) Also, see general directions on page 95.

Scoring: The total weight of the barbell (including the collars) satisfactorily lifted is recorded over body weight. Only the best lift of two trials is recorded. (See Tables 7-3A and B.) The student's strength score is divided by his body weight for the test score.

Safety: The two assistants should stand at each end of the barbell and be ready to catch the bar in the event that the performer over-leans or starts to fall.

Additional Pointers: (a) The performer should sit on the near edge of the bench or mats so that he will not have to rock back and forth to get up. (b) The seat level of bench, mats, or drink cases should be adjusted to the lower patella level before the squat is executed.

Table 7-3A
Raw Score Norms for the Bench Squat Test Prior to Training
Raw Scores Are Figured by Dividing Body Weight into
the Additional Weight Successfully Used in the Test

College Men Scores	Performance Category	College Women Scores
1.61 - Above	Advanced	1.29 - Above
1.38 - 1.60	Adv. Intermediate	1.11 - 1.28
.94 - 1.37	Intermediate	.87 - 1.10
.81 - .93	Adv. Beginner	.68 - .86
.00 - .80	Beginner	.00 - .67

Based on the scores of 80 college men, Corpus Christi State University, Corpus Christi, Tx., 1976.

Based on the scores of 80 college women, Corpus Christi State University, Corpus Christi, Tx., 1976.

Table 7-3B
Raw Score Norms for the Bench Squat Test after Nine Weeks of Training

College Men Scores	Performance Category	College Women Scores
2.09 - Above	Advanced	1.56 - Above
1.76 - 2.08	Adv. Intermediate	1.32 - 1.55
1.19 - 1.75	Intermediate	.92 - 1.31
.91 - 1.18	Adv. Beginner	.71 - .91
.00 - .90	Beginner	.00 - .70

Based on a limited number of scores from physical education weight training classes at Corpus Christi State University, Corpus Christi, Tx., 1976.

Sit-up Test (Knees Bent) (27)

Objective: To measure the strength of the abdominal muscles.

Age Level: Ages twelve through college.

Sex: Satisfactory for both boys and girls.

Reliability: An *r* of .91 was found when scores were recorded on separate days using students familiar with the exercise.

Objectivity: An *r* of .98 was reported by Mary Jane Garcia, 1972.

Validity: Face validity was accepted for this test.

Equipment and Materials: The equipment needed for this test is a mat to lie on, a bar (5 or 6 feet in length), a dumbbell bar, and an assortment of weight plates. A 12-inch ruler and tape are also needed.

Directions: The student may execute the sit-up with either a weight plate, a dumbbell, or, if necessary, a barbell behind the neck. Should a dumbbell or barbell be used, the attached weight plates must not have a greater circumference than standard 5-pound plates. After selecting the desired amount of weight, the performer should place it on a mat so that when he assumes the supine position, he can easily grasp the weight and hold it to the back of the neck. The performer then assumes a supine position and flexes the knees over the 12-inch ruler while sliding the heels as close to the seat as possible. The ruler should be held tightly under the knees until the performer is instructed to slowly slide the feet forward. At the point where the ruler drops to the mat, the tester marks the heel line and *seat line* to indicate how far the feet should remain from the seat during the bent knee sit-up exercise. (See Figure 7-4.) Also, see general directions on page 95.

Scoring: Same as for sit-up test. (See Table 7-4.)

Safety: An assistant should be ready to remove the weight at the completion of the lift.

Additional Pointer: If the ruler is taped along the seat line, the performer can maintain distance between the seat and heel line better.

Bench Press Test (27)

Objective: To measure strength of arm extension in a push-up movement.

Age Level: Ages twelve through college.

Sex: Satisfactory for both boys and girls.

Reliability: An *r* of .93 was found when scores were recorded on separate days using students familiar with the exercise.

Objectivity: An *r* of .97 was reported by Dixie Bennett and Steve Long, 1972.

Validity: Face validity was accepted for this test.

Equipment and Materials: The equipment needed for this test is a bench, a weight bar (5 or 6 feet in length) and enough weight plates to be more than sufficient for the strongest student.

Directions: After adjusting the desired amount of weight on the bar, the student assumes a supine position on the bench, and two assistants place the bar in his hands and across the chest. With the hands approximately

Table 7-4
Raw Score Norms for Sit-up Test (Knees Bent)

College Men		College Women
Scores	Performance Category	Scores
.34 - Above	Advanced	.20 - Above
.29 - .33	Adv. Intermediate	.16 - .19
.18 - .28	Intermediate	.11 - .15
.12 - .17	Adv. Beginner	.06 - .10
.00 - .11	Beginner	.00 - .05

Based on the scores of 111 college men, Corpus Christi State University, Corpus Christi, Tx., 1976.

Based on the scores of 80 college women, Corpus Christi State University, Corpus Christi, Tx., 1976.

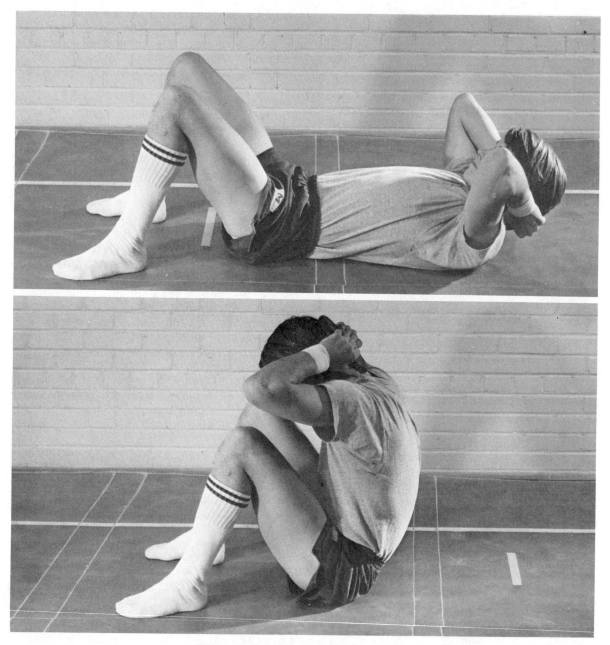

Figure 7-4. Sit-up Test (Knees Bent)

shoulder width apart, the performer should extend the arms, pressing the bar to a "locked out" (elbows straight) position. The two assistants then remove the bar upon completion of the trial. If a second trial is to be taken, the performer may readjust the weight and then repeat the exercise. (See Figure 7-5.) Also, see general directions on page 95.

Scoring: Same as for bench squat test. (See Table 7-5A and B.)

Safety: The two assistants should remain ready to catch the barbell at any time during the trial.

Standing Vertical Arm Press Test (27)

Objective: To measure strength of arm extension in a vertical overhead press movement.

Age Level: Ages twelve through college.

Sex: Recommended for boys only.

Figure 7-5. Bench Press Test

Table 7-5A
Raw Score Norms for Bench Press Test
Prior to Training
Raw Scores Are Figured by Dividing Body Weight into
the Additional Weight Successfully Used in the Test

College Men		College Women
Scores	Performance Category	Scores
1.20 - Above	Advanced	.48 - Above
.99 - 1.19	Adv. Intermediate	.41 - .47
.79 - .98	Intermediate	.30 - .40
.69 - .78	Adv. Beginner	.21 - .29
.00 - .68	Beginner	.00 - .20

Based on the scores of 80 college men, Corpus Christi State University, Corpus Christi, Tx., 1976.

Based on the scores of 65 college women, Corpus Christi State University, Corpus Christi, Tx., 1976.

Table 7-5B
Raw Score Norms for Bench Press Test
after Nine Weeks of Training

College Men		College Women
Scores	Performance Category	Scores
1.33 - Above	Advanced	.57 - Above
1.18 - 1.32	Adv. Intermediate	.52 - .56
.96 - 1.17	Intermediate	.41 - .51
.85 - .95	Adv. Beginner	.37 - .40
.00 - .84	Beginner	.00 - .36

Based on a limited number of scores from physical education weight training classes at Corpus Christi State University, Corpus Christi, Tx., 1976.

Reliability: An r of .98 was found for this test with a group of students who were familiar with the exercise. The best score of two trials, conducted on separate days, was recorded as the test score.

Objectivity: An r of .99 was reported by Charles Prestidge, 1972.

Validity: Face validity was accepted for this test.

Equipment and Materials: The equipment needed is a weight bar (5 or 6 feet in length) and enough weight plates to be more than sufficient for the strongest student.

Directions: After adjusting the desired amount of weight on the bar, the performer assumes a standing position (feet a comfortable distance apart for balance), and two assistants place the bar in the performer's hands at the front chest position. With a forward grasp (palms facing away) the performer should extend the arms upward pressing the bar to a "locked out" (elbows straight) position. The weight should be held steady for a count of three to show control, after which it is lowered to the floor. If a second trial is to be taken, the performer may readjust the weights and then repeat the trial. (See Figure 7-6.) Also, see general directions on page 95.

Figure 7-6. Standing Vertical Arm Press

Scoring: Same as for bench squat test. (See Table 7-6.)

Safety: The two assistants should remain ready to catch the barbell at any time during the trial.

Additional Pointer: The performer must avoid flexing at the knees and hips during the press.

Spring Scale Strength Tests (27)

Objective: To measure strength through a limited range of motion.

Age Level: Ages twelve through college.

Sex: Recommended for girls to correspond to the pull-up test, dip test, and vertical arm press test previously presented for boys only.

Reliability: See each individual test item.

Objectivity: See each individual test item.

Validity: See each individual test item.

Equipment and Materials: All of the equipment needed for the following spring scale tests can be purchased at most hardware stores for a very reasonable price. The equipment and attachments needed are listed as follows: (a) one 160-pound spring scale, (b) two heavy-duty eye hooks, (c) two chain links, (d) two 18-inch chain sections, (e) one 5-foot section of chain, (f) two S hooks, (g) one screw hook, and (h) one wooden bar (2-foot length of hickory). (See Figure 7-7.)

Table 7-6
Raw Score Norms for Standing Vertical Arm Press
Raw Scores Are Figured by Dividing Body Weight into
the Additional Weight Successfully Used in the Test

College Men		
Prior to Training Scores	Performance Category	After 9 Weeks' Training Scores
.92 - Above	Advanced	1.08 - Above
.80 - .91	Adv. Intermediate	.97 - 1.07
.58 - .79	Intermediate	.71 - .96
.47 - .57	Adv. Beginner	.59 - .70
.00 - .46	Beginner	.00 - .58

Based on the scores of 80 college men, Corpus Christi State University, Corpus Christi, Tx., 1976.

Based on a limited number of scores from a physical education weight training class, Corpus Christi State University, Corpus Christi, Tx., 1976.

General Directions: (a) Students should be allowed to become familiar with the three spring scale tests at least several days prior to testing. (b) On each test the student should be allowed two trials (if she so desires) in which she can register the maximum amount of weight possible for that test. (c) The tester should keep his eyes at the same level as the scale in order to determine the maximum amount of weight registered. (d) Students should be allowed to warm up before reporting to the testing station, but they also should be cautioned not to overwork. (e) Foot stance marks should be placed on the floor so that students will assume the same position each time they execute the tests and so that they will be pulling or pushing in a vertical direction.

Scoring: The best score of two trials is recorded as the score for each test. The student's best score for each test is then divided by her body weight and recorded as the test score.

Additional Pointers: If a regular training program is to be conducted, paint marks of different colors along the links of the chain will help each girl to quickly identify her particular link for each exercise. Also, require all students to use a shoulder-width grip on each test.

Spring Scale Test Items

Overhead Pull Test (28)

Objective: To measure the strength of the arms and shoulders in the pull-up movement.

Age Level: Recommended for ages twelve through college.

Sex: Recommended for girls in place of the pull-up test which was presented for boys only.

Reliability: An r of .98 was found for this test when students were tested, allowed a short rest, and then retested.

Objectivity: An objectivity coefficient of .99 was obtained by John Huntsman, 1969.

Validity: Face validity was accepted for this test.

Equipment and Materials: The equipment needed is the spring scale rig as previously described.

Directions: The tester should hook the bar to that part of the chain which will allow each student to start the pull from a straight arm position, but with all the body weight resting on the feet. The feet should be flat on the floor and about 12 inches apart. With a forward grasp on the bar (hands about shoulder width apart) the student should pull the bar downward without any bending of the knees, hips, or turning of the body. The student must bend only at the elbows and keep both feet on the floor while maintaining an erect posture. For girls who are strong enough to pull their body weight or more, it is necessary to have an assistant hold the performer's hips so that the feet will not leave the floor. If a second trial is to be taken, the performer may rest a few seconds and then repeat the exercise. (See Figure 7-8.) Also, see general directions on page 106.

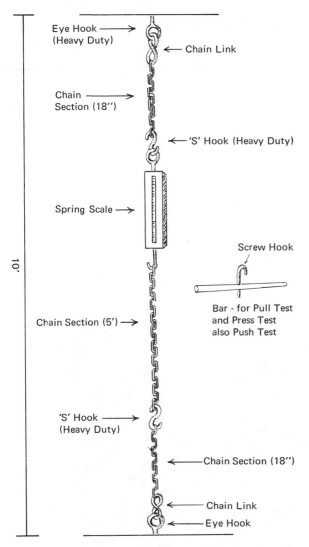

Figure 7-7. Spring Scale Rig

Eye Hook (Heavy Duty)

Chain Link

Chain Section (18″)

'S' Hook (Heavy Duty)

Spring Scale

Screw Hook

Bar - for Pull Test and Press Test also Push Test

Chain Section (5′)

'S' Hook (Heavy Duty)

Chain Section (18″)

Chain Link

Eye Hook

10′

Scoring: Keeping the eyes on the level of the scale, the tester records the greatest number of pounds reached by means of a steady pull. The best score of two trials is recorded over body weight and divided for the test score. (See Table 7-7.)

Additional Pointer: Make sure that each student understands that the pull is to be a steady one rather than a hard or fast jerk.

Two-Hand Push Test (28)

Objective: To measure the strength of the arms and shoulders in a downward push movement.

Age Level: Ages twelve through college.

Sex: Recommended for girls in place of the dip test which was presented for boys only. Satis-

factory for men when 320-pound scale is used.

Reliability: An *r* of .97 was found for this test when students were tested, allowed a short rest, and then retested.

Objectivity: An *r* of .99 was obtained by John Huntsman, 1969.

Validity: Face validity was accepted for this test.

Equipment and Materials: Same as for the previous test.

Directions: The tester should hook the bar attachment to that part of the chain which will allow the bar to run horizontally across the navel of the performer. With the body weight distributed equally over the feet, the performer should push the bar vertically downward by attempting to straighten out the arms. The feet must remain flat on the floor during the test. For some girls it may be necessary to have a classmate hold the hips in order to keep the

Figure 7-8. Overhead Pull Test

Table 7-7
Raw Score Norms for Overhead Pull Test
Raw Scores Are Figured by Dividing Body Weight into the Amount of Weight Registered on the Spring Scale

College	
Scores	Performance Category
1.15 - Above	Advanced
1.04 - 1.14	Adv. Intermediate
.85 - 1.03	Intermediate
.76 - .84	Adv. Beginner
.00 - .75	Beginner

Based on the scores of 80 college women, Corpus Christi State University, Corpus Christi, Tx., 1976.

Table 7-8
Raw Score Norms for Two-Hand Push Test
Raw Scores Are Figured by Dividing Body Weight into the Amount of Weight Registered on the Spring Scale

Men	Performance	Women
Scores	Category	Scores
1.16 - Above	Advanced	.99 - Above
1.07 - 1.15	Adv. Intermediate	.92 - .98
.90 - 1.06	Intermediate	.64 - .91
.81 - .89	Adv. Beginner	.52 - .63
.00 - .80	Beginner	.00 - .51

Based on the scores of 150 college women and 200 college men, Corpus Christi State University, Corpus Christi, Tx., 1977.

Figure 7-9. Two-Hand Push Test

feet down. (See Figure 7-9.) Also, see general directions on page 106.

Scoring: Keeping the eyes on the level of the scale, the tester records the greatest number of pounds reached by means of a steady push. The best score of two trials is recorded over body weight and divided for the test score. (See Table 7-8.)

Additional Pointer: The head of the performer should not be allowed to lean over to the side of the chain but must remain directly in front and in line with it.

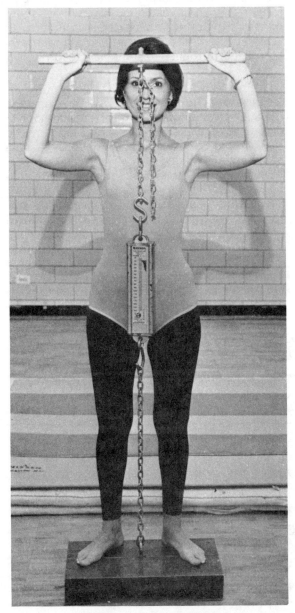
Figure 7-10. Press Test

Table 7-9
Raw Score Norms for Press Test

Raw Scores Are Figured by Dividing Body Weight into the Amount of Weight Registered on the Spring Scale

College Women	
Scores	Performance Category
.56 - Above	Excellent
.48 - .54	Good
.34 - .47	Average
.27 - .33	Poor
.00 - .26	Very Poor

Based on the scores of 100 college women as reported by Ronald Taylor, NLU, Monroe, La., 1972.

Press Test (28)

Objective: To measure the strength of arm extension in a vertical overhead press movement.

Age Level: Ages twelve through college.

Sex: Recommended for girls in place of the standing vertical arm press test with a barbell as previously presented for boys only.

Reliability: An *r* of .96 was found for this test when students were tested, allowed a short rest, and then retested.

Objectivity: An *r* of .99 was obtained by John Huntsman, 1969.

Validity: Face validity was accepted for this test.

Equipment and Materials: Same as for previous test.

Directions: The tester should hook the bar to that part of the chain which will allow each student to start the push with the bar located in front of the forehead (between the eyebrows and the hairline). Keeping the feet flat on the floor, the student should press the bar vertically upward by attempting to straighten out the arms. Palms should be forward on the grasp. If a second trial is to be taken, the performer may rest a few seconds and then repeat the trial. (See Figure 7-10.) Also, see general directions on page 106.

Scoring: Same as for the previous test. (See Table 7-9.)

Additional Pointer: The performer should stand facing the back side of the scale so that the tester can simultaneously observe the body position and the score.

Absolute Strength Tests

Olympic Lifts

The competitive sport of weight lifting was incorporated into the Olympic Games in 1896. It was designed for men, and, until the present time, there is no known record of women ever competing in this sport. For women interested in strength testing, the authors recommend the tests presented under the heading "Practical Tests of Relative Strength." Originally, there were three Olympic lifts, but in recent years the military press lift was dropped from competition due to the difficulty of judging it. The two remaining lifts are presented here. For these two tests, world records are recognized in accordance with body weight categories.

Two-Hands Snatch Lift

General Description: In this test the performer measures his strength by lifting the bar in one movement from the floor to an arms-extended position overhead.

Equipment and Materials: An official weight-lifting barbell of 7 feet in length and 1 inch in diameter is required. Official weights graduated in pounds or kilograms are also required.

Directions: The performer grasps the bar (palms downward) and pulls it in a single movement from the ground to the full extension of the arms vertically above the head, while either splitting or bending the legs. The bar must pass with continuous movement along the body, and no part of the body other than the feet must touch the floor during the lift. The weight must be maintained overhead with arms and legs extended in a steady position for a two-second count. The feet must be aligned during the hold position.

Scoring: The best lift of three trials is recorded as the score. (See Table 7-10.)

Safety: Spotters or assistants should be available to help the performer in the event of difficulty.

Additional Pointers: (1) The turning of the wrists must not take place until the bar has passed the top of the performer's head. (2) The performer may recover from the split or squat phase of the performance at his own time. (3) The lift must meet all international standards for correct performance to stand as a record.

Two-Hands Clean-and-Jerk

General Description: The performer measures his strength in lifting the bar from the floor to his chest, and then, in a second exertion, he extends the bar vertically overhead by the use of the arms and legs.

Equipment and Materials: Same as for the two-hands snatch lift.

Directions: The performer grasps the bar (palms downward) and pulls it in a single movement from the ground to the shoulders, while splitting or bending the legs. The performer shall then recover to an alignment of the feet at his own time. He then bends the legs and extends them as well as the arms so as to push the bar to a vertically extended position over-

Table 7-10
Sample World Class Scores*

Weight Class	Two-Hands Snatch Lift		Clean-and-Jerk Lift	
	Pounds	Kilograms	Pounds	Kilograms
Fly (to 114½ lbs. or 51.3 kg)	233	104.4	308	138.0
Bantam (to 123½ lbs. or 55.3 kg)	259	116.0	333	149.2
Feather (to 132¼ lbs. or 59.2 kg)	277	124.1	349	156.4
Light (to 148¾ lbs. or 66.6 kg)	303	135.7	391	175.2
Middle (to 165¼ lbs. or 74.0 kg)	336	150.5	418	187.3
Light-heavy (to 181¾ lbs. or 81.4 kg)	359	160.8	446	199.8
Middle-heavy (to 198¼ lbs. or 88.8 kg)	386	172.9	471	211.0
Heavy (to 242½ lbs. or 108.6 kg)	391	175.2	493	220.9
Super-heavy (over 242½ lbs. or 108.6 kg)	410	183.7	531	237.9

*These scores are merely sample scores, not necessarily world records.

head. He then returns the feet to the same line again. The performer must hold the weight overhead for a two-second count.

Scoring: The best lift of three trials is recorded as the score. (See Table 7-10.)

Safety: Two assistants should be available to help the performer in the event of difficulty.

Additional Pointers: (1) The performer must hold the weight overhead motionless for the two-second count. (2) The lift must meet all international standards for correct performance to stand as a record.

Power Lifts

Power lifting competition is a relatively new type of weight-lifting competition composed of the squat lift, the bench press, and the dead lift. It was organized in 1965 as a competitive sport for men. For women interested in strength testing, the authors recommend the tests presented under the heading "Tests of Relative Strength." The three power lifts are presented here with sample world class scores. For these three tests, world records are recognized in accordance with body weight categories.

Squat Test

General Description: The performer is measured in his ability to squat downward with a weight resting behind his shoulders and to then return to the standing position.

Equipment and Materials: An official weight-lifting barbell of 7 feet in length and 1 inch in diameter is required. Official weights graduated in pounds or kilograms are also required.

Directions: The performer must assume a motionless upright position with the barbell across the shoulders in a horizontal position, not more than 1 inch below the top of the deltoids, with hands gripping the bar and feet flat on the floor. The performer then must bend the knees, lowering the body until the tops of the thighs are below parallel with the floor. He shall return to the upright standing position at will, without double bouncing. After remaining absolutely motionless for a two-second count, the performer returns the barbell to the rack.

Scoring: The best lift of three trials is recorded as the score. (See Table 7-11.)

Safety: Padding may be applied to the bar, but it must not exceed 30 centimeters in width and 5 centimeters in thickness. Spotters or assistants should be ready to help the performer in the event of difficulty.

Additional Pointers: (1) The use of a wedge at the heels or toes is forbidden. (2) The lifter must not rise on his toes or heels during the performance. (3) There must be no shifting of the bar or the feet during the performance of the lift. (4) Failure to assume an upright position at the start and completion of the lift is a cause for disqualification. (5) The performance must meet all international standards of power lifting competition to stand as a record.

Table 7-11
Sample World Class Scores*

Weight Class	Squat Lift		Bench Press		Dead Lift	
	Pounds	Kilograms	Pounds	Kilograms	Pounds	Kilograms
Fly (to 114½ lbs. or 51.3 kg)	385	172.5	238	106.6	465	208.3
Bantam (to 123½ lbs. or 55.3 kg)	415	185.9	260	116.5	505	226.2
Feather (to 132¼ lbs. or 59.2 kg)	450	201.6	310	138.9	530	237.4
Light (to 148¾ lbs. or 66.6 kg)	510	228.5	325	145.6	615	275.5
Middle (to 165¼ lbs. or 74.0 kg)	585	262.1	355	159.0	635	284.5
Light-heavy (to 181¾ lbs. or 81.4 kg)	600	268.8	378	169.3	650	291.2
Middle-heavy (to 198¼ lbs. or 88.8 kg)	650	291.2	410	183.7	680	304.6
100 kg (to 220½ lbs. or 98.8 kg)	670	300.2	525	235.2	705	315.8
Heavy (to 242½ lbs. or 108.6 kg)	750	336.0	550	246.4	760	340.5
Super-heavy (over 242½ lbs. or 108.6 kg)	825	369.6	600	268.8	882	395.1

*These scores are merely sample scores, not necessarily world records.

Bench Press Lift

General Description: The performer measures the strength of his arm extension by lying on a bench and pressing as heavy a weight as possible upward.

Equipment and Materials: An official barbell and weights as described in the squat test are required. The bench must be flat and level and have a width of between 25 and 30 centimeters.

Directions: The performer must assume either a complete extended supine position on the bench or a position with only the head and trunk (including buttocks) extended on the bench and feet flat on floor. When the bar is resting motionless at the performer's chest, he must press the bar vertically to straight arm's length and hold it motionless for a two-second count. The performer's hands must not be wider than 81 centimeters measured between the forefingers.

Scoring: The best lift of three attempts is recorded as the score. (See Table 7-11.)

Safety: Two or more assistants must be ready to help the performer in the event of difficulty.

Additional Pointers: (1) There must be no raising or shifting of position from the bench or movement of the feet during the lift. (2) There must be no excessive pressure of the bar against the performer's chest or heaving or bouncing of the bar from the chest. (3) The lift must meet all international standards of power lifting competition to stand as a record.

Dead Lift Test

General Description: The performer measures his strength in lifting a barbell from the floor to an erect standing position.

Equipment and Materials: Same as for the squat lift.

Directions: The bar must be laid horizontally in front of the performer's feet. Gripping the bar in an optional grasp with both hands, the performer lifts the bar with one continuous motion until he reaches an erect standing position. At this point, the knees must be locked and the shoulders thrust back. The bar should be held for a two-second count.

Scoring: The best lift of three trials is recorded as the score. (See Table 7-11.)

Safety: Two spotters should be available to assist the performer in the event of loss of balance or inability to control the weight.

Additional Pointers: (1) There must be no raising on the toes or heels or shifting of the feet during the lift. (2) There must be no supporting of the bar on the thighs. (3) The performer must meet all international power lifting standards of competition to attain a record.

Isometric Strength Instruments

Objective: To measure strength without movement of the resistance or the joints involved.

Tensiometer (12, 14, 15): The equipment required for various tests with the tensiometer includes a strap with D ring, a pair of cables with adjusters, a goniometer to establish correct joint angles, and a specially constructed table for various exercise positions. The tensiometer indicates the pounds of pressure exerted up to 300 pounds; however, a smaller tensiometer (for greater precision) is used when measurements are expected below 30 pounds due to the inaccuracy of the lower end of the 300 pound instrument. The smaller tensiometer measures accurately from 0 to 100

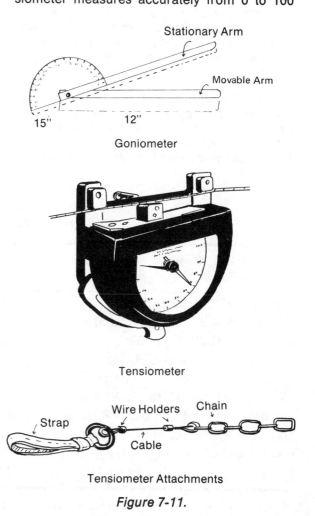

Goniometer

Tensiometer

Tensiometer Attachments

Figure 7-11.

pounds. The reliability of the tensiometer is quite high, since objectivity coefficients for practically all tests were in the .90s. The instrument can be purchased from the Pacific Scientific Company, Inc., of Los Angeles. (See Figure 7-11.)

Grip Dynamometer: The grip dynamometer is used to secure strength scores of the grip of each hand. It has an adjustable handle to fit the size of the hand and a maximum needle indicator for ease of scoring. The scoring dial is marked off in kilograms. Reliability coefficients have been reported in the .90s, which indicates that there is a satisfactory degree of reliability and that the scale does measure from 0 to 100 kilograms. The instrument may be purchased from the C. H. Stoelting Co. of Chicago. (See Figure 7-12.) Norms for both boys and girls were established with the use of the Smedley grip dynamometer. (See Table 7-12.)

Back and Leg Dynamometer. This instrument consists of a scale which measures from 0 to 2500 pounds in 10-pound increments. It is attached to a strong platform and has a chain and bar attachment for individual adjustments according to height. Satisfactory reliability has been reported for tests with this instrument ranging from .86 into the .90s. The main drawback of this instrument is the expense involved for a limited number of exercises. The instrument may be purchased from the Nissen Corporation of Cedar Rapids, Iowa. (See Figure 7-13.)

Heavy Duty Spring Scale. The heavy duty spring scale is seldom used, but can be

Figure 7-13. Back and Leg Dynamometer

employed most effectively in a strength testing program. By placing the scale under an isometric rack, accurate measurements can be recorded for the military press, the bench press, the curl, and other exercises. In any exercise where the student is required to push or lift upward, you simply record the maximum amount read on the scale and then subtract body weight from that figure. For the leg press, a bar may be inserted underneath the scale; then a belt is attached to both ends of the bar and is placed over the subject's hips for the lift. The large scale, which provides motivation, can easily be seen by both the tester and the subject. The reliability for this instrument has been reported in the .90s.

Isokinetic Strength Instruments

Isokinetic strength measurement requires a special machine with an automatic governor to control the resistance and speed at which the subject operates. The advantage of this type of strength training is that it develops strength through the full range of motion for each exercise. In other words, it combines the advantage of isometric and isotonic training. In lifting a barbell or dumbbell (as in isotonic training) the resistance is not equal at each point in the movement due to momentum and coordinating movements. And in isometric training, the muscle receives only one point of maximum

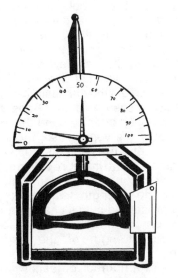

Figure 7-12. Grip Dynamometer

Table 7-12
Norms of Strength of Grip in Kilograms (Smedley)

Age	Boys Right Hand	Left Hand	Girls Right Hand	Left Hand
6	9.21	8.48	8.36	7.74
7	10.74	10.11	9.88	9.24
8	12.41	11.67	11.16	10.48
9	14.34	13.47	12.77	11.97
10	16.52	15.59	14.65	13.72
11	18.85	17.72	16.54	15.52
12	21.24	19.71	18.92	17.78
13	24.44	22.51	21.84	20.39
14	28.42	26.22	24.79	22.92
15	33.39	30.88	27.00	24.92
16	39.37	36.39	28.70	26.56
17	44.74	40.96	29.56	27.43
18	49.28	45.01	29.75	27.66

Based on 2788 boys in Chicago.   Based on 3471 girls in Chicago.

resistance at a time. However, the isokinetic machine adjusts automatically to each exertion throughout its full range.

When isokinetic machines are available, they may be preferred over standard barbells and weight-lifting equipment due to the possibility

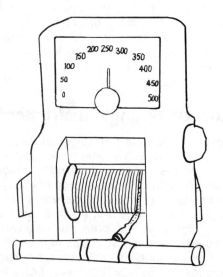

Figure 7-14. Isokinetic Mini Gym, Model 180*

*Mini-Gym Isokinetic Exercise Equipment, P.O. Box 266, 909 West Lexington, Independence, Mo. 64051.

of greater strength development for the time involved. However, standard weight-lifting equipment is still effective and may remain more economical for many years to come.

Problems Associated with Strength Testing

Several of the problems and limitations associated with the measurement of strength are listed and discussed below:

1. The muscular strength tests most frequently used during the past few decades have included some test items of dubious validity. For example, the inclusion of the lung capacity measure in the Rogers Strength Test has been criticized and defended many times over the years. Also, the inclusion of muscular endurance items, such as pull-ups and dips for maximum repetition, have added to the confusion and misinterpretation concerning strength test results. The test items presented in this chapter are believed to be practical measures of isotonic and isometric strength of the large muscle groups.

2. There are a number of tests which provide accurate strength measurement but require expensive equipment; consequently, many

schools have been unable to include such tests in their physical education program. Therefore, the tests presented in this chapter should be of practical value, since all equipment and materials mentioned are well within the budget limits of most schools. Moreover, further attempts should be made to devise inexpensive but reliable and objective strength tests.

3. At the present time, the measurement of abdominal strength has been quite limited. Many of the better-known strength tests have avoided this area entirely, although abdominal strength is important in various activities. The sit-up test with maximum (or near-maximum) resistance behind the neck represents only one attempt at assessing strength in that area. Perhaps another method would be to tie weight to the feet and from a straight arm support on the parallel bars, or from a hand hang under the horizontal bar, lift the legs to a horizontal position and hold for three counts.

4. Different grip widths produce different strength performance results (42C). Thus, it is important to specify a grip of shoulder width in testing.

5. In measuring static strength, it is difficult to establish precisely the same position or angle for certain exercises and for all subjects. Differences in the amount of musculature and fatty tissue, and different lengths of body segments pose special problems for accurate testing. Needless to say, it is imperative that such tests start at the same angle for each student, and from the same reference point on each individual. For example, such phrases as "starting with the elbows at a ninety-degree angle" or "starting with the bar between the eyebrows and the hair line" are absolutely necessary if comparisons are to be made within a group or with established norms. Furthermore, in using any type of gauge such as the scale device that does not have a memory pointer (which remains in place after pressure is released) the tester's eyes must be kept at the same level as the scale in order to secure an accurate reading.

Findings and Conclusions from Strength Measurement and Research

Prior to 1950 it was commonly believed by both coaches and athletes that weight training did not produce the type of strength necessary for superior sports performance and, furthermore, that such training hindered speed of movement. However, starting in 1950 a number of researchers reported that isotonic weight training increased strength and improved speed of movement (2, 7, 9, 21, 39, 54, 56). As a result of such findings, athletes in practically all sports now use weight training as a valuable adjunct to their sports practice.

Although strength is believed to be a major factor in most motor performances, it is not important enough by itself to be predictive for success in very many activities. Berger (4) found the relationship between static (isometric) strength measures and dynamic (isotonic) strength measures to be low. Thus, the value of taking static strength measures to predict ability in any kind of dynamic gross motor activity is questionable. Also, strength is specific by nature, and the amount of strength needed for any sport or dance activity is specific to the activity as well as to the muscles involved (53). Therefore, it is meaningless to use one type of strength test to suggest abilities in skills demanding another type of strength.

Although Elbel (20), in 1928, was probably the first to note that strength could be increased by short static contraction (isometric) exercises, it was not until the highly publicized experiments of Hettinger and Muller (24), 1953, that mass interest was created in this type of training. Since that date numerous studies have indicated that strength can be significantly increased by isometric exercise (3, 22, 33, 41, 48, 55).

Once it was clearly understood that both isometric and isotonic exercises could increase strength, investigators turned their attention to a comparison of the two systems. The results of such endeavors have generally revealed that there is no significant difference in the amount of strength developed by the two programs (1, 10, 23, 32, 43). Usually any difference in the two programs has been specific to the manner in which the strength was tested, either by isotonic means or by isometric measurement.

While one frequently hears of the fantastic strength feats accomplished under hypnosis, a study by Johnson and Kramer (31) failed to reveal that hypnotic conditions were better than non-hypnotic conditions in strength performance.

Concerning the value of strength programs in increasing movement time and reaction time, studies by Meadows (37), Chui (10), and Johnson (25) compared isometric and isotonic training programs and found them to be nearly equal insofar as bringing about increases in speed of movement. In contrast, Swegan's study (43) reported that both isometric and isotonic programs slowed down speed of movement. However, in a recent study by Whitley and Smith (48), it was concluded that regardless of the type of strengthening exercises used, increasing the strength of muscles involved in a particular task makes it possible to execute the movement faster.

Michael (36) found that isometric training increased both speed of movement and reaction time significantly. Crowder (15) further found that isometric and isotonic strength training were equally effective in improving reaction time when the exercises were performed in the same way in which the reaction time measures were taken.

Several studies have indicated that individuals with greater muscular strength usually have greater muscular endurance, although the development of strength endurance is not directly proportional to maximum strength development (4, 6, 19, 50). Two studies even showed strength increases through typical muscular endurance training techniques (10B, 42). Other studies have shown a high relationship between relative strength and relative muscular endurance (29, 46).

In a study of isometric strength and relative isometric endurance. Carlson and McCraw (8) found that weak subjects could hold light weights longer than strong subjects. However, no significant difference was found between the groups when heavy weight loads were used.

Concerning strength and academic achievement, Clarke (12) found that high strength groups had a consistent tendency to have higher means on standard achievement tests and grade point averages, while two studies (49, 51) revealed that persons who had greater strength as measured by grip strength had significantly better grades in physical education courses.

Several studies have indicated the effects of motivation upon strength performance (30, 34, 40). For example, Nelson (40) found that students who exerted more effort under the influence of motivational situations had greater strength decrement and recovered more slowly from their strength loss than those less motivated. Johnson (28) found that motivated isometric training groups significantly increased their strength, whereas a non-motivated isometric training group made little or no gain when tested under conditions of no consciously induced motivation. It was further noted that a special motivational testing situation (which included march music, spectators, photographers, and competition) significantly increased the strength scores of training groups over those scores achieved during training. Thus, strength measures seem to be greatly influenced by the level of motivation present during training and testing.

References and Bibliography

1. Adamson, G. F., "Effects of Isometric and Isotonic Exercise on Elbow Flexor and Spine Extensor Muscle Groups," In Athletic Institute, *Health and Fitness in the Modern World*, Chicago: Athletic Institute, 1961, p. 172.
2. Anderson, Robert W., "The Effect of Weight Training on Total Body Reaction Time" (Unpublished master's thesis, University of Illinois, 1957, p. 66).
3. Barham, Jerry N., "A Comparison of Two Methods of Isometric Exercises on the Development of Muscle Strength" (Unpublished master's thesis, Louisiana State University, 1960).
4. Berger, Richard A., "The Effect of Varied Weight Training Programs on Strength and Endurance" (Microcarded master's thesis, University of Illinois, 1960).
5. _____, "Comparison of Static and Dynamic Strength," *Research Quarterly*, 33:329, October, 1962.
6. Burke, William E., "A Study of the Relationship of Age to Strength and Endurance in Gripping" (Microcarded doctor's thesis, University of Iowa, 1952, p. 49).
7. Capen, Edward K., "The Effect of Systematic Weight Training on Power, Strength, and Endurance," *Research Quarterly*, 21:83-93, May, 1950.
8. Carlson, Robert B., and Lynn W. McCraw, "Isometric Strength and Relative Isometric Endurance," *Research Quarterly*, 42:244-250, October, 1971.
9. Chui, Edward, "Effect of Weight Training on Athletic Power," *Research Quarterly*, 21:188, October, 1950.
10. _____, "Effects of Isometric and Dynamic Weight-Training Exercises upon Strength and Speed of Movement," *Research Quarterly*, 35:246-257, October, 1964.
11. Clark, David H., and G. A. Stull, "Endurance Training as a Determinant of Strength and Fatiguability," *Research Quarterly*, 41:19-26, 1970.

12. Clarke, H. Harrison, "Objective Strength Tests of Affected Muscle Groups Involved in Orthopedic Disabilities," *Research Quarterly*, 19:118-147, May, 1948.

13. _____, and Boyd O. Jarman, "Scholastic Achievement of Boys 9, 12, and 15 Years of Age as Related to Various Strength and Growth Measures," *Research Quarterly*, 32:155, May, 1961.

14. _____, and Richard A. Munroe, "Cable Tension Strength Test Batteries" (Microcarded publication, University of Oregon, 1970).

15. Cotten, Doyice J., and Allen Johnson, "Use of the T-5 Cable Tensiometer Grip Attachment for Measuring Strength of College Men," *Research Quarterly*, 41:454-456, October, 1970.

16. Crowder, Vernon R., "A Comparison of the Effects of Two Methods of Strength Training on Reaction Time" (Unpublished master's thesis, Louisiana State University, 1966).

17. Cureton, T. K., "Analysis of Vital Capacity as a Test of Condition for High School Boys," *Research Quarterly*, 4:80-93, December, 1936.

18. Drury, Francis A., "Strength Through Measurement," Marion, Ind.: Coach's Sporting Goods Corporation, 1963.

19. Eckert, Helen M., and June Day, "Relationship Between Strength and Workload in Push-ups," *Research Quarterly*, 38:380-383, October, 1971.

20. Ebel, Edwin R., "A Study in Short Static Strength of Muscles" (Unpublished master's thesis, International Y.M.C.A. College, July, 1928, p. 64).

21. Endres, John P., "The Effect of Weight Training Exercise Upon the Speed of Muscular Movement" (Microcarded master's thesis, University of Wisconsin, 1953, pp. 29-31).

22. Gardner, Gerald W., "Specificity of Strength Changes of the Exercised and Non-Exercised Limb Following Isometric Training," *Research Quarterly*, 34:99-100, March, 1963.

23. Healy, Alfred, "Two Methods of Weight Training for Children with Spastic Type of Cerebral Palsy," *Research Quarterly*, 29:389-395, December, 1958.

24. Hettinger, T., and E. A. Muller, "Muskelleistung und Muskeltraining," *Arbeitsphysiologie*, 15:111-126, 1953.

25. Johnson, Barry L., "A Comparison of Isometric and Isotonic Exercises Upon the Improvement of Velocity and Distance as Measured by a Vertical Rope Climb Test" (Unpublished master's thesis, Louisiana State University, 1964).

26. _____, "Isometric Strength Tests," (Unpublished study, Northeast Louisiana University, 1966).

27. _____, "Isotonic Strength Tests" (Unpublished study, Northeast Louisiana University, 1966).

28. _____, "Spring Scale Strength Tests: Measuring Strength Through a Limited Range of Motion" (Unpublished study, Northeast Louisiana University, 1966).

29. _____, and Mike D. Morgan, "Relationship of Relative Bench Press Strength to Relative Push-Up Endurance" (Unpublished study, Corpus Christi State University, 1976).

30. _____, and Jack K. Nelson, "The Effects of Applying Different Motivational Techniques During Training and in Testing Upon Strength Performance," *Research Quarterly*, 38:630-636, December, 1967.

31. Johnson, Warren R., and George F. Kramer, "Effects of Stereotyped Non-hypnotic, Hypnotic, and Post-hypnotic Suggestions upon Strength, Power, and Endurance," *Research Quarterly*, 32:522-529, December, 1961.

32. Lorback, Melvin H., "A Study Comparing the Effectiveness of Short Periods of Static Contraction to Standard Weight Training Procedures in the Development of Strength and Muscle Girth" (Microcarded master's thesis, Pennsylvania State University, 1955).

33. Lyne, James, "The Frequency of Static Contraction Exercise Necessary for Strength Level Maintenance" (Microcarded master's thesis, Pennsylvania State University, 1958).

34. Marcel, Norman A., "The Effect of Knowledge of Results as a Motivation on Physical Performance" (Unpublished study, Louisiana State University, 1961).

35. Mathews, D. K., and Robert Kruse, "Effects of Isometric and Isotonic Exercises on Elbow Flexor Muscle Groups," *Research Quarterly*, 28:26, March, 1957.

36. McCloy, C. H., and Norma D. Young, *Tests and Measurements in Health and Physical Education*, New York: Appleton-Century-Crofts, 1954, pp. 130-134.

37. Meadows, P. E., "The Effect of Isotonic and Isometric Muscle Contraction Training on Speed, Force, and Strength" (Microcarded doctoral dissertation, University of Illinois, 1959, pp. 93-95).

38. Michael, Charles E., "The Effects of Isometric Contraction Exercise on Reaction and Speed of Movement Times" (Unpublished doctoral dissertation, Louisiana State University, 1963, p. 61).

39. Mosely, John W., and others, "Weight Training in Relation to Strength, Speed, and Coordination," *Research Quarterly*, 24:308-315, October, 1953.

40. Nelson, Jack K., "An Analysis of the Effects of Applying Various Motivational Situations to College Men Subjected to a Stressful Physical

Performance" (Microcarded doctoral dissertation, University of Oregon, 1962).

41. Rarick, Lawrence, and Gene L. Larson, "Observations on Frequency and Intensity of Isometric Muscular Effort in Developing Muscular Strength," *Research Quarterly*, 29:333-341, October, 1958.

42. Rasch, Phillip J., and Lawrence E. Morehouse, "Effects of Static and Dynamic Exercises on Muscular Strength and Hypertrophy," *Journal of Applied Physiology*, 11:25, July, 1957.

43. _____, "Relationship between Maximum Isometric Tension and Maximum Isotonic Elbow Flexion." *Research Quarterly*, 28:85, March, 1957.

44. Stull, Alan G., and David H. Clarke, "High-Resistance, Low-Repetition Training as a Determiner of Strength and Fatigability," *Research Quarterly*, 41:189-193, May, 1970.

45. Stumiller, Bob, "The Effect of Three Different Grip Widths on Strength Performance" (Unpublished study, Corpus Christi State University, 1976.)

46. _____, and Barry L. Johnson, "The Relationship of Relative Strength to Relative Endurance" (Unpublished study, Corpus Christi State University, 1976).

47. Swegan, Donald B., "The Comparison of Static Contraction with Standard Weight Training in Effect of Certain Movement Speeds and Endurances" (Microcarded doctoral dissertation, Pennsylvania State University, 1957, pp. 137-140).

48. Taylor, William E., "A Study Comparing the Effectiveness of Four Static Contraction Training Methods for Increasing the Contractile Strength of Two Body Movements" (Unpublished master's thesis, Pennsylvania State University, 1954).

49. Tinkle, Wayne F., and Henry J. Montoye, "Relationship Between Grip Strength and Achievement in Physical Education Among College Men," *Research Quarterly*, 32:242, May, 1961.

50. Tuttle, W. W., and others, "Relation of Maximum Back and Leg Strength to Back and Leg Strength Endurance," *Research Quarterly*, 26:96-106, March, 1955.

51. Wessel, Janet A., and Richard C. Nelson, "Relationship Between Grip Strength and Achievement in Physical Education Among College Women," *Research Quarterly*, 32:244, May, 1961.

52. Whitley, Jim D., and Leon E. Smith, "Influence of Three Different Training Programs on Strength and Speed of a Limb Movement," *Research Quarterly*, 37:142, March, 1966.

53. _____, and Lawrence Allan, "A Test of Activation as a General Factor in Strength Performance," *Research Quarterly,* 141:584-587, December, 1970.

54. Wilkin, Bruce M., "The Effect of Weight Training on Speed of Movement," *Research Quarterly*, 23:361-369, October, 1952.

55. Wolbers, Charles P., and Frank D. Sills, "Development of Strength in High School Boys by Static Muscle Contraction," *Research Quarterly*, 27:446, December, 1956.

56. Zorbas, William S., and Peter V. Karpovich, "The Effect of Weight Lifting Upon the Speed of Muscular Contraction," *Research Quarterly*, 22:145-148, May, 1951.

Muscular endurance may be either dynamic or static in nature and concerns the ability of a muscle to repeat identical movements or pressures, or to maintain a certain degree of tension over a period of time. Basically there are three types of muscular endurance tests. Each type may be either *relative* or *absolute*. A *relative* endurance test is one in which the muscles work with a proportionate amount of the maximum strength load of a particular muscle group (54) or with a proportionate amount of the body weight.* An *absolute* endurance test requires a set load for all subjects without a definite relationship to the maximum strength of each individual (54) or to his body weight.

The three types of muscular endurance tests are identified as follows:

Dynamic tests of muscular endurance: The performer executes identical repetitions of a movement through a designated distance and over an unlimited amount of time. The test is scored in terms of the number of correct executions completed. Examples of such tests include barbell exercises with submaximal loads and the frequently used push-ups, pull-ups, and sit-ups.

Repetitive static tests of muscular endurance: The performer executes repetitions of force against a static measuring device, and the test is scored in terms of the number of times the performer registers a force equal to a certain percent of either the maximum strength of the muscles involved or of body weight. An example would be the number of times a performer can squeeze eighty pounds or more on a grip strength dynamometer. The test is usually stopped when the performer either fails to squeeze the prescribed load or when he falls behind the desired cadence. While some writers identify this type test as a dynamic test, it should be noted that movement over a distance is not a factor.

*The authors recommend *relative endurance tests* which are based upon a proportional amount of the body weight since maximum strength is known to fluctuate and to be dependent upon many variables. Body weight is more constant, and the tester can be certain of the maximum body weight measure, whereas he can never know for sure whether he is getting a maximum effort on a strength measure. Moreover, most common muscular endurance tests (chin-ups, dips, push-ups, etc.) are relative endurance tests since each individual is working with his own body weight. Johnson and Garcia (28) have further illustrated this in a Relative Strength—Relative Endurance Continuum.

Chapter Eight

The Measurement of Muscular Endurance

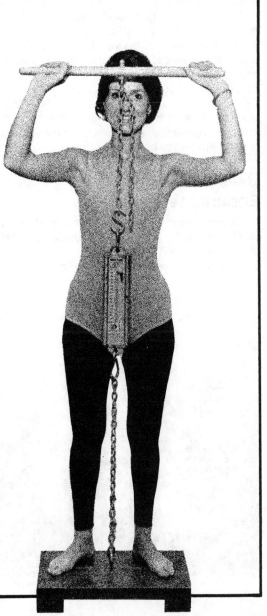

Timed static tests of muscular endurance: The performer maintains one continuous muscle contraction rather than a series of repetitive bouts, and the test is scored in terms of the amount of time the weight was held. An example would be the flexed-arm hang test for girls (1).

Tests of muscular endurance are quite practical for the majority of schools and have been widely used in physical fitness testing programs. Such tests differ from strength tests in that the score is based on the number of repetitions executed (or the length of time a set tension was maintained) and not on the maximum amount of weight lifted or force exerted.

While muscular endurance is closely associated with strength, it is also associated with the number of active capillaries within the working muscles. Because of this association, muscular endurance tests are sometimes confused with circulorespiratory endurance tests. However, muscular endurance tests primarily tax the skeletal muscles involved; whereas the circulorespiratory endurance items primarily tax the efficiency of the heart and lungs.

Uses of Muscular Endurance Tests

Several ways by which muscular endurance tests should be utilized in physical education classes are listed as follows:
1. As a factor in physical fitness tests.
2. As a means to motivate students to improve their status within the class.
3. As a measure for determining achievement and grades when muscular endurance is a specific objective in a physical activity class.
4. As a means to indicate an individual's readiness for vigorous activity.

Practical Tests of Muscular Endurance

Several practical tests of muscular endurance in terms of time, equipment, and cost are presented below:

Sit-ups (Bent Knees) (26)

Objective: To measure the endurance of the abdominal muscles.

Age Level: Ages ten through college.

Sex: Satisfactory as a test for both boys and girls.

Reliability: Has been reported as high as .94.

Objectivity: An *r* of .98 was found for this test.

Validity: Face validity was accepted for this test.

Equipment and Materials: The only equipment required is a mat and yardstick.

Directions: From a lying position on the back, the performer flexes his knees over the yardstick while sliding his heels as close to his seat as possible. The yardstick should be held tightly under the knees until the performer is instructed to slowly slide his feet forward. At the

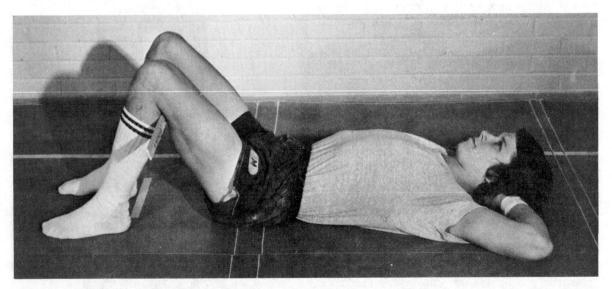

Figure 8-1A. Obtaining Bent-Knee Angle for Sit-up Test

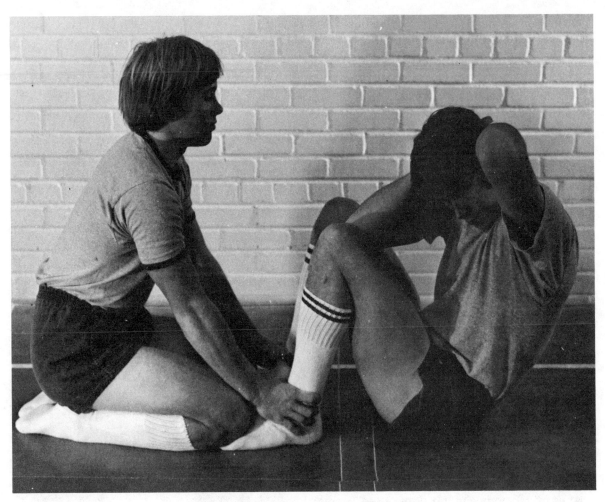

Figure 8-1B. Sit-up Test (Bent Knees)

Table 8-1A
Raw Score Norms for Sit-ups (Bent Knees)
(Prior to Regular Training)

College Men	Performance Level	College Women
66 - Above	Advanced	49 - Above
53 - 65	Adv. Intermediate	37 - 48
34 - 52	Intermediate	21 - 36
25 - 33	Adv. Beginner	13 - 20
0 - 24	Beginner	0 - 12

Based on 85 scores obtained at Corpus Christi State University, Corpus Christi, Tx., 1976.

Based on 80 scores obtained at Corpus Christi State University, Corpus Christi, Tx., 1976.

College Men	Performance Level	College Women
96 - Above	Advanced	57 - Above
79 - 95	Adv. Intermediate	41 - 56
44 - 78	Intermediate	27 - 40
31 - 43	Adv. Beginner	18 - 26
0 - 30	Beginner	0 - 17

Based on 85 scores obtained at Corpus Christi State University, Corpus Christi, Tx., 1976.

Based on 80 scores obtained at Corpus Christi State University, Corpus Christi, Tx., 1976.

point where the yardstick drops to the mat, the tester marks the heel line and seat line to indicate how far the feet should remain from the seat during the bent-knee sit-up exercise. (See Figure 8-1A.) The performer should interlace the fingers behind the neck and perform sit-ups alternating a left elbow touch of the inside right knee and a right elbow touch of the inside left knee. The exercise should be repeated as many times as possible. (See Figure 8-1B.)

Scoring: The total number of repetitions is recorded for the score. However, repetitions should not be counted when fingertips do not maintain contact behind the head, when the knees are not touched, or when the pupil pushes off the floor with the elbow. (See Tables 8-1A and 8-1B.)

Additional Pointers: (a) The feet should rest flat on the floor and may be separated a few inches. (b) The back of the hands should touch the mat each time before curling to the sit-up position. (c) Taping the yardstick to the floor for the seat line helps the performer to maintain proper distance between seat and feet. See Appendix B for AAHPER sit-up test and norms.

Flexed-Arm Hang (1)

Objective: To measure the endurance of the arms and shoulder girdle in the flexed-arm hang position.

Age Level: Ages ten through college.

Sex: This test is presented for girls only.*

*Although the flexed-arm hang test is presented for girls, it can be used quite effectively for boys who cannot chin themselves, thereby enabling the tester to obtain some objective measure of arm and shoulder endurance, as well as providing a record of progress.

Figure 8-2. Flexed-Arm Hang

Table 8-2
Flexed-Arm Hang for Girls (1)
Percentile Scores Based on Age/Test Scores in Seconds

| Percentile | Age | | | | | | | | Percentile |
	9-10	11	12	13	14	15	16	17+	
100th	78	68	84	68	65	83	69	73	100th
95th	42	39	33	34	35	36	31	34	95th
90th	29	30	27	25	29	28	24	28	90th
85th	24	24	23	21	26	25	20	22	85th
80th	21	21	21	20	23	21	17	19	80th
75th	18	20	18	16	21	18	15	17	75th
70th	16	17	15	14	18	15	12	14	70th
65th	14	15	13	13	15	14	11	12	65th
60th	12	13	12	11	13	12	10	10	60th
55th	10	11	10	9	11	10	8	9	55th
50th	9	10	9	8	9	9	7	8	50th
45th	7	8	8	7	8	8	6	7	45th
40th	6	7	6	6	7	7	5	6	40th
35th	5	6	5	5	5	5	4	5	35th
30th	4	5	4	4	5	4	3	4	30th
25th	3	3	3	3	3	4	3	3	25th
20th	2	3	2	2	3	3	2	2	20th
15th	1	2	1	1	2	2	1	2	15th
10th	0	0	1	0	1	1	1	1	10th
5th	0	0	0	0	0	0	0	0	5th
0	0	0	0	0	0	0	0	0	0

Source: AAHPER, *AAHPER Youth Fitness Test Manual,* Revised, Washington, D.C., 1966, pp. 27, 64.

Reliability: Has been reported as high as .90.
Objectivity: An *r* of .99 was obtained for this test.
Validity: Face validity was accepted.
Equipment and Materials: The equipment needed is a horizontal bar (1½ inches in diameter) raised to a height so that the tallest girl cannot touch the ground from the flexed-arm hang position. If standard equipment is not available, a piece of pipe or a doorway gym bar can be used. A stopwatch is also needed for testing.
Directions: With an overhand grasp and the assistance of two spotters, the performer should raise the body off the floor so that the chin is above the bars and the elbows are flexed. The performer should hold this position for as long as possible. (See Figure 8-2.)

Scoring: The number of seconds to the nearest second that the performer maintains the proper position is recorded as the score. (See Table 8-2.)
Additional Pointers: (a) The time should be started as soon as the subject starts in the flexed hang position. (b) The time should be stopped as soon as the chin touches the bar, tilts backward, or drops below the bar. (c) A variation of this test, which is a little easier to score, is to time the individual from the beginning of the flexed hang position until the arms are fully extended. There is no difficulty in determining when the person reaches full extension, which ordinarily occurs suddenly after the subject has hung for a while in a partially flexed position. The time is rarely over 2 minutes for men and is usually under 1 minute for girls.

Table 8-3
Chin-ups (Pull-ups) for Boys (1)
Percentile Scores Based on Age/Test Scores in Number of Pull-ups

Percentile	9-10	11	12	Age 13	14	15	16	17+	Percentile
100th	19	16	18	17	27	20	26	23	100th
95th	9	8	9	10	12	15	14	15	95th
90th	7	6	7	9	10	12	12	13	90th
85th	5	5	6	7	9	11	11	12	85th
80th	4	5	5	6	8	10	10	11	80th
75th	3	4	4	5	7	9	10	10	75th
70th	3	4	4	5	7	9	9	10	70th
65th	2	3	3	4	6	8	8	9	65th
60th	2	3	3	4	5	7	8	8	60th
55th	1	2	2	3	5	7	7	7	55th
50th	1	2	2	3	4	6	7	7	50th
45th	1	1	1	2	4	5	6	6	45th
40th	1	1	1	2	3	5	6	6	40th
35th	1	1	1	2	3	4	5	5	35th
30th	0	1	0	1	2	4	5	5	30th
25th	0	0	0	1	2	3	4	4	25th
20th	0	0	0	0	1	2	3	3	20th
15th	0	0	0	0	1	1	3	2	15th
10th	0	0	0	0	0	1	2	1	10th
5th	0	0	0	0	0	0	1	0	5th
0	0	0	0	0	0	0	0	0	0

Source: AAHPER, *AAHPER Youth Fitness Test Manual*, Revised, Washington D.C., 1966, pp. 34, 65.

Chin-ups (1)

Objective: To measure the muscular endurance of the arms and shoulder girdle in pulling the body upward.

Age Level: Ages ten through college.

Sex: Satisfactory as a test for boys only.

Reliability: An r as high as .87 has been reported for this test when subjects were tested on separate days.

Objectivity: An r of .99 was obtained by Mike Recio, 1972.

Validity: This test has been accepted for its face validity.

Equipment and Materials: The equipment needed is a horizontal bar (1½ inches in diameter) raised to a height so that the tallest performer cannot touch the ground from the hanging position. If standard equipment is not available, a piece of pipe or the rungs of a ladder can be used.

Directions: The performer should assume the hanging position with the overhand grasp (palms forward) and pull his body upward until the chin is over the bar. After each chin-up, he should return to a fully extended hanging position. The exercise should be repeated as many times as possible. (See Figure 8-3.)

Scoring: The score is the number of completed chin-ups. (See Table 8-3).

Additional Pointers: (a) Only one trial is allowed unless it is obvious that the student could do better with a second chance. (b) Swinging and snap-up movements must be avoided. The

Figure 8-3. Chin-up

tester may check this by holding an extended arm across the front of the performer's thighs. (c) The knees must not be flexed during the pull, and kicking motions must be avoided. (d) Although the palms-forward grasp is customarily prescribed in physical fitness batteries, there is no logical reason why this, rather than the reverse (palms-inward) grasp, should be employed other than it is more difficult. As a matter of fact, since the reverse grip yields more repetitions, it might actually be a better measure in terms of distribution of scores. As McCloy (45) pointed out, the overhand grip became standard in World War II when the Armed Forces decreed that it was similar to the grip needed in climbing a fence. McCloy adroitly commented that the reverse grip is the one used in the climbing of a rope.

Half-Squat Jump Test

Objective: To measure the endurance of the muscles of the legs.

The Measurement of Muscular Endurance **125**

Table 8-4
Raw Score Norms for Half-Squat Jump Test

College Men	Performance Level	College Women
86 - Above	Advanced	44 - Above
66 - 85	Adv. Intermediate	34 - 43
37 - 65	Intermediate	22 - 33
19 - 36	Adv. Beginner	15 - 21
0 - 18	Beginner	0 - 14

Based on the scores of 200 college men as reported by M. C. Gomez, Corpus Christi State University, Corpus Christi, Tx., 1974, and on the scores of 100 college women as reported by Charles Prestidge, NLU, Monroe, La., 1972.

Figure 8-4A. Determining Distance for the Half-Squat Jump Test

Age Level: Ages ten through college.

Sex: Satisfactory as a test for both boys and girls.

Reliability: An *r* of .82 was reported by Charles Prestidge, 1972.

Objectivity: An *r* of .99 was reported by Mike Recio, 1972.

Validity: Face validity was accepted for this test.

Equipment and Materials: Adjustable bench, chair, fold-up mats, cold drink cases, or anything that can be stacked to measure to the lower patella (knee-cap) level of your knees.

Directions: (1) Adjust the seat level of bench,

chair, or whatever is available to your lower patella (knee-cap) level. (2) Face about and clasp your hands behind your head and step one foot slightly ahead of the other. (3) Squat down until your seat touches the surface of the seat level and jump upward extending the legs (knees straight) and switch the position of the feet. Repeat for as many repetitions as necessary for your program. (See Figure 8-4B.)

Scoring: One point is scored for each correct repetition. (See Table 8-4.)

Additional Pointers: (a) If the performer stops to rest, the score is terminated at that point. (b) The feet must come off the floor on each jump,

 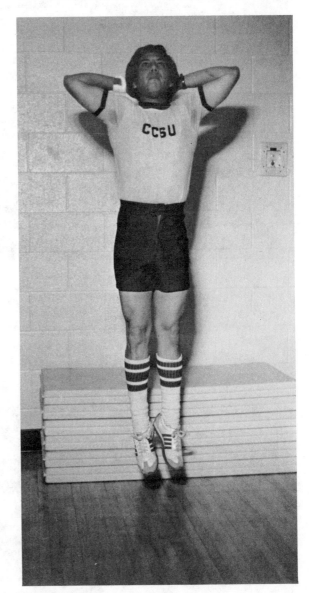

Figure 8-4B. The Half-Squat Jump Test

and the legs must be extended. (c) The performer's buttocks must touch the horizontal seat level on each repetition to be scored.

Push-ups

Objective: To measure the endurance of the arms and shoulder girdle.
Age Level: Ages ten through college.
Sex: Satisfactory for boys only.

Reliability: The authors failed to find a coefficient of reliability reported for this test.
Objectivity: An *r* of .99 was reported by Mike Recio, 1972.
Validity: Face validity was accepted for this test.
Equipment and Materials: A mat on the floor.
Directions: From a straight arm front leaning rest position, the performer lowers the body

Figure 8-5. Push-ups

Table 8-5A
T-Score Norms for Push-ups for Sixth, Seventh, and Eighth Grade Boys

T-Score	6th Grade Raw Score	7th Grade Raw Score	8th Grade Raw Score	T-Score
80	39 Up	40 Up	49 Up	80
75	34 - 38	36 - 39	44 - 48	75
70	30 - 33	32 - 35	39 - 43	70
65	25 - 29	28 - 31	34 - 38	65
60	21 - 24	24 - 27	29 - 33	60
55	16 - 20	20 - 23	24 - 28	55
50	12 - 15	16 - 19	19 - 23	50
45	7 - 11	12 - 15	14 - 18	45
40	3 - 6	8 - 11	9 - 13	40
35	0 - 2	4 - 7	4 - 8	35
30		0 - 3	0 - 3	30

Based on the scores of 161 sixth grade boys, 167 seventh grade boys, and 149 eighth grade boys, Baton Rouge, La., 1972.

Table 8-5B
Scale Point Norms for Push-ups for Men

Scores Men under 30 Years	Scale Points	Scores Men over 30 Years
60	100	50
58	95	48
56	90	46
54	85	44
53	80	43
50	75	40
48	70	38
46	65	36
44	60	34
42	55	32
40	50	30
38	45	28
36	40	26
34	35	24
32	30	22
30	25	20
28	20	18

J. T. Fisher, "Marine Corps Physical Fitness Programs," *Journal of Physical Education*, 65:120, March-April, 1968.

until the chest touches the mat and then pushes upward to the straight arm support. The exercise is continued for as many repetitions as possible without rest. The body must not sag or pike upward but maintain a straight line throughout the exercise. (See Figure 8-5.)

Scoring: The score is the number of correct push-ups executed. (See Tables 8-5A and 5B.)

Additional Pointers: (a) The score is terminated if the performer stops to rest. (b) If the chest does not touch or if the arms are not completely extended on an execution, the trial does not count. (c) In order to rigidly supervise the correct execution of the test, the tester or an assistant should lie on the right side of the performer and place his right hand, palm upward, under the performer's chest. The tester's left hand should be placed lightly on the performer's elbow. In this manner the tester can easily determine if the chest was lowered enough and if the arms reached complete extension.

Modified Push-ups

Objective: To measure the endurance of the arms and shoulder girdle.

Age Level: Ages ten through college.

Sex: Satisfactory for girls only.

Reliability: Has been reported as high as .93.

Validity: Has been reported as high as .72 with the Rogers Short Index (58).

Equipment and Materials: A mat on the floor.

Directions: (See Figure 8-6.) With the knees bent at right angles and the hands on the floor (directly under the shoulders), the performer lowers her body to the floor until the chest touches, and then she pushes back to the starting position. The exercise is continued for as many repetitions as possible without rest. The body must not sag but maintain a straight line throughout the trial.

Scoring: The score is the number of correct push-ups executed. (See Tables 8-6A and 6B.)

Additional Pointers: (a) The score is termi-

Table 8-6A
Raw Score Norms for Modified Push-ups

High School Girls	
Raw Scores	Performance Level
31 — Above	Advanced
25 — 30	Advanced Intermediate
13 — 24	Intermediate
7 — 12	Adv. Beginner
0 — 6	Beginner

Based on the scores of 50 college women, Corpus Christi State University, Corpus Christi, Tx., 1977.

Table 8-6B
Minimum Standard Raw Scores for Modified Push-ups

Girls					
Age 6-7	Age 8-9	Age 10-11	Age 12-13	Age 14-15	Age 16-18
4 times	7 times	9 times	10 times	12 times	14 times

Quaker Oats-American Athletic Union (AAU) Physical Fitness Pentathlon Event. National Standards designed by the AAU for each age group.

Figure 8-6. Modified Push-ups

nated if the performer stops to rest. (b) If the chest does not touch or if the arms are not completely extended on an execution, the trial does not count.

Endurance Dips

Objective: To measure the endurance of the arms and shoulder girdle.

Age Level: Ages ten through college.

Sex: Satisfactory as a test for boys only.

Reliability: An r as high as .90 has been reported for this test when subjects were tested on separate days.

Objectivity: An r of .99 was reported by Mike Recio, 1972.

Validity: Face validity was accepted for this test.

Equipment and Materials: Two parallel bars raised to a height so that all subjects are supported freely above the ground (in a lowered bent arm support) are used.

Directions: The performer should assume a straight arm support between the bars and lower downward until the elbows form a right angle. He should then push back to a straight arm support and continue the exercise for as

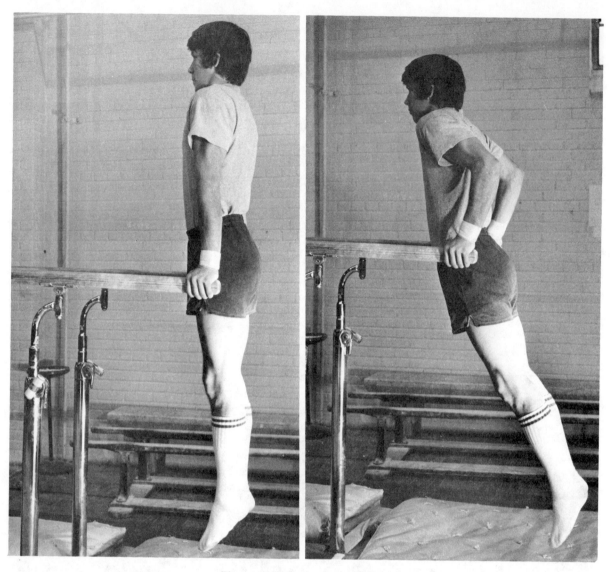

Figure 8-7. Endurance Dips

many repetitions as possible. (See Figure 8-7.)
Scoring: The score is the number of correct repetitions executed. (See Table 8-7.)
Additional Pointers: (a) The score is terminated if the performer stops to rest. (b) The performer should refrain from swinging or kicking in returning to the straight arm support position. (c) The tester should extend his fist upward from inside the bar so that the performer's shoulder will touch it notifying both the student and the tester that the elbows reached the right angle. (d) The tester's other arm can be used to hold across the front of the performer's thighs in the event of swinging, and at other times the tester can lightly grasp the performer's elbow

Table 8-7
Raw Score Norms for Endurance Dips

College Men	Performance Level
25 - Above	Advanced
18 - 24	Adv. Intermediate
9 - 17	Intermediate
4 - 8	Adv. Beginner
0 - 3	Beginner

Based on scores reported from physical education classes at the University of Florida, Gainesville, Fla., and at East Texas State University, Commerce, Tex.

Directions: (See Figure 8-8.) From a standing position (a) bend at the knees and waist and place the hands on the floor in front of the feet, (b) thrust the legs backward to a front leaning rest position, (c) return to the squat position as in the first count, and (d) stand erect. From the signal "go" repeat this exercise at a constant rate of movement for as long as possible.

Scoring: The score is the number of correct repetitions executed. (See Table 8-8.) The score is recorded to the nearest whole number.

Additional Pointers: (a) The score is terminated if the performer stops to rest. (b) Repetitions which are incorrect are not counted toward the score.

Start

b

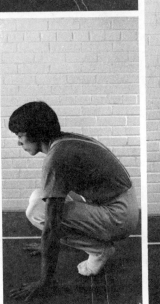

c

d

Figure 8-8. Burpee (Squat Thrust)

to stress full arm extension. (e) If the parallel bars are lower at one end than the other, it facilitates the testing of subjects of different heights.

Burpee (Squat Thrust)

Objective: To measure the general muscular endurance of the body.

Age Level: Ages ten through college.

Sex: Satisfactory as a test for both boys and girls.

Reliability: An *r* of .97 was found for this test when subjects were tested on separate days.

Validity: Face validity was accepted.

Equipment and Materials: Mat on floor.

Table 8-8
Raw Score Norms for Burpee (Squat Thrust) Test

College Men	Performance Level	College Women
94 - Above	Advanced	46 - Above
70 - 93	Adv. Intermediate	38 - 45
39 - 69	Intermediate	20 - 37
22 - 38	Adv. Beginner	12 - 19
0 - 21	Beginner	0 - 11

Based on a limited number of scores from physical education classes at Corpus Christi State University, Corpus Christi, Tx., 1976.

One-Bar Dip Test for Endurance

Objective: To measure the endurance of the arms and shoulder girdle.

Age Level: Ages twelve through college.

Sex: Recommended for girls.

Reliability: An *r* of .81 was found for this test when twenty students were tested on separate days.

Objectivity: An *r* of .96 was obtained when two

Figure 8-9. One-Bar Dip Test for Girls

Table 8-9
Raw Score Norms for One-Bar Dip Test for Girls

Prior to Training Scores	College Women Performance Level	After 9 Weeks' Training Scores
9 - Above	Advanced	25 - Above
7 - 8	Adv. Intermediate	19 - 24
4 - 6	Intermediate	12 - 18
2 - 3	Adv. Beginner	7 - 11
0 - 1	Beginner	0 - 6

Based on the scores of 100 college women as reported by Mike Recio, 1972.

Based on a limited number of scores of college women after nine weeks of training, 1972.

testers independently scored twenty students on the test.

Validity: Face validity was accepted for this test.

Equipment and Materials: The only equipment needed is a single bar raised to a height so that the tallest girl cannot touch the floor when in the lowest position.

Directions: The performer starts from a straight arm support on the bar by lowering downward until the elbows form approximately a right angle. She should then push back to a straight arm support and continue the exercise for as many repetitions as possible. It is permissible to slide the body against the bar during the upward and downward phases of the exercise. (See Figure 8-9.)

Scoring: The total number of repetitions is recorded for the score. However, repetitions should not be counted when the elbows do not bend sufficiently on the lowering phase of the exercise or when they do not fully extend on the press phase. (See Table 8-9.)

Repetitive Press Test with Spring Scale (27)

Objective: To measure the endurance of the arms and shoulders in a mid-military press type exercise.

Age Level: Ages fifteen through college.

Sex: Satisfactory for both boys and girls.

Reliability: An r of .92 was found when girls were tested at one-third of their body weight.

Validity: Face validity was accepted.

Equipment and Materials: The equipment needed is the spring scale, hook and bar,

Table 8-10
Raw Score Norms for the Repetitive
Press Test with Spring Scale

College Men	Performance Level	College Women
47 - Above	Advanced	44 - Above
34 - 46	Adv. Intermediate	31 - 43
18 - 33	Intermediate	11 - 30
7 - 17	Adv. Beginner	2 - 10
0 - 6	Beginner	0 - 1

Based on the scores of 100 college men as reported by Ronald Taylor, 1972.

Based on the scores of 100 college women as reported by Dixie Bennett, 1972.

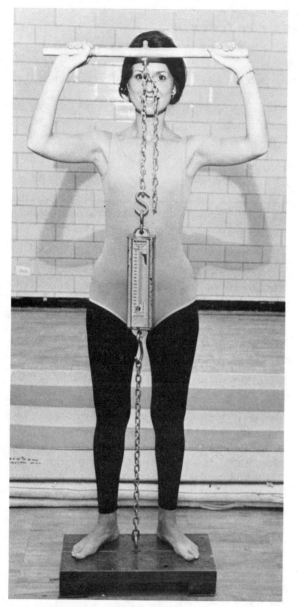

Figure 8-10.
Repetitive Press Test with Spring Scale

score. The tester should maintain the cadence and reset the dial indicator before each press. (See Figure 8-10.)

Scoring: The score is the number of repetitions the performer can register the needle indicator above one-half of his body weight or for girls one-third of her body weight. (See Table 8-10.)

Additional Pointers: (a) The test is terminated on the third successive failure to register the proper score. (b) The score is terminated when the performer is unable to keep up with the cadence. (c) An alternate test would be to use one-half of the performer's maximum strength press (one-third for girls). However, maximum strength is much more variable from day to day than is body weight. Also, we never know for certain when we have secured maximum effort from our students.

Handstand Push-ups Against Wall

Objective: To measure the endurance of the arms and shoulders in pressing the body in a handstand position.

Age Level: Ages twelve through college.

Sex: Recommended for boys only.

Reliability: An *r* of .83 was obtained when testing students on separate days.

Objectivity: An *r* of .98 was obtained when two testers independently scored twenty students.

Validity: This test was accepted for its face validity.

Equipment and Materials: The only equipment needed is a mat placed on the floor and against a smooth-surfaced wall. (See Figure 8-11.)

Directions: The performer should place his hands on the mat (approximately 1 foot from the wall and shoulder-width apart) and kick up-

chains, and a small but sturdy wooden platform to provide better balance during the test. (See Spring Scale Strength Test Items.)

Directions: Same as for the press test under spring scale strength test items except that the performer is required to register at least one-half of his body weight (one-third for girls) on the scale at approximately 2 seconds at a cadence of push-one, push-two, etc., for as many repetitions as possible. The press must be steady each time until it reaches the desired

Table 8-11
Raw Score Norms for Handstand Push-up Test against Wall

College Men	Performance Level
18 - Above	Advanced
11 - 17	Adv. Intermediate
4 - 10	Intermediate
2 - 3	Adv. Beginner
0 - 1	Beginner

Based on the scores of 30 college men, Corpus Christi State University, Corpus Christi, Tx., 1975.

Figure 8-11. Handstand Push-up Test

ward into a handstand with his heels resting against the wall. He then bends at the elbows allowing the body to lower until the tip of the nose touches the mat. He then pushes the body back to its original position by extending the elbows until they lock. The movement is repeated for as many repetitions as possible. A spotter (assistant) should place two fingers against each knee of the performer and assist the performer in maintaining balance as he does the exercise.

Scoring: The score is the number of successful push-ups from a touch of the nose to a lock-out position of the elbows. (See Table 8-11.)

Additional Pointers: (a) A spotter (assistant) should be used to assist the performer in getting into and out of the handstand position. (b) The performer's hands should be flat on the

mat and fingers pointing directly toward the wall during the exercise. (c) The exercise is terminated if the performer hesitates to rest.

Problems Associated with Muscular Endurance Testing

Several of the problems associated with muscular endurance testing are listed as follows:

1. Definite guidelines must be followed when scoring muscular endurance tests, since slight deviations from the correct form and procedure may greatly affect the final results.

2. Since motivational factors greatly influence results, it is most important that the tester standardize as much as possible the

presence of motivation during endurance testing so that all students are scored on the same basis. Furthermore, if the scores are to be used as norms, a notation should be made if a special type of motivation was utilized.

3. Certain muscular endurance tests take a considerable amount of time to administer, and, as a result, a time limit is sometimes placed on them. However, this is not always justifiable, since low correlations are often found between the timed and untimed tests. Perhaps a better approach would be to use barbell plates in terms of a certain percent of each performer's body weight so that the repetitions will not be so numerous. Clarke (13) suggested, in his studies on ergography, that a load and cadence that will accomplish the most work in a relatively short amount of time be considered as a criterion.

4. On some occasions, testers have used dynamic muscular endurance exercises in a training program but have measured their effectiveness with a static endurance test and vice versa. However, it should be recognized that the most valid measure of dynamic endurance training is a dynamic endurance test and that, likewise, the most valid measure of static endurance training is a static endurance test.

5. Many of the norms presently used are out of date or were set up on a limited number of cases. Thus, there is a need for the construction of new norms for both old and new tests.

6. Because of the decided dependence of strength on some endurance items such as push-ups, pull-ups, etc., it is sometimes difficult to defend the use of the term *endurance* in these measures. Obviously, if the individual lacks sufficient strength to do one pull-up, we cannot then validly conclude that he has no endurance. In such instances, measures employing repetitive lifting of submaximal weights or static endurance tests are recommended.

Findings and Conclusions from Muscular Endurance Measurement and Research

Muscular endurance has been measured and studied in various ways. For example, it has been studied by the following methods: (a) repetitive static method where maximal or submaximal contractions are repeated in cadence (usually every two or three seconds) for maximum repetitions (10, 19, 50); (b) the dynamic method by varying the load in proportion to maximum isotonic strength and then performing repetitive isotonic movements (22, 43, 62); (c) the dynamic method by varying the load in proportion to maximum isometric strength and then performing isotonic movements (4, 13, 43, 46); (d) the timed static method by varying the load in proportion to maximum isometric strength and then holding for as long as possible (21, 40, 53, 54, 60).

At the present time, conflicting concepts exist concerning the value of isometric exercises in increasing muscular endurance. One concept indicates that muscle endurance is associated with capillarization and that capillarization is enhanced by rapid contraction movements so that the blood flow in the muscle is increased. Therefore, researchers have indicated that since isometric contraction restricts the flow of blood to the muscle, it is not effective in producing capillarization and the development of endurance (2, 3, 9, 12). A second concept indicates that while endurance is dependent to some extent upon circulation, muscular endurance is also influenced by strength and will improve no matter how strength is developed. There are several studies which support this concept (4, 16, 25, 38, 47).

Research in various exercise programs reveals the following findings concerning muscular endurance:

1. Weight training (dynamic overload) programs will improve performance on muscular endurance exercises (5, 6, 8, 37). Moreover, muscular endurance performance is influenced by the strength of the individual (7, 11, 15, 32, 56, 59).

2. Isotonic exercises are more effective than isometric exercises in the development of muscular endurance (46, 49, 55, 61). Furthermore, a faster rate of repeated contractions produces the greater endurance (36, 46).

3. In contradiction to the above finding, several researchers have found both isometric and isotonic programs to be equally effective in improving muscular endurance (4, 16, 25, 38, 47). While Meadows (47) found both methods significantly increased dipping and chinning endurance, he found the isotonic method superior in the chinning test. In

addition Swegan (55) found that isotonic exercises increased muscular endurance significantly on eight tests, whereas isometric exercises significantly increased such performance in only one of the eight tests.

4. Various types of motivational techniques employed during testing periods will significantly increase muscular endurance performance (18, 20, 26, 30, 31, 48). Two interesting studies by Johnson and Kramer (30, 31) revealed improved endurance performance during hypnosis.

5. Concerning the effect of warming up before endurance performance, no significant effect was observed as a result of passive heating of the muscle (51) or as a result of active warm-ups using hypnosis to control the psychological variable (41).

6. There are conflicting reports concerning the effect of the cross transfer of training on muscular endurance. One study found that both the exercised and non-exercised arm improved in strength, while only the exercised arm significantly improved in endurance (42). However, a more recent study found that when endurance in the trained limb was increased to a high level, the endurance in the untrained limb increased about 28 percent of that level (24).

7. Several studies have indicated that muscular endurance is not directly proportional to the development of maximum strength (44, 59, 63). Thus, a great increase in muscular endurance is not necessarily accompanied by an equal increase in strength itself.

8. Excess weight is a handicap to students in performing relative endurance exercises such as push-ups, pull-ups, and squat jumps (39, 52). Moreover, there is a high relationship between relative strength and relative endurance (29, 57).

Several studies have been conducted to determine proper procedures for endurance testing. The following points should be noted:

1. Since reverse grasp chin-ups give greater results than regular grasp chin-ups, they must not be used interchangeably on chin-up tests (17, 35). Also, hip or kick action should not be allowed, since they will increase chin-up scores (17).

2. Karpovich found low correlations between leg lifts and sit-ups (33) and between timed sit-ups and untimed sit-ups (34), indicating that such items should not be used interchangeably in test batteries.

3. The AAHPER Youth Fitness Test Committee found the flexed-arm hang test more efficient and reliable than the modified pull-up test for girls (1). However, the test directions should specify a straight body position since piking at the hips or bending at the knees can result in significantly higher scores (58).

References and Bibliography

1. AAHPER, *AAHPER Youth Fitness Test Manual,* rev. ed., Washington, D.C.: American Alliance for Health, Physical Education, and Recreation, 1976.
2. Asmussen, E., "Positive and Negative Muscular Work," *Acta Physiol. Scandinavica,* 28:364-382, 1952.
3. _____ , "Training of Muscular Strength by Static and Dynamic Activity," Kongressen *Voredrog, Lingiaden,* Stockholm, 11:22-23, 1949.
4. Baer, Adrian D., and others, "Effects of Various Exercise Programs on Isometric Tension, Endurance, and Reaction Time in the Human," *Archives of Physical Medicine and Rehabilitation,* 36:495-502, 1955.
5. Berger, Richard A., "The Effect of Varied Weight Training Programs on Strength and Endurance" (Microcarded master's thesis, University of Illinois, 1960).
6. Bready, Charles F., "A Study of the Effects of Heavy Resistance Training Upon the Pattern of Muscular Development as Indicated by Strength, Endurance, and Girth of the Right Elbow Flexors" (Microcarded master's thesis, University of Maryland, 1961).
7. Burke, William E., "A Study of the Relationship of Age to Strength and Endurance in Gripping" (Microcarded doctoral thesis, University of Iowa, 1952, p. 49).
8. Capen, Edward K., "The Effect of Systematic Weight Training on Power, Strength, and Endurance, *Research Quarterly,* 21:83-94, May, 1950.
9. Clarke, David H., "Energy Cost of Isometric Exercise," *Research Quarterly,* 31:3-6, March, 1960.
10. _____ , "Strength Recovery from Static and Dynamic Muscular Fatigue," *Research Quarterly,* 33:349-355, October, 1962.
11. Clarke, David H., and Stull, G. A., "Endurance Training as a Determinant of Strength and Fatiguability," *Research Quarterly,* 41:19-26, 1970.
12. Clarke, H. Harrison, "Development of Volitional Muscle Strength as Related to Fitness," In Athletic Institute, *Exercise and Fitness,* Chicago: Athletic Institute, 1959.
13. _____ , and others, "Strength and Endurance (Conditioning) Effects of Exhaustive Exercise

of the Elbow Flexor Muscles," *Journal Assoc. Phy. Ment. Rehabilitation,* 8:184-188, 1954.

14. _____, and others, "Precision of Elbow Flexion Ergography Under Varying Degrees of Muscular Fatigue," *Archives of Physical Medicine,* 33:279-288, May, 1952.

15. Cook, Ellsworth B., and Robert J. Wherry, "Statistical Evaluation of Physical Fitness," *Research Quarterly,* 21:94-111, May, 1950.

16. Dennison, J. D., and others, "Effect of Isometric and Isotonic Exercise Programs Upon Muscular Endurance," *Research Quarterly,* 32:348-353, October, 1961.

17. DeWitt, R. T., "A Comparative Study of Three Types of Chinning Tests," *Research Quarterly,* 15:240-248, October, 1944.

18. Gerdes, Glen R., "The Effects of Various Motivational Techniques Upon Performance in Selected Physical Tests" (Microcarded doctoral dissertation, Indiana University, 1958, pp. 88-92).

19. Grose, Joel E., "Depression of Muscle Fatigue Curves by Heat and Cold," *Research Quarterly,* 29:19-31, March, 1958.

20. Hall, D.M., "Endurance Tests for 4-H Club Members," *Research Quarterly,* 22:48, March, 1951.

21. Hansen, J. W., "The Effect of Sustained Isometric Muscle Contraction on Various Muscle Functions," *Int. Z. Angew, Physiol. Einschl. Arbeilphysiol.,* 19:430-434, 1963.

22. _____, "The Training Effect of Dynamic Maximal Resistance Exercises," *Int. Z. Angew. Physiol. Arbeilphysiol.,* 19:420-424, 1963.

23. Hellebrandt, F. A., and S. J. Hautz, "Mechanisms of Muscle Training in Man," *Physical Therapy Review,* 36:371-383, 1956.

24. Hodgkins, J., "Influence of Unilateral Endurance Training on Contri-lateral Limb," *Journal of Applied Physiology,* 16:991-993, 1961.

25. Howell, Maxwell L., and others, "Effect of Isometric and Isotonic Exercise Programs Upon Muscular Endurance," *Research Quarterly,* 33:539, December, 1962.

26. Johnson, Barry L., "The Effect of Motivational Testing Situations on an Endurance Test" (Laboratory experiment, Northeast Louisiana University, 1963).

27. _____, "Practical Tests of Muscular Endurance" (Unpublished study, Northeast Louisiana University, 1967).

28. _____, and Mary Jane Garcia, *Fitness and Performance for Everyone,* Portland, Tex.: Brown & Littleman Books, 1977, p. 16.

29. _____, and Mike D. Morgan, "The Relationship of Relative Bench Press Strength to Relative Push-Up Endurance," (Unpublished study, Corpus Christi State University, 1976).

30. Johnson, Warren R., and George F. Kramer, "Effects of Different Types of Hypnotic Suggestions Upon Physical Performance," *Research Quarterly,* 32:522-529, December, 1961.

31. _____, "Effects of Stereotyped Non-Hyponotic, Hypnotic, and Post-Hypnotic Suggestions Upon Strength, Power, and Endurance," *Research Quarterly,* 32:522-529, December, 1961.

32. Karpovich, Peter V., "Fatigue and Endurance," Supplement to the *Research Quarterly,* 12:416, May, 1941.

33. _____, and others, "Relation Between Leg-Lift and Sit-up," *Research Quarterly,* 17:21-24, March, 1946.

34. _____, "Studies of the AAF Physical Fitness Test: Selection of a Time Limit for Sit-ups," Project No. 245, Report No. 3, AAF School of Aviation Medicine, Randolph Field, Texas, July, 1944.

35. _____, "The Effect of Reverse and Forward Grips Upon Performance in Chinning," Project No. 178, Report No. 1, AAF School of Aviation Medicine, Randolph Field, Texas, October, 1943.

36. Kincaid, Don. G., "The Specificity of Muscular Endurance Following Different Rates of Training" (Microcarded master's thesis, Pennsylvania State University, 1959, p. 53).

37. Kusinitz, Ivan, and Clifford E. Keeney, "Effects of Progressive Weight Training on Health and Physical Fitness of Adolescent Boys," *Research Quarterly,* 29:294, October, 1958.

38. Lawther, John E., "The Pennsylvania State University Studies on Strength Decrement, Maintenance, and Related Aspects," *61st Annual Proceedings,* College Physical Education Association, 1958.

39. Loveless, James C., "Relationship of the Wartime Navy Physical Fitness Test to Age, Height, and Weight," *Research Quarterly,* 23:347, October, 1952.

40. Martens, Rainer, and Brian J. Sharkey, "Relationship of Phasic and Static Strength and Endurance," *Research Quarterly,* 37:435-436, October, 1966.

41. Massey, Benjamin, and others, "Effect of Warm-up Exercise Upon Muscular Performance Using Hypnosis to Control the Psychological Variable," *Research Quarterly,* 32:63-71, March, 1961.

42. Mathews, Donald K., and others, "Cross Transfer Effects of Training on Strength and Endurance," *Research Quarterly,* 27:206-212, May, 1956.

43. _____, and Robert Kruse, "Effects of Isometric and Isotonic Exercises on Elbow Flexor Muscle Groups," *Research Quarterly,* 28:26-37, 1957.

44. McCloy, C. H., "A New Method of Scoring Chinning and Dipping," *Research Quarterly,* 2:132-143, December, 1931.

45. _____, and Norma D. Young, *Tests and*

Measurements in Health and Physical Education, 3rd ed., New York: Appleton-Century-Crofts, Inc., 1954, p. 168.

46. McCraw, Lynn V., and Stan Burnham, "Resistive Exercises in the Development of Muscular Strength and Endurance," *Research Quarterly*, 37:81, March, 1966.

47. Meadows, P. E., "The Effect of Isotonic and Isometric Muscle Contraction Training on Speed, Force, and Strength" (Microcarded doctoral dissertation, University of Illinois, 1959).

48. Nelson, Jack K., "An Analysis of the Effects of Applying Various Motivational Situations to College Men Subjected to a Stressful Physical Performance" (Microcarded doctoral dissertation, University of Oregon, 1962).

49. Petersen, Flemming B., "Muscle Training by Static, Concentric, and Eccentric Contraction," *Acta Physiol. Scandinavica*, 48:406-416, 1960.

50. Rich, George Q., III, "Muscular Fatigue Curves of Boys and Girls," *Research Quarterly*, 31:485-498, October, 1960.

51. Sedgwick, A. W., and H. R. Wahalen, "Effect of Passive Warm-up on Muscular Strength and Endurance," *Research Quarterly*, 35:45-59, March, 1964.

52. Sills, Frank D., and Peter W. Everett, "The Relationship of Extreme Somatotypes to Performance in Motor and Strength Test," *Research Quarterly*, 21:223-228, May, 1953.

53. Start, K. B., and Rosemary Holmes, "Local Muscle Endurance with Open and Occluded Intramuscular Circulation," *Journal of Appl. Physiology*, 18:804-807, 1963.

54. _____, and J. S. Graham, "Relationship Between the Relative and Absolute Isometric Endurance of an Isolated Muscle Group," *Research Quarterly*, 35:193-194, May, 1964.

55. _____, and Swegan, Donald B., "The Comparison of Static Contraction with Standard Weight Training in Effect on Certain Movement Speeds and Endurances" (Microcarded doctoral dissertation, Pennsylvania State University, January, 1957, pp. 137-140).

56. Stull, G. A., and D. H. Clarke, "High Resistance, Low Repetition Training as a Determiner of Strength and Fatiguability," *Research Quarterly*, 41:189-193, 1970.

57. Stumiller, Bob, and Barry L. Johnson, "The Relationship of Relative Strength to Relative Endurance" (Unpublished study, Corpus Christi State University, 1976).

58. _____, "Effect of Three Different Leg Positions on Flexed-Arm Hang Performance" (Unpublished study, Corpus Christi State University, 1976).

59. Tuttle, W. W., and others, "Relation of Maximum Back and Leg Strength to Back and Leg Strength Endurance," *Research Quarterly*, 26:96-106, March, 1955.

60. _____, "Relation of Maximum Grip Strength to Grip Strength Endurance," *Journal of Appl. Physiology*, 2:663-670, 1950.

61. Wallace, Joseph, "The Development of Muscular Strength and Muscular Endurance through Isotonic and Isometric Exercise," *New Zealand Journal of Physical Education*, 14:3-9, 1958.

62. Walters, C. Etta, and others, "Effect of Short Bouts of Isometric and Isotonic Contractions on Muscular Strength and Endurance," *Am. J. Physical Med.*, 39:131-141, 1960.

63. Wedemeyer, Ross, "A Differential Analysis of Sit-ups for Strength and Muscular Endurance," *Research Quarterly*, 17:40-47, March, 1946.

64. Wilson, Marjorie, "Study of Arm and Shoulder Girdle Strength of College Women in Selected Tests," *Research Quarterly*, 15:258, October, 1944.

Chapter Nine

The Measurement of Cardiovascular Condition

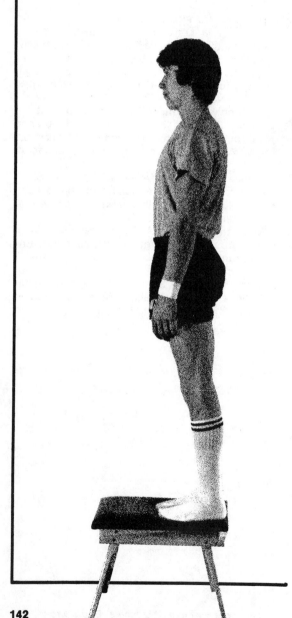

To most people being in *good shape* is exemplified by such feats as climbing several flights of stairs without being red in the face and breathing hard or by the ability to comfortably resume hiking, or cycling, or jogging after a scant few minutes rest. To put it in slightly more technical language, it means the ability of the circulatory and respiratory systems to adjust to and recover from the effects of exercise or work. It is unquestionably one of the key components of physical fitness, and to some physical educators it is the single most indicative measure of a person's physical condition. The most accurate measure of this quality is generally considered to be maximal oxygen uptake, which measures the amount of oxygen consumed per kilogram of body weight per minute of exercise. However, this measurement requires expensive equipment, and the testing is time consuming and rigorous. Therefore, these factors place such a measuring technique out of reach of most schools and colleges.

There have been a number of tests devised to measure cardiovascular function. Some tests simply require the subject to perform a task that calls for sustained total body movement. Usually these tests involve running a prescribed distance, and the subject's cardiovascular endurance is measured by the elapsed time required to cover the distance. This pragmatic approach has been commonly employed in physical fitness test batteries.

Other tests have sought to determine cardiovascular fitness through measures of pulse rate and blood pressure under various conditions involving changes in body position and before and after different degrees of work. Such tests are based on the accepted principle that a physically fit person has more efficient circulatory and respiratory systems than an untrained person. The conditioned individual has a greater stroke volume which enables more blood to be pumped each stroke, thus enabling fewer strokes per minute to do the work. The trained person is also able to achieve fuller oxygen-carbon dioxide exchange, resulting in more available oxygen taken from the air, a slower rate of breathing, and a lower rate of lactic acid formation than is found in the average individual.

Heart rate increases with exercise. The rate of increase is proportional to the work load. The fitness of an individual is reflected by the rate of increase. Generally speaking, the physically fit individual will have a lower heart rate for a specified work load. Or, to view the relationship from another standpoint, at a given heart rate the trained individual will be able to exercise at a higher work load than the untrained person.

Heart rate increases with oxygen consumption, and since the latter is considered to be the most valid measure of cardiorespiratory fitness, this relationship has been utilized in tests to predict oxygen consumption. All in all, heart rate provides a great deal of information about the body's reaction to the stress of exercise, and it is quick and easy to measure. Hence, it can serve as a valuable tool to monitor the strenuousness of an exercise program and provide a valid indicator of an individual's condition in the measurement of cardiovascular fitness.

The systolic pressure of the trained person rises when he stands, and the poorly trained person's systolic pressure does not and, in fact, may even fall. The heart rate, blood pressure, and breathing rate of the person in good physical condition return to the pre-exercise levels more quickly after exercise than do the rates of the individual in poor condition.

Utilization of Cardiovascular Tests

Cardiovascular tests may be given for any of several purposes within the school setting. One purpose, and probably the most common, is as part of a physical fitness test battery in classifying and rating students for assessing status and improvement. In this capacity the test is generally in the form of a distance run or endurance exercise rather than of physiological measurements.

Another purpose may be for screening. A note of caution should be sounded here. Certainly such a test should not be one which requires the subject to exert maximal effort. Furthermore, such a test should not be considered as a substitute for a medical examination.

Cardiovascular tests may be utilized by the physical educator for the purpose of research. This may be in the form of observational research in which measures are taken of status or for establishing norms; or tests may be given before and after a training program in order to measure improvement.

Perhaps one of the most important uses of cardiovascular tests in which pulse rate and blood pressure are measured is as an educational device. The tests may be given in conjunction with a health unit, a biology class, or as a special physical education activity. In any case such tests can be very effective for their motivational properties and for the information that is derived concerning the circulatory and respiratory systems.

While there are quite a number of tests of cardiovascular condition, only a very few will be presented here. The reasons for this are simply that most of the tests are too involved or too time consuming for use in physical education classes or require expensive equipment. The tests presented in this first section can all be administered to students in groups.

Practical Tests of Cardiovascular Fitness

Twelve-Minute (and Nine-Minute) Run-Walk Test

Objective: To measure cardiovascular fitness.
Sex and Age: Satisfactory for both boys and girls of junior high school through college.
Reliability: A test-retest reliability of .94 was reported by Doolittle and Bigbee (19).
Validity: Validity coefficients of .64 to .90 have been obtained when maximum oxygen intake was used as the criterion.
Facilities, Equipment, and Materials. It is suggested that a specific course be measured in distance so that the number of laps completed can be counted and multiplied by the course distance. It is also helpful to divide the course into quarters or eighths by placing markers. This enables the tester to quickly determine the exact distance covered in 12 minutes. A stopwatch, whistle, and distance markers are needed for group testing.
Directions: It is usually most efficient to assign each runner to a spotter. The runners start behind a line and, upon the starting signal, run and/or walk as many laps as possible around the course within the 12 minutes. The spotters maintain a count of each lap, and when the signal to stop is given, they immediately run to the spots at which their runners were at the instant the whistle or command to stop was given.
Scoring: The score in yards is determined by multiplying the number of complete laps times the distance of each lap (e.g., 440 yards), plus the number of segments (quarters, eighths, 10-yard intervals, etc.) of an incomplete lap, plus the number of yards stepped off between a particular segment.

For example, the 12-minute run is given on a 440-yard track sectioned off into eighths. A student completes 5 laps plus 3 one-eighth segments plus 11 yards. The student's score is $5 \times 440 = 2200$; plus 3×55 (each one-eighth segment is 55 yards) = 165; plus 11 yards; i.e., $2200 + 165 + 11 = 2376$ yards covered in 12 minutes.

Additional Pointers: (a) The spotter should be strongly impressed with the necessity of maintaining an accurate count of the number of laps; it is most disconcerting for a runner to exert that amount of effort and then to be given an inaccurate score. (b) For added protection, the runner should also count the number of laps covered. (c) The tester should alert the spotters at least 30 seconds before the end of the 12 minutes. (d) It usually is most efficient to have the spotters remain in the exact spots at which their runners were when the whistle sounded. The tester can then move to each spot and record the scores. (e) The spotter

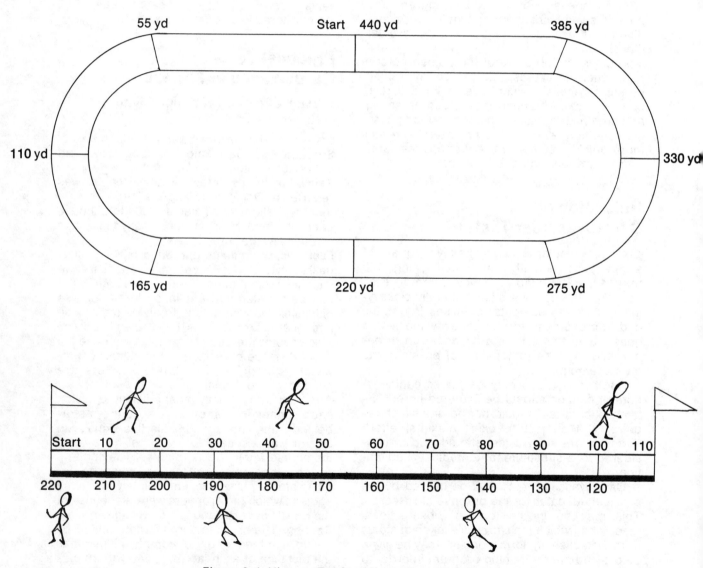

Figure 9-1. Nine- or Twelve-Minute Run-Walk Test
Suggested Test Patterns
(440-yard track marked off in 55-yard intervals or 110-yard straightaway marked off in 10-yard intervals for distance scoring.)

should tell the tester the number of laps, and the tester can then record the number of segments of the incomplete lap and step off the extra yards. This may prove more accurate than relying on the spotters to compute the scores. It is good experience for the spotters to calculate their runners' total yardage, but it is important that the tester be able to check the figures. (f) Although the test can be administered in a variety of settings, such as a 440-yard track, football fields, streets, etc., one should not expect comparable performances on each. It has been demonstrated that the more turns a runner has to make, the more time the runner consumes. While working on the Texas Physi-cal Fitness-Motor Ability Test, Coleman and Jackson (9) recommended two procedures for administering the 9- or 12-minute run: the 440-yard track and the 110-yard straightaway, as shown in Figure 9-1. Coleman and Jackson found no meaningful difference between the two procedures. The norms in *The AAHPER Youth Fitness Test Manual* (Tables 9-1 and 9-2) are from the Texas Physical Fitness-Motor Ability Test. (g) Research has shown that if the 12-minute test is deemed too long for a particular age level or situation, a 9-minute test can be administered in the same way with apparently no significant loss in validity (28). For women, a 6-minute test has also been found to show

Table 9-1
Nine-Minute and Twelve-Minute Run Norms for Girls*

| Percentile | Nine-Minute Run | | | | | | Twelve-Minute Run | | Percentile |
| | 10 Years | | 11 Years | | 12 Years | | 13 Years and Older | | |
	Yards	Meters	Yards	Meters	Yards	Meters	Yards	Meters	
100th	2157	1971	2180	1993	2203	2014	2693	2461	100th
95th	1969	1800	1992	1821	2015	1842	2448	2237	95th
90th	1867	1706	1890	1727	1913	1748	2318	2119	90th
85th	1801	1646	1824	1667	1847	1688	2232	2040	85th
80th	1746	1596	1769	1617	1792	1638	2161	1975	80th
75th	1702	1556	1725	1577	1748	1598	2100	1919	75th
70th	1658	1515	1681	1536	1704	1557	2050	1874	70th
65th	1622	1483	1645	1504	1668	1525	2000	1828	65th
60th	1583	1447	1606	1468	1629	1489	1950	1782	60th
55th	1550	1417	1573	1438	1596	1459	1908	1744	55th
50th	1514	1384	1537	1405	1560	1426	1861	1701	50th
45th	1478	1351	1501	1372	1524	1393	1815	1659	45th
40th	1445	1321	1468	1342	1491	1363	1772	1620	40th
35th	1406	1285	1429	1306	1452	1327	1722	1574	35th
30th	1370	1252	1393	1273	1416	1294	1672	1528	30th
25th	1326	1212	1349	1233	1372	1254	1622	1483	25th
20th	1282	1172	1305	1193	1328	1214	1561	1427	20th
15th	1227	1121	1250	1143	1273	1164	1490	1362	15th
10th	1161	1061	1184	1082	1207	1103	1404	1283	10th
5th	1059	968	1082	989	1105	1010	1274	1164	5th
0	871	796	894	817	917	838	1030	941	0

*Percentile scores taken from AAHPER, *Youth Fitness Test Manual,* Washington, D.C., 1976. Norms were gathered from the Texas Physical Fitness-Motor Ability Test. (Distances in meters are not included in reference.)

comparable validity (16) to the 12-minute test. (h) In administering the 9- or 12-minute tests on the 440-yard track or 110-yard straightaway, it has been recommended that markers be made with the appropriate distances on front and back. For example, on the 110-yard course, the first sign would have "start" on one side and "220" on the other; the second would have "10" on one side and "210" on the other, and so on, until the entire 110 yards have been marked off.

Six-Hundred-Yard Run-Walk Test

Objective: To measure cardiovascular efficiency.

Sex and Age: Satisfactory for both boys and girls of ages six through twelve.

Reliability: A coefficient of .92 was obtained for both boys and girls at the junior high school level (55).

Objectivity: None reported, although obviously an objective measure.

Validity: Validity coefficients of .96, .88, and .76 were found by Biasiotto and Cotten (5) for third, fifth, and seventh grade boys, respectively.

Equipment: A stopwatch and a track, football field, or similar open area are needed to accommodate this test. The *AAHPER Youth Fitness Test Manual* shows diagrams of three suggested areas: (a) A football field on which

Table 9-2
Nine-Minute and Twelve-Minute Run Norms for Boys*

| Percentile | Nine-Minute Run | | | | | | Twelve-Minute Run | | Percentile |
| | 10 Years | | 11 Years | | 12 Years | | 13 Years and Older | | |
	Yards	Meters	Yards	Meters	Yards	Meters	Yards	Meters	
100th	2532	2314	2535	2317	2578	2356	3590	3281	100th
95th	2294	2097	2356	2153	2418	2210	3297	3013	95th
90th	2166	1980	2228	2036	2290	2093	3140	2870	90th
85th	2081	1902	2143	1959	2205	2015	3037	2776	85th
80th	2011	1838	2073	1895	2135	1951	2952	2698	80th
75th	1952	1784	2014	1841	2076	1897	2879	2631	75th
70th	1902	1738	1964	1795	2026	1852	2819	2577	70th
65th	1853	1694	1915	1750	1977	1807	2759	2522	65th
60th	1804	1649	1866	1706	1928	1762	2699	2467	60th
55th	1762	1610	1824	1667	1886	1724	2648	2420	55th
50th	1717	1569	1779	1626	1841	1683	2592	2369	50th
45th	1672	1528	1734	1585	1796	1642	2536	2318	45th
40th	1630	1490	1692	1546	1754	1603	2485	2271	40th
35th	1581	1445	1643	1502	1705	1558	2425	2216	35th
30th	1532	1400	1594	1457	1656	1514	2365	2162	30th
25th	1482	1355	1544	1411	1606	1468	2305	2107	25th
20th	1423	1301	1485	1357	1547	1414	2232	2040	20th
15th	1353	1237	1415	1293	1477	1350	2147	1962	15th
10th	1268	1159	1330	1216	1392	1272	2044	1868	10th
5th	1140	1042	1202	1099	1264	1155	1888	1726	5th
0	901	824	924	845	927	847	1594	1457	0

*Percentile scores taken from AAHPER, *Youth Fitness Test Manual,* Washington, D.C., 1976. Norms were gathered from the Texas Physical Fitness-Motor Ability Test. (Distances in meters are not included in reference.)

four flags are placed at the end line of the end zone 30 yards apart. These markers make a rectangular course 120 x 30 yards, and twice around equals 600. (b) Any open area in the form of a square measuring 50 yards on each side can be used. Three times around measures 600 yards. (c) The inside circumference of a 440-yard track can be used. In this case the tester might start the runners, then walk 160 yards down the track to the finish line.

Directions: It is possible to have as many as a dozen runners at a time in this event. Each runner is assigned a spotter. The subject uses a standing start. The tester gives the commands, "Ready? Go!" The subject is told that he may walk whenever he feels it is necessary. Each spotter positions himself at the finish line where he can hear the timer, who begins counting aloud the times every second as the runners cross the finish line. The spotter watches his partner and remembers his announced time. The spotters must be impressed with the importance of paying close attention and not talking to anyone until they give their partners' time to the recorder.

Scoring: The time in minutes and seconds is recorded as the score. (See Table 9-3.)

Additional Pointers: (a) The same partners should not score each other. (b) Some practice in spotting should be given. (c) The timer must

Table 9-3
Six-Hundred-Yard Run-Walk Scores in Minutes and Seconds
for Boys and Girls Ages Ten, Eleven, and Twelve*

Percentile	Boys			Girls			Percentile
	10	11	12	10	11	12	
100th	1'30''	1'27''	1'31''	1'42''	1'40''	1'39''	100th
95th	1'58''	1'59''	1'52''	2' 5''	2'13''	2'14''	95th
90th	2' 9''	2' 3''	2' 0''	2'15''	2'19''	2'20''	90th
85th	2'12''	2' 8''	2' 2''	2'20''	2'24''	2'24''	85th
80th	2'15''	2'11''	2' 5''	2'26''	2'28''	2'27''	80th
75th	2'18''	2'14''	2' 9''	2'30''	2'32''	2'31''	75th
70th	2'20''	2'16''	2'11''	2'34''	2'36''	2'35''	70th
65th	2'23''	2'19''	2'13''	2'37''	2'39''	2'39''	65th
60th	2'26''	2'21''	2'15''	2'41''	2'43''	2'42''	60th
55th	2'30''	2'24''	2'18''	2'45''	2'47''	2'45''	55th
50th	2'33''	2'27''	2'21''	2'48''	2'49''	2'49''	50th
45th	2'36''	2'30''	2'24''	2'50''	2'53''	2'55''	45th
40th	2'40''	2'33''	2'26''	2'55''	2'59''	2'58''	40th
35th	2'43''	2'36''	2'30''	2'59''	3' 4''	3' 3''	35th
30th	2'45''	2'39''	2'34''	3' 3''	3'10''	3' 7''	30th
25th	2'49''	2'42''	2'39''	3' 8''	3'15''	3'11''	25th
20th	2'55''	2'48''	2'47''	3'13''	3'22''	3'18''	20th
15th	3' 1''	2'55''	2'57''	3'18''	3'30''	3'24''	15th
10th	3' 8''	3' 9''	3' 8''	3'27''	3'41''	3'40''	10th
5th	3'23''	3'30''	3'32''	3'45''	3'59''	4' 0''	5th
0	4'58''	5' 6''	4'55''	4'47''	4'53''	5'10''	0

*Percentile scores taken from AAHPER, *Youth Fitness Test Manual,* Washington, D.C.: AAHPER, 1965.

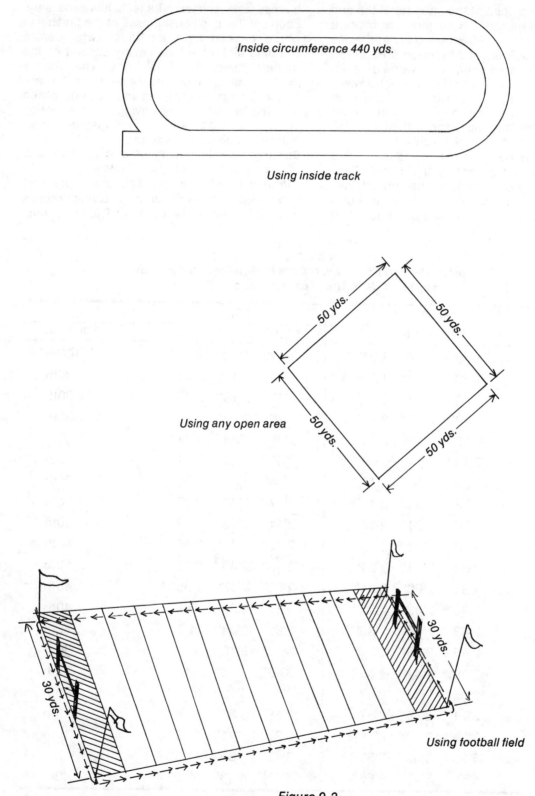

Inside circumference 440 yds.

Using inside track

50 yds.
50 yds.
50 yds.
50 yds.

Using any open area

30 yds.
30 yds.

Using football field

Figure 9-2.
Suggested Areas for Administering AAHPER 600-Yard Run-Walk.

guard against the tendency to stop the watch as soon as the first runner finishes. (d) Each runner should be instructed to listen for his own time as a safeguard against the possibility of a spotter forgetting the time.

One-Mile and Mile-and-One-Half Distance Runs

Objective: To measure cardiovascular fitness.
Sex and Age: Satisfactory for both boys and girls ages ten to adult. In the AAHPER Youth Fitness Test, the 1-mile distance is advised for boys and girls, ages 10 to 12, and the 1.5 dis-tance for both sexes 13 years and older.
Validity: The validity of distance runs of 1 mile and over has been demonstrated in several studies, such as by Disch, Frankiewicz, and Jackson (18).
Equipment: A stopwatch and a track or some type of open area of known dimensions.
Directions: The same directions for the 600-yard run-walk test are appropriate for the 1-mile and 1.5-mile runs.
Scoring: The time in minutes and seconds is recorded (see Tables 9-4 and 9-5).
Additional Pointers: Same as for 600-yard run-walk test.

Table 9-4
One-Mile and Mile-and-One-Half Distance Run Scores for Girls*

Percentile	One-Mile Run 10	11	12	One-and-One-Half-Mile Run 13 and Older	Percentile
100th	6:13	5:42	5:08	10:20	100th
95th	7:28	6:57	6:23	12:17	95th
90th	8:09	7:38	7:04	13:19	90th
85th	8:33	8:02	7:28	14:00	85th
80th	8:57	8:26	7:52	14:34	80th
75th	9:16	8:45	8:11	15:03	75th
70th	9:31	9:00	8:26	15:26	70th
65th	9:51	9:20	8:46	15:50	65th
60th	10:02	9:31	8:57	16:14	60th
55th	10:15	9:44	9:10	16:34	55th
50th	10:29	9:58	9:24	16:57	50th
45th	10:43	10:12	9:38	17:19	45th
40th	10:56	10:25	9:51	17:39	40th
35th	11:07	10:36	10:12	18:03	35th
30th	11:27	10:56	10:22	18:27	30th
25th	11:42	11:11	10:37	18:50	25th
20th	12:01	11:30	10:56	19:19	20th
15th	12:25	11:54	11:30	19:53	15th
10th	12:49	12:18	11:44	20:34	10th
5th	13:30	12:59	12:24	21:36	5th
0	14:45	14:14	13:40	23:33	0

*Percentile scores taken from AAHPER, *Youth Fitness Test Manual,* Washington, D.C., 1976. (Norms were gathered from the Texas Physical Fitness-Motor Ability Test.)

Table 9-5
One-Mile and Mile-and-One-Half Distance Run Scores for Boys*

| Percentile | One-Mile Run | | | One-and-One-Half-Mile Run | Percentile |
	10	11	12	13 and Older	
100th	5:07	4:44	4:21	7:26	100th
95th	5:55	5:32	5:09	8:37	95th
90th	6:38	6:15	5:52	9:15	90th
85th	7:06	6:43	6:20	9:40	85th
80th	7:29	7:03	6:40	10:01	80th
75th	7:49	7:26	7:03	10:19	75th
70th	8:05	7:42	7:19	10:34	70th
65th	8:22	7:59	7:36	10:48	65th
60th	8:38	8:15	7:52	11:02	60th
55th	8:52	8:29	8:06	11:15	55th
50th	9:07	8:44	8:21	11:29	50th
45th	9:22	8:59	8:36	11:42	45th
40th	9:32	9:13	8:50	11:55	40th
35th	9:52	9:29	9:06	12:10	35th
30th	10:09	9:46	9:23	12:24	30th
25th	10:25	10:02	9:39	12:39	25th
20th	10:35	10:22	9:59	12:56	20th
15th	11:08	10:45	10:22	13:17	15th
10th	11:36	11:13	10:50	13:42	10th
5th	12:19	11:56	11:33	14:20	5th
0	14:07	13:44	13:21	15:32	0

*Percentile scores taken from AAHPER, *Youth Fitness Test Manual,* Washington, D.C., 1976. (Norms were gathered from the Texas Physical Fitness-Motor Ability Test.)

Modified OSU Step Test

The Ohio State University Step Test (32) was developed as a submaximal cardiovascular fitness test that was designed to overcome adverse criticisms of the fatigue, muscle soreness, expensive equipment, etc., associated with the methods currently used for assessing cardiovascular fitness such as maximum oxygen consumption, the Balke Treadmill Test, and the Harvard Step Test. The rationale for this test is that the exercise time required to reach a pulse rate of 150 beats per minute is a valid indicator of the subject's capacity for more strenuous work. It employs a split-level bench with an adjustable hand bar. One level of the bench is 15 inches high; the other is 20 inches.

Cotten (12) reported a modification of the Ohio State University Step Test which he felt would be applicable for high school physical education classes. He sought to develop a test that would be suitable for mass testing, be economical in terms of time, require little special equipment, and also require a minimum of student motivation (which is necessary in cardiovascular measures that require strenuous effort to complete the test).

Sex and Age Level: Males grades nine to twelve and adult.

Validity and Reliability: The modified test correlated .84 with the Balke Treadmill Test. Test-retest reliability was .95 with college males as subjects, .75 with high school subjects. However, it was noted that some counting errors may have been responsible for the lower reliability coefficient with the high school students.

Test Equipment and Materials Needed: The test is designed to be given on bleacher steps, which are usually 17 inches high. However, Cotten felt that the test would still be valid for bleacher heights that vary an inch or two from this height. A tape recorder, stopwatch, metronome, and score sheets are the only other recommended equipment and materials.

Directions: The commands and cadences for the eighteen innings should be prerecorded to ensure accuracy. The class is divided into pairs, with the exercising subjects instructed to sit on the bottom bleacher step and the partners behind them on the second row.

The work loads for the three phases of the test are:

Phase I: Six innings—24 steps/minute
Phase II: Six innings—30 steps/minute
Phase III: Six innings—36 steps/minute

At the command to begin, the subject steps up and down for 30 seconds in cadence with the metronome. At the command "stop," he immediately sits down and finds his pulse. After exactly 5 seconds of sitting, the command "count" is given, and after 15 seconds of the rest period, the commands "stop" and "prepare to exercise" are given. The subject records the number of beats counted in the 10-second period. After 5 more seconds, the subject is commanded to start stepping again for another 30-second exercise bout. This procedure is continued for six innings in Phase I or until a pulse count of 25 (which would correspond to a heart rate of 150 beats per minute) is reached. *Each inning consists of 30 seconds of stepping and a 20-second rest period, during which a 10-second pulse count is taken from the fifth to fifteenth seconds.*

Prior to the seventh inning, the subject is informed that the cadence will be increased and to continue the same procedure. Subsequently, prior to the thirteenth inning, the subject is told that the cadence will be increased to 36 steps per minute. The three phases are con-

tinuous. The stepping is performed as a four-count exercise of "up," "up," "down," "down" in which the subject places one, then both, feet onto the platform, straightening his legs and back, and immediately steps down again, one foot at a time. It is normally easier to lead off with the same foot each time; however, alternating feet is permitted if one leg gets tired. No crouching is allowed.

Scoring: The score is the inning in which his pulse count is 25 for the 10-second period (150 beats per minute). If the subject completes the 18 innings, he is given a score of 19.

Additional Pointers: (a) Half of the class can be tested simultaneously using the buddy system. (b) No vigorous exercise should precede the test. (c) A 15-minute rest period should be allowed prior to the test. During this time, instructions should be given and a complete inning demonstrated. (d) Also during this time, the partners should practice finding and counting the pulse rate at the carotid artery. (e) Having the non-exercising partners sitting on the row above the exercising subjects makes it convenient for them to immediately find the pulse at the carotid artery when their partners sit down each time after exercising. (f) Local norms should be established, particularly if the bleacher heights are not 17 inches. (g) To facilitate the cadence, the number of steps should be multiplied by four so that the metronome is set at 96 for 24 steps per minute, 120 for the 30 steps per minute, and 144 for the 36 steps per minute cadence. Thus, each click of the metronome signifies a foot placement.

Queens College Step Test (37)

Objective: To provide a practical, convenient means for assessing cardiorespiratory fitness.

Sex and Age: College women.

Reliability: A reliability coefficient of .92 was reported.

Validity: Using maximal oxygen consumption as the criterion, a correlation of $-.75$ was obtained between the first heart rate recovery score (5-20 seconds after exercise) and max VO_2 expressed in ml/kg/min.

Test Equipment and Materials: Bleachers serve as the stepping bench (16-17 inches). A metronome is used for the cadence. Amplification of the sound of the metronome via loudspeakers is desirable. A stopwatch is used to time the duration of stepping and the pulse-counting interval.

Directions: Half of the class may be tested at one time with the other half serving as partners

Table 9-6
Percentile Norms for Queens College Test (300 College Women)*

Percentile	Pulse Rate (bpm)	Percentile	Pulse Rate (bpm)
100th	128	45th	168
95th	140	40th	170
90th	148	35th	171
85th	152	30th	172
80th	156	25th	176
75th	158	20th	180
70th	160	15th	182
65th	162	10th	184
60th	163	5th	196
55th	164	0	216
50th	166		

*William D. McArdle and others, "Percentile Norms for a Valid Step Test in College Women," *Research Quarterly,* 44:498, December, 1973. Used with permission.

Table 9-7
Percentile Norms for Queens College Test (100 Women Physical Education Majors)*

Percentile	Pulse Rate (bpm)	Percentile	Pulse Rate (bpm)
100th	110	45th	149
95th	119	40th	152
90th	126	35th	154
85th	131	30th	156
80th	134	25th	160
75th	137	20th	163
70th	139	15th	166
65th	141	10th	170
60th	144	5th	177
55th	146	0	188
50th	148		

*Women physical education majors, Louisiana State University, Baton Rouge, La.

to count pulse. Following the explanation of the test and pulse-counting procedures, the counters are allowed several practices in counting their partners' pulse rates for 15-second intervals. The cadence of 22 steps per minute is established by setting the metronome at 88 bpm. A demonstration is given and then the subjects practice at the required cadence for 15 seconds.

The test consists of stepping up and down on the bleacher step for 3 minutes. At the end of the time period, the subjects remain standing while the partners count pulse rate for a 15-second interval beginning 5 seconds after the cessation of exercise. The counters and steppers then exchange places and the other half of the class is tested.

Scoring: The 15-second pulse count is multiplied by 4 to express the score in beats per minute. McArdle and others (36) established norms for 300 women at Queens College (see Table 9-6). Physical education majors were tested and norms constructed at Louisiana State University (see Table 9-7).

Additional Pointers: (a) With practice, subjects can be trained to take their own pulse rates. (b) It should be stressed that the subjects refrain from talking after exercise until the pulse counting is completed. (c) The tester may elect to call out the cadence "up, up, down, down" rather than amplify the metronome, or the entire test procedures and instructions may be recorded on tape.

LSU Step Test (43)

Objective: To measure heart rate response to submaximal exercise and to provide students with a graphic illustration of heart rate adjustments to exercise and recovery.

Sex and Age: Males and females grades 9 to 12 and adults.

Validity and Reliability: Construct validity has been demonstrated through experimental research. The constructs were that resting heart rate, heart rate immediately after exercise, and heart rate during recovery are indicators of cardiorespiratory fitness and may be modified through conditioning. The sensitivity of the test in detecting changes resulting from a conditioning program was evidenced in a study involving university scuba classes in which the subjects trained by swimming a conditioning circuit (44). Significant reductions in heart rate were found for each of the five pulse counts following a six-week conditioning period. A leveling-off effect was also noted between the end of the circuit training and the end of a seven-week period of less strenuous activity.

Test-retest reliability coefficients for the five pulse counts have been reported as follows: before exercise (.86), 5 seconds after exercise (.88), 1 minute after exercise (.85), 2 minutes after exercise (.87) and 3 minutes after exercise (.80).

Test Equipment and Materials Needed: Benches, chairs, or bleachers may be used for the stepping exercise. The height may vary but most chairs and bleachers are approximately 17 or 18 inches. A stopwatch is needed. A metronome is helpful in establishing cadence.

Directions: It is recommended that half of a class or group of subjects be tested at a time so the other half can serve as counters. Subjects should pair up, and practice should be allowed for finding and counting pulse. When bleachers or chairs are used, it is advisable that the counters sit or stand behind the steppers and that they use the carotid artery for the pulse counting. The steppers are also encouraged to count their own pulses using the radial artery.

After the subjects have practiced finding and counting pulse rate for several minutes, the *before exercise* pulse rate is taken. This should be done by taking at least three consecutive 10-second counts until the pulse rate has stabilized and the tester is satisfied that the counters are competent in the pulse-counting procedures.

The steppers then stand in front of the bench and, on the command, begin stepping at the cadence of 24 steps per minute for females and 30 steps per minute for males. The cadence should be established with a metronome by multiplying the desired steps per minute by 4 (i.e., set at 96 for 24 steps per minute and 120 for 30 steps per minute). In this way each step of "up, up, down, down" is synchronized with a click of the metronome. After the 2 minutes of stepping, the commands *"stop, sit down, find your pulse"* are given, and after 5 seconds has elapsed, a 10-second pulse count is taken.

Three recovery pulse counts are then taken (each for 10 seconds) at 1 minute, 2 minutes, and 3 minutes after exercise.

Following the third recovery pulse count, the steppers and counters change places and the test is given again to the new steppers.

Directions to Be Read to Subjects: (You may wish to modify the language in keeping with the level of your subjects).

Today we are going to take a test that is designed to reflect your cardiorespiratory fitness. This refers to your body's ability to adjust to exercise and then recover. You know that when you exercise, such as when you run, play sports, or dance vigorously, your heart beats faster and then it gradually slows down afterward. If you are in good shape—have good cardiorespiratory fitness—you can exercise longer and harder than someone who is not in as good shape, and you also can recover faster.

We will count our pulse rate before exercise, then step up and down on a bench for 2 (or 3) minutes and then count our pulse immediately afterward, then again at 1, 2, and 3 minutes after exercise to see how quickly the pulse rate returns to normal. Talking, laughing, and moving about will cause the heart rate to fluctuate. Therefore, it is very important that you sit down right away after exercise and remain quiet for the 3 minutes during which the pulse counts are taken.

When counting pulse rate, if you feel a beat at the same instant that you are told to begin counting, count that beat as zero.

Later you will plot your pulse rates on a graph so you can see how your heart adjusts to exercise and recovers.

Scoring: The five 10-second pulse counts are recorded on the score sheet. The 10-second counts are then multiplied by 6 in order to express the scores in beats per minute. The beats-per-minute scores are then plotted on each student's graph to provide a picture of the pulse rate adjustments to exercise (see Figure 9-3).

Conditioning effects can be dramatically demonstrated by plotting subsequent test results on the same graph following a conditioning program.

Additional Pointers: (a) As with most step tests, it is advisable to record the entire test on tape. This frees the tester to concentrate on supervisory functions rather than being enslaved by the stopwatch. (b) A 3-minute test can be given if a longer test is deemed more appropriate. However, the correlations between the 2-minute version and 3-minute version have been found to be quite high and no significant differences have been evidenced between the two versions on the construct validity parameters. (c) It is recommended for best results to allow one day for practice and familiarity with procedures and then to test in the next session. (d) The test and analysis of the plotting of scores on the graphs usually stimulates a number of questions. It thus provides a "teachable moment" for discussion of basic exercise physiology. (e) Stress upon the subjects the critical importance of being able to find the pulse rate quickly, especially immediately after the exercise. Also, stress the importance of keeping quiet and not talking, laughing, or getting up from their seats after the exercise. Explain that this will greatly affect the pulse rate and result in their having to take the test again.

Harvard Step Test (6)

Objective: The Harvard Step Test was developed by Brouha for the purpose of measur-

Table 9-8
Average Heart Rates for LSU Step Test of College Women and Men before and after Conditioning*

	Before Exercise	5 Sec. after Exercise	1 Min. after Exercise	2 Min. after Exercise	3 Min. after Exercise
Women (N=70)					
HR before Conditioning	93	175	128	110	103
HR after Conditioning	83	166	113	96	90
Men (N=83)					
HR before Conditioning	85	165	120	108	99
HR after Conditioning	73	152	107	92	86

*Scores gathered at Louisiana State University, Baton Rouge, La.

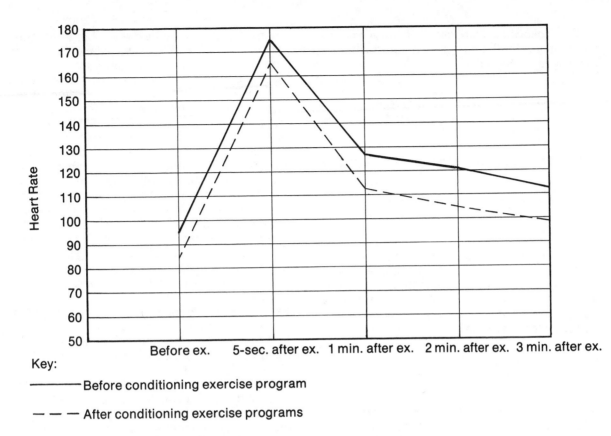

Figure 9-3. Graph for LSU Step Test
Graph depicts improvement in cardiorespiratory fitness as reflected by the LSU Step Test for 70 college women in a 15-week conditioning exercise program (see Table 9-8).

ing physical fitness for muscular work and the ability to recover from work.

Sex and Age Level: The test was originally designed for young men of college age.

Validity: Brouha tested 2200 male students at Harvard in the original validation of the step test. Athletes were found to score considerably higher than non-athletes, and their scores improved with training and decreased after training. Taddonio and Karpovich (53) also found supporting evidence as to its validity.

Test Equipment and Materials Needed: A stable bench or platform 20 inches high and a watch with a second hand are the only equipment needed. A large wall clock with a second hand may be used effectively for group testing.

Directions: The cadence is 30 steps per minute. The body should be erect when the subject steps onto the bench. The subject continues to exercise at the prescribed cadence for 5 minutes, unless he feels that he must stop before

then because of exhaustion. As soon as he stops exercising, he sits down and remains seated and quiet throughout the pulse counts.

There are two forms of the test, the long form and the short form. In the long form the pulse is counted 1 to 1½, 2 to 2½, and 3 to 3½ minutes after exercise. In the short form the pulse is taken only once, 1 to 1½ minutes after exercise.

Scoring: For the long form a Physical Efficiency Index (PEI) is computed with this formula:

$$PEI = \frac{\text{Duration of exercise in seconds} \times 100}{2 \times \text{sum of pulse counts in recovery}}$$

Example: A subject exercises for the full 5 minutes (300 seconds). His pulse counts are 83 for 1 to 1½ minutes; 67 for 2 to 2½ minutes; and 50 for 3 to 3½ minutes after exercise. His PEI score is:

$$PEI = \frac{300 \times 100}{2 \times 200} = \frac{30,000}{400} = 75$$

The Measurement of Cardiovascular Condition   **155**

The following standards of performance were established after testing approximately 8000 college students:

Below 55 ....Poor
55 to 64 ....Low Average
65 to 79 ....High Average
80 to 89 ....Good
Above 90 ....Excellent

For the short form the scoring formula is as follows:

$$PEI = \frac{\text{Duration of exercise in seconds} \times 100}{5.5 \times \text{pulse count for 1 to 1½ minutes after exercise}}$$

A table (Table 9-9) for scoring the short form of the Harvard Step Test has been developed. The score in arbitrary units is based on duration of exercise and the rate of the recovery pulse. The following norms have been established for interpretation:

Below 50 ....Poor
50-80 ....Average
Above 80 ....Good

Additional Pointers: (a) The short form correlates very highly with the long form and in the interest of time may be preferable to the long form. (b) During the exercise, the tester can help the subjects to maintain the cadence by calling out "up, up, down, down." Even more effective is to make a tape recording of the cadence. This allows the tester to supervise all aspects of the testing more closely. (c) When a subject is forced to stop prior to the end of the 5 minutes, it is imperative that his duration of exercise be recorded and that the timing for the pulse taking after exercise be started. A large wall clock with a second hand is very valuable in these cases. It is a simple matter for the counters to record the time at the start of the exercise, to record the time at which the subject is forced to stop, to begin taking the pulse a minute afterwards for 30 seconds, and so on. Trained assistants may also serve in this capacity.

Safety Precautions: (a) The principal safety factor is inherent in the test itself — which is that the test is rather strenuous and might be dangerous for someone in poor health. This underlines the importance of medical examinations for all students and cautions against giving the step test to persons known to have some abnormalities. (b) About the only other safety precaution involves the possibility

Table 9-9
Scoring for the Harvard Step Test*

Duration of Effort (minutes)	Total Heartbeats 1½ Minutes in Recovery											
	40-44	45-49	50-54	55-59	60-64	65-69	70-74	75-79	80-84	85-89	90-94	95-99
	Score (Arbitrary Units)											
0 — ½	6	6	5	5	4	4	4	4	3	3	3	3
½—1	19	17	16	14	13	12	11	11	10	9	9	8
1 —1½	32	29	26	24	22	20	19	18	17	16	15	14
1½—2	45	41	38	34	31	29	27	25	23	22	21	20
2 —2½	58	52	47	43	40	36	34	32	30	28	27	25
2½—3	71	64	58	53	48	45	42	39	37	34	33	31
3 —3½	84	75	68	62	57	53	49	46	43	41	39	37
3½—4	97	87	79	72	66	61	57	53	50	47	45	42
4 —4½	110	98	89	82	75	70	65	61	57	54	51	48
4½—5	123	110	100	91	84	77	72	68	63	60	57	54
5	129	116	105	96	88	82	76	71	67	63	60	56

*From C.F. Conzolazio, R.E. Johnson, and L.J. Pecora, *Physiological Measurements of Metabolic Function in Man,* New York: McGraw-Hill Book Company, 1963. Used by permission of McGraw-Hill Book Company.

Figure 9-4. Proper Form for All Step Tests

of the subject missing his footing and hitting his knee against the bench. Padding of some kind is recommended. Sometimes a mat folded over a bench or bleacher will provide for the exact 20-inch height as well as serve as protective padding.

Cardiovascular Efficiency Test for Girls and Women (26, 50, 51)

Skubic and Hodgkins conducted extensive research with junior and senior high school girls and college women throughout the United States. National norms for cardiovascular efficiency were established.

Sex and Age Level: The test is designed for junior high school girls, senior high school girls, and college women.

Validity and Reliability: The norms were prepared from 686 junior high school girls and 1332 senior high school girls from fifty-five secondary schools, and from 2360 college women from sixty-six colleges. The test successfully differentiated among the sedentary, active, and well-trained subjects. A reliability coefficient of .82 was reported using the test-retest method (50).

Test Equipment and Materials: An 18-inch bench and a stopwatch or wall clock with second hand are all the equipment needed for this test.

Directions: The same basic directions are followed as were described in the Harvard Step Test. The differences are that the cadence is 24 steps per minute instead of 30; the bench is 18 inches instead of 20; and the maximum duration of exercise is 3 minutes instead of 5. Only one pulse count is taken. The pulse rate is felt at the carotid artery and is counted from 1 to 1½ minutes after exercise. The same procedures apply for a subject who stops before the end of the 3 minutes, as in the Harvard Test: the time is noted and the pulse is counted for 30 seconds, starting 1 minute after cessation of stepping.

Scoring: The following formula is employed in computing the subject's cardiovascular efficiency score:

$$\frac{\text{Number of seconds completed} \times 100}{\text{Recovery pulse} \times 5.6}$$

Example: A junior high school girl exercises for the full 3 minutes (180 seconds). Her recovery pulse count measured from 1 to 1½ minutes after exercise is 55. Her cardiovascular efficiency score is:

$$\frac{180 \times 100}{5.6 \times 55} = \frac{18,000}{308} = 58.4 \text{ (round off to 58)}$$

Norms for junior high school girls, senior high school girls, and college women are presented in Table 9-10.

Additional Pointers: Essentially the same as for the Harvard Step Test.

Safety Precautions: Essentially the same as for the Harvard Step Test.

Some Pointers on Pulse Counting

The pulse for step tests is usually taken at the radial or the carotid artery. In both cases two or three fingers should be used to feel the pulse, rather than one's thumb, due to the possible confusion arising from feeling one's own pulse rate transmitted through the thumb. The carotid artery is located immediately below the angle of the jaw. The radial pulse is found in the hollow on the thumb side of the wrist about an inch from the base of the thumb.

It is important that the counter not press too hard on the carotid artery so that a reaction to pressure does not produce an alteration in the beat. In counting pulse it is recommended that the beat felt at the same time as the signal to start counting is given should be designated as "zero." It should be pointed out that a mistake of one pulse count represents a 6-beat error in a 10-second pulse count, 4 beats in a 15-second count, etc.

The person whose pulse is being counted must remain silent and refrain from laughing or talking since this affects pulse rate. If two people are counting the same person's pulse, some criterion needs to be established in cases where the two counters disagree. A maximum

Table 9-10
Norms for Cardiovascular Efficiency Test
for Girls and Women (26, 49)

Rating	Junior H.S. Age Girls		Senior H.S. Age Girls		College Age Girls	
	Cardio-vascular Efficiency Score	30-Sec. Recovery Pulse	Cardio-vascular Efficiency Score	30-Sec. Recovery Pulse	Cardio-vascular Efficiency Score	30-Sec. Recovery Pulse
Excellent	72-100	44 or less	71-100	45 or less	71-100	43 or less
Very Good	62- 71	45-52	60- 70	46-54	60- 70	46-54
Good	51- 61	53-63	49- 59	55-66	49- 59	55-66
Fair	41- 50	64-79	40- 48	67-80	39- 48	67-83
Poor	31- 40	80-92	31- 39	81-96	28- 38	84-116
Very Poor	0- 30	93 and over	0- 30	96 and above	0- 27	117-120

allowable difference might be set (depending on the length of the counting interval). If the difference is more than that set, the subject must be retested. A practical exception would be when one of the counters admits that he or she simply lost count.

Obviously, the keys to accurate testing and pulse counting are orientation to the test and the counting procedures and practice.

Resting Heart Rate

Resting heart rate is difficult to determine. By that we mean that there are many factors which can influence heart rate at any given time. Such factors include temperature, humidity, previous activity, emotions, time since eating, smoking, fatigue, and infection. Resting heart rate is more variable than exercise and recovery heart rates. Therefore, one must use some caution in evaluating pulse counts.

As mentioned previously, it has been observed that resting heart rate is indicative of physical fitness from the standpoint that resting heart rate is usually lowered as a result of conditioning; for example, distance runners tend to have low resting heart rates. Apparently, however, some individuals inherit relatively high or low heart rates that seem to resist changes.

With due recognition of the limitations of resting pulse counts, the following sitting pulse rate test is presented:

A stopwatch or wristwatch with a second-hand is the only equipment needed. The students rest in a sitting position for several minutes while the tester explains pulse-counting procedures. The students are allowed several minutes to practice counting their own and others' pulse rates.

The students are divided into pairs of the same sex. On signal, they count each other's pulse for 1 minute.

A reliability coefficient of .83 was found for college men and women. An objectivity coefficient of .94 was obtained when testers measured the same subjects and recorded the scores independently. Table 9-11 presents some norms for college men and women.

Blood Pressure Measurement

The measurement of systolic and diastolic blood pressure is relatively simple: however, like most testing, it requires considerable practice to become proficient. The cuff of the sphygmomanometer is wrapped around the bare arm above the elbow. With the earphones of the stethoscope in the tester's ears, the bell of the stethoscope is placed on the brachial artery just above the hollow of the elbow. The cuff is pumped up until the artery has been collapsed, i.e., no pulse beat can be heard. Pressure is then slowly released as the tester watches the gauge or mercury column. When the first sound of the pulse is heard, the reading in millimeters of mercury at that instant is recorded as *systolic* pressure. The tester continues to slowly release pressure until a very dull, weak beat is noted. At that instant the pressure in millimeters of mercury is noted, which represents the *diastolic* pressure. The measures are recorded with the systolic pres-

Table 9-11
Resting Heart Rate In Beats per Minute

Men	Performance Level	Women
53 - Lower	Very Low	56 - Lower
60 - 54	Low	64 - 57
65 - 61	Moderate	71 - 65
75 - 66	High	79 - 72
Above - 76	Very High	Above - 80

*Based on the scores of 200 college men and 200 college women, Corpus Christi State University, Corpus Christi, Tx., 1976.

Table 9-12
Systolic-Diastolic Blood Pressure Scale*

Systolic	Level	Diastolic
112 - Lower	Very Low	77 - Lower
120 - 113	Low	80 - 78
129 - 121	Moderate	86 - 81
140 - 130	High	96 - 87
Above - 141	Very High	Above - 97

*Based on accumulated records.

sure first, then the diastolic pressure. A typical reading might be 120/80 or 125/75.

Table 9-12 presents some norms for systolic and diastolic pressures, based upon a physician's records. It is recommended that the pressures be taken after the subject has been sitting quietly for about 30 minutes and that the median of three trials be taken as the score.

Problems Associated with Cardiovascular Fitness Testing

There are so many variables which can affect the pulse rate and blood pressure that it is very difficult to obtain an *average* or *typical* measurement on any given day. Emotions, for example, have a very noticeable effect on cardiorespiratory functions. Physicians often allow for this when they are taking patients' pulse rate and blood pressure during medical examinations.

Besides nervousness, tension, and other emotional manifestations, it has been found that temperature, time of day, exercise, changes in body position, altitude, humidity, digestion, and current state of health also may influence cardiovascular measurements. Consequently, reliability and objectivity coefficients are often low.

The main influencing factors mentioned dictate that great care should be taken in the measurement of pulse rate and blood pressure. If a resting or normal pulse rate is desired, the subject should be allowed to rest for several minutes until the count has stabilized. As has been suggested before, this can be determined by taking consecutive readings until they are similar. It has been observed that a subject's

pulse rate is sometimes lower after mild exercise than when he first entered the laboratory.

Of course, one of the foremost problems associated with cardiovascular fitness testing in physical education classes is the time required for testing. This problem in turn relates to the purposes for which the tests may be used. The group tests are not overly time consuming. Furthermore, these tests are generally most effective in differentiating between different levels of fitness in normal students.

A Brief Summary of Research Findings Concerning Cardiovascular Fitness Tests

There have been differences of opinion expressed concerning the significance of pulse rate measurements before, during, and after exercise. Tuttle (54) contended that it was necessary to obtain a ratio of resting pulse rate to the pulse rate after exercise. Brouha (6), in developing the Harvard Step Test, stated that initial or pre-exercise pulse rate is relatively unimportant and only the recovery pulse rate need be considered. Henry (25) concluded that a decrease in heart rate is an effective measure of changes in athletic conditioning and that the resting pulse rate has validity as an indirect indication of condition. Metz and Alexander (39) found submaximal heart rate to be significantly related to maximal oxygen intake in twelve to fifteen year old boys.

In general, the correlations among various tests of cardiovascular condition have been quite low. Several explanations for this have been suggested, such as the fact that the scoring systems are different. In addition, some use pre-exercise pulse rates, some post-exercise, and some employ both. The differing relations of pre-exercise pulse rate and post-exercise pulse rate following different degrees of work have also been suggested as possible cause for the lack of relationship among tests. Clark (8) found that recovery pulse rate increased in proportion to the duration of exercise up to 2 minutes of exercise. After that point the increase in recovery pulse rate diminished markedly in magnitude. Pollock, Broida, and Kendrick (45) concluded that the palpation technique for estimating heart rate can be used with acceptable accuracy.

Numerous studies have shown that conditioning programs improve scores on cardiovascular fitness tests. This improvement has been in the form of lowered pulse rates, higher resting stroke volumes, and increased resting cardiac output. Among the studies reporting such findings have been Holloszy (27), Henry (25), and Faulkner (22). Conger and MacNab (10) found the pre-exercise heart rate and post-exercise heart rate of women participants in intercollegiate sports were significantly lower than nonparticipants'. Sinning and Adrian (49) reported that the training program during a women's basketball season was not strenuous enough for the subjects to reach maximum physical work capacity. McArdle, Magel, and Kyvallos (38) also reported non-significant changes in body weight, heart rate, and maximum VO$_2$ during a season for a women's college basketball team.

There have also been many studies undertaken to investigate the comparative contributions of different activities in improving cardiovascular fitness. Kozar (30) studied the relative strenuousness of six sports as measured by telemetered heart rates. It was found that while there were no differences among handball, paddleball, tennis, and badminton, these four activities were superior to volleyball and bowling. Volleyball, in turn, produced higher heart rates than bowling. Baker (4) found rope skipping for 10 minutes a day to be as effective in improving cardiovascular efficiency, as measured by the Harvard Step Test, as a 30-minute daily program of jogging.

Pollock and others (46) compared the training effects of running, walking, and bicycling on cardiovascular function. All three programs produced significant improvement. Training effects were independent of mode of training when frequency, duration, and intensity were held constant.

Although many persons stated that isometric exercises could have no beneficial effect in improving one's cardiovascular condition, there have been several studies, Alost (2), Life (33), and Milton (41), which have shown isometrics to be of value insofar as heart rate is an indicator.

Shvartz (48) compared isotonic and isometric exercises on heart rate. He found that isometric exercise performed for 45 seconds at one-half maximum resistance stimulated heart rate to the same extent as isotonic exercise of similar intensity and duration. He also reported that maximum isometric tension resulted in nearly a twofold increase in heart rate.

Dr. Kenneth Cooper (11) did extensive research in an attempt to establish a rating scale for measuring relative values of activities in terms of circulorespiratory conditioning. His research showed the importance of such activities as running, swimming, cycling, walking, handball, basketball, squash, and others in the development of circulorespiratory endurance. Cooper advocates a simple 12-minute run-walk scoring scale for people to evaluate their own condition. Doolittle and Bigbee (19) reported that the 12-minute run-walk correlated .90 with maximum oxygen intake and was thus a highly valid and reliable indicator of cardiorespiratory fitness. Maksud and Coutts (34) found similar reliability (.92) with boys eleven through fourteen and a correlation of .65 between the 12-minute run-walk and aerobic capacity.

The validity of distance runs has been tested in several studies. With college males, Disch, Frankiewicz, and Jackson (18) found through factor analysis that distances longer than 1 mile tended to be loaded almost exclusively on the distance run factor, while shorter distance tests yielded complex factor structures. Jackson and Coleman (28) administered distance runs of 3, 6, 9, and 12 minutes' duration to 866 boys and 803 girls. Factor analysis supported the construct validity of distance runs, with the 9- and 12-minute runs deemed most suitable. Both runs were significantly related to maximum oxygen uptake, with no appreciable difference between the 9- and 12-minute runs.

Running performances of college women for 6, 9, and 12 minutes' duration were correlated with predicted maximal oxygen consumption by Custer and Chaloupka (16). All relationships were significant and of similar magnitude. Consequently, it was concluded that the 6-minute run could be used in place of the 12-minute run.

Santa Maria and others (47) investigated the objectivity, reliability, and validity of the OSU Step Test. It was found that the subject's heart rate determination was less accurate than the investigator's. The test-retest reliability was .69 and validity .47, with maximal oxygen consumption (ml/kg/min) as the criterion.

With maximal oxygen consumption as the criterion, the validity of timed distance runs of 600 yards, three-quarters of a mile, and a mile for 8-year-olds was investigated by Krahenbuhl and others (31). Males exceeded females in maximal oxygen consumption and had faster times in the two longer runs. The mile run was found to be the best predictor of maximal oxygen consumption in males, but none of the three distances were suitable for females.

The intensity, frequency, and duration of exercise are important variables in bringing about improvements in cardiovascular condition. A number of studies have been devoted to the manipulation of these variables. Karvonen (29) concluded that an intensity threshold level of at least 60 percent of the difference between resting and maximum heart rates was necessary for significant improvement in cardiorespiratory condition. Davis and Convertino (17) compared different indices of predicting endurance training intensity. It was found that the Karvonen method yielded more accurate prediction of exercise intensities than using a percentage of maximal heart rate. The latter tended to over-predict exercise intensities.

Gettman and others (24) compared the physiological responses of adult men to 1-, 3- and 5-day per week training programs. Significant improvements were realized in resting and recovery heart rates, treadmill performance time, VO_2 max, maximum O_2 pulse, and V_E max. The degree of improvement was in direct proportion to frequency of training. Moffatt, Stamford, and Neill (42) found significant improvement in aerobic capacity in college men who trained 3 days per week for 10 weeks. There was no difference in the amount of improvement whether the subjects exercised 3 consecutive days per week or whether there was a day separating the exercise days.

Milesis and others (40) measured the effects of 15, 30, and 45 minutes of conditioning on cardiorespiratory fitness variables, body composition, pulmonary function, and serum lipids. Improvements in treadmill performance time, VO_2 max, maximum O_2 pulse, and diastolic blood pressure were in proportion to duration of the training sessions. Crews and Roberts (13) studied the interaction of frequency and intensity of training on the physical work capacity and cardiovascular function of adult males. No interaction effect was noted. However, there were greater training effects for subjects who trained at 150 HR over those training at 120, and both 5- and 3-day-per-week groups had significantly greater gains in work capacity scores than the 1-day group. No difference was found between 5- and 3-days-per-week groups. A bench-stepping exercise was given female subjects by Andzel and Gutin (3) until a heart rate of 140 was achieved. After the exercise the subjects were given no rest, 30 seconds' rest, or 60 seconds' rest before starting a 10-minute stepping task. Performances following the 30- and 60-second rest periods were significantly better than either no prior exercise or no rest following prior exercise. The improvement in performance was attributed to the mobilization of the O_2 transport system.

Burke (7) compared males and females after an 8-week training program in which all subjects exercised at a heart rate of 75 percent to 85 percent maximum with total distance run held equal. It was concluded that while hereditary factors may limit the potential of females in relation to males, the average female can expect relative improvement in aerobic power similar to that of the male. A study by Cunningham and Hill (15) supported the contention that the more sedentary the subjects, the greater the gains in aerobic power. The gains occurred rapidly and were most notable after the initial 9 weeks of training. It was concluded that short-term gains in aerobic power reflect changes in stroke volume, whereas long-term training programs may result in both increased stroke volume and peripheral adaptation. Eisenman and Golding (20) found that the magnitude and rate of improvement in aerobic capacity resulting from a 14-week training program were similar for girls 12 to 13 years of age and for young women 18 to 21 years of age.

Crowder (14) found that a regular program of sauna resulted in significant improvement in cardiovascular efficiency as measured by the Harvard Step Test. Spears (52) reported that exposure to sauna treatments significantly lowered resting pulse rate, blood pressure, body temperature, and metabolism but that these changes were quickly lost when the training program was interrupted. Falls (21) determined that cold showers taken as long as 20 minutes before exercise significantly reduced exercise and recovery heart rates associated with submaximal exercise.

References and Bibliography

1. AAHPER, *AAHPER Youth Fitness Manual,* Washington, D.C.: American Alliance for Health, Physical Education, and Recreation, 1976.

2. Alost, Robert A., "A Study of the Effect of Initial Cardiovascular Condition, Type of Training Program and Frequency of Practice Periods Upon the Cardiovascular Development of College Men" (Unpublished doctoral dissertation, Louisiana State University, 1963).

3. Andzel, Walter D., and Bernard Gutin, "Prior Exercise and Endurance Performance: A Test of the Mobilization Hypothesis," *Research Quarterly,* 47:269-276, May, 1976.

4. Baker, J. A., "Comparison of Rope Skipping and Jogging as Methods of Improving Cardiovascular Efficiency of College Men," *Research Quarterly,* 39:240-243, May, 1968.

5. Biasiotto, Judson, and Doyice Cotten, *Validity of 600 Yard Run-Walk for Elementary School Males* (Unpublished study, Georgia Southern College, 1972).

6. Brouha, Lucien, "The Step Test: A Simple Method of Measuring Physical Fitness for Muscular Work in Young Men," *The Research Quarterly,* 14:31-36, March, 1943.

7. Burke, Edmund J., "Physiological Effects of Similar Training Programs on Males and Females," *Research Quarterly,* 48:510-517, October, 1977.

8. Clark, Jean W., "The Relationship of Initial Pulse Rate, Recovery Pulse Rate, Recovery Index and Subjective Appraisal of Physical Condition After Various Deviations of Work" (Unpublished master's thesis, Louisiana State University, 1966).

9. Coleman, A. Eugene, and Andrew S. Jackson, "Two Procedures for Administering the 12-Minute Run," *JOHPER,* 45:60-62, February, 1974.

10. Conger, Patricia R., and Ross B. J. MacNab, "Strength, Body Composition, and Work Capacity of Participants and Non-Participants in Women's Intercollegiate Sports," *Research Quarterly,* 38:184-192, May, 1967.

11. Cooper, Kenneth H., *Aerobics,* New York: Bantam Books, 1968.

12. Cotten, Doyice J., "A Modified Step Test for Group Cardiovascular Testing," *Research Quarterly,* 42:91-95, March, 1971.

13. Crews, Thad R., and John A. Roberts, "Effects of Interaction of Frequency and Intensity of Training," *Research Quarterly,* 47:48-55, March, 1976.

14. Crowder, Vernon R., "A Study to Determine the Effects of the Sauna Bath on Cardiovascular Efficiency" (Unpublished doctoral dissertation, Louisiana State University, 1969).

15. Cunningham, David A., and J. Stanley Hill, "Effect of Training on Cardiovascular Response to Exercise in Women," *Journal of Applied Physiology,* 39:891-895, December, 1975.

16. Custer, Sally J., and Edward C. Chaloupka, "Relationship Between Predicted Maximal Oxygen Consumption and Running Performance of College Females," *Research Quarterly,* 48:47-50, March, 1977.

17. Davis, James A., and Victor A. Convertino, "A Comparison of Heart Rate Methods for Predicting Endurance Training Intensity," *Medicine and Science in Sports,* 7:295-298, Winter, 1975.

18. Disch, James, Ronald Frankiewicz, and Andrew Jackson, "Construct Validity of Distance Run Tests," *Research Quarterly,* 46:169-176, May, 1975.

19. Doolittle, T. L., and R. Bigbee, "The Twelve-Minute Run-Walk: A Test of Cardiorespiratory Fitness of Adolescent Boys," *Research Quarterly,* 39:491-495, October, 1968.

20. Eisenman, Patricia A., and Lawrence A. Golding, "Comparison of Effects of Training on VO_2 Max in Girls and Young Women," *Medicine and Science in Sports,* 7:136-138, Summer, 1975.

21. Falls, Harold B., "Circulatory Response to Cold Showers: Effect of Varied Time Lapses Before Exercise," *Research Quarterly,* 40:45-49, March, 1969.

22. Faulkner, J. A., "Effect of Cardiac Conditioning on the Anticipatory, Exercise, and Recovery Rates of Young Men," *Journal of Sports Medicine and Physical Fitness,* 4:79-86, June, 1964.

23. Gallagher, J. Roswell, and Lucien Brouha, "A Simple Method of Testing the Physical Fitness of Boys," *Research Quarterly,* 14:24-30, March, 1943.

24. Gettman, Larry R., and others, "Physiological Responses of Men to 1-, 3-, and 5-Day-per-Week Training Programs," *Research Quarterly,* 47:638-646, December, 1976.

25. Henry, Franklin M., "Influence of Athletic Training on the Resting Cardiovascular System," *Research Quarterly,* 25:28-41, March, 1954.

26. Hodgkins, Jean, and Vera Skubic, "Cardiovascular Efficiency Scores for College Women in the United States," *Research Quarterly,* 34:454-461, December, 1963.

27. Holloszy, John V., "Effect of Physical Conditioning on Cardiovascular Function," *American Journal of Cardiology,* 14:761-770, December, 1964.

28. Jackson, Andrew S., and Eugene Coleman, "Validation of Distance Run Tests for Elementary School Children," *Research Quarterly,* 47:86-94, March, 1976.

29. Karvonen, M. J., "Effects of Vigorous Exercise on the Heart," *Work and the Heart,* F. F. Rosenbaum and E. L. Belknap (eds.), New York: Paul B. Hoeber, 1959.

30. Kozar, Andrew J., and Paul Hunsicker, "A Study of Telemetered Heart Rate During Sports Participation of Young Adult Men," *Journal of Sports Medicine and Physical Fitness,* 3:1-5, March, 1963.

31. Krahenbuhl, G. S., and others, "Field Estimation of VO_2 Max in Children Eight Years of Age," *Medicine and Science in Sports,* 9:37-40, Spring, 1977.

32. Kurucz, Robert L., "Construction of the Ohio State University Cardiovascular Fitness Test" (Unpublished doctoral dissertation, Ohio State University, 1967).

33. Life, Mary Louise, "The Effects of Supplementary Isometric Exercises with Swimming and Golf on Selected Physiological Factors of College Women" (Unpublished doctoral dissertation, Louisiana State University, 1964).

34. Maksud, Michael, and Kenneth D. Coutts, "Application of the Cooper Twelve-Minute Run-Walk Test to Young Males," *Research Quarterly,* 42:54-59, March, 1971.

35. Mathews, Donald K., *Measurement in Physical Education,* 4th ed., Philadelphia: W. B. Saunders Company, 1973, pp. 254-256.

36. McArdle, William D., and others, "Percentile Norms for a Valid Step Test in College Women," *Research Quarterly,* 44:498-500, December, 1973.

37. _____ , and others, "Reliability and Interrelationships between Maximal Oxygen Intake, Physical Work Capacity, and Step Test Scores in College Women," *Medicine and Science in Sports,* 4:182-186, Winter, 1972.

38. _____ , John R. Magel, and Lucille C. Kyvallos, "Aerobic Capacity, Heart Rate and Estimated Energy Cost During Women's Competitive Basketball," *Research Quarterly,* 42:178-186, May, 1971.

39. Metz, Kenneth F., and John F. Alexander, "Estimation of Maximal Oxygen Intake from Submaximal Work Parameters," *Research Quarterly,* 42:187-193, May, 1971.

40. Milesis, Chris A., and others, "Effects of Different Durations of Physical Training on Cardiorespiratory Function, Body Composition, and Serum Lipids," *Research Quarterly,* 47:716-725, December, 1976.

41. Milton, George C., "The Effects of Three Programs of Long Distance Running and an Isometric Exercise Program on the Development of Cardiovascular Efficiency" (Unpublished doctoral dissertation, Louisiana State University, 1966).

42. Moffatt, Robert J., Bryant A. Stamford, and Robert D. Neill, "Placement of Tri-Weekly Training Sessions: Importance Regarding Enhancement of Aerobic Capacity," *Research Quarterly,* 48:583-591, October, 1977.

43. Nelson, Jack K., "Fitness Testing as an Educational Process," *Physical Education, Sports and the Sciences,* Jan Broekhoff (ed.), Eugene, Ore.: Microform Publications, 1976.

44. Patterson, Malcolm L., and Jack K. Nelson, "Influence of an Aquatic Conditioning Program on Selected Heart Rate Responses," *Proceedings of the International Conference on Underwater Education,* San Diego, 1976.

45. Pollock, Michael L., Jeffrey Broida, and Zebulon Kendrick, "Validity of the Palpation Technique of Heart Rate Determination and Its Estimation of Training Heart Rate," *Research Quarterly,* 43:77-81, March, 1972.

46. _____ , and others, "Effects of Mode of Training on Cardiovascular Function and Body Composition of Adult Men," *Medicine and Science in Sports,* 7:139-145, Summer, 1975.

47. Santa Maria, D. L., and others, "The Objectivity, Reliability and Validity of the OSU Step Test for College Males," *Research Quarterly,* 47:445-452, October, 1976.

48. Shvartz, Esar, "Effect of Isotonic and Isometric Exercises on Heart Rate," *Research Quarterly,* 37:121-125, March, 1966.

49. Sinning, Wayne E., and Marlene J. Adrian, "Cardiorespiratory Changes in College Women Due to a Season of Competitive Basketball," *Journal of Applied Physiology,* 25:720-724, 1968.

50. Skubic, Vera, and Jean Hodgkins, "Cardiovascular Efficiency Test for Girls and Women," *Research Quarterly,* 34:191-198, May, 1963.

51. _____ , "Cardiovascular Efficiency Test Scores for Junior and Senior High School Girls in the United States," *Research Quarterly,* 35:184-192, May, 1964.

52. Spears, Carolyn D., "Analysis of Physiological Effects on College Women of Two Programs of Regular Exposures to Extreme Heat" (Unpublished doctoral dissertation, Louisiana State University, 1969).

53. Taddonio, Dominick A., and Peter V. Karpovich, "Endurance as Measured by the Harvard Step Test," *Research Quarterly,* 22:381-384, October, 1951.

54. Tuttle, W. W., "The Use of the Pulse-Ratio Test for Rating Physical Efficiency," *Research Quarterly,* 2:5-17, May, 1931.

55. Willgoose, Carl E., and Nathaniel R. Askew, "Reliability of the 600-Yard Run-Walk Test at the Junior High School Level," *Research Quarterly,* 32:264, May, 1961.

Anthropometric measurements have been a part of physical education since its inception in this country. The earliest research was in the area of anthropometry with the emphasis on changes in muscle size brought about through exercise. The modern physical educator is often assigned·the task of measuring height and weight of students. These measures, like any of the other measures taken in school, should be used and not merely recorded and then ignored.

The question is frequently raised, "What do you do with such measures?" "You certainly can't grade on whether a student grows or not." It is indeed true that growth does not constitute a valid criterion upon which a student is graded. However, height, weight, and certain anthropometric measures, used in conjunction with other pertinent data, do represent potentially valuable information. The first portion of this chapter will consider the utilization of these measures under three general headings: classification indexes, the assessment of normal growth and nutrition, and body build classification, otherwise called somatotyping.

Classification Indexes

Physical educators have long realized that the performance of boys and girls is greatly influenced by such factors as age, height, weight, and body structure. It is also acknowledged that persons of the same age will vary considerably in body size and shape; that individuals of the same height will differ greatly in body weight; that persons may weigh the same, but the relative proportion of muscle, fat, and bone will be anything but equal. It is obvious, then, that no single measure by itself is satisfactory for the purposes of classifying students into homogenous groups.

Our school system in the United States is based primarily on a single classification, age. A child starts to school at a specified age, and, if he makes satisfactory progress, he advances a grade each year. The main objection to this system lies in the known differences in maturity within a given chronological age. Clarke (6) tested boys within two months of their tenth birthday and reported differences in skeletal maturity ranging from eight years and less to twelve years and more. Certainly, it is unfair to expect a boy who is at a maturation level of eight years to compete equally with a boy of twelve years. Yet we continually do this as long

Chapter Ten

Anthropometric Measurement, Body Build, and Body Composition

as our only classification index is chronological age.

The assessment of skeletal age, or physical maturity, by X-ray is, of course, not practical for the school situation. Therefore, the physical educator must use other devices if he wishes to classify students into homogenous groupings. Two of the most commonly used classification devices have been the McCloy Classification Index and the Neilson and Cozens Classification Index. Both systems utilize a combination of age, height, and weight.

Before the various classification indices and age-height-weight tables are presented, it may be pertinent to briefly discuss some points that should be considered in measuring height and weight. These measures are so common that occasionally the examiner tends to be too lax and inaccuracies result. Remember that practice and attention to detail are as important here as in any measurement if the results are to have real value.

Measurement of Height

In measuring height, the only equipment and materials necessary are a flat surface against which the subject stands, a measuring tape or marked surface, and an object to place on the subject's head that forms a right angle to the wall or a backboard. If a wall is used, it should not have quarter round or wainscotting so that the subject can stand against it with heels, buttocks, upper back, and back of the head making firm contact.

For permanent mounting, the markings can be painted on the wall or backboard. Most classification devices and nutritional status instruments call for height measured to the nearest ¼ of an inch. Therefore, the scale should be marked in these units. However, for greater versatility and application, it is recommended that a parallel scale be prepared reading in centimeters.

Frequently, weight scales have stadiometers attached consisting of a sliding calibrated rod with hinged top piece. These sometimes are found to be unsatisfactory in cases where the top piece is loose and fails to make a right angle or when the rod sticks or perhaps is too loose.

The subject should be measured without shoes. It has been suggested that standing with the back against a support helps the subject to stretch to his full height. The chin is tucked in slightly and the head is held erect. The object used to form a right angle to the backboard is pressed firmly onto the subject's head. Care should be taken so that the upper surface is horizontal and not tilted and also that this pressure does not cause the subject to slump or alter his position. Finally, the subject bends his knees slightly when he steps away so as not to disturb the angle before the height is recorded.

Measurement of Weight

Generally speaking, scales based on the lever system are more reliable than the spring scales. Both types, however, require periodic inspection and rather delicate handling.

The subject to be weighed should be wearing a minimum amount of clothing, such as only gym shorts. While it may be more accurate for the subjects to be weighed in the nude, it is often not practical nor desirable. Actually, no appreciable accuracy is lost if the amount of clothing is kept consistent. Consistency is the key to all measurements. The subject should be weighed at the same time of day and to the same degree of accuracy—usually the nearest half pound. Smithells and Cameron (46) point out that hair styles may cause variations in weight and that it is somewhat incongruous that hair is pressed down and thus, in a sense, not counted in height measurement, but it is included in body weight.

The teacher should attempt to control the weighing situation so that there is minimal embarrassment on the part of the students. With experience the teacher can acquire the knack of predicting the body weight of students as they step to the scale. This facilitates the process by eliminating much trial and error with regard to jiggling the scale's sliding weights back and forth.

Other Anthropometric Instruments

Instruments other than stadiometers and weight scales for anthropometric measurement include the following:

Shoulder Breadth, Length Caliper: Measures shoulder width and thigh length. (See Figure 10-1.)

Chest Depth Caliper: Measures minimum chest expansion. (See Figure 10-2.)

Compact Indicating Caliper: For direct reading of inside or outside linear measurements to a length of 6 inches. (See Figure 10-3.)

Gulick Tape: Includes spring attachment which permits a slight amount of constant tension on the tape. (See Figure 10-4.)

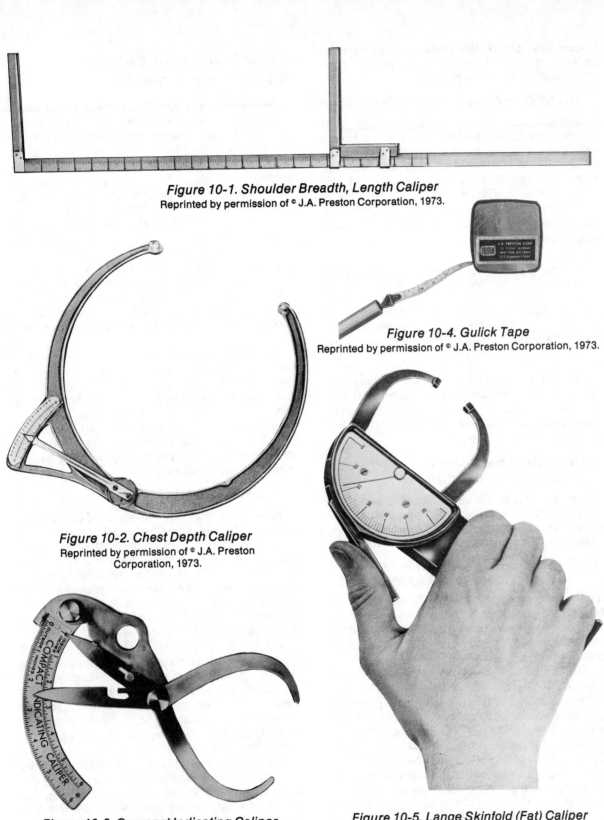

Figure 10-1. Shoulder Breadth, Length Caliper
Reprinted by permission of ® J.A. Preston Corporation, 1973.

Figure 10-4. Gulick Tape
Reprinted by permission of ® J.A. Preston Corporation, 1973.

Figure 10-2. Chest Depth Caliper
Reprinted by permission of ® J.A. Preston Corporation, 1973.

Figure 10-3. Compact Indicating Caliper
Reprinted by permission of ® J.A. Preston Corporation, 1973.

Figure 10-5. Lange Skinfold (Fat) Caliper
Reprinted by permission of ® J.A. Preston Corporation, 1973.

Lange Skinfold (Fat) Caliper: Measures subcutaneous and adipose (fat) tissue with constant tension. (See Figure 10-5.)

The McCloy Classification Index (33)

Despite their limitations, age, height, and weight have been found to correlate highly with valid criteria of competition. Therefore, McCloy believed that, because of their convenience and validity, they should be utilized for classification purposes. On the basis of a statistical study McCloy established three indexes with the following weightings for age, height, and weight:

(For high school)	Classification Index I	20 (age in yrs.) +6 (ht. in inches) +weight in lbs.
(For college)	Classification Index II	6 (ht. in inches) +weight in lbs.
(For elementary grades)	Classification Index III	10 (age in yrs.) +weight in lbs.

McCloy, in recommending the different indices for different age levels, found that age ceased to make a contribution at seventeen years and that height was not an important factor at the elementary level.

The Neilson and Cozens Classification Index (37)

Neilson and Cozens developed two classification indices based on age, height, and weight. However, their second index is the one commonly employed. Its formula is as follows:

Classification Index = 20 (age in yrs.) + 5.55 (ht. in inches) + weight in lbs.

It can be seen that this formula is very similar to McCloy's Classification Index I. As a matter of fact, an r of .98 has been obtained between the two indices, which indicates that either index could be used.

The Neilson and Cozens Classification Index can be quickly and easily determined by consulting a table. The teacher simply finds the exponent value for each of the variables of height, age, and weight. After adding the three exponents, the class, in the form of a letter A, B, C, etc., is established. For the elementary and junior high school students eight classes (A through H) are given. For high school only three classes (A, B, and C) are determined. The *AAHPER Youth Fitness Manual* presents norms based on the Nielson and Cozens Classification Index as well as norms based on age only.

Growth and Nutritional Status Measurement

Many attempts have been made to establish standards for assessing normal growth, desirable body weight, and nutritional status. Tables are available for both sexes at different age levels. Of course, those tables which attempt to take into account differences in body structure are generally more reliable than charts based only on height. Even so, one should exercise reasonable judgment in using such tables because of their inherent limitations. The tables do not differentiate among individuals on the basis of muscular development and relative proportion of muscle and fat. For example, in one table of desirable weights for adult men, the most that a 6-foot man with a large frame should weigh was slightly over 180 pounds.

Nevertheless, age-height-weight tables are of value if used properly. Bogert (3) presents numerous age-height-weight charts as well as comparative descriptions of persons suffering from malnutrition and having good nutrition. The descriptions include the appearance of the skin, hair, muscular development, posture, and other characteristics including sleeping habits, appetite, and disposition.

The Wetzel Grid (52)

One of the most extensively used devices for plotting and evaluating growth in the last quarter century has been the Wetzel Grid (Figure 10-6). This chart and record form was developed by Wetzel on the principle that normal, healthy development proceeds in an orderly manner in keeping with an individual's natural physique. Therefore, the child serves as his own standard of comparison.

Although upon first appearance, the grid gives the impression of being complicated, it actually is quite easy to use. The validity of the grid in detecting growth failures and nutritional disturbances has been well documented. For references see Robert M. Grueninger, *Don't Take Growth for Granted*, N.E.A. Service, Inc., Cleveland, 1961.

Nine general body types were designated by Wetzel. These are identified on the chart by the corresponding channels A_4, A_3, A_2, A_1, M, B_1, B_2, B_3, B_4. The M channel represents the average or medium build; along with A_1 and B_1 it forms a central group of *good physical status*. Channels A_2 and A_3 represent stocky builds.

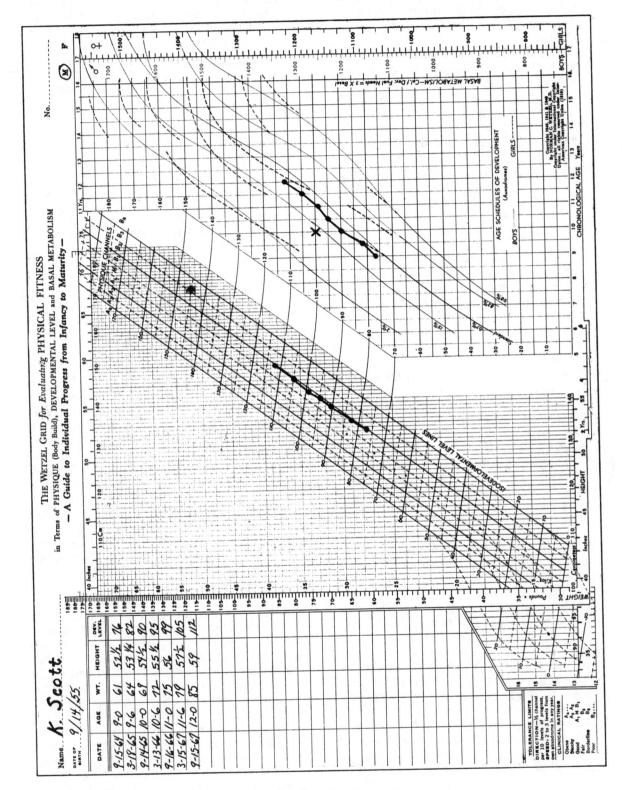

Figure 10-6. The Wetzel Grid

The majority of A_4s are obese. Channels B_2, B_3, and B_4 reflect increasing degrees of thinness, respectively. The procedures for using the grid are as follows:

1. The child's height and weight are recorded and then plotted, thus placing a child in a particular physique channel on the left side of the chart (panel A). The corresponding developmental level is also read off from the horizontal lines crossing the physique channels and then entered in the table. In the example shown in Figure 10-6, the boy's height is 52½ inches and his weight 61 pounds, yielding a point on the border of B_1 and B_2 at level 76.

2. It should be emphasized that the first plotting reveals very little in terms of *quality of growth.* The successive plottings are of primary importance in indicating the character of growth progress. All plots should be checked for accuracy; in case of notable irregularity, weight and height should be re-measured.

3. The child's developmental level is then plotted against age (panel B), e.g., level 76 at age nine.

4. The next measurement, in this instance, is six months later. Height and weight are again plotted, on the channel system and the developmental level in panel B at nine years six months.

5. Subsequent plottings build up the channel and auxodrome trends. These are to be interpreted in relation to the background grid standards of direction and speed of physical development thereby revealing the *quality of individual growth.*

6. Interpretation of a child's advancement in panel B is made by referring to the curved age schedules or auxodromes. The standard of reference for determining whether a child is *normal, advanced, or retarded* in development is the 67-percent auxodrome. To illustrate how this may be used, the X on panel B shows a child, aged ten years, at developmental level 100. This child would be considered 1½ years advanced in development, since the standard auxodrome does not cross the 100 level until the age of 11½ years.

7. The dotted-line curves in panel B (for girls) are seen to level off sooner than the solid line (for boys). This is because of the fact that girls ordinarily mature at an earlier age.

8. Although one shouldn't expect the plotted lines to stay exactly along a particular channel or auxodrome, it has been found that healthy growth and development are remarkably precise, channelwise, as well as along an auxodrome. In the example in Figure 10-6, the boy's growth and development are progressing in a very satisfactory manner.

9. Any child who deviates markedly from his normal channelwise progress or from his own auxodrome should be investigated. Children in A_4 (obese) should be observed closely, and children in B_2 and to the right of the 67-percent auxodrome should be carefully watched also. In his early work with the grid, Wetzel was able to identify 95 percent of the children that had been rated as poor or borderline by physicians.

10. The last two columns are for estimating basal metabolism and daily caloric requirements. Although these standards were announced almost thirty years ago they, nonetheless, correspond with current NRC *recommended allowances.*

Meredith Height-Weight Chart (34)

After much study of growth records of children at various age levels, Meredith was able to construct a zone classification system for height and weight for boys and girls four to eighteen years of age. The charts that were prepared for convenient use by the classroom teacher contain curved zones for height and weight upon which the child's growth progress can be plotted. There are five zones for height: tall, moderately tall, average, moderately short, and short. Similarly, there are five zones for weight: heavy, moderately heavy, average, moderately light, and light. The height zones are at the top of the chart and the weight zones are at the bottom.

When the height and the weight of the child are plotted at the appropriate age column, an immediate check is available to see whether the child's height and weight are in similar zones. It is normally to be expected that a child who is moderately short will be light and a child who is tall will be heavy and so on. When the zones are dissimilar, then it should be determined whether the child's physique accounts for the dissimilarity; for example, if the child is naturally tall and slender or short and stocky, etc. If this is not the case, then further examination is made for possible health problems such as malnutrition, obesity, and illness. Moreover, as successive plottings are made, growth patterns can be observed. It is expected that a child's height and weight will essentially parallel one another, in that they will proceed along their same zones. Any marked deviation from one zone to another is usually cause for referral.

The ACH Index (18)

The ACH Index was developed as a means for screening children in the elementary grades (ages seven to twelve) in need of referral for medical examination with regard to nutritional status. Franzen and Palmer reported that over 10,000 school children had been involved in determining the most significant anthropometric measures for assessing the amount of soft tissue in relation to skeletal build.

Seven measures were selected: hip width, chest depth, chest width, height, weight, arm girth, and subcutaneous tissue over the biceps muscle. It was recognized that these measurements are quite time consuming and require considerable skill. Consequently, a shorter battery was selected from these measures that could be used effectively for screening purposes. These measures are (a) arm girth, (b) chest depth, and (c) hip width.

Franzen and Palmer recommended that the

Table 10-1
The ACH Index of Nutritional Status
(Ages Seven through Twelve)

Boys		Girls	
Width of Hips	Minimum Difference between Arm Girth and Chest Depth	Width of Hips	Minimum Difference between Arm Girth and Chest Depth
Below 20.0	0.0	Below 20.0	.5
20.0-20.4	0.0	20.0-20.4	1.0
20.5-20.9	.4	20.5-20.9	1.6
21.0-21.4	1.0	21.0-21.4	2.1
21.5-21.9	1.6	21.5-21.9	2.6
22.0-22.4	2.2	22.0-22.4	3.0
22.5-22.9	2.7	22.5-22.9	3.4
23.0-23.4	3.3	23.0-23.4	3.8
23.5-23.9	3.8	23.5-23.9	4.2
24.0-24.4	4.2	24.0-24.4	4.5
24.5-24.9	4.7	24.5-24.9	4.8
25.0-25.4	5.1	25.0-25.4	5.1
25.5-25.9	5.6	25.5-25.9	5.4
26.0-26.4	6.0	26.0-26.4	5.6
26.5-26.9	6.3	26.5-26.9	5.8
27.0-27.4	6.7	27.0-27.4	6.0
27.5-27.9	7.0	27.5-27.9	6.1
28.0-28.4	7.3	28.0-28.4	6.2
28.5-28.9	7.6	28.5-28.9	6.3
29.0 over	7.9	29.0 over	6.4

Raymond Franzen, and George Palmer, *The ACH Index of Nutritional Status,* New York: American Child Health Association, 1934.

index be used in either of two ways. It could be employed to screen a quarter of the children for further measurement. These children would then be given the rest of the seven measures. In this manner the authors report that 90 percent of the children would be selected that would have been identified by giving all seven measures to the entire group of children. Another way of using the ACH Index is to set the standards so that a tenth of the group is selected for further measurement. Although some extreme cases may be missed, Franzen and Palmer maintain that it is superior to the age-height-weight method and the speed and simplicity of the measurements justify this system for use in the school situation. The measurement procedures are as follows:

Arm Girth. (a) The child flexes his dominant arm. A skin pencil is used to mark the highest point on the biceps. (b) The child flexes so that the tips of the fingers are touching the shoulder. The girth of the arm at the marked site is measured by a gulick tape to the nearest tenth of a centimeter. In measuring this girth, as in any girth measure, the tape is pulled tight enough so that it is smooth but not producing an indentation in the skin. The tape is crossed to get the point of reading. (c) The child relaxes his arm, letting it hang by the side of his body, and the girth is again measured and recorded.

Chest Depth. (a) A wooden caliper is placed firmly against the chest and back at a point just above the nipple line and just below the angle of the scapula, respectively. (b) Two measures are taken: after normal inspiration and after normal expiration. (c) The measurement is to the nearest tenth of a centimeter.

Hip Width. (a) The wooden caliper is pressed against the widest part of the hips at the greater trochanters. (b) The measurement is read to the nearest tenth of a centimeter.

Scoring. (a) The two arm-girth measures are added, and this figure is subtracted from the total of the two chest-depth measures. (b) From Table 10-1 the child's hip width is located, and the corresponding minimum difference between arm girth and chest depth is found. (c) If the measured difference is equal or less than the figure in the table, the child is referred for further examination.

Body Build Classification (Somatotyping)

The association of certain body builds with personality and behavior patterns, health problems, and physical performance has long been recognized. Most of us have rather stereotyped notions of what the typical fat person is like, the skinny person, and the person who is "all muscle." This concept that a man behaves as he does because of what he is represents the foundation of somatotyping (53).

William H. Sheldon is without doubt the foremost name in the field of somatotyping. He, in turn, was influenced by the work of Kretschmer and others before him. Sheldon and his co-workers (43) concluded that while there are three basic body types, people have varying amounts or degrees of all three. The three primary components are called endomorphy, mesomorphy, and ectomorphy.

Endomorphy is characterized by roundness of body parts with concentration in the center. This is the pear-shaped individual with a large abdomen, round head, short neck, narrow shoulders, fatty breasts, short arms, wide hips, heavy buttocks, and short, heavy legs.

Mesomorphy is evidenced by rugged musculature and large bones. The mesomorph has prominent facial bones, a rather long but muscular neck, wide sloping shoulders, muscular arms and forearms, broad chest, heavily muscled abdomen, low waist and narrow hips, muscular buttocks, and powerful legs.

Ectomorphy is characterized by small bones, with linearity and fragility predominating. The ectomorph has a large forehead, small facial bones, a long skinny neck, narrow chest, round shoulders with winged scapulae, long slender arms, flat abdomen, inconspicuous buttocks, and long, thin legs.

In determining the body build classification, or somatotype, the individual is scaled from 1 to 7 in each component. The somatotype is thus given in a three-number sequence in which the first number represents the endomorphic component; the second, mesomorphy, and the third, ectomorphy. An extreme endomorph is classified as a 7-1-1; an extreme mesomorph is a 1-7-1; and an extreme ectomorph is a 1-1-7.

Most people are dominated by two components. The lesser of the two is usually employed as the adjective in describing the somatotype. For example, a 2-6-4 would be an ectomorphic mesomorph, etc.

Accurate somatotyping for research purposes requires a great amount of training and practice. The specifications and instructions for taking the photographs and the steps and procedures in the somatotyping process are given in detail in Sheldon's *Atlas of Men* (42). Briefly, they are as follows: The subject is photographed, preferably in the nude, from three views — front, side, and back. In order to minimize any changes in body position, a revolving pedestal is used. The subject's height and weight are carefully measured, and the ponderal index is then determined. The ponderal index is the height divided by the cube root of weight (Ht./$\sqrt[3]{\text{wt.}}$). It is the maximal achieved mass over surface area; in other words, it indicates the person's position in relation to ectomorphy. The higher the ponderal index, the more the subject tends toward ectomorphy. A table is consulted showing the possible somatotypes for the obtained ponderal index, and photographs are used for comparative reference.

Recently, Sheldon refined the somatotyping process by making it more objective through the computation of a trunk index. A planimeter is utilized to measure the abdominal and thoracic trunk area on the photograph. Tables have been developed in which the combination of ponderal index, trunk index, and height enable the researcher to accurately identify the subject's somatotype. These tables have not yet been incorporated into the *Atlas*.

Simplified Somatotype Assessment

Willgoose (53) presents a rather comprehensive discussion of somatotyping, its implications, and applications. In his discussion he suggests a method of somatotyping that, while not meant to be as accurate as Sheldon's process, has more practical application for the physical education teacher.

The teacher rates the subject on the primary component on the 1 to 7 scale. Next, he rates the secondary and then the third components in the same manner. The ponderal index is calculated by using the nomograph shown in Figure 10-7. In using the nomograph, the teacher places a ruler on the scale so that it connects the subject's height and weight. The point at which the ruler intersects the middle column is the ponderal index.

The teacher may then consult Sheldon's *Atlas of Men* and study the charts of possible somatotypes and confirm the somatotype

classification. Willgoose maintains that even without the *Atlas* or the ponderal index, one can estimate somatotypes accurately enough for use in the school situation.

Cureton's Subjective Somatotype Form (14)

Cureton has employed a subjective method of estimating somatotype in his research. It consists of studying the five major regions of the body and rating the degree of endomorphy, mesomorphy, and ectomorphy of each region. Then the components are averaged and the somatotype is thus estimated. The rating can be done using the subject himself or posed pictures including front, back, and side views. A summary of the steps are as follows:

Step 1: Using the form in Figure 10-8, rate the amount of each somatotype component on a 1 to 7 scale for Region I (head, face, and neck). The number representing the amount of endomorphy is circled, the number for mesomorphy is circled, and the rating for ectomorphy is circled. For example, 1 for endomorphy, 3 for mesomorphy, and 5 for ectomorphy.

Step 2: The same procedure is followed for Regions II, III, IV, and V.

Step 3: The average endomorphy rating for the five regions is computed. The average mesomorphy and ectomorphy values are also computed. As a further check, it is recommended that the teacher consult Sheldon's table where in the ponderal index values for possible somatotypes for corresponding numbers are indicated.

Step 4: The average scores for the three components are placed in the above order, for example, 2-4-5. The somatotype is then named; in this case, a mesomorphic ectomorph.

A question often raised is, Of what value is somatotyping to the physical education teacher? It certainly wouldn't be practical to consume large blocks of class time for the sole purpose of somatotyping students. On the other hand, it can be done quite efficiently (with practice) on a scheduled individual observation basis. What we are referring to here is a plan in which the teacher makes it a point to observe a particular student(s) each day. Through careful observation, the teacher is able to gain valuable information about each student as to his motor performance, his strengths and weaknesses, and his social adjustment and personality, as well as his posture and his somatotype. This, of course, is not meant to

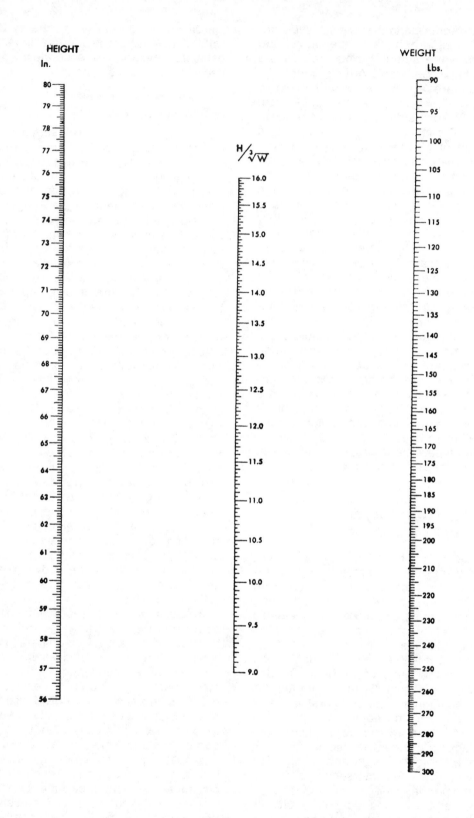

Figure 10-7. Nomograph for Ponderal Index (53)

sound like a one-shot proposition. It should be continuous throughout the year, thereby affording the teacher an opportunity to observe each student in various situations. The main advantage of such a plan is that it ensures that the teacher will consciously study every person in the class rather than just notice the loud ones, the students who misbehave, and the good and bad performers.

Thus, the real value of somatotyping lies in its contribution toward a better understanding of the individual. Better understanding in turn enables the teacher to better meet the needs of each student. The mesomorph's energetic need for physical exercise, excitement, and adventure; the endomorph's inclination toward social activities and relaxing recreational games; and the ectomorph's tendency to shy away from team sports and group activities all present a challenge to the physical educator. The discerning teacher who is able to anticipate the sensitivity of the ectomorph and the endomorph in situations where their physiques and poor physical abilities are apt to evoke ridicule can make a great contribution toward making friends instead of enemies for physical education.

The physical educator and the coach can

Region of the Body	Endomorphy	Mesomorphy	Ectomorphy
I Head, Face, and Neck Notations	1 2 3 4 5 6 7	1 2 3 4 5 6 7	1 2 3 4 5 6 7
II Thoracic Trunk Notations	1 2 3 4 5 6 7	1 2 3 4 5 6 7	1 2 3 4 5 6 7
III Arms, Hands, Shoulders Notations	1 2 3 4 5 6 7	1 2 3 4 5 6 7	1 2 3 4 5 6 7
IV Abdominal Trunk Notations	1 2 3 4 5 6 7	1 2 3 4 5 6 7	1 2 3 4 5 6 7
V Legs and Feet Notations	1 2 3 4 5 6 7	1 2 3 4 5 6 7	1 2 3 4 5 6 7
VI Average Rating	_____	_____	_____

Subject's Name _____ Age_____ Ht._____ Wt._____

Ponderal Index ht./$\sqrt[3]{wt.}$ "t" _____ _____ _____

Estimated Somatotype Number (from VI above)_____

Somatotype Name _____

Figure 10-8. Cureton's Subjective Classification of Body Type

effectively utilize a knowledge of somatotyping along with physical performance measures in predicting potential athletic ability. Since most people are mixtures rather than extremes in a single component, the teacher and coach who are skilled in identifying body structure characteristics will be most likely successful in predicting abilities and channeling students into activities best suited for their needs, interests, and capabilities.

Body Composition

It has been well documented that obesity is a very critical health problem in the United States. It has been shown to be associated with high blood pressure, coronary heart disease, diabetes, respiratory problems, hernias, orthopedic disorders, and various other health problems as well as surgery risks. Understandably, there has been increased concern by the medical professions as to prevention of obesity.

Until rather recently, the bulk of the attention accorded to weight control focused on the adult population. The so-called "creeping obesity" refers to the gradual accumulation of fat over a period of years. To gain 1 or 2 pounds of weight in a year seems inconsequential, but if projected over a 20-year time span it represents a very significant amount of excess fat. Unfortunately, the individual wants to lose the slowly acquired weight overnight. This leads to crash diets until a target amount of weight is lost, then immediate resumption of the regular life style and the resultant gain of weight, and then another crash diet: the "yo-yo" phenomenon. Statistics reporting that 30 to 40 percent of the adult population is obese indicate that the United States is losing the battle of the bulge. Moreover, data gathered through case studies and extensive observations point heavily to the need for more efforts devoted to obesity in children and the preventive role that exercise can play in weight control and fat reduction.

Some of the findings are as follows:

1. Approximately 25 percent of the children in the United States are overfat (54, 10).
2. There is more and more evidence that fat children are not the prototypes of healthy adults; fat children become fat adults (31).
3. Inactivity appears more and more to be the most common denominator in obesity, rather than overeating or glandular disturbances (11).
4. Case studies have revealed that a large percentage of fat adults trace the beginning of their weight problems to the points in their lives when they stopped regular activity (10).
5. Exercise is of value in the loss of fat and in weight control. Severe dieting alone causes a loss of lean body tissue in addition to loss of fat. Exercise programs and exercise plus dieting brings about greater fat reduction without loss of muscle mass (56).
6. Muscle uses more energy than fat. Thus the maintenance of adequate muscle mass through regular exercise can help prevent the accumulation of fat by burning more calories even while at rest. This is one of the primary reasons for weight problems as a person grows older. Due to inactivity and the subsequent reduction of muscle mass, the individual uses fewer calories than before. A paradox develops in that a person with reduced muscle mass and a higher percentage of fat actually has to exercise more and more just to avoid gaining more weight (28).

The problem of obesity and its causes is very complex. There are no simple solutions. Researchers in health, medicine, and exercise physiology have done much to dispel some of the fallacies concerning obesity and the role of exercise. In light of the seriousness of obesity, its medical, psychological, and social implications, and the acknowledged value of exercise in its prevention and treatment, physical educators now generally list weight control and the avoidance of obesity as one of the components of physical fitness.

Measurement of Body Composition

The inclusion of weight control as a component of physical fitness carries with it the obligation of measurement. For years, health educators and physical educators have recognized and sporadically attempted to determine and/ or predict proper or ideal body weight. Differences in body size have long been recognized as important variables in the interpretation of fitness test scores.

Because of the medical risk factors associated with obesity, insurance companies have been concerned with "proper" weight for many years. Their age-height-weight tables with rough classifications of body frame have been widely used as standards for normal weight. The armed services have developed similar scales.

The major flaw in the age-height-weight scales is their inability to account for differences in percentage of lean body weight and fat. Numerous demonstrations of the tables' limitations have been reported. Wilmore (55) cited the case of a 265-pound professional football player who was classified by the insurance tables as being 75 pounds overweight. However, according to body composition measurements, his lean body weight was 225 pounds, and thus in order for him to meet the insurance table's specifications, he would have had to lose 33 pounds of muscle or the equivalent of an arm or a leg! Another frequently cited study involved the comparison of weight classification by U.S. Air Force standards and actual percentage of body fat and lean body weight determined through laboratory methods. It was shown that over 40 percent of the subjects were incorrectly classified by the tables (48).

The only true determination of body composition would be through dissection of a cadaver. One method of assessment that is currently employed to estimate body composition is radiography in which bone, muscle, fat, and skin are quantified by X-ray analysis. Another is the potassium-40 method, which employs the measurement of gamma radiation from the body. This method requires a chamber and elaborate equipment. Still another is the helium dilution method, in which volume differences between volume in a special chamber and subject volume are analyzed.

The most frequently used method of assessing body composition is the underwater weighing technique, in which body density is determined indirectly by the body's loss of weight in water and the application of Archimedes' principle, which states that the loss of weight of the body in water is equal to the weight of the water displaced by the body. A body's density is weight divided by volume. While this may sound rather simple, the method requires equipment, very careful preparatory procedures, and repeated weighings and correction for the volume of the air in the lungs. Another method utilizing the same principle involves measurement of the actual displacement of water caused by the submersion of a body in a water-filled container.

Once density has been estimated, the percentage of fat is calculated, based on the known differences in density of fat and lean tissue. Siri's equation (44) is most often used for converting body density to percentage of fat:

$$\% \text{ fat} = \left(\frac{4.950}{\text{Density}} - 4.500 \right) 100$$

Although the underwater weighing technique is employed rather widely in colleges and university laboratories, it obviously is not applicable for widespread usage in physical education programs. Other simpler measurements such as body girths, diameters, and skinfold thicknesses have thus been employed, and regression equations have been calculated to predict density and relative body fat.

Several of these measurements will be described and some of the equations given. However, widespread practical application of these techniques is limited due to the expense of the equipment (although not especially prohibitive), the time and care needed for the measurements, and the errors of prediction. While these may seem like formidable obstacles and the reader might question the efficacy of including them in a book of this kind, there is increasing evidence that some type of anthropometric measurements are likely to be utilized in the near future as part of the assessment of physical fitness.

Circumference (Girth) Measurements

Circumferences at numerous body sites have been measured and evaluated. From a commonsense standpoint, we tend to incorporate a person's girths of various body segments in our appraisal of his or her body build. Obesity is characterized by large abdominal and hip girths in relation to chest circumference.

The measurement of circumference requires great care. One of the main difficulties is locating the exact body site. The circumferences must be at right angles to the long axis of the body or body segment and not tilted. Another potential source of error is the compression of the skin by the tape. The gulick tape (Figure 10-4) is used widely in research because it has a spring attached to the handle which permits a constant amount of tension that is applied while measuring. A steel or cloth tape may be used.

Some of the body sites most frequently measured are as follows:

Neck: Immediately below the larynx (Figure 10-9).

Chest: At nipple level in males (Figure 10-10). In females, chest measurements are sometimes taken at the level of the breasts (maximum circumference), just above the breast tissue, and just below the breasts. All chest measurements should be taken at the end of normal expiration.

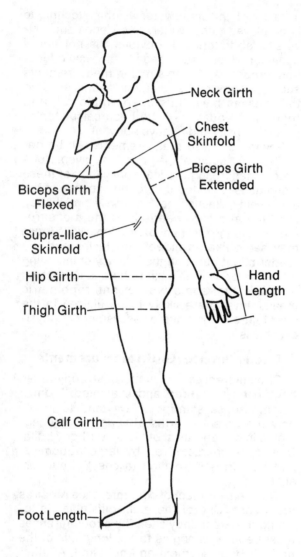

Figure 10-9. Anatomical Landmarks

Labels on figure:
Neck Girth
Chest Skinfold
Biceps Girth Extended
Biceps Girth Flexed
Supra-Iliac Skinfold
Hip Girth
Thigh Girth
Hand Length
Calf Girth
Foot Length

Abdomen: Abdominal girths have been taken at different positions. Three of the sites are:

1. At the level of the umbilicus and iliac crests (Figure 10-10, Abdominal Girth A).
2. At the point of minimal circumference, halfway between the umbilicus and xiphoid process of the sternum between the bottom of the rib cage and iliac crests (Figure 10-10, Abdominal Girth B).
3. At the maximal abdominal girth in women about 2 inches below the umbilicus (Figure 10-10, Abdominal Girth C).

Hips: At a level from the maximal protrusion of the buttocks to the symphysis pubis (Figure 10-9).

Thigh: The point of maximal thigh circumference (Figure 10-9).

Calf: The point of maximal calf circumference (Figure 10-9).

Biceps: (a) Greatest girth when arm is maximally flexed and muscles fully contracted (Figure 10-9). (b) Greatest girth when arm is fully extended and muscles contracted (Figure 10-9).

Body Diameter Measurements

Calipers and anthropometers are employed in diameter measurements. For most measurements the anthropometer is used; it consists of a metric scale with a fixed blade and a movable blade. An anthropometer can be easily made with a meter stick and some type of blades.

The tester should locate the body landmarks with his or her fingers before applying the anthropometer. The blades should be applied with sufficient pressure so as to compress as much of the soft tissue as possible. This makes for greater bone contact and therefore more accurate and reliable measurements.

Anatomical landmarks for diameter measurements include the following:

Head Width: Above the ears at the widest point of the head (Figure 10-11).

Biacromial Diameter: The most lateral margins of the acromial processes with shoulders relaxed and elbows close to the body. Measured from behind the subject (Figure 10-11).

Chest Width: At the nipple line, at the level of fifth and sixth rib with arms at side of body (Figure 10-11).

Bi-Iliac Diameter: Greatest width of the pelvic girdle at the lateral margins of the iliac crests, taken from in front of the subject (Figure 10-11).

Bitrochanteric Diameter: The lateral margins of the greater trochanters (Figure 10-11).

Knee Diameter: With knee flexed to 90°, the widest margins between the lateral and medial epicondyles of the femur (Figure 10-11).

Ankle Diameter: Anthropometer is tilted upward at a 45° angle with blades touching the malleoli (Figure 10-11).

Wrist Diameter: The styloid processes of the radius and ulna (Figure 10-11).

Length Measurements

Standing Height: See page 166.

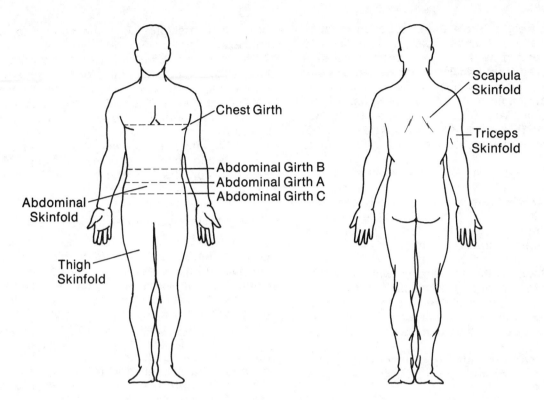

Figure 10-10. Anatomical Landmarks

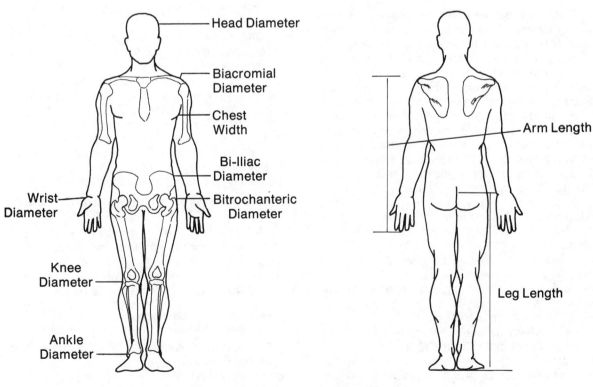

Figure 10-11. Anatomical Landmarks

Sitting Height: Subject is on a bench or table, sitting as erect as possible with legs hanging down and arms resting on thighs. Distance measured from bench to vertex (highest point on top of the head). Subtract height of table top.

Leg Length: From the end of the spinal column to the floor. Also taken from greater trochanter to floor (Figure 10-11). Sometimes the difference between sitting and standing heights is used.

Trunk Length: The standing height minus leg length.

Arm Length: From acromion process to the tip of the third finger (Figure 10-11). It is sometimes measured while subject is holding a wand; measurement is from acromion process to upper surface of wand.

Arm Span: With back against wall, arms are extended horizontally. Distance taken from outstretched fingertips of one hand to the other.

Hand Length: From the tip of the third finger to the base of the thumb (most proximal carpal bone) (Figure 10-9).

Foot Length: From the tip of the most distal toe to the most posterior portion of the heel (Figure 10-9).

Skinfold Measurements

Skinfold measurements require precise calipers that are designed to apply the same tension throughout their range of motion. The tester grasps the skinfold between thumb and index finger and attaches the jaws of the calipers about 1 centimeter from the thumb and finger. The measurements are in millimeters.

Skinfolds provide an indication of subcutaneous fat since the tester's pinch includes the fat contained between the double thickness of skin and excludes the muscle tissue. Therefore, if there is ever a question as to whether the pinch encompasses muscle, the tester should ask the subject to contract the underlying muscle. Measurements are usually taken on the right side of the body with the subject standing.

Some of the anatomical sites that are frequently utilized are as follows:

Scapula: The inferior angle of the scapula. The skinfold is lifted on a 45° diagonal plane parallel to the axillary border (Figure 10-10).

Chest: Midway between the anterior fold of the axilla and the nipple (Figure 10-9).

Triceps: On the back of the arm midway between the acromion process and the olecranon process. The skinfold is taken parallel to the long axis of the arm (Figure 10-10).

Abdomen: About 1 centimeter to the right of the umbilicus, a horizontal fold (Figure 10-10).

Supra-Iliac: Just above the crest of the ilium at the midaxillary line. The fold is lifted diagonally, following the natural line of the iliac crest (Figure 10-9).

Thigh: With the subject's weight on the left foot, a vertical fold on the front of the right thigh halfway between the hip and the knee (Figure 10-10).

Regression Equations

A brief word of caution is warranted concerning regression equations which employ various anthropometric measures such as skinfolds, diameters, and circumferences for the prediction of percentage of fat and lean body weight. Usually, the criterion is body density and fat percentage derived from underwater weighing. There have been quite a number of studies conducted in which predictive equations have been derived. Many of them have been quite accurate in terms of small standard errors. However, they are population specific, which means that their greatest accuracy can only be obtained when applied to samples very similar to those in which the original equations were formulated. Perhaps a national testing program is indicated for widespread application.

Behnke and Wilmore (2) derived several regression equations using hydrostatic weighing determination of body density and lean body weight as criteria. Equations are presented involving skinfolds alone, body diameters and circumferences by themselves, and with all three variables. For example, with only one skinfold measure and body weight, an R of .931 was found for the equation for young men:

Lean Body Weight = 10.260 + .7927 (weight, kg)
      − .3676 (abdominal skinfold)

With all three types of measures an R of .958 was reported for the equation for young men:

Lean Body Weight = 10.138 + .9259 (weight, kg) − .1881 (thigh skinfold) + .6370 (bi-iliac diameter) + .4888 (neck circumference) − .5951 (abdomen circumference taken laterally, at level of the iliac crests, and anteriorly, at the umbilicus)

Behnke and Wilmore (2) also developed several equations for young women such as the following, which uses only skinfolds:

Table 10-2
Height-Weight Rating Scale

Points	Level	Difference Standard
5	Optimal	0 to + or – 4 lbs.
4	Nominal	+ or – 5 lbs. to + or – 9 lbs.
3	Minimal	+ or – 10 lbs. to + or – 14 lbs.
2	Sub-Par	+ or – 15 lbs. to + or – 19 lbs.
1	Low Deficiency	+ or – 20 lbs. to higher

Lean Body Weight = 8.629 + .680 (weight, kg) – .163 (scapula skinfold) – .100 (triceps skinfold) – .054 (thigh skinfold)
$R = .916$

Using all three measures, this equation had an R of .929:

Lean Body Weight = 1.661 + .668 (weight, kg) – .158 (scapula skinfold) – .081 (triceps skinfold + .555 (neck circumference, cm) – .141 (maximum abdominal circumference, cm)

Sloan (45) derived the following equation for predicting body density in young men:

Body Density* = 1.1043 – .00132 (thigh skinfold) – .00131 (scapula skinfold)
$R = .85$

Pollock and others (40) developed an equation for predicting body density for young women as follows:

Body Density* = 1.0852 – .00076 (supra-iliac skinfold) – .00107 (thigh skinfold)
$R = .78$

As stated before, although the equations just cited and others exhibit a high degree of accuracy of prediction, they should not be used for populations other than those from which the data were gathered. Some researchers have simply used the total of several skinfold measures as the criterion of amount of fat and as the dependent variable in studies to assess the amount of fat lost through different exercise programs. Considerable research is currently being done in the area of body composition analysis. It is anticipated that some type of body composition measurements such as circumferences and/or diameters and/or skinfolds will appear in future physical fitness test batteries.

Johnson and Garcia (25) have presented scoring scales for rating one's height and weight and body fat. While these ratings are simple and practical for widespread use, the height and weight rating scale is only a rough estimation at best of an ideal relationship between height and weight. Moreover, skill is of utmost importance in using the skinfold calipers. With these words of caution in mind, the scales are presented as follows:

Height-Weight Rating. Measure your height and weight in regular street clothes. Shoes should have the standard 2-inch heel. Now estimate your body frame size (small, medium, or large) and look at a Metropolitan height-weight table for the difference between your weight and the recommended upper or lower limits (depending on whether you are over- or underweight).

Example: Jane Doe is 5 feet, ½ inch tall and of medium frame. She weighs 125 pounds. According to a Metropolitan height-weight table, the upper limit for her height and frame is 119 pounds. Thus she subtracts 119 from 125 for an excess of 6 pounds. On the basis of information shown in Table 10-2, she determined that her weight is in the nominal level (25).

*Body Density may be converted to percentage of body fat by the Siri formula, (4.950/Body Density – 4.500)100.

Table 10-3
Percent of Body Fat Scale

	Men			Women	
Pts.	Millimeters	% Fat	Rating	Millimeters	% Fat
5	14 - less	15 - Below	Excellent	26 - less	19 - Below
4	24 - 18	18 - 16	Good	38 - 30	23 - 20
3	32 - 26	21 - 19	Average	44 - 40	26 - 24
2	42 - 34	25 - 22	Poor	56 - 48	30 - 27
1	Higher - 44	Higher - 26	Very Poor	Higher - 58	Higher - 31

Body Fat Rating. First, take the skinfold calipers and measure at the triceps on the back of the arm. Second, measure at the supra-iliac crest. Three measures are taken at each point and averaged. The two averages are then added together and compared to the scale in Table 10-3.

Problems Associated with Anthropometric, Body Build, and Body Composition Measurement

Undoubtedly, the major problem in the area of height and weight and body type classification systems is not in their use but rather in their misuse. One only has to look around and it becomes evident that people come in all shapes and sizes. Some individuals seem to be all legs with very small trunk and arms. Others have massive shoulders, arms, and chest and almost puny legs. Still others appear to be evenly proportioned. To judge them all on the same standard, as, for example, to decide whether each is overweight or underweight on the basis of a single factor such as height, is indeed ludicrous.

Growth charts such as the Wetzel Grid and the Meredith graphs can be valuable tools if employed wisely. Obviously, one must recognize that there are wide differences among individuals in height, weight, and body build that are still within the limits of normal growth and maturation. The real value of these devices lies in the recommended emphasis that should be placed on changes in growth patterns detected by the successive plottings. The other recommended feature about these charts is that the child should be evaluated in relation to his own growth pattern rather than be compared favorably or unfavorably with someone else or by some arbitrary standard.

A major criticism of age-height-weight tables is that even though some allow for differences in body framework, they do not account for differences in proportion of muscle, fat, and bone. Some attempts have been made to account for these differences, such as by using the ACH Index, the weight formula developed by Cureton (13), and studies in which the specific gravity of the body is calculated in determining body composition (4). However, specific gravity poses another problem with regard to the reliability of skinfold and girth measurements and certainly in terms of the amount of time required to obtain accurate measurements.

Among the various measures that have been taken and used to indicate nutritional status are chest width, chest depth, chest circumference, bi-iliac hip width, trochanteric hip width, shoulder width, knee width, thigh girth, upper and lower arm girths, wrist girth, and ankle and calf girths. Fat measures are frequently taken at the abdomen, the side, the chest, the back, and the thighs. The length of the body and body segments have been measured to determine standing height, lying height, sitting height, arm length, arm span, leg length, forearm length, hand width, and finger span. There are numerous other anthropometric measurements that have been studied. It is to be recalled that Sargent's profile chart for appraising the physical development of college men contained forty-four anthropometric measurements.

Anthropometry is a science requiring much

knowledge, skill, and especially practice. It is this fact that poses the biggest problem for the use of such measurements by the physical educator. Even in laboratory situations researchers have trouble obtaining repeatable readings. The use of a flesh marking pencil is of considerable value in taking successive measurements within a short period of time. But when measurements are taken days, weeks, or months later, the location of the exact body site must be repeated all over again. Even a difference of several hours can affect nearly all such measurements due to diurnal variation in hydration, etc.

The basic purpose of classification indices is to allow for more equal competition. They are founded on the premise that older, taller, and heavier children should be stronger and more physically mature than children who are smaller and younger. While this is generally true, it should be obvious that these indices are not infallible. Here again body build is an important factor. An endomorph would surely not be an *equal* to a mesomorph of the same age, height, and weight. Wear and Miller (49) suggested that students of excess weight usually are doubly penalized in physical performance tests. First, they must perform while carrying the excess weight, and second, their classification index is higher than a lighter student of comparable age and height. Therefore, they have to do more in order to achieve a similar percentile rank. Perhaps this may serve to stimulate the students to shed excess pounds. On the other hand, it may have negative motivational effects by making their task seem almost hopeless.

A Brief Summary of Research Findings Concerning Anthropometric Measurement, Body Build, and Composition

Kistler (26) reported a correlation of .81 between McCloy's Classification Index and selected track and field events. A lower relationship ($r = .57$) was obtained between certain sports skills and the McCloy Index. In separate studies, Miller found both the Wetzel Grid (36) and the Neilson and Cozens Index to effectively equate college men according to body size.

Wear and Miller (49) studied the relationship of physique and developmental level, as deter-mined by the Wetzel Grid, to performance in fitness tests of junior high school boys. They found subjects who were medium in physique and normal in development to be the best performers, and the subjects of heavy physiques to be the poorest in performance.

In the Medford Growth Study, Clarke and other investigators have utilized the Wetzel Grid as one of the many measures used in this longitudinal study. Clarke and Petersen (9) compared athletes with non-athletes in elementary and junior high school boys as to Wetzel physique channel ratings and found no significant differences. Weinberg (50) obtained significant correlations between Wetzel physique channels and anthropometric and strength tests. He also found a high relationship between Wetzel's developmental level and weight.

Gross and Casciani (22) utilized data from over 13,000 students to determine the value of age, height, and weight as a classification device for the AAHPER Youth Fitness Test. They reported that in all four groups — senior high school girls, junior high school girls, senior high school boys, and junior high school boys — the factors of age, height, and weight had practically no value, singly or in combination, as classifiers for the seven test items. In other words, each group could be considered as a homogeneous group with respect to the effects of these factors on the fitness measures.

Espenschade (17) investigated the relationships of age, height, and weight to the performances of boys and girls on performance tests. Low correlations were found between performances and height and weight when age was held constant. The author recommended the use of age alone as a basis for the development of test norms.

Somatotype ratings and anthropometric measurements were studied by Hebbelinck and Postma (23) as to their relationship to performances on motor fitness tests. Generally, the correlations between body measurements and motor performance were low. The subjects classified as mesomorphs were superior in all motor fitness tests except the 60-yard dash, and the ecto-mesomorphs excelled the endo-mesomorphs except in the shot put event. Garrity (19), in a study involving college women, found a general tendency for the subjects classified as mesomorphic ectomorphs to perform in a more efficient manner on physical fitness tests. The ecto-endomorph group was consistently low in all test items.

Studies utilizing X-ray to determine skeletal maturity have been reported from time to time in the literature. Especially prominent have been those studies conducted as a part of the Medford Growth Study. Clarke and Harrison (8) found the more physically mature group to have a higher mean in all cases where differences in physical and motor traits were significant. A greater difference was observed between mean body weights at all ages than for any other test variable. The greatest differences between means were found at fifteen, twelve, and nine years of age, in that order. Clarke and Degutis (7) compared skeletal ages and selected physical and motor measures with the pubescent development of ten-, thirteen-, and sixteen-year-old boys. Physical maturation was most effectively differentiated by pubescent assessment at thirteen years of age, but it was not as sensitive as was skeletal age. Rarick and Oyster (41) found skeletal maturity to be of little consequence in explaining individual differences in strength and motor proficiency of second grade boys. Of the four physical maturity indicators utilized, chronological age was the most important with regard to variance in strength scores. Alexander (1) failed to find any significant relationships between basketball performance measures of highly skilled women basketball players and somatotype components. As might be expected, height was significantly related to total basketball performance.

Piscopo (38) established norms and compared skinfold and other measurements of 647 Italian, Jewish, and Negro pre-adolescent boys. Among the results revealed were the following: The largest skinfold measurements and upper arm girth, thigh girth, and bi-iliac diameter measurements were found within the Jewish group, followed by the Italian and Negro groups, respectively; thigh girth approximately doubled upper arm girth measurements in all three groups; high correlations were found between skinfold sites within each group; high correlations were found between skinfold and weight, but low correlations were found between skinfold and height. Lane and Mitchem (29) reported anthropometric differences between Negro and white male university students and found the Negro group to have less buoyancy than the white subjects.

In another study pertaining to buoyancy, Malina and Johnston (30) studied age, sex, and maturity differences in the composition of the upper arm. They found fat in the upper arm to be the best predictor of weight in both sexes. Sex differences in the composition of the upper arm were found to arise essentially at adolescence due to the loss of fat in boys.

Mayer (31) provides a cogent summary of the health problems associated with obesity. In the *Physical Fitness Research Digest,* Clarke (5) presents an excellent review of the disadvantages, causes, and determination of obesity, as well as a synopsis of research with regard to the effects of exercise on obesity. Behnke and Wilmore (2) have made a significant contribution to the literature with their monograph, *Evaluation and Regulation of Body Build and Composition.* Both individuals are prominent researchers in the analysis of body composition.

Krzywicki and others (27) compared three techniques to estimate body fat and water. Body density and fat were estimated from the water displacement technique, the potassium (K) estimates, and the deuterium oxide ingestion technique. The estimations of body fat by the three methods did not differ significantly.

Weltman and Katch (51) presented theoretical justification for the use of circumference measurements for estimating total body volume and body density. They concluded that total body volume can be accurately predicted using appropriate circumference measurements. Furthermore, the derived equations for predicting total body volume, when used for calculating percentage of body fat, did not appear to be population specific. Jackson and Pollock (24), however, found systematic prediction errors when body density, lean body weight, and total body volume equations were used with different samples. They concluded that all the equations, including total body volume, are specific to the population being measured. They also concluded that when body density, lean body weight, and total body volume equations were converted to percent fat, the equations were of comparable accuracy.

Several studies have investigated the effects of exercise on body composition changes and the influence of body composition measurements on fitness test scores. Pollock and others (39) found similar reductions in weight and body composition changes for running, walking, and bicycling training regimes. The training effects were therefore independent of the method of training when the frequency, duration, and intensity were similar.

Gettman and others (21) reported a greater loss in fat for the 5-days-per-week exercise program than when subjects exercised only 3 days or 1 day per week. Milesis and others (35) compared the effects of 15-, 30-, and 45-minute exercise sessions on body composition and certain physiological responses. Total skinfold measures were reduced in proportion to the duration of the training sessions.

Mayhew and Gross (32) evaluated the effects of high resistance weight training on the body composition of college women. Measures included total body potassium, skinfolds, girths, and diameters. After the 9-week, 3-days-per-week program, significant increases were found in total body potassium, lean body mass, flexed biceps and forearm girths, and shoulder width. Signficant decreases were reported in relative fat and chest depth.

Dempsey (15) subjected a small group of obese and non-obese men to a vigorous exercise program. He observed that overweight subjects experienced significant losses of body weight and body fat and an increase in muscular mass. Neither fat nor weight loss, however, was dependent upon the initial degree of obesity. In another study, Dempsey (16) employed a multiple regression analysis of height, weight, and body fat data on treadmill performance. He found body fat, fat-free body weight, and relative weight to account for a significant amount of the total variance in step test performance.

Cureton (12) pointed out that a serious limitation in the interpretation of scores on distance run tests for children is the failure to recognize the importance of variations in body composition which are unrelated to age. Consequently, interpretation of distance run scores should recognize the influences of body size, body composition, and running speed as well as cardiovascular-respiratory capacity.

With college women as subjects, Stewart, Williams, and Gutin (47) found that although body composition is a factor in cardiorespiratory endurance, anthropometric factors had a very small influence in this population. Maximal oxygen consumption accounted for the greatest variance in running times.

Getchell and others (20) found that maximal oxygen uptake when expressed as ml/kg/min provided the highest correlation with running times for 1.5 miles, indicating that body fat had relatively little influence for that sample of relatively lean young adult women joggers.

References and Bibliography

1. Alexander, Marion J. L., "The Relationship of Somatotype and Selected Anthropometric Measures to Basketball Performance in Highly Skilled Females," *Research Quarterly,* 47:575-585, December, 1976.
2. Behnke, Albert R., and Jack H. Wilmore, *Evaluation and Regulation of Body Build and Composition,* Englewood Cliffs, N.J.: Prentice-Hall, 1974, pp. 66-67.
3. Bogert, L. Jean, *Nutrition and Physical Fitness,* 6th ed., Philadelphia: W. B. Saunders Company, 1954; 8th ed., 1966.
4. Borzek, J., and A. Keys, "The Evaluation of Leanness-Fitness in Man: Norms and Interrelationships," *British Journal of Nutrition,* 5:194-206, 1951.
5. Clarke, H. Harrison (ed.), *Physical Fitness Research Digest,* Series 5, No. 2, April, 1975.
6. Clarke, H. Harrison, *Application of Measurement to Health and Physical Education,* 4th ed., Englewood Cliffs, N.J.: Prentice-Hall, 1967, p. 79.
7. _____ , and Ernest W. Degutis, "Comparison of Skeletal Age and Various Physical and Motor Factors with the Pubescent Development of 10, 13, and 16 Year Old Boys," *Research Quarterly,* 33:356-368, October, 1962.
8. _____ , and James C. E. Harrison, "Differences in Physical and Motor Traits Between Boys of Advanced, Normal, and Retarded Maturity," *Research Quarterly,* 33:13-25, March, 1962.
9. _____ , and Kay H. Petersen, "Contrast of Maturational, Structural, and Strength Characteristics of Athletes and Nonathletes 10 to 15 Years of Age," *Research Quarterly,* 32:163-176, May, 1961.
10. Corbin, Charles B., Linus J. Dowell, Ruth Lindsey, and Homer Tolson, *Concepts in Physical Education,* 2nd ed., Dubuque, Iowa: Wm. C. Brown Company, 1974, pp. 43-46.
11. _____ , and Philip Pletcher, "Diet and Physical Activity Patterns of Obese and Non-Obese Elementary School Children," *Research Quarterly,* 39:922-928, December, 1968.
12. Cureton, Kirk J., and others, "Determinants of Distance Running Performance in Children: Analysis of a Path Model," *Research Quarterly,* 48:270-279, May, 1977.
13. Cureton, Thomas K., *Physical Fitness Appraisal and Guidance,* St. Louis: C. V. Mosby Company, 1947, Chapter 5.
14. _____ , "Body Build as a Framework of Reference for Interpreting Physical Fitness and Athletic Performance," *Research Quarterly Supplement,* 12:301-330, May, 1941.
15. Dempsey, Jerry A., "Anthropometrical Observations on Obese and Nonobese Young Men Undergoing a Program of Vigorous Physical Exercise," *Research Quarterly,* 35:275-287, October, 1964.
16. _____ , "Relationship Between Obesity and Treadmill Performance in Sedentary and Ac-

tive Young Men," *Research Quarterly,* 35: 288-297, October, 1964.

17. Espenschade, Anna S., "Restudy of Relationships Between Physical Performances of School Children and Age, Height, and Weight," *Research Quarterly,* 34:144-153, May, 1963.

18. Franzen, Raymond, and George Palmer, *The ACH Index of Nutritional Status,* New York: American Child Health Association, 1934.

19. Garrity, H. Marie, "Relationship of Somatotypes of College Women to Physical Fitness Performance," *Research Quarterly,* 37:340-352, October, 1966.

20. Getchell, LeRoy H., Donald Kirkendall, and Gwen Robbins, "Prediction of Maximal Oxygen Uptake in Young Adult Women Joggers," *Research Quarterly,* 48:61-67, March, 1977.

21. Gettman, Larry R., and others, "Physiological Responses of Men to 1-, 3-, and 5-Day-per-Week Training Programs," *Research Quarterly,* 47:638-646, December, 1976.

22. Gross, Elmer A., and Jerome A. Casciani, "Value of Age, Height, and Weight as a Classification Device for Secondary School Students in the Seven AAHPER Youth Fitness Tests," *Research Quarterly,* 33:51-58, March, 1962.

23. Hebbelinck, Marcel, and Johan W. Postma, "Anthropometric Measurements, Somatotype Ratings, and Certain Motor Fitness Tests of Physical Education Majors in South Africa," *Research Quarterly,* 34:327-334, October, 1963.

24. Jackson, Andrew S., and Michael L. Pollock, "Prediction Accuracy of Body Density, Lean Body Weight and Total Body Volume Equations," *Medicine and Science in Sports,* 9:197-201, Winter, 1977.

25. Johnson, Barry L., and Mary Jane Garcia, *Fitness and Performance for Everyone,* Portland, Tex.: Brown and Littleman Books, 1977.

26. Kistler, Joy W., "A Comparative Study of Methods for Classifying Pupils," *Research Quarterly,* 5:42-48, March, 1934.

27. Krzywicki, Harry J., and others, "A Comparison of Methods for Estimating Human Body Composition," *The American Journal of Clinical Nutrition,* 27:1380-1385, December, 1974.

28. Lamb, Lawrence E. (ed.), *The Health Letter,* Vol. 5, No. 4, February 28, 1975.

29. Lane, Elizabeth C., and John C. Mitchem, "Buoyancy as Predicted by Certain Anthropometric Measurements," *Research Quarterly,* 35:21-28, March, 1964.

30. Malina, Robert M., and Francis E. Johnston, "Significance of Age, Sex, and Maturity Differences in Upper Arm Composition," *Research Quarterly,* 38:219-230, May, 1967.

31. Mayer, Jean, *Overweight Causes, Cost and Control,* Englewood Cliffs, N.J.: Prentice-Hall, 1968.

32. Mayhew, J. L., and P. M. Gross, "Body Composition Changes in Young Women with High Resistance Weight Training," *Research Quarterly,* 45:433-439, December, 1974.

33. McCloy, C. H., *The Measurement of Athletic Power,* New York: A. S. Barnes and Company, 1932.

34. Meredith, Howard V., "A Physical Growth Record for Use in Elementary and High Schools," *American Journal of Public Health,* 39:878-885, July, 1949.

35. Milesis, Chris A., and others, "Effects of Different Durations of Physical Training on Cardiorespiratory Function, Body Composition, and Serum Lipids," *Research Quarterly,* 47:716-725, December, 1976.

36. Miller, Kenneth D., "The Wetzel Grid as a Performance Classifier with College Men," *Research Quarterly,* 22:63-70, March, 1951.

37. Neilson, N. P., and Frederick W. Cozens, *Achievement Scales in Physical Education Activities for Boys and Girls in Elementary and Junior High Schools,* New York: A. S. Barnes and Company, 1934.

38. Piscopo, John, "Skinfold and Other Anthropometric Measurements of Pre-adolescent Boys from Three Ethnic Groups," *Research Quarterly,* 33:255-264, May, 1962.

39. Pollock, Michael L., and others, "Effects of Mode of Training on Cardiovascular Function and Body Composition of Adult Men," *Medicine and Science in Sports,* 7:139-145, Summer, 1975.

40. _____, and others, "Prediction of Body Density in Young and Middle-Aged Women," *Journal of Applied Physiology,* 38:745-749, 1975.

41. Rarick, G. Lawrence, and Nancy Oyster, "Physical Maturity, Muscular Strength, and Motor Performance of Young School-Age Boys," *Research Quarterly,* 35:522-531, December, 1964.

42. Sheldon, William H., *Atlas of Men,* New York: Harper and Brothers, 1954.

43. _____, S. S. Stevens, and W. B. Tucker, *The Varieties of Human Physique,* New York: Harper and Brothers, 1940.

44. Siri, W. E., "Gross Composition of the Body," *Advances in Biological and Medical Physics,* (J. H. Lawrence and C. A. Tobias, eds.), New York: Academic Press, 1956.

45. Sloan, A. W., "Estimation of Body Fat in Young Men," *Journal of Applied Physiology,* 23:311-315, 1967.

46. Smithells, Philip A., and Peter E. Cameron, *Principles of Evaluation in Physical Education,* New York: Harper and Brothers, 1962, pp. 334-340.

47. Stewart, Kerry J., Christine M. Williams, and Bernard Gutin, "Determination of Cardiorespiratory Endurance in College Women," *Research Quarterly,* 48:413-419, May, 1977.

48. Wamsley, J. R., and J. E. Roberts, "Body Composition of USAF Flying Personnel," *Aerospace Medicine,* 34:403-405.

49. Wear, C. L., and Kenneth Miller, "Relationship of Physique and Developmental Level to Physical Performance," *Research Quarterly,* 33:615-631, December, 1962.

50. Weinberg, Herbert A., "Structural, Strength and Maturity Characteristics as Related to Aspects of the Wetzel Grid for Boys Nine Through Fifteen Years of Age" (Microcarded doctoral dissertation, University of Oregon, 1964.)

51. Weltman, Arthur, and Victor Katch, "Preferential Use of Casing (Girth) Measures for Estimating Body Volume and Density," *Journal of Applied Physiology,* 38:560-563, March, 1975.

52. Wetzel, Norman C., *The Treatment of Growth Failure in Children,* Cleveland: National Education Association Service, 1948.

53. Willgoose, Carl E., *Evaluation in Health Education and Physical Education,* New York: McGraw-Hill Book Company, 1961, Chapter 13.

54. Wilmore, Jack H., *Athletic Training and Physical Fitness,* Boston: Allyn and Bacon, 1976, p. 202.

55. _____ , "The Role of Health and Physical Education," Symposium on Overweight and Obesity, AAHPER Convention, Anaheim, California, 1974.

56. Zuti, William B., "Effects of Diet and Exercise on Body Composition of Adult Women During Weight Reduction" (Doctoral dissertation, Kent State University, 1972).

Chapter Eleven

Physical Fitness Test Batteries

The preceding chapters of Part Three have presented a variety of specific test items dealing with each phase of physical fitness as visualized by your authors. Now we are ready to look at some of the possible combinations of test items as suggested physical fitness test batteries. Two primary criteria have been used in suggesting the following batteries: (a) that test items not require expensive equipment and (b) that each test battery be composed of at least one item from each of the five areas of physical fitness. This second criterion means that there will be at least one test item from each of the components of *strength, muscular endurance, flexibility, cardiovascular endurance,* and from the height-weight or *body composition* area.

As was pointed out in the introduction to Part Three, we know of no physical fitness battery which has included test items for all five of the areas of physical fitness, and further, a large majority of the attempts to establish physical fitness tests have resulted in a mixture of physical fitness items and motor performance items. Thus, the following batteries are suggested for experimental use at specific school levels during the next few years.

Anyone who attempts to establish a single test battery that purports to encompass several specific abilities is vulnerable to heaps of criticism. Such a person is immediately accused of making value judgments and certain assumptions that are virtually impossible to defend on a strict scientific basis. In the first place, to a certain extent that person is overtly or covertly assuming a generality of abilities or performances which is not supported by research. For example, if only one strength or endurance item is proposed in the battery, is he not assuming that this is representative of "total" body strength or endurance? Furthermore, for every test that is offered, there could be limitless debate over its relative merits and weaknesses, with other tests then offered in its place. Certainly any selection is a reflection of the individual's philosophy and bias. (Your authors by no means agree with each other 100 percent on the various items.)

The proposed test batteries that follow have not been developed through any statistical selection process. Our primary assumption is that each test is a valid and reliable *indicator* of each quality, but certainly not the only one. Furthermore, the components themselves are not mutually exclusive. Muscular endurance, for example, enters into cardiovascular testing, and vice versa; and strength is involved in any measure of fitness, whether it be muscular endurance, flexibility, or cardiovascular endurance. We have tried to remain mindful of the criterion of practical application as well as the other criteria of test evaluation and selection. We have selected tests that have already been described in preceding chapters. The equipment that is needed is inexpensive and easily acquired regardless of budget.

The reader will immediately note that we usually suggest alternatives for each test. This exemplifies our philosophy of measurement and evaluation. We believe a teacher should not feel bound to use only those specific tests that are recommended by his or her department, the school system, state, a particular textbook, or whatever the source might be. *No single test is that good.* Effective evaluation of specific qualities or of a general concept such as physical fitness is dependent upon a number of measurements and judgments, not upon any one test.

Combinations of Tests

Elementary School Physical Fitness Test

Objective: To determine the physical fitness level of elementary school students.
Sex and Age Level: Satisfactory for boys and girls of six to eleven years.
Reliability: See each individual test item.
Objectivity: See each individual test item.
Validity: See each individual test item.
Test Equipment and Materials: See each individual test item.
Test Items:
Strength: Overhead pull test—presented in Chapter 7.
Muscular Endurance: Modified push-ups — presented in Chapter 8. Bent-knee sit-ups — presented in Chapter 8.
Flexibility: Modified sit-and-reach or trunk-and-neck extension—presented in Chapter 6.
Cardiovascular Endurance: Six hundred yard run-walk—presented in Chapter 9.
Scoring: It is recommended that local norms be established and that scoring be patterned in a similar fashion to that appearing in Table 11-4. Limited elementary norms appear in Table 11-1.

Junior High School Physical Fitness Test

Objective: To determine the physical fitness level of junior high school students.
Sex and Age Level: Satisfactory for boys and girls of twelve to fourteen years.
Reliability: See each individual test item.
Objectivity: See each individual test item.
Validity: See each individual test item.
Test Equipment and Materials: See each individual test item.
Test Items:
Strength: Boys—spring scale press test—presented in Chapter 7. Girls—two hand push test (spring scale)—presented in Chapter 7.
Muscular Endurance: Boys—chin-up or spring scale repetitive press test—presented in Chapter 8. Girls—flexed-arm hang or spring scale repetitive press test—presented in Chapter 8. Boys and girls—bent-knee sit-ups—presented in Chapter 8.
Flexibility: Boys and girls—modified sit-and-reach or trunk-and-neck extension—presented in Chapter 6.
Cardiovascular Endurance: Boys—600-yard run-walk or a 6- or 8-minute run-walk test scored in the same manner as the 12-minute run-walk test — presented in Chapter 9. Girls—600-yard run-walk or cardiovascular efficiency test presented in Chapter 9.
Scoring: It is recommended that local norms be established and that scoring be patterned in a similar fashion to that appearing in Table 11-4. Limited junior high norms appear in Table 11-2.

High School and Collegiate Physical Fitness Test

Objective: To determine the overall physical fitness level of high school and college students.
Sex and Age Level: Recommended for boys and girls of the tenth grade through college.
Reliability: See each individual test item.
Objectivity: See each individual test item.
Validity: See each individual test item.
Test Equipment and Materials: See each individual test item.
Test Items:
Strength: Two-hand push test for men and women—presented in Chapter 7.
Flexibility: Modified sit-and-reach test — presented in Chapter 6.

Table 11-1
Average Scores for Fitness Performance (Elementary Students)*

Elementary School Boys

Age	Chin-ups (Reverse Grip)	Age	Sit-and-Reach Test	Age	Bent-Knee Sit-ups	Age	1-Mile Run
7	1 reps	7	15½ inches	7	30 reps	7	10:15 min.
8	1	8	15½	8	34	8	9:54
9	2	9	15½	9	37	9	9:32
10	3	10	15½	10	39	10	9:07
11	4	11	15½	11	43	11	8:45
Source: M. C. Gomez, Corpus Christi, Tx., 1974.		Source: Mary J. Garcia, Corpus Christi, Tx., 1974.		Source: M. C. Gomez, Corpus Christi, Tx., 1974.		Source: M. C. Gomez, Corpus Christi, Tx., 1974.	

Evaluation: These norms reflect only average scores for each age listed. Furthermore, the scores were gathered from students who, in some cases, were not in a high state of physical fitness.

Objective: Parents and teachers should use these norms to determine weak performance areas and to encourage children to train specifically to far exceed the scores listed.

Elementary School Girls

Age	Flexed-Arm Hang	Age	Sit-and-Reach Test	Age	Bent-Knee Sit-ups	Age	1-Mile Run
7	7.30 sec.	7	17¾ inches	7	24 reps	7	12:05 min.
8	6.70	8	18	8	26	8	11:38
9	6.26	9	18¼	9	28	9	11:03
10	6.86	10	18½	10	29	10	10:30
11	6.60	11	18¾	11	32	11	9:59
Source: Dr. Jim DiNucci, S.F.A. Univ., Nacogdoches, Tx.		Source: Same as above.		Source: Same as above.		Source: Same as above.	

*Reproduced by permission of the authors. Source: *Fitness and Performance for Everyone,* by Barry L. Johnson and Mary J. Garcia, Brown & Littleman Books, Portland, Tx., 1977.

Table 11-2
Average Scores for Fitness Performance (Junior High Students)*

Junior High Boys

Age	Chin-ups Test	Age	Sit-and-Reach Test	Age	Bent-Knee Sit-ups	Age	12-Min. Run
12	4 reps	12	16 inches	12	46 reps	12	1.25 miles
13	5	13	16½	13	46	13	1.28
14	6	14	17	14	48	14	1.30
Source: M. C. Gomez, Corpus Christi, Tx., 1974.		Source: Bob Stumiller and Larry Mangum, Corpus Christi, Tx., 1974.		Source: M. C. Gomez, Corpus Christi, Tx., 1974.		Source: M. C. Gomez, Corpus Christi, Tx., 1974.	

Evaluation: These norms reflect only average scores for each age listed. Furthermore, the scores were gathered from students who, in some cases, were not in a high state of physical fitness.

Objective: Parents and teachers should use these norms to determine weak performance areas and to encourage students to train specifically to far exceed the scores listed.

Junior High Girls

Age	Flexed-Arm Hang	Age	Sit-and-Reach Test	Age	Bent-Knee Sit-ups	Age	12-Min. Run
12	6.25 sec.	12	18¾ inches	12	33 reps	12	1.15 miles
13	13.89	13	19	13	35	13	1.18
14	7.74	14	19¼	14	36	14	1.21
Source: Dr. Jim DiNucci, S.F.A. Univ. Nacogdoches, Tx.		Source: M. C. Gomez, Corpus Christi, Tx., 1974.		Source: Same as above.		Source: Same as above.	

*Reproduced by permission of the authors. Source: *Fitness and Performance for Everyone* by Barry L. Johnson and Mary J. Garcia, Brown & Littleman Books, Portland, Tx., 1977.

Table 11-3
Average Scores for Fitness Performance (High School Students)*

High School Boys

Age	Chin-ups Test	Age	Sit-and-Reach Test	Age	Bent-Knee Sit-ups	Age	12-Min. Run
15	6 reps	15	17 inches	15	48 reps	15	1.30 miles
16	7	16	17¼	16	49	16	1.32
17	8	17	17½	17	51	17	1.35
Source: M. C. Gomez, Corpus Christi, Tx., 1974.		Source: Ed. Livsey, Corpus Christi, Tx., 1974.		Source: M. C. Gomez, Corpus Christi, Tx., 1974.		Source: M. C. Gomez, Corpus Christi, Tx., 1974.	

Evaluation: These norms reflect only average scores for each age listed. Furthermore, the scores were gathered from students who, in some cases, were not in a high state of physical fitness.

Objective: Parents and teachers should use these norms to determine weak performance areas and to encourage students to train specifically to far exceed the scores listed.

High School Girls

Age	Flexed-Arm Hang	Age	Sit-and-Reach Test	Age	Bent-Knee Sit-ups	Age	12-Min. Run
15	7.55 sec.	15	19¼ inches	15	26 reps	15	1.18 miles
16	7.65	16	19	16	24	16	1.20
17	11.02	17	19	17	28	17	1.16
Source: Dr. Jim DiNucci, S.F.A. Univ., Nacogdoches, Tx.		Source: Same as above.		Source: Same as above.		Source: Same as above.	

Reproduced by permission of the authors. Source: *Fitness and Performance for Everyone* by Barry L. Johnson and Mary J. Garcia, Brown & Littleman Books, Portland, Tx., 1977.

Muscular Endurance: Chin-up test for men — presented in Chapter 8. Flexed-arm hang test for women—presented in Chapter 8.
Cardiovascular Endurance: Twelve minute run-walk test—presented in Chapter 9.
Body Composition or Ht.-Wt. Rating: Ht.-Wt. Rating Scale presented in Chapter 10.
Scoring: See Table 11-4 for collegiate norms. Limited high school norms are presented in Table 11-3.

Other Physical Fitness Test Batteries

Although the following test batteries do not include all components of physical fitness, they are made up of items which represent two or three of the four components of physical fitness, and they do not include motor performance items.

U.S. Army Physical Fitness Test (3)

Objective: To measure physical fitness.
Sex and Age Level: Recommended for men eighteen years and older.
Reliability: None indicated in the Army guide; however, see individual test items in Chapter 8.
Objectivity: None indicated in the Army guide; however, see individual test items in Chapter 8.
Validity: According to Field Manual 21-20 (October 1957), groups previously deemed to be in excellent condition scored high on this test, while groups previously deemed to be in poor

Table 11-4
High School and Collegiate Physical Fitness Test*

Men

Two-Hand Push

1.16 - Above	=	Excellent
1.07 - 1.15	=	Good
.90 - 1.05	=	Average
.81 - .89	=	Poor
.00 - .80	=	Very Poor

Scoring: Divide body weight into weight lifted

Chin-ups

15 - Above	=	Excellent
12 - 14	=	Good
8 - 11	=	Average
5 - 7	=	Poor
0 - 4	=	Very Poor

Scoring: In repetition

Sit-and-Reach

23¾ - Above	=	Excellent
21¼ - 23½	=	Good
18¾ - 21.0	=	Average
17.0 - 18½	=	Poor
0 - 16¾	=	Very Poor

Scoring: In inches

12-Minute Run-Walk

Miles			Gym Laps
1.75 - Above	=	Excellent	32.2 - Above
1.50 - 1.74	=	Good	27.4 - 32.1
1.25 - 1.49	=	Average	24 - 27.3
1.01 - 1.24	=	Poor	20.4 - 23.6
0 - 1.0	=	Very Poor	0 - 20.3

Scoring: In miles

Ht.–Wt. Rating Scale (For Men and Women)

0 to ±4 lbs.	= Excellent
±5 lbs. to ±9 lbs.	= Good
±10 lbs. to ±14 lbs.	= Average
±15 lbs. to ±19 lbs.	= Poor
±20 lbs. to Higher	= Very Poor

Scoring

Each Excellent	= 5 Pts.
Each Good	= 4 Pts.
Each Average	= 3 Pts.
Each Poor	= 2 Pts.
Each Very Poor	= 1 Pt.

Over-All Rating

Example: Joe Doe

Ht.-Wt. Rating -	Good	= 4
Dip Strength -	Excellent	= 5
Chin-ups -	Average	= 3
Sit-and-Reach -	Poor	= 2
12-Minute Run-Walk -	Good	= 4
	TOTAL	18 pts.
	(Above average)	

23 - 25	= Excellent
18 - 22	= Good
13 - 17	= Average
8 - 12	= Poor
0 - 7	= Very Poor

Women

Two-Hand Push

.99 - Above	=	Excellent
.92 - .98	=	Good
.64 - .91	=	Average
.52 - .63	=	Poor
.00 - .51	=	Very Poor

Scoring: Divide body weight into weight pushed

Flexed-Arm Hang

37 - Above	=	Excellent
25 - 36	=	Good
10 - 24	=	Average
5 - 9	=	Poor
0 - 4	=	Very Poor

Scoring: In seconds

Sit-and-Reach

25¾ - Above	=	Excellent
22½ - 25½	=	Good
20 - 22¼	=	Average
18 - 19¾	=	Poor
0 - 17¾	=	Very Poor

Scoring: In inches

12-Minute Run-Walk

Miles			Gym Laps
1.65 - Above	=	Excellent	29.2 - Above
1.35 - 1.64	=	Good	25.2 - 29.1
1.15 - 1.34	=	Average	20.4 - 25.1
.96 - 1.14	=	Poor	18.0 - 20.3
0 - .95	=	Very Poor	0 - 17.6

Scoring: In miles and fieldhouse laps

*Based on the scores of 250 college men and 200 college women at Corpus Christi State University, 1975.

Table 11-5
U.S. Army Physical Fitness Scale*

Level	Pull-ups	Sq. jumps	Push-ups	Sit-ups	300-yd. run	60-sec. Sq. thrust
Excellent	12-18	77-95	48-60	72-85	50-44	35-41
Good	7-11	53-76	28-47	48-71	58-50.5	30-34
Average	6	52	27	47	58.5	29
Poor	3-5	27-51	10-26	22-46	67-59	22-28
Very Poor	1-2	3-26	1-9	1-21	73.5-67.5	14-21

*Modified from the Dept. of the Army, *Physical Training,* Washington, D.C.: Headquarters, Dept. of Army, Oct., 1957, pp. 197-201.

physical condition scored low on the test. Moreover, the directions and test items meet the criteria for certain components of physical fitness. Basically, this test battery is one of muscular endurance with one item (300-yard run) intended for circulorespiratory endurance. However, the 300-yard run test is of doubtful validity as a circulorespiratory test for adult men, and the 60-second squat thrust test may be substituted for the 300-yard run.

Test Equipment and Materials Needed: See each individual test item in Chapter 8, or in the case of the 300-yard run, look under the distance runs presented in Chapter 9.

Test Items:
Muscular Endurance: Pull-ups—presented in Chapter 8 as chin-ups. Push-ups—presented in Chapter 8. 300-yard run or longer distance runs—presented in Chapter 9. Squat thrusts—presented in Chapter 8.

Scoring: Five out of the six events are totaled for the individual total test score. The 300-yard run test and the 60-second squat thrust (Burpee) test are offered as a choice of one test item to be included with the other four items. Raw scores are converted to point scores by use of the scoring tables. For example, twelve pull-ups equal 78 points. See Table 11-5.

U.S. Navy Physical Fitness Test (4)

Objective: To measure physical fitness.
Sex and Age Level: Recommended for men eighteen years and older.
Reliability: None indicated; however, see individual test items in Chapter 8.
Objectivity: None indicated; however, see individual test items in Chapter 8.
Validity: None reported; however, the test items are acceptable on the basis of face validity as

Table 11-6
T-Scores for Navy Standard Physical Fitness Test*

T-scores	Sq. thrust	Sit-ups	Push-ups	Sq. jumps	Pull-ups
80-100	41-48	100-205	54-89	75-127	23-37
60-79	33-40	51-99	35-53	45-73	13-22
40-59	25-32	25-50	22-34	27-44	6-12
20-39	15-24	13-24	13-21	16-26	2-5
0-19	0-14	0-12	0-12	0-15	0-1

*Modified from the Dept. of the Navy, *Physical Fitness Manual for the U.S. Navy,* Washington, D.C.: Bureau of Navy Personnel, Training Division, Physical Section, 1943, Ch. IV.

muscular endurance items, one of the components of physical fitness.

Test Equipment and Materials: See each individual test item in Chapter 8.

Test Items:

Muscular Endurance: (a) Squat thrusts—see Chapter 8. (b) Sit-ups—see Chapter 8. (c) Push-ups—see Chapter 8. (d) Pull-ups (chin-ups)—see Chapter 8.

Scoring: The number of repetitions for each test item are recorded and compared to a T-score scale. T-scores for the five items may be added and averaged for a total test score. See Table 11-6.

The McCloy Strength Test (6)

The fitness items below were originally selected and used by D. A. Sargent in his Intercollegiate Strength Test. He also included a breathing capacity test which is not included below. These same items were again selected for use by F. R. Rogers with revised scoring for a Strength Index and a Physical Fitness Index (PFI). Then, McCloy revised the scoring and administration to some extent and left out the breathing capacity test.

Objective: To measure muscular endurance and strength as components of physical fitness.

Age and Sex: Recommended for boys and girls eight to eighteen years.

Reliability: Reliability coefficients for the items below have been reported as high as .86 and above.

Objectivity: Objectivity coefficients have been reported as high as .98 for the test items below.

Validity: Each of the items below have been accepted on the basis of face validity since they correspond to one or more of the four components of physical fitness.

Test Equipment and Materials: The grip strength test requires the use of a manuometer; the back lift item and the leg lift item require a dynamometer; the pull-up test requires a horizontal bar; the dip strength test requires a pair of parallel bars; and the push-up test requires a stall bar bench (13 inches high).

Test Items: (a) Grip strength test. (b) Back lift test. (c) Leg lift test. (d) Pull-up test. (e) Dip test. (f) Push-up test.

Scoring: This test takes considerable time to administer, and the equipment is expensive.

Pull-up—Boys Pull-up—Girls Dips—Boys

Figure 11-1. McCloy Strength Test

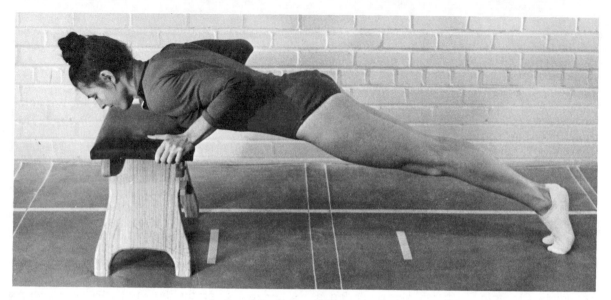

Push-ups—Girls

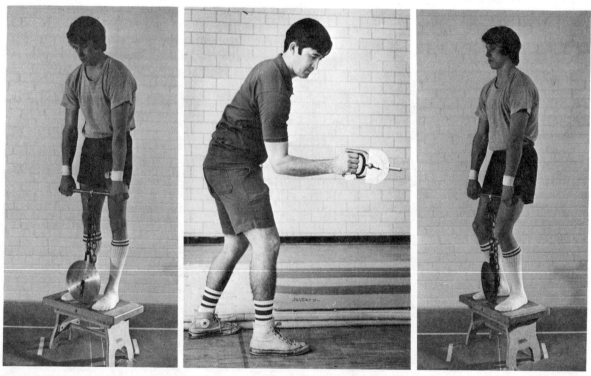

Back Lift
with Dynamometer

Grip Strength

Leg Lift
with Dynamometer

Figure 11-1 (continued). McCloy Strength Test

Since the test is not likely to be used in most high schools, the directions and scoring norms are not presented here. McCloy (4) gives a thorough description of the test along with scoring procedures and norms.

Other Fitness Tests That Include Motor Performance Items

Texas Physical Fitness-Motor Ability Test

The Texas Governor's Commission on Physical Fitness designed a test that separated fitness components from motor performance components. The physical fitness section of the test included the following items:

Chin-ups (for boys) Flexed-Arm Hang (for girls) Dips Bent-Knee Sit-ups	Muscular Endurance Items
12-Minute Run/Walk 1.5-Mile Run/Walk 9-Minute Run or 1-Mile Run (for grades 4-6)	Cardiorespiratory Endurance Items

There were no items which specifically measured flexibility, strength, or body composition (ht./wt. rating). Moreover, a frequent criticism of the test by public school teachers of Texas was that the norm tables were confusing and difficult to understand. A strong point of the test, however, is the fact that it did separate fitness components from motor performance components.

AAHPER Youth Fitness Test (1976 Revision)

The latest revision of the AAHPER Youth Fitness Test continues to be misleading in that half of the test items are motor performance items, not physical fitness items. Thus, the items included in the 1976 revision are divided and identified by your authors as follows:

Test Items	Component	Sex	
Pull-up Test	Muscular End.	M	
Flexed-Arm Hang	Muscular End.	F	Fitness Items
Sit-up (Bent Knees)	Muscular End.	Both	
600-Yard Run*	Cardiorespiratory End.	Both	
Shuttle Run	Agility	Both	
Standing Long Jump	Power	Both	Motor Performance Items
50-Yard Dash	Speed	Both	

*Options offered to the 600-Yard Run Test include the 1-Mile or 9-Minute Run for Ages 10-12 and the 1.5-Mile or 12-Minute Run for ages 13 or older.

References and Bibliography

1. AAHPER, *AAHPER Youth Fitness Test Manual,* Washington, D.C.: American Alliance for Health, Physical Education, and Recreation, 1976.
2. Clarke, H. Harrison, *Application of Measurement to Health and Physical Education,* New York: Prentice-Hall, 1950, pp. 155-85.
3. Department of Army, *Physical Training,* Washington, D.C.: Headquarters, Department of Army, October, 1957, pp. 197-201.
4. Department of Navy, *Physical Fitness Manual for the U.S. Navy,* Washington, D.C.: Bureau of Navy Personnel, Training Division, Physical Section, 1943, Chapter IV.
5. Johnson, Barry L., and Mary J. Garcia, *Fitness and Performance for Everyone,* Portland, Tx.: Brown & Littleman Books, 1977, pp. 127-130.
6. McCloy, Charles H., and Norma D. Young, *Tests and Measurements in Health and Physical Education,* New York: Appleton-Century-Crofts, 1954, pp. 129-41.
7. Texas Governor's Commission on Physical Fitness, *Texas Physical Fitness-Motor Ability Test,* Austin: Texas Governor's Commission on Physical Fitness (no date of publication indicated).

Part Four
Motor
Performance
Measurement

Chapter Twelve

The Measurement of Power

Power may be identified as the ability to release maximum force in the fastest possible time, as is exemplified in the vertical jump, the broad jump, the shot put, and other movements against a resistance in a minimum of time.

The measurement of power in physical education has recently become controversial enough to warrant recognition of two types of such measurement. The two types are identified as follows:

Athletic power measurement: This type of measurement is expressed in terms of the distance through which the body or an object is propelled through space. Such tests as the Sargent jump, broad jump, and vertical arm pull test (distance) are both practical and common tests of athletic power. While such tests involve both force and velocity, other factors also influence testing results. However, the factors of force and velocity are not measured as such; thus, only the resultant distance (inches or feet) is recorded in athletic power measurement.

Work-power measurement: In measuring power for research purposes, special efforts are usually made to eliminate extraneous movements, thus placing maximum effort on the specific muscle group to be studied. Then the result is usually based on computations of work (force × distance) or power (work/time). Examples of this type of measurement are the vertical power jump (28), power lever (31), modified vertical power jump (work) (28), and the vertical arm pull (work) (37).

Athletic power tests are quite practical for the majority of schools and have been widely used in physical fitness and motor ability testing programs. New tests, the modified vertical power jump (work) and the vertical arm pull (work), have also been developed for practical use in physical education programs and for research. Because power includes the important factors of strength and speed of movement, it may become confused with those types of tests. However, strength tests are concerned only with the force exerted or the number of pounds successfully lifted, and speed tests are concerned with the amount of time taken to cover a specified distance or the distance covered in a specified amount of time. In power tests the distance, force, and time factors should be specified, while the resistance is usually either body weight or a specified number of pounds. The 60-yard dash and the 30-yard shuttle run have been used as tests of power and this has caused confusion in an understanding of power measurement. However, since these tests are more characteristic of speed and agility, they should not be considered as power tests.

Uses of Power Tests

Several ways in which power tests can be utilized in physical education classes are listed as follows:

1. As a factor in motor ability tests.
2. As a means to motivate students to improve their status within the class.
3. As a measure for determining achievement and grades when improvement in athletic power is a specific objective in a physical activity class.
4. As a means to indicate an individual's potential for varsity athletics.

Practical Tests of Athletic Power

Several practical tests of athletic power in terms of time, equipment, and cost are presented on the following pages:

Vertical Jump (Sargent Chalk Jump) (51)

Objective: To measure the power of the legs in jumping vertically upward.

Figure 12-1. Vertical Jump Test

Table 12-1
Vertical Jump Scoring Table*

	100	90	80	70	60	50	40	30	20	10	0
Boys and Girls 9-10-11	16	15	14	12	11	10	9	7	4	2	0
Boys 12-13-14	20	18	17	16	14	13	11	9	5	2	0
Girls 12-13-14	16	15	14	13	12	11	10	8	4	2	0
Boys 15-17	25	24	23	21	19	16	12	8	5	2	0
Girls 15-17	17	16	15	14	13	11	8	6	3	2	0
Men 18-34	26	25	24	23	19	16	13	9	8	2	0
Women 18-34	14	13	13	12	10	8	6	4	2	1	0

Source: Harold T. Friermood, "Volleyball Skills Contest for Olympic Development," in United States Volleyball Association, *Annual Official Volleyball Rules and Reference Guide of the U.S. Volleyball Association,* Berne, Ind.: USVBA Printer, 1967, pp. 134-135.

*Raw scores are located in the chart in accordance with age and sex, and percentile scores are located across the top.

Age Level: Satisfactory for ages nine through adulthood.

Sex: Satisfactory for both boys and girls.

Reliability: Has been reported as high as .93.

Objectivity: An objectivity coefficient of .93 was obtained by Jack Clayton, 1969.

Validity: A validity of .78 has been reported with the criterion of a sum of four track and field event scores.

Equipment and Materials: A yardstick, several pieces of chalk, and a smooth wall surface of at least 12 feet from the floor are required.

Directions: The performer should stand with one side toward a wall, heels together, and hold a 1 inch piece of chalk in the hand nearest to the wall. Keeping the heels on the floor, he should reach upward as high as possible and make a mark on the wall. The performer then jumps as high as possible and makes another mark at the height of his jump.

Scoring: The number of inches between the reach and the jump marks measured to the nearest half inch is the score. Three to five trials are allowed and the best trial is recorded as the score. (See Table 12-1.)

Additional Pointers: (a) A double jump or a "crow hop" should not be permitted upon take-off. (b) The chalk should not be extended any further than necessary beyond the fingertips to make the standing and jumping marks. (c) The reliability and validity of the test can be slightly improved if the performer practices the jump until it is correctly executed before being tested. (c) Body weight may be included to score in terms of foot-pounds.

Standing Broad or Long Jump (1)

Objective: To measure the athletic power of the legs in jumping forward.

Age Level: Ages six through college.
Sex: Satisfactory for both boys and girls.
Reliability: Has been reported as high as .963.
Objectivity: An objectivity coefficient of .96 was obtained by Jack Clayton, 1969.
Validity: A validity of .607 has been reported for this test when a pure power test was used as the criterion.
Equipment and Materials: Either a mat or the floor may be used for this test. Marking material (tape or chalk) is needed for the starting line, along with a tape measure to mark off increments of distance along the landing area.
Directions: With the feet parallel to each other and behind the starting mark, the performer bends the knees and swings the arms and jumps as far forward as possible.
Scoring: The number of inches between the starting line and the nearest heel upon landing is the score. Three trials are permitted, and then the best trial is recorded as the score.
Additional Pointers: (a) If the performer falls backwards upon landing, the measurement is made between the starting line and the nearest part of the body touching the landing surface. (b) The jump should be practiced until the movement can be executed correctly, since validity and reliability can be improved thereby.

Vertical Arm Pull Test (Distance) (38)

Objective: To measure the power of the arms and shoulder girdle in a vertical rope pull. This test may be used to indicate potential in pole vaulting and gymnastics.
Age Level: Ages fourteen through college.
Sex: Satisfactory for boys only.

Table 12-2A
Standing Broad (Long) Jump for Boys (1)

	Age								
Percentile	9-10	11	12	13	14	15	16	17+	Percentile
100th	6'5''	8'5''	7'5''	8'6''	9'0''	9'0''	9'2''	9'10''	100th
95th	6'0''	6'2''	6'6''	7'1''	7'6''	8'0''	8'2''	8'5''	95th
90th	5'10''	6'0''	6'3''	6'10''	7'2''	7'7''	7'11''	8'2''	90th
85th	5'8''	5'10''	6'1''	6'8''	6'11''	7'5''	7'9''	8'0''	85th
80th	5'6''	5'9''	6'0''	6'5''	6'10''	7'3''	7'6''	7'10''	80th
75th	5'4''	5'7''	5'11''	6'3''	6'8''	7'2''	7'6''	7'9''	75th
70th	5'3''	5'6''	5'9''	6'2''	6'6''	7'0''	7'4''	7'7''	70th
65th	5'1''	5'6''	5'8''	6'0''	6'6''	6'11''	7'3''	7'6''	65th
60th	5'1''	5'5''	5'7''	6'0''	6'4''	6'10''	7'2''	7'5''	60th
55th	5'0''	5'4''	5'6''	5'10''	6'3''	6'9''	7'1''	7'3''	55th
50th	4'11''	5'2''	5'5''	5'9''	6'2''	6'8''	7'0''	7'2''	50th
45th	4'10''	5'2''	5'4''	5'7''	6'1''	6'6''	6'11''	7'1''	45th
40th	4'9''	5'0''	5'3''	5'6''	5'11''	6'5''	6'9''	7'0''	40th
35th	4'8'	4'11''	5'2''	5'5''	5'10''	6'4''	6'8''	6'10''	35th
30th	4'7''	4'10''	5'1''	5'3''	5'8''	6'3''	6'7''	6'8''	30th
25th	4'6''	4'8''	5'0''	5'2''	5'6''	6'1''	6'6''	6'6''	25th
20th	4'5''	4'7''	4'10''	5'0''	5'4''	5'11''	6'4''	6'4''	20th
15th	4'2''	4'5''	4'9''	4'10''	5'2''	5'9''	6'2''	6'2''	15th
10th	4'0''	4'3''	4'6''	4'7''	5'0''	5'6''	5'11''	5'10''	10th
5th	3'10''	4'0''	4'2''	4'4''	4'8''	5'2''	5'5''	5'3''	5th
0	3'1''	3'0''	3'2''	3'3''	2'0''	2'0''	3'4''	3'0''	0

Table 12-2B
Standing Broad (Long) Jump for Elementary
School Children

Percentile Scores Based on Age/Test Scores in Inches*

Percentile	Sex	Age					
		6	7	8	9	10	11
99th	Boys	56	57	68	67	69	66
	Girls	49	54	58	61	67	62
90th	Boys	47	50	56	60	61	64
	Girls	44	48	52	56	57	61
80th	Boys	44	47	54	56	58	61
	Girls	40	43	48	52	55	59
70th	Boys	42	44	52	54	56	59
	Girls	39	41	47	50	52	55
60th	Boys	41	43	50	53	55	57
	Girls	37	39	44	49	50	53
50th	Boys	40	42	49	51	54	55
	Girls	34	38	42	47	49	50
40th	Boys	40	40	47	50	52	52
	Girls	32	37	41	43	48	49
30th	Boys	39	39	44	48	50	50
	Girls	30	36	40	42	46	48
20th	Boys	38	37	42	46	48	49
	Girls	25	33	38	40	43	47
10th	Boys	35	34	39	43	46	45
	Girls	24	30	37	37	40	46
N	Boys	27	116	126	203	149	50
	Girls	31	101	113	100	82	32

Source: Donald H. Hardin, and John Ramirez, "Elementary School Performance Norms," *TAHPER Journal*, February, 1972, pp. 8-9.

*Measurements were taken to the nearest inch, and the best score of two trials was recorded.

Reliability: An *r* of .97 was found for this test.
Validity: An *r* of .80 was found when the distance score test was correlated with the vertical power pull test (work/time).
Objectivity: An *r* of .99 indicated a high degree of objectivity.
Equipment and Materials: A climbing rope, marking tape, a tape measure, and a chair are required for this test. Students are required to dress in shorts, light shirt, and no shoes.
Directions: Record the performer's name and then have him assume a sitting position on a chair or bench (seat level at least 15 inches off of the floor) and grasp as high up the rope as possible without raising the buttocks from the chair or bench seat. Concerning the grasp, the hand of the preferred arm should be just above the opposite hand. The tester should place a piece of marking tape around the rope just above the uppermost hand. The performer should then pull (without letting the feet touch the floor) and reach as high up the rope as possible and grasp and hold the rope until the tester can again place a piece of marking tape above the uppermost hand. The tester should allow each performer three trials and disregard any trial where the feet touch the floor during the pull. On the third trial, say "This is your last

Table 12-2C
Standing Broad (Long) Jump for Girls (1)

Percentile Scores Based on Age/Test Scores in Feet and Inches and in Centimeters

Percentile	9-10 Ft. & In.	9-10 Cm.	11 Ft. & In.	11 Cm.	12 Ft. & In.	12 Cm.	13 Ft. & In.	13 Cm.	14 Ft. & In.	14 Cm.	15 Ft. & In.	15 Cm.	16 Ft. & In.	16 Cm.	17+ Ft. & In.	17+ Cm.	Percentile
100th	7'11"	241.3	7'0"	213.4	7'0"	213.4	8'0"	243.8	7'5"	226.1	8'0"	243.8	7'7"	231.1	7'6"	228.6	100th
95th	5'10"	177.8	6'0"	182.9	6'2"	188.0	6'5"	195.6	6'8"	203.2	6'7"	200.7	6'6"	198.1	6'9"	205.7	95th
90th	5'8"	172.7	5'9"	175.3	6'0"	182.9	6'2"	188.0	6'5"	195.6	6'3"	190.5	6'3"	190.5	6'6"	198.1	90th
85th	5'5"	165.1	5'7"	170.2	5'9"	175.3	6'0"	182.9	6'3"	190.5	6'1"	185.4	6'0"	182.9	6'3"	190.5	85th
80th	5'2"	157.5	5'5"	165.1	5'8"	172.7	5'10"	177.8	6'0"	182.9	6'0"	182.9	5'11"	180.3	6'2"	188.0	80th
75th	5'2"	157.5	5'4"	162.6	5'6"	167.6	5'9"	175.3	5'11"	180.3	5'10"	177.8	5'9"	175.3	6'0"	182.9	75th
70th	5'0"	152.4	5'3"	160.0	5'5"	165.1	5'7"	170.2	5'10"	177.8	5'9"	175.3	5'8"	172.7	5'11"	180.3	70th
65th	5'0"	152.4	5'2"	157.5	5'4"	162.6	5'6"	167.6	5'8"	172.7	5'8"	172.7	5'6"	167.6	5'10"	177.8	65th
60th	4'10"	147.3	5'1"	154.9	5'2"	157.5	5'5"	165.1	5'7"	170.2	5'6"	167.6	5'6"	167.6	5'9"	175.3	60th
55th	4'9"	144.8	5'0"	152.4	5'1"	154.9	5'4"	162.6	5'6"	167.6	5'6"	167.6	5'4"	162.6	5'7"	170.2	55th
50th	4'8"	142.2	4'11"	149.9	5'0"	152.4	5'3"	160.0	5'4"	162.6	5'5"	165.1	5'3"	160.0	5'5"	165.1	50th
45th	4'7"	139.7	4'10"	147.3	4'11"	149.9	5'2"	157.5	5'3"	160.0	5'3"	160.0	5'2"	157.5	5'4"	162.6	45th
40th	4'6"	137.2	4'8"	142.2	4'10"	147.3	5'1"	154.9	5'2"	157.5	5'2"	157.5	5'1"	154.9	5'3"	160.0	40th
35th	4'5"	134.6	4'7"	139.7	4'9"	144.8	5'0"	152.4	5'1"	154.9	5'1"	154.9	5'0"	152.4	5'2"	157.5	35th
30th	4'3"	129.5	4'6"	137.2	4'8"	142.2	4'10"	147.3	4'11"	149.9	5'0"	152.4	4'10"	147.3	5'0"	152.4	30th
25th	4'1"	124.5	4'4"	132.1	4'6"	137.2	4'9"	144.8	4'10"	147.3	4'11"	149.9	4'9"	144.8	4'11"	149.9	25th
20th	4'0"	121.9	4'3"	129.5	4'5"	134.6	4'8"	142.2	4'9"	144.8	4'9"	144.8	4'7"	139.7	4'9"	144.8	20th
15th	3'11"	119.4	4'2"	127.0	4'3"	129.5	4'6"	137.2	4'6"	137.2	4'7"	139.7	4'6"	137.2	4'7"	139.7	15th
10th	3'8"	111.8	4'0"	121.9	4'2"	127.0	4'3"	129.5	4'4"	132.1	4'5"	134.6	4'4"	132.1	4'4"	132.1	10th
5th	3'5"	104.1	3'8"	111.8	3'10"	116.8	4'0"	121.9	4'0"	121.9	4'2"	127.0	4'0"	121.9	4'1"	124.5	5th
0	1'8"	50.8	2'10"	86.4	3'0"	91.4	3'2"	96.5	3'0"	91.4	3'0"	91.4	2'8"	81.3	3'3"	99.1	0

Figure 12-2. Standing Broad (or Long) Jump

Table 12-3
Vertical Arm Pull Test Distance

High School and College Pole Vaulters and Gymnasts		College Men		High School Boys		Junior High School Boys		Performance Level
In.	Cm.	In.	Cm.	In.	Cm.	In.	Cm.	
31 - 33¾	78.7 - 85.7	28¾ - 30¼	73.0 - 76.8	26 - 29½	66.0 - 74.9	24¼ - 26¼	61.6 - 66.7	Advanced
29 - 30¾	73.7 - 78.1	26¼ - 28½	66.7 - 72.4	24½ - 25¾	62.2 - 65.4	22½ - 23¾	57.2 - 60.3	Adv. Intermediate
25 - 28¾	63.5 - 73.0	19¼ - 26	48.9 - 66.0	19 - 24¼	48.3 - 61.6	15 - 22¼	38.1 - 56.5	Intermediate
20½ - 24¾	52.1 - 62.9	15½ - 19	39.4 - 48.3	15¼ - 18¾	38.7 - 47.6	12 - 14¾	30.5 - 37.5	Adv. Beginner
0 - 20¼	0 - 51.4	0 - 15¼	0 - 38.7	0 - 15	0 - 38.1	0 - 11¾	0 - 29.8	Beginner

Based on the scores of 25 pole vaulters and gymnasts in Louisiana.	Based on the scores of 150 college men in Texas and Louisiana.	Based on the scores of 125 high school boys in Texas and Louisiana.	Based on the scores of 65 junior high school students in Texas and Louisiana.

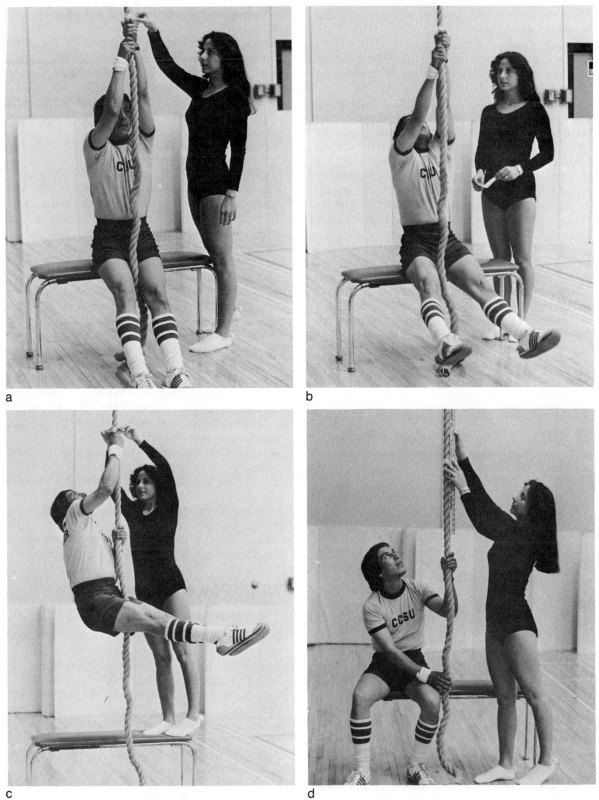

Figure 12-3. Vertical Arm Pull Test (Distance)

pull. Try to beat your last two pulls." (See Figure 12.3.)

Scoring: Record the score of the best pull (distance between the two tape marks) as measured to the nearest quarter inch. (See Table 12-3.)

Additional Pointers: (a) The tester must have marking tape ready to immediately place above the uppermost hand as it grasps the rope. (b) The performer should be instructed to vigorously pike (flex) the hips as he makes the pull. (c) The performer may close his legs in around the rope following his pull and grasp (but not before the uppermost hand makes its grasp). (d) The rope should hang directly downward so that it touches the front edge of the chair between the legs of the performer. (e) As the performer's seat leaves the chair, the tester may step upon the chair to mark the heights of the performer's reach. (f) From the starting position, the uppermost hand will be the pulling hand; the lower hand will become the reaching hand during the pull. Keep in mind that this is a one pull and grasp test, not a climbing sequence test.

Figure 12-4. Two-Hand Medicine Ball Put

Two-Hand Medicine Ball Put (6 lbs)

Objective: To measure the power of the arms and shoulder girdle.

Age Level: Ages twelve through college.

Sex: Satisfactory for boys and girls.

Reliability: An *r* of .81 was found for college girls, while an *r* of .84 was found for college men.

Objectivity: Reported as high as .99 as found by Gene Ford, 1969.

Validity: An *r* of .77 was obtained by correlating distance scores with scores computed by the power formula. However, angle of release was not figured in the correlation, although it is a definite limiting factor affecting the validity!

Equipment and Materials: A 6-pound medicine ball, marking material (chalk or tape), small rope, chair, and a tape measure are needed for this test.

Directions: From a sitting position in a straight-back chair, the performer holds the ball in both hands with the ball drawn back against the chest and just under the chin. He then pushes the ball upward and outward for maximum distance. The rope is placed around the performer's chest and held taut to the rear by a partner in order to eliminate rocking action during the push. The performer's effort should be primarily with the arms.

Scoring: The distance of the best of three trials measured to the nearest foot is recorded as the score. One practice trial may be taken before scoring.

Additional Pointers: (a) Each of three trials should be taken in succession. (b) Distance is measured from the forward edge of the chair to the point of contact of the ball with the floor.

Work-Power Tests

Vertical Arm Pull Test (Work) (37)

Objective: To measure the power of the arms and shoulder girdle in a vertical rope pull.

Age Level: Ages fourteen through college.

Sex: Satisfactory for boys only.

Reliability: An *r* of .94 was found for this test.

Validity: An *r* of .76 was found when the work score (foot pounds) was correlated with the vertical power pull (work/time).

Objectivity: An *r* of .99 indicated a high degree of objectivity.

Equipment and Materials: A climbing rope, marking tape, a tape measure, and weight scales are required for this test. Students are

Table 12-4

Table 12-4
Raw Norms for Medicine Ball Put for College Men and Women

College Men Scores	Performance Level	College Women Scores
26 - Above	Advanced	15 - Above
22 - 25	Adv. Intermediate	13 - 14
14 - 20	Intermediate	8 - 12
10 - 12	Adv. Beginner	5 - 7
0 - 9	Beginner	0 - 4

Based on 100 scores secured from physical education classes at Corpus Christi State University, Corpus Christi, Tx., 1976.

Based on 65 scores secured from physical education classes at Corpus Christi State University, Corpus Christi, Tx., 1976.

required to dress in shorts, light shirt, and no shoes.

Directions: Record the performer's weight and then have him assume a sitting position on a chair or bench (seat level at least 15 inches off of the floor) and grasp as high up the rope as possible without raising the buttocks from the chair or bench seat. Concerning the grasp, the hand of the preferred arm should be just above the opposite hand. The tester should place a piece of marking tape around the rope just above the uppermost hand. The performer should then pull (without letting the feet touch the floor) and reach as high up the rope as possible and grasp and hold the rope until the tester can again place a piece of marking tape above the uppermost hand. The tester should allow each performer three trials and disregard any trial where the feet touch the floor during the pull. On the third trial, say "This is your last pull. Try to beat your last two pulls." (See Figure 11-3.)

Scoring: Using the score of the best pull (distance between the two tape marks), calculate as follows (see Table 12-5):

$$\frac{\text{Distance of pull} \times \text{body weight}}{12} = \text{foot pounds}$$

Additional Pointers: (a) The tester must have marking tape ready to immediately place above the upermost hand as it grasps the rope. (b) The performer should be instructed to vigorously pike (flex) the hips as he makes the pull. (c) The performer may close his legs in

Table 12-5
A-Score Norms for Vertical Arm Pull Test (Work)

College Men Raw Score	Performance Level	High School Boys Raw Score
491 - Higher	Advanced	431 - Higher
392 - 490	Adv. Intermediate	344 - 430
190 - 391	Intermediate	166 - 343
91 - 189	Adv. Beginner	79 - 165
0 - 90	Beginner	0 - 78

Based on the scores of 150 college men and 200 high school boys.

around the rope following his pull and grasp (but not before the uppermost hand makes its grasp). (d) The rope should hang directly downward so that it touches the front edge of the chair between the legs of the performer.

Vertical Power Jump (Work) (28)

Objective: To measure power of the legs in jumping vertically upward.
Age Level: Ages ten through college.
Sex: Satisfactory for both boys and girls.
Reliability: Has been reported as high as .977 for college men.
Objectivity: Was reported as high as .99 by Steve Long, 1972.

Validity: Has been reported as high as .989 with the vertical power jump (horse power) as the criterion with college men.
Equipment and Materials: A jump board marked off in half inches, chalk dust, and weight scales are required for the test. The subject must be dressed in shorts, light shirt, and no shoes.
Directions: Record the performer's weight and then have him assume a standing position facing sideways to the jump board, the preferred arm behind the back (hand grasping top of shorts at the back), and the other arm raised vertically with the hand turned outward and fingers extended. Holding the described posi-

Figure 12-5. Vertical Power Jump (Work)

tion, the performer should stand as tall as possible on the toes so that the height of the extended middle finger of the raised arm can be recorded. Chalk dust is then placed on the middle finger, and the performer adopts a full squat position with head and back erect and body in balance. The performer is then told to jump as high as possible (using only the legs) and to touch the board at the top of the jump. The tester must watch and disregard any jump in which balance or position is lost. The tester should record the height of the chalk mark on the jump board. Each performer is allowed three trials. On the last trial the tester should say, "This is your last jump. Try to beat your last two jumps." (See Figure 12-5.)

Scoring: (See Table 12-6.) Using the measure of the best jump (difference between the reaching height and jumping height), calculate the following formula:

$$\frac{Distance \times body\ weight}{12} = _____\ foot\ pounds$$

Margaria Anaerobic Power Test

See Appendix J.

Problems Associated with Power Testing

Several of the problems associated with power testing are listed as follows:

1. Vigorous activity prior to jumping performance tests seems to have a significantly negative effect upon performance. Therefore, more consideration should be given to rest for participants prior to jumping performance (46, 47, 48, 55).

2. Practice and coaching tips seem to affect the reliability and validity of athletic power tests due to the improved use of extraneous movements rather than of an actual increase in power itself. Thus, it seems necessary to either eliminate the extraneous movements or practice them until all movements are executed correctly before recording scores.

3. The level of motivation must be controlled so that all students are tested under the same conditions. The conditions which are usually considered standard are a knowledge of results, tested in the presence of peers, and the avoidance of cheering and other unusual circumstances.

4. The common tests of athletic power (vertical jump, broad jump, medicine ball put, etc.) are inadequate for use in experimental research since learning to perform could be misinterpreted as increased power. Therefore, such tests as the vertical power jump and the power lever should be used since extraneous movements have been eliminated.

5. There is a need for norms at all grade levels for both boys and girls on certain power tests. The norms for several tests presented in this chapter were based on the scores of local high school and college students.

Table 12-6
Raw Score Norms for Vertical Power Jump (Work)

Performance Level	College Men	College Women	High School Girls
Advanced	301 - Above	134 - Above	119 - Above
Adv. Intermediate	240 - 300	108 - 133	98 - 118
Intermediate	115 - 239	55 - 107	51 - 97
Adv. Beginner	54 - 114	30 - 54	29 - 50
Beginner	0 - 53	0 - 29	0 - 28

Based on the scores of 125 college men, 100 college women, and 100 high school girls.

Findings and Conclusions from Power Measurement and Research

Power has been measured and studied in various ways. For example, it has been studied by the following methods: (a) athletic power method where extraneous movements are not eliminated (8, 13, 22, 42, 50, 54); (b) work-power method where extraneous movements are eliminated (7, 28, 29, 30, 31, 32, 33, 34, 52); and (c) motion photography where recordings of force, distance, and time were collected to calculate power based on its mechanical principle (19, 24, 27, 39).

Studies have shown that systematic weight training can improve athletic power performance (12, 16, 20, 26). However, Muller (45) concluded that strong muscles do not necessarily indicate better performance. Since dynamic (isotonic) training was found to be effective in improving athletic power performance, it was theorized that static (isometric) training might equally be as effective. However, several studies failed to obtain gains in jumping performance to accompany static strength increases at the end of training programs (3, 5, 49, 56), although other studies have found that isometric training improved both strength and speed performance, the two important factors in power performance (15, 17, 36, 43, 44). Obviously, studies are in conflict concerning the effectiveness of isometrics because of variations in testing or training procedures. In isometric training it is important that a measuring device be used each day so that subjects will know how hard they are straining, and it is important to train subjects at the angles where the greatest force is needed in power performance. Otherwise, mediocre results are more than likely to occur.

Several studies have shown that previous activity such as basketball (47) and swimming (46, 47, 48, 55) have a negative effect on jumping tests. Therefore, rest prior to athletic power jump tests should be considered if optimum results are to be achieved.

In studying age, height, weight, and power, the following findings have been reported:

1. The Sargent Jump was found to be a better means of classifying girls for individual athletic performance, since age, height, and weight alone were found to be of little value for such classification (2).
2. Power measures were not found to increase or decrease with the increased age and growth of junior high girls enrolled in un-graded classes (10).
3. Power was found to increase during the early years until the approach of middle age, after which there was a decline in power performance (21).

A number of studies were concerned with the relationship of strength and speed to power. The results of such studies are listed as follows:

1. Two studies found static strength (6, 18, 23) and dynamic strength (6, 18, 41) significantly related to leg power, thus indicating strength as an important variable in power measurement.
2. Several studies indicated that speed was significantly related to power and that it was more important than strength in athletic performance (13, 14, 19, 22).

Concerning physical activities, McCloy (42) found the Sargent jump significantly related to the total point score of select track and field events, and Bushey (11) found a significant relationship between vertical jump scores and modern dance performance.

In studying the effects of various positions on vertical jump performance, Martin and Stull found that the most effective knee angle is approximately 115 degrees, while foot spacings should range between 5 to 10 inches laterally and slightly better than 5 inches anteriorly-posteriorly (40).

References and Bibliography

1. AAHPER, *AAHPER Youth Fitness Test Manual*, Revised ed., Washington, D.C.: American Alliance for Health, Physical Education, and Recreation, 1976.
2. Adams, Eleanore Groff, "The Study of Age, Height, Weight, and Power as Classification Factors for Junior High School Girls," *Research Quarterly*, 5:95-100, May, 1934.
3. Ball, Jerry R., and others, "Effects of Isometric Training on Vertical Jumping Ability," *Research Quarterly*, 35:234, October, 1964.
4. Barrow, Harold M., and Rosemary McGee, *A Practical Approach to Measurement in Physical Education*, Philadelphia: Lea and Febiger, 1964, pp. 147-148.
5. Berger, Richard A., "Effects on Dynamic and Static Training on Vertical Jumping Ability," *Research Quarterly*, 34:423, December, 1963.
6. _____, and Joe M. Henderson, "Relationship of Power to Static and Dynamic Strength," *Research Quarterly*, 37:9, March, 1966.

7. Bilodeau, E. A., "Decrements and Recovery from Decrements in a Single Work Task with Variations in Force Requirements at Different States of Practice," *Journal of Exp. Psychol.,* 44:96-100, 1952.

8. Bovard, J. F., and F. W. Cozens, *The "Leap Meter," An Investigation into the Possibilities of the Sargent Test as a Measure of General Athletic Ability*, Eugene, Ore.: University of Oregon Press, 1928.

9. Burley, Lloyd R., and Roy Anderson, "Relation of Jump and Reach Measures of Power to Intelligence Scores and Athletic Performances," *Research Quarterly,* 28:28-34, March, 1955.

10. _____, Helen C. Dobell, and Betty J. Farrell, "Relations of Power, Speed, Flexibility, and Certain Anthropometric Measures of Junior High School Girls," *Research Quarterly*, 32:443-448, December, 1961.

11. Bushey, Suzane R., "Relationship of Modern Dance Performance to Agility, Balance, Flexibility, Power, and Strength," *Research Quarterly*, 37:313, October, 1966.

12. Capen, Edward K., "The Effect of Systematic Weight Training on Power, Strength, and Endurance," *Research Quarterly*, 21:83-93, May, 1950.

13. Carpenter, Aileen, "A Critical Study of the Factors Determining Strength Tests for Women," *Research Quarterly*, 9:26, December, 1938.

14. _____, "Strength, Power, and Femininity as Factors Influencing the Athletic Performance of College Women," *Research Quarterly*, 9:120-127, May, 1938.

15. Chui, E. F., "Effects of Isometric and Dynamic Weight-Training Exercises Upon Strength and Speed of Movement," *Research Quarterly*, 35:246-257, 1964.

16. _____, "The Effect of Systematic Weight Training on Athletic Power," *Research Quarterly*, 21:188-194, October, 1950.

17. Clarke, David F., "The Effect of Prescribed Exercise on Strength, Speed, and Endurance in Swimming the Crawl Stroke" (Microcarded master's thesis, Central Michigan University, 1965).

18. Costill, David L., S. J. Miller, W. C. Myers, F. M. Kehoe, and W. M. Hoffman, "Relationship Among Selected Tests of Explosive Leg Strength and Power," *Research Quarterly*, 39:785-87, October, 1968.

19. Cureton, T. K., "Elementary Principles and Techniques of Cinematographic Analysis," *Research Quarterly*, 10:3-24, May, 1939.

20. Darling, Donald E., "A Comparative study to determine the Effect of Heel Raises and Deep Knee Bend Exercises on the Vertical Jump" (Microcarded master's thesis, Springfield College, 1960).

21. Dawson, Percy M., "The Influence of Aging on Power and Endurance in Man," *Research Quarterly*, 16:95-101, May, 1945.

22. DiGiavanna, Vincent, "The Relation of Selected Structural and Functional Measures of Success in College Athletics, *Research Quarterly*, 14:213, May, 1943.

23. Eckert, Helen M., "Linear Relationships of Isometric Strength to Propulsive Force, Angular Velocity, and Angular Acceleration in the Standing Broad Jump" (Microcarded doctoral dissertation, University of Wisconsin, 1961).

24. Fletcher, J. G., and others, "Human Power Output: The Mechanics of Pole Vaulting," *Ergonomics*, 3:30, 1960.

25. Fontana, Mickey, "A Comparative Study of Power in the Arm and Shoulder Girdle" (Unpublished study, Northeast Louisiana University, 1970).

26. Garth, R. P. "A Study of the Effect of Weight Training on the Jumping Ability of Basketball Players" (Unpublished master's thesis, State University of Iowa, 1954).

27. Gerrish, P. H., *A Dynamic Analysis of the Standing Vertical Jump*, New York: Columbia University, 1934.

28. Glencross, Dennis J., "The Measurement of Muscular Power; A Test of Leg Power and a Modification for General Use" (Microcarded doctoral dissertation, University of Western Australia, 1960).

29. _____, "The Measurement of Muscle Power on Evaluation of the Validity of Existing Measures of Muscle Power Used in Physical Education" (Microcarded master's thesis, University of Western Australia, 1963, p. 196).

30. _____, "The Nature of the Vertical Jump Test and the Standing Broad Jump," *Research Quarterly*, 37:353-359, October, 1966.

31. _____, "The Power Lever: An Instrument for Measuring Muscle Power," *Research Quarterly*, 37:202, May, 1966.

32. Gray, R. K., K. B. Start, and D. J. Glencross, "A Test of Leg Power," *Research Quarterly*, 33:44-50, March, 1962.

33. _____, and others, "A Useful Modification of the Vertical Power Jump," *Research Quarterly*, 33:230-235, May, 1962.

34. _____, K. B. Start, and A. Walsh, "Relationship Between Leg Speed and Leg Power," *Research Quarterly,* 33:395-400, October, 1962.

35. Hofmann, James A., "A Comparison of the Effect of Two Programs of Weight Training on Explosive Force" (Microcarded master's thesis, South Dakota State College, 1959, p. 48).

36. Johnson, Barry L., "A Comparison of Isometric and Isotonic Exercises Upon the Improvement of Velocity and Distance as Measured by a Vertical Rope Climb Test" (Unpublished master's thesis, Louisiana State University, 1964).

37. _____, "The Establishment of a Vertical Arm Pull Test (Work)," *Research Quarterly*, 40:237-239, March, 1969.

38. _____, "A Screening Test for Pole Vaulting and Selected Gymnastic Events," *JOHPER*, 44:71-72, May, 1973.

39. Koepke, C. A., and L. S. Whitson, "Power and Velocity Developed in Manual Work," *Mech. Eng.*, 62:383-389, 1940.

40. Martin, Thomas P., and G. Alan Stull, "Effects of Various Knee Angle and Foot Spacing Combinations on Performance in the Vertical Jump," *Research Quarterly*, 40:324-331, May, 1969.

41. McClements, Lawrence C., "Power Relative to Strength of Leg and Thigh Muscles," *Research Quarterly*, 37:71, March, 1966.

42. McCloy, C. H., "Recent Studies in the Sargent Jump," *Research Quarterly*, 3:35, May, 1932.

43. Meadows, P. E., "The Effect of Isotonic and Isometric Muscle Contraction Training on Speed, Force, and Strength" (Microcarded doctoral dissertation, University of Illinois, 1959, pp. 93-95).

44. Michael, Charles E., "The Effects of Isometric Contraction Exercise on Reaction and Speed of Movement Times" (Unpublished doctoral dissertation, Louisiana State University, 1963, p. 61).

45. Muller, E. A., "The Regulation of Muscular Strength," *Journal Assoc. Phy. and Ment. Rehabilit.*, 11:41-47, 1957.

46. Nelson, Dale O., "Effect of a Single Day's Swimming on Selected Components of Athletic Performance," *Research Quarterly*, 32:389-393, October, 1961.

47. _____, "Effects of Swimming and Basketball on Various Tests of Explosive Power," *Research Quarterly*, 33:586, December, 1962.

48. _____, "Effect of Swimming on the Learning of Selected Gross Motor Skills," *Research Quarterly*, 28:374-378, December, 1957.

49. Newlin, Bruce, "The Relation of Isometric Strength to Isotonic Strength Performance" (Unpublished master's thesis, University of California, 1959).

50. Sargent, D. A., "The Physical Test of a Man," *American Physical Education Review*, 25:188-194, April, 1921.

51. Sargent, L. W., "Some Observations in the Sargent Test of Neuro-Muscular Efficiency," *American Physical Education Review*, 29:47-56, 1924.

52. Start, K. B., and others, "A Factorial Investigation of Power, Speed, Isometric Strength, and Anthropometric Measures in the Lower Limb," *Research Quarterly*, 37:553-558, December, 1966.

53. United States Volleyball Association, *1967 Annual Official Volleyball Rules and Reference Guide of the U.S. Volleyball Association*, Berne, Inc.: USVBA Printer, 1967, pp. 134-135.

54. Van Dalen, Deobold, "New Studies in the Sargent Jump," *Research Quarterly*, 11:114, May, 1940.

55. Whitaker, R. Russell, "Effect of Swimming on the Learning of Selected Gross Motor Skills When the Skills and Swimming Are Performed on the Same Day" (Unpublished master's thesis, Utah State University, 1960).

56. Wolbers, Charles P., and Frank D. Sills, "Development of Strength in High School Boys by Static Muscle Contraction," *Research Quarterly*, 27:446-450, November-December, 1956.

Introduction

Agility may be defined as the physical ability which enables an individual to rapidly change body position and direction in a precise manner. Agility is an important ability in many sports activities, as exemplified in a fast game of badminton by two experienced players or by the trampolinist executing a triple twisting back somersault. By the proper use of tests which rate high in validity and reliability, it is possible for the physical education teacher to determine which individuals in class are most agile and which ones need work in agility in order to better perform the particular activity.

Uses of Agility Tests

Several ways by which agility tests are utilized in physical education classes are listed as follows:
1. As an element for predicting potential in different sports activities.
2. As a measure for determining achievement and grades when agility is a specific objective in the teaching unit.
3. As a factor in general motor ability tests.
4. As a means to evaluate results obtained from activities and methods of instruction. For example, if you were to measure agility before and after a unit of instruction in weight training, you could evaluate weight training as to whether it is beneficial or not in agility improvement.

Practical Tests of Agility

Tests of agility which are practical in terms of time, equipment, and cost are presented on the following pages.

Burpee Test (or Squat Thrust)*

Objective: To measure the rapidity by which body position can be changed.
Age Level: Ages ten through college.
Sex: Satisfactory for both boys and girls.
Reliability: Has been reported as high as .921.
Objectivity: An *r* of .99 was obtained by Doyle Hammons, 1969.
Validity: With the criterion of general athletic

*To the best of the authors' knowledge this test was first presented by Royal H. Burpee and first checked for reliability and validity by C. H. McCloy.

Chapter Thirteen

The Measurement of Agility

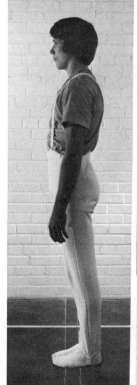

Start

and returning to the standing position is four. (See Table 13-1.)

Penalty: There is a one-point penalty for the following faults: (a) if the feet move to the rear before the hands touch the floor, (b) if there is excessive sway or pike of the hips in the rearward position, (c) if the hands leave the floor before the feet are drawn up in position number three, and (d) if the stand is not erect with the head up.

Side Step Test*

Objective: To measure the rapidity by which lateral movement can be made and changed to the opposite direction.

*This test is the authors' modification of the sidestep test proposed by H. D. Edgren in the March, 1932, issue of Research Quarterly.

Figure 13-1. Burpee Test (or Squat Thrust)

ability, an *r* of .553 has been reported for boys and .341 for girls.

Equipment and Materials: Stopwatch or wristwatch with a second hand.

Directions: (See Figure 13-1.) From a standing position (a) bend at the knees and waist and place the hands on the floor in front of the feet, (b) thrust the legs backward to a front leaning rest position, (c) return to the squat position, and (d) rise to a standing position. From the signal "go" repeat this movement as rapidly as possible until the command "stop" is given.

Scoring: The test is scored in terms of the number of parts executed in 10 seconds. For example, squatting and placing the hands on the floor is one part, thrusting legs to the rear is two, returning to squat-rest position is three,

Table 13-1
Raw Score Norms for Burpee (Squat Thrust) Test

Performance Level	College Men	High School and College Girls and Women	High School Boys
Advanced	34 - Higher	30 - Higher	32 - Higher
Adv. Intermediate	29 - 33	26 - 29	28 - 31
Intermediate	17 - 28	14 - 25	16 - 27
Adv. Beginner	12 - 16	10 - 13	12 - 15
Beginner	0 - 11	0 - 9	0 - 10

Based on the scores of 125 college men, 150 high school girls and college women, and 125 high school boys from Texas and Louisiana, 1976.

Age Level: Ages 10 through college.
Sex: Satisfactory for both boys and girls.
Reliability: Has been reported as high as .89.
Objectivity: An *r* of .91 was obtained by Mike Vining, 1969.
Validity: Has been reported as high as .70.
Equipment and Materials: Marking tape and a stopwatch or wristwatch with a second hand.
Directions: (See Figure 13-2.) From a standing position astride the center line, (a) the performer sidesteps on the signal "go" to the right until his foot has touched or crossed the outside line. (b) He then sidesteps to the left until his left foot has touched or crossed the outside line to the left. (c) He repeats these movements as rapidly as possible for 10 seconds.
Scoring: A 1-foot tick mark should be placed between the center line and each outside line to facilitate the spreading of scores. Each trip from the center line across a marker counts as one. For example, moving to the right the performer crosses a tick mark for one point, the outside marker for two, back across the tick mark for three, across the center marker for four, across the left tick mark for five, across the outside marker for six, and so on until he hears the signal to stop at the end of 10 seconds. (See Table 13-2.)
Penalty: There is a one point penalty for each time one foot is crossed over the other and for each failure to get the proper foot on or across the outside marker.

Shuttle Run (1)

Objective: To measure the agility of the performer in running and changing direction.

Table 13-2
Raw Score Norms for Side Step Test

Performance Level	College Men	College Women	High School Girls	High School Boys
Advanced	30 - Above	24 - Above	25 - Above	30 - Above
Adv. Intermediate	26 - 29	20 - 23	21 - 24	26 - 29
Intermediate	16 - 25	14 - 19	14 - 20	15 - 25
Adv. Beginner	12 - 15	10 - 13	10 - 13	11 - 14
Beginner	0 - 11	0 - 9	0 - 9	0 - 10

Based on the scores of 125 college men, 125 college women, 125 high school girls, and 125 high school boys from Texas and Louisiana, 1976.

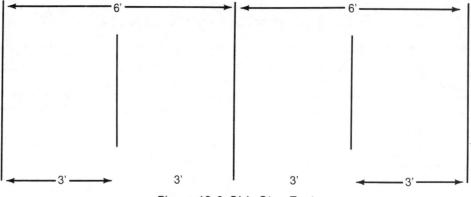

Figure 13-2. Side Step Test

Age Level: Ages 9 through college.
Sex: Satisfactory for both boys and girls.
Reliability: Not reported in test booklet.
Objectivity: Not reported in test booklet.
Validity: Not reported in test booklet.
Equipment and Materials: Marking tape, stopwatch and two blocks of wood (2" x 2" x 4").
Directions: (See Figure 13-3.) The performer starts behind the starting line on the signal "go" and runs to the blocks, picks up one, returns to the starting line, and places block behind the line; he then repeats the process with the second block. Allow some rest between the two trials.
Scoring: The score for each performer is the length of time required (to the nearest tenth of a second) to complete the course. (See Tables 13-3 A and B.) Record only the best trial.

Additional Pointers: (a) Stress importance of running as hard as possible across the finish line with second block. (b) Marking tape should be used to designate the starting and finishing line. (c) A person may touch behind the line and not use blocks since blocks may be tumbled, dropped, kicked, or thrown and thus require an additional testing or problems in standardization.

Quadrant Jump*

Objective: To measure the agility of the performer in changing body position rapidly by jumping.

---

*This test is the first author's modification of a similar one once demonstrated by a colleague in a measurements class.

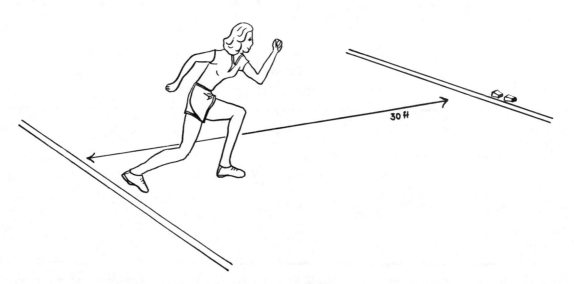

Figure 13-3. Shuttle Run

Table 13-3A
Shuttle Run for Boys (1)

Percentile	Age								Percentile
	9-10	11	12	13	14	15	16	17+	
100th	9.2	8.7	6.8	7.0	7.0	7.0	7.3	7.0	100th
95th	10.0	9.7	9.6	9.3	8.9	8.9	8.6	8.6	95th
90th	10.2	9.9	9.8	9.5	9.2	9.1	8.9	8.9	90th
85th	10.4	10.1	10.0	9.7	9.3	9.2	9.1	9.0	85th
80th	10.5	10.2	10.0	9.8	9.5	9.3	9.2	9.1	80th
75th	10.6	10.4	10.2	10.0	9.6	9.4	9.3	9.2	75th
70th	10.7	10.5	10.3	10.0	9.8	9.5	9.4	9.3	70th
65th	10.8	10.5	10.4	10.1	9.8	9.6	9.5	9.4	65th
60th	11.0	10.6	10.5	10.2	10.0	9.7	9.6	9.5	60th
55th	11.0	10.8	10.6	10.3	10.0	9.8	9.7	9.6	55th
50th	11.2	10.9	10.7	10.4	10.1	9.9	9.9	9.8	50th
45th	11.5	11.0	10.8	10.5	10.1	10.0	10.0	9.9	45th
40th	11.5	11.1	11.0	10.6	10.2	10.0	10.0	10.0	40th
35th	11.7	11.2	11.1	10.8	10.4	10.1	10.1	10.1	35th
30th	11.9	11.4	11.3	11.0	10.6	10.2	10.3	10.2	30th
25th	12.0	11.5	11.4	11.0	10.7	10.4	10.5	10.4	25th
20th	12.2	11.8	11.6	11.3	10.9	10.5	10.6	10.5	20th
15th	12.5	12.0	11.8	11.5	11.0	10.8	10.9	10.7	15th
10th	13.0	12.2	12.0	11.8	11.3	11.1	11.1	11.0	10th
5th	13.1	12.9	12.4	12.4	11.9	11.7	11.9	11.7	5th
0	17.0	20.0	22.0	16.0	18.6	14.7	15.0	15.7	0

Age Level: Ages 10 through college.

Sex: Satisfactory for both boys and girls.

Reliability: An r of .89 was found for this test when the best of two trials administered on different days was correlated.

Objectivity: An r of .96 was obtained by Larry Malone, NLU, La., 1969.

Validity: Face validity was accepted.

Equipment and Materials: Marking tape, and a stopwatch or wristwatch with a second hand.

Directions: (See Figure 13-4.) The performer begins behind the small starting tick mark and jumps both feet into 1, then into 2, 3, 4, and back to 1 again. The pattern is continued until the signal "stop" is given.

Scoring: The score for each performer is the number of times the feet land in a correct zone in 10 seconds. The best score of two trials is recorded as the test score. (See Table 13-4.)

Penalty: There is a half point penalty for each time the feet land on a line or in an improper zone.

Additional Pointers: (a) The two cross lines should each be 3 feet long. (b) One assistant should count the number of errors. The half point errors should then be totaled and subtracted from the number of jumps. (c) A performer who stops or who could obviously do better should be retested. (d) Each zone may be identified by tick marks with marking tape.

SEMO Agility Test (12)

Objective: To measure the general agility of the body in maneuvering forward, backward, and sideward.

Age Level: High school and college.

Table 13-3B
Shuttle Run for Girls (1)

Percentile	9-10	11	12	13	14	15	16	17+	Percentile
				Age					
100th	8.0	8.4	8.5	7.0	7.8	7.4	7.8	8.2	100th
95th	10.2	10.0	9.9	9.9	9.7	9.9	10.0	9.6	95th
90th	10.5	10.3	10.2	10.0	10.0	10.0	10.2	10.0	90th
85th	10.9	10.5	10.5	10.2	10.1	10.2	10.4	10.1	85th
80th	11.0	10.7	10.6	10.4	10.2	10.3	10.5	10.3	80th
75th	11.1	10.8	10.8	10.5	10.3	10.4	10.6	10.4	75th
70th	11.2	11.0	10.9	10.6	10.5	10.5	10.8	10.5	70th
65th	11.4	11.0	11.0	10.8	10.6	10.6	10.9	10.7	65th
60th	11.5	11.1	11.1	11.0	10.7	10.9	11.0	10.9	60th
55th	11.6	11.3	11.2	11.0	10.9	11.0	11.1	11.0	55th
50th	11.8	11.5	11.4	11.2	11.0	11.0	11.2	11.1	50th
45th	11.9	11.6	11.5	11.3	11.2	11.1	11.4	11.3	45th
40th	12.0	11.7	11.5	11.5	11.4	11.3	11.5	11.5	40th
35th	12.0	11.9	11.7	11.6	11.5	11.4	11.7	11.6	35th
30th	12.3	12.0	11.8	11.9	11.7	11.6	11.9	11.9	30th
25th	12.5	12.1	12.0	12.0	12.0	11.8	12.0	12.0	25th
20th	12.8	12.3	12.1	12.2	12.1	12.0	12.1	12.2	20th
15th	13.0	12.6	12.5	12.6	12.3	12.2	12.5	12.5	15th
10th	13.8	13.0	13.0	12.8	12.8	12.6	12.8	13.0	10th
5th	14.3	14.0	13.3	13.2	13.1	13.3	13.7	14.0	5th
0	18.0	20.0	15.3	16.5	19.2	18.5	24.9	17.0	0

Table 13-4
Raw Score Norms for Quadrant Jump

College Men	Performance Level	College Women
31 - Above	Advanced	33 - Above
25 - 30	Adv. Intermediate	27 - 32
13 - 24	Intermediate	14 - 26
7 - 12	Adv. Beginner	8 - 13
0 - 6	Beginner	0 - 7

Based on the scores of 75 college men and 75 college women at Corpus Christi State University, Corpus Christi, Tx., 1976.

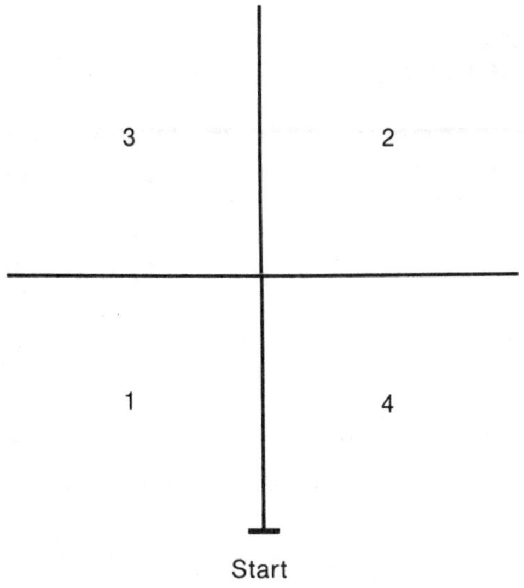

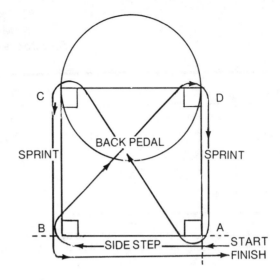

Figure 13-4. Quadrant Jump

Figure 13-5. SEMO Agility Test

Sex: Satisfactory for boys and girls.

Reliability: Using trials one and two, an r of .88 was found for high school boys and college men.

Objectivity: An r of .97 was found when the scores from two test administrators were correlated.

Validity: An r or .63 was found when the SEMO test was correlated with the AAHPER Shuttle Run Test.

Equipment and Materials: This test was designed to utilize the free throw lane of a basketball court, but any smooth area 12 by 19 feet with adequate running space around it will suffice. Four plastic cones (9- by 9-inch base with 12-inch height) or suitable substitute objects and a stopwatch are needed. The cones are placed squarely in each corner of the free throw lane as seen in Figure 13-5.

Directions: The students line up outside the free throw lane (at A). With his back to the free throw line, the performer waits for the signals "ready, go." The student should side step from A to B and pass outside the corner cone. He should then backpedal from B to D and pass to the inside of the corner cone. He then should sprint forward from D to A and pass outside the corner cone. He should then backpedal from A to C and pass to the inside of the corner cone. He should then sprint forward from C to B and pass outside of the corner cone. He should then side step from B to the finish line at A.

Scoring: The best of two trials (recorded to the nearest 1/10 second) is recorded as the score.

Additional Pointers: (a) In performing the side step, the crossover step cannot be used. (b) In performing the backpedal, the student must keep his back perpendicular to an imaginary line connecting the corner cones. (c) Although incorrect procedure constitutes an unscored trial, the student should be tested until he completes one legal trial. (d) At least one practice trial should be given.

Right-Boomerang Run (9)

Objective To measure the agility of the performer in running and changing direction.

Age Level: Ages ten through college.

Sex: Satisfactory for both boys and girls.

Reliability: Has been reported as high as .93 for boys and .92 for girls.

Objectivity: An r of .98 was obtained by Steve Long, 1972.

Validity: Has been reported as high as .82 for boys and .72 for girls using the sum of T-scores for sixteen and fifteen tests of agility, respectively, as the criterion.

Equipment and Materials: One jumping standard or chair for the center station, four Indian clubs or small similar objects for the outside stations, one stopwatch, and marking tape.

Directions: (See Figure 13-6.) Upon hearing the signal "go," the performer runs to the center

Table 13-5
SEMO Agility Test
Raw Score Performance Scale

College Men	Performance Level	College Women
10.72 — Less	Excellent	12.19 — Less
11.49 — 10.73	Good	12.99 — 12.20
13.02 — 11.50	Average	13.90 — 13.00
13.79 — 13.03	Poor	14.49 — 13.91
Above — 13.80	Very Poor	Above — 14.50

Based on scores of college men obtained by Ronald Kirby, Southwest Missouri State, 1971. Scores for women were limited to a small group tested at Corpus Christi State University, Corpus Christi, Tx., 1976.

Table 13-6A
T-Score Norms for Right-Boomerang Run
Scores Are Recorded to the Nearest 1/10 of a Second

Junior High School Boys (7th and 8th Grade)

Raw Scores	—	T-Scores	Raw Scores	—	T-Scores	Raw Scores	—	T-Scores
10.9	—	72	13.0	—	55	15.2	—	38
11.0	—	71	13.1	—	54	15.3	—	37
11.1	—	70	13.3	—	53	15.5	—	36
11.2	—	69	13.4	—	52	15.6	—	35
11.3	—	68	13.5	—	51	15.7	—	34
11.4	—	67	13.7	—	50	15.9	—	33
11.6	—	66	13.8	—	49	16.0	—	32
11.7	—	65	13.9	—	48	16.1	—	31
11.8	—	64	14.0	—	47	16.3	—	30
12.0	—	63	14.2	—	46	16.4	—	29
12.1	—	62	14.3	—	45	16.5	—	28
12.2	—	61	14.4	—	44	16.6	—	27
12.4	—	60	14.6	—	43	16.8	—	26
12.5	—	59	14.7	—	42	16.9	—	25
12.6	—	58	14.8	—	41	17.0	—	24
12.7	—	57	14.9	—	40	17.2	—	23
12.9	—	56	15.1	—	39	17.3	—	22

Based on the scores of 100 subjects from East Baton Rouge Parish Schools, Baton Rouge, La.

Table 13-6B
Right-Boomerang Run Scoring Scale

College Men	College Women	Performance Level
10.79 — And Less	12.60 — Less	Advanced
11.49 — 10.80	12.99 — 12.61	Adv. Intermediate
12.60 — 11.50	14.59 — 13.00	Intermediate
13.90 — 12.61	15.99 — 14.60	Adv. Beginner
Above — 13.91	Above — 16.00	Beginner

Based on the scores of a limited number of men and women at Corpus Christi State University, Corpus Christi, Tx., 1977.

station making a quarter right turn and continues through the course.

Scoring: The score is determined by the time taken to complete the course. Time is recorded to the nearest tenth of a second. (See Tables 13-6A and B.)

Penalty: There is a 1/10 second penalty for each object touched at the various stations.

Additional Pointers: (a) Stress running as hard as possible across the finish line. (b) Stress importance of not touching the object at each station. (c) Retest a performer when it is obvious that he could have done better. (d) Allow the students to jog through it once to become familiar with the pattern.

LSU Agility Obstacle Course

Objective: To measure various kinds of agility in one test involving zigzag, dodging and shuttle running, and squat thrusts. Due to the specificity of agility, it is believed that the inclusion of several different types of agility in one test provides a more accurate assessment of overall agility performance.

Age Level: Ages 10 through college.

Sex: Satisfactory for both boys and girls.

Reliability: Through intraclass correlation the reliability of two trials was .91.

Objectivity: An intraclass correlation of .98 was obtained by two testers with college men and women.

Validity: Face validity and construct validity are assumed.

Equipment and Materials: A badminton court without the net, seven traffic cones and a stopwatch are required. No markings are needed.

Directions: (See Figure 13-7.) The subject lies on his back with feet behind end line. When

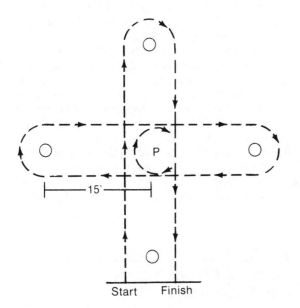

Figure 13-6. Right-Boomerang Run

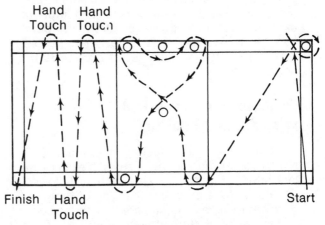

Figure 13-7. LSU Agility Obstacle Course

The Measurement of Agility **223**

Table 13-7
LSU Agility Obstacle Course Norms

	Scores in Seconds	
College Men	Performance Level	College Women
21.1 and Under	Excellent	23.0 and Under
22.3 - 21.2	Good	25.1 - 23.1
23.6 - 22.4	Average	27.4 - 25.2
24.8 - 23.7	Poor	29.5 - 27.5
24.9 and Above	Very Poor	29.6 and Above

Scores from 65 male university physical education majors and 84 females at Louisiana State University, Baton Rouge.

ready, the subject scrambles to his feet and runs to the left and all the way around cone 1. The subject performs one squat thrust, then runs to the left of cone 2, to the right of cone 3, etc., as shown in the figure. After passing cone 7, the runner performs two squat thrusts, then races to the opposite sideline and touches his hand to the floor just over the line. The subject shuttles back and forth, touching the floor twice more (three hand touches in all); the subject then races across the finish line.

Scoring: The tester starts the watch when the performer begins to scramble to his feet. The time is stopped when the subject crosses the finish line. The score is in seconds to the nearest tenth of a second. A penalty of .5 seconds is added to the score each time a subject fails to perform the squat thrust in the correct four-count sequence.

Additional Pointers: (a) The students should practice the test several times for familiarization prior to testing as scores tend to improve over the first three trials. (b) Stress the point that they must not "short cut the squat thrusts." (c) No penalty is assessed if a cone is hit accidentally.

Problems Associated with Agility Testing

Concerning agility testing, there are several problems and limitations which exist in the laboratory situation. They are listed as follows:
1. The surface area and the type of footwear seem to have a definite bearing on the scoring ability of students in certain tests such as the side step test. Perhaps this problem could be overcome by using a nonslip surface and by requiring all students to either go barefooted or wear the same type shoes.
2. It requires considerable time to administer certain agility tests to large groups. Two or more test stations are advised.
3. Too many of the tests concerning agility involve running ability or the ability to change body position rapidly as initiated by the legs. In the opinion of the authors there is a need for more tests which make use of various body parts.
4. Several of the agility tests do not scatter scores widely enough to give a definite distinction between good and poor performance. Thus, further efforts are needed to overcome this problem.
5. The side step test possibly gives the taller student an unfair advantage, since he has to take fewer steps to cross the side lines than the shorter student. Perhaps this could be overcome by varying the side lines from the center line in accordance with each subject's height.
6. Agility is quite specific to the type of agility being measured. In other words, one type of agility such as the shuttle run does not correlate highly with another such as the squat thrust.

Findings and Conclusions from Agility Measurement and Research

In the past it was generally believed that agility was almost entirely dependent upon one's heritage; however, measurement and research revealed that it could be improved through practice, training, and instruction (3, 5, 14, 20).

Seils (24), in testing primary-grade children, found a moderately high positive correlation between physical growth and agility performance in boys and girls. Espenschade (8) noted that both boys and girls increase in agility performance up to 14 years of age, after which girls seem to decline while boys rapidly gain in agility performance.

Concerning body types, there is general agreement among investigators that endomorphs (fatty types) have the least potential of the somatotypes concerning performance in agility (4, 7, 21, 25). However, some disagreement exists concerning whether mesomorphs (muscular types) are superior to ectomorphs (thin types). While Sills (25) found the mesomorphs superior, Bookwalter (4) noted that thin boys of average size perform better than medium physique boys of average size. Moreover, Solley (26) found no significant evidence to support the claim that boys who are big for their age or small for their age may be expected to perform better or worse on agility items.

Numerous investigators have indicated the importance of agility as a factor in the prediction of motor ability and/or sports ability (6, 9, 10, 11, 15, 16, 17). Agility seems to be fundamental to skill in certain sports activities (2, 19, 22). Mohr and Haverstick (19) found significant associations between volleying skill in volleyball and agility, while Hoskins (10), Lehsten (16), and Johnson (11) found agility important to basketball performance.

For many years, physical educators and coaches generally felt that muscular development associated with weight training was harmful to skill coordination. However, in recent years, investigators have elicited results which indicate that progressive resistance exercises tend to affect favorably the coordination of performers (5, 13, 20).

References and Bibliography

1. AAHPER, *AAHPER Youth Fitness Test Manual,* Washington, D.C.: American Alliance for Health, Physical Education, and Recreation, 1976, pp. 32, 40, 48.
2. Beise, Dorothy, and Virginia Peasely, "The Relation of Reaction Time, Speed, and Agility of Big Muscle Groups to Certain Sports Skills," *Research Quarterly,* 18:133-142, March, 1937.
3. Bennett, Colleen L., "Relative Contributions of Modern Dance, Folk Dance, Basketball, and Swimming to Motor Abilities of College Women," *Research Quarterly,* 27:256-257, October, 1956.
4. Bookwalter, Karl W., and others, "The Relationship of Body Size and Shape to Physical Performance," *Research Quarterly,* 23:279, October, 1952.
5. Calvin, Sidney, "Effects of Progressive Resistive Exercises on the Motor Coordination of Boys," *Research Quarterly,* 30:387, December, 1958.
6. Carruth, Wincie Ann, "An Analysis of Motor Ability and Its Relationship to Constitutional Body Patterns of College Women" (Unpublished doctoral dissertation, New York University, 1952).
7. Cureton, Thomas, K., "Body Build and a Framework for Interpreting Physical Fitness and Athletic Performance," *Research Quarterly,* 12:301-330, March, 1941.
8. Espenschade, Anna, "Development of Motor Coordination in Boys and Girls," *Research Quarterly,* 18:30-43, March, 1947.
9. Gates, D. P., and R. P. Sheffield, "Tests of Change of Direction as Measurement of Different Kinds of Motor Ability in Boys of the 7th, 8th, and 9th Grades," *Research Quarterly,* 11:3, 136-147, October, 1940.
10. Hoskins, Robert N., "The Relationships of Measurements of General Motor Capacity to the Learning of Specific Psycho-Motor Skills," *Research Quarterly,* 5:63-72, March, 1934.
11. Johnson, L. William, "Objective Basketball Tests for High School Boys" (Unpublished master's thesis, University of Iowa, 1934).
12. Kirby, Ronald F., "A Simple Test of Agility," *Coach and Athlete,* June, 1971, pp. 30-31.
13. Kurt, Charles P., "The Effect of Weight Training on Hand-Eye Coordination, Balance, and Response Time" (Microcarded master's thesis, State University of Iowa, 1956, p. 26).
14. Lafuze, Marion, "A Study of the Learning of Fundamental Skills by College Freshmen Women of Low Motor Ability," *Research Quarterly,* 22:149-157, May, 1951.
15. Lerson, Leonard, "A Factor Analysis of Motor Ability Variables and Tests, with Tests for College Men," *Research Quarterly,* 12:499-517, October, 1941.
16. Lehsten, Nelson, "A Measure of Basketball Skills for High School Boys," *Physical Educator,* 5:103-109, December, 1948.
17. McCloy, Charles H., "Blocks Test of Multiple Response," *Psychometrika,* 7:165-169, September, 1942.
18. _____, and Norma D. Young, *Tests and Measurements in Health and Physical Education,* Appleton-Century-Crofts, New York, 1954, p. 78.
19. Mohr, Dorothy R., and Martha L. Haverstick,

"Relationship between Height, Jumping Ability and Ability to Volleyball Skill," *Research Quarterly,* 27:74, March, 1956.

20. Moseley, J. W., A. Hairaedian, and D. N. Donelson, "Weight Training in Relation to Strength, Speed, and Co-ordination," *Research Quarterly,* 24:308-315, October, 1953.

21. Perbis, Joyce A., "Relationships Between Somatotype and Motor Fitness in Women," *Research Quarterly,* 25:84, March, 1954.

22. Rarick, Lawrence, "An Analysis of the Speed Factor in Simple Athletic Events," *Research Quarterly,* 8:89, December, 1937.

23. Scott, Gladys, M., and Esther French, *Measurement and Evaluation in Physical Education,* Dubuque, Iowa: Wm. C. Brown Company, 1959.

24. Seils, L. G., "Agility-Performance and Physical Growth," *Research Quarterly,* 22:244, May, 1951.

25. Sills, Frank, "The Relationship of Extreme Somatotypes to Performance in Motor and Strength Tests," *Research Quarterly,* 24:223-228, May, 1953.

26. Solley, Wm. H., "Ratio of Physical Development as a Factor in Motor Coordination of Boys Ages 10-14," *Research Quarterly,* 28:295-303, October, 1957.

Introduction

The two types of tests of balance which are in common use in physical education are tests of static balance and tests of dynamic balance. Static balance may be defined as that physical ability which enables an individual to hold a stationary position. On the other hand, dynamic balance is the ability to maintain balance during vigorous movement, as in walking a fence or leaping from stone to stone while crossing a brook. There is evidence to indicate that the ability to balance easily, whether statically or dynamically, depends upon the function of the mechanisms in the semicircular canals; the kinesthetic sensations in the muscles, tendons, and joints; visual perception while the body is in motion; and the ability to coordinate these three sources of stimuli (1). Balance is an important ability which is used in our everyday activities, such as in walking and standing, as well as in most games and sports.

Uses of Balance Tests

Balance tests may be utilized in physical education classes as follows:
1. As a measure for determining achievement when balance is a specific objective in the teaching unit.
2. As an element for assessing potential in gymnastics, diving, and other individual and team activities.
3. As a means of diagnosis to determine whether there has been injury or damage to one or more of the kinesthetic receptors in the body or its parts.
4. As a factor in general motor ability tests.

Practical Tests of Balance

Several practical tests of balance in terms of time, equipment, and cost are presented on the following pages.

Static Balance Tests

Stork Stand

Objective: To measure the static balance of the performer while supported on the ball of the foot of the dominant leg.
Age Level: Ages ten through college.
Sex: Satisfactory for both boys and girls.
Reliability: An *r* of .87 was found for this test when the best trial of the initial test was cor-

Chapter Fourteen

The Measurement of Balance

Table 14-1
Raw Score Norms for Stork Stand

College Men	Performance Level	College Women
51 - Higher	Advanced	28 - Higher
37 - 50	Adv. Intermediate	23 - 27
15 - 36	Intermediate	8 - 22
5 - 13	Adv. Beginner	3 - 6
0 - 4	Beginner	0 - 2

Based on the scores of 50 college men and 50 college women, Corpus Christi State University, Corpus Christi, Tx., 1976.

related with the best trial of the second test, which were administered on different days.

Objectivity: Reported as high as .99 as determined by Jim Knox, 1969.

Validity: Face validity was accepted for this test.

Equipment and Materials: One stopwatch or a wristwatch with a second hand.

Directions: (See Figure 14-1.) From a stand on the foot of the dominant leg, place the other foot on the inside of the supporting knee and place the hands on the hips. Upon a given signal, raise the heel from the floor and maintain the balance as long as possible without moving the ball of the foot from its initial position or letting the heel touch the floor.

Scoring: The score is the greatest number of seconds counted between the time the heel is raised and the balance is lost on three trials with the preferred foot. (See Table 14-1.) Only the highest score is recorded.

Additional Pointers: (a) Students may be tested in pairs, with one performing while the other takes note of how long the performer balanced as the number of seconds are counted off (aloud) by the timer. (b) Students who failed to get started on time are retested. (c) The performer cannot remove his hands from his hips during the test.

Bass Stick Test (Crosswise) (1)

Objective: To measure the static balance of the performer while supported on a narrow surface on the ball of the foot.

Table 14-2
Raw Score Norms for Bass Stick Test (Crosswise)

College Men	Performance Level	College Women
225 - Higher	Advanced	180 - Higher
165 - 224	Adv. Intermediate	140 - 179
65 - 164	Intermediate	60 - 139
15 - 64	Adv. Beginner	15 - 59
0 - 14	Beginner	0 - 14

Based on the scores of 50 college men and 50 college women, Corpus Christi State University, Corpus Christi, Tx., 1976.

Figure 14-1. Stork Stand

stopwatch, or wristwatch with a second hand, and (c) adhesive tape are needed for this test.

Directions: (See Figure 14-2.) Arrange several performers in one line and an observer for each performer in an opposite line. Each performer should place the ball of the foot crosswise on the stick and (upon a given signal) lift the opposite foot from the floor holding the balance for as long as possible up to a maximum of 60 seconds. As the timer counts aloud, each observer takes note of how long his performer maintains balance. Have each performer execute the test six times (three times on right leg and three times on left leg).

Scoring: The score for the test is the sum of the times for all six trials. (See Table 14-2.)

Additional Pointers: (a) Tape the sticks to the floor. (b) If either the heel or the toe of the per-

Figure 14-2. Bass Stick Test (Crosswise)

Age Level: Ages ten through college.
Sex: Satisfactory for both boys and girls.
Reliability: Has been reported as high as .90.
Validity: Has been accepted for its obvious face validity.
Equipment and Materials: (a) Several sticks 1 inch wide, 1 inch high, and 12 inches long, (b) a

nating a long and short shot until the whistle blows at the end of 1 minute. He cannot run with the ball, he must dribble it regardless of how far he must go to retrieve it. He may shoot the short shot from anywhere — it does not have to be a lay-up; the long shot has to be shot from behind the restraining line. Two complete trials are given with a short rest in between.

Scoring: The watch is started on the signal to begin and is stopped at the end of one minute. A long shot counts two points and a short shot counts one point. The score is the total number of points made in the two trials.

Additional Pointers: (a) The distance from the basket for the long shot can be varied depending upon the age level and the type of shot being stressed. (b) The type of shot may be varied; for example, the teacher or coach may want the subjects to shoot a jump shot, then rush in and recover and shoot a lay-up or a short jump shot. (c) Or, the arc may be shortened to test shooting left handed, then right handed, or vice-versa, depending upon the particular student's dominant hand, with the higher point value given for baskets made with the non-dominant hand. (d) The test works well as a drill and provides for individual competition among the players while practicing, much like the familiar game of Twenty-one.

Bowling

The game of bowling is, in itself, objective measurement. Consequently, most of the work done in this area has been the construction of norms. Phillips and Summers (54) developed norms for college women based on initial levels of ability. Ratings were established for the different levels of ability as to progress at various stages up through twenty-five lines of bowling. Martin and Keogh (52) recently published bowling norms for college men and women in elective physical education classes. The bowlers were classified as experienced or non-experienced. Separate norms as to superior, good, average, poor, and inferior performance were constructed for men and women for experienced and non-experienced bowlers.

Football

The AAHPER Football Skills Tests (55)

Ten tests have been presented as part of the AAHPER Sports Skills Tests Project to measure the fundamental skills of football. Each test purports to measure a single basic skill.

The tests are the following ones: (a) forward pass for distance, (b) 50-yard dash with football, (c) blocking, (d) forward pass for accuracy, (e) football punt for distance, (f) ball-changing zigzag run, (g) catching the forward pass, (h) pull-out, (i) kick-off, and (j) dodging run. All the tests except the blocking test may also be used to evaluate basic skills in touch or flag football. (See norms on the following pages.)

Forward Pass for Distance. The test is administered and scored in the same manner as the softball throw for distance in the *Youth Fitness Manual* and the *Softball Skills Test Manual*. (Best of three trials, 6-foot restraining area, distance measured to the last foot passed, and measured at right angles to the throwing line — not arcing from the point from which the throw was made.)

Fifty Yard Dash with Football. The subject runs as fast as he can for 50 yards carrying a football. Two trials are given with a rest in between the two trials. *Scoring:* When the starter shouts "go" and simultaneously swings a white cloth down with his arm, the timer starts the watch. The time is stopped when the runner crosses the finish line. The score is to the nearest tenth of a second. The better score of the two trials is used as the score.

Blocking. On the signal to "go," the subject runs forward and executes a cross-body block against a blocking bag. He immediately recovers and charges toward a second bag placed 15 feet directly to the right of the first bag. After cross-body blocking that bag clear to the ground, he scrambles to his feet and races toward the third bag. The third bag is 15 feet

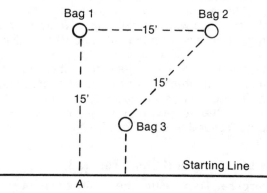

Figure 16-9. Diagram for AAHPER Football Blocking Test

former's supporting foot touches the floor, the observer should terminate the count for that trial. (c) Performers who lose their balance within the first 3 seconds of a trial should be retested due to a bad start. (d) Although a large number of trials increase reliability, the authors have found that not a great deal of reliability is lost when the subjects are given only three trials on the preferred leg. In the interest of time and application of test results, the instructor might consider shortening this test.

Bass Stick Test (Lengthwise) (1)
Objective: Same as for previous test, except place the foot on the stick lengthwise. (See Table 14-3). In this test, only the ball of the foot is allowed to rest on the stick while attempting to balance.

Progressive Inverted Balance Test (Long Form and Short Form) (15)
Objective: To measure the ability to balance in an inverted position. These test items are probably most appropriate for a gymnastics unit or self-testing activities unit.
Age Level: Ages nine through college.
Sex: Satisfactory for both boys and girls.
Reliability: An *r* of .82 was found for this test when subjects were tested on separate days.
Validity: Face validity was accepted for this test.
Equipment and Materials: One stopwatch and a tumbling mat.
Directions: The inverted balance test consists of five inverted balance stunts. Each is described and illustrated below:

1. *Tripod Balance.* From a squatting position, place the hands shoulder width apart with the fingers pointing straight ahead. Lean forward bending at the elbows and place the inside of the knees against and slightly above the outside of the elbows. Continue to lean forward until the feet come off the floor and the forehead rests on the mat. Balance in this position for as many counts as possible up to a maximum of 5 seconds. (See Figure 14-4A.)

2. *Tip-up Balance.* Same as for the tripod balance except do not allow the head to rest on the mat, but balance with the face several inches from the floor. (See Figure 14-4B.)

3. *Head Balance.* Place the forehead on the mat several inches ahead of the hands and kick upward one foot at a time and maintain the balance with the back slightly arched, legs straight and together, and toes pointed. Body weight should be primarily on the hands with some weight on the forehead. Balance in this position for as many counts as possible up to a maximum of 5 seconds. To get out of this position push with the hands, duck the head, and roll forward, or step down one foot at a time. (See Figure 14-4C.)
   Safety Tip: A partner may grasp the performer's legs and assist him to the proper position before the balance begins.

4. *Head and Forearm Balance.* Place the forearms on the mat and bring the hands

Table 14-3
Raw Score Norms for Bass Stick Test (Lengthwise)

College Men	Performance Level	College Women
346 - Higher	Advanced	336 - Higher
306 - 345	Adv. Intermediate	301 - 335
221 - 305	Intermediate	206 - 300
181 - 220	Adv. Beginner	166 - 205
0 - 180	Beginner	0 - 165

Based on the scores of 50 college men and 50 college women, Corpus Christi State University, Corpus Christi, Tx., 1976.

Figure 14-3. Bass Stick Test (Lengthwise)

close enough together for the thumbs and forefingers to form a cup for the head to fit into. Place the back of the head in the cup formed by the thumbs and fingers and kick upward one foot at a time and balance

between the tripod support formed by the head and forearms. (See Figure 14-4D.) Balance in this position for as many counts as possible up to a maximum of 5 seconds. *Safety Tip:* Same as for the head balance.

5. *Handstand.* Bend forward and place the hands on the mat about shoulder width apart. Lean the shoulders over the hands and separate the feet so that one foot is ahead of the other. With the eyes looking forward of the fingertips, swing the rear foot upward as the front foot pushes from the mat, and maintain a balanced position with the feet overhead for as many counts as possible up to a maximum of 5 seconds. (See Figure 14-4E.)

Safety Tip: Same as for the head balance.

Scoring for Long Form: The above balances carry the following weights:

Tripod—weight of one.
Tip-up—weight of two.
Head balance—weight of three.
Head and forearm—weight of four.
Handstand—weight of five.

Each balance may be held for a maximum of five points (one point for each second). To figure the total score, multiply the weight of the balance by the number of seconds it was held and then add the five scores together for the final score. The maximum raw score possible is seventy-five points. If a student cannot balance or fails to try a particular balance, his score is zero for that balance.

Scoring for Short Form: Same as for the long form except that the student chooses only one of the five balances to perform. For example, if a student chose the head balance with a weight of three and held the position for 5 seconds, his score would be fifteen points. The maximum score possible for the short form test is twenty-five points.

Short Form—Scoring Scale		
Score		Performance Level
25	—	Excellent
20	—	Good
15	—	Average
10	—	Poor
5	—	Very Poor

Figure 14-4A. Tripod Balance

Figure 14-4B. Tip-up Balance

Figure 14-4C. Head Balance

Figure 14-4D.
Head and Forearm Balance

Figure 14-4E. Handstand

Table 14-4
T-Score Norms for Progressive Inverted Balance Test (Long Form)

College Men	Performance Level	College Women
70 - Higher	Advanced	64 - Higher
59 - 69	Adv. Intermediate	49 - 63
28 - 58	Intermediate	22 - 48
17 - 27	Adv. Beginner	7 - 21
0 - 16	Beginner	0 - 6

Based on the scores of 50 college men and 50 college women, Corpus Christi State University, Corpus Christi, Tx., 1976.

Modified Bass Test
of Dynamic Balance (1, 16)

Objective: To measure the ability to jump accurately and maintain balance during movement and after movement.

Age Level: High school and college.

Sex: Boys and girls.

Reliability: An *r* of .75 was found for this test when subjects were tested on separate days.

Validity: An *r* of .46 was found when this test was correlated with the Bass Test of Dynamic Balance.

Objectivity: An *r* of .97 was found when two testers scored twenty-five subjects independently on the test.

Equipment and Materials: The equipment and materials needed are stopwatches, ¾-inch marking tape, and yardsticks. Cut eleven 1-by-¾-inch pieces of marking tape and tape them in the proper pattern to the floor. (See the proper pattern in Figure 14-5.)

Directions: Standing with the right foot on the starting mark, the performer leaps to the first tape mark with the left foot and tries to hold a steady position on the ball of his left foot for as many seconds as possible up to 5 seconds. He then leaps to the second tape with the right foot, and so on, alternating the feet from tape to tape. He should remain on each tape mark for as many seconds as possible up to a maximum of 5 seconds, and his foot must completely cover the tape so that it cannot be seen.

Scoring: The score for each mark successfully landed on is five points, and, in addition, one point is awarded for each second the balance is held up to 5 seconds per mark. Thus, a performer may earn a maximum of ten points per

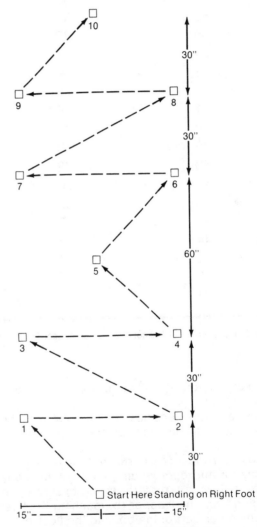

Figure 14.5. Floor Pattern for
Modified Bass Dynamic Test

Table 14-5
T-Score Norms for Modified Bass Dynamic Test

T-Scores		Raw Scores	T-Scores		Raw Scores
67	—	100	40	—	60
66	—	98	39	—	59
65	—	97	38	—	57
64	—	95	37	—	56
63	—	94	36	—	54
62	—	93	35	—	53
61	—	91	34	—	51
60	—	90	33	—	50
59	—	88	32	—	48
57	—	85	31	—	47
56	—	84	30	—	45
55	—	82	29	—	44
54	—	81	28	—	42
53	—	79	27	—	41
52	—	78	26	—	39
51	—	76	25	—	38
50	—	75	24	—	36
49	—	73	23	—	35
48	—	72	22	—	34
47	—	70	20	—	32
46	—	69	19	—	30
45	—	67	18	—	29
44	—	66	17	—	27
43	—	64	16	—	26
42	—	63	15	—	24
41	—	62	14	—	23

Based on the scores of 100 college women at East Texas State University, Commerce, Tex.

marker or a total of 100 points for the test. (See Table 14-5.)

Penalties: The penalties for this test may be classified into landing errors and balance errors.

Landing errors—The performer sacrifices five points for improper landing if he commits any of the following errors: (a) failing to stop upon landing from the leap, or (b) touching the heel or any other part of the body to the floor other than the ball of the supporting foot upon landing, or (c) failing to completely cover the marker with the ball of the foot. The performer is allowed to reposition himself for the 5-second balance on the ball of the foot after making a landing error (25).

Balance errors—If the performer commits any of the balance errors below prior to the completion of the 5 seconds, he sacrifices the remaining points at the rate of one point per second: (a) touching any part of the body to the floor other than the ball of the supporting foot, or (b) moving the foot while in the balance position. When the performer loses his balance, he must step back on the proper marker and then leap to the next marker (25).

Additional Pointers: (a) The seconds of each balance attempt should be counted aloud for the performer. (b) The landing score and the balance score should be recorded for each marker.

Dynamic Test of Positional Balance (17)

Objective: To measure the ability to land accurately and to balance while in various precarious positions.

Age Level: Ages ten through college.

Sex: Satisfactory for boys and girls.

Reliability: An r of .76 was found for this test when the subjects were scored on separate days.

Validity: Face validity was accepted for this test.

Objectivity: An r of .94 was found when two different testers scored twenty-five subjects.

Equipment and Materials: The equipment and materials needed are stopwatches, tape measures or yardsticks, and marking tape. Cut four 1-by-¾-inch pieces of marking tape and tape them in the proper pattern to the floor. (See the proper pattern in Figure 14-6.)

Directions: (a) Standing on the left foot behind the starting mark, the performer leaps to marker A, landing on the right foot, and balances in a stork stand for as many seconds as possible up to 5 seconds. (b) The performer leaps from marker A to marker B, landing on the ball of the left foot and immediately lowering into a front scale position where the trunk is tilted forward and the nonsupporting leg is raised upward (parallel to floor) in the rear. The arms should be extended horizontally to the sides while the head and chest are held high. The supporting leg should be straight as the balance is held for as many seconds as possible up to 5 seconds. (c) Return to an upright position on one foot and leap from marker B to marker C, landing on the left foot, and

Table 14-6
T-Score Norms for Dynamic Test of Positional Balance

T-Scores		Raw Scores	T-Scores		Raw Scores
84	—	50	42	—	32
81	—	49	39	—	31
79	—	48	37	—	30
77	—	47	35	—	29
74	—	46	32	—	28
72	—	45	30	—	27
70	—	44	28	—	26
67	—	43	25	—	25
65	—	42	23	—	24
63	—	41	21	—	23
60	—	40	18	—	22
58	—	39	16	—	21
56	—	38	14	—	20
53	—	37	11	—	19
51	—	36	9	—	18
49	—	35	7	—	17
46	—	34	4	—	16
44	—	33	2	—	15

Based on the scores of 100 college men at East Texas State University, Commerce, Tex.

B. Front Scale. Balance on ball of foot.

A. Stork Stand.
   Eyes open, foot flat.

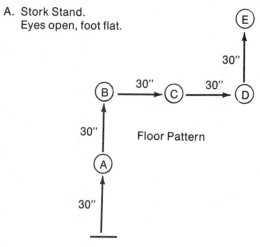

Figure 14-6. Dynamic Test of Positional Balance

C. Side Scale. Foot
flat on floor.

D. One Foot Balance.
On ball of foot.

E. Knee Scale.
One for each
knee. Foot of
supporting leg held up.

lower into a side scale position by leaning to the right side and by lifting the right leg until it is parallel to the floor. The left arm is extended along the side of the body with the hand resting on the thigh, while the right arm is extended forward. The head should be leaned close to the extended right arm. Keeping the supporting leg straight, hold the position for as many seconds as possible up to 5 seconds. (d) Return to an upright position on one foot and leap from marker C to marker D, landing on the ball of the left foot. Maintain a position on the ball of the foot for as many seconds as possible up to 5 seconds. (e) Turn and drop to the floor so that the hands will be resting on each side of marker E. Draw the left leg under the trunk and place the knee on marker E. The performer then balances on the knee as the hands and the opposite leg are lifted from the floor. The balance should be held for as many seconds as possible up to 5 seconds. (f) Exchange knees and repeat the knee balance on the opposite knee.

Scoring: The score for each marker successfully landed on is five points except for marker E, where there is no landing skill involved. There is a total of twenty points possible for correct landings. For balance, one point is awarded for each second that each of the six balances are held. Five seconds is maximum per balance. Thus, a performer may earn a maximum of thirty points for balance. The grand total for the test is fifty points. The best of three trials is recorded as the test score.

Penalties: The penalties for this test may be classified into landing errors and balance errors.

Landing Errors—The performer sacrifices five points for improper landings if he commits the following errors: (a) failing to stop upon landing from the leap, or (b) failing to completely cover the marker with the foot. The performer is allowed to reposition himself for the 5-second balance after making a landing error.

Balance Errors—If the performer commits the following errors prior to the completion of the 5 seconds, he sacrifices the remaining points at the rate of one point per second: (a) touching any part of the body to the floor other than the point of support or (b) moving the foot while in the balance position. When the performer loses his balance, he must step back on the proper marker and then leap to the next marker (25).

Additional Pointers: (a) The seconds of each balance attempt should be counted aloud for the performer. (b) The landing score and the balance score should be recorded for each marker.

Modified Sideward Leap Test (30)

Objective: To measure the ability to land accurately and to balance during and after movement.

Age Levels: Ages ten through college.

Sex: Satisfactory for both boys and girls.

Reliability: Has been reported between .66 and .88 at various grade levels.

Validity: Has been accepted for its obvious face validity.

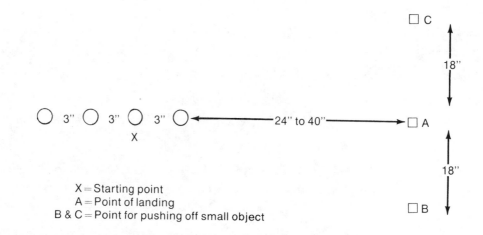

X = Starting point
A = Point of landing
B & C = Point for pushing off small object

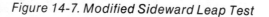

Figure 14-7. Modified Sideward Leap Test

Equipment and Materials: The equipment and materials needed for this test are stopwatches, tape measures, chalk markers, and several small objects such as the cork heads cut off of old badminton birds.

Directions: (See Figure 14-7.) Place a small object on spot B and measure the student's leg from the hip joint to the floor in order to determine the spot on the floor from which the subject will begin his leap. This spot should be the nearest X which corresponds most closely in distance to the length of the leg. The performer then places the left foot on the proper X mark and leaps sideward landing on spot A with the ball of right foot. He then immediately leans forward and pushes the small object off of spot B and maintains his balance for 5 seconds. Each performer executes two trials to the left and two trials to the right.

Scoring: (See Table 14-7.) On each trial the performer is awarded five points for covering spot A on the landing, five points for immediately lowering and pushing the cork from spot B (this must be accomplished within 2 seconds from time foot landed on spot A), and one point for each second the balance is held up to 5 seconds. The total possible score for the four trials is sixty points.

Penalty: (a) If the performer fails to cover spot A with the ball of his foot upon landing or fails to maintain a steady position, he sacrifices the five points for correct landing, but he may reassume the correct position and immediately lower (within 2 seconds) and push the object from point B or C and continue for the balance of 5 seconds. (b) If the performer takes longer than 2 seconds to remove the object from B or C, he sacrifices five points, but he may continue

for the balance of 5 seconds. (c) If the performer loses his balance before the 5 seconds is up, his score for that part of the test is the number of seconds the balance was held.

Additional Pointers: (a) Several patterns should be drawn on the floor so that students can be tested faster. (b) The student should be timed on the 5 second balance from the time he assumes a steady position on the ball of one foot at spot A. Thus, if it takes him 2 seconds to push the object from B or C, he would have only 3 seconds left to maintain position. (c) The timer should count the seconds aloud.

The Nelson Balance Test (22)

Objective: To measure both static and dynamic balance in a single test.

Age Level: Ages nine through college.

Sex: Satisfactory for both boys and girls.

Reliability: Test-retest coefficients of .91, .90, and .68 were obtained for fourth, fifth, and sixth grade boys, respectively.

Validity: The test has face validity as a measure of balance. Moreover, a coefficient of .77 was found when the test was correlated with the combined score of several standard balance measures.

Equipment and Materials: The following equipment and materials are needed: (a) Seven small wooden blocks, 2 by 4 by 8 inches. A 10-foot wooden balance beam, 2 by 4 inches. The beam is held edgewise by three triangular shaped supports. (See Figure 14-8A.) (b) In order to prevent the blocks from sliding or tipping, pieces of rubber are glued to the bottom of each block. This also protects the gymnasium floor. Four of the blocks are painted red or in some way marked differently. (c)

Table 14-7
T-Score Norms for Modified Sideward Leap Test

College Men	Performance Level	College Women
58 - 60	Advanced	58 - 60
53 - 57	Adv. Intermediate	51 - 57
42 - 52	Intermediate	39 - 50
37 - 41	Adv. Beginner	33 - 38
0 - 36	Beginner	0 - 32

Based on the scores of 50 college men and 70 college women at Corpus Christi State University, Corpus Christi, Tx., 1976.

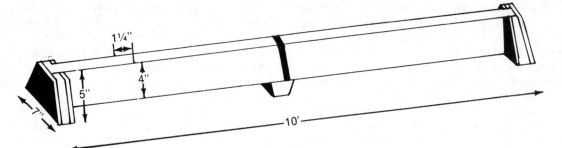

Figure 14-8A. Balance Beam

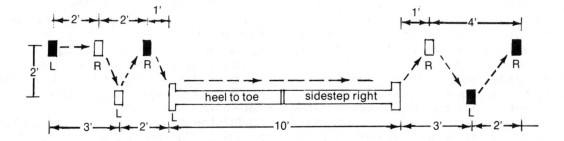

Figure 14-8B. Nelson Balance Test Phase 1

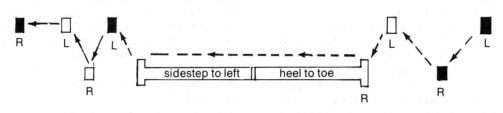

Figure 14-8C. Nelson Balance Test Phase 2

Stopwatch, tape measure, and possibly chalk or tape to mark the position of the blocks on the floor.

Directions: Two lines may be drawn 24 inches apart and 20 feet long. The blocks are placed crosswise; the blocks and balance beam are positioned as shown in Figure 14-8B.

First Phase: When ready, the subject steps onto the first block on the ball of the left foot. The tester starts the watch and counts aloud "1-2-3-4-5" to signify 5 seconds. (This count is repeated as the subject mounts each red block but not when he mounts others.)

The performer then proceeds along the route indicated in Figure 14-8B, leaping from one block to the next, alternating feet each time.

The subject tries to go as fast as he can, but without making mistakes. There are four red 5-second-hold blocks where the subject must balance on one foot while the tester calls out the 5 seconds. When crossing the balance beam in the first phase of the test, the performer walks heel-to-toe the first half of the beam; at the halfway point he turns and sidesteps to his *right* the remainder of the distance. He steps off on his *right* foot and completes the first phase of the test.

Second Phase: As soon as the subject steps off the last block, he turns and steps back upon the block on the ball of his left foot, holds for 5 seconds, leaps to next block onto his right foot, and proceeds according to the diagram in Figure 14-8C. The subject walks across the first half of the balance beam (heel-to-toe), then turns and sidesteps to his *left* the last half of the beam. He steps off with his *left* foot and completes the remainder of the course.

Scoring: The score is entirely based on cumulative time to the nearest 1/10 second for the completion of both phases of the test. The stopwatch is started when the subject steps upon the first block and stops when he steps off the seventh block at the end of the first phase. *The watch is not reset.* It is then started again as soon as he steps back upon the block and is stopped at the completion of the second phase.

Penalties: Any time the performer's foot touches the floor, he must get back onto the block at the place at which he fell off and proceed from that point. If the subject should leave one of the "hold" blocks before the 5 seconds has elapsed, he must return and "hold" for the remaining seconds (i.e., if the subject should leave a red block after 3 seconds, he would have to return and hold for 2 seconds to satisfy the 5-second requirement for the red blocks).

Similarly, if the subject should fall off, or deviate from the heel-toe or sidestep walk across the balance board, he must return to that point at which the fault occurred and resume the walk across the board.

In all cases the watch continues to run until the end of the last 5-second-hold count at the end of the course.

Problems Associated with Balance Testing

Several of the problems and limitations associated with the testing of balance are listed and discussed below:

1. Strength seems to have a considerable influence on certain tests of balance. This is especially noticeable in the Bass stick tests and the progressive inverted balance test.
2. Although research reveals controversy on this point, it seems logical to the authors that moderate to severe fatigue affects the balance scores of a student. Thus, it would seem logical to conduct balance skills prior to the more strenuous tests that may be given during a testing program (23).
3. Because of the exact position required (and

Table 14-8
T-Scale for Nelson Balance Test for Fourth, Fifth, and Sixth Grade Boys
Raw Scores in Seconds

T-Score	Grade 4	Grade 5	Grade 6	T-Score
80	48.7-Up	45.0-Up	45.7-Up	80
75	53.2-48.8	48.5-45.1	48.2-45.8	75
70	57.7-53.3	52.0-48.6	50.7-48.3	70
65	62.2-57.8	55.5-52.1	53.2-50.8	65
60	66.7-62.3	59.0-55.6	55.7-53.3	60
55	71.2-66.8	62.5-59.1	58.2-55.8	55
50	75.7-71.3	66.0-62.6	60.7-58.3	50
45	80.2-75.8	69.5-66.1	63.2-60.8	45
40	84.7-80.3	73.0-69.6	65.7-63.3	40
35	89.2-84.8	76.5-73.1	68.2-65.8	35
30	93.7-89.3	80.0-76.6	70.7-68.3	30
25	98.2-93.8	83.5-80.1	73.2-70.8	25
20	102.7-98.3	87.0-83.6	75.7-73.3	20

display of force to get in that position), it may be necessary to allow students as many as three trials on certain tests in order to get their best score. This, of course, requires more time.

4. Norms in this area of testing are limited primarily to the college level. There is a need for norms to be constructed at the elementary, junior high, and high school levels for both boys and girls.

5. Since static balance is positional or specific in nature, a student may show up poorly in one aspect of balance and yet be quite proficient in other aspects. Perhaps motor ability tests which include static balance items should have several balance items of similar difficulty from which to choose.

6. Certain balance tests require not only expensive equipment but also excessive amounts of time to administer. Therefore, the tests presented in this chapter should be of practical value when several stations are set up and students are rotated between stations. Moreover, further attempts should be made to devise inexpensive balance tests for the average school situation.

Findings and Conclusions from Balance Measurement and Research

It is frequently heard, and inaccurately so, that girls have better balance than boys because of their lower center of gravity. However, in an upright position a female's center of gravity is not enough lower than the male's to overcome the greater strength factor which rests in favor of the male. Moreover, in the inverted position the male assumes the lower center of gravity, plus the fact that he still has the strength factor in his favor. Therefore, the findings of Smith (32) and Hoffman (14) that boys are superior to girls of compatible ages in balance activities seem most logical and valid.

Another fallacy frequently heard is that balance is inherited and that there is very little the average person can do to improve his balance. While the ability to balance may be inherited to a certain extent, it can be significantly improved upon as determined in studies by Espenschade (8), Lafuze (19), Smith (32), Gunden (13), and Garrison (10). Furthermore, Espenschade (8) found that balance improved with an increase in chronological age between

the ages of eleven and sixteen years, but the rate of gain between the ages of thirteen and fifteen was noticeably retarded among boys.

Concerning mental ability, Hoffman (14) has stated that fast learning groups for each sex and grade tend to be superior to slow learning groups on balance tests.

Concerning the relationship of balance and kinesthesis, Scott (29) has stated that specific balance tests should be a part of any kinesthesis battery since the balance leap and the balance stick tests were consistently reliable and valid in her study.

In identifying factors of balance, Whelan (33) found four factors which corresponded with the findings of Bass (1). They were general static balance kinesthetic response, vertical semi-circular canals, general ampular sensitivity, and convergence of the eyes. Whelan (33) also found that very little difference existed between the blind and the sighted in balance ability and that balance ability in the blind probably does not over-compensate for the loss of sight as do other factors such as hearing and touch. Furthermore, Padden (24) found that poor balance groups among deaf students made significantly poorer showings in the ability to orient themselves under water than better balance groups among deaf students when the eyes were blindfolded. However, in Padden's study (24) the groups were not equated in swimming ability, and there is a possibility that lack of experience, and not poor balance, brought about the results.

Some controversy exists among physical educators concerning whether or not fatigue reduces balance control. While Scott and French (30) have maintained that excessive fatigue reduces balance control, Culane (4) has reported that fatigue has no noticeable effect upon balance. However, in the opinion of the authors, it seemed that Culane should have used the terms "slight fatigue" or "warm-up" to specify the degree of fatigue, since the exercises she used were not severe enough to cause "moderate" or "severe" fatigue to the average student. It has been noted by gymnastic coaches and performers that moderate to severe fatigue usually has an adverse effect on static balance. Moreover, Johnson (18) found that squat thrusts performed for maximum repetition significantly decreased static balance performance as measured by the stork stand (heel-up) test.

If balance is of importance in athletic activities, it is logical to assume that athletes would perform better than non-athletes on tests of balance. Lessl (20) found scientific evidence to this effect when he compared college athletes with average college students. Other investigators have found similar results. Slater-Hammel (31) found varsity athletes significantly better than physical education majors, and Reynolds' Balance Test showed that physical education majors were significantly better than liberal arts majors. Mumby (21) found that good wrestlers were somewhat better than poor wrestlers in the ability to balance and to learn to balance. Gross (12) concluded that good swimmers have better dynamic balance than poor swimmers.

Several investigators have attempted to determine the contribution of physical education activities to improvement in balance. Greenlee (11) conducted a study in which a significant relationship was found between dynamic balance and bowling performance. Bennett (2) concluded at the end of sixteen weeks of participation that there were no significant differences among the activities of modern dance, swimming, folk dance, and basketball concerning balance as measured by the Bass Leap Test. It should be pointed out, however, that since an initial test was not given before participation, the author was unable to assess the amount of improvement that was made. Consequently, it was not known whether or not initial differences among groups might have masked any differences in improvement in balance brought about by the activities. Gunden (13) found that participation in basketball, tumbling, tennis, and volleyball resulted in improvement in the balance ability of college women.

A number of researchers have reported a positive relationship between static balance and ability in gross motor activity (3, 5, 6, 8, 9, 28, 34). However, Drowatzky and Zuccato (7) found low inter-correlations among balance tests which suggested that each balance test measured a different type of balance. Sandborn and Wyrick (27) also found little relationship among balance tests used in their study. However, they did find that the most effective combination of predictors of balance beam skill were two tests of dynamic balance, the sideward leap and the modified sideward leap. Wyrick (36) further found that balance performance was a general ability and not specific to task height.

References and Bibliography

1. Bass, Ruth I., "An Analysis of the Components of Tests of Semi-Circular Canal Function and of Static and Dynamic Balance," *Research Quarterly*, 10:33, May, 1939.
2. Bennett, Colleen L., "Relative Contributions of Modern Dance, Folk Dance, Basketball, and Swimming to Motor Abilities of College Women," *Research Quarterly*, 27:261, October, 1956.
3. Carruth, Wincie A., "An Analysis of Motor Ability and Its Relationship to Constitutional Body Patterns" (Microcarded doctor's dissertation, New York University, 1952).
4. Culane, Mary J., "The Effect of Leg Fatigue Upon Balance" (Microcarded master's thesis, State University of Iowa, 1956).
5. Cumbee, Frances J., "A Factorial Analysis of Motor Coordination," *Research Quarterly*, 25:420, December, 1954.
6. _____, and others, "Factorial Analysis of Motor Co-ordination Variables for Third and Fourth Grade Girls," *Research Quarterly*, 28: 107-108, May, 1957.
7. Drowatzky, John N., and Jay C. Zuccato, "Interrelationships Between Selected Measures of Static and Dynamic Balance," *Research Quarterly*, 38:509, October, 1967.
8. Espenschade, A., and others, "Dynamic Balance in Adolescent Boys," *Research Quarterly*, 24:270, October, 1953.
9. Estep, Dorothy O., "Relationship of Static Equilibrium to Ability in Motor Activities," *Research Quarterly*, 28:5, March, 1957.
10. Garrison, Levon E., "An Experiment in Improving Balance Ability Through Teaching Selected Exercises" (Unpublished master's thesis, State University of Iowa, 1943).
11. Greenlee, Geraldine A., "The Relationship of Selected Measures of Strength, Balance, and Kinesthesis to Bowling Performance" (Unpublished master's thesis, State University of Iowa, 1958).
12. Gross, Elmer A., and Hugh L. Thompson, "Relationship of Dynamic Balance to Speed and Ability in Swimming," *Research Quarterly*, 28:346, December, 1957.
13. Gunden, Ruth E., "The Effect of Selected Sports Activities Upon the Balance Ability of College Women" (Microcarded master's thesis, State University of Iowa, 1956).
14. Hoffman, Virginia, "Relation of Selected Traits and Abilities to Motor Learning" (Microcarded doctor's dissertation, Indiana University, 1955).
15. Johnson, Barry L., "A Progressive Inverted Balance Test" (Unpublished study, Northeast Louisiana University, 1966).
16. _____, and John Leach, "A Modification of the Bass Test of Dynamic Balance" (Unpublished

study, East Texas State University, 1968).

17. _____, and Jeff Fitch, "Dynamic Test of Positional Balance" (Unpublished study, East Texas State University, 1968).

18. _____, and others, "The Effect of Fatigue Upon Balance," *Abstracts of Research Papers 1968 AAHPER Convention*, Washington, D.C.: American Association for Health, Physical Education, and Recreation, 1968, p. 118.

19. Lafuze, Marion, "A Study of the Learning of Fundamental Skills by College Freshmen Women of Low Motor Ability," *Research Quarterly*, 22:156, May, 1951.

20. Lessl, Robert F., "The Development of a New Test of Balance and Its Use in Comparing College Athletes and Average College Students in their Ability to Balance" (Microcarded master's thesis, University of Wisconsin, 1954).

21. Mumby, Hugh H., "Kinesthetic Acuity and Balance Related to Wrestling Ability," *Research Quarterly*, 24:334, October, 1953.

22. Nelson, Jack K., "The Nelson Balance Test" (Unpublished study, Louisiana State University, 1968).

23. _____, and Barry L. Johnson, "Effects of Local and General Fatigue on Static Balance," *Perpetual and Motor Skills*, 37:615-618, 1973.

24. Padden, Don A. "Ability of Deaf Swimmers to Orient Themselves When Submerged in Water," *Research Quarterly*, 30:225, May, 1959.

25. Reagh, Hubbard C., Jr., "Construction of Norms for the Revised Nelson Balance Test" (Unpublished study, Louisiana State University, 1971).

26. Russell, Carrice, "A Study of the Relationship Between the Bass Test of Dynamic Balance and the Modified Bass Test of Dynamic Balance" (Unpublished study, Northeast Louisiana University, 1970).

27. Sandborn, Carla, and Waneen Wyrick, "Prediction of Olympic Balance Beam Performance from Standardized and Modified Tests of Balance," *Research Quarterly*, 40:174-184, March, 1969.

28. Scott, M. Gladys, "Motor Ability Tests for College Women," *Research Quarterly*, 14:402, December, 1943.

29. _____, "Measurement of Kinesthesis," *Research Quarterly*, 26:337, October, 1955.

30. _____, and Esther French, *Measurement and Evaluation in Physical Education*, Dubuque, Iowa: Wm. C. Brown Company, Publishers, 1959.

31. Slater-Hammel, A. T., "Performance of Selected Groups of Male College Students on the Reynold's Balance Test," *Research Quarterly*, 27:351, October, 1956.

32. Smith, Jean A., "Relation of Certain Physical Traits and Abilities to Motor Learning in Elementary School Children," *Research Quarterly*, 27:228, May, 1956.

33. Whelan, Thomas P., "A Factor Analysis of Tests of Balance and Semicircular-Canal Function" (Microcarded doctor's dissertation, State University of Iowa, 1955).

34. Wiebe, Vernon R., "A Study of Tests of Kinesthesis" (Unpublished master's thesis, State University of Iowa, 1951).

35. Witte, Faye, "A Factorial Analysis of Measures of Kinesthesis" (Doctor's dissertation, Indiana University, 1953).

36. Wyrick, Waneen, "Effect of Task Height and Practice on Static Balance," *Research Quarterly*, 40:215-221, March, 1969.

Chapter Fifteen

The Measurement of Speed and Reaction

Speed of movement and quick reactions are prized qualities in athletics. Coaches are frequently heard to praise certain players or an entire team for their *quickness*. In football a player who is extremely fast poses a constant threat to break away for the long run; in baseball the fast runner causes hurried throws and adjustments in pitching and defensive strategy; the full-court press is a potent weapon in basketball if a team has the speed to make it effective; and, of course, in track speed is the essence of the sport.

However, despite these commonplace observations, the study of speed of movement and speed of reaction is much more complex than it might appear. Speed of movement, for example, entails much more than mere running speed. The speed with which a wrestler executes a reversal, the lightning flash of a boxer's jab, the explosive spring of the shot putter's move across the throwing circle, and the graceful swiftness of the swimmer and skater are but a few of the many different kinds of movement speeds that are involved in physical performance. *Speed of movement shall thus be defined as the rate at which a person can propel his body, or parts of his body, through space.*

Reaction time is the interval of time between the presentation of the stimulus and the initiation of the response. While reaction time was initially thought to be a rather simple and easily measured phenomenon, it has been shown to be influenced by a number of variables. Strictly speaking, an individual cannot be described as having a single reaction time without specifying the conditions under which he is being tested. Some of the factors which have been found to influence reaction time are the following: the sense organ involved, the intensity of the stimulus, the preparatory set, general muscular tension, motivation, practice, the response required, fatigue, and one's general state of health.

Analysis of speed of movement and reaction time when combined together is even more complex. It has been fairly well established that some individuals react quickly but move slowly; and some react slowly but are able to run or move very rapidly once they get started. However, even though speed of movement and speed of reaction may not show a significant relationship when these traits are measured separately and then correlated with each other, they cannot be separated in actual performance. A linebacker in football, for instance,

might react quickly in diagnosing the play, but he still has to move fast enough to be able to make the tackle if he is to be a successful performer.

Therefore, while it may be highly desirable to measure each factor separately for diagnostic purposes and for research, it would seem more practical for the coach and physical educator to measure them together in test situations that duplicate response-movements that are required in the activity in question. Speed and reaction time are considered to be largely innate abilities; however, both can be improved through practice and training. Consequently, it would seem only logical that the practice and training would be performed with reaction time and speed of movement combined in a *gamelike* sequence of movements.

Generally, speed has been measured by short dashes. Distances of over 100 yards are usually not recommended because endurance then becomes a factor. Naturally, the age, sex, and characteristics of the subjects should be the major consideration in selecting tests of speed.

Reaction time has usually been more complicated and more expensive to measure because of the timing device that has been employed. The device usually has a stimulus-presenting mechanism, such as a light or buzzer, and a switch that the subject presses or releases in response to the stimulus. A precise timer then measures the interval of time from the stimulus to the response. Recently, Nelson developed a measuring device that is both simple and inexpensive. The Nelson Reaction Timer* is based on the law of constant acceleration of free falling bodies and consists of a stick that is scaled to read in time as computed from the following formula:

$$\text{Time} = \sqrt{\frac{2 \times \text{Distance the stick falls}}{\text{Acceleration due to gravity}}}$$

Utilization of Tests

Speed of movement and reaction time measures may be utilized by physical educators in a number of ways, some of which are suggested below:
1. As a factor in motor ability tests, motor fitness tests, and sport skills tests.

*The Nelson Reaction Timer, Model RT-2, Copyright 1965 by Fred B. Nelson, P.O. Box 51987, Lafayette, La.

2. For diagnosis prior to specific practice and conditioning work.
3. For classification into homogeneous groups for certain activities.
4. For motivation and information purposes in conjunction with health, safety, and driver education units.

Practical Tests of Speed and Reaction

The physical educator is ordinarily not able to justify the purchase of an expensive timing device. Therefore he is somewhat limited in his measurement of speed of movement and, particularly, in his measurement of reaction time. Nevertheless, armed with only a stopwatch and imagination, the physical educator can obtain valuable measures of both of these traits which are both meaningful and sufficiently accurate.

The tests that are presented here include a hand reaction test, a foot reaction test, several dashes, and a choice-response accuracy test. None of the tests require expensive timing devices or elaborate equipment.

The Nelson Hand Reaction Test (38)

Objective: To measure the speed of reaction with the hand in response to a visual stimulus.
Age Level: Any age from kindergarten upward. The only limiting factor would be the subject's ability to catch the falling stick with the fingers.
Sex: Boys and girls.
Validity: The validity of the timing device is inherent, since the earth's gravitational pull is consistent; therefore, the timer falls at the same rate of acceleration each time.
Reliability: A reliability coefficient of .89 was obtained using average scores taken on two separate test administrations.
Test Equipment and Materials: Nelson Reaction Timer, table and chair, or desk chair.
Directions: The subject sits with his forearm and hand resting comfortably on the table (or desk chair). The tips of the thumb and index finger are held in a *ready to pinch* position about 3 or 4 inches beyond the edge of the table. (See Figure 15-1.) The upper edges of the thumb and index finger should be in a horizontal position. The tester holds the stick-timer near the top, letting it hang between the subject's thumb and index finger. The Base Line should be even with the upper surface of the subject's thumb (Figure 15-2).

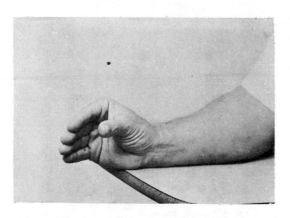

Figure 15-1. Position of Hand and Fingers for the Nelson Hand Reaction Test

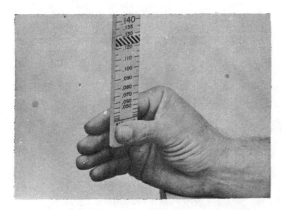

Figure 15-2. Ready Position with Thumb as Base Line for Nelson Hand Reaction Test

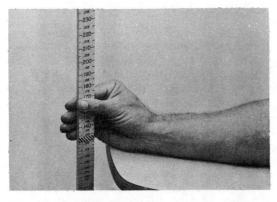

Figure 15-3. Example of Scoring the Nelson Hand Reaction Test (.170 seconds in this example)

The subject is directed to look at the *Concentration Zone* (which is a black shaded zone between the .120 and .130 lines) and is told to react by catching the stick (by pinching the thumb and index finger together) when it is released. The subject should not look at the tester's hand; nor is he allowed to move his hand up or down while attempting to catch the falling stick. Twenty trials are given. Each drop is preceded by a preparatory command of "ready."

Scoring: When the subject catches the timer, the score is read just above the upper edge of the thumb. (See Figure 15-3.) The five slowest and the five fastest trials are discarded, and an average of the middle ten is recorded as the score. Numbers on the timer represent thousandths of a second. Scores may be recorded to the nearest 5/1000 of a second.

Safety Precautions: None.

Additional Pointers: (a) The testing environment should be such that the subject is able to concentrate. (b) Allow the subject three or four practice trials to make sure he understands the procedures and becomes familiar with the task. (c) The interval of time between the preparatory command of "ready" and the release is extremely important. It should be varied in order to prevent the subject from becoming accustomed to a constant pattern. On the other hand, this interval should remain within a range of not less than one-half second nor longer than approximately 2 seconds. If too short, it catches the subject before he is ready, and if the interval is too long the subject loses his optimal state of readiness. For standardization the tester could have a specific order of these intervals. For example, on the first trial he could say "ready," then count to himself 1,001, then release; on the second trial, after "ready," he might mentally say, "one," then release, etc. (d) Obvious anticipations should be discarded and should not be counted as one of the twenty trials. (e) The tester must be careful that the subject's thumb or index finger is not touching the timer. (f) If the subjects are young children, the test should be conducted like a challenging game. (g) The subject's dominant hand should be used if only one hand is to be tested. (h) The thumb and index finger should not be more than 1 inch apart at the start.

Norms are not complete at this time. With college men, the average reaction time is around .16 with a range of .13 to .22. With small children (first graders), the average is about .26.

The Nelson Foot Reaction Test (38)

Objective: To measure the speed of reaction with the foot in response to a visual stimulus.

Age and Sex: Same as with the hand reaction test.

Validity: Face validity. Same as with the hand reaction test.

Reliability: A reliability coefficient of .85 was obtained with college men as subjects.

Test Equipment and Materials: Nelson Reaction Timer, table or bench, wall space.

Directions: The subject sits on a table (or bench) which is about 1 inch from the wall. With his shoe off, the subject positions his foot so that the ball of the foot is held about 1 inch from the wall with the heel resting on the table about 2 inches from the edge. The tester holds the reaction timer next to the wall so that it hangs between the wall and the subject's foot with the Base Line opposite the end of the big toe. The subject looks at the *Concentration Zone* and is told to react, when the timer is dropped, by pressing the stick against the wall with the ball of his foot. Twenty trials are given. (See Figure 15-4.)

Scoring: The reaction time for each trial is the line just above the end of the big toe when the foot is pressing the stick to the wall. The slowest five trials and the fastest five trials are discarded, and the average of the middle ten trials is recorded.

Safety Precautions: None.

Additional Pointers: Same as with hand reaction test.

Norms are incomplete. The average reaction time for college men is approximately .21.

The Nelson Speed of Movement Test (38)

Objective: To measure combined reaction and speed of movement of the hands.

Age and Sex: Same as with reaction tests.

Validity: Face validity as long as no attempt is made to separate reaction time and speed of movement.

Reliability: A reliability coefficient for college men was found to be .75.

Test Equipment and Materials: Nelson Reaction Timer, table and chair, chalk or tape and ruler.

Directions: The subject sits at a table with his hands resting on the edge of the table. The palms are facing one another with the inside border of the little fingers along two lines which are marked on the edge of the table 12 inches

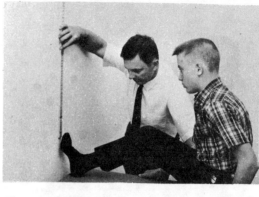

Figure 15-4. Ready Position with End of Big Toe at Base Line for Nelson Foot Reaction Test

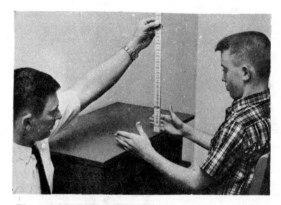

Figure 15-5. Ready Position with Hands 12 Inches Apart for Nelson Speed of Movement Test

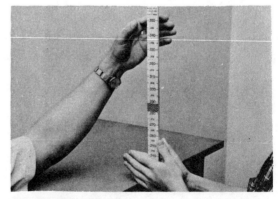

Figure 15-6. Example of Scoring the Nelson Speed of Movement Test (.240 seconds in this example)

apart. The tester holds the timer near its top so that it hangs midway between the subject's palms. The Base Line should be positioned so it is level with the upper borders of the subject's hands. (See Figure 15-5.)

After the preparatory command "ready" is given, the timer is released and the subject attempts to stop it as quickly as possible by clapping the hands together. The subject must be careful not to allow his hands to move up or down when he is clapping the hands together. Twenty trials are given.

Scoring: The score for the combined response-movement is read from the timer at the point just above the upper edge of the hand after the catch (Figure 15-6). The average of the middle ten trials, after the slowest and fastest five trials have been discarded, is recorded.

Safety Precautions: None.

Additional Pointers: (a) The pointers listed for the hand reaction time test are applicable for this test. (b) After the subject has his hands in the ready position, a 12-inch ruler should be utilized to make sure the hands are the correct distance apart. (c) A small mark exactly between the two marks should be made to facilitate the positioning of the timer prior to release. (d) The subject should remove any rings to prevent the denting or marring of the timer's surface.

Norms are incomplete at this time. Average time has been found to be about .24 for college men.

Four-Second Dash

(See Scott Motor Ability Test, Chapter 19, for directions.) This test could be utilized for junior high school, high school, and college men.

Six-Second Dash (33)

Objective: Although this event has been used as a measure of running endurance, it would seem to be appropriate as a test of speed, at least for older students. Except for the extremely fast high school or college student, the distance covered would rarely be over 50 yards, and endurance should not be a factor.

Age Level: There are only norms for high school and college students, but the test could be used for junior high students.

Sex: Satisfactory for both boys and girls.

Validity: Face validity is accepted.

Reliability: No figures given.

Test Equipment and Materials: Stopwatch, whistle, running space of at least 70 yards to allow for a gradual stop, and approximately fourteen markers placed at 2-yard intervals from 34 to 60 yards.

Directions: The subject starts from a standing position with both feet behind the end line. The starter uses the preparatory commands of "get set" and "go." On the command to go the subject runs in a straight line as fast as possible until the whistle is blown at the end of 6 seconds. The subject does not have to come to a sudden stop at the sound of the whistle, he merely begins to slow down at his own rate. Two trials are given, 5 minutes apart.

Scoring: A spotter is assigned to each runner and is positioned about 45 yards from the starting line. At the sound of the whistle the spotter immediately runs to the place where the runner was at the time the whistle was blown. This point is then measured from the nearest marker (or line, if lines are drawn across the running lane). The score is recorded to the

Table 15-1
Raw Score Norms for Four-Second Dash

Scores in Feet—Measured Indoors on Gym Floor		
College Men	Performance Level	College Women
93 - Higher	Advanced	76 - Higher
88 - 92	Adv. Intermediate	72 - 75
82 - 87	Intermediate	65 - 71
70 - 81	Adv. Beginner	59 - 64
0 - 69	Beginner	0 - 58

Based on the scores of 43 college men and 43 college women, Corpus Christi State University, Corpus Christi, Tx., 1977.

Table 15-2
Scoring Table for Six-Second Run

College Men	College Women	Performance Level	High School Boys	High School Girls
54 - Above	45 - Above	Excellent	51 - Above	43 - Above
51 - 53	42 - 44	Good	48 - 50	40 - 42
42 - 50	35 - 41	Average	43 - 47	35 - 39
37 - 41	29 - 34	Poor	40 - 42	32 - 34
0 - 36	0 - 28	Very Poor	0 - 39	0 - 31

Based on the scores of fifty students for each category as reported by Leroy Scott, NLU, Monroe, La., 1973.

Table 15-3
Fifty-Yard Dash Norms for Elementary Children

Percentile	Sex	Age 6	7	8	9	10	11
99th	Boys	8.3	8.4	7.6	7.5	7.3	7.4
	Girls	9.2	8.6	8.0	7.7	7.7	7.5
90th	Boys	8.8	8.6	7.9	7.8	7.6	7.7
	Girls	9.4	8.9	8.4	8.0	7.8	7.6
80th	Boys	9.0	8.8	8.1	8.0	7.8	7.9
	Girls	9.7	9.1	8.7	8.2	8.0	7.8
70th	Boys	9.3	9.1	8.4	8.1	8.0	8.1
	Girls	9.9	9.4	8.9	8.5	8.4	8.0
60th	Boys	9.4	9.2	8.6	8.3	8.2	8.3
	Girls	10.1	9.5	9.1	8.7	8.6	8.1
50th	Boys	9.5	9.5	8.7	8.4	8.3	8.4
	Girls	10.2	9.9	9.3	9.0	8.8	8.5
40th	Boys	9.5	9.7	9.0	8.7	8.5	8.6
	Girls	10.5	10.0	9.5	9.2	9.1	9.0
30th	Boys	9.9	10.1	9.2	8.9	8.7	8.8
	Girls	10.9	10.2	9.9	9.5	9.4	9.4
20th	Boys	10.6	10.5	9.7	9.4	9.0	9.4
	Girls	11.5	10.8	10.5	10.0	9.8	9.7
10th	Boys	12.5	12.3	12.6	11.4	10.5	9.8
	Girls	13.4	14.8	17.5	12.5	11.4	10.8
N	Boys	27	116	126	203	149	50
	Girls	31	101	113	100	82	32

Source: Donald H. Hardin, and John Ramirez, "Elementary School Performance Norms," *TAHPER Journal*, February, 1972, pp. 8-9.

nearest yard, and the best of the two trials is used. (See Table 15-2.)

Safety: Precautions should be taken to allow sufficient warm-up to avoid strained muscles. Adequate space should be provided along the sides of the running lanes and at the end of the lanes. Proper footwear should be insisted upon.

Additional Pointers: (a) The main advantage of this type of run is that several subjects can be tested with one stopwatch. Therefore, it is recommended that more than one runner be tested at a time. Otherwise, running a specific distance for time is a more precise measure. (b) Each spotter must be impressed with the necessity of watching only his runner and not look to see who is winning. (c) In judging the exact spot at which the runner was when the whistle sounded, the spotter should use the subject's chest as the point of reference. (d) The tester (or timer) should keep his eyes on the watch and not on the runners. He should count loudly the seconds 3, 4, and 5 to alert the spotters as to the approximate point at which their runners will be. (e) Chalk or painted lines across the running lanes at the 2-yard intervals will facilitate scoring. (f) Although a period of 5 minutes is suggested as the interval between trials, more time should be allowed if fatigue is adjudged to be a possible influence on the second trial.

Fifty-Yard Dash (1)

Objective: To measure speed.
Age Level: Ages six through seventeen.
Sex: Satisfactory for both boys and girls.
Reliability: None reported.
Objectivity: None reported.
Validity: Face validity is accepted.
Equipment: Two stopwatches, or a watch with a split-second timer is needed. A suitable running area to allow the fifty-yard run plus extension for stopping is also required.
Directions: It is advised that two subjects run at

the same time. Both start from a standing position. The commands, "Are you ready?" and "Go!" are given. At the command to go the starter drops his arm so that the timer at the finish line can start the timing. The subjects run as fast as possible across the finish line.

Scoring: The elapsed time from the starting signal until the runner crosses the finish line is measured to the nearest tenth of a second. (See Tables 15-3 and 15-4 A and B.)

Nelson Choice-Response-Movement Test (39)

Objective: To measure ability to react and move quickly and accurately in accordance with a choice stimulus. It was believed that this type of test simulated movement patterns found in a number of sports.
Age Level: Satisfactory for ages ten through college.
Sex: Satisfactory for both boys and girls.
Validity: Face validity is accepted.
Reliability: A reliability coefficient of .87 was found for college men, using the test-retest method.
Objectivity: An objectivity coefficient of .83 was obtained with two testers scoring the same individuals. However, much of the disagreement was believed to be due to the difficulty of synchronizing the start with two watches.
Test Equipment and Materials: Stopwatch, measuring tape, and marking equipment. See Figure 15-7 for diagram of test markings.
Directions: The subject faces the tester while crouching in an on-guard position at a spot exactly between the two side lines. The tester holds the stopwatch in his upraised hand. The tester then abruptly waves his arm to either the left or right and simultaneously starts the watch. The subject responds to the hand signal and attempts to run as quickly as possible, in the indicated direction, to the boundary line. The watch is stopped when the subject crosses the correct line. If the subject should start to

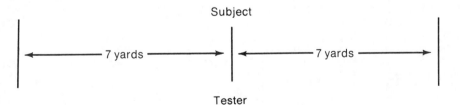

Figure 15-7. Diagram for Nelson Choice-Response-Movement Test

Table 15-4A
AAHPER Youth Fitness Test
50-YARD DASH FOR BOYS

Percentile Scores Based on Age/Test Scores in Seconds and Tenths

Percentile	Age								Percentile
	10	11	12	13	14	15	16	17	
100th	6.0	6.0	6.0	5.8	5.8	5.6	5.6	5.6	100th
95th	7.0	7.0	6.8	6.5	6.3	6.1	6.0	6.0	95th
90th	7.1	7.2	7.0	6.7	6.4	6.2	6.1	6.0	90th
85th	7.4	7.4	7.0	6.9	6.6	6.4	6.2	6.1	85th
80th	7.5	7.5	7.2	7.0	6.7	6.5	6.3	6.2	80th
75th	7.6	7.6	7.3	7.0	6.8	6.5	6.3	6.3	75th
70th	7.8	7.7	7.5	7.1	6.9	6.6	6.4	6.3	70th
65th	8.0	7.8	7.5	7.2	7.0	6.7	6.5	6.4	65th
60th	8.0	7.8	7.6	7.3	7.0	6.7	6.5	6.5	60th
55th	8.1	8.0	7.8	7.4	7.0	6.8	6.6	6.5	55th
50th	8.2	8.0	7.8	7.5	7.1	6.9	6.7	6.6	50th
45th	8.3	8.0	7.9	7.5	7.2	7.0	6.7	6.7	45th
40th	8.5	8.1	8.0	7.6	7.2	7.0	6.8	6.7	40th
35th	8.5	8.3	8.0	7.7	7.3	7.1	6.9	6.8	35th
30th	8.7	8.4	8.2	7.9	7.5	7.1	6.9	6.9	30th
25th	8.8	8.5	8.3	8.0	7.6	7.2	7.0	7.0	25th
20th	9.0	8.7	8.4	8.0	7.8	7.3	7.1	7.0	20th
15th	9.1	9.0	8.6	8.2	8.0	7.5	7.2	7.1	15th
10th	9.5	9.1	8.9	8.4	8.1	7.7	7.5	7.3	10th
5th	10.0	9.5	9.2	8.9	8.6	8.1	7.8	7.7	5th
0	12.0	11.9	12.0	11.1	11.6	12.0	8.6	10.6	0

Table 15-4B
AAHPER Youth Fitness Test
50-YARD DASH FOR GIRLS

Percentile Scores Based on Age/Test Scores in Seconds and Tenths

Percentile	Age								Percentile
	10	11	12	13	14	15	16	17	
100th	6.0	6.0	5.9	6.0	6.0	6.4	6.0	6.4	100th
95th	7.0	7.0	7.0	7.0	7.0	7.1	7.0	7.1	95th
90th	7.3	7.4	7.3	7.3	7.2	7.3	7.3	7.3	90th
85th	7.5	7.6	7.5	7.5	7.4	7.5	7.5	7.5	85th
80th	7.7	7.7	7.6	7.6	7.5	7.6	7.5	7.6	80th
75th	7.9	7.9	7.8	7.7	7.6	7.7	7.7	7.8	75th
70th	8.0	8.0	7.9	7.8	7.7	7.8	7.9	7.9	70th
65th	8.1	8.0	8.0	7.9	7.8	7.9	8.0	8.0	65th
60th	8.2	8.1	8.0	8.0	7.9	8.0	8.0	8.0	60th
55th	8.4	8.2	8.1	8.0	8.0	8.0	8.1	8.1	55th
50th	8.5	8.4	8.2	8.1	8.0	8.1	8.3	8.2	50th
45th	8.6	8.5	8.3	8.2	8.2	8.2	8.4	8.3	45th
40th	8.8	8.5	8.4	8.4	8.3	8.3	8.5	8.5	40th
35th	8.9	8.6	8.5	8.5	8.5	8.4	8.6	8.6	35th
30th	9.0	8.8	8.7	8.6	8.6	8.6	8.8	8.8	30th
25th	9.0	9.0	8.9	8.8	8.9	8.8	9.0	9.0	25th
20th	9.2	9.0	9.0	9.0	9.0	9.0	9.0	9.0	20th
15th	9.4	9.2	9.2	9.2	9.2	9.0	9.2	9.1	15th
10th	9.6	9.6	9.5	9.5	9.5	9.5	9.9	9.5	10th
5th	10.0	10.0	10.0	10.2	10.4	10.0	10.5	10.4	5th
0	14.0	13.0	13.0	15.7	16.0	18.0	17.0	12.0	0

Table 15-5
Norms for Nelson Choice-Response-Movement Test

College Men	Performance Level	College Women
1.30 - Less	Advanced	1.60 - Less
1.60 - 1.35	Adv. Intermediate	1.90 - 1.65
2.40 - 1.65	Intermediate	2.55 - 1.95
2.70 - 2.45	Adv. Beginner	2.85 - 2.60
Higher - 2.75	Beginner	Higher - 2.90

Data gathered from 200 college men, Louisiana State University, Baton Rouge, La., 1968, and 45 college women, Corpus Christi State University, Corpus Christi, Tx., 1976.

move in the wrong direction, the watch continues to run until the subject reverses directions and reaches the correct side line. Ten trials are given, five to each side, but in a random sequence. A rest interval of 20 seconds is provided between each trial.

Scoring: The time for each trial is read to the nearest tenth of a second. The average score is then recorded. (See Table 15-5.)

Safety: The teacher should insist upon adequate footwear and should provide warm-up exercises. The testing area must be kept free from obstructions.

Additional Pointers: (a) Several practice trials should be given to acquaint the subjects with the test procedures. (b) The tester should practice the starting signals to attain proficiency in synchronizing his hand signal with the start of the watch. (c) In selecting the sequence of direction, the tester can simply put five slips with *right* on them and five slips with *left* on them in a hat for a random draw. This procedure prevents the subject from anticipating the direction from one trial to the next. However, the *subject should not be told* that he will have five trials in each direction. In fact, the subject should probably be told that this is not the case—that the distribution of trials is entirely based on random selection and may have more in one direction than another. There should be several prepared sequences so that students waiting to be tested cannot memorize the order of directions. (d) This test could be adapted so as to be more applicable to the specific activity in question. For example, tackling dummies could be placed at each sideline that the subject must hit to stop the clock. (e) As in all speed and reaction tests, the interval between the command, "ready," and

the starting signal should be within a range of approximately ½ to 2 seconds.

Problems Associated with Speed of Movement and Reaction Time Testing

Some of the problems and limitations that are associated with speed and reaction time measurement were mentioned in the first part of the chapter. It was pointed out that equipment would be a major obstacle if the physical educator wished to secure very precise measures for a variety of response-movements. Quite obviously the need for elaborate equipment would depend upon the purposes for which the measures were to be used.

When speed of movement and reaction time are to be studied separately, the specificity of each must be considered, as well as how each may operate in relation to the movements involved and the task. In other words, it would not make much sense to measure reaction time by having the subject release a telegraph key device upon hearing a buzzer and speed of movement by the 100-yard dash, and then attempt to make conclusions regarding the reaction and movement speed of a defensive lineman in football. The tasks are too unrelated. It would be much more meaningful and accurate to have the subject react to the movement of the ball on an actual pass from the center and have the subject then move to hit a dummy some distance away. To get both reaction and speed of movement on the same trial would require a timing device with two clocks. One clock would start when the ball was moved and would stop when the subject started to move (such as if he lifted his hand from a switch on the ground). This would measure reaction time. A second clock would start when the subject started to move and would stop when contact was made with the dummy, which would measure his movement time.

The meaningfulness and challenge of the test, the testing position, the skill and past experience of the subject are all important points to be considered. The reaction of a football player may be much faster in the above situation than in an artificial setting such as was described earlier using a telegraph key and a buzzer. As in all tests the tester must carefully evaluate the nature of the performance that is being measured. In a great many sports, for example, the crucial speed that is required is but for a very few yards. The abilities to perceive the meaning of the stimulus, react correctly, and move to the required spot just a few feet away are of vital importance in tennis, badminton, handball, football, basketball, baseball, softball, and many other sports. The speed at which a person can run 100 yards is not nearly so important in those activities.

The use of a standing start as opposed to the crouched sprinter's stance is ordinarily recommended in physical education class testing. This is due to the fact that persons who have not practiced crouched starts would be at a definite disadvantage. This disadvantage would be even more pronounced if they were given their choice and elected to start from the crouched position without any training. The untrained individual's first move from the sprinter's stance is usually to stand up—then start running—which, of course, is wasted motion.

Concentration and the individual's state of readiness to react are essential for speed and reaction measurement, and therefore the testing situation should be conducive for optimum performance. The importance of the proper interval between the preparatory command and the signal to respond has already been discussed in the descriptions of the tests. The tester must be ever conscious of this foreperiod and guard against the tendency to give the same interval each time. As was recommended earlier, it is best to have a definite sequence established.

The consumption of class time is not a limiting factor if the measures utilized consist only of dashes. However, if the physical educator wishes to measure functional response-movements, then a sufficient number of trials involves considerable time for testing.

Findings and Conclusions from Speed and Reaction Time Measurement and Research

There has been a vast amount of research done in psychology, physiology, and physical education on speed of movement and reaction time. Despite the voluminous literature on the subject, much research is still needed.

A misconception held for years by many coaches and physical educators was that strength-building exercises would be detrimental to speed of movement. However, research has shown quite convincingly that just the opposite is true. Zorbas and Karpovich (53), Wilkin (51), Masley (32), Endres (13), and Chui (7) all found that weight training improved speed of movement. Meadows (34) and Johnson (27) further found that both isotonic and isometric exercises improved speed of movement, while Crowder (10) reported isotonic and isometric exercises produced significant improvement in reaction time. Michael (35), dealing only with isometric exercises, found significant gains in both speed of movement and reaction time. Dintiman (12) reported that a combination of flexibility and weight training programs, given as supplements to spring training, improved speed significantly more than the spring training program alone.

Several studies have reported low correlations between reaction time and movement time. Representative of such studies are those by Owens (42), Henry (22), and Clarke (8).

Magill and Powell (31) investigated the often reported finding that reaction time and movement time are totally unrelated. The authors concluded that the significance of the relationship is highly dependent on the experimental situation. In other words, by manipulation of certain variables such as age, sex, set, and amount of practice, significant or nonsignificant relationships between reaction time and movement time may be attained.

Smith (45) found that reaction time and velocity of the arm when in a state of stretch was not significantly faster than when the arm was relaxed or tensed. But when the prime movers of the limb were stretched, significantly faster performances resulted. The results of another study by Smith (46) gave further support to the theory of specificity, in that differences in movement time of a limb involving a single joint are largely independent of strength measures of that limb and joint.

Motivation has been shown to be quite effective in bringing about faster speed of movement and reaction. Henry (23) found that a motivated simple response transferred its increase in speed to a more complex response. Fairclough (14) reported that motivated improvement in speed in one part of the body could be transferred to another body part.

Levitt and Gutin (30) administered five-choice reaction time and movement time tests while the subjects walked on a treadmill at heart rates of 80, 115, 145, and 175 beats per minute. The choice reaction time performance was best at 115 and poorest at 175, whereas the movement time improved linearly with increases in heart rate. They concluded that reaction time and movement time are affected differently by physical exertion.

Reynolds (43) tested physically conditioned and unconditioned subjects on reaction time while they were exposed to stress. Reaction time was not significantly affected by stress.

The intensity of the stimulus is a factor, as was revealed in Vallerga's (50) study in which a loud sound was found to produce faster speed of movement and more forceful contraction than soft or medium sounds. Studies by Henry (23), Hipple (25), Howell (26), and others have shown that devices such as electric shock, suggested failure, etc., result in increased tension and thus increased speed of response. Wilson (52) and Thompson and others (49) reported that rhythmic starting signals improved reaction time performance. Minter (36) found no difference in reaction time to a visual stimulus between deaf and normal college students. The deaf were superior in a complex reaction-movement task.

Athletes were found to be superior to non-athletes in reaction time in studies by Keller (28), Sigerseth and York (44), Burpee and Stroll (4), and Olsen (41). In a study by Davis (11) women physical education majors had faster hand reaction and foot reaction times than non-majors as measured by the Nelson Hand and Foot Reaction Time. P. Smith (47) found athletes to be faster than non-participants at three different ages in total-body and arm reaction time. Total-body completion time was shown to be the most significant differentiator for successful athletic performance.

Reaction times and movement times of males and females aged 9 to 17 were analyzed by Fulton and Hubbard (16). Speed of reaction improved significantly with age, with females showing consistently faster times. Movement times also improved markedly with age, and males were faster.

Botwinick and Thompson (2) found that elderly subjects were significantly slower in reaction time than young athletes, but they were not significantly slower than young non-athletes. Spirduso (48) found support for the association of activity and reaction time, concluding that reaction time and movement time are functions of both age and physical activity level. She reported that men 50 to 70 years of age who were highly active had faster central nervous system processing times and faster muscular movements than less active men. Chema (5) investigated the response time of elderly subjects. Response times were fractionated into premotor reaction time, motor reaction time, and movement time. Elderly subjects evidenced slower premotor reaction times under all conditions of the study. It was concluded that a central nervous system deficit was the most plausible premise regarding slowed response times in elderly individuals.

Christina (6) tested the hypothesis advanced by Henry in conjunction with his Memory Drum Theory that a sensory set would evoke faster reaction times than a motor set (21). The sensory set concentrates on the stimulus, while the motor set concentrates on the movement to be performed. Henry had hypothesized that concentration on the movement would interfere with the memory mechanism, resulting in slower reaction and movement. Christina's study found support for the sensory set with reaction time performance but no significant differences were found for the movement time scores.

Norrie (40) found support for Henry's Memory Drum Theory in that the decision-making process in simple movement tasks takes place before the start of the movement. She also found that as the numbers of choice conditions increased, the reaction time effect of increased complexity of movement lessened.

In comparing four variations of the upright stance with knees straight or bent and weight on the balls of the feet or with flat feet, Cotten and Denning (9) concluded that optimum reaction-movement time results from a knees-bent, feet-flat stance.

Specific training in sprint starting was found

to improve reaction performance in studies by Gibson (17) and Gottshall (18). A conditioning exercise program was also found to result in improved reaction time in Gottshall's study.

Krahenbuhl (29) compared speed of movement on synthetic turf versus natural grass and also the relative effects of three types of footwear on movement speed on the two surfaces. Movement times were faster on synthetic turf regardless of the footwear employed. Tennis shoes or soccer-style shoes on synthetic turf produced the fastest movement times.

Nakamura (37) studied the foreperiod between the preparatory command and the signal to go and found the optimum time interval to be 1.5 seconds. Bresnahan and others (3) concur and recommend that a foreperiod of 1.4 to 1.6 seconds yields the fastest reaction times.

Haywood and Teeple (20) analyzed reaction time and movement time scores over 35 trials. It was concluded that a minimum of 8 trials, using the first 2 trials as practice, yields a representative score of performance for the 35 trials with little deviation in mean scores, reliability, or standard error.

References and Bibliography

1. AAHPER, *AAHPER Youth Fitness Test Manual,* rev. ed., Washington, D.C.: American Alliance for Health, Physical Education, and Recreation, 1965.
2. Botwinick, J., and L. Thompson, "Age Difference in Reaction Time: An Artifact?," *The Gerontologist,* 8:25-28, 1968.
3. Bresnahan, George T., W. W. Tuttle, and Francis X. Cretzmeyer, *Track and Field Athletics,* 4th ed., St. Louis: C. V. Mosby Company, 1956, p. 79; 6th ed., 1964.
4. Burpee, Royal H., and Wellington Stroll, "Measuring Reaction Time of Athletes," *Research Quarterly,* 7:110-118, March, 1936.
5. Chema, Hope M., "Reaction and Movement Times of the Elderly in Relation to Peripheral Nerve Conduction and the Central Nervous System" (Master's thesis, Florida State University, Tallahassee, 1977).
6. Christina, Robert W., "Influence of Enforced Motor and Sensory Sets on Reaction Latency and Movement Speed," *Research Quarterly,* 44:483-487, December, 1973.
7. Chui, Edward, "Effect of Systematic Weight Training on Athletic Power," *Research Quarterly,* 21:188-194, October, 1950.
8. Clarke, David H., "Correlation Between the Strength/Mass Ratio and the Speed of an Arm Movement," *Research Quarterly,* 31:570-574, December, 1960.
9. Cotten, Doyice J., and Donald Denning, "Comparison of Reaction-Movement Times from Four Variations of the Upright Stance," *Research Quarterly,* 41:196-199, May, 1970.
10. Crowder, Vernon R., "A Comparison of the Effects of Two Methods of Strength Training on Reaction Time" (Unpublished master's thesis, Louisiana State University).
11. Davis, Cleo, Jr., "Reaction Time of Women Physical Education Majors and Non-Majors," (Unpublished master's thesis, North Carolina Central University, 1969).
12. Dintiman, George B., "Effects of Various Training Programs on Running Speed," *Research Quarterly,* 35:456-463, December, 1964.
13. Endres, John P., "The Effect of Weight Training Exercise Upon the Speed of Muscular Movements" (Microcarded master's thesis, University of Wisconsin, 1953.)
14. Fairclough, R. H., "Transfer of Motivated Improvement in Speed of Reaction and Movement," *Research Quarterly,* 23:20-27, March, 1952.
15. Ford, Gene L., "A Study of Reaction Times Among Black and White Students" (Unpublished study, Northeast Louisiana University, 1970).
16. Fulton, Clifton D., and Alfred W. Hubbard, "Effects of Puberty on Reaction and Movement Times," *Research Quarterly,* 46:335-344, October, 1975.
17. Gibson, Dennis A., "Effect of a Special Training Program for Sprint Starting on Reflex Time, Reaction Time and Sargent Jump" (Microcarded master's thesis, Springfield College, 1961).
18. Gottshall, Donald R., "The Effects of Two Training Programs on Reflex Time, Reaction Time and the Level of Physical Fitness" (Microcarded master's thesis, Springfield College, 1962).
19. Hardin, Don H., and John Ramirez, "Elementary School Performance Norms," *TAHPER Journal,* February, 1972, pp. 8-9.
20. Haywood, Kathleen M., and Janet B. Teeple, "Representative Simple Reaction and Movement Time Scores," *Research Quarterly,* 47:855-856, December, 1976.
21. Henry F. M., and D. E. Rogers, "Increased Response Latency for Complicated Movements and a 'Memory Drum' Theory of Neuromotor Reaction," *Research Quarterly,* 31:448-458, 1960.
22. _____ , "Reaction Time-Movement Time Correlations," *Perceptual and Motor Skills,* 12:63-66, February, 1961.
23. _____ , "Increase in Speed of Movement by Motivation and by Transfer of Motivated Improvement," *Research Quarterly,* 22:219-228, May, 1951.
24. _____ , "Independence of Reaction and Movement Times and Equivalence of Sensory Mo-

tivators of Faster Response," *Research Quarterly,* 23:43-53, March, 1952.

25. Hipple, Joseph E., "Racial Differences in the Influence of Motivation on Muscular Tension, Reaction Time, and Speed of Movement," *Research Quarterly,* 25:297-306, October, 1954.

26. Howell, Maxwell L., "Influence of Emotional Tension of Speed on Reaction and Movement," *Research Quarterly,* 24:22-32, March, 1953.

27. Johnson, Barry L., "A Comparison of Isometric and Isotonic Exercises Upon the Improvement of Velocity and Distance as Measured by the Rope Climb Test" (Unpublished study, Louisiana State University, January, 1964).

28. Keller, L. F., "The Relation of Quickness of Bodily Movement to Success in Athletics," *Research Quarterly,* 13:146-155, May, 1942.

29. Krahenbuhl, Gary S., "Speed of Movement with Varying Footwear Conditions on Synthetic Turf and Natural Grass," *Research Quarterly,* 45:28-33, March, 1974.

30. Levitt, Stuart, and Bernard Gutin, "Multiple Choice Reaction Time and Movement Time During Physical Exertion," *Research Quarterly,* 42:405-410, December, 1971.

31. Magill, Richard A., and Frank M. Powell, "Is the Reaction Time-Movement Time Relationship 'Essentially Zero'?," *Perceptual and Motor Skills,* 41:720-722, December, 1975.

32. Masley, John W., Ara Hairabedian, and Donald N. Donaldson, "Weight Training in Relation to Strength, Speed, and Coordination," *Research Quarterly,* 24:308-315, October, 1953.

33. McCloy, C. H., and Norma D. Young, *Tests and Measurements in Health, and Physical Education,* 3rd ed., New York: Appleton-Century-Crofts, 1954, p. 186.

34. Meadows, P. E., "The Effect of Isotonic and Isometric Muscle Contraction Training on Speed, Force, and Strength" (Microcarded doctor's dissertation, University of Illinois, 1959).

35. Michael, Charles E., "The Effects of Isometric Contraction Exercise on Reaction and Speed of Movement Times" (Unpublished doctoral dissertation, Louisiana State University, 1963).

36. Minter, Martin C., "A Comparison of Reaction Time and Movement Time in Deaf and Hearing Freshmen Male College Students" (Unpublished master's thesis, University of Maryland, 1969).

37. Nakamura, H., "An Experimental Study of Reaction Time of the Start in Running a Race," *Research Quarterly Supplement,* 5:33-45, March, 1934.

38. Nelson, Fred B., "The Nelson Reaction Timer," Instruction leaflet, P. O. Box 51987, Lafayette, La.

39. Nelson, Jack K., "Development of a Practical Performance Test Combining Reaction Time, Speed of Movement and Choice of Response" (Unpublished study, Louisiana State University, 1967).

40. Norrie, Mary Lou, "Effects of Movement Complexity on Choice Reaction and Movement Times," *Research Quarterly,* 45:154-161, May, 1974.

41. Olsen, Einar A., "Relationship Between Psychological Capacities and Success in College Athletics," *Research Quarterly,* 27:79-89, March, 1956.

42. Owens, Jack A., "Effect of Variations in Hand and Foot Spacing on Movement Time and on Force of Charge," *Research Quarterly,* 31:75, March, 1960.

43. Reynolds, Harriet L., "The Effects of Augmented Levels of Stress on Reaction Time in the Peripheral Visual Field," *Research Quarterly,* 47:768-775, December, 1976.

44. Sigerseth, Peter O., and Norman N. York, "A Comparison of Certain Reaction Times of Basketball Players and Non-Athletes," *The Physical Educator,* 11:51-53, May, 1954.

45. Smith, Leon E., "Effect of Muscular Stretch, Tension, and Relaxation Upon the Reaction Time and Speed of Movement of a Supported Limb," *Research Quarterly,* 35:546-553, December, 1964.

46. _____ , "Specificity of Individual Differences of Relationship Between Forearm 'Strengths' and Speed of Forearm Flexion," *Research Quarterly,* 40:191-197, March, 1969.

47. Smith, Peter E., "Investigation of Total-Body and Arm Measures of Reaction Time, Movement Time, and Completion Time for Twelve, Fourteen, and Seventeen Year Old Athletes and Nonparticipants" (Unpublished master's thesis, University of Oregon, 1968).

48. Spirduso, Waneen, "Reaction and Movement Time as a Function of Age and Physical Activity Level," *Journal of Gerontology,* 30:435-440, 1975.

49. Thompson, Clem W., Francis J. Nagle, and Robert Dobias, "Football Starting Signals and Movement Times of High School and College Football Players," *Research Quarterly,* 29:222-230, May, 1958.

50. Vallerga, John M., "Influence of Perceptual Stimulus Intensity on Speed of Movement and Force of Muscular Contraction," *Research Quarterly,* 29:92-101, March, 1958.

51. Wilkin, Bruce M., "The Effect of Weight Training on Speed of Movement," *Research Quarterly,* 23:361-369, October, 1952.

52. Wilson, Don J., "Quickness of Reaction and Movement Related to Rhythmicity or Non-Rhythmicity of Signal Presentation," *Research Quarterly,* 30:101-109, March, 1959.

53. Zorbas, William S., and Peter V. Karpovich, "The Effect of Weight Lifting upon the Speed of Muscular Contraction," *Research Quarterly,* 22:145-148, May, 1951.

Chapter Sixteen

The Measurement of Sports Skills

One of the major objectives of physical education is the development of neuromuscular skills. It naturally follows then that physical educators should strive to construct precise and meaningful measuring devices to help evaluate the extent to which this objective is being met. Much of the total physical education program is devoted to the acquisition of sports skills. Thus, it is doubly important that continued efforts be made to scientifically construct valid, reliable, and objective tests in the various sports activities.

Utilization of Sports Skills Tests

There are many ways in which the teacher and the student may use skill tests. Some of these purposes of measurement are the same as for tests in other areas. But again, because sports activities represent such a major part of the physical education program, these performance tests are especially applicable to the instructional phase. Some specific uses of skills tests are suggested below:

1. The tests may be used to measure achievement in the particular sports activity.
   a. This information may be used to help evaluate the instructional program in terms of the effectiveness of the teaching methods and the strengths and weaknesses of the course's content.
   b. Achievement measures may also be utilized, in conjunction with other information, for grading purposes.
2. Skill tests can, and should, play an important role as a teaching aid to supplement instruction and to be used for practice. This would apply to the coach as well as to the teacher.
3. Skill tests enable each student to objectively plot his individual progress throughout the course and, conceivably, from one year to the next.
4. Skill tests can be used for diagnostic purposes by pointing out needs for special emphasis at each particular grade level in which a sport is taught. This is one way to avoid the needless repetition and lack of progression that characterize many physical education programs.
5. In some cases skill test items can, in themselves, be used for competition in intramural programs and for rainy day activities.
6. Skill tests have been used effectively as one of the means of interpreting the program to

the administration, the parents, and the public.

7. Skill tests can and should serve as excellent motivational devices.

Some Practical Sports Skills Tests

In this section some practical tests for measuring sports skills are presented. The reader is cautioned not to rely too heavily on one test or any battery of tests. Except in those sports such as archery, bowling, golf, certain track events, etc., in which the actual score itself is essentially an objective measure of achievement, skill tests can only measure certain aspects of performance in a particular sport. Furthermore, even in those sports mentioned above there are many factors such as environmental conditions, emotional pressure, and daily variations in performance that greatly influence one's score. It is suggested that the teacher think of skills tests more as instructional aids and motivational devices for the students rather than as valid measures of the students' ability to play a particular sport. In addition, the teacher should be especially alert to use these tests in developing local norms which are applicable and meaningful to the individual situation with regard to the factors of age, sex, interests, and socio-economic setting.

Sound tests have not been constructed for all sports. The authors have selected the following tests on the basis of their practicability in terms of the time required to administer them, the limited equipment needed, the ease of scoring, and their ability to measure at least certain aspects of performance in that sport. In some cases only one or two items have been

Table 16-1
AAHPER Archery Test
Percentile Scores Based on Age/Test Scores in Points

| | | Boys | | | | | | | | | | | | | | | | | | | |
| | Age | 12-13 | | | | 14 | | | | 15 | | | | 16 | | | | 17-18 | | | |
	Yards	10	20	30	Tot.	10	20	30	Tot.	10	20	30	Tot.	10	20	30	Tot.	10	20	30	Tot.
	100	91	70	45	195	96	75	50	210	100	90	81	270	100	100	95	270	100	95	85	270
	95	83	53	28	156	88	61	34	179	97	77	50	215	99	78	56	220	98	78	64	222
	90	78	44	24	138	80	48	28	160	94	70	41	195	97	71	47	205	96	72	53	206
	85	73	38	22	128	78	45	24	150	90	66	35	187	96	67	43	197	93	67	47	197
	80	70	34	18	122	75	41	21	146	88	63	31	177	91	63	40	189	90	63	42	190
	75	67	31	16	112	72	38	18	143	84	58	28	167	90	59	36	181	88	59	39	184
	70	64	28	14	103	70	36	16	139	80	54	25	158	88	56	32	173	86	55	37	176
	65	61	26	12	98	68	33	15	136	78	51	22	149	86	54	30	163	84	52	35	166
	60	59	24	11	93	67	30	13	130	76	47	20	140	84	51	28	160	82	49	31	158
	55	57	23	9	87	65	28	11	124	73	42	17	130	80	48	25	154	79	46	28	151
	50	54	22	8	81	63	26	10	119	69	39	15	120	79	46	23	148	77	43	26	144
	45	50	20	7	74	60	24	8	114	65	36	14	114	77	43	22	142	74	40	24	136
	40	48	18	6	67	57	22	7	110	62	34	13	107	75	41	20	136	71	37	21	130
	35	45	16	4	60	55	20	5	106	59	31	12	100	72	39	18	129	68	34	20	125
	30	42	14	0	54	52	18	4	98	55	28	11	94	70	36	16	123	63	32	17	119
	25	38	12	0	47	45	16	0	87	51	24	10	87	67	33	13	117	59	29	16	112
	20	34	10	0	38	40	14	0	77	48	21	9	79	61	28	11	110	55	25	11	109
	15	31	8	0	28	36	12	0	69	43	18	7	70	51	25	9	103	48	20	9	96
	10	26	6	0	21	31	10	0	61	36	15	6	62	50	20	6	80	40	17	6	86
	5	16	3	0	15	25	6	0	43	25	9	2	43	40	14	2	61	27	11	3	65
	0	0	0	0	0	0	0	0	0	0	0	0	0	0	0	0	0	0	0	0	0

Percentile (vertical axis label)

taken from a particular battery; in other cases the entire battery is briefly described. The reader should consult the original reference if a more complete description of a specific test is desired.

Archery

AAHPER Archery Test (1)

As a part of the Sports Skills Tests Project of the AAHPER, an archery test is available that is designed to measure skill in shooting at the standard 48-inch target from different distances for boys and girls ages twelve through eighteen.

Directions: It is recommended that the class be organized into squads of four, with one squad shooting at one target. Each archer shoots two ends of six arrows each (total of twelve arrows) at each distance, except that archers who do not score at least ten points at one distance may not advance to the farther distance.

As each subject finishes shooting, an assistant withdraws the arrows and records the score for each arrow. Each subject is given four practice shots at each distance. Distances are 10, 20, and 30 yards for boys and 10 and 20 yards for girls.

Scoring: (a) The standard 48-inch archery target is used with the point values nine, seven, five, three, and one for the respective circles from the center outward. (b) The total point value of the twelve arrows (two ends) is the score for each distance. Norms are presented for boys and girls.

Table 16-2
AAHPER Archery Test
Percentile Scores Based on Age/Test Scores in Points

		Girls													
Age		12 - 13			14			15			16			17 - 18	
Yards	10	20	Tot.	10	20	Tot.	10	20	Tot.	10	20	Tot.	10	20	Tot.
100	85	60	129	89	70	159	96	81	160	100	91	161	100	95	180
95	69	40	100	74	47	109	82	55	130	87	58	134	87	71	149
90	60	29	89	68	38	99	75	47	112	80	50	115	80	60	129
85	50	22	81	63	35	89	70	43	103	73	44	107	73	52	123
80	46	19	69	58	32	84	66	39	96	67	40	100	69	47	116
75	41	17	64	54	28	79	63	34	89	64	36	96	66	42	109
70	38	15	60	50	25	75	60	32	85	60	32	91	62	40	104
65	35	13	55	48	23	70	56	29	80	56	29	87	58	36	100
60	34	12	50	46	21	66	53	27	77	53	27	80	55	32	95
55	32	10	46	43	20	62	51	25	73	49	25	76	52	29	91
50	30	9	42	41	18	58	49	23	70	46	22	72	48	26	85
45	27	7	38	38	16	54	46	22	66	43	20	67	46	24	78
40	24	6	35	35	14	50	43	20	62	41	18	63	42	21	73
35	22	1	32	33	12	47	40	18	59	38	16	60	40	19	68
30	19	0	28	30	10	45	37	16	55	33	14	56	38	18	64
25	16	0	25	28	8	42	34	13	51	31	12	52	35	16	60
20	14	0	22	25	7	40	31	11	45	29	10	47	31	14	53
15	12	0	17	22	0	34	27	8	40	25	8	41	28	12	45
10	10	0	12	19	0	28	21	6	33	21	6	36	24	9	38
5	6	0	5	12	0	22	13	0	25	16	0	26	19	0	30
0	0	0	0	0	0	0	0	0	0	0	0	0	0	0	0

(Percentile Scores — vertical label at left)

Badminton

The Badminton Set-up Machine is an inexpensive device used for testing and training in the sport of badminton. It provides for overhead stroke practice and has pitch-out capabilities. Models may be either automatic or manual.

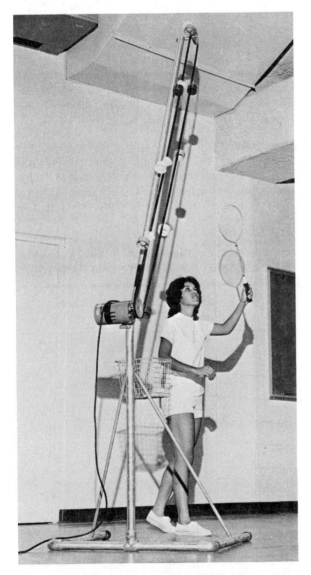

Figure 16-1. Inexpensive Badminton Set-up Machine* (Automatic Model) Shown in Use with the Overhead Smash Test

*The Badminton Set-up Machine, Model A-1, Patent Pending—1972, by Barry L. Johnson, Corpus Christi State University, Corpus Christi, Tx. 78411. (See Appendix K for plans.)

Badminton Smash Test

Objective: To measure ability in the overhead smash skill in badminton utilizing the Johnson Badminton Set-up Machine.

Age Level: Junior high school through college.

Sex: Satisfactory for both boys and girls.

Reliability: An *r* of .77 was reported by Bill Parker, 1973.

Objectivity: An *r* of .94 was obtained between the scoring of an experienced tester and an inexperienced tester.

Validity: Face validity was accepted for this test.

Equipment and Floor Markings: A Johnson Badminton Set-up Machine (motor or manual) is needed along with a tightly strung badminton racket and several birdies. Figure 16-2 shows lines and points that should be marked with chalk or tape on the court. The machine should be placed 13 feet from the net, with the arm rotating belt parallel to the net.

Directions: The subject will stand below the dropping point of the machine and facing the

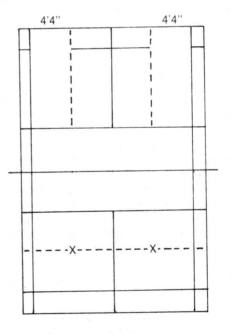

Target area is between the dotted line and the singles side line. Subjects may use either target area (left or right).

Figure 16-2. Court Markings for Smash Test

Table 16-3
Badminton Smash Test
Percentile Scores Based on Sex

	Sex		
Percentile	Boys	Girls	Percentile
100th	10	10	100th
95th	7	8	95th
90th	6	7	90th
80th	5	6	80th
70th	4	5	70th
60th	4	5	60th
50th	3	4	50th
40th	2	4	40th
30th	2	3	30th
20th	1	2	20th
10th	1	1	10th
0	0	0	0

Based on scores of 50 college men and 52 college women as reported by Bill Parker, 1973.

Reliability: Reliability coefficients from .51 to .89 have been obtained by using the odd-even method and the Spearman-Brown Prophecy Formula. The amount of playing experience apparently inversely influences the size of the reliability coefficient.

Equipment and Floor Markings: A clothesline rope should be stretched above the net, on the same standards, at a distance of 20 inches from the top of the net. A tightly strung badminton racket is needed, and at least five serviceable shuttles should be available for each player. Markings 2 inches wide in the form of arcs are drawn on the floor at distances of 22, 30, 38, and 46 inches from the midpoint of the intersection of the center line and the short service line of the right service court. (See Figure 16-3.) The distances include the width of the 2-inch lines.

Directions: The subject stands in the service court diagonally opposite from the target. Twenty serves are attempted, either consecutively or in groups of ten. The subject tries to send the shuttle *between* the net and the net. After seven practice trials, the student is to smash the bird into the scoring areas along either side line. Trials taken without reasonable speed and force are incorrect and must be repeated for scoring purposes.

Scoring: Ten trials are allowed for score and the maximum score possible is ten points. (See scoring table.)

Additional Pointers: (a) The student should be informed immediately when an incorrect stroke is to be repeated. (b) If a repeated trial is also incorrect, the trial is scored as zero. (c) The shuttle skirt should be placed skirt down in the cups of the machine so as to allow the bird a quick rotation to the tip down position for the smash shot.

French Short Serve Test (17)

Purpose: To measure accuracy of placement and ability in the low, short serve in badminton.

Age and Sex: College women (but can be used equally well with men).

Validity: With tournament rankings as a criterion, coefficients from .41 to .66 have been reported.

Table 16-4
Norms for the French Short Serve Test (18)

T-Score	Short Serve*	Short Serve**	T-Score
80	68	86	80
75	66	79	75
70	59	73	70
65	53	66	65
60	44	59	60
55	37	52	55
50	29	46	50
45	22	39	45
40	13	32	40
35	8	26	35
30	4	19	30
25	1	12	25
20	0	6	20

*Based on the performance of 385 college women after a 25-lesson beginning course in badminton.
**Based on the performance of 46 college women after a 30-lesson beginning course in badminton.

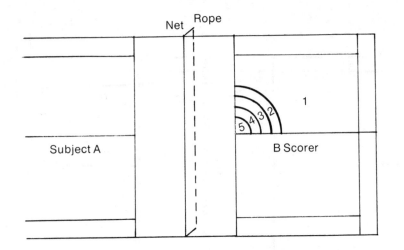

Figure 16-3. Court Markings for French Short Serve Test

rope. The scorer stands nearer the center of the left service court, facing the target (designated as B in Figure 16-3.) The subject tries to hit the target area nearest the intersection of the center line and short service line. Shuttles which hit on a line are given the higher point value.

Scoring: The zones are given point values of five, four, three, two, and one as indicated in Figure 16-3. The value of the area in which each shuttle hits is recorded as the score for each trial. Any trial which does not pass between the net and rope counts as zero; similarly, any trial landing out of bounds, either to the side or short of the short service line is zero. If the shuttle hits the rope, it is reserved and no trial counted.

Additional Pointers: (a) It is recommended that the test not be given until the students have had adequate practice. The test tends to be unreliable for beginning players until a certain degree of skill has been attained. (b) It is time consuming to administer unless there are several courts so that the testing does not interfere with regular play. (c) In keeping with a realistic game situation the subject should probably be instructed to serve from a point no closer than 2 or 3 feet from the short service line in his court.

The Poole Long Serve Test (16)

Purpose: To measure ability to serve high and deep to the rear of the court.

Sex and Age Level: Test may be used with high school and college students of both sexes.

Validity: The test correlated .51 with the results of tournament play.

Reliability: The test-retest reliability coefficient was .81.

Equipment and Court Markings: The court is marked as shown in Figure 16-4. Four lines have to be drawn which are indicated by the dotted lines in the figure. One line is drawn 2 inches behind and parallel to the back boundary line. A second line is drawn parallel to and 16 inches closer to the net than the first *drawn* line. This places the second drawn line 14 inches from the back boundary line and 16 inches in back of the doubles long service line. The third line is drawn 16 inches closer to the net and parallel to the doubles long service line. The fourth line is drawn 16 inches in depth as indicated in Figure 16-4. It should be noted that the 5-point zone extends 2 inches beyond the back boundary line. A 15-by-15-inch square is drawn 11 feet from the net in the middle of

Table 16-5
Poole's Long Serve Test
Scoring Scale

Preliminary Skill Test	Performance Level	Final Skill Test
26-Above	Advanced	30-Above
17-25	Intermediate	20-29
0-16	Beginner	0-19

Based on a limited number of beginner course students.

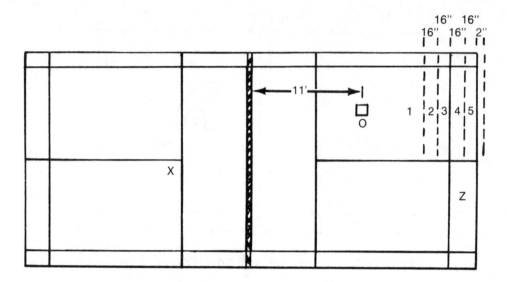

Figure 16-4. Court Markings for the Poole Long Serve Test

the service court (O). Two rackets and preferably twelve shuttles, in good condition, are needed for the test.

Directions: The subject stands anywhere in the right service court (X) and serves twelve shuttles. The server attempts to serve over the extended racket of a student who stands in the square (O) in the target court. This student acts as the "opponent" and assists in the scoring by yelling "low" for any shuttle which does not go over his racket.

Scoring: The scorer stands at point Z in the figure. Each serve is scored according to the zone in which the shuttle hits. The best ten out of twelve serves are totaled. A perfect score would be fifty. Shuttles hitting on the line are given the higher point values. One point is deducted for any shuttle that fails to clear the upheld racket of the player at O.

Additional Pointers: (a) Only legal serves are scored. (b) The height of the player O who extends the racket over his head is of little consequence. Naturally, extremes should be avoided. (c) Poole believed that this represented a more gamelike situation than the use of a rope and that it sacrificed very little objectivity. In addition, it facilitates the test administration in terms of equipment and economy of time. If the tester wishes to use a rope, Poole recommends that it be 9 feet high

and placed 11 feet from the net. (d) The 2-inch zone beyond the back boundary line was included in the maximum point zone because it was believed that an opponent would ordinarily play any shot that close to the base line. (e) In order to expedite the test administration, the test could be shortened to the best six out of eight trials. It was found that this scoring method correlated .95 with the ten out of twelve scoring system.

The Poole Forehand Clear Test (16)

Purpose: To measure the player's ability to hit the forehand clear from his back court high and deep into the opponent's court.

Sex and Age Level: The test may be used with high school and college students of both sexes.

Validity: The test correlated .70 with the results of tournament play.

Reliability: The test-retest reliability coefficient was .90.

Equipment and Court Markings: The court with scoring zones is marked as shown in Figure 16-5. One line is drawn parallel to and halfway (6½ feet) between the short service line and the doubles long service line. Another line is marked 6 inches beyond the back boundary line. A 15-by-15-inch square is drawn 11 feet from the net astride the center line (O in Figure 16-5). On the other side of the court a 15-by-15

Table 16-6
Poole's Forehand Clear
Scoring Scale

Preliminary Skill Test	Performance Level	Final Skill Test
20 - Above	Advanced	24 - Above
13 - 19	Intermediate	16 - 23
0 - 12	Beginner	0 - 15

Based on a limited number of beginner course students.

inch square is drawn at the intersection of the doubles long service line and the center line (X in Figure 16-5). Two rackets and preferably twelve shuttles in good condition are needed.

Directions: The subject stands with his right foot in the X square (assuming he is right-handed), holding his racket face up. The shuttle is placed feathers down on the forehand side of the racket. He then tosses the shuttle into the air and hits an overhead forehand clear of his opponent's racket and deep into the opponent's court. His right foot should stay in contact with the X square until the shuttle has been struck. A player stands at point O with his racket extended overhead. He calls out "low" if any shuttle does not go over his racket. Twelve clears are attempted.

Scoring: The point value of the zone in which the shuttle hits is recorded on the score sheet for each attempt. The best ten out of twelve shots are totaled. A perfect score would be forty. Shuttles hitting on the line are given the higher point values. One point is deducted for any shuttle which fails to clear the racket of the player O.

Additional Pointers: (a) Most of the pointers listed for the long service test apply also for this test. (b) The tossing of the shuttle by the subject is a skill that needs some practice; however, it has been demonstrated that any beginner can quickly acquire this skill. It was felt that this feature of the test (not utilizing a second person to serve shuttles to the subject) increases the objectivity of the test considerably and also facilitates the test administration. (c) The tossing and hitting of the shuttle also serves as a drill that the student can practice by himself on or off the court from the first day of class. (d) If desired, the test can be shortened to the best six out of eight trials. This correlated .96 with the best ten out of twelve score.

The Poole Backhand Clear Test (16)

Purpose: To measure the player's ability to hit a backhand clear from his back court high and deep into the opponent's court.

Sex and Age Level: High school and college males and females.

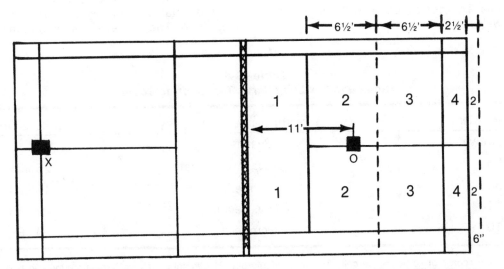

Figure 16-5. Court Markings for the Poole Forehand and Backhand Clear Tests

Table 16-7
Poole's Backhand Clear Test Scoring Scale

Preliminary Skill Test	Performance Level	Final Skill Test
16 - Above	Advanced	22 - Above
9 - 15	Intermediate	11 - 21
0 - 8	Beginner	0 - 10

Based on a limited number of beginner course students.

Validity: The test correlated .56 with the results of tournament play.
Reliability: The test-retest reliability coefficient was .78.
Equipment and Court Markings: Same as for the forehand clear test. (See Figure 16-5.)
Directions: Same as for the forehand clear with the following exception: The subject stands with his left foot in the X square. He places the shuttle on the forehand side of the racket, tosses it into the air, and then executes a backhand clear shot deep into the opponent's court. Twelve trials are given.
Scoring: Same as for the forehand clear test.
Additional Pointers: (a) Same as for the forehand clear test. The tossing skill needs practice. It was found that placing it on the forehand side of the racket was easier to perform for the backhand clear than placing it on the backhand side of the racket. (b) If desired, the test can be shortened to the best six out of eight trials. This correlated .94 with the best ten out of twelve score.

Scott and Fox
Long Serve Test (18)

Purpose: To measure ability to serve high and deep to the rear of the court.
Age and Sex: May be used for both sexes. College and/or high school level.
Validity: The test correlated .54 with subjective ratings by judges on forty-five university women.
Reliability: Reliability coefficients of .68 and .77 were obtained by Scott and Fox using the odd-even trials method and the Spearman-Brown Prophecy Formula.
Equipment and Floor Markings: Extra standards are needed from which a rope can be stretched across the court at a height of 8 feet and at a distance of 14 feet from the net. A tightly strung racket and at least five shuttles in good condition are needed for the test.

With chalk or washable paint, arcs are drawn outward from the intersection of the left singles side line and the long service line. The arcs are drawn at distances of 22, 30, 38, and 46 inches from the mid-point. Each distance includes the width of the 2-inch lines. (See Figure 16-6.)
Directions: The subject (A) stands in the service court diagonally opposite the target and attempts to serve over the rope into the corner of the court containing the target zones. The shuttle must pass over the rope in order to score points. Only legal serves count as trials. The target zones are marked according to the point values shown in Figure 16-6. Twenty shuttles are served.
Scoring: Any shuttle falling on a line is given the higher point value. The score for the entire test is the total of the twenty trials. Fouls are repeated. The scorer (B) should stand so that

Table 16-8
Scott and Fox Long Serve Test Scoring Scale

College Men	Performance Level	College Women
39 - Above	Advanced	33 - Above
31 - 38	Adv. Intermediate	26 - 31
22 - 30	Intermediate	14 - 25
17 - 21	Adv. Beginner	9 - 13
0 - 16	Beginner	0 - 8

Based on the scores of 70 beginning college male students and 91 beginning college female students in badminton as reported by Steve Long, 1972.

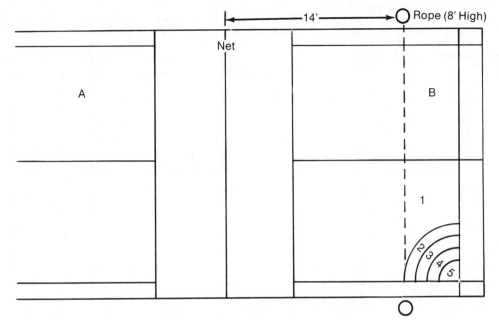

Figure 16-6. Court Markings for Scott and Fox Long Serve Test.

he can determine whether or not the shuttle passed over the rope as well as to see where the shuttles hit. Scores are called out to a recorder.

French Clear Test (18)

Purpose: To measure power necessary to successfully execute the clear shot in badminton.

Age and Sex: College women (but can be used with men).

Validity: The validity coefficient was reported to be .60 when correlated with tournament rankings.

Reliability: The odd-even method stepped up by the Spearman-Brown Prophecy Formula resulted in a correlation of .96.

Equipment and Materials Needed: A clothesline rope is stretched across the court at a height of 8 feet, at a distance of 14 feet from the net. At least five shuttlecocks, a tightly strung racket, and floor markings with lines 1½ inches wide drawn on the floor as shown in Figure 16-7.

Directions: The subject (A) stands behind the short service line on the court opposite the target. Small marks are drawn in each service court 11 feet from the net and 3 feet from the

Table 16-9
French High Clear Test Scoring Scale

College Men	Performance Level	College Women
84 - Above	Advanced	74 - Above
77 - 83	Adv. Intermediate	57 - 73
64 - 76	Intermediate	23 - 56
53 - 63	Adv. Beginner	4 - 22
0 - 52	Beginner	0 - 3

Based on the scores of 83 beginning college male students in badminton and 100 beginning college female students in badminton as reported by Dixie Bennett, 1972.

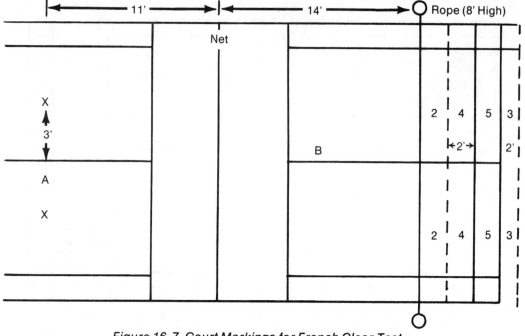

Figure 16-7. Court Markings for French Clear Test

center line. An experienced player (B) (or perhaps the instructor) serves to the subject who stands between the two marks. A total of twenty shuttles are served to each subject, who attempts to return each shuttle with a clear shot that goes over the rope and, preferably, lands near the end line. The twenty shuttles may be given consecutively or in groups of ten. A serve to the subject should fall between the two marks. If it does not go that far, or falls outside the marks, the subject is not supposed to return it. Thus, the subject does not have to play a poorly placed shuttle; only those shuttles played by the subject count as trials. The subject repeats any trial in which a foul is committed, such as when a stroke is *carried* or *slung,* or in the event that the shuttle hits the rope. The instructor demonstrates, and two practice trials are then given. The target extends from side to side, thus the subject does not have to confine his shots to half the court. The point values are shown in Figure 16-7.

Scoring: The server also acts as the scorer, calling out the point value for each shuttle. The score is the total points for the twenty trials. An assistant records the scores. Any shuttle landing on a line receives the higher point value. Only those shuttles passing over the rope count for score.

Basketball

The AAHPER Basketball Skill Test (20, 21)

Front Shot:* The subject shoots from a marked spot to the left of the free throw line just outside the circle. Any method of shooting is permitted, and the player attempts to make the shot without hitting the backboard. A total of fifteen trials are given in series of five at a time. He must leave the spot after each five shots. *Scoring:* A basket made counts two points; one point is awarded for a shot that hits the rim but does not go in (provided that it does not hit the backboard before it hits the rim). A total of thirty points is possible.

Side Shot: A line is drawn near the corner of the court at each side of the basket—20 feet for boys, 15 feet for girls—measured from the center of the basket. The subject shoots ten shots from each side, using any type shot. *Scoring:* Each basket counts two points, and one point is given for balls that hit the rim but do not go in. In this case it doesn't matter whether or not the backboard is hit. A total of forty points is possible.

*Norms for all items follow.

Table 16-10
AAHPER Basketball

FRONT SHOT (BOYS)

Percentile Scores Based on Age/Test Scores in Points

Percentile	Age								Percentile
	10	11	12	13	14	15	16	17-18	
100th	23	26	27	27	27	29	29	30	100th
95th	17	17	18	21	22	22	22	24	95th
90th	15	16	18	19	20	21	21	22	90th
85th	13	15	17	18	20	20	20	21	85th
80th	12	14	16	17	19	20	20	20	80th
75th	11	13	15	16	18	19	19	19	75th
70th	10	12	14	16	17	18	18	18	70th
65th	9	12	14	15	17	17	17	18	65th
60th	9	11	13	15	16	17	17	17	60th
55th	8	10	12	14	16	16	16	17	55th
50th	7	9	11	14	15	16	16	16	50th
45th	7	9	11	13	15	15	15	16	45th
40th	6	8	10	12	14	15	15	15	40th
35th	5	7	9	12	13	14	14	14	35th
30th	4	6	9	11	12	14	14	14	30th
25th	4	6	8	10	12	13	13	13	25th
20th	3	5	7	10	11	12	12	12	20th
15th	2	4	6	8	10	11	11	11	15th
10th	1	2	5	7	9	10	10	10	10th
5th	0	1	3	5	7	7	8	8	5th
0	0	0	0	0	0	3	3	3	0

FRONT SHOT (GIRLS)

Percentile	Age							Percentile
	10-11	12	13	14	15	16	17-18	
100th	21	21	30	30	30	30	30	100th
95th	14	15	17	18	18	18	18	95th
90th	12	13	15	16	16	17	17	90th
85th	11	12	14	15	15	15	16	85th
80th	10	11	13	14	14	14	15	80th
75th	9	10	12	13	13	14	14	75th
70th	8	9	11	12	13	13	13	70th
65th	7	9	10	11	12	12	13	65th
60th	6	8	9	10	11	12	12	60th
55th	6	8	9	9	10	11	11	55th
50th	5	7	8	9	9	10	11	50th
45th	4	6	7	8	9	9	10	45th
40th	3	6	6	8	8	9	9	40th
35th	3	5	6	7	7	8	9	35th
30th	2	4	6	6	7	8	8	30th
25th	1	4	5	5	6	7	7	25th
20th	1	3	4	4	5	6	6	20th
15th	1	2	3	3	4	5	5	15th
10th	0	1	2	2	3	4	4	10th
5th	0	0	1	1	2	2	3	5th
0	0	0	0	0	0	0	0	0

Table 16-11

SIDE SHOT (BOYS)

Percentile Scores Based on Age/Test Scores in Points

Percentile	Age 10	11	12	13	14	15	16	17-18	Percentile
100th	27	29	32	33	35	35	35	36	100th
95th	17	18	21	25	26	26	26	26	95th
90th	14	16	20	21	24	24	25	25	90th
85th	13	14	17	20	22	22	22	24	85th
80th	11	13	17	19	21	21	21	22	80th
75th	9	12	15	17	20	20	20	21	75th
70th	8	11	14	16	19	19	19	21	70th
65th	7	10	13	15	18	18	18	20	65th
60th	6	9	12	14	17	17	17	19	60th
55th	5	8	12	14	16	16	16	18	55th
50th	5	7	11	13	16	16	16	18	50th
45th	4	6	10	12	15	15	15	17	45th
40th	3	5	9	11	15	15	15	16	40th
35th	3	5	8	10	14	14	14	15	35th
30th	2	4	7	9	13	13	13	14	30th
25th	1	3	6	8	12	12	12	13	25th
20th	1	2	5	7	11	11	11	12	20th
15th	0	2	4	6	10	10	10	11	15th
10th	0	2	3	5	7	7	9	9	10th
5th	0	2	2	3	5	5	7	7	5th
0	0	0	0	1	1	2	2	2	0

SIDE SHOT (GIRLS)

Percentile	Age 10-11	12	13	14	15	16	17-18	Percentile
100th	25	26	29	30	31	31	32	100th
95th	16	16	19	21	22	23	22	95th
90th	13	15	17	18	20	20	20	90th
85th	12	13	15	17	18	18	18	85th
80th	11	12	14	16	17	17	17	80th
75th	9	11	13	15	16	16	16	75th
70th	8	10	12	14	15	15	15	70th
65th	7	9	11	13	14	14	14	65th
60th	6	8	11	12	13	13	13	60th
55th	5	7	10	12	12	12	12	55th
50th	4	6	9	11	12	12	12	50th
45th	4	6	8	10	11	11	11	45th
40th	3	5	7	9	10	10	10	40th
35th	2	4	6	8	9	9	9	35th
30th	1	3	6	8	8	8	8	30th
25th	1	3	5	7	7	7	7	25th
20th	0	2	4	6	6	6	6	20th
15th	0	1	3	5	5	5	5	15th
10th	0	0	1	3	3	3	3	10th
5th	0	0	0	1	2	1	1	5th
0	0	0	0	0	0	0	0	0

Table 16-12

FOUL SHOT (BOYS)

Percentile Scores Based on Age/Test Scores in Number of Baskets Made

| Percentile | Age | | | | | | | | Percentile |
	10	11	12	13	14	15	16	17-18	
100th	13	16	17	20	20	20	20	20	100th
95th	7	8	10	12	13	16	16	16	95th
90th	5	7	8	10	11	13	13	13	90th
85th	4	6	7	9	10	12	12	12	85th
80th	4	5	7	8	10	11	11	11	80th
75th	3	5	6	7	9	10	10	10	75th
70th	3	4	6	7	8	9	9	9	70th
65th	3	4	5	6	8	8	8	9	65th
60th	2	3	5	6	7	8	8	8	60th
55th	2	3	4	5	7	8	8	8	55th
50th	2	3	4	5	6	8	8	8	50th
45th	2	3	4	5	6	7	7	7	45th
40th	1	2	3	4	5	7	7	7	40th
35th	1	2	3	4	5	6	6	6	35th
30th	1	1	3	3	4	5	5	5	30th
25th	0	1	2	3	4	5	5	5	25th
20th	0	1	2	2	4	4	4	4	20th
15th	0	1	1	2	3	4	4	4	15th
10th	0	0	1	1	2	3	3	3	10th
5th	0	0	0	1	2	2	2	2	5th
0	0	0	0	0	0	0	0	0	0

FOUL SHOT (GIRLS)

| Percentile | Age | | | | | | | Percentile |
	10-11	12	13	14	15	16	17-18	
100th	20	20	20	20	20	20	20	100th
95th	7	8	9	9	9	10	10	95th
90th	5	6	7	7	8	9	9	90th
85th	4	5	6	6	7	8	8	85th
80th	4	5	5	5	6	7	7	80th
75th	3	4	5	5	6	6	6	75th
70th	3	4	4	4	5	6	6	70th
65th	2	3	4	4	5	5	5	65th
60th	2	3	3	3	4	5	5	60th
55th	2	2	3	3	4	4	5	55th
50th	1	2	3	3	4	4	4	50th
45th	1	2	2	3	3	4	4	45th
40th	1	2	2	2	3	3	4	40th
35th	0	1	2	2	3	3	3	35th
30th	0	1	1	2	2	3	3	30th
25th	0	1	1	2	2	2	3	25th
20th	0	1	1	1	2	2	2	20th
15th	0	0	1	1	1	1	2	15th
10th	0	0	0	1	1	1	2	10th
5th	0	0	0	0	0	0	1	5th
0	0	0	0	0	0	0	0	0

Table 16-13

UNDER BASKET SHOT (BOYS)

Percentile Scores Based on Age/Test Scores in Number of Baskets Made

Percentile	Age								Percentile
	10	11	12	13	14	15	16	17-18	
100th	14	23	23	23	23	29	33	34	100th
95th	10	11	13	15	16	18	19	20	95th
90th	9	10	11	13	15	17	17	18	90th
85th	7	9	10	12	14	16	17	17	85th
80th	7	8	10	12	14	15	15	16	80th
75th	6	8	9	11	13	15	15	15	75th
70th	6	7	9	10	12	14	14	15	70th
65th	6	6	8	10	12	13	14	14	65th
60th	6	6	8	10	12	13	14	14	60th
55th	5	6	7	9	11	13	13	14	55th
50th	5	6	7	8	10	11	12	13	50th
45th	4	5	7	8	10	11	12	12	45th
40th	4	5	5	6	9	10	11	11	40th
35th	4	4	5	6	9	9	10	11	35th
30th	3	4	5	6	8	9	9	10	30th
25th	3	4	4	5	8	8	9	10	25th
20th	3	3	4	5	7	8	8	9	20th
15th	2	3	4	5	6	7	7	8	15th
10th	2	2	3	3	4	6	6	7	10th
5th	1	1	2	2	3	4	5	6	5th
0	0	1	1	1	1	1	1	1	0

UNDER BASKET SHOT (GIRLS)

Percentile	Age							Percentile
	10-11	12	13	14	15	16	17-18	
100th	15	15	16	16	18	19	20	100th
95th	8	10	10	11	11	13	13	95th
90th	7	8	8	10	10	11	11	90th
85th	6	7	8	9	9	10	10	85th
80th	5	7	7	8	8	9	9	80th
75th	5	6	7	8	8	8	8	75th
70th	5	6	7	7	7	8	8	70th
65th	5	5	6	7	7	7	7	65th
60th	4	5	6	6	6	7	7	60th
55th	4	5	6	6	6	6	6	55th
50th	4	4	5	6	6	6	6	50th
45th	4	4	5	5	5	5	5	45th
40th	3	4	5	5	5	5	5	40th
35th	3	4	4	5	5	5	5	35th
30th	3	3	4	4	4	4	4	30th
25th	2	3	4	4	4	4	4	25th
20th	2	3	3	4	4	4	4	20th
15th	2	2	3	3	3	3	3	15th
10th	1	2	2	3	3	3	3	10th
5th	1	1	1	2	2	2	2	5th
0	0	0	0	1	1	1	1	0

Table 16-14

SPEED PASS (BOYS)
Percentile Scores Based on Age/Test Scores in Seconds and Tenths

Percentile	Age								Percentile
	10	11	12	13	14	15	16	17-18	
100th	10.0	8.5	5.5	5.5	5.5	4.5	4.5	4.5	100th
95th	11.6	10.5	8.5	7.8	7.6	7.4	7.3	6.8	95th
90th	11.6	11.2	9.7	8.3	8.0	7.8	7.7	7.2	90th
85th	12.2	11.6	10.1	8.8	8.3	8.0	7.9	7.5	85th
80th	12.5	11.9	10.4	9.3	8.6	8.3	8.1	7.8	80th
75th	12.8	12.2	10.7	9.8	8.9	8.5	8.4	8.0	75th
70th	13.1	12.4	11.1	10.0	9.0	8.7	8.6	8.2	70th
65th	13.3	12.7	11.4	10.3	9.2	8.9	8.7	8.3	65th
60th	13.6	12.9	11.7	10.6	9.4	9.1	8.9	8.6	60th
55th	13.9	13.2	11.7	10.8	9.6	9.3	9.1	8.8	55th
50th	14.2	13.4	12.2	11.1	9.9	9.4	9.2	9.0	50th
45th	16.6	13.7	12.5	11.4	10.2	9.6	9.4	9.2	45th
40th	14.9	14.0	12.7	11.8	10.4	10.0	9.6	9.4	40th
35th	15.2	14.3	13.0	12.2	10.6	10.2	9.9	9.6	35th
30th	15.6	14.6	13.3	12.6	11.0	10.5	10.2	9.9	30th
25th	16.0	14.9	13.6	13.0	11.3	10.9	10.5	10.2	25th
20th	16.5	15.3	14.2	13.4	11.7	11.3	11.1	10.5	20th
15th	17.3	15.7	14.9	14.2	12.2	12.0	11.6	11.1	15th
10th	18.1	16.3	15.5	15.1	13.0	12.8	12.5	11.9	10th
5th	19.3	17.5	16.9	16.6	14.4	14.1	14.0	13.4	5th
0	26.0	26.5	25.0	21.4	20.4	20.4	20.3	20.0	0

SPEED PASS (GIRLS)

Percentile	Age							Percentile
	10-11	12	13	14	15	16	17-18	
100th	7.5	7.5	7.5	7.5	7.5	6.5	6.5	100th
95th	11.9	10.5	10.4	10.0	9.5	9.5	9.5	95th
90th	12.6	11.1	11.1	10.7	10.2	10.1	10.0	90th
85th	12.9	11.7	11.7	11.1	10.7	10.6	10.4	85th
80th	13.2	12.0	12.0	11.5	11.0	10.9	10.7	80th
75th	13.5	12.4	12.4	11.8	11.3	11.2	11.0	75th
70th	13.9	12.8	12.7	12.1	11.6	11.5	11.3	70th
65th	14.2	13.1	13.0	12.4	11.9	11.8	11.6	65th
60th	14.5	13.4	13.2	12.7	12.2	12.1	11.9	60th
55th	14.9	13.7	13.5	13.0	12.5	12.4	12.2	55th
50th	15.3	14.0	13.8	13.4	12.8	12.7	12.5	50th
45th	15.6	14.4	14.2	13.7	13.1	13.0	12.8	45th
40th	15.9	14.8	14.5	14.0	13.5	13.4	13.1	40th
35th	16.3	15.1	14.9	14.4	13.9	13.6	13.4	35th
30th	16.7	15.5	15.3	14.8	14.3	14.1	13.8	30th
25th	17.2	16.1	15.8	15.1	14.8	14.5	14.4	25th
20th	17.7	16.8	16.4	15.5	15.3	15.1	15.0	20th
15th	18.3	17.6	17.1	16.2	16.1	15.7	15.7	15th
10th	19.1	18.4	18.2	17.3	17.0	16.6	16.6	10th
5th	20.3	21.1	20.0	19.2	18.6	18.0	17.9	5th
0	25.5	25.4	25.4	25.4	25.4	25.4	24.4	0

Table 16-15

JUMP AND REACH (BOYS)

Percentile Scores Based on Age/Test Scores in Inches

Percentile	10 In.	10 Cm.	11 In.	11 Cm.	12 In.	12 Cm.	13 In.	13 Cm.	14 In.	14 Cm.	15 In.	15 Cm.	16 In.	16 Cm.	17-18 In.	17-18 Cm.	Percentile
100th	18	46	22	56	25	64	29	74	29	74	31	79	31	79	34	86	100th
95th	14	36	16	41	18	46	20	51	22	56	24	61	24	61	26	66	95th
90th	13	33	15	38	17	43	19	48	21	53	22	56	23	58	25	64	90th
85th	13	33	14	36	16	41	18	46	21	53	21	53	22	56	24	61	85th
80th	12	30	14	36	16	41	17	43	20	51	21	53	21	53	24	58	80th
75th	12	30	13	33	15	38	17	43	19	48	20	51	21	53	23	58	75th
70th	12	30	13	33	15	38	17	43	19	48	20	51	21	53	23	58	70th
65th	11	28	12	30	14	36	16	41	18	46	19	48	20	51	22	56	65th
60th	11	28	12	30	14	36	16	41	18	46	19	48	20	51	22	56	60th
55th	11	28	12	30	13	33	15	38	17	43	18	46	19	48	21	53	55th
50th	10	25	11	28	13	33	15	38	17	43	18	46	19	48	20	51	50th
45th	10	25	11	28	13	33	14	36	16	41	17	43	18	46	20	51	45th
40th	10	25	11	28	13	33	14	36	16	41	17	43	18	46	19	48	40th
35th	10	25	10	25	12	30	14	36	15	38	17	43	18	46	19	48	35th
30th	9	23	10	25	12	30	13	33	15	38	16	41	17	43	18	46	30th
25th	9	23	10	25	11	28	13	33	14	36	16	41	17	43	18	46	25th
20th	9	23	9	23	10	25	11	28	13	33	14	36	15	38	16	41	20th
15th	8	20	9	23	10	25	11	28	13	33	14	36	14	36	15	38	15th
10th	8	20	8	20	10	25	11	28	13	33	13	33	14	36	15	38	10th
5th	6	15	7	18	9	23	9	23	12	30	12	30	13	33	14	36	5th
0	4	10	4	10	5	13	5	13	7	18	7	18	8	20	13	33	0

JUMP AND REACH (GIRLS)

Percentile	10-11 In.	10-11 Cm.	12 In.	12 Cm.	13 In.	13 Cm.	14 In.	14 Cm.	15 In.	15 Cm.	16 In.	16 Cm.	17-18 In.	17-18 Cm.	Percentile
100th	18	46	21	53	24	61	24	61	25	64	25	64	25	64	100th
95th	15	38	16	41	17	43	18	46	18	46	18	46	18	46	95th
90th	14	36	15	38	16	41	16	41	17	43	17	43	17	43	90th
85th	13	33	14	36	15	38	15	38	16	41	16	41	16	41	85th
80th	12	30	14	36	15	38	15	38	16	41	16	41	16	41	80th
75th	12	30	13	33	14	36	14	36	15	38	15	38	15	38	75th
70th	11	28	13	33	14	36	14	36	15	38	15	38	15	38	70th
65th	11	28	13	33	13	33	14	36	14	36	14	36	14	36	65th
60th	11	28	12	30	13	33	13	33	14	36	14	36	14	36	60th
55th	10	25	12	30	12	30	13	33	14	36	14	36	14	36	55th
50th	10	25	12	30	12	30	13	33	13	33	13	33	13	33	50th
45th	10	25	11	28	12	30	12	30	13	33	13	33	13	33	45th
40th	10	25	11	28	11	28	12	30	13	33	13	33	13	33	40th
35th	9	23	11	28	11	28	12	30	12	30	12	30	12	30	35th
30th	9	23	10	25	11	28	11	28	12	30	12	30	12	30	30th
25th	9	23	10	25	10	25	11	28	11	28	11	28	12	30	25th
20th	9	23	9	23	10	25	10	25	11	28	11	28	11	28	20th
15th	8	20	9	23	9	23	10	25	10	25	10	25	11	28	15th
10th	8	20	9	23	9	23	9	23	10	25	10	25	10	25	10th
5th	7	18	8	20	8	20	9	23	9	23	9	23	9	23	5th
0	5	13	5	13	5	13	5	13	7	18	7	18	7	18	0

Table 16-16

OVERARM PASS FOR ACCURACY (BOYS)

Percentile Scores Based on Age/Test Scores in Points

| Percentile | Age | | | | | | | | Percentile |
	10	11	12	13	14	15	16	17-18	
100th	18	27	27	27	29	31	31	31	100th
95th	14	18	20	20	22	24	24	25	95th
90th	13	15	18	19	21	22	22	23	90th
85th	11	14	17	18	20	21	21	22	85th
80th	10	12	16	17	19	20	20	21	80th
75th	8	11	15	16	18	19	19	20	75th
70th	7	11	14	16	18	19	19	19	70th
65th	6	10	13	15	17	17	18	18	65th
60th	6	9	12	15	17	17	17	17	60th
55th	5	8	12	14	16	17	17	17	55th
50th	4	7	11	13	16	16	16	16	50th
45th	3	6	10	12	15	15	15	15	45th
40th	2	5	10	12	14	15	15	15	40th
35th	2	4	9	11	14	14	14	14	35th
30th	1	3	8	10	13	13	13	13	30th
25th	0	2	7	9	12	12	12	12	25th
20th	0	2	6	9	10	11	11	11	20th
15th	0	1	5	8	10	10	11	11	15th
10th	0	1	3	6	9	9	9	9	10th
5th	0	0	2	4	7	7	8	8	5th
0	0	0	0	0	0	0	0	0	0

OVERARM PASS FOR ACCURACY (GIRLS)

| Percentile | Age | | | | | | | Percentile |
	10-11	12	13	14	15	16	17-18	
100th	27	29	30	30	30	30	30	100th
95th	23	24	25	25	26	26	26	95th
90th	22	23	24	24	25	25	25	90th
85th	21	22	23	23	24	24	24	85th
80th	19	21	22	22	23	23	23	80th
75th	18	20	21	21	22	22	22	75th
70th	17	19	20	20	22	22	22	70th
65th	16	18	19	20	21	21	21	65th
60th	14	17	18	19	20	21	20	60th
55th	13	16	18	18	20	20	19	55th
50th	12	15	17	18	19	19	19	50th
45th	11	15	17	17	18	18	18	45th
40th	10	14	15	16	17	17	17	40th
35th	8	13	14	15	17	17	15	35th
30th	7	12	13	15	16	16	14	30th
25th	5	11	12	14	15	15	13	25th
20th	4	9	11	13	13	14	11	20th
15th	2	7	9	11	12	12	10	15th
10th	0	4	7	9	9	9	8	10th
5th	0	1	4	6	6	6	5	5th
0	0	0	0	0	0	0	0	0

Table 16-17

PUSH PASS FOR ACCURACY (BOYS)

Percentile Scores Based on Age/Test Scores in Points

Percentile	Age 11	12	13	14	15	16	17-18	Percentile
100th	29	29	29	29	29	30	30	100th
95th	19	22	24	25	27	27	29	95th
90th	17	20	22	24	25	26	28	90th
85th	14	18	21	23	24	25	28	85th
80th	12	16	20	21	23	24	27	80th
75th	11	14	19	21	23	23	27	75th
70th	9	13	18	20	22	23	26	70th
65th	8	12	17	19	21	22	26	65th
60th	7	11	16	18	21	21	26	60th
55th	5	10	15	18	20	21	25	55th
50th	4	9	13	17	19	20	24	50th
45th	3	8	13	16	19	19	24	45th
40th	2	7	12	15	18	18	23	40th
35th	1	5	11	14	17	18	23	35th
30th	1	4	10	14	16	17	22	30th
25th	1	3	9	12	15	16	21	25th
20th	1	2	7	11	14	15	20	20th
15th	0	2	5	10	13	14	18	15th
10th	0	1	2	8	11	12	17	10th
5th	0	1	1	4	6	9	14	5th
0	0	0	1	1	2	4	5	0

PUSH PASS FOR ACCURACY (GIRLS)

Percentile	Age 10-11	12	13	14	15	16	17-18	Percentile
100th	29	30	30	30	30	30	30	100th
95th	26	27	28	28	29	29	29	95th
90th	24	26	27	28	28	28	28	90th
85th	23	25	26	27	27	27	27	85th
80th	22	24	25	26	27	27	27	80th
75th	21	23	24	25	26	26	26	75th
70th	21	22	24	25	25	26	26	70th
65th	20	22	23	24	25	25	25	65th
60th	19	21	22	23	24	25	25	60th
55th	18	20	22	23	24	24	24	55th
50th	17	19	21	22	23	24	24	50th
45th	16	19	21	22	23	23	23	45th
40th	15	18	20	21	22	22	23	40th
35th	13	17	19	20	22	22	22	35th
30th	12	16	18	19	21	21	21	30th
25th	10	14	17	18	20	20	20	25th
20th	8	12	15	17	19	19	19	20th
15th	7	10	13	15	18	17	17	15th
10th	4	8	11	13	16	12	13	10th
5th	2	4	7	10	12	8	9	5th
0	0	0	0	0	0	0	0	0

Table 16-18

DRIBBLING (BOYS)
Percentile Scores Based on Age/Tests Scores in Seconds and Tenths

Percentile	10	11	12	13	14	15	16	17-18	Percentile
100th	12.0	10.5	6.5	6.5	6.5	5.5	5.5	5.5	100th
95th	13.0	12.0	10.3	9.8	9.7	9.5	9.5	8.8	95th
90th	13.7	12.8	11.3	10.4	10.1	9.8	9.8	9.5	90th
85th	14.1	13.0	11.7	10.8	10.7	10.1	10.0	9.9	85th
80th	14.6	13.3	12.1	11.2	10.9	10.3	10.3	10.3	80th
75th	14.8	13.6	12.3	11.6	11.1	10.6	10.5	10.5	75th
70th	15.1	13.9	12.6	11.9	11.3	10.9	10.8	10.8	70th
65th	15.3	14.1	12.9	12.2	11.5	11.1	11.0	11.0	65th
60th	15.5	14.4	13.2	12.4	11.8	11.4	11.3	11.2	60th
55th	15.8	14.7	13.4	12.7	12.0	11.7	11.5	11.5	55th
50th	16.0	15.0	13.7	13.0	12.3	12.0	11.8	11.7	50th
45th	16.3	15.3	14.1	13.3	12.6	12.3	12.1	11.8	45th
40th	16.5	15.6	14.4	13.6	12.9	12.6	12.3	12.0	40th
35th	16.9	16.0	14.7	13.9	13.2	12.9	12.6	12.3	35th
30th	17.2	16.3	15.0	14.2	13.6	13.2	12.9	12.6	30th
25th	17.6	16.8	15.3	14.4	13.9	13.5	13.2	13.0	25th
20th	18.0	17.2	15.8	14.9	14.3	14.0	13.4	13.3	20th
15th	18.4	17.9	16.5	15.3	14.8	14.5	13.8	13.7	15th
10th	19.4	18.8	17.3	16.1	15.6	15.2	14.2	14.2	10th
5th	21.4	20.4	18.7	18.3	17.4	16.5	14.7	14.6	5th
0	26.0	26.5	26.5	23.0	22.0	22.0	21.6	21.5	0

DRIBBLING (GIRLS)

Percentile	10-11	12	13	14	15	16	17-18	Percentile
100th	9.5	9.5	9.5	9.5	9.5	8.5	7.5	100th
95th	13.7	12.0	11.7	11.7	11.7	10.9	10.8	95th
90th	14.5	12.9	12.8	12.6	12.3	11.7	11.7	90th
85th	14.9	13.5	13.3	13.0	12.8	12.1	12.0	85th
80th	15.2	14.0	13.7	13.4	13.1	12.5	12.4	80th
75th	15.6	14.3	14.0	13.7	13.4	12.7	12.7	75th
70th	15.9	14.6	14.4	14.0	13.6	13.0	13.0	70th
65th	16.2	14.9	14.7	14.3	13.8	13.2	13.2	65th
60th	16.5	15.2	14.9	14.5	14.0	13.5	13.4	60th
55th	16.8	15.5	15.1	14.8	14.2	13.7	13.6	55th
50th	17.1	15.8	15.4	15.0	14.5	14.0	14.0	50th
45th	17.5	16.2	15.7	15.2	14.7	14.3	14.3	45th
40th	17.8	16.5	16.1	15.5	15.0	14.6	14.5	40th
35th	18.2	16.9	16.4	15.8	15.3	14.9	14.7	35th
30th	18.5	17.3	16.7	16.2	15.6	15.2	15.0	30th
25th	19.0	17.7	17.1	16.5	16.0	15.5	15.2	25th
20th	19.5	18.2	17.5	17.0	16.3	16.0	15.5	20th
15th	20.4	18.7	18.0	17.5	16.9	16.5	16.3	15th
10th	21.1	20.5	18.2	17.8	17.2	17.1	17.0	10th
5th	22.4	21.2	20.6	19.8	18.9	18.4	18.0	5th
0	29.0	24.5	24.5	24.5	24.5	24.5	24.5	0

Foul Shot: The subject shoots twenty free throws in series of five at a time. He must leave the spot after each five shots. Any method of shooting is permitted. *Scoring:* One point is given for each basket made regardless of how it goes in. A total of twenty points is possible.

Under Basket Shot: The subject stands with the ball under the basket. On the signal to begin he starts making as many lay-up shots as possible within 30 seconds. Any method of shooting is permitted; the subject must recover the ball each time. Two complete trials are given. *Scoring:* One point is given for each basket made. The number of baskets made in 30 seconds in the better of the two trials is the score.

Speed Pass: The subject stands behind a line drawn 9 feet from the wall. On the signal to begin, he passes the ball against the wall as rapidly as possible until ten passes have hit the wall. All passes have to be made from behind the line, and the subject must recover his pass each time. Two complete trials are given. *Scoring:* The watch is started as soon as the first pass hits the wall and is stopped when the tenth ball hits. The time to the nearest tenth of a second of the better of the two trials is recorded as the score.

Jump and Reach: The usual procedures for this test are followed. The subject holds a piece of chalk ¾ inch long to make the standing and jumping marks. Two trials are given. *Scoring:* The score is the difference between the standing and jumping marks of the better of two trials to the nearest inch.

Overarm Pass for Accuracy: The subject, using a one armed throw, passes the ball at a distance—35 feet for boys, 20 feet for girls—away from the target, which is circular and consists of three circles. The inner circle is 18 inches in diameter, the second circle is 38 inches, and the outer circle is 58 inches in diameter. The bottom of the outer circle is 3 feet from the floor. Ten passes are made, and all must be made from behind the restraining line. *Scoring:* The point values for the inner, middle, and outer circles are three, two, and one, respectively. Any pass hitting a line is given the higher score. A maximum of thirty points is possible.

Push Pass for Accuracy: The subject passes from behind a line—25 feet for boys, 15 feet for girls—from the same target as used in the overarm pass. A two hand push pass is used. Ten trials are given. *Scoring:* The same scoring procedures are used as in the overarm pass. A total of thirty points is possible.

Dribble: Six chairs are placed in a straight line. The first chair is 5 feet from the starting line; the rest of the chairs are 8 feet apart. The subject stands behind the starting line, and on the command "go" he begins to dribble around the right side of the first chair, then to the left of the second, and so on alternately around the rest of the chairs and back to the starting line. He may dribble the ball with either hand, but he must use only legal dribbles. He must dribble at least once as each chair is passed. Two trials are allowed. *Scoring:* The better score of the two trials to the nearest tenth of a second is recorded. The time starts at the signal "go" and stops as the subject crosses the starting line on his return.

LSU Basketball Passing Test (38)

Purpose: To measure ability to pass and recover the ball accurately while moving.

Equipment and Floor Markings: A basketball, stopwatch, smooth wall surface, and tape or paint for marking are required for this test. Six squares are painted or marked by tape as shown in Figure 16-8. The bottoms of the low targets are 3 feet from the floor; the bottoms of the high targets are 5 feet from the floor. Each target is 2 by 2 feet (the dimensions include the widths of the lines). The targets are spaced 2 feet apart. A restraining line is drawn 10 feet from the wall. *Note:* The height of the targets should be lowered for upper elementary and junior high school players. The bottoms of the low and high targets are 2 and 4 feet, respectively, and the restraining line is drawn 7 feet from the wall.

Directions: The subject stands with the ball behind the restraining line facing the target on

Table 16-19
LSU Basketball Passing Test Scoring Scale

College Men	Performance Level	College Women
47 - Above	Advanced	44 - Above
43 - 46	Adv. Intermediate	40 - 43
37 - 42	Intermediate	34 - 39
33 - 36	Adv. Beginner	32 - 33
0 - 32	Beginner	0 - 31

Based on a limited number of college men and college women from Louisiana State University, Baton Rouge, La., and Corpus Christi State University, Corpus Christi, Tx., respectively, 1973 and 1976.

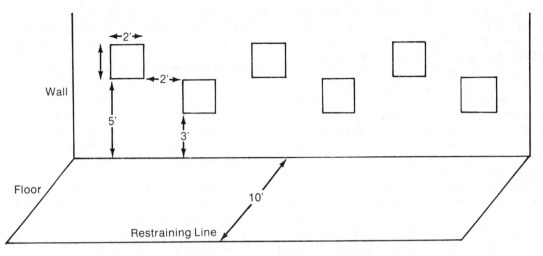

Figure 16-8. Wall Markings for LSU Basketball Passing Test

the far left. On the signal to begin, he passes the ball to the target, recovers the rebound, passes to the second target as he moves to the right. After passing at the last target at the right, he passes again at that target and begins moving to his left. He does this as many times as possible in 30 seconds. He must keep moving, and he is not allowed to pass at any target twice in succession, except for the targets at either end while changing directions. He must pass from behind the restraining line, although he may go in front to retrieve a loose ball. Two trials are given. If the ball gets completely away from the subject, a new trial is given. This only is allowed once. *Scoring:* The time starts when the first pass hits the wall and stops at the end of 30 seconds. Each target that is hit counts one point. Any part of the target that is hit by the ball counts. The score is the total number of points for both trials.

Additional Pointers: (a) Variations can be added. The teacher or coach may want to have the players pass with the right hand while moving to the right and with the left hand while moving to the left. (b) The scoring of the test can be modified in that the subject *must* hit each target in turn until three or four trips are traversed and the score then is in elapsed seconds. In this version the subject may have to pass at one target several times before being able to move along.

LSU Long and Short Test (38)

Purpose: To measure the ability to shoot long and short shots in basketball and, to a certain extent, ball handling and dribbling skills.

Equipment and Floor Markings: The equipment needed includes a basketball, stopwatch, regulation basket and backboard, and a string and chalk for marking the floor. A string is stretched from directly under the basket to the top of the free throw circle. Keeping the string taut, an arc is made with chalk from the top of the free throw circle to the end line on either side of the basket. This is the restraining line for the long shots.

Directions: The subject stands with the ball in back of the restraining line. On the signal to begin he shoots from behind the restraining line, then rushes in to get the rebound, and shoots a short shot. After attempting the lay-up, he runs back behind the restraining line and shoots a long shot, recovers the ball, and shoots a short shot. He thus continues, alter-

Table 16-20
LSU Long and Short Test
Scoring Scale

College Men	Performance Level	College Women
18 - Above	Advanced	14 - Above
14 - 17	Adv. Intermediate	12 - 13
7 - 13	Intermediate	4 - 11
3 - 6	Adv. Beginner	2 - 3
0 - 2	Beginner	0 - 1

Based on the scores of a limited number of men and women students, Corpus Christi State University, Corpus Christi, Tx., 1976.

away in the direction of the starting line, but at a 45-degree angle to the line from bags 1 and 2. (This places the bag about 5 feet from the starting line.) The subject blocks this third bag to the ground with a cross-body block and then runs across the starting line. Two trials are given. The blocking bags must be blocked clear to the ground. (See Figure 16-9 for diagram of bag placement.) *Scoring:* The time from the signal "go" until he crosses back over the line is measured to the nearest tenth of a second. The better of the two trials constitutes the subject's score.

Forward Pass for Accuracy. A target is painted on a 8-by-11-foot canvas which is hung from the crossbar of the goal posts. The center circle is 2 feet in diameter, the middle circle 4 feet, and the outer circle 6 feet in diameter. The bottom of the outer circle is 3 feet from the ground. It is recommended that a wooden or metal bar be inserted in a channel sewn along the bottom of the canvas, and then the channel be tied to the goal posts to keep the canvas stretched taut. A restraining line is drawn 15 yards from the target. The player takes two or three small running steps along the line, hesitates, then throws at the target. The player may go either to the right or to the left, but he must stay behind the restraining line. He should pass the ball with good speed. Ten trials are given. *Scoring:* The target circles score three, two, and one for the inner, middle, and outer circles, respectively. Passes hitting on a line are given the higher value. The point total for the ten trials is the score.

Football Punt for Distance. The player takes one or two steps within the 6-foot kicking zone and punts the ball as far as possible. The administration and scoring are the same as for the forward pass for distance. (See also softball throw for distance in *Youth Fitness Manual.*)

Ball-Changing Zigzag Run. Five chairs are placed in a line, 10 feet apart, and all facing away from the starting line. (See Figure 16-10.) The first chair is 10 feet in front of the starting line. Holding a football under his right arm, the subject starts from behind the starting line on the signal "go." He runs to the right of the first chair, then changes the ball to his left arm as he runs to the left of the second chair. He continues running in and out of the chairs in this manner, changing the position of the ball to the outside arm as he passes each chair. The inside arm should be extended as in stiff-arming. He circles around the end chair and runs in and out of the chairs back to the starting line. He is not allowed to hit the chairs. Two timed trials are given. *Scoring:* The time from the signal "go" until he passes back over the starting line is recorded to the nearest tenth of a second. The better of the two trials constitutes the subject's score for this test.

Catching the Forward Pass. A scrimmage line is drawn with two *end* marks located 9 feet to the right and to the left of the center. (See Figure 16-11.) At a distance of 30 feet in front of these marks are *turning points.* The subject lines up on the right *end* mark facing the *turning point* 30 feet directly in front of him. On the signal "go" he runs straight ahead, cuts around

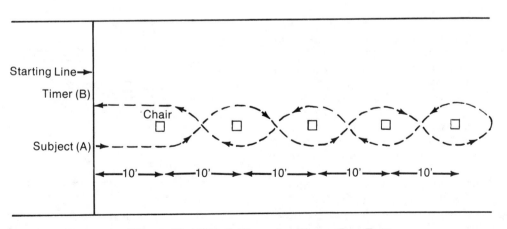

Figure 16-10. Ball-Changing Zigzag Run Test

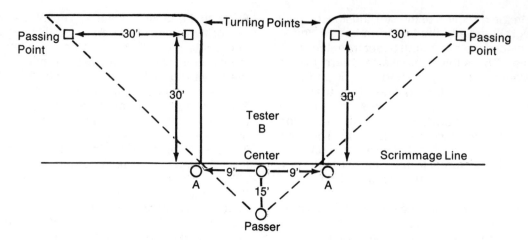

Figure 16-11. Diagram for AAHPER Football Forward Pass-Catching Test

the *turning point*, and runs to receive the pass 30 feet away at the *passing point*. On the signal "go" the center snaps the ball 15 feet to the passer, who takes one step, then passes the ball directly over the *passing point* above head height. The passer must be able to pass the ball in a mechanical manner to the passing point without paying attention to the receiver. A similar passing point is located 30 feet to the left of the left turning point. Ten trials are given to the right and ten trials are given to the left. The player need not try for poorly thrown passes, but he must go around the turning point before proceeding to the passing point. *Scoring:* One point is scored for each pass caught. The sum of passes caught from both sides is recorded as the score for this test. *Note:* Considerable practice and skill are needed on the part of the passer to be able to time his pass so as to enable the subject to reach the passing point in a controlled manner and get his hands on the ball.

Pull-out. The subject lines up in a set position halfway between two goal posts. On the signal "go" he pulls out and runs parallel to the imaginary line of scrimmage, cuts around the right hand goal post and races straight ahead across a finish line 30 feet from and parallel to the goal posts. Two timed trials are given. *Scoring:* The score is the better of the two trials, measured from the signal "go" until he crosses the finish line in seconds and tenths of seconds.

Kick-off. A kicking tee is placed in the center of one of the lines running across the field. The ball is positioned so that it tilts slightly back toward the kicker. The player takes as long a run as he wants and kicks the ball as far as possible. Three trials are given. *Scoring:* Same as for the forward pass and the punt for distance.

Dodging Run. The Frederick W. Cozens Dodging Test is used, with the only exception being that the subject carries a football. The course is laid out as is shown in Figure 16-12. The player starts from behind the line to the right of the first hurdle, which is on the starting line. On the signal "go," he runs to the left of the second hurdle and follows the course as shown in the diagram. Two complete round trips constitute a run; two runs are given. The ball does not have to be changed from side to side. *Scoring:* The time is measured to the nearest tenth of a second. The better of the two runs is recorded as the score.

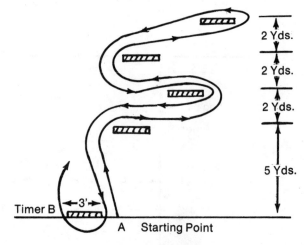

Figure 16-12.
Diagram for AAHPER Dodging Run Test

Table 16-21
AAHPER Football Test

FORWARD PASS FOR DISTANCE

Percentile Scores Based on Age/Test Scores in Feet

Percentile	Age 10 Ft.	10 M.	11 Ft.	11 M.	12 Ft.	12 M.	13 Ft.	13 M.	14 Ft.	14 M.	15 Ft.	15 M.	16 Ft.	16 M.	17-18 Ft.	17-18 M.	Percentile
100th	96	29.3	105	32.0	120	36.6	150	45.7	170	51.8	180	54.9	180	54.9	180	54.9	100th
95th	71	21.6	83	25.3	99	30.2	115	35.1	126	38.4	135	41.2	144	43.9	152	46.3	95th
90th	68	20.7	76	23.2	92	28.1	104	31.7	118	36.0	127	38.7	135	41.2	143	43.6	90th
85th	64	19.5	73	22.3	87	26.5	98	29.9	114	34.8	122	37.2	129	39.3	137	41.8	85th
80th	62	18.9	70	21.3	83	25.3	95	29.0	109	33.2	118	36.0	126	38.4	133	40.6	80th
75th	61	18.6	68	20.7	79	24.1	91	27.7	105	32.0	115	35.1	123	37.5	129	39.3	75th
70th	59	18.0	65	19.8	77	23.5	88	26.8	102	31.1	111	33.8	120	36.6	127	38.7	70th
65th	58	17.7	64	19.5	75	22.9	85	25.9	99	30.2	108	32.9	117	35.7	124	37.8	65th
60th	56	17.1	62	18.9	73	22.3	83	25.3	96	29.3	105	32.0	114	34.8	121	36.9	60th
55th	55	16.8	61	18.6	71	21.6	80	24.4	93	28.4	102	31.1	111	33.8	117	35.7	55th
50th	53	16.2	59	18.0	68	20.7	78	23.8	91	27.7	99	30.2	108	32.9	114	34.8	50th
45th	52	15.9	56	17.1	66	20.1	76	23.2	88	26.8	97	29.6	105	32.0	110	33.5	45th
40th	51	15.5	54	16.5	64	19.5	73	22.3	85	25.9	94	28.7	103	31.4	107	32.6	40th
35th	49	14.9	51	15.5	62	18.9	70	21.3	83	25.3	92	28.1	100	30.5	104	31.7	35th
30th	47	14.3	50	15.2	60	18.3	69	21.0	80	24.4	89	27.1	97	29.6	101	30.8	30th
25th	45	13.7	48	14.6	58	17.7	65	19.8	77	23.5	85	25.9	93	28.4	98	29.9	25th
20th	44	13.4	45	13.7	54	16.5	63	19.2	73	22.3	81	24.7	90	27.4	94	28.7	20th
15th	41	12.5	43	13.1	51	15.5	61	18.6	70	21.3	76	23.2	85	25.9	89	27.1	15th
10th	38	11.6	40	12.2	45	13.7	55	16.8	64	19.5	71	21.6	79	24.1	80	24.4	10th
5th	33	10.1	36	11.0	40	12.2	46	13.1	53	16.2	62	18.9	70	21.3	67	20.4	5th
0	14	4.3	25	7.6	10	3.0	10	3.0	10	3.0	20	6.1	30	9.1	20	6.1	0

50-YARD DASH WITH FOOTBALL

Percentile Scores Based on Age/Test Scores in Seconds and Tenths

Percentile	10	11	12	13	14	15	16	17-18	Percentile
100th	7.3	6.8	6.2	5.5	5.5	5.8	5.5	5.0	100th
95th	7.7	7.4	7.0	6.4	6.4	6.2	6.0	6.0	95th
90th	7.9	7.6	7.2	6.8	6.6	6.3	6.1	6.1	90th
85th	8.1	7.7	7.4	6.9	6.8	6.4	6.3	6.2	85th
80th	8.2	7.8	7.5	7.0	6.9	6.5	6.4	6.3	80th
75th	8.3	7.9	7.5	7.1	7.0	6.6	6.5	6.3	75th
70th	8.4	8.0	7.6	7.2	7.1	6.7	6.6	6.4	70th
65th	8.5	8.1	7.7	7.3	7.2	6.8	6.6	6.5	65th
60th	8.6	8.2	7.8	7.4	7.2	6.9	6.7	6.6	60th
55th	8.6	8.3	7.9	7.5	7.3	7.0	6.8	6.6	55th
50th	8.7	8.4	8.0	7.5	7.4	7.0	6.8	6.7	50th
45th	8.8	8.5	8.1	7.6	7.5	7.1	6.9	6.8	45th
40th	8.9	8.6	8.1	7.7	7.6	7.2	7.0	6.8	40th
35th	9.0	8.7	8.2	7.8	7.7	7.2	7.1	6.9	35th
30th	9.1	8.8	8.3	8.0	7.8	7.3	7.2	7.0	30th
25th	9.2	8.9	8.4	8.1	7.9	7.4	7.3	7.1	25th
20th	9.3	9.1	8.5	8.2	8.1	7.5	7.4	7.2	20th
15th	9.4	9.2	8.7	8.4	8.3	7.7	7.5	7.3	15th
10th	9.6	9.3	9.0	8.7	8.4	8.1	7.8	7.4	10th
5th	9.8	9.5	9.3	9.0	8.8	8.4	8.0	7.8	5th
0	10.6	11.0	12.0	12.0	12.0	11.0	10.0	10.0	0

Table 16-22

BLOCKING
Percentile Scores Based on Age/Test Scores in Seconds and Tenths

Percentile	Age 10	11	12	13	14	15	16	17-18	Percentile
100th	6.9	5.0	5.5	5.0	5.0	5.0	5.0	5.0	100th
95th	7.5	6.6	6.6	5.9	5.8	6.0	5.9	5.5	95th
90th	7.7	7.1	7.3	6.5	6.2	6.2	6.1	5.7	90th
85th	7.9	7.5	7.6	6.7	6.6	6.3	6.3	5.8	85th
80th	8.1	8.0	7.7	6.9	6.8	6.5	6.5	6.0	80th
75th	8.3	8.3	7.9	7.2	7.0	6.7	6.7	6.2	75th
70th	8.5	8.6	8.1	7.4	7.1	6.9	7.0	6.3	70th
65th	8.9	9.1	8.4	7.6	7.3	7.0	7.2	6.5	65th
60th	9.3	9.5	8.6	7.7	7.5	7.2	7.4	6.7	60th
55th	9.6	9.7	8.8	7.9	7.7	7.4	7.6	7.0	55th
50th	9.8	9.9	9.0	8.1	7.8	7.5	7.8	7.2	50th
45th	10.1	10.2	9.2	8.3	8.0	7.8	8.0	7.4	45th
40th	10.5	10.4	9.4	8.4	8.1	7.9	8.3	7.6	40th
35th	10.7	10.6	9.6	8.6	8.3	8.2	8.6	7.8	35th
30th	11.0	10.9	9.7	8.9	8.5	8.3	8.8	8.0	30th
25th	11.3	11.1	9.9	9.1	8.7	8.5	9.1	8.2	25th
20th	11.6	11.3	10.2	9.4	9.0	8.8	9.5	8.5	20th
15th	12.0	11.6	10.5	9.8	9.2	9.0	9.0	9.0	15th
10th	12.8	12.0	10.9	10.2	9.5	9.4	10.6	9.4	10th
5th	14.4	13.1	11.6	11.2	10.3	10.4	10.7	10.8	5th
0	17.5	18.0	15.0	15.0	15.0	13.0	15.0	14.0	0

FORWARD PASS FOR ACCURACY
Percentile Scores Based on Age/Test Scores in Points

Percentile	Age 10	11	12	13	14	15	16	17-18	Percentile
100th	18	26	26	28	26	26	28	28	100th
95th	14	19	20	21	21	20	21	22	95th
90th	11	16	18	19	19	19	20	21	90th
85th	10	15	17	18	18	18	18	19	85th
80th	9	13	16	17	17	17	17	18	80th
75th	8	12	15	16	16	16	16	18	75th
70th	8	11	14	15	15	15	15	17	70th
65th	6	10	13	14	14	14	15	16	65th
60th	5	9	12	13	13	13	14	15	60th
55th	4	8	11	13	13	13	13	15	55th
50th	3	7	11	12	12	12	13	14	50th
45th	2	6	10	11	11	11	12	13	45th
40th	2	5	9	11	10	11	12	12	40th
35th	1	5	8	10	9	9	11	12	35th
30th	0	4	7	9	8	9	10	11	30th
25th	0	3	6	8	8	8	9	10	25th
20th	0	2	5	7	7	7	8	9	20th
15th	0	1	4	5	5	6	7	8	15th
10th	0	0	3	4	4	5	6	7	10th
5th	0	0	1	2	2	3	4	5	5th
0	0	0	0	0	0	0	0	0	0

Table 16-23

FOOTBALL PUNT FOR DISTANCE
Percentile Scores Based on Age/Test Scores in Feet

Percentile	Age 10 Ft.	M.	11 Ft.	M.	12 Ft.	M.	13 Ft.	M.	14 Ft.	M.	15 Ft.	M.	16 Ft.	M.	17-18 Ft.	M.	Percentile
100th	87	26.5	100	30.5	115	35.1	150	45.7	160	48.8	170	51.8	160	48.8	180	54.9	100th
95th	75	22.9	84	25.6	93	28.4	106	32.3	119	36.3	126	38.4	140	42.7	136	41.5	95th
90th	64	19.5	77	23.5	88	26.8	98	29.9	110	33.5	119	36.3	126	38.4	128	39.0	90th
85th	61	18.6	75	22.9	84	25.6	94	28.7	106	32.3	114	34.8	120	36.6	124	37.8	85th
80th	58	17.7	70	21.3	79	24.1	90	27.4	103	31.4	109	33.2	114	34.8	120	36.6	80th
75th	56	17.1	68	20.7	77	23.5	87	26.5	98	29.9	105	32.0	109	33.2	115	35.1	75th
70th	55	16.8	66	20.1	75	22.9	83	25.3	96	29.3	102	31.1	106	32.3	110	33.5	70th
65th	53	16.2	64	19.5	72	22.0	80	24.4	93	28.4	99	30.2	103	31.4	107	32.6	65th
60th	51	15.5	62	18.9	70	21.3	78	23.8	90	27.4	96	29.3	100	30.5	104	31.7	60th
55th	50	15.2	60	18.3	68	20.7	75	22.9	87	26.5	94	28.7	97	29.6	101	30.8	55th
50th	48	14.6	57	17.4	66	20.1	73	22.3	84	25.6	91	27.7	95	29.0	98	29.9	50th
45th	46	14.1	55	16.8	64	19.5	70	21.3	81	24.7	89	27.1	92	28.1	96	29.3	45th
40th	45	13.7	53	16.2	61	18.6	68	20.7	78	23.8	86	26.2	90	27.4	93	28.4	40th
35th	44	13.4	51	15.5	59	18.0	64	19.5	75	22.9	83	25.3	86	26.2	90	27.4	35th
30th	42	12.8	48	14.6	56	17.1	63	19.2	72	22.0	79	24.1	83	25.3	86	26.2	30th
25th	40	12.2	45	13.7	52	15.9	61	18.6	70	21.3	76	23.2	79	24.1	81	24.7	25th
20th	38	11.6	42	12.8	50	15.2	57	17.4	66	20.1	73	22.3	74	22.6	76	23.2	20th
15th	32	9.8	39	11.9	46	13.1	52	15.9	61	18.6	69	21.0	70	21.3	70	21.3	15th
10th	28	8.5	34	10.4	40	12.2	44	13.4	55	16.8	62	18.9	64	19.5	64	19.5	10th
5th	22	6.7	27	8.2	35	10.7	33	10.1	44	13.4	54	16.5	56	17.1	53	16.2	5th
0	11	3.4	9	2.7	10	3.0	10	3.0	10	3.0	10	3.0	10	3.0	10	3.0	0

BALL CHANGING ZIGZAG RUN
Percentile Scores Based on Age/Test Scores in Seconds and Tenths

Percentile	10	11	12	13	14	15	16	17-18	Percentile
100th	7.2	7.4	7.0	6.0	6.5	6.0	6.0	6.0	100th
95th	9.9	7.7	7.8	8.0	8.7	7.7	7.7	8.4	95th
90th	10.1	8.1	8.2	8.4	9.0	8.0	8.0	8.7	90th
85th	10.3	8.6	8.5	8.7	9.2	8.3	8.4	8.8	85th
80th	10.5	9.0	8.7	8.8	9.4	8.5	8.6	8.9	80th
75th	10.7	9.3	8.8	9.0	9.5	8.6	8.7	9.0	75th
70th	10.9	9.6	9.0	9.2	9.6	8.7	8.8	9.1	70th
65th	11.1	9.8	9.1	9.3	9.7	8.8	8.9	9.2	65th
60th	11.2	10.0	9.3	9.5	9.8	8.9	9.0	9.3	60th
55th	11.4	10.1	9.5	9.6	9.9	9.0	9.1	9.4	55th
50th	11.5	10.3	9.6	9.7	10.0	9.1	9.3	9.6	50th
45th	11.6	10.5	9.8	9.8	10.1	9.2	9.4	9.7	45th
40th	11.8	10.6	10.0	10.0	10.2	9.4	9.5	9.8	40th
35th	11.9	10.9	10.1	01.2	10.4	9.5	9.7	9.9	35th
30th	12.2	11.1	10.3	10.3	10.5	9.6	9.9	10.1	30th
25th	12.5	11.3	10.5	10.3	10.7	9.9	10.1	10.3	25th
20th	12.8	11.6	10.8	10.8	10.9	10.1	10.3	10.5	20th
15th	13.3	12.1	11.1	11.1	11.2	10.3	10.6	10.9	15th
10th	13.8	12.9	11.5	11.4	11.5	10.6	11.2	11.4	10th
5th	15.8	14.2	12.3	12.1	12.0	11.5	12.2	12.1	5th
0	24.0	15.0	19.0	20.0	14.5	20.0	17.0	15.0	0

Table 16-24

CATCHING THE FORWARD PASS

Percentile Scores Based on Age/Test Scores in Number Caught

| Percentile | Age | | | | | | | | Percentile |
	10	11	12	13	14	15	16	17-18	
100th	20	20	20	20	20	20	20	20	100th
95th	19	19	19	20	20	20	20	20	95th
90th	17	18	19	19	19	19	19	19	90th
85th	16	16	18	18	18	19	19	19	85th
80th	14	15	18	17	18	18	18	18	80th
75th	13	14	16	17	17	18	18	18	75th
70th	12	13	16	16	16	17	17	17	70th
65th	11	12	15	15	15	16	16	16	65th
60th	10	12	14	15	15	16	16	16	60th
55th	8	11	14	14	14	15	15	15	55th
50th	7	10	13	13	14	15	15	15	50th
45th	7	9	12	13	13	14	14	14	45th
40th	6	8	12	12	12	13	13	13	40th
35th	5	7	11	11	11	12	12	13	35th
30th	5	7	10	10	10	11	11	12	30th
25th	4	6	10	9	9	10	10	11	25th
20th	3	5	8	8	8	9	9	10	20th
15th	2	4	7	7	8	8	8	9	15th
10th	1	3	6	6	6	7	6	8	10th
5th	1	1	5	4	4	6	4	6	5th
0	0	0	0	0	0	0	0	0	0

PULL-OUT

Percentile Scores Based on Age/Test Scores in Seconds and Tenths

| Percentile | Age | | | | | | | | Percentile |
	10	11	12	13	14	15	16	17-18	
100th	2.5	2.2	2.2	2.4	2.2	2.0	2.0	1.8	100th
95th	2.9	2.5	2.8	2.8	2.7	2.5	2.5	2.6	95th
90th	3.2	2.7	3.0	2.9	2.8	2.6	2.6	2.7	90th
85th	3.3	2.8	3.0	3.0	2.9	2.7	2.7	2.8	85th
80th	3.4	2.9	3.1	3.0	3.0	2.8	2.9	2.8	80th
75th	3.5	2.9	3.1	3.1	3.0	3.0	2.9	2.9	75th
70th	3.5	3.0	3.2	3.1	3.0	3.0	3.0	2.9	70th
65th	3.6	3.1	3.3	3.2	3.1	3.0	3.0	3.0	65th
60th	3.6	3.2	3.3	3.2	3.1	3.1	3.1	3.0	60th
55th	3.7	3.3	3.4	3.3	3.2	3.1	3.1	3.1	55th
50th	3.8	3.4	3.4	3.3	3.2	3.2	3.2	3.1	50th
45th	3.8	3.5	3.5	3.4	3.3	3.2	3.2	3.1	45th
40th	3.9	3.6	3.5	3.4	3.3	3.3	3.3	3.2	40th
35th	3.9	3.7	3.6	3.5	3.4	3.3	3.3	3.2	35th
30th	4.0	3.8	3.7	3.5	3.4	3.4	3.3	3.2	30th
25th	4.0	3.9	3.8	3.6	3.5	3.5	3.4	3.3	25th
20th	4.1	4.0	3.9	3.7	3.5	3.6	3.5	3.4	20th
15th	4.2	4.1	3.9	3.8	3.6	3.7	3.7	3.5	15th
10th	4.3	4.2	4.1	3.9	3.7	3.9	3.9	3.6	10th
5th	4.4	4.4	4.2	4.0	4.0	4.1	4.3	3.9	5th
0	5.5	5.0	5.0	5.0	5.0	5.0	5.0	5.0	0

Table 16-25

KICK-OFF

Percentile Scores Based on Age/Test Scores in Feet

Percentile	10 Ft.	10 M.	11 Ft.	11 M.	12 Ft.	12 M.	13 Ft.	13 M.	14 Ft.	14 M.	15 Ft.	15 M.	16 Ft.	16 M.	17-18 Ft.	17-18 M.	Percentile
100th	88	26.8	110	33.5	120	36.6	129	39.3	140	42.7	160	48.8	160	48.8	180	54.9	100th
95th	69	21.0	79	24.1	98	29.9	106	32.3	118	36.0	128	39.0	131	39.9	138	42.1	95th
90th	64	19.5	72	22.0	83	25.3	97	29.6	108	32.9	120	36.6	125	38.1	129	39.3	90th
85th	59	18.0	68	20.7	78	23.8	92	28.1	102	31.1	114	34.8	119	36.3	124	37.8	85th
80th	58	17.7	64	19.5	74	22.6	86	26.2	97	29.6	108	32.9	114	34.8	119	36.3	80th
75th	55	16.8	60	18.3	70	21.3	81	24.7	94	28.7	104	31.7	108	32.9	113	34.5	75th
70th	53	16.2	58	17.7	67	20.4	78	23.8	90	27.4	100	30.5	104	31.7	108	32.9	70th
65th	50	15.2	56	17.1	65	19.8	75	22.9	86	26.2	96	29.3	99	30.2	105	32.0	65th
60th	47	14.3	54	16.5	64	19.5	72	22.0	84	25.6	93	28.4	97	29.6	103	31.4	60th
55th	46	14.1	52	15.9	60	18.3	69	21.0	81	24.7	90	27.4	95	29.0	98	29.9	55th
50th	45	13.7	50	15.2	57	17.4	67	20.4	77	23.5	87	26.5	93	28.4	95	29.0	50th
45th	43	13.1	48	14.6	54	16.5	64	19.5	74	22.6	83	25.3	90	27.4	92	28.1	45th
40th	40	12.2	46	14.1	52	15.9	62	18.9	71	21.6	79	24.1	87	26.5	88	26.8	40th
35th	39	11.9	44	13.4	48	14.6	59	18.0	68	20.7	76	23.2	83	25.3	84	25.6	35th
30th	37	11.3	42	12.8	45	13.7	56	17.1	65	19.8	72	22.0	79	24.1	79	24.1	30th
25th	35	10.7	40	12.2	42	12.8	52	15.9	62	18.9	69	21.0	75	22.9	74	22.6	25th
20th	32	9.8	37	11.3	38	11.6	48	14.6	58	17.7	64	19.5	70	21.3	70	21.3	20th
15th	30	9.1	34	10.4	34	10.4	42	12.8	52	15.9	59	18.0	65	19.8	64	19.5	15th
10th	26	7.9	30	9.1	29	8.8	36	11.0	45	13.7	50	15.2	60	18.3	57	17.4	10th
5th	21	6.4	24	7.3	22	6.7	26	7.9	38	11.6	40	12.2	47	14.3	43	13.1	5th
0	5	1.5	10	3.0	0	0.0	0	0.0	0	0.0	10	3.0	10	3.0	10	3.0	0

DODGING RUN

Percentile Scores Based on Age/Test Scores in Seconds and Tenths

Percentile	10	11	12	13	14	15	16	17-18	Percentile
100th	21.0	18.0	18.0	17.0	16.0	16.0	16.0	16.0	100th
95th	24.3	20.4	23.8	23.3	22.6	22.4	22.3	22.2	95th
90th	25.8	21.6	24.6	24.2	23.9	23.5	23.3	23.2	90th
85th	26.3	22.5	25.0	24.8	24.6	24.1	23.9	23.7	85th
80th	26.4	23.5	25.2	24.9	24.7	24.6	24.3	24.1	80th
75th	27.5	24.0	25.3	25.3	25.2	24.9	24.7	24.4	75th
70th	27.8	25.0	25.8	25.7	25.2	25.2	25.0	24.7	70th
65th	28.1	25.7	26.3	26.1	26.1	25.5	25.3	25.0	65th
60th	28.4	26.3	26.6	26.5	26.3	25.8	25.5	25.3	60th
55th	28.7	26.9	26.9	26.8	26.6	26.1	25.8	25.6	55th
50th	28.9	27.4	27.3	27.2	26.9	26.4	26.1	26.0	50th
45th	29.3	28.0	27.6	27.5	27.2	26.7	26.3	26.3	45th
40th	29.7	28.3	27.9	27.9	27.5	27.0	26.7	26.6	40th
35th	30.1	28.8	28.4	28.3	27.9	27.4	27.0	26.9	35th
30th	30.5	29.2	28.8	28.7	28.3	27.8	27.3	27.2	30th
25th	30.9	29.8	29.2	29.1	28.7	28.2	27.7	27.6	25th
20th	31.3	30.4	29.8	29.5	29.3	28.6	28.1	28.0	20th
15th	31.8	31.1	30.4	30.1	29.9	29.1	28.8	28.7	15th
10th	32.7	32.0	31.3	30.8	30.7	29.8	29.6	29.2	10th
5th	33.6	33.5	33.0	32.3	31.8	31.0	30.6	30.4	5th
0	40.0	40.0	41.0	40.0	36.0	36.0	36.0	36.0	0

Golf

Clevett's Putting Test (60)

Clevett devised four tests of golf utilizing the brassie, midiron, mashie, and putter. The putting test is described here.

Equipment and Materials: A smooth carpet 20 feet long and 27 inches wide is marked as shown in Figure 16-13. Each zone is 9 inches square. The *10* square represents the hole. A putter and at least ten golf balls in good condition are required.

Directions: The subject putts at a distance of 15 feet from the *hole*. It can be seen in Figure 16-13 that the subject is encouraged to putt for the hole rather than leave it short. Ten trials are taken.

Scoring: The point at which the ball stops is the score for that putt. The total of the ten trials is the score. Balls resting on a line are given the higher point value.

Additional Pointers: (a) The test can be decidedly improved by cutting an actual hole in the carpet. Several moveable putting surfaces can be constructed using carpeting stretched over plywood, thus enabling a hole to be formed. The scoring areas should then be altered, slightly reducing somewhat the point values for going beyond the hole. (b) To make the test more functional, the distances could be varied. (c) The use of synthetic grass would undoubtedly improve the test also.

The Nelson Pitching Test (64)

Purpose: To measure the ability of a golfer to use the short irons in pitching close to the pin.

Age and Sex: Suitable for both boys and girls at the secondary and college levels.

Validity: A correlation of .86 was obtained with judges' ratings of ability. An *r* of .79 was found between the test scores and golf scores.

Reliability: Using odd-even trials and the Spearman-Brown Prophecy Formula, a coefficient of reliability of .83 was found with men and women college students.

Equipment and Materials: The equipment needed include the following items: the appropriate golf club that is being used, usually the eight iron, nine iron or wedge; preferably four baskets, each with thirteen balls in good condition (although two baskets will suffice if only one person is being tested at a time); a flag stick for the center of the target, two flags or markers for the restraining line; tape measure and lime or other field marking materials. The target is marked as shown in Figure 16-14. The inner circle is 6 feet in diameter. Proceeding out from the center, each circle's radius is 5 feet wider than the previous one. The diameters are 6, 16, 26, 36, 46, 56, and 66 feet. The target is divided into equal quadrants. A restraining line is marked 20 yards from the flag, and the hitting line is 40 yards from the flag. The numbers for the particular sectors of each circle are as shown in the figure.

Directions: Preferably two students are tested at a time, taking turns hitting. A spotter is assigned for each subject. The instructor acts as the recorder. The instructor and the spotters stand near the target. The subject is given three practice shots, then ten trials, attempting to have each ball come to rest as near the flag as possible. The ball must be airborne until it passes the restraining line in order to be a good shot and to prevent rolling the ball all the way. If the subject swings and misses, it counts as a trial. Any swing, regardless of how far the ball goes, counts as a trial. After the subjects have finished, they retrieve their balls, and the spotters prepare to be tested next. Two new spotters are then called.

Scoring: The point value for the area in which the ball comes to rest is called out to the recorder. The spotter calls out his subject's name and score—for example, "Smith, seven." The recorder enters each score. It is not difficult for the recorder to see every score, but the spotters aid in double checking and in avoiding errors in entering scores for the proper person. A ball resting on a line is given

Start		1	1	1	1	2	2	2	2	6	7	7	5	5	3	3	3
		1	1	1	1	2	2	2	6	6	10	8	8	8	4	4	4
		1	1	1	1	2	2	2	2	6	7	7	5	5	3	3	3

←——— 8' ———→

Figure 16-13. Markings for Clevett's Golf Putting Test

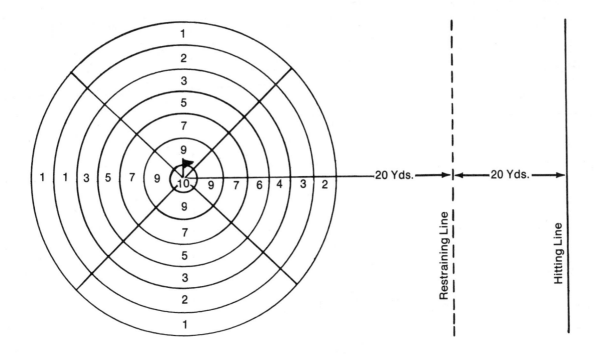

Figure 16-14. Target for the Nelson Pitching Test

the higher point value. The score is the total point value for the ten trials.

Additional Pointers: (a) Using different colored golf balls, three subjects can easily be tested at a time without requiring the services of spotters. The instructor then stands back at the hitting line. After all have finished, he goes to the target area to record the scores for each subject by noting the zone in which each particular colored ball is resting. (b) The subjects must take turns hitting so as not to bother one another. If a subject is particularly slow in hitting, he may be tested by himself at the end or with another equally slow player. (c) Balls that hit before passing the restraining line are immediately removed so that they will not be mistakenly counted if they should roll onto the target. (d) It sometimes aids the subject to call out his score if, because of uneven ground, he cannot see the exact position of the previous shot. (e) The test works well as a practice drill, enabling each student to have an objective record of his progress. For this reason it is best to have the circles permanently marked by burning the lines in the grass or etching the lines in the ground. (f) The hitting distance can be varied for more functional practice and more effective testing. (g) If time is pressing, very little reliability is lost by having the student hit ten

balls and the instructor discard the three lowest trials from them and then total the remaining seven.

Plastic Ball Golf Iron Test (62)

Purpose: To measure the ability to hit the irons in golf.

Sex and Age Level: Both sexes, high school and college.

Validity: The test with the three, five, seven, and nine irons correlated .82 with judge's ratings and tee-to-green scores. The seven iron alone correlated .75 with judge's ratings and .76 with tee-to-green scores.

Reliability: The test-retest reliability coefficients were .72, .69, .72, and .70 for the three, five, seven, and nine irons, respectively. Reliability coefficients were also determined for wind conditions for each iron. The coefficients ranged from .74 to .96, which indicated that the battery could be used effectively under wind conditions.

Equipment and Target Markings: A sufficient number of plastic whiffle golf balls (at least ten for each station) and appropriate golf club(s) are needed for each station. The target grid is divided into twelve sections (see Figure 16-15) with a point value assigned for each section. The three grid sections farthest from the sub-

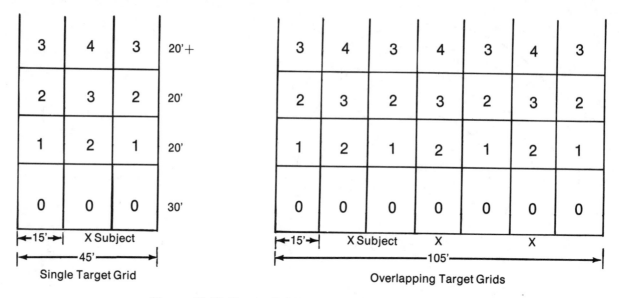

Figure 16-15. Target Grid for Plastic Ball Golf Iron Test

ject have no distance limits. Each section is 15 feet wide. From the hitting line to the first scoring section is 30 feet. More than one testing station may be set up using adjacent or overlapping target grids (Figure 16-15). A flag or target object may be placed in the center of the four-point section.

Directions: The subject is given ten swings with each iron. Preferably, more than one student can be tested at a time. A scorer for each subject should be stationed at the rear of the four-point section of the target grid. If the subject swings and misses, it counts as a trial.

Scoring: (a) Each ball receives the value of the grid section in which it first strikes the ground, not the point to which it rolls. (b) However, a topped ball that rolls into the scoring area receives one point less than the value of the section in which it stops. (c) A ball hitting a line receives the higher point value. (d) A ball that doesn't reach the scoring area receives no points; nor does a ball that hits to the left or right of the grid. (e) A missed swing counts as a trial and receives no points. (f) The score is the cumulative points for the ten trials. A perfect score is forty for each iron.

Additional Pointers: (a) In order to conserve time for testing, the seven iron alone could be used since the addition of the other iron scores did not raise the predictive value of the test battery significantly above that of the seven iron alone. (b) The existing markings of a football field may be used conveniently for the 15-foot widths of the target grid. (c) The test could be given indoors in a gymnasium, hitting from golf mats.

Table 16-26
Plastic Ball Golf Iron Test Scoring Scale

No. Seven Iron Test	Performance Level	Total of All Four Irons
25	Advanced	94
20	Adv. Intermediate	76
15	Intermediate	58
10	Adv. Beginner	40
5	Beginner	22

Based on the scores of 70 boys and girls as reported by Doyice Cotten and Jerry Thomas at Georgia Southern College, Statesboro, Ga., 1971.

Gymnastics

Difficulty Rating Scale for Beginner Stunts for Women (75)

Objective: To measure individual stunt performance.

Age Level: Junior high school through college.

Sex: Satisfactory for boys and girls as per event.

Evaluation: These beginner stunts were rated for difficulty on a 5-point scale. Experienced men and women students from four different classes rated the stunts independently of each other. Statistical treatment revealed that the difficulty ratings of the four classes were significantly related. Moreover, the relationship between the instructor's ratings and the average ratings of the students was also significant.

Equipment and Materials: A complete gymnastic facility for boys and girls or the specific equipment for selected events in gymnastics.

Directions: Each stunt below is presented with its average difficulty rating and a suggested upper and lower limit as based on a 5-point scale. Allow students to select two stunts for presentation from each of the five events.

Scoring: When a student performs a stunt poorly, deductions may be made from the average difficulty rating score to the lower limit. On the other hand, when a student performs a stunt exceedingly well, additions may be made up to the upper limit of the rating score. The maximum score possible on a ten stunt test would be 99.75.

Additional Pointers: (a) This test should be given only after adequate instruction and practice. (b) It is recommended that students be allowed to choose the stunts they wish to present.

Table 16-27
Scoring Scale for Gymnastic Stunts

Free Exercise			
Tumbling	Lower Limit	Average	Upper Limit
1. Forward Roll	1.50	1.75	2.00
2. Shoulder Roll	2.25	2.50	2.75
3. Dive Roll	2.50	3.00	2.75
4. Backward Roll	3.25	3.50	3.75
5. Cartwheel	3.25	3.50	3.75
6. Cartwheel 1/4 Turn	3.75	4.00	4.25
7. Kip-up	3.75	4.00	4.25
8. Forward Roll to Straddle Stand	3.25	3.50	3.75
9. Headspring	4.25	4.50	4.75
10. Handspring	4.50	4.75	5.00
11. Front Walkover	4.50	4.75	5.00
12. Back Walkover	4.50	4.75	5.00
Balance and Flexibility Skills			
1. Tripod Balance	.75	1.00	1.25
2. Tip-up Balance	2.00	2.25	2.50
3. Headstand	2.75	3.00	3.25

Balance and Flexibility Skills (cont.)	Lower Limit	Average	Upper Limit
4. Head and Forearm Balance	3.25	3.50	3.75
5. Forearm Balance	3.75	4.00	4.25
6. Handstand	4.00	4.50	5.00
7. "V" Seat Balance	3.25	3.50	3.75
8. "L" Balance	3.50	3.75	4.00
9. Front Scale	3.00	3.25	3.50
10. Side Scale	3.25	3.50	3.75
11. Front Splits	3.50	4.00	4.50
12. Side Splits	4.00	4.50	5.00

Vaulting			
1. Front Vault	2.25	2.50	2.75
2. Flank Vault	2.25	2.50	2.75
3. Rear Vault	3.25	3.50	3.75
4. Thief Vault	4.25	4.50	4.75
5. Squat Vault	3.00	3.25	3.75
6. Straddle Vault	4.00	4.25	4.50
7. Wolf Vault	3.25	3.50	3.75
8. Stoop Vault	4.50	4.75	5.00
9. Straddle Vault 1/2 Turn	4.00	4.50	5.00
10. Front Vault 1/2 Turn Outward	4.00	4.50	5.00
11. Rear Vault 1/2 Turn Inward	4.00	4.50	5.00

Trampoline			
1. Tuck Bounce	1.25	1.50	1.75
2. Pike Bounce	1.50	1.75	2.00
3. Straddle Bounce	1.50	1.75	2.00
4. Seat Drop	1.00	1.25	1.50
5. Knee Drop	1.50	1.75	2.00
6. Hands and Knee Drop	2.25	2.50	2.75
7. Knee Drop—Front Drop	2.75	3.00	3.25
8. Front Drop	3.25	3.50	3.75
9. Back Drop	3.25	3.50	3.75
10. Half Twist to Back Drop	3.75	4.00	4.25
11. Half Twist to Front Drop	3.75	4.00	4.25
12. Combination Front Drop to Back Drop	4.00	4.25	4.50

Trampoline (cont.)	Lower Limit	Average	Upper Limit
13. Combination Back Drop to Front Drop	4.00	4.25	4.50
14. Seat Drop 1/2 Twist to Feet	2.50	2.75	3.00
15. Seat Drop 1/2 Twist to Seat Drop	4.00	4.25	4.50
16. Back Drop 1/2 Twist to Feet	3.25	3.50	3.75
17. Back Drop 1/2 Twist to Seat Drop	4.25	4.50	4.75
18. Back Drop 1/2 Twist to Back Drop	4.00	4.50	5.00
19. One-half Turntable	4.00	4.50	5.00
20. Front Somersault	4.00	4.50	5.00
21. Back Pullover	4.00	4.50	5.00

Balance Beam	Lower Limit	Average	Upper Limit
1. Front Support Mount to "L" Position	2.00	2.25	2.50
2. Fence Vault Mount	2.75	3.00	3.25
3. Crotch Seat Mount	3.25	3.50	3.75
4. Pivot to Stand from "L" Position	3.00	3.25	3.50
5. Cast to Knee Scale and Return to Stand	2.75	3.00	3.25
6. Squat Rise from "V" Seat Position	3.50	4.00	4.50
7. Walk	1.00	1.25	1.50
8. Step Turn	2.00	2.25	2:50
9. Pirouette Turn	3.00	3.25	3.50
10. Arabesque Turn	2.00	2.25	2.50
11. Squat Turn	2.25	2.50	2.75
12. Skip Step	2.00	2.25	2.50
13. Cat Leap	3.00	3.50	4.00
14. Leap	3.75	4.25	4.75
15. Squat Leap	3.50	3.75	4.00
16. Scissor Leap	3.75	4.25	4.75
17. Front Scale	2.75	3.00	3.25
18. Attitude	2.25	2.50	2.75
19. "V" Seat Balance	2.25	2.75	3.25
20. Splits	4.50	4.75	5.00
21. Straddle-Touch Dismount	4.00	4.25	4.50
22. Pike-Touch Dismount	4.00	4.25	4.50
23. Front Dismount	3.25	3.50	3.75
24. Forward Roll	4.00	4.50	5.00
25. Back Shoulder Roll	4.25	4.50	4.75
26. Backward Roll	4.00	4.50	5.00
27. Roundoff or Cartwheel Dismount	4.00	4.50	5.00

Uneven Bars	Lower Limit	Average	Upper Limit
1. German Hang	2.25	2.50	2.75
2. Crotch Seat Mount	3.00	3.25	3.50
3. German Hang with Simple Turn	3.25	3.50	3.75
4. One-Leg Squat Rise and Combination Movements	1.50	1.75	2.00
5. Back Pullover (Low Bar)	3.25	3.50	3.75
6. Knee Kip-up	3.50	3.75	4.00
7. Swan Balance	2.75	3.00	3.25
8. Back Pullover (High Bar)	3.50	3.75	4.00
9. Help-Kip	3.75	4.00	4.25
10. Forward Roll to Knee Circle Dismount	3.00	3.25	3.50
11. Underswing Dismount	3.75	4.00	4.25
12. Underswing Dismount over Low Bar	4.00	4.25	4.50
13. Underswing Dismount 1/4 Turn over Low Bar	4.25	4.50	4.75
14. Half Turn from Low Bar to High Bar	1.75	2.00	2.25
15. Back Hip Circle	4.00	4.25	4.50
16. Forward Hip Circle	4.00	4.50	5.00
17. Forward Roll Down 1/2 Turn to Low Bar	3.50	3.75	4.00
18. Quarter-Turn Dismount over Low Bar	4.00	4.50	5.00

Horizontal Bar			
1. German Hang	1.25	1.50	1.75
2. German Hang—Full Turn	2.50	2.75	3.00
3. Back Pullover	3.00	3.25	3.50
4. Knee Kip-up	3.00	3.25	3.50
5. Underswing Dismount	3.25	3.50	3.75
6. Pick-up Swing and Simple Back Dismount	3.25	3.50	3.75
7. Kip-up	4.00	4.50	5.00
8. Drop Kip	4.25	4.50	5.00
9. Back-Hip Circle	4.00	4.25	4.50
10. Forward Hip Circle	4.25	4.50	4.75
11. Circus Kip	4.50	4.75	5.00
12. Back Uprise	4.00	4.50	5.00
13. Back Kip-up	4.50	4.75	5.00
14. Pike Seat Rise	4.50	4.75	5.00
15. Back Leanover Dismount	4.25	4.50	4.75
16. Underswing Dismount ½ Turn	4.25	4.50	4.75

Parallel Bars	Lower Limit	Average	Upper Limit
1. Cross-Straddle Seat Travel	1.00	1.25	1.50
2. Front Dismount	3.00	3.25	3.50
3. Rear Dismount	3.00	3.25	3.50
4. Front Dismount—Half Turn	4.00	4.25	4.50
5. Rear Dismount—Half Turn	4.25	4.50	4.75
6. Single-Leg Cut and Catch	3.50	3.75	4.00
7. Flank Cut and Catch	4.50	4.75	5.00
8. Straddle Cut and Catch	4.50	4.75	5.00
9. Straddle Dismount	4.00	4.25	4.50
10. Flank Mount	4.00	4.25	4.50
11. Forward Roll in Straddle Position	3.75	4.00	4.25
12. Shoulder Stand	4.25	4.50	4.75
13. Single-Leg Cut—Half Turn	4.25	4.50	4.75
14. Back Uprise	4.00	4.25	4.50
15. Hip-Kip Straddle	3.75	4.00	4.25
16. Hip-Kip-up	4.00	4.25	4.50
17. Drop Kip	4.50	4.75	5.00
18. Single-Leg Cut and Catch (Center of Bars)	4.50	4.75	5.00
19. "L" Position	4.00	4.25	4.50

Still Rings	Lower Limit	Average	Upper Limit
1. German Hang	.75	1.00	1.25
2. Bird's Nest	.75	1.00	1.25
3. Inverted Hang	1.00	1.25	1.50
4. Single-Leg Cut Dismount	3.00	3.25	3.50
5. Single-Leg Straddle Dismount	3.00	3.50	4.00
6. Double-Leg Cut Dismount	4.00	4.50	5.00
7. Double-Leg Straddle Dismount	4.00	4.50	5.00
8. Single-Leg Kip-up	4.25	4.50	4.75
9. Dislocate	4.50	4.75	5.00
10. Inlocate	4.50	4.75	5.00
11. Muscle-up	4.00	4.50	5.00
12. Double-Leg Kip-up	4.50	4.75	5.00
13. "L" Position	4.00	4.25	4.50
14. Single-Leg Front Lever	4.50	4.75	5.00
15. Beginner's Cross	4.50	4.75	5.00
16. Shoulder Stand	4.50	4.75	5.00
17. Swinging to Tuckover Dismount	3.75	4.00	4.25

Side Horse	Lower Limit	Average	Upper Limit
1. Squat Mount to "L"	2.25	2.50	2.75
2. Feint Swings	2.00	2.25	2.50
3. Single-Leg Half-Circles	3.00	3.50	4.00
4. Single-Leg Full Circle	3.25	3.75	4.25
5. Double-Leg Half-Circles	3.50	4.00	4.50
6. Double-Leg Half-Cut Mount to Single-Leg Half-Circles	4.00	4.25	4.50
7. Single Rear Dismount	3.75	4.00	4.25
8. Single-Leg Travel	4.00	4.25	4.50
9. Double Rear Dismount	4.00	4.50	5.00
10. Front Scissors	4.00	4.50	5.00
11. Rear Scissors	4.00	4.50	5.00
12. Beginner's Baby Moore	4.50	4.75	5.00
13. Baby Loop Mount	4.25	4.50	4.75
14. Hop Turn Travel	4.50	4.75	5.00

Handball

Cornish Handball Test (80)

Cornish constructed a test for the measurement of handball ability. Five test items were selected: the 30-second volley, the front-wall placement, the back-wall placement, the service placement, and the power test.

Age and Sex: College men.

Validity: A criterion consisting of the total points scored by each student minus the points scored by his opponents was used in the statistical procedures for test selection. The r for the five tests with the criterion was .694. The power test singly correlated highest with the criterion ($r=.58$). This test along with the 30-second volley correlated nearly as high with the criterion (.667) as did the five items. Consequently, in the interests of time and ease of administration, these two tests are recommended.

Equipment and Court Markings: Only the power test and 30-second volley will be described here. Other markings are needed for the three placement tests. Several handballs in good condition are required. All should be comparable with regard to their liveliness. The service line is the only marking necessary for the volley test. For the power test, a line is drawn on the front wall at a height of 6 feet.

Lines are also drawn on the floor as follows: the first line is 18 feet from the front wall; the second line is 5 feet behind the first; the third, fourth, and fifth lines are each 5¾ feet apart. These lines form six scoring zones. The area from the front wall to the first line scores one point, as does the first of the five zones behind. The second, third, fourth, and fifth zones score two, three, four, and five points, respectively. A stopwatch is needed for the volley test.

Directions: *Power Test.* The subject stands in the service zone and throws the ball against the front wall, letting it hit the floor on the rebound before striking it. He then hits the ball as hard as possible, making sure that it strikes the front wall *below* the 6-foot line. He throws the ball against the wall prior to each power stroke. Five trials are given with each hand. A retrial is allowed for any attempt in which the subject steps into the front court or fails to hit the wall below the 6-foot line. *Scoring.* The value of the scoring zone in which each trial first touches the floor is recorded. The score is the total points for the ten trials. *Thirty-Second Volley.* The subject stands behind the service line, drops the ball, and begins volleying it against the front wall for 30 seconds. The subject should hit all strokes from behind the service line. In case the ball fails to return past this line, the subject is allowed to step into the front

court to hit the ball, but he must get back behind the line for the succeeding stroke. If he should miss the ball, he is handed another ball by the instructor, and he continues volleying.
Scoring. The score is the total number of times the ball hits the front wall in 30 seconds.

Pennington and others (83) constructed a test of handball ability consisting of service placement, a total wall volley score, and back-wall placement tests. These were selected by the Wherry-Doolittle test selection method from seventeen strength, motor ability, and handball skill test items. This test was constructed while using a larger ball than regulation, with fewer rebound characteristics, and on a smaller than regulation court. For this reason it is not described here. However, because of its high validity coefficient, it is recommended that these items be studied as to their applicability with the regulation court and ball.

Soccer

McDonald Soccer Test (90)

Purpose: To measure general soccer ability.
Age and Sex: College men and women.
Validity: Validity coefficients were computed for college varsity players, junior varsity players, freshman varsity players, and for the combined groups. The scores of the above groups were correlated with coaches' ratings and the resulting coefficients were .94, .63, .76, and .85, respectively.
Equipment and Materials: A wall or backboard 30 feet wide and 11½ feet high is needed. A restraining line is drawn 9 feet from the wall. A stopwatch and three soccer balls, properly inflated and in good condition, are required.
Directions: At the signal "go," the subject

begins kicking the ball from behind the 9 foot restraining line against the wall as many times as possible in 30 seconds. The subject may kick it on the fly or on the bounce. He may retrieve the ball using his hands or by kicking it, but in order to count as a hit, the kick must be made from behind the restraining line. If the ball gets out of control, the subject has the option of playing one of the spare balls instead of retrieving the loose ball. He may use his hands in getting a spare ball in position. The two spare balls are placed 9 feet behind the restraining line. Four trials are allowed.
Scoring: The score is the highest number of legal kicks in any of the four trials.

Johnson Soccer Test (88)

Purpose: To measure general soccer ability by a single-item test.
Age and Sex: College men.
Validity: A coefficient of correlation between test scores and ratings by the investigator of .98 was found for physical education service class students; an *r* of .94 was obtained for physical education majors; and correlations of .58, .84, and .81 were found for varsity players on the first, second, and third teams.
Reliability: A reliability coefficient of .92 was found for consecutive trials.
Equipment and Materials: Soccer balls, stopwatch, and a backboard 24 feet wide and 8 feet high are required. This target has the same dimensions as a regulation soccer goal. A restraining line is marked 15 feet from the wall. A ball box for spare balls is located 15 feet in back of the restraining line.
Directions: The subject holds a soccer ball while standing behind the restraining line. On the signal to begin, the subject kicks the ball

Table 16-28
McDonald Soccer Test

College Men	Performance Level	College Women
24 - Above	Advanced	18 - Above
20 - 23	Adv. Intermediate	15 - 17
11 - 19	Intermediate	7 - 14
8 - 10	Adv. Beginner	2 - 6
0 - 7	Beginner	0 - 1

Based on the scores of 50 students in each category as reported by Leroy Scott, 1973.

against the backboard (either on the fly or after bouncing it). He attempts to kick the ball against the backboard as many times as possible in 30 seconds. The ball must be kicked from behind the restraining line; regulation soccer rules pertaining to kicking the ball are followed. Assistants retrieve the loose balls if the subject elects to use a spare ball instead of chasing the loose ball. Three 30 second trials are given.

Scoring: The score is the total number of legal hits on the three trials.

Speedball

The Buchanan Speedball Skill Test (86)

Buchanan developed a four-item test designed to measure the fundamental skills in speedball. The four items are the following: lift to others, throwing and catching, dribbling and passing, and kick-ups. A complete description, along with diagrams and achievement scales may be found in Weiss and Phillips (95).

Lift to Others: A net (volleyball, tennis, or badminton) is stretched between two standards so that the top of it is 2½ feet from the ground. Standing behind a line 6 feet from the net, the subject attempts to lift the ball with either foot and pass it so that it crosses the net and lands within a 3-foot square diagonally opposite from the subject. Ten trials are given, one point being scored for each pass that lands in the proper square. The test is designed for partners to score one another and alternate turns from each side of the net.

Throwing and Catching: A restraining line is drawn 6 feet from, and parallel to, an unobstructed wall space. On the signal "ready, go," the subject throws the ball and catches the rebound as many times as possible in 30 seconds. The score is the average number of catches made in five trials.

Dribbling and Passing: A starting line is marked 60 yards from the end line of the field. Five Indian clubs or other objects are placed in a line 10 yards apart. At the end line two goal areas are marked, one to the right and one to the left of the dribbling course. The goal areas are 6 yards long, and their inner borders are 4 feet to the left and 4 feet to the right of the dribbling line. The subject stands behind the starting line, and on the signal "ready, go" starts dribbling down the field. The subject dribbles to the right of the first Indian club and to the left of the second, etc. Immediately after dribbling to the

right of the last club, the subject attempts to kick the ball to the left into the goal area. Ten trials are given, five to the right and five to the left. Three scores are obtained: The combined score is the sum of the scores in seconds on the ten trials minus ten times the number of accurate passes to the goal on the ten trials; the dribbling score is the sum of the ten trials in seconds; the passing score is the number of accurate passes made in ten trials.

Kick-ups: Each testing station for this test item consists of a 2-foot square, with the inner side 3 feet from the side line. A starting line is drawn 4 feet from the outside corner of the square, following an imaginary extension of the diagonal of the square. Partners are used for this test, whereby one student throws the ball from behind the side line directly opposite the square. The thrower tosses the ball from overhead so that it lands in the 2-foot square. The subject stands behind the starting line until the thrower releases the ball; at that instant the subject runs forward and executes a kick-up to herself. The score is the number of successful kick-ups in ten trials.

Softball and Baseball

Generally, the tests suggested for the AAHPER Softball Skill Tests represent items that have been employed in previous tests. Test descriptions, diagrams, and percentile norms are provided by the *Manuals*. The items are briefly presented here.

AAHPER Softball Skills Test (96, 97)

Purpose: To measure fundamental skills of softball for boys and girls.

Validity and Reliability: Evidently, face validity was accepted. In the criteria for the Sports Skills Test Project, it was decided that the reliability coefficients should not be less than .80 on events scored on distance and not less than .70 for events scored on the basis of accuracy and form.

Test Items: (a) Overhand throw for accuracy, (b) underhand pitching, (c) speed throw, (d) fungo hitting, (e) base running, (f) fielding ground balls, and (g) softball throw for distance. The items are identical for both boys and girls except that the throwing distances for the throw for accuracy and underhand pitching are shorter for girls. (See norms in this chapter.)

Overhand throw for accuracy. The subject throws ten throws from a distance of 65 feet for boys, 40 feet for girls, at a target with the following dimensions: three concentric circles with 1-inch lines, the center circle measuring 2 feet in diameter, the next circle 4 feet, and the outer circle 6 feet in diameter. The bottom of the outer circle is 3 feet from the floor. The target may be marked on a wall, or, preferably, in order to conserve softballs, on canvas against a mat hung on the wall. (This target is the same as used in the AAHPER football battery.) The subject is given one or two practice throws prior to the ten trials. *Scoring:* The center circle counts three points, the second circle counts two points, the outer circle counts one point. The total points made on ten throws is the score. Balls hitting a line are given the higher point value.

Underhand pitching. The target is rectangular in shape, representing the strike zone. The bottom of the target is 18 inches from the floor. The outer lines are 42 inches long and 29 inches wide. An inner rectangle is drawn 30 inches by 17 inches. A 24-inch pitching line is drawn 46 feet from the target for boys, 38 feet for girls. The subject takes one practice pitch, then pitches fifteen underhand trials to the target. He must keep one foot on the pitching line while delivering the ball, but he can take a step forward. Only legal pitches are scored. A mat behind the target helps prevent damage to the softballs. *Scoring:* Balls hitting the center area or its boundary line count two points, balls hitting the outer area count one point. The score is the sum of the points made on fifteen pitches.

Speed throw: The subject, holding a softball, stands behind a line drawn on the floor 9 feet from a smooth wall. On the signal to go he throws the ball overhand against the wall and catches the rebound and repeats this as rapidly as possible until fifteen hits have been made against the wall. Balls that fall between the wall and the restraining line can be retrieved, but the subject must get back of the line before continuing. If the ball gets entirely away, the subject may be given one new trial. A practice trial is allowed and two trials are then given for time. *Scoring:* The watch is started when the first ball hits the wall and is stopped when the fifteenth throw hits the wall. The score is in time to the nearest tenth of a second on the better of the two trials.

Fungo hitting. The subject selects a bat and stands behind home plate with a ball in his hand. When ready, he tosses the ball up and tries to hit a fly ball into right field. He then hits the next ball into left field. He alternates hitting to right and left fields until ten balls have been hit in each direction. Every time the ball is touched by the bat it is considered as a trial. Regardless of where the ball goes, he must hit the next ball to the opposite (right or left) field. Practice trials are allowed to each side. Hits to a specific side must cross the base line between second and third, or first and second base. *Scoring:* If a player completely misses two balls in a row, it is considered as a trial; otherwise a complete miss is not counted. A fly ball that goes to the proper field counts two points, a ground ball counts one point. No score is given for a ball that lands in the wrong field. The point value for each trial is recorded and summed at the end. The maximum is forty points.

Base running. All subjects stand holding a bat in the right-hand batter's box. On the signal to hit, the subject swings at an imaginary ball, then drops the bat and races around the bases. He must not throw or carry the bat, and he must take a complete swing before beginning to run. Each base must be touched in proper sequence. A practice and two timed trials are given. *Scoring:* The watch is started on the signal "hit" and is stopped when the runner touches home plate. The better time of the two trials to the nearest tenth of a second is the score.

Fielding ground balls. A rectangular area 17 by 60 feet is marked off as shown in Figure 16-16. Two lines are drawn across the area 25 and 50 feet from the front, or throwing, line. This results in three areas being drawn. The subject stands in the 17-by-10-foot area at the end of the rectangle. The thrower stands behind the throwing line with a basket of ten balls. On the signal to begin the thrower begins throwing ground balls at exactly 5-second intervals into the first 17-by-25-foot zone. The throw is made in an overhand manner with good speed. Each throw must hit the ground inside the first area for at least one bounce. Some variation in direction is desirable, but the thrower should not try to deliberately make the subject miss. A throw that does not land as specified should be taken over. The subject attempts to field each ball cleanly, holds it momentarily, then tosses it aside. The subject starts back of the 50-foot line, but thereafter he may field the ball anywhere in back of the 25-foot line. A practice trial and then twenty trials for score are given. *Scoring:* The scoring is on a pass or fail basis. Each throw scores one point or zero. The maximum score is twenty.

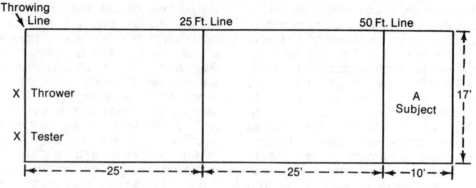

Figure 16-16. Diagram for AAHPER Fielding Ground Balls Test

Softball Throw for Distance

Purpose: To measure skill and coordination.

Equipment: Softball (preferably several in good condition), tape measure, and small metal or wooden marking stakes are needed. A football field that is marked in 5-yard intervals serves nicely for this event.

Directions: The subject must throw from within a 6-foot restraining area which is drawn parallel to the 5-yard field markers. The ball's point of contact is marked. If his second or third throw is farther, the marker is moved. Three trials are given. It is advised that a group of approximately five students be tested together, and after completing the third throw, each subject should jog out and stand at his marker while the measurements are being taken. In this way the possibility of recording the wrong score is reduced.

Scoring: The distance to the nearest foot of the best of three trials is the score. The measurement is made at right angles from the point of landing to the restraining line. In other words, the tape is not swung in an arc for each throw.

Elrod Fielding and Throwing Test (98)

Purpose: To measure skill in fielding grounders and throwing accurately to first base.

Sex and Age Level: Could be given to both sexes, junior high school, high school, and college.

Validity and Reliability: The validity coefficient was .67 with judges' ratings as the criterion. The test-retest correlation was .69 for reliability.

Equipment: A regulation softball diamond or any area sufficiently large to simulate a triangular area of home plate to shortstop position to first base. A target with a 6-by-6-foot frame covered with canvas. The canvas should be marked with a 3-by-3-foot square in the center. The target is placed upright at first base. Regulation softballs and bat or fungo are also needed.

Directions: The subject stands at a distance from home plate and first base that would correspond to the normal shortstop position. The tester hits ten ground balls, three to the subject's left, three to his right, and four directly at him. These are done in a random order. The subject fields each grounder and throws to the target area at first base. As soon as he throws or if he misses the grounder, he immediately returns to his position for the next trial.

Scoring: Two separate scores may be obtained, or they can be combined into one score. For *fielding:* (a) A score of two points is awarded for each ball cleanly fielded; (b) one point is given if the ball is knocked down but is then thrown to first base within a 5-second period from the time the ball is batted; (c) a score of zero is given if the subject misses the ball or knocks it down but cannot make the play within the 5-second period; (d) a perfect score for ten trials would be twenty. For *throwing:* (a) A score of three points is given for a ball that hits within the 3-by-3-foot center area (or lines that outline the square); (b) two points are given if the ball hits the target outside the 3-by-3-foot center area; (c) one point is given if the ball hits anywhere on the target on the first bounce; (d) a perfect score for ten trials would be thirty. A perfect score for the combined fielding and throwing score would be fifty.

Additional Pointers: (a) The subject is informed about the 5-second time period. It is explained that in a game it is sometimes possible to throw a runner out even when the ball is not

Percentile	Sex	Age											
		6		**7**		**8**		**9**		**10**		**11**	
		Ft.	M.	Ft.	M.	Ft.	M.	Ft.	M.	Ft.	M.	Ft.	M.
99th	Boys	69	21.0	93	28.4	115	35.1	121	36.9	123	37.5	130	39.6
	Girls	39	11.9	72	21.9	58	17.7	102	31.1	101	30.8	90	27.4
90th	Boys	60	18.3	74	22.6	88	26.9	101	30.8	110	33.5	115	35.1
	Girls	38	11.6	41	12.5	49	14.9	66	20.1	79	24.1	86	26.2
80th	Boys	53	16.2	66	20.1	81	24.7	95	29.0	102	31.1	110	33.5
	Girls	28	8.5	35	10.7	45	13.7	59	18.0	65	19.8	80	24.4
70th	Boys	50	15.2	62	18.9	75	22.9	90	27.4	96	29.3	103	31.4
	Girls	25	7.6	31	9.5	42	12.8	53	16.2	58	17.7	76	23.2
60th	Boys	43	13.1	60	18.3	71	21.6	85	25.9	92	28.1	98	29.9
	Girls	24	7.3	28	8.5	39	11.9	49	14.9	53	16.2	70	21.3
50th	Boys	40	12.2	54	16.5	65	19.8	81	24.7	88	26.8	95	28.9
	Girls	23	7.0	27	8.2	36	11.0	45	13.7	51	15.5	62	18.9
40th	Boys	34	10.4	49	14.9	62	18.9	75	22.9	85	25.9	90	27.4
	Girls	20	6.1	24	7.3	32	9.8	42	12.8	50	15.2	60	18.3
30th	Boys	31	9.5	45	13.7	58	17.7	70	21.3	80	24.4	85	25.9
	Girls	17	5.2	22	6.7	30	9.1	39	11.9	46	14.0	54	16.5
20th	Boys	29	8.8	42	12.8	52	15.9	63	19.2	72	22.0	73	22.3
	Girls	15	4.6	20	6.1	28	8.5	34	10.4	41	12.5	49	14.9
10th	Boys	28	8.5	36	11.0	46	14.0	54	16.5	66	20.1	65	19.8
	Girls	13	4.0	17	5.2	25	7.6	26	7.9	36	11.0	41	12.5
N	Boys	27	8.2	116	35.4	126	38.4	203	61.9	149	45.4	50	15.2
	Girls	31	9.5	101	30.8	113	34.5	100	30.5	82	25.0	32	9.8

*Measurements were made to the nearest foot and the best score of two was recorded by Donald H. Hardin and John Ramirez, University of Texas at El Paso, 1972.

fielded cleanly. (b) The 5-second time period is counted by an assistant or by the tester. (c) The target may be held by assistants or braced so that it stands by itself. (d) Any ball that cannot be fielded due to a bad bounce or that is poorly hit does not count and is taken over. Tentative norms for this combined fielding and throwing test are given in Table 16-37.

Elrod Batting Test (98)

Purpose: To measure skill in batting pitched balls.

Sex and Age Level: Boys, high school and college. Scoring zones could be adjusted for girls and younger boys.

Validity and Reliability: The validity coefficient was .61 with judges' ratings. A reliability coefficient of .57 was reported on test-retest.

Equipment and Facilities: The equipment and area needed include: (a) a softball diamond with at least foul lines, home plate, and pitching rubber indicated; (b) a stake and 300-foot ball of cord; (c) approximately three dozen small markers, such as tongue depressors; (d)

Table 16-30
AAHPER Softball Test

SOFTBALL THROW FOR DISTANCE (BOYS)
Percentile Scores Based on Age/Test Scores in Feet

	Age														
	10-11		12		13		14		15		16		17-18		
Percentile	Ft.	M.	Ft.	M.	Ft.	M.	Ft.	M.	Ft.	M.	Ft.	M.	Ft.	M.	Percentile
100th	200	61.0	208	63.4	200	61.0	230	70.1	242	73.8	247	75.3	255	77.7	100th
95th	154	47.0	163	49.7	185	56.4	208	63.4	231	70.4	229	69.8	229	69.8	95th
90th	144	43.9	152	46.3	175	53.4	203	61.9	205	62.5	219	66.8	222	67.7	90th
85th	127	38.7	146	44.5	167	50.9	191	58.2	198	60.4	213	64.9	216	65.9	85th
80th	121	36.9	140	42.7	160	48.8	184	56.1	192	58.5	208	63.4	213	64.9	80th
75th	118	36.0	135	41.2	154	47.0	178	54.3	187	57.0	202	61.6	207	63.1	75th
70th	114	34.8	132	40.2	150	45.7	173	52.7	182	55.5	196	59.8	204	62.2	70th
65th	111	33.8	129	39.3	145	44.2	168	51.2	178	54.3	193	58.8	199	60.7	65th
60th	109	33.2	125	38.1	142	43.3	163	49.7	174	53.1	190	57.9	196	59.8	60th
55th	106	32.3	122	37.2	138	42.1	159	48.5	170	51.8	186	56.7	192	58.5	55th
50th	103	31.4	118	36.0	135	41.2	154	47.0	167	50.9	183	55.8	188	57.3	50th
45th	100	30.5	115	35.1	131	39.9	152	46.3	165	50.3	180	54.9	185	56.4	45th
40th	98	29.9	113	34.5	128	39.0	148	45.1	161	49.1	174	53.1	182	55.5	40th
35th	95	29.0	109	33.2	125	38.1	144	43.9	157	47.9	171	52.1	178	54.3	35th
30th	92	28.1	106	32.3	122	37.2	140	42.7	154	47.0	167	50.9	173	52.7	30th
25th	91	27.7	102	31.1	117	35.7	137	41.8	148	45.1	164	50.0	169	51.5	25th
20th	85	25.9	98	29.9	113	34.5	133	40.6	143	43.6	159	48.5	163	49.7	20th
15th	80	24.3	93	28.4	107	32.6	129	39.3	138	42.1	152	46.3	153	46.6	15th
10th	72	22.0	85	25.9	101	30.8	123	37.5	133	40.6	146	44.5	147	44.8	10th
5th	62	18.9	76	23.2	97	29.6	113	34.5	119	36.3	140	42.7	140	42.7	5th
0	24	7.3	31	9.5	60	18.3	105	32.0	93	28.4	135	41.2	90	27.4	0

SOFTBALL THROW FOR DISTANCE (GIRLS)

	Age														
	10-11		12		13		14		15		16		17-18		
Percentile	Ft.	M.	Ft.	M.	Ft.	M.	Ft.	M.	Ft.	M.	Ft.	M.	Ft.	M.	Percentile
100th	120	36.6	160	48.8	160	48.8	160	48.8	200	61.0	200	61.0	200	61.0	100th
95th	99	30.2	113	34.5	133	40.6	126	38.4	127	38.7	121	36.9	120	36.6	95th
90th	84	25.6	104	31.7	112	34.1	117	35.7	116	35.4	109	33.2	109	33.2	90th
85th	76	23.2	98	29.9	105	32.0	109	33.2	108	32.9	103	31.4	102	31.1	85th
80th	71	21.6	94	28.7	98	29.9	104	31.7	103	31.4	98	29.9	97	29.6	80th
75th	68	20.7	89	27.1	94	28.7	99	30.2	97	29.6	94	28.7	93	28.4	75th
70th	66	20.1	85	25.9	90	27.4	95	29.0	93	28.4	91	27.7	89	27.1	70th
65th	62	18.9	81	24.7	86	26.2	92	28.1	88	26.8	87	26.5	87	26.5	65th
60th	60	18.3	77	23.5	83	25.3	88	26.8	85	25.9	84	25.6	84	25.6	60th
55th	57	17.4	74	22.6	81	24.7	85	25.9	80	24.4	81	24.7	82	25.0	55th
50th	55	16.8	70	21.3	76	23.2	82	25.0	77	23.5	79	24.1	80	24.4	50th
45th	53	16.2	67	20.4	73	22.3	79	24.1	75	22.9	76	23.2	77	23.5	45th
40th	50	15.2	64	19.5	70	21.3	76	23.2	72	22.0	73	22.3	74	22.6	40th
35th	48	14.6	61	18.6	68	20.7	73	22.3	70	21.3	70	21.3	72	22.0	35th
30th	45	13.7	58	17.7	64	19.5	69	21.0	67	20.4	67	20.4	69	21.0	30th
25th	43	13.1	55	16.8	62	18.9	66	20.1	64	19.5	63	19.2	66	20.1	25th
20th	41	12.5	51	15.5	60	18.3	61	18.6	61	18.6	60	18.3	63	19.2	20th
15th	38	11.6	48	14.6	56	17.1	57	17.4	58	17.7	56	17.1	60	18.3	15th
10th	34	10.4	43	13.1	51	15.5	52	15.9	54	16.5	51	15.5	55	16.8	10th
5th	31	9.5	37	11.3	43	13.1	43	13.1	49	14.9	45	13.7	50	15.2	5th
0	20	6.1	20	6.1	20	6.1	20	6.1	20	6.1	10	3.1	10	3.1	0

Table 16-31

OVERHAND THROW FOR ACCURACY (BOYS)
Percentile Scores Based on Age/Test Scores in Points

| Percentile | Age | | | | | | | Percentile |
	10-11	12	13	14	15	16	17-18	
100th	22	22	23	25	25	27	25	100th
95th	14	17	18	19	20	20	21	95th
90th	12	15	16	17	17	18	19	90th
85th	11	13	15	16	16	17	18	85th
80th	9	12	13	15	15	16	17	80th
75th	8	11	12	14	14	15	16	75th
70th	8	11	12	13	13	14	15.	70th
65th	7	10	11	12	12	14	15	65th
60th	6	9	10	11	11	13	14	60th
55th	5	9	10	11	11	12	13	55th
50th	5	8	9	10	10	11	13	50th
45th	4	7	8	10	10	11	12	45th
40th	4	6	7	9	9	10	11	40th
35th	3	6	7	8	9	9	11	35th
30th	3	5	6	8	8	8	10	30th
25th	2	4	5	7	7	8	9	25th
20th	1	3	4	6	7	7	8	20th
15th	1	3	3	6	6	6	7	15th
10th	0	2	2	5	5	5	6	10th
5th	0	0	1	3	3	4	4	5th
0	0	0	0	0	0	1	0	0

OVERHAND THROW FOR ACCURACY (GIRLS)

| Percentile | Age | | | | | | | Percentile |
	10-11	12	13	14	15	16	17-18	
100th	24	26	26	26	30	30	26	100th
95th	17	17	18	19	19	22	20	95th
90th	14	16	16	17	18	20	18	90th
85th	13	14	15	15	16	18	17	85th
80th	12	13	14	14	15	17	16	80th
75th	11	12	13	13	14	16	15	75th
70th	10	11	12	12	13	15	14	70th
65th	9	10	11	11	12	13	13	65th
60th	8	9	10	11	11	12	12	60th
55th	7	9	9	10	11	12	11	55th
50th	6	8	9	9	10	11	10	50th
45th	5	7	8	9	9	10	9	45th
40th	4	6	7	8	8	9	8	40th
35th	4	5	6	7	8	8	7	35th
30th	3	4	6	6	7	7	6	30th
25th	2	4	5	5	6	6	5	25th
20th	1	3	4	4	5	5	4	20th
15th	1	2	3	3	3	4	3	15th
10th	0	1	1	2	2	2	2	10th
5th	0	0	0	1	1	1	1	5th
0	0	0	0	0	0	0	0	0

Table 16-32

UNDERHAND PITCH (BOYS)
Percentile Scores Based on Age/Test Scores in Points

| Percentile | Age | | | | | | | Percentile |
	10-11	12	13	14	15	16	17-18	
100th	18	23	21	22	24	25	25	100th
95th	12	14	15	16	18	19	19	95th
90th	10	12	13	15	16	17	17	90th
85th	9	11	11	14	15	15	16	85th
80th	8	9	10	12	14	14	15	80th
75th	7	9	10	12	13	13	14	75th
70th	7	8	9	11	12	12	13	70th
65th	6	7	8	10	11	12	12	65th
60th	6	7	8	9	10	11	12	60th
55th	5	6	7	9	10	10	11	55th
50th	4	6	7	8	9	9	10	50th
45th	4	5	6	7	8	9	10	45th
40th	3	4	5	7	7	8	9	40th
35th	3	4	5	6	7	8	8	35th
30th	2	3	4	6	6	7	8	30th
25th	2	3	4	5	5	6	7	25th
20th	1	2	3	4	4	5	6	20th
15th	1	2	3	4	4	4	5	15th
10th	1	1	2	3	3	3	4	10th
5th	0	0	1	2	2	2	3	5th
0	0	0	0	0	0	0	0	0

UNDERHAND PITCH (GIRLS)

| Percentile | Age | | | | | | | Percentile |
	10-11	12	13	14	15	16	17-18	
100th	23	22	24	24	26	27	26	100th
95th	12	14	16	17	16	19	21	95th
90th	10	13	14	15	15	16	18	90th
85th	8	11	12	14	13	14	17	85th
80th	7	10	11	13	12	12	15	80th
75th	6	9	10	12	11	12	14	75th
70th	6	8	9	11	10	11	13	70th
65th	5	7	9	10	9	10	12	65th
60th	5	6	8	9	8	10	11	60th
55th	4	6	7	8	7	9	10	55th
50th	4	5	7	8	6	8	9	50th
45th	3	5	6	7	6	8	9	45th
40th	3	4	6	6	5	7	8	40th
35th	2	4	5	5	4	6	7	35th
30th	2	3	4	5	4	5	6	30th
25th	1	2	4	4	3	5	5	25th
20th	1	2	3	3	2	4	5	20th
15th	0	1	2	3	2	3	4	15th
10th	0	0	2	2	1	2	3	10th
5th	0	0	1	1	0	0	2	5th
0	0	0	0	0	0	0	0	0

Table 16-33

SPEED THROW (BOYS)
Percentile Scores Based on Age/Test Scores in Seconds and Tenths

| Percentile | Age | | | | | | | Percentile |
	10-11	12	13	14	15	16	17-18	
100th	13.1	11.0	10.0	9.0	13.0	10.0	10.0	100th
95th	16.1	15.3	14.9	13.0	13.5	12.5	12.1	95th
90th	17.1	16.1	14.9	14.0	13.8	13.2	12.8	90th
85th	17.6	16.8	15.7	14.6	14.2	13.7	13.2	85th
80th	18.0	17.3	16.2	15.1	14.5	14.1	13.3	80th
75th	18.6	17.6	16.8	15.6	14.9	14.5	13.9	75th
70th	19.1	18.0	16.9	15.9	15.6	14.8	14.2	70th
65th	19.7	18.4	17.3	16.3	15.9	15.1	14.5	65th
60th	20.2	18.9	17.6	16.6	16.0	15.5	14.8	60th
55th	20.8	19.5	17.9	17.1	16.4	15.8	14.9	55th
50th	21.3	19.8	18.4	17.3	16.7	16.4	15.3	50th
45th	21.8	20.4	19.1	17.7	17.1	16.6	15.6	45th
40th	22.6	21.0	19.3	18.1	17.5	17.1	16.2	40th
35th	23.6	21.5	19.8	18.5	17.9	17.4	16.7	35th
30th	24.6	22.2	20.6	19.0	18.3	18.2	17.2	30th
25th	25.7	23.1	12.2	19.5	18.9	18.8	17.6	25th
20th	26.7	23.9	21.9	20.2	19.5	19.4	18.3	20th
15th	28.2	25.4	23.0	21.3	20.2	19.9	18.9	15th
10th	30.1	27.8	24.2	22.5	20.9	20.9	19.9	10th
5th	34.7	29.5	26.4	25.1	22.2	23.0	21.2	5th
0	43.1	36.0	29.3	28.2	24.9	25.5	26.1	0

SPEED THROW (GIRLS)

| Percentile | Age | | | | | | | Percentile |
	10-11	12	13	14	15	16	17-18	
100th	10.0	12.0	12.0	12.0	12.0	14.0	14.0	100th
95th	20.1	13.8	13.0	13.0	15.6	15.8	15.0	95th
90th	21.4	15.8	16.3	13.9	16.6	16.9	15.0	90th
85th	22.8	17.7	17.8	15.3	17.6	17.6	15.6	85th
80th	24.1	18.8	18.6	16.5	18.1	18.1	16.1	80th
75th	25.2	19.8	19.4	17.6	18.6	18.5	17.6	75th
70th	26.0	20.8	20.0	18.2	19.1	18.9	18.0	70th
65th	27.0	21.6	20.6	18.7	19.6	19.4	18.5	65th
60th	27.4	22.3	21.3	19.3	20.1	20.0	18.9	60th
55th	28.8	23.1	21.9	19.9	20.6	20.7	19.3	55th
50th	29.8	24.1	22.7	20.7	21.1	21.4	19.8	50th
45th	30.9	25.2	23.4	21.1	21.7	22.2	20.3	45th
40th	31.9	26.2	24.3	21.8	22.6	22.9	20.8	40th
35th	33.0	27.5	25.4	22.5	23.3	23.7	21.4	35th
30th	34.1	28.6	26.4	23.5	24.3	24.8	22.3	30th
25th	35.9	29.8	27.5	24.6	25.4	26.1	23.3	25th
20th	38.0	31.3	28.9	25.8	26.9	27.8	24.1	20th
15th	41.0	33.1	30.9	27.4	28.7	30.4	25.0	15th
10th	46.1	36.7	33.0	30.2	31.5	33.0	26.1	10th
5th	55.2	40.8	38.5	33.5	37.4	36.9	28.9	5th
0	105.0	66.0	52.0	50.0	50.0	52.0	40.0	0

Table 16-34

FUNGO HITTING (BOYS)

Percentile Scores Based on Age/Test Scores in Points

| Percentile | Age | | | | | | | Percentile |
	10-11	12	13	14	15	16	17-18	
100th	40	40	39	36	40	40	40	100th
95th	35	36	38	35	39	38	39	95th
90th	32	33	34	35	37	36	37	90th
85th	29	31	33	33	34	34	36	85th
80th	27	30	31	31	33	33	35	80th
75th	26	29	30	30	31	33	34	75th
70th	24	28	29	29	30	32	32	70th
65th	22	27	28	28	29	30	31	65th
60th	21	26	27	27	28	29	30	60th
55th	20	25	25	26	26	28	29	55th
50th	19	23	24	24	24	26	28	50th
45th	17	22	23	23	23	25	26	45th
40th	16	20	21	21	21	23	25	40th
35th	14	19	19	19	19	21	23	35th
30th	13	17	18	18	17	19	21	30th
25th	11	15	16	16	16	17	19	25th
20th	10	13	15	15	14	15	17	20th
15th	8	11	14	13	12	13	15	15th
10th	6	10	12	12	11	11	13	10th
5th	3	7	9	11	9	9	11	5th
0	0	0	1	9	1	0	3	0

FUNGO HITTING (GIRLS)

| Percentile | Age | | | | | | | Percentile |
	10-11	12	13	14	15	16	17-18	
100th	30	38	38	38	38	38	38	100th
95th	21	28	30	31	30	30	31	95th
90th	18	24	26	30	27	27	28	90th
85th	15	22	23	26	25	25	26	85th
80th	14	20	22	23	23	24	25	80th
75th	13	18	20	21	22	22	23	75th
70th	12	17	19	20	20	21	22	70th
65th	12	16	18	19	19	19	20	65th
60th	11	15	17	18	18	18	19	60th
55th	9	14	16	17	17	17	18	55th
50th	9	13	14	15	16	16	17	50th
45th	8	12	13	14	15	15	16	45th
40th	7	11	13	13	14	14	15	40th
35th	6	10	12	12	13	13	14	35th
30th	6	9	11	11	12	12	14	30th
25th	5	8	10	10	11	11	13	25th
20th	4	7	8	9	10	10	12	20th
15th	3	5	7	8	8	9	10	15th
10th	2	4	6	6	7	8	8	10th
5th	0	2	4	3	4	5	6	5th
0	0	0	0	0	0	0	0	0

Table 16-35

BASE RUNNING (BOYS)

Percentile Scores Based on Age/Test Scores in Seconds and Tenths

Percentile	Age							Percentile
	10-11	12	13	14	15	16	17-18	
100th	10.1	9.6	9.4	9.7	10.0	10.0	10.0	100th
95th	12.9	12.4	11.7	11.5	11.6	11.3	11.1	95th
90th	13.5	12.5	12.2	11.9	11.9	11.6	11.4	90th
85th	13.9	13.3	12.7	12.2	12.2	11.8	11.6	85th
80th	14.1	13.5	12.9	12.5	12.4	12.0	11.8	80th
75th	14.3	13.7	13.2	12.7	12.5	12.1	11.9	75th
70th	14.5	13.9	13.4	12.9	12.7	12.3	12.0	70th
65th	14.8	14.1	13.6	13.0	12.8	12.4	12.2	65th
60th	14.9	14.3	13.8	13.1	13.0	12.5	12.3	60th
55th	15.1	14.5	13.9	13.3	13.1	12.6	12.4	55th
50th	15.2	14.7	14.1	13.4	13.2	12.8	12.6	50th
45th	15.4	14.8	14.3	13.5	13.3	12.9	12.7	45th
40th	15.6	15.0	14.5	13.7	13.5	13.0	12.8	40th
35th	15.8	15.2	14.7	13.9	13.6	13.2	12.9	35th
30th	16.0	15.4	14.9	14.1	13.7	13.3	13.0	30th
25th	16.2	15.7	15.1	14.2	13.9	13.6	13.2	25th
20th	16.5	15.9	15.4	14.5	14.0	13.8	13.4	20th
15th	17.0	16.2	15.7	14.8	14.3	14.1	13.6	15th
10th	17.4	16.5	15.9	15.2	14.5	14.4	13.9	10th
5th	18.2	17.4	16.7	15.8	15.0	15.3	14.9	5th
0	23.0	20.6	17.2	17.2	15.8	18.0	17.8	0

BASE RUNNING (GIRLS)

Percentile	Age							Percentile
	10-11	12	13	14	15	16	17-18	
100th	11.0	11.0	12.0	12.0	12.0	12.0	12.0	100th
95th	13.1	13.4	12.6	12.7	12.9	13.2	13.6	95th
90th	13.8	13.7	13.1	13.1	13.5	13.7	13.9	90th
85th	14.3	14.0	13.5	13.5	13.7	14.0	14.3	85th
80th	14.7	14.3	13.7	13.7	13.9	14.4	14.6	80th
75th	14.9	14.5	13.9	13.8	14.1	14.6	14.8	75th
70th	15.2	14.7	14.1	14.0	14.3	14.8	14.9	70th
65th	15.4	14.9	14.3	14.2	14.5	14.9	15.1	65th
60th	15.6	15.0	14.5	14.4	14.7	15.1	15.3	60th
55th	15.8	15.2	14.7	14.5	14.9	15.3	15.5	55th
50th	16.0	15.3	14.8	14.8	15.0	15.5	15.7	50th
45th	16.2	15.5	15.0	14.9	15.2	15.6	15.9	45th
40th	16.4	15.7	15.2	15.1	15.4	15.8	16.1	40th
35th	16.7	15.8	15.4	15.3	15.5	15.9	16.3	35th
30th	17.0	16.0	15.6	15.5	15.8	16.0	16.5	30th
25th	17.3	16.2	16.0	15.7	16.1	16.2	16.9	25th
20th	17.7	16.5	16.3	16.0	16.3	16.3	17.1	20th
15th	18.2	16.9	16.6	16.4	16.7	16.4	17.6	15th
10th	18.8	17.4	17.2	16.9	17.3	17.8	18.2	10th
5th	19.9	18.2	18.0	17.8	18.1	18.4	19.2	5th
0	27.0	20.0	22.0	23.0	28.0	31.0	32.0	0

Table 16-36

FIELDING GROUND BALLS (BOYS)

Percentile Scores Based on Age/Test Scores in Points

Percentile	Age 10-11	12	13	14	15	16	17-18	Percentile
100th	20	20	20	20	20	20	20	100th
95th	19	20	20	20	20	20	20	95th
90th	18	19	19	19	19	20	20	90th
85th	18	19	19	19	19	20	20	85th
80th	17	18	18	18	18	19	19	80th
75th	17	18	18	18	18	19	19	75th
70th	16	17	17	17	18	19	19	70th
65th	16	17	17	17	17	18	18	65th
60th	15	16	16	16	16	18	18	60th
55th	15	16	16	16	16	17	17	55th
50th	14	15	15	15	15	17	17	50th
45th	13	15	14	14	15	16	17	45th
40th	13	14	14	14	14	16	16	40th
35th	12	14	13	13	13	15	16	35th
30th	11	13	13	12	12	14	15	30th
25th	10	12	12	10	11	13	14	25th
20th	9	11	11	10	10	10	12	20th
15th	8	9	10	9	9	9	10	15th
10th	6	8	8	8	8	9	9	10th
5th	4	6	6	6	7	8	9	5th
0	0	0	1	1	1	5	6	0

FIELDING GROUND BALLS (GIRLS)

Percentile	Age 10-11	12	13	14	15	16	17-18	Percentile
100th	20	20	20	20	20	20	20	100th
95th	18	20	20	20	20	20	20	95th
90th	17	19	19	19	20	20	20	90th
85th	16	19	19	19	19	19	19	85th
80th	15	18	19	19	19	19	19	80th
75th	15	18	18	18	18	19	19	75th
70th	14	17	18	18	18	18	18	70th
65th	13	16	17	17	18	18	18	65th
60th	13	15	17	17	17	18	18	60th
55th	12	15	16	17	17	17	17	55th
50th	11	14	16	16	16	17	17	50th
45th	10	13	15	15	16	17	17	45th
40th	10	12	15	15	15	16	16	40th
35th	9	10	14	14	15	16	16	35th
30th	8	10	13	13	14	15	15	30th
25th	8	9	12	12	13	14	14	25th
20th	7	9	11	10	12	13	14	20th
15th	6	8	10	10	11	12	13	15th
10th	5	7	9	9	10	10	11	10th
5th	3	5	8	8	9	8	9	5th
0	0	0	0	0	0	0	0	0

Table 16-37
T-Scale Norms for Elrod Fielding and Throwing Test and Batting Test

T-Score	Fielding and Throwing Raw Score	Batting Raw Score
80	48-50	38-40
75	44-47	35-37
70	41-43	33-34
65	37-40	30-32
60	34-36	28-29
55	30-33	25-27
50	27-29	23-24
45	23-26	20-22
40	20-22	18-19
35	16-19	15-17
30	13-15	13-14
25	9-12	10-12
20	6- 8	8- 9

Norms based on 100 high school boys.

regulation softballs and bats; and (e) ribbon or tape to mark 80-foot intervals on cord.

Directions: The tester or an assistant who can consistently pitch balls across the plate pitches to the subject for ten trials. The subject attempts to hit the ball into the outfield. Each swing counts as a trial, but he does not have to swing at a bad pitch. Spotters place a marker at the spot at which each hit lands in fair territory.

Scoring: A stake is driven behind home plate and serves as a pivot point. The cord is attached to the stake and is stretched from home plate to the outfield. One ribbon or a piece of tape or other type of marker is attached to the cord 80 feet from home plate, and another is attached 80 feet beyond the first.

When the subject has had ten trials, an assistant grabs the far end of the cord and walks from one foul line to the other. As the outstretched cord passes over each marker, the point value for that marker is called out. The scoring zones are two points for a ball that hits in the first 80-foot zone, three points for the second 80-foot zone and four points for a ball beyond that zone. One point is given for a foul ball. A swing and a miss counts as a trial and

receives a zero. The maximum score for the ten trials would be forty.

Additional Pointers: (a) In order to facilitate the testing and prevent the batter from being too selective, a trial is counted if the subject allows two pitches to go by in the strike zone without swinging; (b) the stake and cord method greatly facilitates the testing in eliminating the need for elaborate field markings; (c) the use of a pitcher does detract from the objectivity, but it is felt that the only way batting skill can be tested accurately is to hit a pitched ball; (d) tentative norms are shown in Table 16-37.

Swimming and Diving

Swimming Achievement Scales

Hewitt constructed achievement scales for college men (113) and for high school boys and girls (114) for the purposes of classifying students into homogeneous swimming groups and measuring improvement in performance. The test items for the College Swimming Achievement Scales are as follows:

Fifteen-minute endurance swim. The subject

swims for 15 minutes, counting the number of lengths of the pool covered. The lengths are converted into yards. No score is given if subject fails to swim for 15 minutes.

Twenty- and twenty-five-yard underwater swims. From a regulation start, using any type of stroke, the subject swims the entire distance underwater. Time is to the nearest tenth of a second.

Twenty-five-yard and fifty-yard swims using the crawl, breast, and back-crawl strokes. From a regulation start the swims are scored to the nearest tenth of a second.

Fifty-yard glide relaxation swims using elementary back stroke, side stroke, and breast stroke. The score for each of these events is the number of strokes taken to cover the distance. All starts are made in the water.

The items for the High School Swimming Achievement Scales are as follows:

Fifty-yard crawl. Using a racing dive, this crawl stroke event is scored in time to the nearest second.

Twenty-five-yard flutter kick with polo ball. The subject holds on to the side with one hand and the ball with the other until given the signal to go. He then pushes off and kicks to the other end (25 yards) of the pool. The score is time to the nearest tenth of a second.

Twenty-five-yard glide relaxation using the elementary back stroke, side stroke, and breast stroke. Same testing procedures as in the college test except for the distance. The score is the number of strokes taken.

Rosentsweig's Revision of the Fox Swimming Test (117)

Objective: To measure form and power on five basic strokes of swimming.

Age Level: This test could be used in junior high school through college.

Sex: Satisfactory for boys and girls.

Reliability: The test-retest reliability was found to be satisfactory for each of the five strokes with r's ranging from .89 to .96.

Validity: While face validity is acceptable for this test, the author reported r's of .63 to .83 between the best power scores and the judges' ratings. These correlations were not intended as a validity measure.

Equipment and Materials: Marking tape and string stretched the length of the pool and marked off in 1-yard units beginning 8 feet from the shallow end are needed. The first marker is the starting line and the tape markers are stapled to the string.

Directions: A partner stands to the side of the performer and, with one of the forearms, cradles the legs of the performer up to the surface of the water. The shoulders are lined up on the first deck marker (starting line). The performer is allowed to scull or float in the starting position until taking the first arm stroke. If a kick is made prior to the first arm stroke, the trial is immediately stopped. The performer is to take twelve arm strokes or six cycles depending upon the type of stroke measured. The teacher rates the performer on a five-point scale (A-F) and then takes note of distance covered in the twelve strokes by again using the shoulders as a reference point with the distance marker.

Scoring: The two measures of form and distance are combined into a grade for each student.

Tennis

Overhead Smash Test (135)

Objective: To measure the effectiveness of the overhead smash stroke.

Age Level: Junior high school through college age level.

Sex: Satisfactory for both boys and girls.

Reliability: An r of .96 was reported by Stan Johnson, 1973.

Objectivity: An r of .98 was reported by Mike Recio and Charles Prestidge, 1972.

Validity: Since the overhead smash is one of the most vital shots in tennis, this test is accepted for its face validity.

Table 16-38
Raw Score Norms for Overhead Smash Test with Johnson's Tennis and Badminton Machine

College Men	Performance Level
9 - 10	Advanced
7 - 8	Adv. Intermediate
5 - 6	Intermediate
3 - 4	Adv. Beginner
0 - 2	Beginner

Based on the scores of a limited number of college men as reported by Mike Recio and Charles Prestidge, 1972.

Equipment and Materials: The tennis and badminton machine, several tennis balls, and a tennis racket are needed for the test.

Directions: The machine is placed in a position where the ball will fall at the junction of the center service line and the service line. The subject assumes the proper position for the smash and strikes the ball as it drops from the top pulley of the machine. The subject is allowed three practice trials, and then ten trials are administered for the test. The student tries to smash the ball across the net and into the singles playing court.

Scoring: The subject scores one point for each successful smash into the opposing playing court. The maximum score is ten points.

Additional Pointers: (a) Do not count trials where the subject fails to execute satisfactory form and force for a smash. Have the subject repeat each improper trial. (b) The test can be administered on a backboard with the net line drawn. This procedure is especially recommended for practice sessions while in the class period. (c) If a repeated trial is also incorrect, the trial is scored as a zero.

The Tennis Set-up Machine is an inexpensive device used for testing and training purposes in the sport of tennis. It provides for overhead stroke practice and has pitch-out capabilities. Models may be either automatic or manual.

Hewitt's Revision of the Dyer Backboard Tennis Test (128)

Purpose: For classification of beginning and advanced tennis players.

Age and Sex: May be used for both sexes at the college and high school levels.

Validity: Rank order correlations were computed using the results of round-robin tournaments and scores made on the Hewitt revision test for beginning and advanced tennis players. Rho's were converted to r's and were found to range from .68 to .73 for the beginner classes and .84 to .89 for the advanced classes.

Reliability: Using the test-retest method, the reliability coefficients were .93 for the advanced players and .82 for the beginners.

Equipment and Materials: A wall 20 feet high and 20 feet wide is needed for the test. The required equipment includes a tennis racket, a stopwatch, a basket with at least a dozen new tennis balls, and masking tape for marking lines. A line 1 inch wide is marked on the wall at a height of 3 feet and 20 feet long to simulate the net. A restraining line 20 feet long and 1 inch wide is marked 20 feet from the wall.

Directions: The subject starts with two tennis balls behind the 20-foot restraining line and serves the ball against the wall. Any type of serve may be used. The watch is started when the served ball hits above the net line on the wall. The subject then rallies from behind the restraining line against the wall using any type of stroke. If the ball should get away from the student, he may take another ball from the basket. However, each time he takes a new ball, it must be started with a serve again. The hitting continues for 30 seconds. Three trials are given.

Scoring: One point is counted for each time the ball hits above the 3-foot net line. No score is counted when the subject steps over the restraining line or for balls that hit below the net line. Balls that hit the line are counted. The average of the three trials is the score.

Figure 16-17. Inexpensive Tennis Set-up Machine*shown in use indoors with a shag net.

*The Tennis Set-up Machine, Model M4, Patent Pending—1972, by Barry L. Johnson, Corpus Christi State University, Corpus Christi, Tx. 78411. (See Appendix K for plans.)

Table 16-39
Scoring Scale for Hewitt's Service Placement Test

College Men	Performance Level	College Women
20 - 60	Advanced	14 - 60
16 - 19	Adv. Intermediate	10 - 13
7 - 15	Intermediate	4 - 9
3 - 6	Adv. Beginner	1 - 3
0 - 2	Beginner	0

Based on a limited number of beginning students in tennis as reported by Stan Johnson, 1973.

Hewitt's Tennis Achievement Test (129)

Hewitt constructed an achievement test for measuring the service and forehand and backhand drives. Beginners, advanced, and varsity tennis players were utilized in validating the test and establishing achievement scales.

Validity coefficients ranged from .52 to .93, and reliability coefficients from .75 to .94. It was found that the service placement test had the highest predictive value for the varsity players; the revised Dyer wall test had highest validity for the advanced players; and the speed of service test had the highest validity coefficient for beginners.

Hewitt recommends the revised Dyer test as being the best test because of its simplicity and ease of administration. Its validity coefficients

were .87, .84, and .73 for varsity, advanced, and beginning players, respectively. If no wall is available, Hewitt suggests that the Hewitt Tennis Achievement Test be used.

The service placement test, the speed of service test, and the forehand and backhand drive tests are briefly described here. Complete descriptions are provided in the original reference.

Hewitt's Service Placement Test. This test was found to have the highest validity coefficient for varsity players.

Court Markings: The right service court is marked as shown in Figure 16-18. The point values from 1 to 6 are also shown in the figure. A quarter-inch rope is stretched above the net at a height of 7 feet.

Directions: After a demonstration by the in-

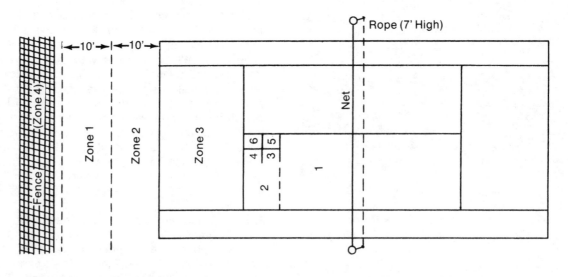

Figure 16-18. Court Markings for Hewitt's Service Placement and Speed of Service Tests

structor and 10-minute warm-up on another court, the subject serves ten balls into the marked right service courts. He must serve the ball between the net and the rope.

Scoring: The point value for the zone in which each ball hits constitutes the score. The points are added for the ten trials. Balls going over the rope are given a score of zero.

Hewitt's Speed of Service Test. Hewitt found that the distance the ball bounced after it hit the service court was a good indication of the speed of service. The type of serve had little effect on this distance. This test had the highest validity coefficient for beginners.

Court Markings: Four zones are formed. Zone 1 is the backcourt area to the base line; zone 2 is the area 10 feet beyond the base line; zone 3 consists of the area from 10 to 20 feet beyond the base line; and zone 4 is the area 20 feet beyond the base line or the fence in most courts. (See Figure 16-18.)

Directions: This test can be scored at the same time as the service placement test. For each of the good serve placements (in other words, those that hit in the service court), the zone in which the ball hits on the second bounce is noted.

Scoring: The point values for zones 1, 2, 3, and 4 are 1 point, 2 points, 3 points, and 4 points, respectively.

Hewitt's Forehand and Backhand Drive Tests.

Court Markings: With the service line as one of the lines for the test, three chalk lines are drawn 4½ feet apart between the service line and the base line. Figure 16-19 shows the court markings and the point value for each zone. A quarter-inch rope is stretched above the net at a height of 7 feet.

Directions: The subject stands at the center mark of the base line. With a basket of balls the instructor takes a position across the net at the intersection of the center line and the service line. The instructor hits five practice balls to the student just beyond the service court. Then ten trials are given for the forehand and ten for the backhand. The student may choose which ten balls to hit forehand and backhand. The student tries to hit the ball between the net and the rope so that the ball goes deep into the court. The same instructor should hit to all students to standardize the testing as much as possible. A ball-throwing machine, if available, would be very effective. Net balls are repeated.

Scoring: The point values for the scoring zones in which the forehand and backhand trials hit are recorded. Balls that pass over the rope receive half the point value of the respective zones.

Volleyball

The Volleyball Set-up Machine is an inexpensive device used for testing and training purposes in the sport of volleyball. It can be used as the thrower on the AAHPER Volleyball Passing Test and Set-up Test. It is also an ideal set-up device for spiking tests since each set-up delivery is identical.

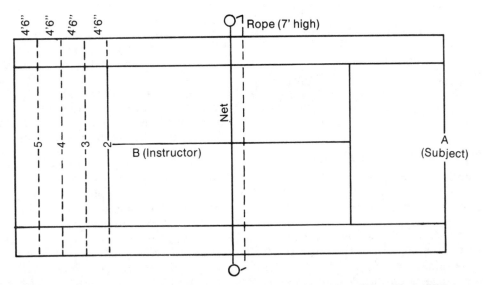

Figure 16-19. Court Markings for Hewitt's Forehand and Backhand Drive Tests

Figure 16-20. Inexpensive Volleyball Set-up Machine for Spike Test*

*The Volleyball Set-up Machine, Model M-2, Patent Pending—1972, by Barry L. Johnson, Corpus Christi State University, Corpus Christi, Tx. 78411. (See Appendix K for plans.)

AAHPER Volleyball Skills Test (138)

The manual contains four tests: volleying, serving, passing, and set-ups. The tests are designed to cover the fundamental skills of volleyball.

Volleying: This test is essentially the same as the Brady Wall Volley except that the line on the wall is 11 feet above the floor, 5 feet long, and vertical lines extend upward from each end of the line 3 or 4 feet. The subject volleys the ball against the wall as many times as possible in 1 minute. Scores over fifty are not recorded.

Serving: The server is given ten trials. The score is the total points made according to the value of the zone in which the serve lands. (See Figure 16-21.) For children below 12 years of age, the serving line should be 20 feet from the net instead of 30.

Passing: A thrower (T in Figure 11-22) tosses a high pass to the passer (P in diagram) who attempts to execute a legal volleyball pass over the rope onto the marked area. Twenty trials are given alternately to the right and left. The trial counts but no points are given for any ball which hits the rope or net or falls outside the target area. Maximum score is twenty.

Set-up: A thrower (T in Figure 11-23) tosses a high pass to the subject (S in diagram) who executes a set-up over the rope and onto the target area. Two subjects can be tested simultaneously, one setting up to the right and the other to the left. Ten trials are given to the right and ten to the left. Any ball that touches the rope or net or doesn't hit the target receives zero for that trial. Any throw from T that doesn't fall into the 6-by-5-foot area is to be repeated. Maximum score is twenty.

(Norms for boys and girls ages ten through eighteen for each test are presented in this chapter.)

Problems in Sports Skills Measurement

In any sport there are a number of skills and abilities involved which make for successful performance. Even though the fundamental components can be identified, they can never be measured separately and then summed up to represent actual performance. Here, as in many phases of human performance, the whole is greater than the sum of the parts. The successful teacher must recognize this and strive to select those tests which will provide the student and the teacher with the most accurate information of the student's progress and achievement.

The basic concepts and criteria of test construction and selection which were discussed in Chapter 4 are especially pertinent in the area of sports skills measurement. Criteria such as ease of administration, needed equipment, time required to administer the tests, need for trained testers, the meaningfulness of the test items, and the ease and objectivity of scoring

Table 16-40
AAHPER Volleyball Test Norms

	Volleying Test (Boys)							Volleying Test (Girls)							
	Percentile Scores Based on Age / Test Scores in Points							Percentile Scores Based on Age / Test Scores in Points							
Percentile	10-11	12	13	14	15	16	17-18	10-11	12	13	14	15	16	17-18	Percentile
100	40	42	44	50	50	50	50	47	49	49	50	50	50	50	100
95	24	31	35	39	42	44	45	21	29	31	32	37	40	40	95
90	19	28	30	36	40	41	42	13	24	25	26	31	36	38	90
85	17	24	28	33	36	38	42	10	19	20	21	24	28	31	85
80	15	22	26	31	34	36	41	8	16	17	19	21	25	27	80
75	13	19	24	29	32	34	40	6	13	15	17	18	22	23	75
70	12	18	22	27	30	33	39	5	11	13	14	16	20	20	70
65	11	17	21	26	29	32	37	4	10	11	13	15	18	18	65
60	9	16	19	24	28	30	36	3	8	10	12	13	16	16	60
55	8	15	18	23	27	28	34	3	7	9	11	12	14	14	55
50	7	13	17	21	25	26	32	2	6	8	10	11	12	12	50
45	6	12	15	19	24	25	29	2	5	7	9	10	11	11	45
40	5	11	14	18	22	23	27	1	4	6	8	9	9	9	40
35	4	9	12	17	20	21	24	1	3	5	7	8	8	8	35
30	3	8	11	15	18	19	23	1	2	4	6	7	7	7	30
25	3	7	9	13	17	18	20	0	2	3	5	6	6	6	25
20	2	6	8	11	15	16	19	0	1	1	4	5	5	5	20
15	1	4	7	9	13	15	17	0	1	1	3	4	4	4	15
10	0	3	5	7	10	12	14	0	0	0	1	2	3	3	10
5	0	2	3	5	6	11	11	0	0	0	0	1	2	2	5
0	0	0	0	0	0	0	0	0	0	0	0	0	0	0	0

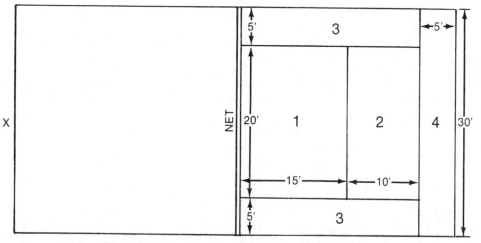

Figure 16-21. AAHPER Volleyball Serving Test

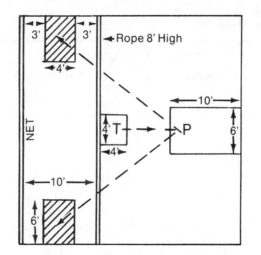

Figure 16-22. AAHPER Volleyball Passing Test

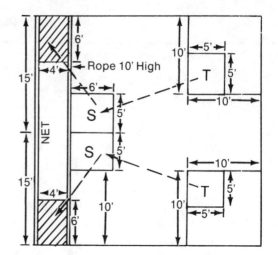

Figure 16-23. AAHPER Volleyball Set-up Test
(Two Stations for Right and Left)

Table 16-41
AAHPER Volleyball Test Norms

| | Serving Test (Boys) | | | | | | | Serving Test (Girls) | | | | | | | |
| | Percentile Scores Based on Age / Test Scores in Points | | | | | | | Percentile Scores Based on Age / Test Scores in Points | | | | | | | |
Percentile	10-11	12	13	14	15	16	17-18	10-11	12	13	14	15	16	17-18	Percentile
100	39	40	40	40	40	40	40	36	38	40	40	40	40	40	100
95	29	31	32	34	36	37	37	24	26	26	28	30	31	32	95
90	27	28	29	31	33	33	33	20	22	23	26	26	26	26	90
85	25	26	27	29	32	32	32	18	20	20	23	23	24	24	85
80	23	24	26	27	30	30	31	16	18	18	21	21	22	23	80
75	22	23	24	25	28	29	30	15	16	17	20	20	21	21	75
70	21	21	23	24	28	29	30	14	15	15	18	19	20	20	70
65	20	20	22	23	27	28	29	13	14	14	17	17	19	19	65
60	18	19	21	22	25	27	27	12	13	13	15	16	18	18	60
55	17	18	20	21	24	25	26	11	12	12	14	15	17	17	55
50	16	16	19	20	22	23	24	10	11	11	13	14	16	16	50
45	15	15	18	19	21	22	22	9	10	10	11	13	15	15	45
40	14	14	17	18	20	21	21	8	9	9	10	12	14	14	40
35	13	13	16	17	19	19	20	7	8	8	9	11	13	14	35
30	12	12	15	16	18	19	19	6	6	7	8	10	13	13	30
25	11	11	13	15	16	17	17	5	5	5	7	9	11	11	25
20	9	10	12	14	15	15	16	4	4	4	6	8	10	10	20
15	8	9	10	12	12	13	14	2	3	3	5	6	8	9	15
10	7	8	8	10	11	12	12	1	1	1	3	4	7	7	10
5	4	5	5	8	9	10	11	0	0	0	1	2	4	4	5
0	0	3	3	5	6	6	7	0	0	0	0	0	0	0	0

Table 16-42
AAHPER Volleyball Test Norms

| | Passing Test (Boys) | | | | | | | Passing Test (Girls) | | | | | | | |
| | Percentile Scores Based on Age / Test Scores in Points | | | | | | | Percentile Scores Based on Age / Test Scores in Points | | | | | | | |
Percentile	10-11	12	13	14	15	16	17-18	10-11	12	13	14	15	16	17-18	Percentile
100	19	19	19	20	20	20	20	19	19	20	20	20	20	20	100
95	12	14	16	17	17	17	17	10	12	12	13	13	14	15	95
90	10	13	14	16	16	16	16	8	10	10	11	11	12	13	90
85	9	12	13	15	15	15	15	7	8	9	10	10	11	12	85
80	8	11	12	14	14	14	14	6	7	8	9	9	10	11	80
75	7	10	12	13	13	13	13	5	6	7	8	8	8	9	75
70	6	9	11	12	12	12	13	4	6	6	7	7	8	9	70
65	5	8	10	12	12	12	13	3	5	5	6	6	8	8	65
60	4	8	9	11	11	12	12	3	4	4	6	6	7	8	60
55	4	7	9	10	10	12	12	2	4	4	5	5	6	7	55
50	3	6	8	10	10	11	11	2	3	4	5	5	6	6	50
45	3	5	7	9	9	10	10	1	3	3	4	4	5	6	45
40	2	4	7	8	8	9	9	1	2	3	4	4	4	5	40
35	2	4	6	8	8	9	9	0	2	2	3	3	4	4	35
30	1	3	5	7	7	8	8	0	1	2	3	3	3	4	30
25	1	2	4	6	6	7	8	0	1	1	2	2	3	3	25
20	0	2	4	5	5	6	7	0	0	1	1	2	2	3	20
15	0	1	3	4	4	5	6	0	0	0	1	1	2	2	15
10	0	0	2	3	3	4	4	0	0	0	0	1	1	1	10
5	0	0	1	2	2	2	2	0	0	0	0	0	0	0	5
0	0	0	0	0	0	0	0	0	0	0	0	0	0	0	0

are all very much interrelated. Singly and in combination, they also greatly contribute to or detract from the basic concepts of validity, reliability, and objectivity. Much of the discussion in Chapter 4 utilized skill tests in the examples; therefore it would be redundant to discuss these problems again. However, there are a few points that appear to the authors to be so crucial that they deserve some reiteration. One of these concerns objective scoring versus realism and validity. Test makers frequently attempt to eliminate the influence of a second person on the performance of the subject being measured. Consequently, in tennis, for example, some test items require the subject to drop the ball, then stroke it, rather than to stroke a ball that has been hit to him by another person. Similarly, in softball tests, the subject is tested by throwing at a target instead of a person, and he bats the ball from a batting tee, or tosses the ball to himself instead of hitting a pitched ball. Furthermore, when a second person is involved in certain test items, that person's role is often out of context with regard to actual performance. Using tennis and softball again as examples, the second person in some tests may stand at the net and throw tennis balls to the subject; and in softball, the second person is sometimes used to throw ground balls and/or fly balls to the subject being tested.

Obviously, the reasons for using test items such as these relate to the objectivity of scoring and, presumably, greater consistency in the test administration. But let us examine these practices with regard to the performance they are supposed to measure. First, though, we should hasten to say that tennis and softball are certainly not the only sports in which these problems exist. All sports skills tests are faced with the problem of including only realistic, functional test items.

Table 16-43
AAHPER Volleyball Test Norms

	Set-up Test (Boys) Percentile Scores Based on Age / Test Scores in Points							Set-up Test (Girls) Percentile Scores Based on Age / Test Scores in Points							
Percentile	10-11	12	13	14	15	16	17-18	10-11	12	13	14	15	16	17-18	Percentile
100	16	18	20	20	20	20	20	19	20	20	20	20	20	20	100
95	10	14	16	16	16	17	17	11	13	14	14	14	15	15	95
90	9	12	14	15	15	15	15	9	11	11	12	12	12	14	90
85	8	11	13	13	13	14	15	7	9	10	10	11	11	12	85
80	7	10	12	12	12	13	14	6	8	9	10	10	10	11	80
75	6	9	11	11	11	12	13	5	7	8	9	9	9	10	75
70	6	8	10	10	10	10	11	5	6	7	8	8	8	8	70
65	5	8	9	9	9	9	11	4	6	7	7	7	7	7	65
60	5	7	8	8	8	9	10	4	5	6	6	6	7	7	60
55	4	7	7	8	8	8	10	3	5	5	6	6	6	6	55
50	4	6	7	7	7	7	9	3	4	5	5	5	6	6	50
45	3	6	6	6	6	6	9	2	4	4	4	4	5	5	45
40	3	5	6	6	6	6	8	2	3	4	4	4	5	5	40
35	3	5	5	5	5	5	7	2	3	3	3	3	4	4	35
30	2	4	4	5	5	5	7	1	2	3	3	3	3	4	30
25	2	4	4	4	4	4	6	1	2	2	2	2	3	3	25
20	2	3	3	4	4	4	6	1	2	2	2	2	2	3	20
15	1	3	3	3	3	3	5	0	1	1	1	1	2	2	15
10	0	1	1	2	2	2	2	0	0	1	1	1	1	1	10
5	0	1	1	1	1	1	2	0	0	0	0	0	1	1	5
0	0	0	0	0	0	0	1	0	0	0	0	0	0	0	0

In some tennis tests, there is a definite skill involved in being able to drop the ball and then successfully hit it with a forehand (and particularly a backhand) stroke that is not called for in the actual game of tennis. The perception, timing, and footwork that are necessary in being able to execute a forehand or backhand drive are not involved in such a test.

In softball and similar sports, throwing at a target may be viewed as violating the well-established teaching and coaching point that the player should not *aim* his throw. The height of the target should also be examined. The softball and baseball player usually throws to a relatively low target, such as to the first baseman who stretches to meet the throw or to the catcher who must make the tag low on the sliding runner. In batting, hitting from a tee is quite different from hitting a pitched ball. A batting tee is usually just employed in practice to help correct *hitches* in the swing and other fundamental faults in the stance and swing. The validity of fungo hitting as a measure of batting skill may also be questioned. During practice sessions the pitchers spend a large amount of time hitting fly balls to other players, but as a group they are notoriously poor hitters. There does not seem to be much point continuing to question other test items, such as whether or not fielding ground balls or catching fly balls is different when the ball is thrown or batted, etc. The question essentially becomes that of how much deviation from the actual skill the teacher is willing to sacrifice in order to increase the objectivity of the test item.

It is hoped that the test items would be usable for practice drills and serve as motivation and provide indications of progress for the student. This is one very important way in which tests may serve several functions and thereby justify their use in terms of time spent for testing. Permanent testing stations and mobile test equipment are extremely valuable in this respect.

The scoring of the test should be such that it is able to distinguish among persons of different levels of ability. Decisions must be made as to target size, whether or not to give a score for hitting just behind the boundary lines, and whether or not the nature of the test encourages poor form. While it is of considerable value and interest for a test to possess national norms, the physical education teacher should always be urged to construct and utilize local norms.

Finally, the teacher should exercise great care in regard to the proportion of a student's grade that is determined by performance in skills tests. The teacher must continually evaluate the degree to which performance on a specific test reflects the ability to play the game. Certain activities, of course, lend themselves to more precise evaluation than others. The performance in some sports like golf, bowling, etc., is measured by the scores themselves. Relative ability in certain activities like handball, badminton, and others can be assessed quite accurately through round-robin tournaments. While in still others, such as in swimming, diving, and gymnastics, the performance must almost always invoke subjective judgment. Performance in team sports like touch football, basketball, volleyball, and others is sometimes more difficult to determine. Here, as in all sports, skills tests can be used to good advantage for grading, provided that they are combined with careful subjective evaluation of the subject's actual performance in that sport.

Findings and Conclusions from Sports Skills Measurement and Research

The literature concerning sports skills generally pertains to methodology utilized in sports skills acquisition and measurement or to analysis of performance in sports. Needless to say, there have been countless studies conducted that could conceivably fall under the heading of sports skills. The following is a sampling of research done since 1960 in this field.

Zabik and Jackson (189) concluded that the modified Chicago Round and the modified Flint Round were reliable measures of archery achievement of college men. Furthermore, the relationship between the two rounds was sufficiently low to warrant using both measures. Eckert and Wendt (171) found no relationship between kinesthetic perception of a comfortable pull and the actual pull required to comfortably draw the bow.

In a study by Burdeshaw and others (168), the evidence failed to support the concept that a basic skills course in a specific sport facilitates subsequent performance. The study involved two groups of college women of low motor ability. One group participated in badminton while the control group took part in another sport. Both groups then received badminton instruction. There was no difference in performance despite the prior badminton experience of the one group. Gray and Brumbach (6) reported that daylight viewing of loop films of specific skills appeared to accelerate learning in beginning badminton, although the learning advantage was not maintained as the subjects continued to play.

McArdle and others (178) found no significant improvement in aerobic capacity of women basketball players during the season despite the fact that relatively high heart rates were maintained during games.

In a study on somatotypes of football players, Carter (169) generally supported Sheldon's observations but also found that some of the rare somatotypes were well-suited to football, especially if tall and heavy. There were significant somatotype differences between backs and linemen.

Alderman (165) compared two grips in teaching beginning golf and reported no differences in range, angle of impact, and velocity after six weeks of instruction. Purdy and Stallard (182) found the whole method of learning to be more effective in improving accuracy and general golf ability, and the overlapping grip to be more effective when the whole method was used. DeBacy (170) concluded that self-viewing by video tapes is beneficial in improving accuracy of self-assessment in beginning golf. A study by Thompson (187) revealed that immediate external feedback through the use of the graph-check-sequence facilitated learning of golf skills. Bowen (59) concluded that putting success for beginning golfers was not related to the use of a particular point of aim.

Johnson (175) conducted a twenty-year follow-up study on objectivity of gymnastics judging and recommended re-evaluation of the rules, judging procedures, and selection of skills for compulsory routines to permit greater discrimination between performances.

Asprey and others (166) reported no adverse effects on swimming performances in the 1-mile freestyle from eating a meal of cereal and milk at times of ½ hour, 1 hour, or 2 hours prior to swimming. Maglischo and Maglischo (176) compared three racing starts in competitive swimming and reported evidence favoring the circular-backswing start. Groves and Roberts (173) identified the optimum angle of projection for the racing start to be 13 degrees downward from the horizontal. Separate studies in swimming by Burdeshaw (167) and Mitchem and Lane (180) both concluded that Negroes had less bouyancy than whites. McCatty (179) concluded that the use of a flotation device does not accelerate the learning process for non-swimmers.

Cotten and Nixon (122) failed to find any evidence in support of the hypothesis that learning to serve in beginning tennis would be facilitated by initially practicing closer to the net. Surbury (186) found that the presentation of audio, visual, and audio-visual instructions in conjunction with mental practice significantly improved performance in the forehand drive in tennis. Mariani (177) compared the command and task methods of teaching in tennis and concluded that the task method was superior in teaching the backhand and that it was superior in retention for both the forehand and backhand. Neuman and Singer (181) compared traditional and programmed methods on various measures of tennis skills. There was no difference in general skill level of the groups, although the traditionally taught group made significant improvement in general skills while the programmed group did not. Better subjective rating scores on form were obtained by the programmed group. Farrell (172) also found apparently equal effectiveness in using programmed and teacher-directed instruction; therefore, it was concluded that programmed instruction is an effective teaching device for beginning tennis. Woods (188) investigated the comparative effectiveness of emphasizing velocity and accuracy in a tennis skill. Equal and simultaneous emphasis was found to be most desirable. Initial emphasis on velocity followed by accuracy was deemed to be superior to an initial emphasis on accuracy.

In the measurement of sprint running, Jackson and Baumgartner (174) reported that the greatest source of measurement error existed in the first 20 yards. Hence, in order to secure reliable scores, more than two trials are necessary. Shick (184) investigated the effects of mental practice on selected volleyball skills. Inconsistent results were obtained with regard to the effectiveness of mental practice in the serve and wall volley.

Singer and Weiss (185) concluded that wrestlers may lose up to 7 percent of body weight without adverse effects on selected anthropometric, physical, and performance measures. Ribisl and Herbert (183) reported that a 5 percent loss in body weight within 48 hours due to dehydration significantly reduced the physical working capacity of wrestlers. However, rehydration restored working capacity.

References and Bibliography

Archery   References and Sources

1. AAHPER, *Skills Test Manual: Archery,* David Brace, Test consultant, Washington, D.C.: American Alliance for Health, Physical Education, and Recreation, 1967.
2. Hyde, Edith I., "An Achievement Scale in Archery," *Research Quarterly,* 8:109, May, 1937.
3. Bohn, Robert W., "An Achievement Test in Archery" (Unpublished master's thesis, University of Wisconsin, 1962).

Badminton   References and Sources

4. Davis, Phillis R., "The Development of a Combined Short and Long Badminton Service Skill Test" (Unpublished master's thesis, University of Tennessee, 1968).
5. French, Ester, and Evelyn Stalter, "Study of Skill Tests in Badminton for College Women," *Research Quarterly,* 20:257-72, October, 1949.
6. Gray, Charles A., and Wayne B. Brumbach, "The Effect of Daylight Projection of Film Loops on Learning Badminton," *Research Quarterly,* 38:562-569, December, 1967.
7. Hicks, Joanna V., "The Construction and Evaluation of a Battery of Five Badminton Skill Tests" (Unpublished doctoral dissertation, Texas Woman's University, 1967).
8. Hale, Patricia Ann, "Construction of a Long Serve for Beginning Badminton Players" (Microcarded master's thesis, University of Wisconsin, 1970).
9. Johnson, Rose Marie, "Determination of the Validity and Reliability of the Badminton Placement Test" (Unpublished master's thesis, University of Oregon, 1967).
10. Kowert, Eugene A., "Construction of a Badminton Ability Test for Men" (Unpublished master's thesis, University of Iowa, 1968).

11. Lockhart, Aileene, and Frances A. McPherson, "Development of a Test of Badminton Playing Ability," *Research Quarterly,* 20:402-405, December, 1949.

12. Lucey, Mildred A., "A Study of the Components of Wrist Action as They Relate to Speed of Learning and the Degree of Proficiency Attained in Badminton" (Unpublished doctoral dissertation, New York University, 1952).

13. McDonald, E. Dawn, "The Development of a Skill Test for the Badminton High Clear" (Unpublished master's thesis, Southern Illinois University, 1968).

14. Miller, Frances A., "A Badminton Wall Volley Test," *Research Quarterly,* 22:208-213, May, 1951.

15. Poole, James, *Badminton,* Pacific Palisades, Cal.: Goodyear Publishing Company, 1969, pp. 30-32.

16. Poole, James, and Jack Nelson, "Construction of a Badminton Skills Test Battery" (Unpublished study, Louisiana State University, 1970).

17. Scott, M. Gladys, Aileen Carpenter, Esther French, and Louise Kuhl, "Achievement Examinations in Badminton," *Research Quarterly,* 12:242-53, May, 1941.

18. Scott, M. Gladys, and Ester French, *Measurement and Evaluation in Physical Education,* Dubuque, Iowa: Wm. C. Brown Company, Publishers, 1959, Chapter VI.

19. Washington, Jean, "Construction of a Wall Volley Test for the Badminton Short Serve, and the Effect of Wall Practice on Court Performance" (Unpublished master's thesis, North Texas State University, 1968).

Basketball   References and Sources

20. AAHPER, *Skills Test Manual: Basketball for Boys,* David K. Brace, Test consultant, Washington, D.C.: American Alliance for Health, Physical Education, and Recreation, 1966.

21. AAHPER, *Skills Test Manual: Basketball for Girls,* David K. Brace, Test consultant, Washington, D.C.: American Alliance for Health, Physical Education, and Recreation, 1966.

22. Barrow, Harold M., "Basketball Skill Test," *Physical Educator,* 16:26-27, March, 1959.

23. Bonner, Donald A., "A Comparative Study of the Ability of High School Basketball Players to Perform Basic Skills at Three Stages of the Season" (Unpublished master's thesis, North Carolina Central University, 1963).

24. Cunningham, Phyllis, "Measuring Basketball Playing Ability of High School Girls" (Unpublished doctoral dissertation, University of Iowa, 1964).

25. Edgren, H. D., "An Experiment in the Testing of Ability and Progress in Basketball," *Research Quarterly,* 3:159, March, 1932.

26. Elbel, E. R., and Forrest C. Allen, "Evaluating Team and Individual Performance in Basketball," *Research Quarterly,* 5:538-55, October, 1941.

27. Gilbert, Raymond R., "A Study of Selected Variables in Predicting Basketball Players" (Unpublished master's thesis, Springfield College, 1968).

28. Jacobson, Theodore V., "An Evaluation of Performance in Certain Physical Ability Tests Administered to Selected Secondary School Boys" (Unpublished master's thesis, University of Washington, 1960).

29. Johnson, L. W., "Objective Test in Basketball for High School Boys" (Unpublished master's thesis, State University of Iowa, 1934).

30. Jones, Edith, "A Study of Knowledge and Playing Ability in Basketball for High School Girls" (Unpublished master's thesis, State University of Iowa, 1941).

31. Kay, H. Kenner, "A Statistical Analysis of the Profile Technique for the Evaluation of Competitive Basketball Performance" (Unpublished master's thesis, University of Alberta, 1966).

32. Knox, Robert D., "Basketball Ability Test," *Scholastic Coach,* 17:45, 1947.

33. Lehsten, Nelson, "A Measure of Basketball Skills in High School Boys," *The Physical Educator,* 5:103-109, December, 1948.

34. Leilich, Avis, "The Primary Components of Selected Basketball Tests for College Women" (Unpublished doctoral dissertation, Indiana University, 1952).

35. Matthews, Leslie E., "A Battery of Basketball Skills Test for High School Boys" (Unpublished master's thesis, University of Oregon, 1963).

36. Miller, Wilma K., "Achievement Levels in Basketball Skills for Women Physical Education Majors," *Research Quarterly,* 25:450-55, December, 1954.

37. Mortimer, Elizabeth M., "Basketball Shooting," *Research Quarterly,* 22:234-43, May, 1951.

38. Nelson, Jack K. "The Measurement of Shooting and Passing Skills in Basketball" (Unpublished study, Louisiana State University, 1967).

39. Peters, Gerald V., "The Reliability and Validity of Selected Shooting Tests in Basketball" (Unpublished master's thesis, University of Michigan, 1964).

40. Pimpa, Udom, "A Study to Determine the Relationship Between Bunn's Basketball Skill Test and the Writer's Version of That Test" (Unpublished master's thesis, Springfield College, 1968).

41. Plinke, John F., "The Development of Basketball Physical Skill Potential Test Batteries by Height Categories" (Unpublished doctoral dissertation, Indiana University, 1966).

42. Schwartz, Helen, "Achievement Tests in Girls Basketball at the Senior High School Level," *Research Quarterly,* 8:143-56, March, 1937.

43. Stroup, Francis, "Relationship Between Measurement of Field of Motion Perception and Basketball Ability in College Men," *Research Quarterly,* 28:72-76, March, 1950.

44. Stubbs, Helen C., "An Explanatory Study of Girls Basketball Relative to the Measurement of Ball Handling Ability" (Unpublished master's thesis, University of Tennessee, 1968).

45. Thornes, Ann B., "An Analysis of a Basketball Shooting Test and Its Relation to Other Basketball Skill Tests" (Unpublished master's thesis, University of Wisconsin, 1963).

46. Voltmer, E. F., and Ted Watts, "A Rating Scale for Player Performance in Basketball," *Journal of Health and Physical Education,* 2:94-95, February, 1947.

47. Walton, Ronald J., "A Comparison Between Two Selected Evaluative Techniques for Measuring Basketball Skill" (Unpublished master's thesis, Western Illinois University, 1968).

48. Wilbur, Carol D., "Construction of a Simple Skills Test," in *Basketball Guide—1959-60,* Washington, D.C.: American Alliance for Health, Physical Education, and Recreation, 1959, pp. 30-33.

49. Young, Genevieve, and Helen Moser, "A Short Battery of Tests to Measure Playing Ability in Women's Basketball," *Research Quarterly,* 5:3-23, May, 1934.

Bowling   References and Sources

50. Johnson, Norma Jean, "Tests of Achievement in Bowling for Beginning Girl Bowlers" (Unpublished master's thesis, University of Colorado, 1962).

51. Martin, Joan L., "A Way to Measure Bowling Success," *Research Quarterly,* 31:113-116, March, 1960.

52. Martin, Joan, and Jack Keogh, "Bowling Norms for College Students in Elective Physical Education Classes," *Research Quarterly,* 35:325-327, October, 1964.

53. Olson, Janice, and Marie R. Liba, "A Device for Evaluating Spot Bowling Ability," *Research Quarterly,* 38:193-201, May, 1967.

54. Phillips, Marjorie, and Dean Summers, "Bowling Norms and Learning Curves for College Women," *Research Quarterly,* 21:377-385, December, 1950.

Football   References and Sources

55. AAHPER, *Skills Test Manual: Football,* David K. Brace, Test consultant, Washington, D.C.: American Alliance for Health, Physical Education, and Recreation, 1965.

56. Brace, David K., "Validity of Football Achievement Tests as Measures of Learning as a Partial Basis for the Selection of Players," *Research Quarterly,* 14:372, December, 1943.

57. Cowell, C. C., and A. H. Ismail, "Validity of a Football Rating Scale and Its Relationship to Social Integration and Academic Ability," *Research Quarterly,* 33:461-67, December, 1961.

58. Lee, Robert C., "A Battery of Tests to Predict Football Potential" (Unpublished master's thesis, University of Utah, 1965).

Golf   References and Sources

59. Bowen, Robert T., "Putting Errors of Beginning Golfers Using Different Points of Aim," *Research Quarterly,* 39:31-35, March, 1968.

60. Clevett, Melvin A., "An Experiment in Teaching Methods of Golf," *Research Quarterly,* 2:104-106, December, 1931.

61. Cochrane, June F., "The Construction of an Indoor Golf Skills Test as a Measure of Golfing Ability" (Unpublished master's thesis, University of Minnesota, 1960).

62. Cotten, Doyice J., Jerry R. Thomas, and Thomas Plaster, "A Plastic Ball Test for Golf Iron Skill" (Paper presented at AAHPER National Convention, Houston, Texas, March 24, 1972).

63. McKee, Mary E., "A Test for the Full-Swing Shot in Golf," *Research Quarterly,* 21:40-46, March, 1950.

64. Nelson, Jack, "An Achievement Test for Golf" (Unpublished study, Louisiana State University, 1967).

65. Roberts, Jane A., "The Effect of a Particular Practice Technique on the Golf Swing" (Unpublished thesis, University of Iowa, 1966.)

66. Reece, Patsy A., "A Comparison of the Scores Made on an Outdoor and the Scores Made on an Indoor Golf Test by College Women" (Unpublished master's thesis, University of Colorado, 1960).

67. Vanderhoof, Ellen R., "Beginning Golf Achievement Tests" (Unpublished master's thesis, State University of Iowa, 1956).

68. Watts, Harriet, "Construction and Evaluation of a Target on Testing the Approach Shot in Golf" (Unpublished master's thesis, University of Wisconsin, 1942).

69. West, Charlotte, and Jo Anne Thorpe, "Construction and Validation of an Eight-Iron Approach Test," *Research Quarterly,* 39:1115-1120, December, 1968.

Gymnastics   References and Sources

70. Amateur Athletic Union (AAU), *Gymnastics Guide,* AAU, 231 W. 58th St., New York (Publication updated regularly).

71. Bowers, Carolyn O., "Gymnastic Skill Test For Beginning to Low Intermediate Girls and

Women" (Unpublished master's thesis, Ohio State University, 1965).

72. Division of Girls' and Women's Sports (DGWS), *Gymnastic Guide,* Washington, D.C.: American Alliance for Health, Physical Education, and Recreation (Publication updated regularly).

73. Harris, J. Patrick, "A Design for a Proposed Skill Proficiency Test in Tumbling and Apparatus for Male Physical Education Majors at the University of North Dakota" (Unpublished master's thesis, University of North Dakota, 1966).

74. Johnson, Barry L., "A Screening Test for Pole Vaulting and Selected Gymnastic Events," *Journal of Health, Physical Education, and Recreation,* 44:71-72, May, 1973.

75. Johnson, Barry L., and Mary J. Garcia, *Gymnastics for the Beginner,* Manchala, Tx.: Sterling Swift Publishing Company, 1976, pp. 134-138.

76. Landers, Daniel M., "A Comparison of Two Gymnastic Judging Methods" (Unpublished master's thesis, University of Illinois, 1965).

77. National Collegiate Athletic Association (NCAA), *Official Gymnastics Rules,* NCAA, 394 East Thomas Rd., Phoenix, Ariz. (Publication updated regularly).

78. Schwarzkoph, Robert J. "The Iowa-Brace Test as a Measuring Instrument for Predicting Gymnastic Ability" (Unpublished master's thesis, University of Washington, 1962).

79. United States Gymnastic Federation (USGF), *Age Group Workbook,* USGF, P.O. Box 4699, Tucson, Ariz. (Publications updated regularly).

Handball References and Sources

80. Cornish, Clayton, "A Study of Measurement of Ability in Handball," *Research Quarterly,* 20:215-222, May, 1949.

81. Griffith, Malcolm A., "An Objective Method of Evaluating Ability in Handball Singles" (Unpublished master's thesis, University of North Carolina, 1949).

82. McCachren, James R., "A Study of the University of Florida Handball Skill Test" (Unpublished master's thesis, University of North Carolina, 1949).

83. Montoye, H. J., and J. Brotzman, "An Investigation of the Validity of Using the Results of a Doubles Tournament as a Measure of Handball Ability," *Research Quarterly,* 22:214-18, 1951.

84. Pennington, G. Gary, James A. P. Day, John N. Drowatsky, and John F. Hanson, "A Measure of Handball Ability," *Research Quarterly,* 38:247-253, May, 1967.

Soccer and Speedball References and Sources

85. Bontz, Jean, "An Experiment in the Construc-

tion of a Test for Measuring Ability in Some of the Fundamental Skills Used by Fifth and Sixth Grade Children in Soccer" (Unpublished master's thesis, State University of Iowa, 1942).

86. Buchanan, Ruth E., "A Study of Achievement Tests in Speedball for High School Girls" (Unpublished master's thesis, State University of Iowa, 1942).

87. Crew, Vernon N., "A Skill Test Battery for Use in Service Program Soccer Classes at the University Level" (Unpublished master's thesis, University of Oregon, 1968).

88. Johnson, Joseph R., "The Development of a Single-Item Test as a Measure of Soccer Skill" (Microcarded master's thesis, University of British Columbia, 1963).

89. MacKenzie, John, "The Evaluation of a Battery of Soccer Skill Test as an Aid to Classification of General Soccer Ability" (Unpublished master's thesis, University of Massachusetts, 1968).

90. McDonald, Lloyd G., "The Construction of a Kicking Skill Test as an Index of General Soccer Ability" (Unpublished master's thesis, Springfield College, 1951).

91. Mitchell, J. Reid, "The Modification of the McDonald Soccer Skill Test for Upper Elementary School Boys" (Unpublished master's thesis, University of Oregon, 1963).

92. Schaufele, Evelyn F., "The Establishment of Objective Tests for Girls of the Ninth and Tenth Grades to Determine Soccer Ability" (Unpublished master's thesis, State University of Iowa, 1940).

93. Smith, Gwen, "Speedball Skill Tests for College Women" (Unpublished study, Illinois State University, 1947).

94. Streck, Bonnie, "An Analysis of the McDonald Soccer Skill Test as Applied to Junior High School Girls" (Unpublished master's thesis, Fort Hayes State College, 1961).

95. Weiss, Raymond A., and Marjorie Phillips, *Administration of Tests in Physical Education,* St. Louis: C. V. Mosby Company, 1954, pp. 253-257.

Softball and Baseball References and Sources

96. AAHPER, *Skills Test Manual: Softball for Boys,* David K. Brace, Test consultant, Washington, D.C.: American Alliance for Health, Physical Education, and Recreation, 1966.

97. AAHPER, *Skills Test Manual: Softball for Girls,* David K. Brace, Test consultant, Washington, D.C.: American Alliance for Health, Physical Education, and Recreation, 1966.

98. Elrod, Joe M., "Construction of a Softball Skill Test Battery for High School Boys" (Unpublished master's thesis, Louisiana State University, 1969).

99. Everett, Peter W., "The Prediction of Baseball

Ability," *Research Quarterly,* 23:15-19, March, 1952.

100. Finger, Margaret N., "A Battery of Softball Skill Tests for Senior High School Girls" (Unpublished master's thesis, University of Michigan, 1961).

101. Fox, Margaret G., and Olive G. Young, "A Test of Softball Batting Ability," *Research Quarterly,* 25:26-27, March, 1954.

102. Hardin, Donald H., and John Ramirez, "Elementary School Performance Norms," *TAHPER Journal,* February, 1972, pp. 8-9.

103. Hooks, G. Eugene, "Prediction of Baseball Ability Through an Analysis of Measures of Strength and Structure," *Research Quarterly,* 30:38-43, March, 1959.

104. Kehtel, Carmen H., "The Development of a Test to Measure the Ability of a Softball Player to Field a Ground Ball and Successfully Throw It at a Target" (Unpublished master's thesis, University of Colorado, 1958).

105. Kelson, Robert E., "Baseball Classification Plan for Boys," *Research Quarterly,* 24:304-309, October, 1953.

106. O'Donnell, Doris J., "Validation of Softball Skill Tests for High School Girls" (Unpublished master's thesis, Indiana University, 1950).

107. Shick, Jacqueline, "Battery of Defensive Softball Skills Tests for College Women," *Research Quarterly,* 41:82-37, March, 1970.

Swimming and Diving
References and Sources

108. Arrasmith, Jean L., "Swimming Classification Test for College Women" (Unpublished doctoral dissertation, University of Oregon, 1967).

109. Bennett, LaVerne M., "A Test of Diving for Use in Beginning Classes," *Research Quarterly,* 13:109-115, March, 1942.

110. Burris, Barbara J., "A Study of the Speed-Stroke Test of Crawl Stroking Ability and Its Relationship to Other Selected Tests of Crawl Stroking Ability" (Unpublished master's thesis, Temple University, 1964).

111. Durrant, Sue M., "An Analytical Method of Rating Synchronized Swimming Stunts," *Research Quarterly,* 35:126-34, May, 1964.

112. Fox, Margaret G., "Swimming Power Test," *Research Quarterly,* 28:233-237, October, 1957.

113. Hewitt, Jack E., "Swimming Achievement Scale Scores for College Men," *Research Quarterly,* 12:282-289, December, 1948.

114. _____ , "Achievement Scale Scores for High School Swimming," *Research Quarterly,* 20:170-179, May, 1949.

115. Kilby, Emelia Louise J., "An Objective Method of Evaluating Three Swimming Strokes" (Unpublished doctoral dissertation, University of Washington, 1956).

116. Munt, Marilyn R., "Development of an Objective Test to Measure the Efficiency of the Front Crawl for College Women" (Unpublished master's thesis, University of Michigan, 1964).

117. Rosentsweig, Joel, "A Revision of the Power Swimming Test," *Research Quarterly,* 39:818-19, October, 1968.

118. Scott, M. Gladys, and Esther French, *Measurement and Evaluation in Physical Education,* Dubuque, Iowa: Wm. C. Brown Company, Publishers, 1959, Chapter VI.

119. Wilson, Marcia R., "A Relationship Between General Motor Ability and Objective Measures of Achievement in Swimming at the Intermediate Level for College Women" (Unpublished master's thesis, University of North Carolina, 1962).

Tennis   References and Sources

120. Broer, Marian R., and Donna Mae Miller, "Achievement Tests for Beginning and Intermediate Tennis," *Research Quarterly,* 21:303-321, October, 1950.

121. Cobane, Edith, "Test for the Service," in AAHPER, *Tennis and Badminton Guide— June 1962-June 1964,* Washington, D.C.: American Alliance for Health, Physical Education, and Recreation, pp. 46-47.

122. Cotten, Doyice J., and Jane Nixon, "A Comparison of Two Methods of Teaching the Tennis Serve," *Research Quarterly,* 39:929-31, December, 1968.

123. DiGennaro, Joseph, "Construction of Forehand Drive, Backhand Drive, and Serve Tennis Tests," *Research Quarterly,* 40:496-501, October, 1969.

124. Dyer, Joanna T., "Revision of the Backboard Test of Tennis Ability," *Research Quarterly,* 9:25-31, March, 1938.

125. Edwards, Janet, "A Study of Three Measures of the Tennis Serve" (Unpublished master's thesis, University of Wisconsin, 1965).

126. Fonger, Sandra J., "The Development of a Reliable Objective and Practical Tennis Serve Test for College Women" (Unpublished master's thesis, University of Michigan, 1963).

127. Hewitt, Jack E., "Classification Tests in Tennis," *Research Quarterly,* 39:552-555, October, 1968.

128. _____ , "Revision of the Dyer Backboard Tennis Test," *Research Quarterly,* 36:153-157, May, 1965.

129. _____ , "Hewitt's Tennis Achievement Test," *Research Quarterly,* 37:231-237, May, 1966.

130. Hubbell, Nancy C., "A Battery of Tennis Skill Tests for College Women" (Unpublished master's thesis, Texas Woman's University, 1960).

131. Johnson, Joann, "Tennis Serve of Advanced Women Players," *Research Quarterly,* 28:123-131, May, 1957.

132. Jones, Shirley K., "A Measure of Tennis Serv-

ing Ability" (Unpublished master's thesis, University of California, 1967).

133. Kemp, Joann, and Marilyn F. Vincent, "Kemp-Vincent Rally Test of Tennis Skill," *Research Quarterly,* 29:1000-04, December, 1964.

134. Malinak, Nina R., "The Construction of an Objective Measure of Accuracy in the Performance of the Tennis Serve" (Unpublished master's thesis, University of Illinois, 1961).

135. Recio, Michael, and Charles Prestidge, "The Overhead Smash Test Utilizing the Johnson Tennis and Badminton Machine" (Unpublished study, Northeast Louisiana University, 1972).

136. Ronnings, Hilding E., "Wall Tests for Evaluating Ability" (Unpublished master's thesis, Washington State University, 1959).

137. Timmer, Karen L., "A Tennis Test to Determine Accuracy in Playing Ability" (Unpublished master's thesis, Springfield College, 1965).

Volleyball   References and Sources

138. AAHPER, *Skills Test Manual: Volleyball,* Clayton Shay, Test consultant, Washington, D.C.: American Alliance for Health, Physical Education, and Recreation, 1969.

139. Blackmon, Claudia J., "The Development of a Volleyball Test for the Spike" (Unpublished master's thesis, Southern Illinois University, 1968).

140. Brady, George F., "Preliminary Investigations of Volleyball Playing Ability," *Research Quarterly,* 16:14-17, March, 1945.

141. Brumbach, Wayne B., Carl M. McGowan, and Berge A. Borrevik, *Beginning Volleyball,* Eugene, Ore.: Wayne Brumbach (Distributed by University of Oregon Cooperative Store), 1972.

142. Camp, Billie Ann, "The Reliability and Validity of a Single-Hit Repeated Volleys Test in Volleyball and the Relationship of Height to Performance on the Test" (Unpublished master's thesis, University of Colorado, 1963).

143. Chaney, Dawn S., "The Development of a Test of Volleyball Ability For College Women" (Unpublished master's thesis, Texas Woman's University, 1966).

144. Clifton, Marguerite A., "Single Hit Volley Test for Women's Volleyball," *Research Quarterly,* 33:208-211, May, 1962.

145. Crogan, Corrinne, "A Simple Volleyball Classification Test for High School Girls," *Physical Educator,* 4:34-37, October, 1943.

146. Cunningham, Phyllis, and Joan Garrison, "High Wall Volley Test for Women's Volleyball," *Research Quarterly,* 39:480-490, October, 1968.

147. French, Ester L., and Bernice I. Cooper, "Achievement Tests in Volleyball for High School Girls," *Research Quarterly,* Vol. 8, No. 2, May, 1937.

148. Jackson, Patricia, "A Rating Scale for Discriminating Relative Performance of Skilled Female Volleyball Players" (Unpublished master's thesis, University of Alberta, 1967).

149. Johnson, Judith A., "The Development of a Volleyball Skill Test for High School Girls" (Unpublished master's thesis, Illinois State University, 1967).

150. Jones, Richard N., "The Development of a Volleyball Skills Test for Adult Males" (Unpublished master's thesis, Springfield College, 1964).

151. Kissler, Adrian A., "The Validity and Reliability of the Sandefur Volleyball Spiking Test" (Unpublished master's thesis, California State College, 1968).

152. Kronqvist, Robert A., and Wayne B. Brumbach, "A Modification of the Brady Volleyball Skill Test for High School Boys," *Research Quarterly,* 39:116-120, March, 1968.

153. Lamp, Nancy A., "Volleyball Skills for Junior High School Students as a Function of Physical Size and Maturity, *Research Quarterly,* 25:189, May, 1954.

154. Liba, Marie R., and Marilyn R. Stauff, "A Test for the Volleyball Pass," *Research Quarterly,* 34:56-63, March, 1963.

155. Lopez, Delfina, "Serve Test," in Division of Girl's and Women's Sports (DGWS), *Volleyball Guide—1957-1959,* Washington, D.C.: American Alliance for Health, Physical Education, and Recreation, 1957, pp. 29-30.

156. Michalski, Rosalie A., "Construction of an Objective Skill Test for the Underhand Volleyball Serve" (Unpublished master's thesis, University of Iowa, 1963).

157. Mohr, Dorothy R., and Martha V. Haverstick, "Repeated Volleys Test for Women's Volleyball," *Research Quarterly,* 26:179, May, 1955.

158. Petry, Kathryn, "Evaluation of a Volleyball Serve Test," (Unpublished master's thesis, Los Angeles State College, 1967).

159. Russel, Naomi, and Elizabeth Lange, "Achievement Tests in Volleyball for Junior High School Girls," *Research Quarterly,* 11:33-41, December, 1940.

160. Ryan, Mary F., "A Study of Tests for the Volleyball Serve" (Unpublished master's thesis, University of Wisconsin, 1969).

161. Shaw, John H., "A Preliminary Investigation of a Volleyball Skill Test' (Unpublished master's thesis, University of Tennessee, 1967).

162. Shavely, Marie, "Volleyball Skill Tests for Girls," in Division of Girl's and Women's Sports (DGWS), *Selected Volleyball Articles,* Washington, D.C.: American Alliance for Health, Physical Education, and Recreation, 1960, pp. 77-78.

163. Suttinger, Joan, "A Proposal Predictive Index of Volleyball Playing Ability for College Wom-

en," (Unpublished study, University of California, May, 1957).

164. West, Charlotte, "A Comparative Study Between Height and Wall Volley Test Scores as Related to Volleyball Playing Ability of Girls and Women" (Unpublished master's thesis, University of North Carolina, June, 1957).

Other Sources

165. Alderman, Richard B., "A Comparative Study on the Effectiveness of Two Grips for Teaching Beginning Golf," *Research Quarterly,* 38: 3-9, March, 1967.

166. Asprey, Gene M., Louis E. Alley, and W. W. Tuttle, "Effect of Eating at Various Times on Subsequent Performances in the One-Mile Freestyle Swim," *Research Quarterly,* 39:231-234, May, 1968.

167. Burdeshaw, Dorothy, "Acquisition of Elementary Swimming Skills by Negro and White College Women," *Research Quarterly,* 39:872-879, December, 1968.

168. _____, Jane E. Spragens, and Patricia A. Weis, "Evaluation of General Ability," *Research Quarterly,* 41:472-477, December, 1970.

169. Carter, J. E. Lindsay, "Somatotypes of College Football Players," *Research Quarterly,* 39: 476-481, October, 1968.

170. DeBacy, Diane, "Effect of Viewing Video Tapes of a Sport Skill Performed by Self and Others on Self-assessment," *Research Quarterly,* 41:27-31, March, 1970.

171. Eckert, Helen M., and Dorothy M. Wendt, "Relationship Between Perception of Pull and Draw in Archery," *Research Quarterly,* 38: 544-549, December, 1967.

172. Farrell, Joan E., "Programmed Versus Teacher-Directed Instruction in Beginning Tennis for Women," *Research Quarterly,* 41:51-58, March, 1970.

173. Groves, Richard, and John A. Roberts, "A Further Investigation of the Optimum Angle of Projection for the Racing Start in Swimming," *Research Quarterly,* 41:167-173, May, 1972.

174. Jackson, Andrew S., and Ted A. Baumgartner, "Measurement Schedules of Sprint Running," *Research Quarterly,* December, 1969, pp. 708-711.

175. Johnson, Marvin, "Objectivity of Judging at the National Collegiate Athletic Association Gymnastic Meet: A Twenty-Year Follow-up Study," *Research Quarterly,* 42-454-455, December, 1971.

176. Maglischo, Cheryl W., and Ernest Maglischo, "Comparison of Three Racing Starts Used in Competitive Swimming," *Research Quarterly,* 39:604-609, October, 1968.

177. Mariani, Tom, "A Comparison of the Effectiveness of the Command Method and the Task Method of Teaching the Forehand and Backhand Tennis Strokes," *Research Quarterly,* 41:171-174, May, 1970.

178. McArdle, William D., John R. Magel, and Lucille C. Kyvallos, "Aerobic Capacity, Heart Rate and Estimated Energy Cost During Women's Competitive Basketball," *Research Quarterly,* 42:178-185, May, 1971.

179. McCatty, Cressy A. M., "Effects of the Use of a Flotation Device in Teaching Non-Swimmers," *Research Quarterly,* 39:621-626, October, 1968.

180. Mitchem, John C., and Elizabeth C. Lane, "Bouyancy of College Women as Predicted by Certain Anthropometric Measures," *Research Quarterly,* 39:1032-1036, December, 1968.

181. Neuman, Milton C., and Robert N. Singer, "A Comparison of Traditional Versus Programmed Methods of Learning Tennis," *Research Quarterly,* 39:1044-1048, December, 1968.

182. Purdy, Bonnie J., and Mary L. Stallard, "Effect of Two Learning Methods and Two Grips on the Acquisition of Power and Accuracy in the Golf Swing of College Women," *Research Quarterly,* 38:474-479, October, 1967.

183. Ribisl, Paul M., and William G. Herbert, "Effects of Rapid Weight Reduction and Subsequent Rehydration upon the Physical Working Capacity of Wrestlers," *Research Quarterly,* 41: 536-541, December, 1970.

184. Shick, Jacqueline, "Effects of Mental Practice on Selected Volleyball Skills for College Women," *Research Quarterly,* 41:88-94, March, 1970.

185. Singer, Robert N., and Steven A. Weiss, "Effects of Weight Reduction on Selected Anthropometric, Physical and Performance Measures of Wrestlers," *Research Quarterly,* 39:361-368, May, 1968.

186. Surbury, Paul R., "Audio, Visual and Audio-Visual Instruction with Mental Practice in Developing the Forehand Tennis Drive," *Research Quarterly,* 39:728-734, October, 1968.

187. Thompson, Donnis Hazel, "Immediate External Feedback in the Learning of Golf Skills," *Research Quarterly,* 40:589-594, October, 1969.

188. Woods, John B., "The Effect of Varied Instructional Emphasis Upon the Development of a Motor Skill," *Research Quarterly,* 38:132-141, March, 1967.

189. Zabik, Roger M., and Andrew S. Jackson, "Reliability of Archery Achievement," *Research Quarterly,* 40:254-255, March, 1969.

Evaluation in the area of rhythm and dance has depended mainly on rating scales. This dependence on rating scales has been of necessity since there are very few tests in this area which can be used in the classroom. Authorities in this field have found rhythm as difficult to define as it is to measure. Existing definitions of rhythm from various sources have consistently mentioned such terms as flow, movement, repetition, and beat. Thus, rhythm may be thought of as the flow of movement with the regular repetition of beat in grouping movements for the successful execution of a pattern or a skill. Physical educators frequently think of rhythm as that pattern which makes performance, even difficult performance, look easy and graceful. Rhythm is closely associated with kinesthesis, speed, and agility and is important in any skill which requires a series of successive movements. In the execution of a dance the individual moves his body as he listens to music. Dance is therefore complicated in that movement of the individual is related to a rhythmic pattern of the music. Some instructors insist that the student move in time with the music, while other instructors feel that a student should not be penalized for the inability to pick up a rhythmic pattern of music.*

Uses of Rhythm and Dance Tests

Tests of rhythm and dance may be utilized in physical education in the following ways:

1. As a means to further the learning process by stimulating students to devote their maximum effort toward rhythmic interpretation and performance. This type of use should be followed by a critique so that the student will benefit from his mistakes.
2. As a means to help students recognize rhythmic patterns in sports activities or in improving fundamental skills such as walking, running, and jumping.
3. As a measure for determining achievement and grades in dance classes. Rhythmic action is also a point to consider in grading gymnastics stunts and swimming skills.
4. As a means for evaluating prospective members of physical education exhibition

*The authors are indebted to Professor I. F. Waglow, University of Florida, Gainesville, Fla., for assistance in writing the above section.

Chapter Seventeen

The Measurement of Rhythm and Dance

groups in such activities as synchronized swimming, gymnastics, and dance.

Practical Tests of Rhythm and Dance

Since tests of rhythm and dance are quite limited, the following items are submitted as the most practical found at the present time. Moreover, the word *practical* is used somewhat apologetically for this section. For directions in each of the various types of dance areas, it is important for the instructor to inform the student as to what the instructor is looking for as he rates the performer. Also, the rating scale to be used should be understood by the student. A few of the criteria and ideas that should be considered in various types of dance were suggested by Waglow* as follows:

1. *Folk Dance.* In folk dancing the following three criteria should be considered in rating students: (a) the style of execution of the movement, (b) the execution of the dance in a pattern as related to the music — in general, the student would have memorized this movement — and (c) the rhythm of the student as related to the music.
2. *Modern dance.* If the instructor uses set patterns of movement (exercises) in preparing the student for self-expression in modern dance, these movements could be used to evaluate the student. A second area in which the student could be evaluated is in the performance of a dance, whether it be to a poem or music. In judging an original composition of the student, the instructor might look for difficulty, combination of movements, and judge the execution and form. Many instructors find it desirable to bring in other experts in the area of dance to judge the performance of students.
3. *Social dance.* In social dance the instructor may require students to execute a series of variations while they are being rated. This series of variations is often memorized, and the instructor is provided with a statement as to what variations the students will do. Another way of judging the student would be to require the student to make up variations which were not learned in class, and then as the student performs these variations, he or she could be evaluated. In evaluating the student in social dance, it is important that the student dance in time with the rhythm pattern of the music and that the style of movement be appropriate for the rhythm that is being played.

4. *Square dance.* As the student performs square dance movements, the following three criteria should be considered: (a) How well does the performer respond to the caller? (b) How well does the performer execute the movement that is called for? (c) Does the dancer move according to the rhythm pattern of the music? The instructor could make use of a record with a caller on it in evaluating, or the instructor could be the caller and have other instructors do the evaluating.
5. *Tap dancing.* In evaluating a student in tap dancing, the following three areas should be considered: (a) Are the movements executed properly? (b) Is the memorized routine of the dance performed correctly? (c) Is the dance performed in rhythm with the music that is being played?

Waglow's Social Dance Test (34)

Objective: The objective of this test is to measure the ability of a student to execute a dance step in time with music.

Age Level: Satisfactory for the secondary and college level.

Sex: Satisfactory for both boys and girls.

Reliability: Recent refinements have raised the reliability of this test to $r = .82$. This is considerably higher than the reliability indicated in the original report in the literature.

Validity: The validity for this test has been found to be .76 in recent studies. The criterion was the combined subjective ratings of two judges.

Equipment and Materials: In administering the test, it is necessary to have music transcribed from records to a tape. Students will need chalk to mark a spot on the floor and also small score cards and pencils for keeping score.

Directions to Tester: The tape is made by indicating the rhythm that is being played. With the tape recorder turned on, the rhythm is identified. It is then indicated how many measures the student will wait before starting to move. For example, the tape would say "waltz," a short pause, and then "six measures," a short pause; and then the tape would record the number of measures which are desired. In making the tape, the instructor would have to make up his mind as to how many measures of music he would want the students to dance.

*Submitted by I. F. Waglow, University of Florida, Gainesville, Fla.

Table 17-1
T-Score Norms for the Waglow Social Dance Test at the College Level

(Raw Scores are based on Performance Deviations)

T-Scores	—	Raw Scores	T-Scores	—	Raw Scores	T-Scores	—	Raw Scores
71	—	.5	48	—	4.5	38	—	8.5
67	—	1.0	47	—	5.0	36	—	9.5
62	—	1.5	45	—	5.5	34	—	10.5
58	—	2.0	43	—	6.0	33	—	11.0
55	—	2.5	42	—	6.5	32	—	11.5
53	—	3.0	41	—	7.0	31	—	12.0
52	—	3.5	40	—	7.5	30	—	12.5
50	—	4.0	39	—	8.0	29	—	13.0

Source: I.F. Waglow, University of Florida, Gainesville, Fla.

When that number of measures had gone by, the tape recorder would then cease to record. There would be a 15-second pause, and the above procedure would then be repeated for another rhythm.

Directions to Students: The students should be instructed to listen for the rhythm that is to be played and also the number of measures they are to wait before beginning to move. As the tape is played, the students are informed that they are not to move until the end of the introductory measures, and then they are to continue moving until the music stops. The forward and backward pattern is to be followed where applicable.

Scoring: The students must be paired up, and it doesn't make any difference whether there are two males or two females together. The student performing must make a mark on the floor, and the partner must be seated in front of the performer with a score card and pencil. The scorer should count the number of times that the performer leaves and returns to the chalk mark. Each time the performer returns to the chalk mark he receives a score of one. When the music has stopped, the scorer totals up the score and computes the difference between that score and the correct number of measures for that rhythm. Plus and minus signs are disregarded in scoring. For example, if the correct answer is four and the student performed three steps, the score would be minus one; whereas if the student performed five steps, the score would be plus one. However, the positive and negative scores are added together, disregarding the signs, for a composite score. When the scores are added, the performers with the lowest deviations from the true score would be the better performers. (See Table 17-1.)

Additional Pointers: (a) In practicing to take the test, the students should be told to practice doing the steps as neatly as possible so that there will not be any question in the minds of the scorers as to whether the performer left the chalk mark or not. (b) Music used during the teaching of the course should be used to construct the test. (c) It is possible for the performer to finish away from the chalk mark, in which case the score would be at a half count. For example, if there were exactly eight measures of waltz music played and a box step performed, a correct score would be four. If the student performed too fast and completed five box steps, it would indicate that he danced two measures too fast. If he completed three steps, it would indicate that he performed too slow. In such cases one score is as bad as the other.

The Tempo Test (17)

Objective: To measure the ability to repeat a given tempo.

Age Level: Ages ten through college.

Sex: Satisfactory for both boys and girls.

Reliability: Reliability was not reported for this test. Thus, there is a need for a study on the reliability of the scoring procedure presented below.

Validity: This test was accepted at face validity.

Table 17-2
Raw Score Norms for the Tempo Test

College Students	
Total Deviation Scores	Performance Level
2 - 0	Excellent
4 - 3	Good
7 - 5	Average
9 - 8	Poor
Above - 10	Very Poor

Based on the scores of 100 college students with minimal rhythm training in 1970 and with similar results with 35 students in 1976.

Equipment and Materials: One metronome and either a stopwatch or a wristwatch with a second hand are needed.

Directions: Three tempos are sounded on the metronome with settings of 64, 120, and 184 so that the three speeds will give 12, 22, and 32 beats, respectively, in 10 seconds. The performer should listen to the metronome at each speed and then step as nearly as possible in the same tempo while the partner counts the steps for 10 seconds. The metronome is not in use during each 10-second testing.

Scoring: The score is the total number of deviations from the specified beats for the three speeds. (See Table 17-2.)

Ashton's Practical Rhythm Test (2)

Objective: To measure ability to perform

Musical Excerpts

Form #1	Meas.	MM.	Time (Sec.)
Section 1			
Walk—*Wisconsin Blueprint*	12	112	21.9
Skip—Davies	16	192	19.7
Run—Huerter—*Fire Dance*	24	192	29.3
Section 2			
Skip—*Kerry Dance*	20	208	21.6
Run—Concone—*Study*	16	208	24.8
Fast Walk—Prokofiev	32	132	29.0
Slow Walk—Beethoven—Waterman ABC—p. 108	16	104	33.1
Skip—*New Mown Hay*	24	192	37.2
Run—Reinhold—*Gnomes*	32	208	27.6
Section 3			
Schottische—*Jubilee*	16	192	24.7
Slow Waltz—Tschaikowsky—*Waltz from Sleeping Beauty*	32	138	36.1
Mod. Waltz—Schubert, No. 7	32	168	29.0
Polka—Lichner	32	208	24.3
Form #2	**Meas.**	**MM.**	**Time (Sec.)**
Section 1			
Walk—Davies	12	128	20.3
Skip—*Queen of Sheba*	16	208	32.5
Run—*Wisconsin Blueprint*	12	184	14.4
Section 2			
Skip—Schumann—*Sicilianish*	24	132	21.8
Run—Moszkowski—*Scherzino*	12	208	22.3
Fast Walk—Handel—*Joshua*	16	196	21.0
Slow Walk—*Hollaender March*	17	116	31.6
Skip—*Marche Lorraine*	32	132	28.8
Run—Delibes—*Passapied*	24	208	25.5
Section 3			
Schottische—*Faust-up-to-Date*	24	168	35.1
Slow Waltz—Gurlit—*First Dance*	32	138	35.7
Mod. Waltz—Tschaikowsky—*Waltz of the Flowers*	32	168	27.2
Polka—*Plantation Dance*	24	200	25.3

rhythmical movement in response to selected musical excerpts.

Age Level: Ages twelve through college.

Sex: Satisfactory for both boys and girls.

Reliability: Has been reported as high as .86.

Validity: Face validity was accepted for this test.

Equipment and Materials: The tester should make a tape recording of the musical excerpts listed on page 330 or record similar excerpts.

Directions: Students are informed that the first part of the recording has music for walking, running, and skipping. Since each musical excerpt is played twice, students should listen to the first one and perform as it is replayed until the music stops.

During the musical excerpts on the second part of the record, students are to show any movement which they feel will fit the music. Students may restrict their movements to walking, running, and skipping; however, they should show their best movement, since any

Table 17-3
Raw Score Norms for the Ashton Rhythm Test

College Students	
Total Points	Performance Level
92 - Above	Excellent
66 - 91	Good
40 - 65	Average
14 - 39	Poor
0 - 13	Very Poor

Scoring scale projected on basis of a zero to four point scale with twenty-six measured items.

movement will be accepted and judged for its value.

The third part of the recording has music for the schottische, waltz, and polka with more than one piece of music being played for some

Rhythm Rating Scale

0—No response or incorrect response.
   Correct beat and accent only through chance.
   Step and rhythm incorrect.
   Attempts to start self in motion; undecided as to correct step. Starts a preliminary faltering movement; then stops.

1—Correct step but not correct beat (unable to pick up new beat or tempo).
   Correct movement only by imitation of another student.
   Awkward, uncoordinated movement.
   Ability to start self in movement maintained only for a measure or two.
   Difficulty in changing direction.

2—Step and rhythm pattern correct. Reaction time slow. Movement uncertain — lapses occasionally into incorrect beat.
   Movements are consistently heavy; shows tension.
   Maintenance of movement is short; phrase.
   Movement is forced; mechanical. Lacking in style.
   It is prosaic—no variety.

3—Uses correct step, beat, and accent. If student loses the accent and gets off the beat, is aware of it and able to get back on the beat.
   Ability to maintain movement throughout excerpt.
   Varies direction with effort but is able to maintain movement.
   Student shows ability in simple movement. Movement has direction but is not alive and spirited.

4—Immediate response with correct step, beat, and accent.
   Ability to maintain movement throughout excerpt.
   Ability to vary movement (turns, etc.).
   Confidence shown in movement. Movements are definite, spirited, and easily accomplished. Student is relaxed.

movements. Students are told what to do by the tester's voice on the recording.

Scoring: The rhythm rating scale on page 302 is used for all parts of the test. The final score is a total of points made on the test. (See Table 17-3.)

Dance Leap Test

Objective: To determine the power of the legs in performing a dance leap for horizontal distance.

Age Level: Junior high school through college ages.

Sex: Satisfactory for girls and women.

Reliability: An *r* of .89 was found when the subjects were tested on separate days by Alita Robnak, 1971.

Objectivity: An *r* of .99 was obtained when the subjects were tested by Sara Stockard and Alita Robnak, 1971.

Validity: Face validity was accepted for this test.

Equipment and Materials: Tape measure and marking material.

Directions: Starting with the toes of the right foot behind a starting line, the performer swings the left leg from the rear forward and leaps from the right leg as far forward as possible. Thus, the leap is made from one foot to the other foot while the performer splits the legs in the air. The landing on the left foot should be

Table 17-4
Raw Score Norms for the Dance Leap Test

Scores		Performance Level
College Women		
Inches	Centimeters	
64¼ - Above	163.2 - Above	Excellent
54 - 64	137.2 - 162.6	Good
42¼ - 53¾	107.3 - 136.5	Average
35 - 42	88.9 - 106.7	Poor
0 - 34¾	0 - 88.3	Very Poor

Based on the scores of 100 college women as reported by Elizabeth Greenwood, 1972.

cushioned by landing on the ball of the foot giving in to the heel and by bending the knee. The right foot should then be brought forward to save the balance.

Scoring: The measurement is made from the starting line to the back of the heel of the left foot. The best of three trials as measured to the nearest quarter of an inch is recorded as the score. A penalty of 1 inch is assessed from the score for each occurrence of the following errors: (a) failure to extend the legs and point the toes during the leap, (b) failure to make a steady landing, and (c) landing flat footed.

Figure 17-1. Dance Leap Test

Rhythm Run Dance Test

Objective: To measure a dancer's coordination and control in running a given distance at one level.

Age Level: Junior high school through college.

Sex: Girls and women.

Reliability: An *r* of .85 was determined when the test was administered on two separate days by Alita Robnak, 1971.

Objectivity: An *r* of .89 was obtained by Sara Stockard and Alita Robnak.

Validity: Face validity was accepted for this test.

Equipment and Materials: One roll of crepe paper (2 inches wide), marking tape, and two poles or standards are needed. The crepe paper is tied between the two poles or standards which are 40 feet apart. The marking tape is used to mark off every 10 feet on the floor under the crepe paper.

Directions: The crepe paper should be stretched so that it is at eye level at the center between the two poles. The crepe paper should be adjusted evenly on both sides or be kept as straight as possible between the two poles. The performer starts at one standard (pole) and performs a low run under the length of the crepe paper.

Scoring: There are 100 points possible on the test. A loss of points occurs as follows: (a) For each 10-foot zone that the performer tilts her head forward while running, there is a ten-point penalty. (b) There is a ten-point penalty for stepping rather than running for each 10-foot

Table 17-5
Raw Score Norms for Rhythm Run Dance Test

College Women	
Score (Points)	Performance Level
96 - 100	Excellent
83 - 95	Good
61 - 82	Average
48 - 60	Poor
0 - 47	Very Poor

Based on the scores of 100 college women as reported by Pam Carmichael Holt, 1972.

Figure 17-2. Rhythm Run Dance Test

a

c

dimension. (c) There is a five-point penalty for each time the performer touches her head to the crepe paper. (See Table 17-5.)

Additional Pointers: (a) The performer should keep the knees flexed at all times during the rhythm run. (b) The performer should start the extension of the leg from the hip to avoid stepping. (c) The use of a drumbeat is helpful to students during the test.

Fall and Recovery Test of Dance Agility

Objective: To determine the agility of dance students in falling and recovering in dance movement.

Age Level: Junior high school through college ages.

b

d

Figure 17-3. Fall and Recovery Test of Dance Agility

Table 17-6
Raw Scores for Fall and Recovery Test

College Women	
Score	Performance Level
15 - Above	Excellent
12 - 14	Good
10 - 11	Average
6 - 9	Poor
0 - 5	Very Poor

Based on the scores of 100 college women as reported by Beth Greenwood, 1973.

Sex: Satisfactory for women students.
Reliability: An *r* of .92 was found when the subjects were tested on separate days by Alita Robnak, 1971.
Objectivity: An *r* of .68 was obtained when the subjects were tested by Sara Stockard and Alita Robnak, 1971.
Validity: Face validity was accepted for this test.
Equipment and Materials: Stopwatch and mat.
Directions: (a) The performer begins from a front standing position and pushes off from the right foot, extending it as the left leg flexes and turns out. The arms are extended overhead. This completes phase one. (b) The performer brings the left knee behind the right knee while allowing the right to bend, thus lowering herself to the floor on the left thigh. (c) The performer continues to a complete extended position on the left side (on floor). This completes phase two. (d) Phase three is the recovery phase, where the performer sits up and brings the right leg over the left and then returns to a standing position.
Scoring: The performer is timed for 15 seconds and receives one point for each phase of the movement performed correctly (see scoring scale above).
Additional Pointers: (a) To assume extension in phase one, the performer must push off the right leg (in flexion) to an extended position. (b) To prevent injury to the knee cap in phase two, the performer lowers herself to the floor, rotating the leg outward, thus sliding onto the leg rather than on the knee itself. (c) To get a better score, the performer should immediately go from phase three to phase one without hesitating.

Problems and Limitations of Rhythm and Dance Measurement

The problems and limitations that have existed in the measurement of rhythm and dance are identified and briefly discussed below:

1. Most of the testing accomplished in the area of rhythm and dance has pertained to gathering facts and data for research purposes rather than for developing practical tests for the measurement of rhythm and dance ability in the classroom. Thus there appears to be a greater need for objective rhythm and dance tests which are practical for use by the classroom teacher. Graduate students and professional researchers should be encouraged to give greater consideration to the devotion of time and effort for innovating simple tests of rhythm and dance for this purpose.

2. Certain rhythmic tests are limited in use because of the necessity of complicated and/or expensive equipment. Also, since commercial recordings are impractical for use due to lack of variety and proper arrangement, it has taken considerable time and expense to make recordings for testing purposes. However, greater use should be made of the tape recorder for developing suitable recordings for testing purposes.

3. Some of the well-known rhythmic tests require only small muscle response, which renders them to limited use in physical education dance classes. Tapping tests and tests which require only a written response fall into this category.

4. Another problem which has been perplexing to the tester is that some students do not do their best when rated in front of a group due to embarrassment. Also, rating students one at a time takes considerable class time. On the other hand when several students are rated at the same time, the poor student has an opportunity to get cues from the more adept ones.

Findings and Conclusions from Rhythm and Dance Measurement and Research

The Seashore test, a frequently used test of rhythm, has been correlated with various measures of motor performance (1, 4, 9, 17). Such correlations ranged from $-.10$ to .48. Two investigators concluded that written sensory tests are not adequate for the type of rhythm emphasized in physical education classes (17, 28).

Several investigators have tested the hypothesis that the rhythm found in music has a positive effect on the learning and performance of physical skills (9, 10, 11, 18). While the findings of such studies have revealed a positive effect, Nelson (23) found that pure rhythmical tones, or music intensity, had no favorable or unfavorable effect on an endurance performance test.

Two studies have shown that, when music is used in conjunction with the presence of other people and with competition, endurance and strength performance is improved (14, 15). Nelson (23) suggested that the same might be true of pure rhythmical tones or musical intensity.

It has been frequently assumed that Negroes are superior to whites in motor rhythm. Several investigators have tested this hypothesis, and the consensus of results indicates that Negroes do not show a statistically significant superiority in rhythm to whites (16, 22, 25, 26, 30).

Concerning the use of rhythm for faster reaction time and movement time, Miles and Graves (21), Thompson (33), and Wilson (35) found faster starts when a stimulus was presented in a rhythmic rather than a nonrhythmic series. It was further noted that the speed of movement initiated by reaction is not influenced by rhythmicity or non-rhythmicity (33).

Controversy exists among investigators concerning the question as to whether rhythm is innate or acquired. McCristal (19) and Swindle (32) concluded that rhythm increases with the amount of training acquired and is not an inherited quality. On the other hand, studies by Haight (12) and Lemon and Sherbon (17) revealed results which indicated rhythmic ability to be more the result of innate tendencies. Other studies indicated the importance of practice and development to the improvement of motor rhythm. For example, Muzzey (22) concluded that motor rhythm is a function of school age with each grade showing superiority to the previous one, while Annett (1) found that the earlier a child begins activities related to motor rhythm, everything else being equal, the better he will become as a dancer. Thus, from a study of previous research, it appears that rhythm is innate to a certain extent, but can be greatly improved through consistent practice and training.

Contrary to popular belief, there are tests and measurements instruments which will enable the tester to objectively evaluate a student's rhythm performance. A number of tests involve specially constructed apparatus which is not only complicated but is rarely found in physical education departments (3, 6, 7, 13, 24, 28, 29). Other objective tests have been devised which are practical from the standpoint of equipment involved but take too much time to administer (20, 27).

Benton (4), testing the hypothesis that dance movement involves more than just rhythm, found that other elements involved are static balance, motor educability, agility, and strength. While no single measure was found of value in predicting dance skill, a combination of several motor tests revealed a high relationship with criterion ratings (sum of three judges' scores for each subject) of dance movement technique.

Bond (6) found that several of the senses (tactile, aural, and visual) are capable of experiencing rhythmic patterns but failed to find a significant relationship between scores from sensory rhythmic perception tests and measures of motor performance.

References and Bibliography

1. Annett, Thomas, "A Study of Rhythmic Capacity and Performance in Motor Rhythm in Physical Education Majors," *Research Quarterly,* 3:190, May, 1932.
2. Ashton, Dudley, "A Gross Motor Rhythm Test," *Research Quarterly,* 24:253-260, October, 1953.
3. Baldwin, B. T., and L. I. Stecher, *The Psychology of the Pre-School Child,* New York: D. Appleton and Company, 1924, pp. 141-145.
4. Benton, Rachel J., "The Measurement of Capacities for Learning Dance Movement Techniques," *Research Quarterly,* 15:139-140, May, 1944.
5. Blake, Patricia Ann, "Relationship Between Audio-Perceptual Rhythm and Skill in Square Dance," *Research Quarterly,* 31:231, May, 1960.
6. Bond, Marjorie H., "Rhythmic Perception and Gross Motor Performance," *Research Quarterly,* 30:259, October, 1959.
7. Buck, Nadine, "A Comparison of Two Methods of Testing Response to Auditory Rhythms," *Research Quarterly,* 7:37-43, October, 1936.
8. Cooper, John M., and Ruth B. Glassow, *Kinesiology,* St. Louis: C. V. Mosby Company, 1963, pp. 278-279.

9. Dillon, Evelyn K., "A Study of the Use of Music as an Aid in Teaching Swimming," *Research Quarterly,* 23:8, March, 1952.

10. Diserens, C. M., *The Influence of Music on Behavior,* Princeton, N.J.: Princeton University Press, 1926, p. 224.

11. Estep, Dorothy P., "The Relationship of Static Equilibrium to Ability in Gross Motor Activities" (Unpublished master's thesis, University of California, 1958).

12. Haight, Edith C., "Individual Differences in Motor Adaptations to Rhythmic Stimuli," *Research Quarterly,* 15:42, March, 1944.

13. Heinlein, C. P., "A New Method of Studying Rhythmic Responses of Children Together with an Evaluation of the Method of Simple Observation," *Journal of Genetic Psychology,* 26(2): 205-229, June, 1929.

14. Johnson, Barry L., "The Effect of Applying Different Motivational Techniques During Training and in Testing Upon Strength Performance" (Microcarded doctoral dissertation, Louisiana State University, 1965).

15. _____ , "The Effect of Motivational Testing Situations on an Endurance Test" (Laboratory experiment, Northeast Louisiana University, 1963).

16. Johnson, Guy B., "A Summary of Negro Scores on the Seashore Music Talent Tests," *Journal of Comparative Psychology,* 11:383-393, 1931.

17. Lemon, Eloise, and Elizabeth Sherbon, "A Study of the Relationship of Certain Measures of Rhythmic Ability and Motor Ability in Girls and Women," *Research Quarterly Supplement,* 5:85, March, 1934.

18. Loewenthal, Evelyn, "Rhythmic Training," *Journal of Health Physical Education Recreation,* 19(7):474, 1948.

19. McCristal, K. J., "Experimental Study of Rhythm in Gymnastics and Tap Dancing," *Research Quarterly,* 4:74-75, May, 1933.

20. McCulloch, Margaret Lorraine, "The Development of a Test of Rhythmic Response Through Movement of First Grade Children" (Microcarded doctoral dissertation, University of Oregon, 1955).

21. Miles, W. R., and B. J. Graves, "Studies in Physical Exertion: III. Effect of Signal Variation on Football Charging," *Research Quarterly,* 2:31, October, 1931.

22. Muzzey, Dorothy M., "Group Progress of White and Colored Children in Learning a Rhythm Pattern," *Research Quarterly,* 4:62-70, October, 1933.

23. Nelson, Dale O., "Effect of Selected Rhythms and Sound Intensity on Human Performance as Measured by the Bicycle Ergometer," *Research Quarterly,* 34:488, May, 1963.

24. Patterson, D. G., and others, *Minnesota Mechanical Ability Tests,* Minneapolis: University of Minnesota, 1930.

25. Peterson, J., and L. H. Lanier, "Studies in the Comparable Abilities of Whites and Negroes," *Mental Measurement Monograph 5,* No. 4, 1929, p. 156.

26. Sanderson, Helen E., "Differences in Musical Ability in Children of Different National and Racial Origin," *Journal of Genetic Psychology,* 42:100-120, 1933.

27. Shambaugh, Mary E., "The Objective Measurement of Success in the Teaching of Folk Dancing to University Women," *Research Quarterly,* 6:52, March, 1935.

28. Simpson, Shirley E., "Development and Validation of an Objective Measure of Locomotor Response to Auditory Rhythmic Stimuli," *Research Quarterly,* 29:342, October, 1958.

29. Smoll, Frank L., "A Rhythmic Ability Analysis System," *Research Quarterly,* 44:232, May, 1973.

30. Streep, R. L., "A Comparison of White and Negro Children in Rhythm and Consonance," *Journal of Applied Psychology,* 15:52-71, 1931.

31. Stupp, Lillian L., "A Correlation of Musical Ability and Dancing Ability" (Unpublished master's thesis, University of Wisconsin, 1922, p. 43).

32. Swindle, P. F., "On the Inheritance of Rhythm," *American Journal of Psychology,* 24:180-203, April, 1913.

33. Thompson, Clem W., and others, "Football Starting Signals and Movement Times of High School and College Football Players," *Research Quarterly,* 29:230, May, 1953.

34. Waglow, I. F., "An Experiment in Social Dance Testing," *Research Quarterly,* 24:100-101, March, 1953.

35. Wilson, Don J., "Quickness of Reaction and Movement Related to Rhythmicity or Nonrhythmicity of Signal Presentation," *Research Quarterly,* 30:109, March, 1959.

36. Young, Glenda Sue, "Teacher-Made Tests of Rhythm" (Unpublished study, Northeast Louisiana University, 1964).

Chapter Eighteen

Perceptual Motor Performance and Kinesthesis

Although theories advocating the value of motor activity experiences in the child's perceptual development are by no means new, there has been a great upsurge of interest recently among physical educators in the relationship between basic motor patterns and intellectual growth. Much of this interest has been stimulated by the work of Kephart (22) and Delacato (9) who utilized motor therapy with children with language and reading readiness problems.

Much controversy has ensued as to the relative merits of the various therapeutic programs which emphasize developmental movement experiences and the practice of basic locomotor activities. The evidence has been contradictory, due in large part to a lack of objective evidence. The instruments used in assessing movement behavior and perceptual functions have been questioned with regard to their validity and reliability (44). Other facets of the controversy concern the appropriate age level, whether all children should be involved or just the slow learners, and the kinds of motor activities that should be incorporated in the programs.

In studies concerning the slow learner, many of the children were found to be of normal and above normal intelligence, yet they were found to perform poorly on motor ability test items. According to Kephart, poor motor coordination involving laterality and directionality must be overcome through practice of various movement patterns if the child is to be able to cope with the more complex activities of reading, writing, and arithmetic.

It has been said that the children of today are denied many of the opportunities to climb, run, jump, explore, and manipulate their environment that were afforded children of previous generations. Hence, some workers in this area maintain that a real need exists for a wide variety of movement experiences for all pre-school and primary grade children.

Space does not permit us to present an adequate discussion of the rationale behind the perceptual-motor "movement" and the research evidence supporting and discounting the claims that cognitive functioning can be improved through motor activities. It will suffice to say that there is general agreement that a child's self-image and level of aspiration may be aided through improved motor skills and that, because of the interaction between perception and motor functions, certain parts of the overall educational program may be affected positively through movement activities (6). Therefore, although there may be disagreement as to the extent of direct and indirect enhancement of intellectual functioning as a result of movement, we can conclude that perceptual-motor activities should be provided for all young children.

The stated objectives in the various perceptual-motor programs may differ in terms of emphasis, but essentially they seek to provide the child experiences in the following areas (4):

1. To develop and utilize skills of locomotor movement such as walking, running, jumping, hopping, sliding, skipping, climbing, etc.
2. To develop and utilize eye-hand and foot-hand coordination skills of throwing, catching, striking, and kicking.
3. To develop skills basic to movement and gross motor performance such as balance, agility, flexibility, strength, and endurance.
4. To develop a functional concept of body size and space requirements in terms of height, depth, and breadth for one's body to perform in a variety of situations.
5. To provide opportunities for the child to utilize various sense modalities, auditory, visual, tactual, and proprioceptive, in gross motor activities.

As was mentioned before, one of the problems in establishing evidence of the effectiveness of perceptual-motor programs is the lack of precise measuring devices for evaluation. This is certainly understandable, since the teacher is interested in the quality of the movements perhaps more so than the quantity. In other words, the evaluative criteria may stress the "how" of performance as well as the "what." The teacher is interested in observing the child as he performs in terms of his confidence, coordination, relaxation, etc., and not just how quickly he negotiates the task. Subsequently, the assessment of quality is by necessity largely subjective. The child's performance has generally been scored either as "pass" or "fail" or on a "good," "average," "fair," or "failure" basis.

We are not condemning these evaluation methods; on the contrary, subjective judgment is fundamental in teaching motor skills. It, of course, necessitates a skilled examiner, which in turn requires preparation and practice. In view of the dearth of tests in the area of perceptual motor performance, we can only present some tests that have been utilized and in so do-ing perhaps prompt the interested individual to modify the existing tests and devise better ones.

In this first part of the chapter, some tests are presented under the heading Kinesthetic Perception Measurement. This may be too limited in terms of the objectives of a perceptual-motor program. This would seem to involve only the proprioceptive sensory modality, whereas the teacher is interested in visual, auditory, and tactual as well. However, with some adjustments in administration and scoring, assessment of these modalities can be incorporated into some of the kinesthetic perception tests. Also, the use or modification of tests presented in other chapters, such as some of the agility, balance, strength, and sports skill tests, can provide information on specific skills in question. Herkowitz (15) described a number of perceptual-motor training activities for pre-school children which emphasized the various sensory modalities and gave suggestions for evaluation of performance. She strongly cautions that there is yet no evidence that training on the different equipment will transfer to performance on other motor tasks. More will be said about the specificity of kinesthesis later in the chapter.

Kinesthetic Perception Measurement

Kinesthetic perception, the ability to perceive the position, effort, and movement of parts of the body or the entire body during muscular action is sometimes referred to as the sixth sense. In reality, we have more than just six senses; in fact, kinesthetic sense could be considered as several senses within itself. The term *proprioceptive sense* is also used to refer to this sense. The sources of proprioceptive or kinesthetic perception are presumably located in the joints, muscles, and tendons.

Physical educators have long recognized the importance of kinesthesis. Steinhaus (47) declared that our muscles see more than our eyes. Individuals who can observe a demonstration and perceive the significance of the sequence of movements are able to develop a physical empathy which enables them to learn a movement much faster than others whose kinesthetic ability is not as highly developed. Kinesthetic perception can be improved through practice. Physical educators and coaches constantly urge performers to be aware of the "feel" of the correct movement, the amount of effort or force involved, and the position of the body part, racket, club, etc., at various points in the movement.

Uses of Kinesthetic Perception Tests

Some of the ways physical educators might utilize tests of kinesthetic perception are as follows:

1. As a form of practice in establishing the *feel* of certain movements.
2. As a means for diagnostic and interpretive purposes.
3. As a method of providing students with experiences in utilizing this sense modality by itself and in combination with other sensory modalities.
4. As variables in demonstrating or exploring the specificity and/or generality of kinesthesis in research projects.

Tests of Kinesthetic Perception

Distance Perception Jump (39)

Objective: To measure ability to perceive distance by concentrating on the effort involved in a jump.

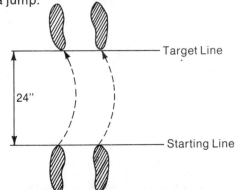

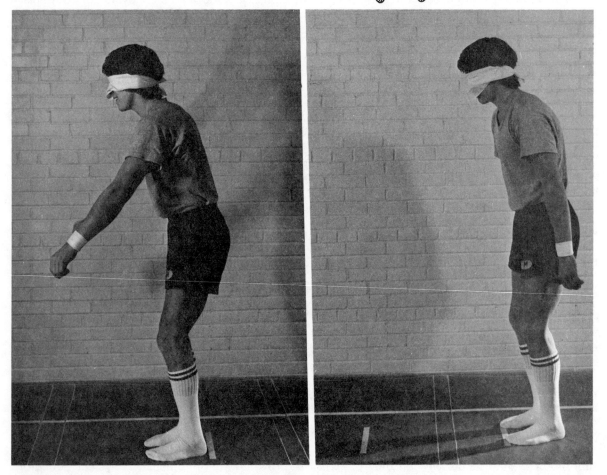

Figure 18-1. Distance Perception Jump

Table 18-1
Excellent, Average, and Very Poor Performance Scores
on the Distance Perception Jump Test
for Junior and Senior High School Boys

School Level	Very Poor Scores		Average Scores		Excellent Scores	
	In.	Cm.	In.	Cm.	In.	Cm.
Junior High School	10¼	26	5½	13	¾	2
Senior High School	10¼	26	5¼	13	½	1

Score deviations are in inches and centimeters and are based on a limited number of subjects from physical education classes in East Baton Rouge Parish, Baton Rouge, La. The above scores are based on a total of only two trials.

Age Level: Pre-school and up. The distance is immaterial; therefore, if the 24-inch distance is too great for the younger children, it can be reduced to 18 inches, 15, 12, etc.
Sex: Both.
Validity: With the eyes closed, face validity is acceptable.
Reliability: The reliability is increased with increased trials. A coefficient of .44 was obtained with seventh and eighth grade boys on test-retest using the total of two trials as the score. A coefficient of .61 was found with seventh and eighth grade boys using the total of ten trials as the score (31).
Objectivity: An r of .99 was reported by Elaine Wyatt, 1969.
Equipment and Materials: Yardstick or tape measure, blindfold, and chalk.
Directions: The performer is instructed to sense the distance between the two lines without a practice trial. The blindfold is then put on and the subject jumps from behind the starting line trying to land with the heels as close to the target line as possible (see Figure 18-1). He is allowed to see where he lands on each trial. Ten trials are given. *Note:* This is a modification of the original distance perception jump in which only two trials were allowed. Another variation of the test is to allow the subject to jump first with his eyes open. Then he is blindfolded to measure his ability to duplicate the amount of effort required. However, very few can jump perfectly on the first trial; therefore, it again becomes a matter of interpreting the feedback from each jump.
Scoring: For each jump the distance to the

nearest ¼ inch from the target line to the farthest heel is measured and recorded. The score is the total for ten jumps.

The Shuffleboard Distance Perception Test (18)

Objective: To measure the ability to perceive distance by concentrating on the effort involved in pushing a disc.
Age Level: The distance could be modified to be suitable for pre-school and primary grade children as well as older children. The distance utilized below was found satisfactory for ages nine and up.
Sex: For both boys and girls.
Validity: With the eyes closed, face validity is acceptable.
Reliability: An r of .71 was obtained on test-retest, using seventh and eighth grade boys. An r of .66 was found with fourth grade girls on test-retest.
Equipment and Floor Marking: Shuffleboard cue sticks, discs, chalk or tape, blindfolds, and tape measure. The floor is marked as shown in Figure 18-2. There are three phases of the test, each from a different distance to the target (5, 10, and 15 feet from beginning of target scoring zones). The distance between each scoring zone is 6 inches.
Directions: The subject is initially given four or five practice trials away from the target to get acquainted with the shuffleboard pushing motion and the movement of the disc on the floor surface. He is then taken to the target and positioned at the starting line 1 (5 feet from beginning of target zones) and told to sense the

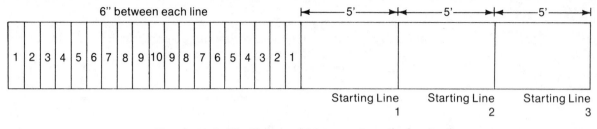

Figure 18-2. Shuffleboard Distance Perception Test

Table 18-2
Raw Scores of College Students Limited to Ten
Trials (Blindfolded) from the 15 Foot Line to the First Zone

College Men	Performance Level	College Women
95-100	Excellent	95-100
65-75	Average	70-80
30-40	Poor	40-50

Based on the scores of 100 college men and 100 college women as reported by Roosevelt Johnson and Dalton LeBlanc, 1967.

distance to the 10-point target zone. He is then blindfolded and given ten trials. After each trial he is allowed to see where the disc came to rest. The blindfold is then repositioned, and he executes his next trial. After 10 trials at that distance he is moved to starting line 2 and instructed to try to sense the distance to the 10-point zone. He is again blindfolded, and ten trials are given. The same procedures are repeated at starting line 3.

Scoring: The zone in which the disc stops is recorded as the score for each trial. The total points from the three distances (thirty trials) are recorded as the score.

Additional Pointers: (a) The test can be given on cement and other hard surfaces. (b) The nature of the feedback can be altered by calling out the score on each trial, such as "seven over" or "eight under," etc. (c) The order of testing from the different starting lines could be altered such as 15, 10, then 5 or in a random order. (d) Some aspects of transfer could be studied by having the subjects practice at distances different from the distance tested, etc.

(e) Several targets can be established to expedite the administration of the test. (f) Performance with eyes open may be assessed if the instructor wishes to evaluate depth perception.

Kinesthetic Obstacle Test (19)

Objective: To measure ability to predict position during movement without the use of the eyes.

Age Level: Ages ten through college.

Sex: Satisfactory for both boys and girls.

Reliability: An r of .30 was found for college women when test 1 was correlated with test 2. For men, an r of .53 was found using the same procedure.

Validity: Without the use of the eyes, there is obvious face validity.

Equipment and Materials: The equipment and materials required are twelve chairs (or similar objects), material for blindfolds, chalk markers or a tape marker, and tape measures.

Directions: Arrange 12 chairs in accordance with the floor pattern shown in Figure 18-3. Each performer is allowed one practice trial

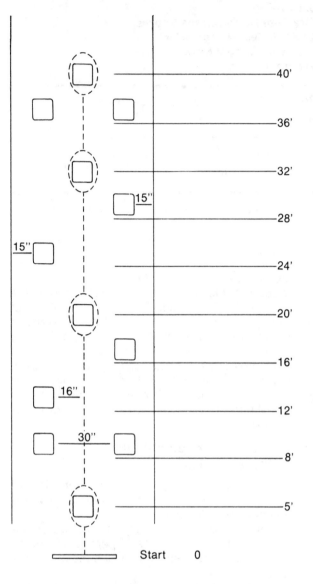

Figure 18-3. Kinesthetic Obstacle Test

walk through the course without a blindfold and one walk through the course blindfolded for a score.

Scoring: The performer scores 10 points for each station he successfully clears without touching. There are 10 stations for a maximum score of 100 points. (See Table 18-3.)

Penalty: (a) There is a 10-point penalty for touching any part of the body against any part of a chair. When such a penalty occurs, the performer is directed to the center line and one step ahead of the station where the penalty occurred. (b) There is a 5-point penalty for each occurrence of getting outside of the line or pattern of the chairs. Upon such occurrences, the performer is directed back into the center of the pattern at the nearest point from which he went astray.

Additional Points: (a) The dotted line merely shows the ideal walking path and need not be drawn on the floor. (b) The two outside lines are boundary lines and should be indicated on the floor. (c) Further experimentation with scoring systems is needed, since the reliability of the test was found to be quite low.

Bass Kinesthetic Stick Test (Lengthwise) (55)

Objective: To measure the kinesthetic ability to maintain balance on a small narrow surface.

Age Level: Ages ten and up. (See additional pointers.)

Sex: Satisfactory for both boys and girls.

Reliability: A test-retest correlation of .36 was found with sixth grade boys.

Validity: With the eyes closed, this test has obvious face validity.

Equipment and Materials: The equipment and materials needed are stopwatches, several sticks cut to 1 inch by 1 inch by 12 inches, tape,

Table 18-3
Raw Score Norms for Kinesthetic Obstacle Test

Men	Performance Level	Women
90-100	Excellent	80-90
65-50	Average	60-70
40-50	Poor	30-40

Based on the scores of 100 college men and 100 college women as reported by Barbara Bogivest Dunn and Dorothy Washington, 1967.

Table 18-4
Excellent, Average, and Very Poor Performance Scores
on the Bass Kinesthetic Stick Test (Lengthwise)
for Junior and Senior High School Boys
(Scores based on one trial)

School Level	Very Poor Scores	Average Scores	Excellent Scores
Junior High School	3	9	15
Senior High School	3½	10	16

Scores are in seconds and are based on a limited number of subjects from physical education classes in East Baton Rouge Parish, Baton Rouge, La.

and blindfolds. Several stations may be set up to save time.

Directions: The subject is instructed to place his dominant foot lengthwise on a balance stick and to raise his opposite foot from the floor to see how long he can maintain his balance. Each subject is given one preliminary trial and is then blindfolded for the test. The subject is timed from the moment he raises his opposite foot from the floor until balance is lost. Ten trials are given.

Scoring: The score is recorded to the nearest ½ second for each trial; the score is the total number of seconds for the ten trials.

Additional Pointers: (a) This task is quite difficult even for adults. The test could be modified to make it more suitable for younger children by increasing the width of the stick. A block of wood 1 inch high by 3 inches by 3 inches should be sufficient to make the child balance on the ball of one foot. (b) The Bass Stick Test can be done crosswise also, but it is even more difficult and the scores are usually quite low.

Perceptual Motor Test Batteries

A few batteries of simple to complex activities have been devised to assess perceptual-motor performance. Some are scored on a pass-fail basis, others on a rating scale of the quality of the performance, and still others on a more objective basis. Some investigators have established obstacle courses in order to appraise the child's ability to solve the

perceptual-motor "problems" that are placed in his path as he moves through the course. Such courses have the advantage of being motivating in that they present a challenge to the child and of providing a knowledge of results as to his improvement over previous performances. A variety of tasks can be provided in a test battery, and the tester can evaluate the child's abilities as he performs the different types of movement patterns required.

Uses of Perceptual-Motor Test Batteries

Some of the ways in which batteries of perceptual-motor tests can be used by the teacher are as follows:

1. As a means of establishing objective evidence of the values of perceptual-motor program experiences in which the child participates.
2. As motivation for the child by allowing him to see his improvement in performing the different tasks and negotiating the obstacle course.
3. As a means for diagnosis and interpretation.
4. As a means for practice and evaluation of specific factors of perceptual-motor performance such as laterality, directionality, balance, eye-hand coordination, locomotor skills, and problem solving ability.

Test Batteries

The following batteries are presented as examples of tests that provide an objective score even though a number of the items may be evaluated subjectively.

Dayton Sensory Motor Awareness Survey for Four- and Five-Year-Olds (8)

Date of Test _____

Name _____ Sex _____ Birth _____ Center _____

Body Image. One-half point for each correct part; nine points possible.

_____ 1. Ask the child to touch the following body parts:

Head _____	Ankles _____	Ears _____	Stomach _____
Toes _____	Nose _____	Legs _____	Chin _____
Eyes _____	Feet _____	Mouth _____	Waist _____
Wrists _____	Chest _____	Fingers _____	Shoulders _____
Back _____	Elbows _____		

Space and Directions. One-half point for each correct direction; five points possible.

_____ 2. Ask the child to point to the following directions:

Front _____ Back _____ Up _____ Down _____ Beside you _____
Place two blocks on a table about 1 inch apart. Ask the child to point:
Under _____ Over _____ To the top _____ To the bottom _____
Between _____

Balance. Score two points if accomplished.

_____ 3. Have the child stand on tiptoes, on both feet, with eyes open for 8 seconds.

Balance and Laterality. Score two points for each foot; four points possible.

_____ 4. Have the child stand on one foot, eyes closed, for 5 seconds. Alternate feet.

Laterality. Score two points if the child keeps his feet together and does not lead off with one foot.

_____ 5. Have the child jump forward on two feet.

Rhythm and Neuromuscular Control. Score two points for each foot if accomplished six times; four points possible.

_____ 6. Have the child hop on one foot. Hop in place.

Rhythm and Neuromuscular Control. Score two points.

_____ 7. Have the child skip forward. Child must be able to sustain this motion around the room for approximately 30 feet.

Integration of Right and Left Sides of the Body. Score two points if cross-patterning is evident for each.

_____ 8. Have the child creep forward.

_____ 9. Have the child creep backwards.

Eye-Foot Coordination. Score two points if done the length of tape or mark.

_____ 10. Use an 8 foot tape or chalk mark on the floor. The child walks in a crossover step the length of the tape or mark.

Fine Muscle Control. Score two points if paper is completely crumpled. Score one point if paper is partially crumpled. Score zero points if child needs assistance or changes hands.

_____ 11. Using a half sheet of newspaper, the child picks up the paper with one hand and puts the other hand behind his back. He then attempts to crumple the paper in his hand. He may not use his other hand, the table, or his body for assistance.

Form Perception. Score one point for each correct match.

_____ 12. Using a piece of paper with 2 inch circles, squares, and triangles, ask the child to point to two objects that are the same.

Form Perception. Score one point if circle is identified correctly. Score two points if the triangle and square are identified correctly.

_____ 13. Ask the child to identify by saying, "Point to the circle." "Point to the square." "Point to the triangle."

Hearing Discrimination. Score one point if the child taps correctly each time.

_____ 14. Ask the child to turn his back to you. Tap the table with a stick three times. Ask the child to turn around and tap the sticks the same way. Ask the child to turn his back to you. Tap the table again with the sticks (two quick taps, pause, then two more quick taps). Have the child turn back to you and tap out the rhythm.

Eye-Hand Coordination. Score one point for each successful completion.

_____ 15. A board is used with three holes in it. The holes are ¾, ⅝ and ½ inch in diameter. The child is asked to put his finger through the holes without touching the sides.

The Fisher Motor Performance Test (11)

Objective: To measure various aspects of motor performance of pre-school and primary grade children.
Age Level: Kindergarten and primary grades.
Sex: Both boys and girls.
Reliability: An r of .82 was found on test-retest with kindergarten children.
Equipment and Materials: The test consists of 10 stations as shown in Figure 18-4. In Fisher's study, the children were told to imagine that a wild animal was chasing them, and consequently the various test stations represented rivers, tunnels, mountains, cliffs, etc. Considerable ingenuity was manifested in the construction and painting of the test stations. This of course is not necessary for the accomplishment of the tasks.

The equipment and materials are described along with the test directions at the different stations.

Station 1. Ball Bounce
Equipment and Materials: A 10-inch playground ball and stopwatch.
Directions: The child must bounce the ball ten times before proceeding on to next station. If the ball gets away he must retrieve it and continue bouncing. *Note:* Stopwatch is started when child bounces the ball the first time and continues to run until the child crosses the finish line (station 10).

Station 2. Balance Beam
Equipment and Materials: A 4-inch balance beam, 8 feet long and about 6 inches above the ground.
Directions: The child has to run from station 1 a distance of 35 feet and cross the "river" as quickly as he can being careful not to fall into the "water." If he falls off, he gets back up at that point and continues across.

Station 3. Tunnel Crawl
Equipment and Materials: A cloth tunnel 10 feet long, approximately 2 feet wide and 2 feet high.
Directions: The child runs from station 2 a distance of 19 feet and must crawl on hands and knees as quickly as he can through the tunnel.

Station 4. Accuracy Throw
Equipment and Materials: A target made of poster paper 28 by 36 inches in size. In Fisher's study, the target was a tiger drawn on the paper, the bottom of which was 54 inches from the ground. At least two 10-inch playground balls are needed. A restraining line 6 feet from the target and another line 15 feet from the target are drawn with chalk or made by ropes or string.
Directions: The child runs 36 feet from station 3 and is told to throw the ball at the target from behind the 6-foot restraining line. He tries to hit the target three times, but, if he is unsuccessful, a maximum of six trials are given. The second line 15 feet from the target is the out-of-bounds line. If the ball, rebounding from the target, stays between the 6-foot and 15-foot lines, the

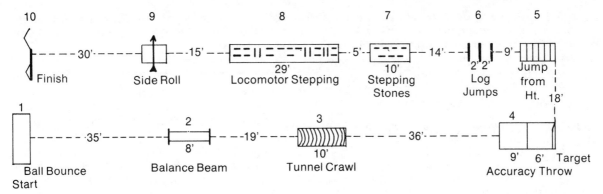

Figure 18-4. Fisher Motor Performance Test

child must retrieve it and run back to the 6 foot line to throw again. If the ball gets away beyond the lines, he is handed another ball.

Station 5. Jump from Height

Equipment and Materials: A ramp about 3 feet wide and 8 feet long made of boards sloping up to a height of 2 feet. In Fisher's study, a set of four stairs was constructed up to a platform 4 feet square.

Directions: The child runs 18 feet from station 4 and must run up the ramp and jump to the ground.

Station 6. Log jump

Equipment and Materials: Three "logs" approximately 6 inches high are spaced 2 feet apart. The "logs" can be either cardboard, metal, or wood.

Directions: The child runs 9 feet from station 5 and must jump three times in succession over the "logs." He is instructed to use both feet for take-off and landing on each jump.

Station 7. Stepping Stones

Equipment and Materials: Nine blocks approximately 2 inches high and 4 by 7 inches in size are staggered in two lines each equidistant across a 10-foot space. (See Figure 18-4.)

Directions: The subject runs 14 feet from station 6 and is instructed to walk across the "river" stepping on each "stone" as quickly as possible without falling off. If the child falls off, he gets back up on that block and continues across.

Station 8. Locomotor Stepping

Equipment and Materials: A paper cloth or canvas 29 feet long is needed. Right and left footprints are drawn on this in such a manner that the child must jump and hop turning right and left.

Directions: The child runs 5 feet from station 7 and is instructed to "do what the feet tell you to

do as quickly as you can." The object of the test is to have the child jump and hop on one and two feet, turning left and right as he moves along as rapidly as he can. If he should slightly miss a footprint, he is not stopped, but, if he fails to execute the prescribed jump or if he goes completely off the sheet, he must start at that point and continue on.

Station 9. Side Roll

Equipment and Material: A small mat and a board of sufficient length supported by two sawhorses which place the board 21 inches above the mat are needed for this task.

Directions: The child runs 15 feet from station 8 and must roll on his side (either right or left, or tester can specify) under the board as quickly as he can and scramble up to run to finish line.

Station 10. Finish Line

Equipment and Materials: A chalk line is all that is needed. In Fisher's study, a doorway was built to represent a house and "safety" from the pursuing animal.

Directions: The child runs as fast as he can the 30 feet from station 9 to cross the finish line. The stopwatch is stopped at the moment he crosses the line.

Scoring: The score is the elapsed time to the nearest tenth of a second from the first ball bounce at station 1 to the finish line at station 10. The total distance is approximately 250 feet. The average of four trials is the score.

Additional Pointers: (a) It is desirable to have a couple assistants to the tester, one to assist at the accuracy throw and the other between the two ends of the course to encourage the children. (b) It is possible to start a second subject when the first subject finishes throwing at the accuracy throw. Of course, two watches are needed. (c) Considerable imagination can be utilized in devising the test stations to help motivate and challenge the children. (d) Strict adherence to the exact distances between test stations is not of great importance. The distances established by Fisher were determined by several factors such as the configuration of the grounds and the nature and space requirements of the individual test stations.

Perceptual-Motor Obstacle Course (32)

The following is an example of an obstacle course that can be utilized for practice and the appraisal of various types of perceptual-motor performance for pre-school and primary grade children. Validity and reliability coefficients and norms are not yet available.

Directions: The child is instructed to proceed through the course as quickly and correctly as he can. The stopwatch is started when the child leaves the starting line and stopped when he crosses the finish line.

Scoring: The score can be in terms of elapsed time for completion of the entire course. A scoring system combining errors and time is also being considered.

Station 1. Foot-Eye Coordination

Equipment and Materials: A canvas, sheet, or paper with footprints or some type marking to denote the foot placement pattern. The pattern could be painted on a blacktop or concrete play area. The footprints are about 12 to 15 inches apart. (See Figure 18-5.)

Directions: The child is told to hop according to the footprints as quickly as possible.

Scoring: If errors are to be counted, the number of times he fails to hit the indicated footprints is recorded. If time only is considered, he must start again at the point at which he missed.

Station 2. Over and Under (Body Space)

Equipment and Materials: Barriers and hurdles are constructed with light wood, preferably in such a way that the crossbar falls off easily when bumped. The barriers are approximately 2½ feet from the ground, and the hurdles are 12 inches high. (See Figure 18-5.)

Directions: The child is instructed to stoop under and jump over the barriers and hurdles as quickly as possible.

Scoring: Same as station 1.

Station 3. Form Discrimination

Equipment and Materials: A pattern of squares, triangles, and circles is drawn on a canvas or surface. Each figure is about 12 inches in diameter and the distance between similar forms is about 15 inches. (See Figure 18-5.)

Directions: The child is told to jump placing both feet on the specified form, i.e., a triangle, or square, or circle. The specific form can vary with different trials.

Scoring: Same as station 1.

Station 4. Ball Transfer (Eye-Hand Coordination)

Equipment and Materials: Two boxes or other containers large enough to hold at least five 10-inch playground balls. Distance between boxes should be at least 15 feet.

Directions: The child takes the balls out of the box one at a time on the left and places them in the box at the right. The manner in which he deposits the ball in the box depends on the nature and level of skill desired. The teacher may want the child to: (a) simply place the balls in the basket, (b) toss it from a specified distance, (c) toss it over a barrier, (d) bounce it in, (e) bank it in, etc. The size and number of balls can be altered also.

Scoring: The score can be the number of correct trials or the elapsed time for a certain number of trials, etc.

Station 5. Balance and Locomotor Movement

Equipment and Materials: Three balance beams, made from 2x4's, each about 8 feet in length. The beams may be set up on edge or placed flat to vary the width of the beam depending on the age and skill level of the children. The height of the beams from the ground can also be varied.

Directions: The child is instructed to cross the first beam in a sideward sliding movement either right or left, then cross the second beam forward (or backward) and the third is a sliding sideward movement in the opposite direction as on the first beam. The child is encouraged to move as quickly as he can safely. The manner in which the child crosses the beams can be varied in accordance with the desired objectives.

Scoring: Same as in station 1.

Station 6. Agility Tire Run

Equipment and Materials: Seven automobile tires are staggered with their sides touching as shown in Figure 18-5.

Directions: The child is to run through the tires as quickly as he can. He may be instructed to put his feet in the center of the tires or just to land on the sides of each tire, depending on the wishes of the tester.

Scoring: Same as in station 1.

Station 7. The Maze

Equipment and Materials: A maze pattern is drawn or taped onto canvas or floor surface; or, if sufficient folding mats are available, a

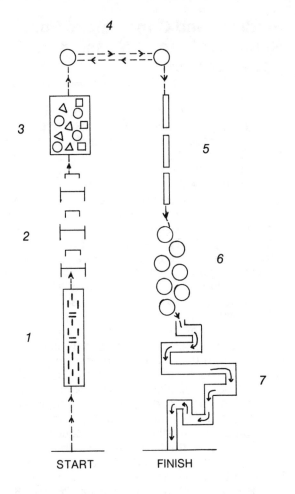

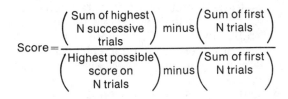

Figure 18-5. *Perceptual Motor Obstacle Course*

challenging maze can be constructed with the mats placed upright. The lane is 2 feet in width. An example of possible dimensions is shown in Figure 18-5.

Directions: The child is instructed to negotiate his way through the maze as quickly as possible without touching the boundary lines and then run to the finish line.

Scoring: Same as in station 1.

Problems Associated with Perceptual-Motor and Kinesthesis Testing

Some of the problems and limitations associated with the measurement of perceptual-motor performance, including kinesthesis testing, are as follows:

1. The problem of specificity is a major factor confronting perceptual-motor training programs. As was mentioned earlier, there is yet no evidence that experiences in one type of gross motor skill will transfer to another. This problem pervades in any attempts to measure perceptual-motor abilities. The results are thus limited in that the performance being assessed is specific. However, most research evidence indicates this is true with any measurement. A possible approach is the utilization of a problem solving test in which the child must negotiate a series of tasks or type of obstacle course which is comprised of tasks similar to the specific items that were practiced.

2. Since quality of performance is of great importance in perceptual-motor evaluation, the scoring of tests in this area is made more complicated. Research is needed to devise scoring scales which might combine ratings or errors along with quantitative measures such as distance and time.

3. It would seem that practice trials might also be interwoven into the measurement of perceptual-motor performance. Perhaps some scoring system could be developed such as discussed by McCraw (29) in which improvement is related to possible improvement such as

$$Score = \frac{\left(\begin{array}{c} Sum\ of\ highest \\ N\ successive \\ trials \end{array}\right) minus \left(\begin{array}{c} Sum\ of\ first \\ N\ trials \end{array}\right)}{\left(\begin{array}{c} Highest\ possible \\ score\ on \\ N\ trials \end{array}\right) minus \left(\begin{array}{c} Sum\ of\ first \\ N\ trials \end{array}\right)}$$

McCraw found the total score and the percent gain of possible gain methods to be the most valid ones for measuring improvement on learning tests.

4. Crafts (5) made some observations about perceptual-motor assessment instruments concerning validity. She cautioned that perhaps, in some tests, the ability of the child to learn in general involving various patterns of behavior, the ability to interpret feedback and then correct errors, attention span, confidence, and other factors may be what is actually being reflected in the score rather than perceptual-motor ability.

5. Norms for perceptual-motor performance, including kinesthetic perception, are practically non-existent. If certain basic skills could be agreed upon by clinicians in this

area, some norms for different age levels would be of great help for teachers of preschool and elementary school children.

6. Many investigators have failed to recognize the influence of tactual stimulation involved in the more traditional tests of kinesthesis (42). For example, Chernikoff (3) has pointed out that, when a subject exerts force against a scale, body contact produces tactual stimulation. Moreover, when the subject is blindfolded and is required to move a body part to a designated point in space, the tester commonly moves the subject's body part in the preliminary trial, and this also produces tactual stimulation.

7. Many kinesthetic tests (including those in this chapter) which have been used are still in the exploratory stage and are of questionable reliability and validity. However, concerning validity, Henry (14) stated that a test in which *muscle sense* is the only possible cue for a successful response should be acknowledged as a valid test of some aspect of kinesthetics. Concerning reliability, investigators frequently show kinesthetic tests to be reliable by using the split half technique when stepped up by the Spearman-Brown formula, but then they recommend a different scoring system when testing other than for reliability. In checking such recommended scoring systems by the test-retest method on separate days, the authors and their assistants found considerably lower *r*'s. Thus, there is a need for further experimentation to establish reliable scoring systems which will also be practical for use.

8. Since most writers on the topic of kinesthesis agree that it is specific to the test and body part rather than general, it would seem appropriate to devise tests of kinesthesis with that thought in mind. For example, if a coach is trying to emphasize *touch* in basketball goal shooting, he might experiment with having a player shoot blindfolded. After each shot, the performer receives verbal feedback and then tries to adjust by *feel*. The use of skill tests while blindfolded as a form of practice in certain activities may have considerable value in trying to establish more reliance on proprioceptive cues and achieve consistency of performance such as in *grooving* a golf swing. Needless to say, common sense must prevail; nevertheless, there may be merit in this procedure.

Findings and Conclusions from Perceptual-Motor Measurement and Research

Several investigators have concluded that there is no general kinesthetic ability but rather a number of factors specific to the task and the particular part of the body involved in the performance (7, 39, 46, 52).

Although the evidence is by no means conclusive, studies have shown that the skilled performer in a specific activity tends to score higher on kinesthetic tests than the less skilled (30, 35, 41, 52). Two studies found no significant difference between boys and girls in kinesthetic perception (42, 54). Athletes score higher in kinesthetic performance than nonathletes (51); however, most studies have failed to find any appreciable relationship between kinesthesis and ability in sports such as gymnastics (50), bowling (13), and basketball (48).

Laszlo (24) utilizing a blood pressure cuff to reduce kinesthetic sensation induced decreased tapping efficiency. She found that the impairment produced by the cuff on the arm resulted in loss of tactile sense of the fingers first, passive kinesthetic sense second, and then active kinesthetic sense.

In general, low relationships have been found between kinesthesis and motor performance (13, 30, 33), motor learning (26, 36, 38), and certain psychological and physiological factors (14, 43, 46).

The following studies reported a positive relationship between motor performance and intellectual functioning. Ismail and Gruber (17) found highest correlations between the Otis Short Form of Mental Ability and tests of coordination and balance. Strength, speed, and power items had lower predictive power. They concluded that organized physical education had a favorable effect on academic achievement scores. Kagerer (21) reported substantial and consistent correlations between activities designed to measure ability to move within a posture and achievement in school. Oliver (34) administered physical and mental pre- and post-tests to two matched groups of educationally subnormal boys. The experimental group subjects who were given a ten-week course of systematic and progressive physical conditioning made marked gains in both the physical and mental measures. Kulcinski (23) found a definite and positive relationship between intelligence of fifth and sixth grade boys and girls and their ability to learn fundamental muscular skills.

Leithwood (25) correlated simple and complex motor measures of sixty four-year-old children with eight dimensions of intellectual functioning and a multidimensional scale of psychosocial adjustment. He reported several significant relationships with twice as many significant correlations of cognitive abilities with complex motor tasks as with simple motor tasks. However, although significant, the correlations were quite low, the highest being .44. Herndon (16) also found a significant relationship between intelligence and perceptual ability of kindergarten-age children. In Lipton's (27) study, a twelve-week perceptual-motor program was found to be superior to a conventional physical education program in improving perceptual-motor performance, visual perception, and reading readiness of first grade children.

McCormick and others (28) studied the effect of perceptual-motor training upon improvement in reading achievement of first graders. They concluded such training could contribute to the child's capacity for academic achievement and that such activities are more effective for underachievers than average or above-average children. Several researchers have indicated that children who have achieved skill in motor performance evidence better social adjustment and fewer negative personality traits than children less skilled in motor activities (37, 45, 49).

On the other hand, a number of studies have found no relationship between motor performance and intellectual achievement. Singer (40) reported very low correlations between intelligence tests and physical and perceptual-motor tests with sixth graders. Jones (20) also found practically no correlation between intelligence and motor performance.

Brown (2) investigated the effects of a perceptual-motor skills program on reading readiness for first grade children. While significant improvement in motor skills was evidenced, the perceptual-motor program had little effect on reading performance.

In a study with kindergarten children, Fisher (11) compared the motor ability, intelligence, and academic readiness of one group who participated in a sequential, individualized perceptual-motor program with a group who received the traditional supervised free play and games. Although both groups gained

significantly in all measures, there was no significant difference between the groups.

Espenschade (10) concluded that the only association between mental and motor abilities was at the very low end of the mental range. Goodenough (12) claimed that the tests utilized for the measurement of motor ability and intelligence had enough in common that one could expect a certain degree of relationship between them and that what correlation is found is usually among persons of lower intelligence.

References and Bibliography

1. Bass, Ruth I., "Analysis of the Components of Tests of Semi-circular Canal Functions and of Static and Dynamic Balance," *Research Quarterly,* 10:33-52, May, 1939.
2. Brown, Roscoe C., Jr., "The Effect of a Perceptual-Motor Education Program on Perceptual-Motor Skills and Reading Readiness" (Paper presented at Research Section, AAHPER Convention, St. Louis, April, 1968).
3. Chernikoff, R., and F. V. Taylor, "Reaction Time to Kinesthetic Stimulation Resulting from Sudden Arm Displacement," *Journal of Experimental Psychology,* 43:1-8, 1952.
4. Clifton, Marguerite, "A Developmental Approach to Perceptual-Motor Experiences," *Journal of Health Physical Education Recreation,* 41:34-37, April, 1970.
5. Crafts, Virginia R. (Comments reported by Robert E. McAdam), "Perceptual-Motor Assessment Instruments," in AAHPER, *Foundations and Practices in Perceptual Motor Learning—A Quest for Understanding,* Washington, D.C.: American Alliance for Health, Physical Education, and Recreation, 1971, p. 52.
6. Cratty, Bryant J., *Movement Activities for Neurologically Handicapped and Retarded Children and Youth,* Freeport, N.Y.: Educational Activities, 1967, p.3.
7. _____ , "Comparison of Learning a Time Motor Task with Learning a Similar Gross Motor Task Using Kinesthetic Cues," *Research Quarterly,* 33:220, May, 1962.
8. *Dayton Sensory Motor Awareness Survey,* William Braley, Dayton Public Schools, 348 W. First St., Dayton, Ohio.
9. Delacato, C. H., *The Diagnosis and Treatment of Speech and Readiness Problems,* Springfield, Ill.: Charles C. Thomas, Publisher, 1963.
10. Espenschade, Anna, "Perceptual-Motor Development in Children," *Academy Papers,* 1:14-20, 1967.
11. Fisher, David H., "Effects of Two Different Types of Physical Education Programs Upon Skills

Development and Academic Readiness of Kindergarten Children" (Unpublished doctoral dissertation, Louisiana State University, 1970).

12. Goodenough, Florence L., *Mental Testing: Its History, Principles and Applications,* New York: Rinehart and Company, Publishers, 1949, p. 371.

13. Greenlee, Geraldine A., "The Relationship of Selected Measures of Strength, Balance, and Kinesthesis to Bowling Performance" (Microcarded master's thesis, State University of Iowa, 1958).

14. Henry, F. M., "Dynamic Kinesthetic Perception and Adjustment," *Research Quarterly,* 24:176-187, May, 1953.

15. Herkowitz, Jacqueline, "A Perceptual-Motor Training Program to Improve the Gross Motor Abilities of Preschoolers," *Journal of Health Physical Education Recreation,* 41:38-42, April, 1970.

16. Herndon, Daisy E., "The Relationship of Perceptual Motor Ability and Intellectual Ability in Kindergarten-Age Children" (Unpublished master's thesis, Texas Women's University, 1970).

17. Ismail, A. H., and J. J. Gruber, *Motor Aptitude and Intellectual Performance,* Columbus, Ohio: Charles E. Merrill Books, 1967, p. 190.

18. Johnson, Barry L., "The Shuffle Board Control of Force Test" (Unpublished study, Northeast Louisiana University, September, 1966), and Jack K. Nelson, "Modification of Shuffleboard and Bean Bag Kinesthesis Tests" (Unpublished study, Louisiana State University, 1971).

19. _____ , "A Kinesthetic Obstacle Test" (Unpublished study, Northeast Louisiana University, September, 1966).

20. Jones, H. E., *Motor Performance and Growth,* Berkeley, Cal.: University of California Press, 1949, pp. 165-167.

21. Kagerer, R. L., "The Relationship Between the Kraus-Weber Test for Minimum Muscular Fitness and School Achievement" (Unpublished master's thesis, Purdue University, 1958).

22. Kephart, Newell C., *The Slow Learner in the Classroom,* Columbus, Ohio: Charles E. Merrill Books, 1960.

23. Kulcinski, Louis E., "The Relationship of Intelligence to the Learning of Fundamental Muscular Skills," *Research Quarterly,* 16:266-276, October, 1945.

24. Laszlo, Judith I., "The Performance of a Simple Motor Task with Kinesthetic Sense Loss," *Quarterly Journal of Experimental Psychology,* 18:1-8, 1966.

25. Leithwood, Kenneth A., "Motor, Cognitive, and Affective Relationships Among Advantaged Preschool Children," *Research Quarterly,* 42:47-53, March, 1971.

26. Linsay, D., "Relationship Between Measures of Kinesthesis and the Learning of a Motor Skill" (Unpublished master's thesis, University of California, 1952).

27. Lipton, Edward D., "A Perceptual-Motor Development Program's Effect on Visual Perception and Reading Readiness of First Grade Children," *Research Quarterly,* 41:402-5, October, 1970.

28. McCormick, Clarence C., Janice N. Schnobrick, and S. Willard Footlik, "The Effect of Perceptual-Motor Training on Reading Achievement," *Academic Therapy,* 4:171-176, March, 1969.

29. McCraw, L. W., "Comparative Analysis of Methods of Scoring Tests of Motor Learning," *Research Quarterly,* 26:440-453, December, 1955.

30. Mumby, H. Hugh, "Kinesthetic Acuity and Balance Related to Wrestling Ability," *Research Quarterly,* 24:334, October, 1953.

31. Nelson, Jack K., "The Reliability of Selected Measures of Kinesthetic Perception with Grade School Children" (Unpublished study, Louisiana State University, 1972).

32. _____, "The Construction of a Perceptual-Motor Performance Obstacle Course for Preschool and Primary Grade Children" (Unpublished study, Louisiana State University, 1972).

33. Norrie, M. L., "The Relationship Between Measures of Kinesthesis and Motor Performance" (Unpublished master's thesis, University of California, 1952).

34. Oliver, James N., "The Effects of Physical Conditioning Exercises and Activities on the Mental Characteristics of Educationally Sub-Normal Boys," *British Journal of Educational Psychology,* 28:155-65, June, 1958.

35. Phillips, Bernath Eugene, "The Relationship Between Certain Phases of Kinesthesis and Performance During the Early Stages of Acquiring Two Perceptuo-Motor Skills" (Microcarded master's thesis, Pennsylvania State College, 1941).

36. Phillips, Marjorie, and Dean Summers, "Relation of Kinesthetic Perception to Motor Learning," *Research Quarterly,* 25:456-469, December, 1954.

37. Rarick, G. Lawrence, and Robert McKee, "A Study of Twenty Third-Grade Children Exhibiting Extreme Levels of Achievement on Tests of Motor Proficiency," *Research Quarterly,* 20:142-152, May, 1949.

38. Roloff, Louise L., "Kinesthesis in Relation to the Learning of Selected Motor Skills," *Research Quarterly,* 24:210-217, May, 1953.

39. Scott, M. Gladys, "Tests of Kinesthesis," *Research Quarterly,* 26:234-241, October, 1955.

40. Singer, Robert N., "The Inter-relatedness of Physical, Perceptual-Motor, and Academic

Achievement Variables in Elementary School Children" (Paper presented at AAHPER Convention, St. Louis, April, 1968).

41. Slater-Hammel, A. T., "Measurement of Kinesthetic Perception of Muscular Force with Muscle Potential Changes," *Research Quarterly,* 28:153-159, May, 1957.

42. _____, "Comparisons of Reaction-Time Measures to a Visual Stimulus and Arm Movement," *Research Quarterly,* 26:470-479, December, 1955.

43. Slocum, Helen M., "The Effect of Fatigue Induced by Physical Activity on Certain Tests in Kinesthesis" (Microcarded doctoral dissertation, State University of Iowa, 1952, pp. 39-40).

44. Smith, Hope M., "Motor Activity and Perceptual Development," *Journal of Health Physical Education Recreation,* 39:28-33, February, 1968.

45. Sperling, Abraham P., "The Relationship Between Personality Adjustment and Achievement in Physical Education Activities," *Research Quarterly,* 13:1-7, December, 1942.

46. Start, K. B., "Kinesthesis and Mental Practice," *Research Quarterly,* 35:316-319, October, 1964.

47. Steinhaus, Arthur H., "Your Muscles See More than Your Eyes," *Journal of Health Physical Education Recreation,* 37:38, September, 1966.

48. Taylor, William J., "The Relationship Between Kinesthetic Judgement and Success in Basketball" (Unpublished master's thesis, Pennsylvania State College, 1933).

49. Thorpe, Louis P., *Child Psychology and Development,* New York: Ronald Press Company, 1946, p. 417.

50. Wettstone, Eugene, "Tests for Predicting Potential Ability in Gymnastics and Tumbling," *Research Quarterly,* 9:115-125, December, 1938.

51. Wiebe, Vernon R., "A Factor Analysis of Tests of Kinesthesis" (Microcarded doctoral dissertation, State University of Iowa, 1956, pp. 66-67).

52. _____, "A Study of Tests of Kinesthesis," *Research Quarterly,* 25:222-227, May, 1954.

53. Witte, Fae, "Relation of Kinesthetic Perception to a Selected Motor Skill for Elementary School Children," *Research Quarterly,* 33:476, October, 1962.

54. _____, "A Factorial Analysis of Measures of Kinesthesis" (Microcarded doctoral dissertation, Indiana University, 1953).

55. Young, Olive G., "A Study of Kinesthesis in Relation to Selected Movements," *Research Quarterly,* 16:277, May, 1945.

Chapter Nineteen

Motor Performance Test Batteries

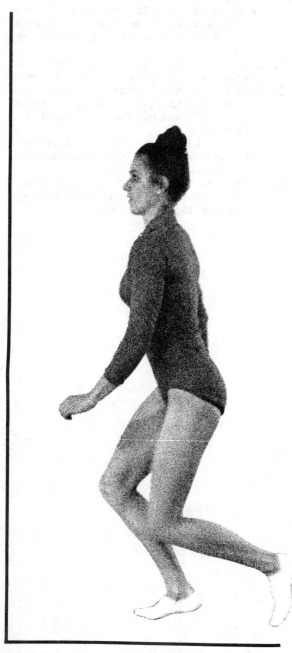

A comprehensive motor performance test battery would theoretically represent all the factors that enter into various types of physical performance. Not only would this be beyond the scope of any one test, but by and large, research has failed to adequately support the theory of "generality" of motor skills. Nevertheless, physical educators have continued to speak in terms of general athletic ability and have sought ways of measuring it.

It is not our intention to enter into the argument of specificity versus generality but merely to present some of the test batteries that have been frequently used as measures of motor performance. Motor performance batteries have been devised with a specific purpose in mind. For example, there are those designed to measure *general athletic ability* (one's present ability to excel in various sports events); to measure *general motor ability* (one's acquired and innate ability to display fundamental motor skills rather than highly specialized sports events); to measure *motor capacity* (one's inborn ability to learn complex motor performance; to measure *motor educability* (one's ability to quickly learn unfamiliar motor skills; and to measure *motor fitness* (one's ability to perform efficiently basic motor skills involving such elements as power, agility, speed, and balance). However, it should be noted that, while motor performance batteries have been designed with a specific purpose in mind, the items selected and/or the manner in which they were administered and scored were not always conducive to the original purpose of the test.

Those qualities which are considered as motor performance qualities and which make up the majority of the test items for motor performance test batteries include *speed, power, agility, reaction time, hand* and *eye coordination,* and *balance.* Although *reaction time* is recognized as a separate quality, it has not been measured as such in motor performance tests, but rather it has remained combined with *speed.* Other test items which are sometimes included are strength and endurance, although they more properly belong classified as physical fitness factors. It is recognized that motor factors may be improved with practice, but essentially they are considered relatively stable. Despite the fact that most studies have found motor ability to be task specific, perhaps more generality would be found with sufficient practice. In other words, if a person possesses considerable ability in basic skills that are thought to underlie motor performance and are represented by the test items in the general motor ability tests, then he should perform well in a variety of physical tasks if given enough practice to overcome initial inhibitions and to establish the specific neuromotor patterns. Cratty (20) has proposed an interesting three-level theory of perceptual-motor behavior that is pertinent to this topic.

Uses of Motor Performance Test Batteries

Although more research is indicated as to the efficacy and predictability of certain motor performance tests, the following uses have been suggested:

1. As a means for preliminary classification of students into homogeneous groups.
2. As a tool for diagnosis of weaknesses in particular areas of motor performance.
3. As a form of motivation in which the students are able to assess their own status.
4. As one of a number of measures for prognostic purposes.
5. As a test of physical achievement.

Barrow Motor Ability Test (4)

Objective: To measure motor ability for purposes of classification, guidance, and achievement.

Age and Sex: College men, junior and senior high school boys.

Validity: Twenty-nine test items measuring eight factors were administered to 222 college men. Through multiple correlation and regression equations, two test batteries were established. The first test contained six items which yielded an r of .950 with the criterion. This figure was the total score from the twenty-nine items. The shorter test battery, containing three items (which are included in the six-item battery), was found to have an r of .920 with the criterion.

Reliability: Using the test-retest method, reliability for each test item was computed. Objectivity was also established by having two persons score each subject on each test item. The test item, the motor ability factor it represents, reliability coefficient, objectivity coefficient, and the correlation of that item with the criterion are presented in Table 19-1.

Equipment and Materials: The equipment and space needed for the six test items are as follows: (a) *Standing broad jump:* A mat 5 by 12 feet and a measuring tape if the mat is not marked off. (b) *Softball throw:* Several 12-inch inseam softballs, a target area of about 100 yards. A football field marked off in 5-yard intervals is ideal for this test. (c) *Zigzag run:* Stopwatch, five standards or obstacles, and space enough to accommodate the 16-by-10-foot course. (d) *Wall pass:* Regulation basketball, stopwatch, wall space. (e) *Medicine ball put:* Space approximately 90 by 25 feet and tape measure. (f) *Sixty-yard dash:* Stopwatch, whistle, smooth surface at least 80 yards long with start and finish lines.

Standing Broad Jump. (Same as the standing broad jump presented in Chapter 12.)

Table 19-1
Test Item Data for the Barrow Motor Ability Test for College Men

Test Item	Factor*	Reliability	Objectivity	Correlation with Criterion
Standing Broad Jump	Power	.895	.996	.759
Softball Throw	Arm-Shoulder Coord.	.928	.997	.761
Zigzag Run	Agility	.795	.996	.736
Wall Pass	Hand-eye Coord.	.791	.950	.761
Medicine Ball Put	Strength	.893	.997	.736
60-Yard Dash	Speed	.828	.997	.723

*Balance and flexibility were also identified as motor ability factors, but no test item for either factor was found to have a high enough coefficient of correlation with the criterion to be included in the final battery.

Softball Throw

Directions: The subject is allowed three trials in which he attempts to throw the softball as far as possible. A short run is allowed, but the subject must not step over the restraining line.

Scoring: The best of three trials is recorded. Distance is measured to the nearest foot.

Safety: Students who are assisting with marking and measuring of the throws must be warned to keep their eyes on the ball when it is thrown. The subject should not be allowed to throw until the field is clear. Adequate warm-up should be provided.

Additional Pointers: (a) Student helpers can be utilized effectively in marking each throw, measuring, and retrieving the balls. If a football field is used, markers can be prepared, reading in feet, and placed at each 5-yard line. (b) One of the student helpers should be assigned to immediately run and stand at the spot at which the ball lands while another brings the subject's marker. A decision can then be made whether the subject has a better throw. (c) Measuring from the nearest 5-yard line facilitates the process as opposed to the use of a tape measure from the point of the throw.

Zigzag Run

Directions: The student begins from a standing start on the command to go. He runs the prescribed pattern shown in Figure 19-1 as quickly as he can without grasping or moving the standards. Three complete circuits are run. The stopwatch is started when the command to go is given and stopped when the subject crosses the finish line.

Scoring: The elapsed time to the nearest tenth of a second is recorded. If the student should grasp or move a standard, run the wrong pattern, or otherwise fail to follow the directions, he should run again after a suitable rest period.

Safety: The subjects should wear proper fitting shoes with good traction to avoid blisters and slipping. Other students should be kept well away from the perimeter of the obstacle course and, especially, away from the finishing area. Sufficient warm-up should be allowed.

Additional Pointers: (a) The instructor should demonstrate the pattern of the course and stress the point that three complete circuits are to be made. (b) The students should be allowed to jog through the course. (c) If any student believes he can improve his score he should be given another trial after he has rested.

Wall Pass

Directions: The subject stands behind a restraining line that is drawn 9 feet from the wall. On the signal to begin he passes the ball against the wall in any manner he chooses. He attempts to catch the rebound and pass it again as many times as possible for 15 seconds. For the pass to be legal, both of the subject's feet must remain behind the restraining line. If he should lose control of the ball, he must retrieve it and return to the line and continue passing.

Scoring: The score is the number of times the ball hits the wall in the 15 seconds.

Safety: There are no special safety hazards with this test.

Additional Pointers: (a) The teacher should consider the possible variations in the cases where a subject loses control of the ball. He may wish to standardize the distance behind the subject by having students line up to block the ball, or have a wall of rolled mats, etc. (b) The teacher should stress the fact that the sub-

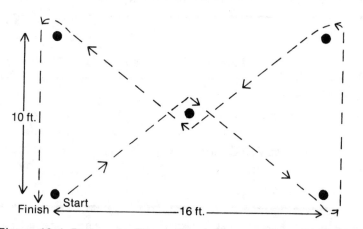

Figure 19-1. Pattern for Zigzag Run in Barrow Motor Ability Test

ject must maintain control of the ball and that he won't be thrown a new ball if he misses the rebound.

Six-Pound Medicine Ball Put

Directions: The subject stands between two restraining lines which are 15 feet apart. He then attempts to propel the medicine ball out as far as possible without stepping on or over the restraining line. He should hold the ball at the junction of his neck and shoulder and thrust it away from his body at an angle of approximately 45 degrees. He is given three throws.

Scoring: The best of three throws is recorded. The distance is computed to the nearest foot. A throw in which the subject commits a foul is not scored. However, if all three trials are fouls, he should try until he makes a fair put.

Additional Pointers: (a) Two students are needed at all times to assist in marking and measuring the throws. It is helpful to also have a student assigned to retrieve the ball. One student should quickly run to the exact spot where the ball lands while another comes to mark (or measures) it. (b) Any of several plans could be followed in measuring the individual throws. Since the test is conducted on the gymnasium floor, small pieces of tape could be used to quickly mark each of the three trials. (c) Another approach is to leave the tape stretched out from the restraining line and then measure each throw. One disadvantage to this method is that each throw must be recorded unless, of course, the succeeding throw(s) is not as far. The tape should be swung in an arc in order to be sure that the distance from the point of the throw to the spot of landing is obtained. (d) Still another method is to have arcs marked on the floor 5 or 10 feet apart. In this way the measuring tape would not have to be as long, and it

may facilitate testing. (e) The tester may wish to dust the ball with powdered chalk before each throw in order to obtain the exact point of landing. This procedure is ordinarily not too practical because of the time consumed and the necessity of continually wiping away the chalk marks.

The 60-Yard Dash

Directions: The subject starts from a standing position on the signal to go and runs as rapidly as possible to the finish line. One trial is given.

Scoring: The score is recorded in seconds to the nearest tenth of a second. The time begins when the command "go" is given. In 60 yards there should be no appreciable time lag due to the relative speed of sound versus the speed of light.

Safety: The most important safety precaution has to do with pulled muscles. The teacher should make it a point to provide a thorough warm-up. The other safety features concern footwear, running surface, and adequate space beyond the finish line.

Additional Pointers: (a) The timer should be stationed parallel to the finish line to make sure he obtains an accurate score. (b) The starter should standardize the preparatory commands such as "ready," "get set," "go." If an arm signal is employed for starting, the movement of the arm must be practiced to synchronize it with the verbal command to "go."

Scoring for Total Battery: A regression equation utilizing weighted standard scores is provided to determine the total General Motor Ability Test score (GMAS). The equation is as follows:

GMAS = 2.2 (standing broad jump) + 1.6 (softball throw) + 1.6 (zigzag run) + 1.3 (wall pass) + 1.2 (medicine ball put) + 60 yard dash.

Table 19-2
General Motor Ability Test Scores for College Men

P. E. Majors			Non-Majors	
Six Items	Three Items		Six Items	Three Items
586 Up	197 Up	Excellent	550 Up	185 Up
534-585	180-196	Good	481-549	163-184
480-533	161-179	Average	410-480	138-162
428-479	143-160	Poor	341-409	116-137
427 Down	142 Down	Inferior	340 Down	115 Down

Table 19-3
T-Scores for College Men

T-Score	Standing Broad Jump (Inches)	Zigzag Run (Seconds)	Medicine Ball Put (Feet)	T-Score
80	113 Up	20.8 Up	58 Up	80
75	109-112	21.6-20.9	55-57	75
70	105-108	22.4-21.7	52-54	70
65	101-104	23.1-22.5	48-51	65
60	97-100	23.9-23.2	45-47	60
55	93-96	24.7-24.0	42-44	55
50	89-92	25.5-24.8	39-41	50
45	85-88	26.3-25.6	35-38	45
40	81-84	27.1-26.4	32-34	40
35	77-80	27.8-27.2	29-31	35
30	73-76	28.6-27.9	26-28	30
25	69-72	29.4-28.7	23-25	25
20	68 Down	29.5 Up	22 Down	20

Table 19-4
**Standing Broad Jump T-Scores for High School
and Junior High School Boys**

Grade	7	8	9	10	11	
T-Score						T-Score
80	90 Up	97 Up	103 Up	105 Up	112 Up	80
75	86-89	92-96	98-102	101-104	107-111	75
70	82-85	88-91	93-97	97-100	103-106	70
65	77-81	83-87	88-92	92-96	97-102	65
60	73-76	78-82	83-87	88-91	93-96	60
55	69-72	73-77	79-82	83-87	88-92	55
50	65-68	69-72	74-78	79-82	83-87	50
45	61-64	64-68	69-73	75-78	78-82	45
40	56-60	59-63	64-68	71-74	74-77	40
35	52-55	54-58	59-63	66-70	69-73	35
30	48-51	50-53	54-58	62-65	64-68	30
25	44-47	45-49	49-53	58-61	59-63	25
20	43 Down	44 Down	48 Down	57 Down	58 Down	20

Table 19-5
Zigzag Run T-Scores for High School and Junior High School Boys

Grade	7	8	9	10	11	T-Score
T-Score						
80	20.1 Down	17.8 Down	20.2 Down	21.6 Down	21.5 Down	80
75	21.4 - 20.2	19.5 - 17.9	21.3 - 20.3	22.7 - 21.7	22.6 - 21.6	75
70	22.7 - 21.5	21.2 - 19.6	22.4 - 21.4	23.8 - 22.8	23.7 - 22.7	70
65	24.0 - 22.8	22.8 - 21.3	23.5 - 22.5	24.8 - 23.9	24.7 - 23.8	65
60	25.2 - 24.1	24.5 - 22.9	24.6 - 23.6	25.8 - 24.9	25.8 - 24.8	60
55	26.5 - 25.3	26.2 - 24.6	25.7 - 24.7	26.9 - 25.9	26.8 - 25.9	55
50	27.8 - 26.6	27.8 - 26.3	26.8 - 25.8	27.9 - 27.0	27.8 - 26.9	50
45	29.0 - 27.9	29.5 - 27.9	27.9 - 26.9	28.9 - 28.0	28.9 - 27.9	45
40	30.3 - 29.1	31.2 - 29.6	29.0 - 28.0	29.9 - 29.0	29.9 - 29.0	40
35	31.6 - 30.4	32.8 - 31.3	30.1 - 29.1	31.0 - 30.0	31.0 - 30.0	35
30	32.8 - 31.7	34.5 - 32.9	31.2 - 30.2	32.1 - 31.1	32.0 - 31.1	30
25	34.1 - 32.9	36.2 - 34.6	32.3 - 31.3	33.1 - 32.2	33.0 - 32.1	25
20	34.2 Up	36.3 Up	32.4 Up	33.2 Up	33.1 Up	20

Table 19-6
Medicine Ball Put T-Scores for High School and Junior High School Boys

Grade	7	8	9	10	11	T-Score
T-Score						
80	43 Up	45 Up	49 Up	50 Up	54 Up	80
75	38-42	43-44	46-48	47-49	51-53	75
70	35-37	40-42	44-45	44-46	48-50	70
65	33-34	37-39	41-43	42-43	46-47	65
60	30-32	34-36	38-40	39-41	43-45	60
55	27-29	31-33	35-37	37-38	40-42	55
50	25-26	28-30	32-34	34-36	37-39	50
45	22-24	25-27	29-31	32-33	34-36	45
40	19-21	23-24	27-28	29-31	31-33	40
35	17-18	20-22	24-26	27-28	28-30	35
30	14-16	17-19	21-23	24-26	25-27	30
25	12-13	14-16	18-20	22-23	22-24	25
20	11 Down	13 Down	17 Down	21 Down	21 Down	20

Barrow recommends that the users of the test establish their own norms. In the original source, the author offered the following norms based on a sample of college students and a group of physical education majors. Barrow adapted this motor ability test to include junior and senior high school boys (5). Using the three-item indoor battery consisting of the standing broad jump, medicine ball put, and zigzag run, norms are presented for grades seven through eleven as well as for college men. It should be remembered that this shortened version loses very little in predictive power when compared to the six-item test. The small loss is compensated for by the tremendous increase in administrative economy. It is also significant to point out that the order of testing is unimportant, which enables the teacher to employ three testing stations.

The norms for college men are shown in Table 19-3. The norms for boys in grades 7 through 11 for each test item are presented in Tables 19-4, 19-5, and 19-6.

Scott Motor Ability Test (63, 64)

Objective: To measure general motor ability in order to determine the individual needs of students and to assist in the sectioning of classes.

Age and Sex: College women and high school girls.

Validity: Two test batteries were devised

Table 19-7
Validity and Reliability Data
for Scott Motor Ability Test Items (63, 65)

Test Item	Validity	Reliability
1. Basketball Throw	.79 when correlated with the McCloy general motor ability test, total points scored from running, throwing, and jumping, and .78 with composite criterion of total points, other sport items, and subjective ratings.	An *r* of .89 on successive trials with 200 University of Iowa women.
2. Dash	Utilizing the same criteria as the basketball throw, *r*'s of .71 and .62 were obtained, respectively.	.62 with 88 University of Iowa women.
3. Wall Pass	Using the same criteria as above, coefficients of .47 and .54 were found, respectively.	.62 with 188 college women, .75 for 185 high school girls.
4. Broad Jump	Using same criteria as above, the coefficients were .79 and .78, respectively.	.79 for 252 college women, .92 for 144 high school girls.
5. Obstacle Race	When correlated with the longer, but similar test, an *r* of .94 was found. The older test used the same criteria as described above, and the coefficients were .65 and .58, respectively.	.91 when taken on two successive days.

through the use of subjective ratings of sports ability, skill items common to sports, the McCloy general motor ability test items for girls, and a composite score made up of the above criteria.

Validity was established for each test battery. The criterion that was used was a composite score comprised of ratings by experts, T-scores from a variety of sport skills, and an achievement score composed of three fundamental activities. Validity coefficients of .91 and .87 were found for Battery 1 and Battery 2, respectively. (See Table 19-7 for validity coefficients for each test item.)

Reliability: The reliability coefficients for individual test items ranged from .62 to .91. (See Table 19-7 for reliability coefficients for each test item.)

Test Battery 1 is made up of the following test items: the basketball throw, dash, wall pass, and broad jump.

Test Battery 2 has three items: basketball throw, broad jump, and obstacle race. This battery is much easier to administer and may be preferable because of this factor. It differs very little from the larger battery in validity. Scott has found it to be accurate in predicting rate of achievement in physical education skills, and it has been used effectively for screening purposes in locating individuals needing special help in motor ability development.

Equipment and Materials: (a) *Basketball Throw:* three or four regulation basketballs, (although one could suffice), measuring tape. Chalk or tape is desirable to mark off the floor. (b) *Dash:* stopwatch and whistle. Tape or chalk or other marking materials are also needed. (c) *Wall pass:* regulation basketball, stopwatch, and unobstructed wall space. (d) *Broad jump:* gymnasium mat, measuring tape (or mat marked in inches), beat board (or 2-foot solid board). (e) *Obstacle race:* stopwatch, jump standard, a 6-foot crossbar and supports, and chalk or tape for marking.

Basketball Throw

Directions: This test is intended to measure arm and shoulder girdle strength and coordination. The subject attempts to throw the basketball as far as she can without stepping on or across the restraining line. The student has three trials. The directions emphasize that no demonstration should be given. Any technique of throwing is allowed, but the teacher is not to specify any particular one.

Scoring: The distance from the restraining line

to the spot where the ball lands is measured to the nearest foot. The best of the three trials is used as the score for this event.

Safety: There are no particular hazards connected with this test. Sufficient warm-up should be provided, and the throwing area should be kept clear of traffic. On each trial, the student should not be allowed to throw until the marker and scorer are ready.

Additional Pointers: The students can be utilized to help with the testing as they proceed from one station to another. One student should be utilized as a spotter to work the landing point while another is utilized to watch for fouls at the throwing line.

Dash

Directions: On the command to go the student starts running down the lane as fast as possible until the whistle blows. The student does not have to stop on the whistle, but simply slows down and stops at her own pace. The student should be told that the running time will be 4 seconds, and only one trial is given. The student stands behind the starting line in any position she wishes.

Scoring: The running course is marked and numbered in 1-yard zones. The zone in which the student was at the sound of the whistle is quickly marked by an assistant. The distance in yards is then noted and recorded as the score for this event.

Safety: There are several factors that should be considered with regard to safety. Pulled muscles and other injuries can easily occur without adequate warm-up. Another precaution the teacher must take is to provide ample space at the end of the course to accommodate a gradual stop. Without sufficient space it is not only a safety hazard, but it will affect the validity of the test as well if the performer starts to slow down prior to the whistle.

Adequate footwear is another factor that should be insisted upon by the teacher in the interests of safety (and again validity). Of course, all obstructions must be removed from the running lane. The width of the lane itself should be at least 4 feet, and additional space along the sides of the lane should be kept clear.

Additional Pointers: (a) The first 10 yards need not be marked off in 1-yard intervals. The numbers can either be painted (or chalked) on the floor, or cards can be prepared and placed along the side of the running lane. The latter is preferable since it has to be done only once and the cards can then be used again. (b) More than one student can be tested at the same time if provisions are made for judges. If this procedure is followed, the judges must be impressed with the importance of keeping their eyes on their assigned runners. The judges must guard against the tendency to watch to see who is ahead. At the sound of the whistle each judge should run out and stand on the spot at which her assigned runner was when the whistle sounded. (c) The tester must be careful not to glance up at at the runner(s) and thereby let the watch run past the 4 seconds.

Wall Pass. (Same as wall pass test previously presented in the Barrow Motor Ability Test.)

Broad Jump. (Same as for the standing broad jump test previously presented in Chapter 12.)

Obstacle Race

Directions: This test was modified from the earlier form (64). It was designed to measure speed, agility, and general body coordination. The student starts in a back-lying position on the floor with her heels at the starting line. When given the command to go, the student scrambles to her feet and runs to the first square that is marked on the floor (see Figure 17-2). She must step on this square, and on each of the next two squares, with both feet. She then runs twice around the jump standard and proceeds to the crossbar, gets up and runs to the end line, touches it with her hand, runs back to line F, touches it, runs and touches the end line, runs back to line F, then sprints across the end line. One trial is given.

Scoring: The stopwatch is started when the signal to go is given and stopped when the student sprints across the end line. The score is the number of seconds, to the nearest tenth of a second, that is required to complete the course.

Safety: As is true in all speed and agility tests, the subject's footwear is an important consideration. Another possible source of injury is the part of the test in which the student must crawl or roll under the crossbar. This sometimes results in a scraped knee, and the teacher might consider the use of knee guards for this test. The crossbar itself should be made of very light material so as not to pose any danger when it is knocked down. The teacher should keep onlookers well away from the course boundaries, and particularly away from the finishing area. Adequate warm-up should be provided.

Additional Pointers: (a) It is suggested that all the class be given the directions at the same time in order to avoid needless repetition. (b) The teacher should walk through the test and make sure the students understand what is meant by stepping with both feet in the squares. It is not necessary to call the student back if the toe or heel is not completely inside the square. (c) It should not be considered a foul if the subject happens to bump and dislodge the crossbar as she passes under it. (d) The student cannot grasp the jump standard as she runs around it. (e) The teacher should emphasize the method of circling the jump standard and also stress the number of times the student must touch behind the end line and line F, as this procedure can result in some confusion if not thoroughly understood. (f) It is suggested that two timers and watches could be utilized to reduce the testing time. In this arrangement, the second girl is started when

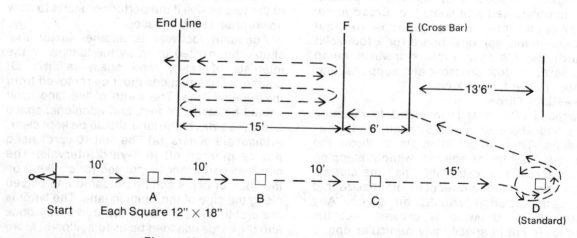

Figure 19-2. Obstacle Race for Scott Motor Ability Test

Table 19-8
T-Scales for High School Girls
on Scott Motor Ability Test

T-Score	Wall Pass (410)*	Basketball Throw (Ft.) (310)*	Broad Jump (In.) (287)*	4-Sec. Dash (Yd.) (398)*	Obstacle Race (Sec.) (374)*	T-Score
80	16	71				80
79			96			79
78						78
77	15	68	94	27		77
76		66			18.5-18.9	76
75		65				75
74		64	92			74
73	14	63				73
72		61				72
71		59	90	26		71
70		55	88		19.0-19.4	70
69	13	54				69
68		52	86	25		68
67		51			19.5-19.9	67
66		50				66
65		49				65
64		48	84	24	20.0-20.4	64
63	12	47				63
62		46	82		20.5-20.9	62
61			80			61
60		45		23		60
59		44	78		21.0-21.4	59
58	11	43				58
57		42	76		21.5-21.9	57
56		41				56
55		40	74	22		55
54					22.0-22.4	54
53		39				53
52	10		72			52
51		37			22.5-22.9	51
50		36		21		50

*Indicates the number of subjects on which the scale is based.

Table 19-8 (continued)

T-Score	Wall Pass (410)*	Basketball Throw (Ft.) (310)*	Broad Jump (In.) (287)*	4-Sec. Dash (Yd.) (398)*	Obstacle Race (Sec.) (374)*	T-Score
49		35	70			49
48			68		23.0-23.4	48
47		34	66			47
46	9	33			23.5-23.9	46
45		32	64	20		45
44		31			24.0-24.4	44
43			62			43
42		30			24.5-24.9	42
41	8	29	60	19		41
40		28				40
39			58		25.0-25.4	39
38		27	56			38
37	7		54		25.5-25.9	37
36		26			26.0-26.4	36
35			52	18	26.5-26.9	35
34		25	50		27.0-27.4	34
33						33
32		24	47		27.5-27.9	32
31	6	23				31
30			44		28.0-28.4	30
29		22		17	28.5-28.9	29
28					29.0-29.4	28
27		21			29.5-29.9	27
26			40		30.0-30.4	26
25	5	20				25
24				16	30.5-31.4	24
23		19	36		31.5-32.4	23
22				15	32.5-34.9	22
21		16				21
20	4			14	35.0-36.0	20

*Indicates the number of subjects on which the scale is based.

Table 19-9
T-Scales for College Women on
Scott Motor Ability Test

T-Score	Basketball Throw	Passes	Broad Jump	Obstacle Race	T-Score
85	75	18	86	17.5-17.9	85
84					84
83	71	17		18.0-18.4	83
82					82
81		16	85		81
80	70	15			80
79	69			18.5-18.9	79
78	68	14	84		78
77	67		83		77
76	66				76
75	65		82	19.0-19.4	75
74	64		81		74
73	62		80		73
72	61	13	79	19.5-19.9	72
71	59				71
70	58		78	20.0-20.4	70
69	57		77		69
68	56		76		68
67	55		75	20.5-20.9	67
66	54	12	74		66
65	52				65
64	51		73	21.0-21.4	64
63	50		72		63
62	48		71	21.5-21.9	62
61	47				61
60	46		70		60
59	45	11	69	22.0-22.4	59
58	44		68		58
57	43		67	22.5-22.9	57
56	42				56
55	41		66	23.0-23.4	55
54	40		65		54
53	39		64	23.5-23.9	53
52	38	10	63		52
51	37			24.0-24.4	51
50	36		62		50
49	35		61	24.5-24.9	49
48			60		48
47	34		59	25.0-25.4	47
46	33		58		46

Table 19-9 (continued)

T-Score	Basketball Throw	Passes	Broad Jump	Obstacle Race	T-Score
45	32	9	57	25.5-25.9	45
44	31				44
43			56	26.0-26.4	43
42	30		55		42
41			54	26.5-26.9	41
40	29		53	27.0-27.4	40
39	28	8	52		39
38				27.5-27.9	38
37	27		51	28.0-28.4	37
36	26		50		36
35			49	28.5-28.9	35
34	25		48	29.0-29.4	34
33			47	29.5-29.9	33
32		7	46	30.0-30.4	32
31			45	30.5-30.9	31
30	24		44	31.0-31.4	30
29			43	31.5-31.9	29
28	23		42	32.0-32.4	28
27	21		41	32.5-32.9	27
26		6	40	33.0-33.4	26
25	20		39	33.5-33.9	25
24			38	34.0-34.4	24
23		5	37	34.5-34.9	23
22			36		22
21	19			35.0-35.4	21
20					20
19			35	35.5-35.9	19
18					18
17	18	4			17
16					16
15					15
14				43.5-43.9	14
13			30	45.5-45.9	13

the first girl finishes circling the jump standard. *Norms:* T-scales are available for each test item and for the composite scores (GMAS) for each test battery for high school girls and college women. These norms are presented in Tables 19-8 and 19-9.

Two methods are suggested for computing the composite score. One method is to obtain an average T-score by adding the T-score values for the three or four tests given and dividing this sum by the appropriate number. For example, on Test Battery 1, a high school girl has the following T-scores: forty-five for the basketball throw, fifty-five for the dash, fifty-two for the wall pass, and forty-eight for the broad jump. The mean of these T-scores is thus fifty, which indicates that the student's overall performance on this test battery was exactly average.

Another method is to utilize the regression equation for the appropriate test battery, as follows:

Test Battery 1 (four items) .7 (basketball throw) + 2.0 (dash) + 1.0 (wall pass) + .5 (broad jump)

Test Battery 2 (three items) 2.0 (basketball throw) + 1.4 (broad jump) − (obstacle race)

To illustrate, a college girl has the following raw scores on the three-item test battery:

Basketball throw	47 feet
Broad jump	72 inches
Obstacle race	20.6 seconds

The raw scores are multiplied by their proper weightings and the products are added as follows:

$$2.0(47) + 1.4(72) - 20.6 = 174.2$$

This value is then found to represent a T-score of sixty-three, which indicates that this girl is considerably above average in motor ability.

Latchaw Motor Achievement Tests for Fourth, Fifth, and Sixth Grade Boys and Girls (44,45)

Objective: To measure general motor achievement.

Age and Sex: Fourth, fifth, and sixth grade girls and boys.

Validity: Face validity was accepted for each test.

Reliability: The reliability coefficients for the individual test items ranged from .77 to .97. Students from twenty elementary schools in two states were tested.

Equipment and Materials: The special equipment and the space needed for each of the test items are: (a) *Basketball wall pass:* stopwatch, regulation basketball, tape or marking equipment, and wall space to accommodate a target that is 8 feet long, 4 feet high, and drawn 3 feet from the floor. Restraining line is 8 feet long and 4 feet from wall. (See Figure 19-3.) (b) *Volleyball wall volley:* stopwatch, regulation volleyball, and a target identical to basketball wall pass test (Figure 19-3). (c) *Vertical jump:* forty-eight 1-inch cloth strips, cut so that, when suspended from a horizontal bar, the longest strip is 5 feet from the floor and each succeeding one is 1 inch shorter, with the shortest strip being 8 feet 11 inches from the floor. Forty-eight pennies are needed so that the bottom of each strip is weighted to provide even hanging. (d) *Standing broad jump:* a mat and measuring tape unless mat is marked in inches. (e) *Shuttle run:* stopwatch, floor markings, as follows: two ½-inch lines parallel to each other and 20 feet apart. The lines are at least 20 feet long. The test requires space to permit the 20-foot shuttle run as well as an equal distance to allow for slowing down after crossing the finish line. (f) *Soccer wall volley:* stopwatch, regulation soccer ball, marking material, and wall and floor space to accommodate a wall target 4 by 2½ feet and a 4-by-2½-foot floor area. (See Figure 19-4.) (g) *Softball repeated throws:* stopwatch, regulation softball (12-inch inseam), marking material, and wall and floor space to accommodate a wall target 10 feet high and 5½ feet wide, with the bottom of the target 6 inches above the floor. A 5½-foot square is marked as the throwing area, 9 feet from the wall. A backstop 15 feet behind throwing area should be 12 feet long and at least 2½ feet high (Figure 19-5).

Basketball Wall Pass

Reliability:

Boys, Grade four = .91
Grade five = .84
Grade six = .78

Girls, Grade four = .94
Grade five = .89
Grade six = .83

Directions: The student must stand behind the restraining line, which is 4 feet from the wall. When the teacher gives the signal to begin, the student throws the ball against the wall inside the target as many times as possible in 15 seconds. The ball must be thrown from behind the restraining line in order to count, and it must hit completely inside the target. Balls which touch the line do not count. The student does not have to catch the ball first in order for it to be a successful hit. In other words, he could catch it in the air, catch it on the bounce, or have to run to retrieve it before he throws. If he loses control of the ball, he must recover it

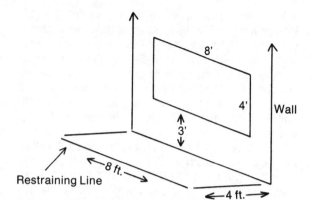

Figure 19-3. Wall and Floor Markings for Basketball Wall Pass and Volleyball Wall Volley Tests.

himself. A 10-second practice period is allowed, then two 15-second trials are given.

Scoring: The score is the number of correct hits in the 15-second period. The best of the two trials is recorded as the score.

Safety: There are no particular safety hazards connected with this test. The area should be kept free from traffic and obstacles which might be in the way of a subject who loses control of the ball.

Additional Pointers: (a) Make sure that the subject understands that he must hit inside the target area and that he must throw from behind the line. (b) It should also be stressed that he doesn't have to catch the ball in the air on the rebound and that, if he loses it, he must retrieve it as quickly as possible, since the time keeps running. (c) It makes for much easier testing if the person keeping the time does not have to simultaneously count hits and watch for faults.

Volleyball Wall Volley

Reliability:

Boys, Grade four =.85
Grade five =.89
Grade six =.91

Girls, Grade four =.88
Grade five =.92
Grade six =.93

Directions: On the signal to begin, the subject throws the ball (from behind the restraining line) against the wall. He then must hit it as it bounces off the wall so that it hits inside the target. He must hit from behind the restraining line, and, if the ball gets away, he must recover it. Any time that he must start again, he may throw the ball against the wall and then continue to hit it. Balls that are thrown or *carried* are not counted, nor are balls which hit the lines of the target. One 10-second practice test is given, then the subject has four 15-second trials.

Scoring: The best of the four trials is counted, with the score being the number of legal hits inside the target.

Safety: Same as in basketball wall pass.

Additional Pointers: (a) The teacher should be sure to explain the difference between a hit and a throw or *carry.* (b) Other procedures are the same as the basketball wall pass.

Vertical Jump. (Same as for vertical jump presented in Chapter 12, except cloth strips are used and unlimited trials are allowed.)

Standing Broad Jump. (Same as for the standing broad jump test previously presented in Chapter 12.)

Shuttle Run

Reliability:

Boys, Grade four =.89
Grade five =.89
Grade six =.89

Girls, Grade four =.84
Grade five =.85
Grade six =.79

Directions: The student stands behind the starting line with one foot against the line. On the command to go, he runs to the other line and places at least one foot on the line. He then returns to the other side, touches that line with at least one foot, returns, and so on back and forth until three round trips have been completed. He thus finishes by crossing the same line at which he started. The student is stopped if at any time he does not at least touch one of the lines. He may step beyond a line, of course. If he is stopped, he is given no score for the trial and, after a short rest, is tested again. If he fails again to follow directions, he is given a score of zero for that trial. Two trials are given in this test.

Scoring: The better of two trials is taken as the score for this test, measured in seconds to the nearest tenth of a second.

Safety: All subjects should be required to wear suitable shoes to prevent injury to their feet. Warm-up is recommended, and the area should be kept clear beyond both lines and especially at the finish line.

Additional Pointers: (a) Spotters at both ends could be assigned to watch for foot faults;

Table 19-10
Latchaw Achievement Scales for Fifth-Grade Boys

T-Scores	Basketball Wall Pass	Volleyball Wall Volley	Vertical Jump	Standing Broad Jump	Shuttle Run	Soccer Wall Volley	Softball Repeated Throws	Percentile
	27							
75	26		17"	6'3"	11.2	16		99
70	22	20	16	6-2	11.4	15	14	97
	21	19		6-0	11.5	14	13	
65	20	17	15	5-8	11.8	13	12	92
						12		
60	19	14	14	5-3	12.2	11	11	81
	18	13						
		11	13					
55	17	10		5-0	12.5		10	69
		8						
50	16		12	4-9	12.8	10	9	50
45	15	7	11	4-5	13.3	9	8	30
	14	6						
	13	5						
40	12	4	10	4-0	13.7	8	7	15
	11							
35			9	3-9	14.0	7		6
	10		8					
30	9	3	7	3-8	14.8		6	2
	8				15.1			
25	6	2		3-7	15.9	5	5	1

Modified for economy of space. By permission of author and M. Gladys Scott and Esther French, *Measurement and Evaluation in Physical Education*, Dubuque, Iowa: Wm. C. Brown Company, 1959.

Table 19-11
Latchaw Achievement Scales for Fifth-Grade Girls

T-Scores	Basketball Wall Pass	Volleyball Wall Volley	Vertical Jump	Standing Broad Jump	Shuttle Run	Soccer Wall Volley	Softball Repeated Throws	Percentile
75		18	16	5'8"	11.6	15	10	99
70	20	17, 13	15	5-7	11.8	14, 13	9	97
65	19	12, 11	14	5-4	12.2	12, 11		92
60	18, 17, 16, 15	9, 8	13, 12	4-10	12.5	10		81
55		7		4-5	13.0	9	8	69
50	14	6, 5	11, 10	4-1	13.4, 13.5	8	7	50
45	13	4		3-10	13.7	7		30
40	12, 11, 10, 9	3	9, 8	3-8, 3-7	14.0, 14.1	6	6	15
35	8, 7	2	7	3-3	14.4, 14.5	5	5	6
30	6	1		2-11	15.1	4	4	2
25			6	2-8	15.9, 16.0		3	1

Modified for economy of space. By permission of author and M. Gladys Scott and Esther French, *Measurement and Evaluation in Physical Education*. Dubuque, Iowa: Wm. C. Brown Company, 1959.

however, the tester can usually do the timing, watching, and recording quite easily by himself in such a small area. (b) When the student sprints across the end line at the finish of the race, the timer should be parallel to that line in order to get the most accurate score. (c) If subjects are tested in pairs, the factor of fatigue can be well handled by testing student A, then B, then A again, and finally B. Short rest periods between the two trials are thus provided without any lag in the testing. (d) If a large number of students are to be tested, chalk is unsuitable for marking the lines, as it rubs off. White washable tempera paint is recommended.

Soccer Wall Volley

Reliability:

Boys, Grade four = .82
Grade five = .89
Grade six = .88

Girls, Grade four = .77
Grade five = .83
Grade six = .77

Directions: The subject stands behind the restraining line, which is an extension of 1 foot on either side of the 4-foot line on the floor area farthest from the wall. He places the ball at any place he chooses behind the line. When the teacher gives the signal to begin, the subject kicks the ball toward the wall in an attempt to hit inside the target. When the ball rebounds from the wall, the student attempts to kick it again inside the target. If the ball gets away from the student, he must recover it and bring it back into position to kick again. When the student is attempting to retrieve a ball that is within the 4-by-2½-foot floor area between the restraining line and the wall, he may not use his hands. However, if he must recover a loose ball outside that area, he is allowed to use his hands. To be counted, all kicks must be made from behind the restraining line, and the ball must be completely within the target area without touching any line. A practice period of 15 seconds is allowed, then four 15-second trials are given.

Scoring: The number of legal kicks is a 15-second trial is counted, and the best of the four trials is used as the score. A penalty of one point is deducted for each time a subject touches the ball with his hands while in the rectangular floor area.

Safety: All subjects should wear shoes, and the area should be kept unobstructed.

Additional Pointers: (a) While a kick made from

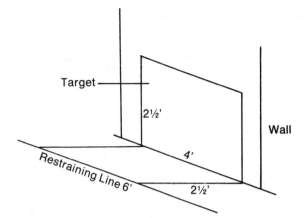

Figure 19-4. Wall and Floor Markings for Soccer Wall Volley Test

within the 6-by-2½-foot floor area is not counted as a legal score, the student may certainly kick a ball from within this area and then kick the ball on the rebound from behind the restraining line. In this way the student can recover the ball quickly and not use his hands. This point should be stressed. (b) The suggestions that were mentioned for the basketball wall pass and volleyball wall volley also apply for this item. In all three events the teacher may wish to regulate the degree of ball control loss. For example, if there is a large open area behind the subject, the student could not hope to recover a loose ball and return before the trial was over. Therefore, the teacher may wish to standardize it by having the students who are waiting to be tested stand in a line at a prescribed distance in back of the restraining line. Then, if the student loses control, the line of students could allow the ball to hit them and be kept from rolling far, but they must not do anything to help or hinder the performer.

Softball Repeated Throws

Reliability:

Boys, Grade four = .82
Grade five = .81
Grade six = .85

Girls, Grade four = .80
Grade five = .82
Grade six = .85

Directions: The student may stand anywhere within the 5½-foot square throwing area. On the command to go he throws the ball at the target with an overhand throwing motion. He attempts

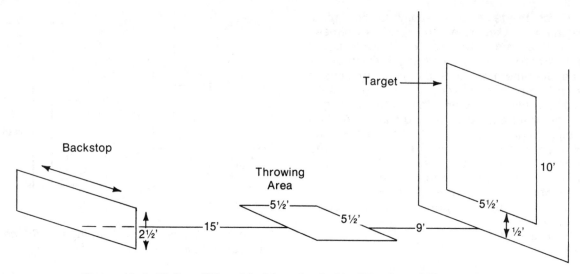

Figure 19-5. Wall and Floor Markings for Softball Repeated Throws Test

to catch the ball as it rebounds in the air or on the bounce, so that he may throw it again as many times as possible in 15 seconds. Each ball must be thrown from within the throwing area in order to be legal, and the ball must strike the wall completely within the target boundaries. Balls that hit the target lines do not count. If the student loses control of the ball, he must retrieve it as quickly as possible, rush back to the throwing area, and continue throwing. A practice period of 10 seconds is provided, and then two 15-second trials are given.

Scoring: The better score of the two 15-second trials is recorded. The score is the number of correct throws in the 15-second period.

Safety: All persons should be kept well away from the target area. The entire testing area from the wall to the backstop and with ample lateral distance should be kept free of obstructions and people.

Additional Pointers: (a) The backstop may be a rolled mat, an ordinary table turned on its side, or an actual wall. (b) A wall volley test with a softball quickly softens and alters the shape of the ball. This, of course, can influence subsequent performance, and it should be considered when administering the test. The tester may wish to bring out new balls periodically or rotate them in some manner. At any rate it can be expensive, but with children of this age it is not nearly as serious a problem as with older students.

Norms: Norms are available in the form of T-scores and percentile scores for each of the seven tests. The T-scales provide for separate norms for boys and girls at the fifth grade level. These norms are presented in Tables 19-10 and 19-11.

AAHPER Youth Fitness Test (1)

Since this test battery cuts across both fitness and motor performance components, we will mention only the motor performance test items.

Shuttle Run. See Chapter 13 (Agility).

Fifty-Yard Dash. See Chapter 15 (Speed and Reaction Time).

Standing Broad Jump. See Chapter 12 (Power).

For the AAHPER test items that your authors consider to be fitness components, see Chapter 11.

Johnson Indoor Motor Performance Test

Objective: To provide a screening test in motor performance for students pursuing a degree in physical education. Hopefully, students who are not highly skilled or active in selected sports but who desire to major in physical education can demonstrate an average or higher level of ability and, thus, show competency in this area of physical performance.

Age and Sex: Intended for college-age students (male and female). The test can also be used for purposes of classification, guidance, and achievement with other school levels when satisfactory norms are established at each respective level.

Validity: The intent of the test constructor was to include items of static balance, hand-eye coordination, agility, power, and speed/reaction time. Tests designed to measure these components were accepted on face validity. Moreover, this battery includes a wider variety of general motor performance components than previously published test batteries.

Reliability: All items were found to have satisfactory reliability when the best of three trials for each test was correlated from two separate days of testing.

Objectivity: All items were found to be satisfactory in objectivity when two different testers scored the same group of students.

Equipment and Materials: See each individual test item.

Inverted Balance Test for Static Balance (Short Form)

Directions: The student selects one of the five balances presented in Chapter 14 and attempts to hold the balance for a maximum of 5 seconds. Each balance has its own difficulty value, which is multiplied times the number of seconds held (up to 5 seconds) for the score. The balances and values are as follows:

Tripod balance .... 1 point per second
Tip-up balance .... 2 points per second
Headstand .... 3 points per second
Head and forearm .... 4 points per second
Handstand .... 5 points per second

Thus, if a student selects the headstand and holds it for 4 seconds, the score would be $3 \times 4 = 12$ points. However, a score of 15 points is considered the minimal accepted standard for men and women majors.

Softball Overhand Throw for Accuracy (Hand-eye Coordination)

Directions: Men throw at a target from a 65-foot line while women throw from a 40-foot line. Each student is allowed two practice throws prior to ten trials. The target is of the same dimensions as the AAHPER softball overhand throw for accuracy in Chapter 16. Scoring is as follows:

Center circle—3 points
Second circle—2 points
Outer circle—1 point

Balls hitting a line are given the higher value. A score of 13 points is the minimal accepted level for men while a score of 16 points is required for women.

Basketball Dribble Test (Agility)

Directions: This test is the same as the AAHPER dribble test in Chapter 16. A score of 11.7 sec-

onds is required for men majors and 14.0 seconds for women majors. The equipment and materials required include eight chairs and a stopwatch.

Standing Broad Jump (Athletic Power)

Directions: Same as for the standing broad jump test in Chapter 12. Men must jump 7 feet 3 inches or better while women must jump 5 feet 4 inches or better to meet minimal standards.

Four-Second Dash (Speed and Reaction Time)

Directions: Each performer starts behind the starting line and on the signal "go" races as far down a field-marking tape as possible. For indoor testing, it is best to race from one gym corner toward another to give maximum space for running. A spotter judges the distance covered by the performer upon the timer's signal to stop at 4 seconds. This test is the same as that described in the Scott Motor Ability Test presented earlier in this chapter.

Scoring: See Table 19-12 for accumulating scores for a grand total.

JCR Test (56)

Objective: The JCR Test is a three-item test battery designed to measure ability to perform fundamental motor skills such as jumping, climbing, running, and dodging. The test is intended to assess total ability rather than the basic elements which make up total ability.

Sex and Age Level: College men. Could be also used for high school. Test was developed using men from the U.S. Air Force.

Reliability and Validity: Reliability coefficients of .91 and .94 were obtained for the total battery using different groups. Individual item reliability coefficients ranged from .80 to .95. Validity was established using a twenty-five-variable criterion in which an *r* of .81 was obtained. An *r* of .90 was found for the test with a nineteen-item criterion of physical fitness.

Test Equipment Materials Needed: A vertical jump board or wall surface, chalk for the fingers, chinning bar, stopwatch, and bankboards for the shuttle run are needed to administer this test. The bankboards are about 12 inches wide and set at an angle of 40 degrees with the floor. The bankboards are 10 yards apart with each lane measuring 6 feet in width. Exact instructions are given in the original reference.

Vertical Jump

Directions: The jump is performed in the typical manner. Three trials are given. The best of three trials is used for scoring.

Table 19-12

Raw Score Norms for Johnson Indoor Motor Performance Test

Men

Inverted Balance Test—Short Form	Throw for Accuracy Overhand	Dribble Test	Standing Broad Jump	Four-Second Dash
25 = Excellent	20 - Above = Excellent	9.4 - Less = Excellent	8'4 - Above = Excellent	93 - Higher = Excellent
20 = Good	17 - 19 = Good	10.5 - 9.5 = Good	7'9 - 8'3 = Good	88 - 92 = Good
15 = Average	12 - 16 = Average	12.6 - 10.6 = Average	6'11 - 7'8 = Average	82 - 87 = Average
10 = Poor	7 - 11 = Poor	14.2 - 12.7 = Poor	6'1 - 6'10 = Poor	70 - 81 = Poor
5 = Very Poor	0 - 6 = Very Poor	Above - 14.3 = Very Poor	0 - 6'0 = Very Poor	0 - 69 = Very Poor
Scores in rating points. Source: See Chapter 14 of this text, p. 231.	Scores in points from 65 feet. From males at Corpus Christi State University, 1976. Source: AAHPER Sports Skills Project, 1966.	Scores in seconds. Source: AAHPER Sports Skills Project, 1966.	Scores in feet and inches. Source: AAHPER Youth Fitness Test, 1966.	Scores in feet. From males at Corpus Christi State University, 1976. Source: Scott Motor Ability Test.

Overall Rating

28 - 25 = Excellent
18 - 22 = Good
13 - 17 = Average
8 - 12 = Poor
0 - 7 = Very Poor

Directions for Score

Each Excellent = 5 pts.
Each Good = 4
Each Average = 3
Each Poor = 2
Each Very Poor = 1

Example: Jane Doe

Inverted Balance - Excellent =	5 pts.
Throw for Accuracy - Average =	3 pts.
Dribble Test - Good =	2 pts.
Standing Broad Jump - Good =	4 pts.
4-Second Dash - Average =	3 pts.
Total	17 pts.

Women

Inverted Balance Test—Short Form	Throw for Accuracy Overhand	Dribble Test	Standing Broad Jump	Four-Second Dash
25 = Excellent	23 - Above = Excellent	11.6 - Less = Excellent	6'5 - Above = Excellent	76 - Higher = Excellent
20 = Good	21 - 22 = Good	12.7 - 11.7 = Good	5'10 - 6'4 = Good	72 - 75 = Good
15 = Average	14 - 20 = Average	15.0 - 12.8 = Average	4'11 - 5'9 = Average	65 - 71 = Average
10 = Poor	9 - 13 = Poor	17.0 - 15.1 = Poor	4'4 - 4'10 = Poor	59 - 64 = Poor
5 = Very Poor	0 - 8 = Very Poor	Above - 17.1 = Very Poor	0 - 4'3 = Very Poor	0 - 58 = Very Poor
Scores in rating points. Source: See Chapter 14 of this text, p. 231.	Scores in points from 40 feet. From females at Corpus Christi State University, 1976. Source: AAHPER Sports Skills Project, 1966.	Scores in seconds. Source: AAHPER Sports Skills Project, 1966.	Scores in feet and inches. Source: AAHPER Youth Fitness Test, 1966.	Scores in feet. From females at Corpus Christi State University, 1976. Source: Scott Motor Ability Test.

Chinning

Directions: The usual directions for chinning should be followed. Half chins are not counted.

Shuttle Run

Directions: The subject's starting position is standing inside the starting line with one foot in contact with the bankboard. On the signal to begin he runs as fast as he can to the opposite bankboard, touches it, and runs back to the starting bankboard. He should spring from the bankboards and not bounce off them. Five complete round trips are made for a total distance of 100 yards. He thus finishes at the same line from which he started, stepping over the board at the finish.

Scoring: The elapsed time to the nearest half second is recorded as the score for this event.

Additional Pointers: (a) Several lanes can be constructed to facilitate group testing. Several students can be tested with only one watch as follows: the tester begins counting aloud in half seconds ("20-hup, 21-hup, 22-hup," etc.) as the first runner nears the finish line and continues counting until the last runner has finished.

Students or assistants are assigned a subject to watch and listen for his time as he crosses the finish line. (b) The tester should practice counting this way silently for a few seconds before he counts aloud in order to establish the proper rhythm. (c) The subject must touch the bankboard each time. If he does not, he should be stopped and given a brief rest, then retested. (d) The subjects should be given a short practice period in which to become accustomed to the bankboard turns. (e) The subjects should be told the number of laps they have completed as they are running and be given additional instructions, such as "two more to go," etc.

Safety Precautions: (a) The floor surface should be smooth and free from obstructions. (b) The bankboards should be well braced to prevent movement or collapse. (c) The subjects should be given ample warm-up. (d) It must be stressed that each runner stay within his running lane.

Norms are provided in Table 19-13. Phillips suggested that each tester construct his own norms.

Table 19-13
The JCR Test

JCR Test Scoring Tables

Jump	Chin	Run	JCR Sum*	Score	Rating	Jump	Chin	Run	JCR Sum*	Score	Rating
28	18	19	246	100		––	––	––	221	85	
––	––	––	243	99		––	––	20.5	219	84	
––	––	––	242	98		––	––	––	218	83	
27	17	––	240	97	E	––	13	––	216	82	E
––	––	19.5	239	96	X	––	––	––	213	81	X
––	––	––	237	95	C	24	––	––	212	80	C
––	16	––	236	94	E	––	––	––	210	79	E
––	––	––	234	93	L	––	12	21	209	78	L
26	––	––	233	92	L	––	––	––	207	77	L
––	––	––	231	91	E	––	––	––	206	76	E
––	15	20	228	90	N	––	––	––	204	75	N
––	––	––	227	89	T	23	11	––	203	74	T
––	––	––	225	88		––	––	––	201	73	
––	––	––	224	87		––	––	21.5	198	72	
25	14	––	222	86		––	––	––	197	71	

*Sum of scores for jump, chin, and run.

Table 19-13 (continued)

JCR Test Scoring Tables

Jump	Chin	Run	JCR Sum*	Score	Rating	Jump	Chin	Run	JCR Sum*	Score	Rating
—	10	—	195	70		—	—	—	111	34	P
—	—	—	194	69		—	3	25	109	33	O
22	—	—	192	68		16	—	—	108	32	O
—	—	—	191	67		—	—	—	107	31	R
—	—	22	189	66	G	—	—	—	105	30	
—	9	—	188	65	O						
—	—	—	186	64	O	—	—	—	103	29	
—	—	—	183	63	D	—	—	25.5	102	28	
21	—	—	180	62		—	2	—	99	27	
—	—	—	177	61		15	—	—	97	26	
—	8	22.5	174	60		—	—	—	96	25	
—	—	—	171	59		—	—	26	94	24	
—	—	—	168	58		—	—	—	93	23	
—	—	—	167	57		—	—	—	91	22	
20	—	—	165	56		—	1	—	90	21	
—	7	—	164	55		14	—	26.5	88	20	
—	—	23	162	54		—	—	—	87	19	V
—	—	—	159	53	A	—	—	—	84	18	E
—	—	—	156	52	V	—	—	—	82	17	R
—	—	—	153	51	E	—	—	27	81	16	Y
19	6	—	150	50	R	—	—	—	79	15	
—	—	—	147	49	A	13	—	—	78	14	P
—	—	23.5	144	48	G	—	0	—	76	13	O
—	—	—	141	47	E	—	—	27.5	75	12	O
—	—	—	138	46		—	—	—	73	11	R
—	5	—	136	45		—	—	—	72	10	
18	—	—	135	44		—	—	—	69	9	
—	—	24	133	43		12	—	28	67	8	
—	—	—	132	42		—	—	—	66	7	
—	—	—	129	41		—	—	—	64	6	
—	—	—	126	40		—	—	—	63	5	
—	4	—	123	39	P	—	—	28.5	61	4	
17	—	24.5	120	38	O	11	—	—	60	3	
—	—	—	117	37	O	—	—	—	58	2	
—	—	—	114	36	R	—	—	29	57	1	
—	—	—	112	35		10	—	29.5	54	0	

*Sum of scores for jump, chin, and run.

Division of Girls' and Women's Athletics (DGWS) Physical Performance Test (51)

Objective: The Research Committee of the National Section on Women's Athletics (NSWA), now the Division of Girls' and Women's Sports (DGWS), selected eight tests for the purpose of assessing muscular control and coordination, speed and agility, and strength.

Sex and Age Level: High school girls.

Validity: The items were selected by the Research Committee on an empirical basis. Therefore, the items are assumed to have face validity. Some of the items were chosen to evaluate general motor ability, such as the standing broad jump, the basketball throw, and the potato race. Agility measures include the 10-second squat thrust as well as the potato race. The strength of the arm and shoulders is represented by performance in the pull-ups or push-ups, and the abdominal muscle strength is measured by sit-ups. Endurance is assessed by the 30-second squat thrust. No reliability figures were given; however, the test items were administered to over 20,000 girls, and scoring scales were constructed based on data gathered from the twenty-five schools showing the best performances.

Test Items: The eight items are as follows: standing broad jump, basketball throw, potato race, pull-ups, push-ups, sit-ups, 10-second squat thrust, and 30-second squat thrust. The committee recommends that, if it is not feasible to administer all eight of the tests, the battery may be shortened to the following:

> Standing broad jump
> Basketball throw
> Potato race *or* 10-second squat thrust
> Sit-ups
> Push-ups *or* pull-ups

Standing Broad Jump

Directions: Performed in the usual manner, scored in feet and inches.

Basketball Throw

Directions: The floor should be marked off in 5-foot intervals to facilitate scoring. The subject stands behind the restraining, or zero line, and throws a regulation basketball as far as possible. She may take one step in throwing, but she must not step over the restraining line. Any method of throwing may be used. Two trials are given.

Scoring: Spotters are employed to stand along the throwing lanes at a distance the girl has thrown in practice. As soon as the ball hits, the spotters immediately stand at that point. The marked zone is noted and the distance to the nearest foot is recorded. The best of two trials is the score.

Potato Race.

Directions: The same procedures are followed as were described for the shuttle race in the AAHPER Youth Fitness Test. Two trials are given.

Scoring: The best score of the two trials to the nearest fifth of a second is recorded.

Sit-ups

Directions: Same as for AAHPER Youth Fitness Test, except that the girls do not stop at fifty.

Scoring: The maximum number is recorded.

Push-ups

Directions: The girl assumes a position in which the hands are placed on the mat, shoulder width apart; the knees are in contact with the mat with feet raised; and the body is kept straight from head to knees. The subject bends her arms to touch the chest to the floor and pushes up again, keeping the body as straight as possible thoughout. The arms must come to complete extension, and only the chest is allowed to touch the floor. The subject repeats the exercise with no rest for as long as possible.

Scoring: The maximum number of repetitions is recorded.

Pull-ups

Directions: A horizontal bar is adjusted at a height of 3½ feet from the floor. The subject grips the bar and moves under it so that her arms are completely extended, her knees are bent to right angles, and her body is straight from the shoulders to the knees and parallel with the floor. All of her weight should be borne by hands and feet. The subject then pulls upward, using only her arms (no leg action) until her chest touches the bar. The body moves from the knees with no bending at the hips or rounding of the back, nor is resting allowed. The arms must be completely extended after each touching of the chest.

Scoring: The maximum number of repetitions is recorded.

Squat Thrusts

Directions: The squat thrusts are performed in the usual manner as described in Chapter 13. Emphasis is placed on making each of the four parts of the exercise distinct—(a) squat, (b) front leaning rest, (c) squat, (d) return to standing position—and the subject's body should be straight with no sway or bend when in the front leaning rest position.

Table 19-14
Norms for DGWS Physical Performance Test

Scale Score	Standing Broad Jump	Basket-ball Throw	Potato Race	Pull-ups	Push-ups	Sit-ups	10-Second Squat Thrust	30-Second Squat Thrust	Scale Score
100	7-9	78	8.4	47	61	65	9-1	24	100
95	7-7	75	8.6	45	58	61	9	23	95
90	7-4	72	8.8	42	54	57	8-3	22	90
85	7-2	68	9.0	39	51	54	8-1	21	85
80	6-11	65	9.4	37	47	50	8	20	80
75	6-9	62	9.6	34	43	46	7-3	19	75
70	6-7	59	10.0	32	39	43	7-1	18-2	70
65	6-4	56	10.2	29	36	39	7	18	65
60	6-2	53	10.4	26	32	36	6-2	17	60
55	6-0	50	10.6	24	28	33	6-1	16	55
50	5-9	46	11.0	21	25	29	6	15	50
45	5-7	43	11.2	18	21	25	5-2	14-2	45
40	5-5	40	11.6	16	17	22	5-1	14	40
35	5-2	37	11.8	13	13	18	4-3	13	35
30	5-0	34	12.0	10	10	15	4-2	12	30
25	4-9	31	12.4	8	6	11	4	11	25
20	4-7	27	12.6	5	2	7	3-3	10	20
15	4-4	24	13.0	3	1	3	3-2	9	15
10	4-2	21	13.2	1	0	1	3	8-2	10
5	4-0	18	13.4	0	0	0	2-3	7-2	5
0	3-9	15	13.6	0	0	0	2-2	7	0

Source: Eleanor Metheny, Chairman, "Physical Performance Levels for High School Girls," *Journal of Health and Physical Education*, June, 1945, p. 309.

Scoring: The number of complete movements, plus extra quarter-movements performed in the 10-second or 30-second time period.

Additional Pointers for the DGWS Test Battery: (a) The committee recommends that the test should not be given to any students who have not been given medical approval for strenuous exercise, and no girl should be tested during her menstrual period. (b) Form should be stressed instead of all-out maximum performance. No more than two tests should be given in one day; furthermore, no more than two tests that are to be used for official records should generally be given in one week. (c) The test scores should be employed to evaluate the program with respect to selecting activities which provide balanced development. (d) Girls who score very poorly on the tests should be given special attention as to cause and remedial work.

Norms: The scoring table with the scale based on three standard deviations above and below the mean is given in Table 19-14.

Other Tests of Motor Performance

Space does not permit the description of other motor performance tests. Brief mention is made here of some of these. The reader is referred to the individual references for test descriptions and norms.

McCloy (49, 50) devised tests which were described as being measures of general motor achievement. These tests included track and field events and strength tests. The test items for boys consisted of pull-ups, a 50- or 100-yard dash, running or standing broad jump, running high jump, and a shot put, basketball, or baseball throw for distance. For girls the items were modified pull-ups, a dash, a broad jump, and a throw. Through the use of his tables the General Motor Ability Score (GMAS) is obtained with the following formulas for boys and girls:

GMAS (Boys) = .1022 (total track and field points) + .3928 (chinning strength)

GMAS (Girls) = .42 (total track and field points) + (number of chins)

Cozen's General Athletic Ability Test (19) has been used for measuring motor ability of college men for a number of years. Through a study of forty activities, seven tests were selected. The test items are dips, baseball throw for distance, football punt for distance, bar snap, standing broad jump, dodging run, and quarter mile run. These items, which were selected as measuring the elements of general motor ability, are weighted and totaled. Then, through the use of a classification scale which takes into account body size, the score for the test battery is interpreted as superior, above average, average, below average, and inferior. The validity and reliability coefficients have been very high. The principal disadvantage to this test is the space and time requirements for administration.

Larson (43) developed a motor ability test for college men through factor analysis which has both an indoor and an outdoor form. The indoor test battery includes a dodging run, chinning, dipping, vertical jump, and the bar snap. The outdoor test has the baseball throw for distance, bar snap, chinning, and the vertical jump. The raw scores are converted to T-scores, which are weighted and totaled in order to be used for classification. High validity and reliability have been reported.

The Humiston Motor Ability Test (33) was devised to measure the present status in motor ability of college women for the primary purpose of classifying them for intramurals and physical education. It contains seven test items consisting of a dodging run, sideward roll on a mat, climb over a box, turn around in a circle, run between two barriers, throwing of a basket-ball over a rope and catching it, and 60-foot sprint. These items are arranged in the form of an obstacle course set up on a gymnasium floor. The items must be executed in sequence, and the score is the elapsed time to the nearest tenth of a second.

The Newton Motor Ability Test for high school girls was developed by Powell and Howe (58). The test is made up of three items: the standing broad jump; a hurdle race in which the girl jumps over five 15-inch hurdles, runs around an Indian club and back over the hurdles; and a scramble, which involves getting to her feet from a supine position and running to tap a bell twice, then returning to the starting position, clapping her hands twice on the floor, and, finally, repeating the task until the fourth double tap of the ball. The authors recommend that the test be given again on successive days and an average taken for each item in order to increase reliability.

Iowa-Brace Motor Educability Test (48, 49)

The Iowa-Brace Test represents McCloy's revision of the original Brace Test. With twenty-one items, ten of which were from the Brace Test, students are scored on ten stunts without practice. Scoring is on a pass or fail basis with two trials allowed. If the person does it correctly on the first trial, he receives two points. If he fails on the first trial, he immediately tries again and, if successful, receives one point. If he fails on this attempt, he receives a zero.

Several sample items are presented below.
Stork stand: Stand on left foot. Hold the bottom of right foot against the inside of the left knee. Place the hands on the hips. Close the eyes and hold this position for 10 seconds without shifting the left foot about on the floor. It is a failure: (a) to lose the balance, (b) not to keep the right foot against the knee, and (c) to open the eyes or remove hands from the hips.
Double heel click: Jump upward and clap the feet together twice and land with the feet apart (any distance). It is a failure: (a) not to click the feet together twice, and (b) to land with the feet touching each other.
Full right turn: Stand with both feet together. Jump up and make a full turn to the right, landing on about the same spot. Do not lose the balance upon landing, causing the feet to move. It is a failure: (a) not to make a full right turn and land facing in the original direction, and (b) to lose the balance and have to move the feet after they touch the floor.

Adams Sports-Type Educability Test (2)

Adams developed a sports-type educability test with two rather unusual items that fit the concept of testing with unfamiliar skills. The two items (from a battery of four items) are presented below.

Lying Tennis Ball Catch: The subject lies on his back and tosses a tennis ball in the air and catches it with either hand. The ball must go at least 6 feet in the air, and he must maintain the lying position. Ten trials are given. The score is the number of correct tosses. A perfect score would be ten.

Ball Bounce Test: The subject stands in a circle that is 6 feet in diameter. Holding a softball bat one hand length from the thick end, he attempts to bounce a volleyball on the top end of the bat for ten consecutive bounces. Ball must bounce at least 6 inches off top of bat. Each attempt, whether successful or not, is a trial. Ten trials are given. A perfect score would be 100.

Carpenter Motor Ability Test (15, 16)

The Carpenter Motor Ability Test was developed for boys and girls of grades one, two, and three. The measurements taken include the broad jump in distance, the (4-pound) shot put in distance, and body weight to the nearest pound. The scores are computed with the following formula:

GMAS (Boys)=Standing broad jump+2.5 shot put+.5 weight

GMAS (Girls)=Standing broad jump+1.5 shot put+.05 weight

Johnson-Metheny Motor Educability Test (52)

A canvas, 15 feet long, is marked as shown in Figure 19-6. In the middle of the canvas, a lane 24 inches wide is divided into 10 equal sections. Every other line is 3 inches wide; the narrow lines are ¾ inch wide. The centers of the lines are 18 inches apart. A ¾-inch line is then drawn down the center of the 24-inch lane, running the length of the canvas. The canvas should be placed over a mat with the ends and sides tucked under so that the canvas is stretched taut. Of course, the lines could be painted or chalked directly on a mat.

Two of the four test items are presented as samples below. The numbers in parentheses refer to the number of the test item in the original Johnson test battery.

Front Roll (Test No. 5): The subject starts from a standing position at one end of the 24-inch lane. He performs one front roll within the limits of the first half of the lane; he then does another front roll within the limits of the second half of the lane. Each roll is worth five points. Points are deducted as follows: (a) For each roll, two points are deducted if the subject strays beyond the left boundary, and a similar penalty is imposed if he overreaches the right boundary. (b) One point is deducted for each roll if the subject does not complete the roll within the designated half of the lane. (c) Five points are deducted for failure to perform a true roll. If the subject fails on the first attempt, he is allowed to try a second roll in the last half of the lane.

Jumping Half Turn (Test No. 8): Standing on the first 3-inch line the subject jumps upward and executes a half turn in either direction, landing on the second 3-inch line. He is now facing the starting line. He then jumps upward making a half turn in the opposite direction from which the first jump was done. He proceeds in this manner, alternating directions of the turns, until he has completed four jumps. Perfect execution is worth ten points. Two points are deducted for each jump in which the subject does not land on the line with both feet or turns in the wrong direction. Only two points are deducted for each jump.

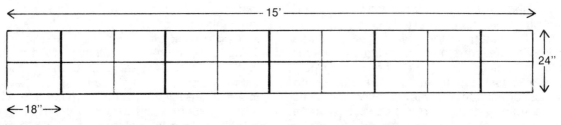

Figure 19-6. Canvas Markings for Johnson-Metheny Test

California Physical
Performance Tests (12)

There are five test items for boys and girls from ten to eighteen years of age in the California Physical Performance Tests. The items are: pull-ups for boys, knee push-ups for girls, standing broad jump, knee-bent sit-ups for time, 50-yard dash, and softball throw for distance. Nearly all the test items have been described previously. It should be noted that several of the AAHPER Youth Fitness Test items were taken from this test. The knee push-ups are performed as outlined in the NSWA test except that the maximum is fifty. Some of the unique features of the knee-bent sit-ups for time should be mentioned.

Knee-bent Sit-ups for Time: The sit-up is accomplished in the manner described in Chapter 8. The hands are clasped behind the head, and the subject raises the trunk by lifting first the head, then the shoulders, and then the back. Each student must show that he or she can do this exercise by performing five sit-ups for the testers before proceeding with the time trials. The following time limits are observed: 30 seconds for boys and girls ten and eleven; 60 seconds for boys twelve, thirteen, and fourteen and for all girls fifteen and over; and 90 seconds for boys twelve and above.

The revised norms for the test battery are in percentiles and are based on only sex and age. Espenschade (23) found that height and weight did not significantly affect performance any more than age alone.

Oregon Motor Fitness Test (54)

The Oregon State Department of Education provides a manual of motor fitness test batteries and norms for three age groups: intermediate boys and girls, grades four, five, six; junior high school boys and girls, grades seven, eight, nine; and senior high school boys and girls, grades ten, eleven, twelve. For boys in grades four through six the items include the standing broad jump, floor push-ups, and sit-ups. The junior and senior high school tests are pull-ups, jump and reach, and the 160-yard potato race. All of the foregoing test items, except the potato race, have been described previously.

The 160-yard potato race is conducted in an area requiring 70 feet for running, plus some space for finishing. Three circles are drawn on the floor in a line; each circle is 1 foot in diameter. The first circle is drawn immediately behind the starting line. The second circle is 50 feet, and the third is 70 feet away. A small block or eraser 2 by 4 inches is placed in circle two and another in circle three. The subject runs to circle two, picks up the block and runs to place it in the first circle. He then runs to circle three, picks up the block, and places it in circle one. As soon as he has placed it in the circle, he grabs the first block and returns it to circle two, runs back and gets the remaining block, and carries it to circle three. He finishes the race by dashing across the finish line. The score is in seconds.

The girls' battery also contains three items. They are: the standing broad jump, hanging in arm-flexed position, and crossed-arm curl-ups. The hanging in arm-flexed position test is similar to the flexed-arm hang for girls in the AAHPER Youth Fitness Test except that the timing continues as long as there is some flexion in the elbow. The time stops as soon as the elbow straightens.

The crossed-arm curl-ups are done with the knees bent at about a 90-degree angle and with the soles of the feet flat on the floor. The feet are held down by a partner. The subject folds her arms across her chest and raises to a sitting position without using the arms in any way to help. The subject then returns to a lying position and repeats the exercise as many times as possible. It is not permissible to bounce back up, or to rest at any time.

Problems Associated with Motor Performance Testing

The problems that are involved in the testing of general motor ability are primarily the problems that are associated with the testing of the separate qualities which make up the total battery. In other words, if the motor ability test contains measures of agility, balance, power, etc., the same problems are involved that are associated with agility testing, balance testing, power testing, etc. However, the problems are not necessarily additive. Some of the limitations of the individual measures are actually remedied when the tests are used as part of a battery that purports to measure general motor ability. For example, the standing broad jump might be questioned as a strict measure of leg power because of the arm and trunk action. However, for general motor ability, the inclusion of this coordination of the arms, trunk, and legs is desirable.

An obvious problem in motor ability testing is the question of whether or not physical fitness factors should be included in motor ability batteries. Such factors as cardiovascular capacity, strength, muscular endurance, and flexibility are essential to a satisfactory fitness level, whereas power, agility, coordination, reaction time, balance, and speed are factors primarily essential to motor performance and not to physical fitness. The authors have found the criteria set up for this distinction by Johnson and associates (36) most satisfactory.

If this distinction is accepted by the majority of the members of our profession, then we can safely state that there is a need for new motor ability tests based on the factors identified above as motor ability factors.

The physical educator must make the decision concerning the efficacy of motor ability tests based on his own particular situation. Obviously, if only a few activities are offered in the program, then testing for purposes of classification should involve tests for those specific activities. On the other hand, if a large number and wide variety of activities are taught, then task-specific testing is normally not feasible. In this case, the use of general motor ability tests would appear to be applicable. In all cases the teacher should utilize tests in conjunction with his own knowledge and subjective evaluation of the attitudes and the individual needs and interests of the students.

A number of authorities in the areas of anatomy and kinesiology have objected to the performance of sit-ups with straight legs. Sit-ups done in this manner are said to involve the iliopsoas more so than the abdominal muscles, and it has been observed that the iliopsoas muscle does not ordinarily require additional exercise. More important, however, is the possible harm that can be done to the back in persons with weak abdominal muscles. Because of the attachment of the iliopsoas to the lumbar vertebrae, straight-leg sit-ups are said to cause excessive pull and possible strain in the lumbar area. Thus, bent-knee sit-ups are recommended since they reduce the effects of the iliopsoas and are directed more to the abdominal muscles. Despite these objections many motor fitness tests, including the AAHPER test (1), use the straight-leg sit-ups.

Most of the motor fitness tests require very little equipment, which is a good point in their favor. They are also relatively easy to administer. Each local setting, whether it be a single school or county or state, should strive to establish standardized testing procedures. Through clinics and workshops, the various fine points of administration that are not covered in the directions should be agreed upon. This is, of course, the principal value of the laboratory portion of a class in tests and measurements. Without actually going through the tests and discussing the procedures, it is impossible to attain the rigid standardization that is necessary for accurate and worthwhile results. For the same reasons the teacher should exercise good judgment in using national norms. These norms are intended only for general reference. It should be obvious that under varied conditions for testing that are allowable in a test such as the AAHPER Youth Fitness Test the results will also vary. For example, if some testers administer the shuttle race out of doors and others use a gymnasium floor, their scores would hardly be comparable. Similarly, if the 50-yard dash is given in one instance on a track and another on the grass, variation in scores will result. In most cases the makers of tests recommend that local norms be constructed. In any case, the norms should be made available to the students so as to have maximum interpretative and motivational values. We repeat once more, a test should be used for evaluation on the part of the teacher, the students, the parents, the administration, and the general public.

Findings and Conclusions from Motor Performance Measurement and Research

Studies related to the topic of motor performance are so numerous that this brief summary can only be considered as a sampling at best. Furthermore, only studies on motor ability reported in the literature since 1950 are presented here, although a great deal of research in this area was done prior to that time. In fact, most of the motor ability tests were developed in the thirties and forties. However, the sprinkling of studies that are mentioned here is merely intended to acquaint the reader with some of the current information pertaining to this topic.

Although some of the test makers have proceeded on the assumption that motor ability is basically stable, Lafuze (41) found that general motor ability can be significantly improved through specific practice. Glassow and Krause (28) observed that while changes did occur, individuals tended to remain in the same relative position from year to year. Broer (10) studied the improvement in general motor ability of students of low ability. She concluded that basic instruction is more beneficial than participation in a regular activity program and should precede participation in the regular program. In a somewhat contradictory study Dohrmann (22) concluded that throwing and kicking training programs, performed in addition to the regular physical education programs, did not result in greater improvement in throwing and kicking ability than did the regular physical education program alone.

Burdeshaw and others (11) studied the effects of specific versus general instruction of badminton skills to college women classified as low in motor ability, as measured by the Scott Motor Ability Test. The results supported the theory of specificity in learning motor skills and cast doubt on the worth of a basic skills course in facilitating subsequent performance in specific skills. Gallagher (26) compared athletically high-skilled and low-skilled subjects on the learning of six novel motor skills. He found that the high-skilled group had significantly better improvement scores on only two of the six tasks. The two tasks were athletically oriented, which again supported specificity.

Miller (53) did not find any differences in motor ability, as measured by the Barrow Motor Ability Test, as a result of individual and team sports physical education programs. Patterson (55) compared subjects participating in a physical education soccer class with subjects who also received supplementary exercises and found all three programs to be equally effective in significantly improving scores on the Barrow Motor Ability Test.

Some findings that are particularly relevant to the subject of testing and motor ability are those by Smith and Bozymowski (71), Ryan (61), and Singer (68). Smith and Bozymowski concluded that subjects who viewed warm-up as being desirable performed better when warm-up preceded performance in an activity, such as an obstacle race. Subjects who had less favorable attitudes toward warm-up did not improve significantly following warm-up. Ryan studied the relationship between motor performance and arousal and found indications that arousal precedes performance. Singer found that non-athletes performed significantly better on a gross motor task than athletes in the presence of spectators.

Landiss (42) found that, of eight activities studied, tumbling, gymnastics, and wrestling appeared most effective in developing those abilities measured in the Larson Test of Motor Ability. In a study with college women Bennett (8) investigated the relative effectiveness of four activities in developing specific and general motor ability. The subsequent ratings were swimming and modern dance first, basketball second, and folk dance third.

Boys were found to be superior to girls on all motor ability-educability tests and practically all physical skills by Smith (70) and Hoffman (31). Bachman (3), however, concluded that the rate of learning in large muscle skills was independent of age and sex over the range of six to twenty-six years and that no sex differences were found in motor learning ability in that age range.

Lockhart and Mott (46) concluded that superior performers benefit by being segregated into homogeneous ability groupings and that the majority of subjects involved preferred participation in classes composed of persons of similar ability. Walters (73) found that the above average bowlers had higher motor ability scores than the below average bowlers. Roloff (60), Hoffman (31), and Phillips and Summers (57) all found positive relationships between motor ability tests and kinesthesis. Athletes were found to be superior to non-athletes in performance on test items related to general motor ability and motor capacity by Shelley (66) and by Girolamo (27). Coleman and others (18) reported a strong positive relationship between motor ability scores and both peer acceptance and social adjustment with boys experiencing learning difficulties.

The literature in the area of motor fitness is so extensive that it would fill volumes. There have been numerous studies reported on constructing tests, on the contribution of various activities in developing fitness, and the relationship of fitness to other traits and types of performance. In this brief review of literature the term *physical fitness* is sometimes used by the writers of the studies, but the measuring devices employed are motor fitness tests as the term is used in this text.

Wilbur (74) compared two types of activity programs, a sports program and an apparatus program, in developing motor fitness. The sports program was found to be superior for developing arm and shoulder strength, body coordination, agility, and control. The programs were equal in improving leg speed and strength and endurance. In a somewhat similar study Landiss (42) investigated the contributions of eight selected physical education activities in developing fitness. It was found that the combined activities of tumbling and gymnastics were most effective in developing motor fitness and motor ability and that tennis, swimming, and boxing ranked lowest.

Davis (21) found that a training and conditioning program for the 200-yard crawl stroke in swimming brought about significant improvement in motor fitness tests. Campbell (13) studied the effects of supplemental weight training given to members of football, basketball, and track squads with regard to improving motor fitness performance. His findings showed that weight training produced a significantly greater increase in fitness than the normal conditioning program alone. A program of creative activities was found by Estes (24) to produce increases in muscular fitness, strength, balance, and flexibility.

Keogh (37) compared a daily physical education program with a program which met twice a week on the development of motor fitness in third and fifth grade children. The actual time spent in class was the same for both programs, since the daily program lasted for four weeks and the two-day-a-week program continued for ten weeks. Both programs were equally effective in improving motor fitness. Fabricius (25) found that a physical education program for fourth grade boys and girls in which calisthenics were added to the normal program improved fitness, as measured by the Oregon Motor Fitness Test, to a greater degree than the program without added calisthenics. Wireman (75) concluded from his study that a knowledge of results of performance in calisthenics, games, and sports facilitated improvement in motor fitness.

Harkness (29) compared the physical education program with an ROTC program on improvement in motor fitness as measured by the JCR Test. The physical education program was significantly superior to the ROTC program in the development and maintenance of motor fitness.

A number of studies have shown that programs of conditioning will produce gains in fitness (32, 40, 67). In contradiction to this, Campney and Wehr (14) concluded that a ten-week training period utilizing the exercises advocated by the President's Council on Physical Fitness was not likely to produce significant improvements in any of the fitness components studied except in flexibility. Kirby (39) investigated the effects of different amounts of extra exercise performed in addition to the regular physical education activities on improvement of college men on the JCR Test. He found that the gains in the JCR scores were inversely proportional to the number of additional exercises. He concluded that the intensity of performing the exercises in a short time was more influential than the number of exercises performed.

References and Bibliography

1. AAHPER, *AAHPER Youth Fitness Test Manual,* Revised ed., Washington, D.C.: American Alliance for Health, Physical Education, and Recreation, 1976.
2. Adams, Arthur R., "A Test Construction Study of Sport-Type Motor Educability for College Men" (Microcarded doctor's dissertation, Louisiana State University, 1954).
3. Bachman, John C., "Motor Learning and Performance as Related to Age and Sex in Two Measures of Balance Coordination," *Research Quarterly,* 32:123-137, May, 1961.
4. Barrow, Harold M., "Test of Motor Ability for College Men," *Research Quarterly,* 25:253-260, October, 1954.
5. _____, *Motor Ability Testing for College Men,* Minneapolis: Burgess Publishing Company, 1951.
6. _____, and Rosemary McGee, *A Practical Approach to Measurement in Physical Education,* Philadelphia: Lea and Febiger, 1964.
7. Baumgartner, Ted. A., and Andrew S. Jackson, "Measurement Schedules for Tests of Motor Performance," *Research Quarterly,* 41:10, March, 1970.
8. Bennett, Colleen L., "Relative Contributions of Modern Dance, Folk Dance, Basketball, and Swimming to Motor Abilities of College Women," *Research Quarterly,* 27:253-261, October, 1956.
9. Brace, David K., *Measuring Motor Ability,* New York: A. S. Barnes and Company, 1927.
10. Broer, Marion R., "Evaluation of a Basic Skills Curriculum for Women Students of Low Motor Ability at the University of Washington," *Research Quarterly,* 26:15-27, March, 1955.
11. Burdeshaw, Dorothy, Jane E. Spragens, and Patricia A. Weis, "Evaluation of General Versus Specific Instruction of Badminton Skills to Women of Low Motor Ability," *Research Quarterly,* 41:472-477, December, 1970.
12. *California Physical Performance Tests,*

Sacramento, Cal.: Bureau of Health Education, Physical Education, and Recreation, California State Department of Education, 1962.

13. Campbell, Robert L., "Effects of Supplemental Weight Training on the Physical Fitness of Athletic Squads," *Research Quarterly*, 33:343-355, October, 1962.

14. Campney, Harry K., and Richard W. Wehr, "Effects of Calisthenics on Selected Components of Physical Fitness," *Research Quarterly*, 36:393-402, December, 1965.

15. Carpenter, Aileen, "Strength Testing in the First Three Grades," *Research Quarterly*, 13:328-335, October, 1942.

16. _____, "The Measurements of General Motor Capacity and General Motor Ability in the First Three Grades," *Research Quarterly*, 13:444-465, December, 1942.

17. Clarke, H. Harrison, *Application of Measurement to Health and Physical Education*, 4th ed., Englewood Cliffs, N.J.: Prentice-Hall, 1967, Chapter 7.

18. Coleman, James C., Jack F. Keogh, and John Mansfield, "Motor Performance and Social Adjustment among Boys Experiencing Serious Learning Difficulties," *Research Quarterly*, 34:516-517, December, 1963.

19. Cozens, F. W., *Achievement Scales in Physical Education Activities for College Men*, Philadelphia: Lea and Febiger, 1936.

20. Cratty, Bryant J., "A Three Level Theory of Perceptual Motor Behavior," *Quest*, Monograph VI, May, 1966, pp. 3-10.

21. Davis, J. F., "Effects of Training and Conditioning for Middle Distance Swimming Upon Various Physical Measures," *Research Quarterly*, 30:399-412, December, 1959.

22. Dohrmann, Paul, "Throwing and Kicking Ability of 8-Year-Old Boys and Girls," *Research Quarterly*, 35:464-471, December, 1964.

23. Espenschade, Anna S., "Restudy of Relationships Between Physical Performances of School Children and Age, Height, and Weight," *Research Quarterly*, 34:144-153, May, 1963.

24. Estes, Mary M., "The Role of Creative Play Equipment in Developing Muscular Fitness" (Microcarded doctoral dissertation, State University of Iowa, 1959).

25. Fabricius, Helen, "Effect of Added Calisthenics on the Physical Fitness of Fourth Grade Boys and Girls," *Research Quarterly*, 35:135-140, May, 1964.

26. Gallagher, James D., "Motor Learning Characteristics of Low-Skilled College Men," *Research Quarterly*, 41:59-67, March, 1970.

27. Girolamo, Carmen G., "A Comparison of General Motor Capacity of Athletes and Non-Athletes" (Microcarded master's thesis, State University of Iowa, 1956).

28. Glassow, Ruth B., and Pauline Krause, "Motor Performance of Girls Age 6 to 14 Years," *Research Quarterly*, 31:432-433, October, 1960.

29. Harkness, William W., "The Contributions of AFROTC and Physical Education Experiences to Selected Components of Fitness of College Men" (Microcarded doctoral dissertation, Stanford University, 1957).

30. Henry, Franklin M., "Evaluation of Motor Learning When Performance Levels Are Heterogeneous," *Research Quarterly*, 27:176-181, May, 1956.

31. Hoffman, Virginia, "Relation of Selected Traits and Abilities to Motor Learning" (Microcarded doctoral dissertation, Indiana University, 1955).

32. Hughes, B. O., "Test Results of the University of Michigan Physical Conditioning Program June 15 through September 26, 1942," *Research Quarterly*, 13:498-511, December, 1942.

33. Humiston, Dorothy A., "A Measurement of Motor Ability in College Women," *Research Quarterly*, 8:181-185, May, 1937.

34. Jackson, Andrew S., "Factor Analysis of Selected Muscular Strength and Motor Performance Tests," *Research Quarterly*, 42:164, May, 1971.

35. Johnson, Granville B., "Physical Skill Tests for Sectioning Classes into Homogeneous Units," *Research Quarterly*, 3:128-134, March, 1932.

36. Johnson, Perry B., Wynn F. Updyke, Donald C. Stolberg, and Maryellen Schaefer, *Physical Education — A Problem Solving Approach to Health and Fitness*, Chicago: Holt, Rinehart and Winston, 1966, pp. 20-27.

37. Keogh, Betty J., "The Effects of a Daily and Two Day Per Week Physical Education Program Upon Motor Fitness of Children" (Microcarded doctoral dissertation, State University of Iowa, 1962).

38. Keogh, Jack F., "Motor Performance Test Data for Elementary School Children," *Research Quarterly*, 41:600-602, December, 1970.

39. Kirby, Ronald F., "The Effects of Various Exercise Programs Involving Different Amounts of Exercise on the Development of Certain Components of Physical Fitness" (Unpublished doctoral dissertation, Louisiana State University, 1966).

40. Kistler, Joy W., "A Study of the Results of Eight Weeks of Participation in a University Physical Fitness Program," *Research Quarterly*, 15:23-28, March, 1944.

41. Lafuze, Marion, "A Study of the Learning of Fundamental Skills by College Freshmen Women of Low Motor Ability," *Research Quarterly*, 22:149-157, May, 1951.

42. Landiss, Carl W., "Influence of Physical Education Activities on Motor Ability and Physical

Fitness of Male Freshmen," *Research Quarterly,* 26:295-307, October, 1955.

43. Larson, Leonard A., "A Factor Analysis of Motor Ability Variables and Tests, with Tests for College Men," *Research Quarterly,* 12:499-517, October, 1941.

44. Latchaw, Marjorie, "Measuring Selected Motor Skills in Fourth, Fifth, and Sixth Grades," *Research Quarterly,* 25:439-449, December, 1954.

45. _____ , and Camille Brown, *The Evaluation Process in Health Education, Physical Education and Recreation,* Englewood Cliffs, N.J.: Prentice-Hall, 1962, pp. 84-104.

46. Lockhart, Aileene, and Jane A. Mott, "An Experiment in Homogeneous Grouping and Its Effect on Achievement in Sports Fundamentals," *Research Quarterly,* 22:58-62, March, 1951.

47. Martens, Rainer, "Internal-External Control and Social Reinforcement Effects on Motor Performance," *Research Quarterly,* 42:307, October, 1971.

48. McCloy, C. H., "An Analytical Study of the Stunt Type Test as a Measure of Motor Educability," *Research Quarterly,* 8:46-55, October, 1937.

49. _____ , "The Measurement of General Motor Capacity and General Motor Ability," *Research Quarterly Supplement,* 5:46-61, March, 1934.

50. _____ , and Norma D. Young, *Tests and Measurements in Health and Physical Education,* 3rd ed., New York: Appleton-Century-Crofts, 1954, Chapter 17.

51. Metheney, Eleanor, "Physical Performance Levels for High School Girls," *Journal of Health and Physical Education,* 16:32-35, June, 1945.

52. _____ , "Studies of the Johnson Test as a Test of Motor Educability," *Research Quarterly,* 9:105-114, December, 1938.

53. Miller, David K., "A Comparison of the Effects of Individual and Team Sports Programs on the Motor Ability of Male College Freshmen" (Unpublished doctoral dissertation, Florida State University, 1970).

54. *Motor Fitness Tests for Oregon Schools,* Salem, Oregon: State Department of Education, 1962.

55. Patterson, Malcolm L., "A Comparison of Two Methods of Training on the Improvement of General Motor Ability Performance" (Unpublished doctoral dissertation, Louisiana State University, 1970).

56. Phillips, B. E., "The JCR Test," *Research Quarterly,* 18:12-29, March, 1947.

57. Phillips, Marjorie, and Dean Summers, "Relation of Kinesthetic Perception to Motor Learning," *Research Quarterly,* 25:456-468, December, 1954.

58. Powell, Elizabeth, and E. C. Howe, "Motor Ability Tests for High School Girls," *Research Quarterly,* 10:81-88, December, 1939.

59. Roberts, Glyn C., and Rainer Martens, "Social Reinforcement and Complex Motor Performance," *Research Quarterly,* 41:175, May, 1970.

60. Roloff, Louise L., "Kinesthesis in Relation to the Learning of Selected Motor Skills," *Research Quarterly,* 24:210-215, May, 1953.

61. Ryan, Dean E., "Relationship Between Motor Performance and Arousal," *Research Quarterly,* 33:279-287, May, 1962.

62. Schmidt, Richard A., "Retroactive Interference and Amount of Original Learning in Verbal and Motor Tasks," *Research Quarterly,* 42:314, October, 1971.

63. Scott, M. Gladys, "Motor Ability Tests for College Women," *Research Quarterly,* 14:402-405, December, 1943.

64. _____ , "The Assessment of Motor Abilities of College Women Through Objective Tests," *Research Quarterly,* 10:63-83, October, 1939.

65. _____ , and Esther French, *Measurement and Evaluation in Physical Education,* Dubuque, Iowa: Wm. C. Brown Company, Publishers, 1959, pp. 344-350.

66. Shelley, Morgan E., "Maturity, Structure, Strength, Motor Ability, and Intelligence Test Profiles of Outstanding Elementary School and Junior High School Athletes" (Microcarded master's thesis, University of Oregon, 1960).

67. Sills, F. D., "Special Conditioning Exercises for Students with Low Scores on Physical Fitness Tests," *Research Quarterly,* 25:333-337, October, 1954.

68. Singer, Robert N., "Effect of Spectators on Athletes and Non-Athletes Performing a Gross Motor Task," *Research Quarterly,* 36:473-482, December, 1965.

69. _____ , Jack Llewellyn, and Ellington Darden. "Placebo and Competition Placebo Effects on Motor Skill," *Research Quarterly,* 44:51, March, 1973.

70. Smith, Jean A., "Relation of Certain Physical Traits and Abilities to Motor Learning in Elementary School Children," *Research Quarterly,* 27:220-228, May, 1956.

71. Smith, Judith L., and Margaret F. Bozymowski, "Effect of Attitude toward Warm-up on Motor Performance," *Research Quarterly,* 36:78-85, March, 1965.

72. Thorpe, Joanne, Charlotte West, and Dorothy Davies, "Learning Under a Traditional and an Experimental Schedule Involving Master Classes," *Research Quarterly,* 42:83, March, 1971.

73. Walters, Etta C., "Motor Ability and Educability Factors of High and Low Scoring Beginning

Bowlers," *Research Quarterly,* 30:94-100, March, 1959.

74. Wilbur, E. A., "A Comparative Study of Physical Fitness Indices as Measured by Two Programs of Physical Education: The Sports Method and the Apparatus Method,"

Research Quarterly, 14:326-332, October, 1943.

75. Wireman, Billy O., "Comparison of Four Approaches to Increasing Physical Fitness," *Research Quarterly,* 31:658-666, December, 1960.

Part Five
Other Areas
of Measurement

Chapter Twenty

The Measurement of Social Qualities and Attitudes

Part I—Social Qualities

Introduction

Social development is considered by most physical educators to be one of the major objectives of physical education. Unfortunately, social concepts such as character, sportsmanship, adjustment, personality, leadership, behavior, and acceptance are very difficult to measure objectively. Because these concepts cannot be easily measured, some critics have argued that this area should not be included as one of our objectives. However, as we have mentioned before, attempts at developing scientific measures in this area are still in a relatively immature stage. It is certainly logical to assume that better evaluative techniques will be developed.

It seems appropriate to also point out that these concepts do exist and that they can be appraised. It is too often assumed that desirable changes automatically come about through athletic and physical education participation. However, we must recognize that games and other physical activities under poor leadership can breed undesirable social change. Therefore, regardless of the fact that our measuring tools are somewhat crude, a systematic, conscientious effort should be made to evaluate this aspect of the student's development just as in the more tangible area of organic efficiency and skills.

Uses of Social Measurement Instruments

Social measurement instruments are utilized in physical education in the following ways:
1. To assist in the evaluation of social behavior.
2. To determine the degree of acceptance or the status of individuals within the group.
3. To identify group leaders and the degree to which students perceive the best course in getting along with others.
4. To provide the information necessary for guidance or referral to professional personnel.

Practical Measurements of Social Factors

Measurements of social factors are identified in three sections.* Section I is Social Behavior and Adjustment Scales, where the attempt is to measure the changes in habits or the behavior which is exhibited in association with others. Section II deals with sociometric measures to determine the status or degree of acceptance of students within their group. Section III is concerned with leadership and ability to perceive getting along with others.

I. Social Behavior and Adjustment Scales

Blanchard Behavior Rating Scale (8)

Objective: To measure the character and personality of students.

Age Level: Satisfactory for ages twelve through seventeen.

*The authors are indebted to Dr. Marion Johnson, Southeastern Louisiana University, for his assistance.

Sex: Satisfactory for both boys and girls.
Reliability: The reliability has been reported as high as $r = .71$.
Validity: A validity of .930 was found when intercorrelations of one trait action were made with the rest of the items in its category.
Directions: The teacher rates each student on the basis of the following scale items. Individual items are then analyzed for specific weaknesses.
Scoring: The scale below was modified so that the maximum score possible would be 100 points. The higher the score, the better the evaluation of character and personality.

Cowell's Social Adjustment Index (20)

Objective: To determine the degree of social adjustment or maladjustment of students within their social groups.
Age Level: Satisfactory for ages twelve through seventeen.

Blanchard Behavior Rating Scale
(Modified by authors of text)

	No Opportunity to Observe	Never	Seldom	Fairly Often	Frequently	Extremely Often	Score
1. He is popular with classmates		1	2	3	4	5	
2. He seeks responsibility in the classroom		1	2	3	4	5	
3. He shows intellectual leadership in the classroom		1	2	3	4	5	
4. He shows initiative in assuming responsibility in unfamiliar situations		1	2	3	4	5	
5. He is alert to new opportunities		1	2	3	4	5	
6. He shows keenness of mind		1	2	3	4	5	
7. He volunteers ideas		1	2	3	4	5	
8. He grumbles over decisions of classmates	5	4	3	2	1		
9. He takes a justified criticism by teacher or classmate without showing anger or pouting		1	2	3	4	5	
10. He is loyal to his group		1	2	3	4	5	
11. He discharges his group responsibilities well		1	2	3	4	5	
12. He is cooperative in his attitude toward the teacher		1	2	3	4	5	
13. He makes loud-mouthed criticisms and comments	5	4	3	2	1		
14. He respects the rights of others		1	2	3	4	5	
15. He is truthful		1	2	3	4	5	
16. He is dependable and trustworthy		1	2	3	4	5	
17. He has good study habits		1	2	3	4	5	
18. He is liked by others		1	2	3	4	5	
19. He makes a friendly approach to others in the group		1	2	3	4	5	
20. He is friendly		1	2	3	4	5	

Cowell's Social Adjustment Index (20)

Positive Behavior Trends (Form A)	Markedly (+3)	Somewhat (+2)	Only Slightly (+1)	Not at All (+0)
1. Enters heartily and with enjoyment into the spirit of social intercourse _____				
2. Frank; talkative and sociable, does not stand on ceremony _____				
3. Self-confident and self-reliant, tends to take success for granted, strong initiative, prefers to lead _____				
4. Quick and decisive in movement, pronounced or excessive energy output _____				
5. Prefers group activities, work or play; not easily satisfied with individual projects _____				
6. Adaptable to new situations, makes adjustments readily, welcomes change _____				
7. Is self-composed, seldom shows signs of embarrassment _____				
8. Tends to elation of spirits, seldom gloomy or moody _____				
9. Seeks a broad range of friendships, not selective or exclusive in games and the like _____				
10. Hearty and cordial, even to strangers, forms acquaintanceships very easily _____				

The authors modified the scoring for Form A since Form B was not to be presented.

Sex: Satisfactory for both boys and girls.
Reliability: The reliability was reported as high as .82.
Validity: With Pupil Who's Who Ratings as the criterion, an r of .628 was obtained with the Social Adjustment Index.
Direction: The teacher rates each student on the basis of the scale items shown above.
Scoring:* To score form A (positive behavior trends), merely add up the points and compute an average to compare to the descriptive scale categories for the overall rating.

*The original reference should be consulted for greater test accuracy.

II. Sociometric Measures of Acceptance

Breck's Sociometric Test of Status (10)

Objective: To measure the status of students within a group concerning acceptance for team membership and friendship.
Age Level: Satisfactory for ages twelve through college.
Sex: Satisfactory for both boys and girls.
Reliability: The reliability of the skill status test was reported as $r = .894 \pm .01$. The reliability of the friendship status test was reported as $r = .79 \pm .01$.

Validity: Face validity has been accepted for the two items.

Materials: Cards or paper and pencils are needed for this test.

Directions: Students are asked to print in order of preference the names of five students they would most prefer to have as members of their team and the five they would least like to have as members of their team. Also, the students are directed to list the names they would most prefer to have as friends and the five they would least like to have as friends.

Scoring: For team membership the number of choices received by each student, minus the number of rejections by classmates, is calculated. For friendship the number of choices received by each student is merely tabulated.

Cowell's Personal Distance Scale (20)

Objective: To determine a student's degree of acceptance by his social group.

Age Level: Satisfactory for ages twelve through college.

Sex: Satisfactory for both boys and girls.

Reliability: The reliability has been reported as high as .93.

Validity: With Pupil's Who's Who Rating as the criterion, an *r* of .844 was obtained with Pupil's Personal Distance Scale.

Direction: Each student is directed to rate fellow students on the basis of the scale items shown below.

Scoring: Add each subject's total weighted scores given by fellow students and divide by the total number of respondents. Division is carried to two places and the decimal point is dropped. The lower the score, the greater the degree of acceptance.

III. Measures of Leadership and Ability to Perceive Getting Along

Modified Nelson Sports Leadership Questionaire (63)

Objective: To determine athletic leaders as identified by the players.

Age Level: Satisfactory for junior high through college.

Sex: Satisfactory for both boys and girls.

Reliability: An *r* of .96 was reported by Lloyd Williams with ninth grade football players, Monroe, La., 1973. An *r* of .78 was reported by

Cowell's Personal Distance Ballot

What To Do:	I would be willing to accept him:						
If you had full power to treat each student on this list as you feel, just how would you consider him? How near would you like to have him to your family? Check each student in *one* column as to your feeling toward him. Circle your own name.	Into my family as a brother	As a very close "pal" or "chum"	As a member of my "gang" or club	On my street as a "next-door neighbor"	Into my class at school	Into my school	Into my city
	1	2	3	4	5	6	7

1. _____

2. _____

3. _____

4. etc. _____

Modified Nelson Sports Leadership Questionnaire

A._____
B._____ 1. If you were on a trip and had a choice of the players you would share the hotel room with, who would they be?

A._____
B._____ 2. Who are the most popular members of the team?

A._____
B._____ 3. Who are the best scholars on the team?

A._____
B._____ 4. Which players know the most about the sport, in terms of strategy, rules, etc?

A._____
B._____ 5. If the coach were not present for a workout, which athletes would be the most likely to take charge of the practice?

A._____
B._____ 6. Which players would you listen to first if the team appeared to be disorganized during a crucial game?

A._____
B._____ 7. When the team is behind in a close match and there is still a chance to win, who is the most likely teammate to score the winning points?

A._____
B._____ 8. Of all of your teammates, who exhibits the most poise during crucial parts of the match?

A._____
B._____ 9. Who are the most valuable players on the team?

A._____
B._____ 10. Who are the players who play "most for the team"?

A._____
B._____ 11. Who are the most consistent point makers for the team?

A._____
B._____ 12. Who are the most respected performers on the team?

A._____
B._____ 13. Which teammates have the most overall ability?

A._____
B._____ 14. Which teammates train the hardest to improve their performance off season?

A._____
B._____ 15. Who are the most likeable players on the team?

A._____
B._____ 16. Which players have most favorably influenced you?

A._____
B._____ 17. Which players have actually helped you the most?

A._____
B._____ 18. Which teammates do you think would make the best coaches?

A._____
B._____ 19. Which teammates do you most often look to for leadership?

A._____
B._____ 20. Who are the hardest workers during regular practice hours?

Pam Holt with varsity college basketball players, Monroe, La., 1973.

Objectivity: An *r* of .98 was reported by Lloyd Williams and Pam Holt, NLU, Monroe, La., 1973.

Validity: Face validity was accepted for this instrument.

Materials: Pencils and questionnaires must be available.

Directions: Do not sign your name to the questionnaire. Fill in the name or names of the squad members that, in your opinion, best fit the question. Give your first and second choice in all cases. *Do not use your own name* on any of the answers. The names of the same athletes can be used any number of times and your answers will be kept confidential.

Scoring: Five points are awarded each time a player's name appears in the response A blank, and three points are awarded to names appearing in the response B blank.

Getting Along Appraisal (53)

Objective: To determine the extent to which students get along with themselves, with others, and with their surroundings.

Age Level: Grades seven, eight, and nine.

Sex: Satisfactory for both boys and girls.

Reliability: The range was .79 to .84 for form A and .73 to .83 for form B.

Objectivity: None reported.

Validity: High correlations were found between social adjustment ratings and raw scores.

Materials: Pencils and the test questions and answer sheets are needed.

Directions: Do not open the booklet until told to do so. There are forty-five items in the test. Each item has two pictures with information about them. At the right of each pair of pictures you will find a sentence with three possible answers. Read the sentence carefully and choose the answer you think is best. Note the letter of the answer (a, b, c). (See sample below.)

Problems Associated with Social Measurement

Several of the problems associated with social measurement are listed as follows:
1. Since many physical educators are not trained observers of character and per-

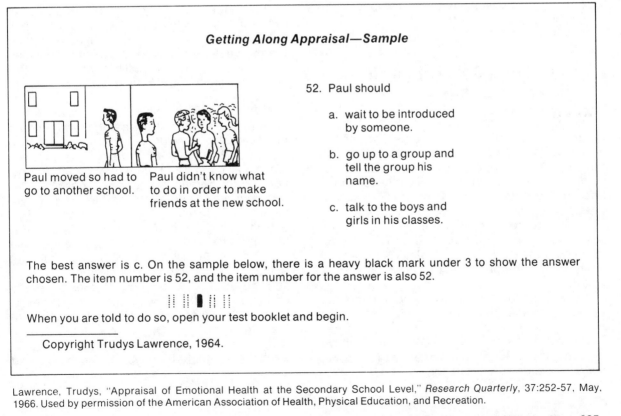

Getting Along Appraisal—Sample

52. Paul should

    a. wait to be introduced by someone.

    b. go up to a group and tell the group his name.

    c. talk to the boys and girls in his classes.

Paul moved so had to go to another school.

Paul didn't know what to do in order to make friends at the new school.

The best answer is c. On the sample below, there is a heavy black mark under 3 to show the answer chosen. The item number is 52, and the item number for the answer is also 52.

When you are told to do so, open your test booklet and begin.

Copyright Trudys Lawrence, 1964.

Lawrence, Trudys, "Appraisal of Emotional Health at the Secondary School Level," *Research Quarterly*, 37:252-57, May, 1966. Used by permission of the American Association of Health, Physical Education, and Recreation.

sonality traits, the validity of their evaluations may be questioned. Thus, it seems most important for such measurement to include pupil evaluations in conjunction with teacher evaluation.

2. The physical and mental condition of the teacher frequently affects the type of ratings students get. For example, a teacher who is ill or unduly tired at the time of the rating may not give the same ratings as would be given at a time when the same teacher was feeling well or in high spirits. Also, the personality of the teacher may have a bearing on the ratings, in that the teacher may rate students who exhibit behavior patterns similar to his own as *good* and students of an opposite nature as *poor.*

3. Although sociometric tests are quite reliable and valid for the purpose they serve, they are limited in the types of information they can provide.

4. Results may not be too valid when sociometric tests are given without consideration for feelings toward the opposite sex. Usually it is best to have boys rate boys, girls rate girls, and then have each rate members of the opposite sex. Otherwise, certain students may indicate only members of the opposite sex as the ones they would like to work with or have as friends.

Findings and Conclusions from Social Measurement and Research

Numerous studies have found that various physical measures (motor ability, physical fitness, physically active, athletic ability, height, weight, health, etc.) were significantly related to social measures (leadership ability, well adjusted, popularity, etc.) (5, 71, 77, 83, 84, 93).

Concerning the characteristic of being physically active, Cowell (22), Tryon (88), Kuhlen and Lee, (51) and Hanley (34) all found it to be an important factor in social acceptance.

Physical educators have long contended that physical education activity participation brings about desirable traits or closer social integration within the group. Several studies have found support for such a contention (7, 18, 80, 95). While desirable changes in social status

have been reported, it is feasible that physical activity participation under the wrong leadership could breed undesirable social change. Perhaps differences in leadership or in emphasis on social goals was the reason why Blanchard (7) found girls' activity classes to be significantly superior to boys' activity classes in the acquisition of wholesome character and personality traits.

Two studies have investigated the effects of motivated activity participation upon social acceptance (64, 90). Walters (90) found motivated groups to be more closely knit than non-motivated groups in bowling classes and students to become more closely integrated socially as a result of acquaintance and group participation. Nelson and Johnson (64) further found that motivated participation brought about positive changes in social ratings when anti-cohesive pairs were induced to work together.

Several studies have found that individuals do not radically shift from one position to a very different position concerning social standings, thus revealing the stability of sociometric testing (11, 37, 64). Such testing has been used to show objective relationships between physical education and the development of groups (11, 60, 97) and the closer integration of individuals constituting those groups (11, 60, 75). Moreover, some studies have concerned themselves with the relationships between sociometric status and skill in specific activities such as volleyball, swimming, and dancing (10, 31, 80).

Members of athletic teams were found to have higher social status than boys who could not make the team or were not members of a team (6, 22, 30, 58, 66). Trapp (87) and Cowell and Ismail (22) further noted that social integration in a football squad was positive and remained so or increased as the playing time together increased.

Concerning the relationship of physical fitness and strength to social prestige, Clarke (17), Yarnell (96), Jones (40, 41), and Popp (69) found that boys who scored higher in strength and physical fitness enjoyed greater social prestige than those who did not. However, Haines (32) did not find such a relationship with fifth grade students. On the other hand, Cowell and Ismail (22) and Rarick (70) found students who scored high in physical measures and motor achievement to be the most popular.

Part II—Attitudes

Introduction

Attitudes are ideas or feelings that one may have about something as a result of past experience or as a result of imaginative likes and dislikes. Moreover, attitudes may change as often as we sometimes hear that a woman may change her mind. When conditions or changes in the environment occur, whether for better or worse, we can usually expect to see a change in attitudes. In physical education, we are concerned with the attitudes of students toward the physical education activity program as well as toward individual activities within the program. It is important to measure attitudes to see what effect various types of programs, administrative procedures, and methods of instruction have upon a student's feelings. When such measurement is objectively conducted, avenues of approach are opened up so that desirable changes can be logically brought about.

Uses of Attitude Tests

Several ways by which attitude tests may be utilized in physical education classes are listed as follows:
1. To assist in determining whether objectives are being reached.
2. As a means for assembling information in a survey for administrative planning and curriculum development.
3. To evaluate the effectiveness of teaching methods in helping students to enjoy physical education.

Scoring Attitude Scales

The two methods most commonly used in scoring attitude scales are the Thurston and Chave method and the Likert method. A study by Adams (1) shows how each method is applied to measuring attitude toward physical education.

In the *Thurston and Chave method*, the statements would appear as follows on the student statement list:

10. Physical education is a necessary subject.
     Agree ( ) Disagree ( )

Thus, to score the items, the teacher merely considers the statements marked as "agree." The other items are ignored. On the teacher's master statement list will appear statement marks which were derived from judges' scores representing the average position of each statement along a favorable-unfavorable continuum ranging from eleven to one. An example of a statement as it appears on the teacher's copy follows:

10. Physical education is a necessary subject. (8.65)

Thus, if "agree" is checked for statement number 10, the score awarded is 8.65, and the final score is the sum of all of the statement scores divided by the number of "agree" items checked. Statement scores should never appear on the student's questionnaire copy.

In the *Likert method*, each statement is followed by a line of "boxes" as follows:

10. Physical education is a necessary subject.
$$\boxed{+3} \ \boxed{+2} \ \boxed{+1} \ \boxed{0} \ \boxed{-1} \ \boxed{-2} \ \boxed{-3}$$

The numbers are interpreted as follows:

+3 = Very strongly agree
+2 = Strongly agree
+1 = Agree
0 = Neither agree nor disagree

−1 = Disagree
−2 = Strongly disagree
−3 = Very strongly disagree

Positive statements are weighted so that a favorable response will result in a higher score than an unfavorable one as seen below:

10. Physical education is a necessary subject.
$$\boxed{+3} \ \boxed{+2} \ \boxed{+1} \ \boxed{0} \ \boxed{-1} \ \boxed{-2} \ \boxed{-3}$$

Weighted Pts.	6	5	4	3	2	1	0

For negative statements, the entire procedure is reversed as follows:

15. Physical education is of no value to students.
$$\boxed{+3} \ \boxed{+2} \ \boxed{+1} \ \boxed{0} \ \boxed{-1} \ \boxed{-2} \ \boxed{-3}$$

Weighted Pts.	0	1	2	3	4	5	6

General Physical Education Attitude Scales

Several practical attitude scales directed toward general physical education include those by Wear, Carr, and Adams.

Wear's Attitude Scale with Equivalent Forms (91)

Objective: To measure changes in attitude toward physical eduction as a result of special experiences in which students might be involved.

Age Level: College.

Reliability: The reliability of form A was reported as .94 and the reliability of form B was .96. The product correlation between scores on the two forms was .96.

Validity: Face validity has been accepted for the two scales.

Directions: Students are directed to consider physical education only from the standpoint of its place as an activity course taught during a regular class period and to check the response which best expresses the feeling about each statement. Students are also told to let their own personal experiences determine their answers and that their answers will in no way affect their grade in any course.

Scoring: The five possible responses to each inventory item are as follows: strongly agree, agree, undecided, disagree, and strongly disagree. The responses are scored five-four-three-two-one when the item is worded positively and one-two-three-four-five when worded negatively. Thus, a high score would indicate a favorable attitude toward physical education. (See the original source for form B.)

Form A

1. If for any reason a few subjects have to be dropped from the school program, physical education should be one of the subjects dropped.
2. Physical education activities provide no opportunities for learning to control the emotions.
3. Physical education is one of the more important subjects in helping to establish and maintain desirable social standards.
4. Vigorous physical activity works off harmful emotional tensions.
5. I would take physical education only if it were required.
6. Participation in physical education makes no contribution to the development of poise.
7. Because physical skills loom large in importance in youth, it is essential that a person be helped to acquire and improve such skills.
8. Calisthenics taken regularly are good for one's general health.
9. Skill in active games or sports is not necessary for leading the fullest kind of life.
10. Physical education does more harm physically than it does good.
11. Associating with others in some physical education activity is fun.
12. Physical education classes provide situations for the formulation of attitudes which will make one a better citizen.
13. Physical education situations are among the poorest for making friends.
14. There is not enough value coming from physical education to justify the time consumed.
15. Physical education skills make worthwhile contributions to the enrichment of living.
16. People get all the physical exercise they need in just taking care of their daily work.
17. All who are physically able will profit from an hour of physical education each day.
18. Physical education makes a valuable contribution toward building up an adequate reserve of strength and endurance for everyday living.
19. Physical education tears down sociability by encouraging people to attempt to surpass each other in many of the activities.
20. Participation in physical education activities makes for a more wholesome outlook on life.
21. Physical education adds nothing to the improvement of social behavior.
22. Physical education class activities will help to relieve and relax physical tensions.
23. Participation in physical education activities helps a person to maintain a healthful emotional life.
24. Physical education is one of the more important subjects in the school program.
25. There is little value in physical education as far as physical well-being is concerned.
26. Physical education should be included in the program of every school.
27. Skills learned in a physical education class do not benefit a person.
28. Physical education provides situations for developing character qualities.
29. Physical education makes for more enjoyable living.
30. Physical education has no place in modern education.

Sample

Agree	Disagree	
_____	_____	1. Being a leader is a fine responsibility.
_____	_____	2. I feel as if I am learning something when I play with someone who plays better than I do.
_____	_____	3. I prefer playing outdoors when the weather is good.
_____	_____	4. I like to bathe after playing hard.
_____	_____	5. I like to set a goal for my own improvement and want to practice until I reach that goal.
_____	_____	6. I like to talk to my teachers as that makes them seem like friends.
_____	_____	7. I prefer to play in a playsuit as I feel I can play more freely.
_____	_____	8. I like games that have lots of vigorous activity in them.
_____	_____	9. I like to have a place to keep my own things.
_____	_____	10. Playing games with a group is more fun than playing alone.

Carr Physical Education Attitude Scale (16)

Objective: To determine the attitudes of girls as they relate to physical education.

Age Level: High school.

Sex: Satisfactory for girls.

Reliability: Reliability was not reported for this scale.

Validity: Face validity was accepted in addition to following selected criteria in establishing the scale.

Directions: The student is directed to indicate her attitude be either agreeing or disagreeing with each statement.

Scale: Place a check mark in the desired space before each statement.

Scoring: The first thirty-seven statements are indicated as desirable attitudes and the remaining forty-seven statements as undesirable attitudes. The final score is determined by subtracting the percentage of undesirable attitudes indicated from the percentage of desirable attitudes checked. (See original source for complete list of statements.)

Adams Physical Education Attitude Scale (1)

Objective: To provide a means for assessing individual and group attitudes toward physical education.

Age Level: High school and college.

Sex: Satisfactory for both boys and girls.

Reliability: An *r* of .71 was obtained using the Thurstone and Chave scoring scale.

Validity: An *r* of .77 was obtained when correlating the Thurston (set 1) scoring scale against the Likert scoring scale.

Directions: This is a questionnaire to measure your attitude toward physical education as a college subject. There are a number of statements about physical education below, each one followed by a pair of brackets under two headings, "Agree" and "Disagree." You are asked to check one of these brackets to show whether you agree or disagree with the statement. Please consider each statement carefully, and in your answer indicate your present feelings about physical education as you know it.

Sample: Physical education encourages moral improvement. Agree ( ) Disagree ( )

Scoring: Consider only the "agree" item checked. The final score is the sum of all of the statement scores divided by the number of "agree" items checked. Thus, if "agree" is checked for items 7, 8, 9, and 12, the corresponding statement values of 8.64, 8.0, 7.71, and 10.6 are added up and divided by 4.

Additional Pointers: (a) Statement scores should never be printed on the questionnaire itself. (b) A cardboard straight-edge with the appropriate numbers printed and spaced to correspond with brackets in the questionnaire helps with scoring.

Set I*
Sample of Twelve Items

Agree	Disagree		
————	————	1. Physical education gets very monotonous.	3.50
————	————	2. I only feel like doing physical education now and then.	5.95
————	————	3. Physical education should be disposed of.	1.58
————	————	4. Physical education is particularly limited in its value.	4.50
————	————	5. I suppose physical education is all right but I don't much care for it.	5.03
————	————	6. Physical education is the most hateful subject of all.	1.02
————	————	7. I do not want to give up physical education.	8.64
————	————	8. On the whole I think physical education is a good thing.	8.0
————	————	9. People who like physical education are nearly always good to know.	7.71
————	————	10. Anyone who likes physical education is silly.	2.65
————	————	11. Physical education has some usefulness.	6.45
————	————	12. Physical education is the ideal subject.	10.66

*See original source for complete scale.

Attitude Scales toward Physical Activity

Scales by Kenyon, McPherson and Yuhansz, and Richardson are examples of scales directed toward attitudes dealing with physical activity and physical fitness.

Kenyon's Six Attitude Scales toward Physical Activity (43,44)

Objective: To determine attitudes toward physical activity. The author recommends that the scales be restricted to use for research purposes.

Age Level: College.

Reliability: Hoyt reliabilities ranged from .72 to .89 for the six scales.

Validity: Scale scores differentiated satisfactorily between strong and weak preference groups in the predicted direction for all scales except "catharsis" (recreation and relaxation).

Directions: The directions and scales may be ordered as follows:*

ADI Auxiliary Publications Project
Photoduplication Service
Library of Congress
Washington, D.C. 20540

*Cite document number 9983 and enclose $1.25 for photoprints. Make checks or money orders payable to: Chief, Photoduplication Service, Library of Congress.

The six dimensions developed include:**
1. Physical Activity as a Social Experience.
2. Physical Activity as Health and Fitness.
3. Physical Activity as the Pursuit of Vertigo.
4. Physical Activity as an Aesthetic Experience.
5. Physical Activity as Catharsis.
6. Physical Activity as an Ascetic Experience.

An example of an item from the vertigo scale is as follows: "I would enjoy engaging in those games and sports that require a defiance of danger."

Scoring: Likert type scoring is used. Order photoprints for details.

Exercise and Physical Activity Scale (61)

Objective: To measure the attitude of students toward exercise and physical activity.

Age Level: High school through adulthood.

**A seventh dimension was more recently developed along with a semantic differential approach for all seven scales. For details, the reader is referred to the following:
Values Held for Physical Activity by Selected Urban Secondary School Students in Canada, Australia, England and the United States.
This publication can be obtained from ERIC Document Reproduction Service, P. O. Drawer O, Bethesda, Md. 20014, U.S.A. Please quote accession #ED 019709. The cost for microfiche copy is 65¢ and for hard copy $13.16. This report contains considerable data and also complete instructions on the use of the scales.

Sample Inventory Questions

Strongly Disagree	Disagree	Neutral	Agree	Strongly Agree		
( )	( )	( )	( )	( )	1.	Physical exercise is beneficial to the human body.
( )	( )	( )	( )	( )	2.	Exercise helps to work off emotional tensions and anxieties.
( )	( )	( )	( )	( )	3.	Adults get all the physical activity they need in their daily work.
( )	( )	( )	( )	( )	4.	Exercise is of little value in maintaining desirable body weight.
( )	( )	( )	( )	( )	5.	Regular physical activity makes one feel better.
( )	( )	( )	( )	( )	6.	Physical education should be a required subject for elementary and secondary school children.
( )	( )	( )	( )	( )	7.	Exercise does more harm than good.
( )	( )	( )	( )	( )	8.	Those who are physically able should take part in a daily period of physical activity.
( )	( )	( )	( )	( )	9.	An individual has all the strength and stamina he needs without participating in an exercise program.
( )	( )	( )	( )	( )	10.	Exercise does little to improve a person's sense of well-being.

Reliability: An r of .72 was reported on a test-retest basis.

Validity: A significant difference at the .01 level occurred between a criterion group presumed to have favorable attitudes and a criterion group presumed to have unfavorable attitudes.

Directions: Students are asked to respond to the fifty statements expressing common opinions, beliefs, attitudes, and fallacies about exercise and physical activity.

Scoring: A five-point Likert-type scale is used. The scores on each item are summed, and the total score indicates the intensity of the subject's attitude toward exercise and physical activity. (Contact the authors of the original source for further details.)

Richardson Physical Fitness and Attitude Scale (73)

Objective: To measure the attitude of students toward physical fitness and exercise.

Age Level: College, but it could be adapted for the high school students.

Richardson Scale (73)

Form A*
Sample of 10 Items**

(1.1) Physical fitness activity is the lowest type of activity indulged in by man.
(1.3) Man has outgrown the need for physical fitness programs.
(1.5) Physical fitness activity programs are necessary only in wartime.
(1.7) Physical fitness activities are the least civilized of man's activities.
(1.9) Physical activity should not be stressed so much in our present culture.
(2.1) Planned physical activity programs have limited value.
(2.3) Physical fitness activity is unnecessary.
(2.5) The values of physical activity are debatable.
(2.7) Physical fitness activity should be left to the individual.
(2.9) Physical fitness programs are too soft.

*The scale values indicated in parentheses to the left of each test item are listed with decimal points only for presentation purposes here. When using the instrument in testing, items are given three numbers (without decimals) for convenience in scoring. The first of the three refers to item number on the test; the last two numbers indicate scale values. Thus, the subject upon testing sees the numbers, 111, 113, 115, 117, etc., to the left of each item. This method of numbering was utilized to minimize the possibility of a suggested response pattern for the subject.

**See original source for complete scale.

Sex: Satisfactory for both boys and girls.
Reliability: A reliability coefficient derived from test-retest samplings was .83±.06.
Validity: Based upon authoritative opinion and expert judgment.
Directions: Read each item carefully and circle the number opposite each item with which you agree. *Make no marks* on the numbers opposite the items with which you disagree. There is no time limit but mark rapidly.
Scoring: The subject's score is the median value of numerical scale values of the statements marked. For example, if the subject indicated an agreement with seven items having scale values of 2.5, 2.7, 3.5, 4.1, 4.5, and 4.7, the value of 3.7 would be his score.

Psycho/Social Constructs (Sportsmanship Scales)

The following scales by Johnson and Lakie pertain to the sensitivity that a student has in dealing with his own needs and rights and those of other people.

Johnson Sportsmanship Scale (39)

Example: A pitcher in a baseball game threw a fastball at the batter to scare him.

STRONGLY APPROVE   APPROVE   DISAPPROVE   STRONGLY DISAPPROVE

(If you strongly approve of this action by the pitcher you would circle the first response category as shown.)

Sample of Ten Items
(Request complete scales from the original author)

1. After a basketball player was called by the official for traveling, he slammed the basketball onto the floor.

    STRONGLY APPROVE   APPROVE   DISAPPROVE   STRONGLY DISAPPROVE

2. A baseball player was called out as he slid into home plate. He jumped up and down on the plate and screamed at the official.

    STRONGLY APPROVE   APPROVE   DISAPPROVE   STRONGLY DISAPPROVE

3. After a personal foul was called against a basketball player, he shook his fist in the official's face.

    STRONGLY APPROVE   APPROVE   DISAPPROVE   STRONGLY DISAPPROVE

4. A basketball coach talked very loudly in order to annoy an opponent who was attempting to make a very important free throw shot.

    STRONGLY APPROVE   APPROVE   DISAPPROVE   STRONGLY DISAPPROVE

5. After a baseball game, the coach of the losing team went up to the umpire and demanded to know how much money had been paid to "throw" the game.

    STRONGLY APPROVE   APPROVE   DISAPPROVE   STRONGLY DISAPPROVE

6. A basketball coach led the spectators in jeering at the official who made calls against his team.

    STRONGLY APPROVE   APPROVE   DISAPPROVE   STRONGLY DISAPPROVE

7. After two men were put out on a double play attempt, a baseball coach told the players in his dugout to boo the umpire's decision.

    STRONGLY APPROVE   APPROVE   DISAPPROVE   STRONGLY DISAPPROVE

8. As the basketball coach left the gymnasium after the game, he shouted at the officials, "You lost me the game; I never saw such lousy officiating in my life."

    STRONGLY APPROVE   APPROVE   DISAPPROVE   STRONGLY DISAPPROVE

9. A basketball coach put sand on the gym floor to force the opponents into traveling penalties.

    STRONGLY APPROVE   APPROVE   DISAPPROVE   STRONGLY DISAPPROVE

10. A football coach left the bench to change the position of a marker dropped by an official to indicate where the ball went out of bounds.

    STRONGLY APPROVE   APPROVE   DISAPPROVE   STRONGLY DISAPPROVE

Johnson Sportsmanship Attitude Scales (39)

Objective: To measure attitudes toward sportsmanship.
Age Level: Ages twelve through fourteen.
Sex: Satisfactory for both boys and girls.
Reliability: A reliability of .86 was found between scores of form A and form B for a single test administration.
Validity: Empirical validity coefficients ranging from -.01 to .43 were found between test scores and behavior ratings.
Directions: This booklet contains several statements describing events that happen in sports and games. Read each statement carefully and decide whether you approve or disapprove of the action taken by the person. Circle the ONE response category that tells the way you feel. PLEASE COMPLETE *EVERY* ITEM. (See page 402.)

Lakie's Attitudes Toward Athletic Competition Scale (52)

Objective: To determine to what degree the "win-at-any-cost" attitude exists among students and groups.
Age Level: College level.
Sex: Satisfactory for both men and women.
Reliability: A reliability of .81 was reported.
Validity: Face validity was accepted for this scale.
Directions: Students are directed to circle the category that indicates their feelings toward the behavior described in each of the situations below:
Scoring: Except for item 6, where points should be figured in reverse order, add the points as scored. The lower the scores, the greater the student agrees with a "win-at-any-cost" attitude.

Problems Associated with Attitude Testing

Several of the problems associated with attitude testing are listed as follows:
1. Each statement must be worded carefully to

Lakie's Scale (52)

Sample of Ten Items*

(1) Strongly Approve (2) Approve (3) Undecided (4) Disapprove (5) Strongly Disapprove

1 2 3 4 5   1. During a football game team A has the ball on its own 45-yard line, fourth down and 1 yd. to go for a first down. The coach of team A signals to the quarterback the play that he wants the team to run.

1 2 3 4 5   2. Team A is the visiting basketball team and each time a member of the team is given a free shot the home crowd sets up a continual din of noise until the shot has been taken.

1 2 3 4 5   3. Tennis player A frequently calls out, throws up his arms, or otherwise tries to indicate that his opponent's serve is out of bounds when it is questionable.

1 2 3 4 5   4. In a track meet team A enters a man in the mile run who is to set a fast pace for the first half of the race and then drop out.

1 2 3 4 5   5. In a football game team B's quarterback was tackled repeatedly after handing off and after he was out of the play.

1 2 3 4 5   6. Sam, playing golf with his friends, hit a drive into the rough. He accidentally moved the ball with his foot; although not improving his position, he added a penalty stroke to his score.

1 2 3 4 5   7. A basketball player was caught out of position on defense, and rather than allow his opponent to attempt a field goal he fouled him.

1 2 3 4 5   8. Player A during a golf match made quick noises and movements when player B was getting ready to make a shot.

1 2 3 4 5   9. School A has a powerful but quite slow football team. The night before playing a smaller but faster team, they allowed the field sprinkling system to remain on, causing the field to be heavy and slow.

1 2 3 4 5   10. A basketball team used player A to draw the opponent's high scorer into fouling situations.

---

*Consult the original source for the complete scale.

secure the actual attitude response and to avoid giving away the desired response.

2. There is an obvious lack of stability of attitudes of young people, especially those below the high school level. It is quite common for students to change their attitudes rapidly after exposure to new experiences. Therefore, attitude results must not be regarded as permanent.

3. The validity associated with attitude scales is sometimes questionable. If students have had limited experience with certain aspects of a program, obviously they cannot make intelligent responses concerning them.

Findings and Conclusions from Attitude Measurement and Research

Numerous studies have reported that students generally have favorable attitudes toward physical education as an activity course (3, 4, 12, 13, 42). Brumbach (13) further found that students who participated in a high school athletic program or who attended a small school (enrollment under 300) were apt to have a wholesome attitude toward physical education. Moreover, both Bell (4) and Brumbach (13) found that the university students with the most favorable attitudes toward physical education were the ones who had had more years of physical education in high school.

Physical educators who are concerned with the social and ethical values of activities often question the contributions of varsity athletics toward such values. Both Kistler (47) and Richardson (74) found that varsity athletes had poorer attitudes about sportsmanship than did those students who either had not participated at the varsity level or had engaged in the less publicized sports.

While Kistler (47) found that only a small number of students were aware of the benefits concerning social and ethical values received from participation in physical education classes, Keogh (46) reported that students endorsed the social, physical, and emotional values of physical education, and Vincent (89) found that college women expressed greatest appreciation for the physiological-physical values of physical education.

Dotson and Stanley (27) studied the values of physical activities perceived by male students and found that students of gymnastics expressed the highest positive attitude, with students of badminton, archery, and bowling the lowest. They also found that physical activity as pursuit of vertigo (thrills and excitement) and catharsis (recreation and relaxation) were the strongest perceived values, while aesthetic experience was the lowest of the six values studied.

Carr (16) and Vincent (89) found that attitudes held by girls do influence their success in physical education. Wessel and Nelson (94) further found that strength among college women is significantly related to attitudes toward physical activity.

Several studies have measured attitudes of various groups toward athletic competition. The results of such studies are listed as follows:

1. Scott (76) found that a majority of the parents, teachers, and administrators surveyed tended to favor intensive competition at the elementary school level.

2. McGee (59) found that parents and coaches are significantly more in favor of intensive athletic competition for high school girls than are administrators.

3. Leyhe (54) reported that a majority of the women members of AAHPER believed that girl participants in varsity sports are happier and better adjusted than non-participants.

References and Bibliography

1. Adams, R. S., "Two Scales for Measuring Attitude Toward Physical Education," *Research Quarterly*, 34:91-94, 1963.

2. Alderman, K. B., "A Sociopsychological Assessment of Attitude Toward Physical Activity in Champion Athletes," *Research Quarterly*, 41:1-9, 1970.

3. Baker, Mary C., "Factors Which May Influence the Participation in Physical Education of Girls and Women," *Research Quarterly*, 11:126-131, 1940.

4. Bell, Margaret, and C. Etta Walters, "Attitudes of Women at the University of Michigan Toward Physical Education," *Research Quarterly*, 24:379, December, 1953.

5. Betz, Robert L., "A Comparison Between Personality Limits and Physical Fitness Tests of Males 26-60" (Unpublished master's thesis, University of Illinois, 1956).

6. Biddulph, Lowell G., "Athletic Achievement and Personal-Social Adjustment of High School Boys," *Research Quarterly*, 25:1-7, 1954.

7. Blanchard, B. E., "A Comparative Analysis of Secondary School Boys' and Girls' Character and Personality Traits in Physical Education

Classes," *Research Quarterly,* 17:33-39, March, 1946.

8. _____ , "A Behavior Frequency Rating Scale for the Measurement of Character and Personality in Physical Education Classroom Situations," *Research Quarterly,* May, 1936, pp. 56-66.

9. Bovyer, George, "Children's Concepts of Sportsmanship in the Fourth, Fifth, and Sixth Grades," *Research Quarterly,* 34:282-87, 1963.

10. Breck, June, "A Sociometric Test of Status as Measured in Physical Education Classes" (Unpublished master's thesis, University of California, 1947).

11. Breck, Sabina June, "A Sociometric Measurement of Status in Physical Education Classes," *Research Quarterly,* 21:75-82, May, 1950.

12. Broer, Marion, and others, "Attitudes of University of Washington Women Students Toward Physical Education Activity," *Research Quarterly,* 36:378-384, December, 1955.

13. Brumbach, Wayne B., and J. A. Cross, "Attitudes Toward Physical Education of Male Students Entering the University of Oregon," *Research Quarterly,* 36:10, March, 1965.

14. Campbell, Donald E. "Students' Attitudes Toward Physical Education," *Research Quarterly,* 39:456-62, 1968.

15. _____ , "Wear Attitude Inventory Applied to Junior High School Boys," *Research Quarterly,* 39:888-893, December, 1968.

16. Carr, Martha G., "The Relationship Between Success in Physical Education and Selected Attitudes Expressed by High School Freshman Girls," *Research Quarterly,* 16:176-191, October, 1945.

17. Clarke, H. Harrison, and David H. Clarke, "Social Status and Mental Health of Boys as Related to Their Maturity, Structural, and Strength Characteristics," *Research Quarterly,* 32:326, October, 1961.

18. Clevett, Melvin A., "An Experiment in Physical Education Activities Related to the Teaching of Honesty and Motor Skills," *Research Quarterly,* 3:121-127, March, 1932.

19. Corbin, C., and Tolson, H., "Attitudes of College Males toward Physical Activity" (Unpublished paper, Texas A & M University, 1970).

20. Cowell, Charles C., "Validating an Index of Social Adjustment for High School Use," *Research Quarterly,* March, 1958, pp. 7-18.

21. _____ , "An Abstract of a Study of Differentials in Junior High School Boys Based on the Observation of Physical Education Activities," *Research Quarterly,* 6:129-136, December, 1935.

22. _____ , and A. H. Ismail, "Relationships Between Selected Social and Physical Factors," *Research Quarterly,* 33:4 , March, 1962.

23. _____ , "Validity of a Football Rating Scale and Its Relationship to Social Integration and Academic Ability," *Research Quarterly,* 32:461-467, December, 1961.

24. Cratty, Bryant J., *Movement Behavior and Motor Learning,* Philadelphia: Lea and Febiger, 1967.

25. Darden, Ellington, "Sixteen Personality Factor Profiles of Competitive Body Builders and Weightlifters," *Research Quarterly,* 43:142-47, May, 1972.

26. Dawley, Dorothy J., Maurice Troyer, and John H. Shaw, "Relationship Between Observed Behavior in Elementary School Physical Education and Test Responses," *Research Quarterly,* 22:70-76, March, 1951.

27. Dotson, Charles O., and W. J. Stanley, "Values of Physical Activity Perceived by Male University Students," *Research Quarterly,* 43:148-56, May, 1972.

28. Dowell, Linus J., "A Study of Selected Psychological Dimensions and Athletic Achievement of Entering College Freshmen" (Paper presented at Southern District Convention of AAHPER, Memphis, 1969).

29. Drinkwater, Barbara L., "Development of an Attitude Inventory to Measure the Attitudes of High School Girls Toward Physical Education as a Career for Women," *Research Quarterly,* 31:575-580, December, 1960.

30. Flowtow, Ernest A., "Charting Social Relationships of School Children," *Elementary School Journal,* 46:498, May, 1946.

31. Fulton, Ruth E., "Relationship Between Teammate Status and Measures of Skill in Volleyball," *Research Quarterly,* 21:274-276, October, 1950.

32. Haines, James E., "The Relationship of Kraus-Weber Minimal Muscular Fitness and Rogers' Physical Fitness Index Tests with Social Acceptance, Teacher Acceptance, and Emotional Stability in Selected Fifth Grade Pupils" (Unpublished doctoral dissertation, Springfield College, 1957).

33. Hale, Patricia W., "Proposed Method for Analyzing Sociometric Data," *Research Quarterly,* 27:152-61, May, 1956.

34. Hanley, Charles, "Physique and Reputation of Junior High School Boys," *Child Development,* 22:247, 1951.

35. Harres, Bea, "Attitudes of Students Toward Women's Athletic Competition," *Research Quarterly,* 39:278-284, May, 1968.

36. Jaeger, Eloise, "An Investigation of a Projective Test in Determining Attitudes of Prospective Teachers of Physical Education" (Unpublished doctoral dissertation, State University of Iowa, 1952).

37. Jennings, Helen H., "Sociometry and Social Theory," *American Sociological Review,* 6:512-522, 1941.

38. Johnson, Alvin D., "An Attempt at Change in Inter-Personal Relations," *Sociometry,* 2:43-49.

39. Johnson, Marion L., "Construction of Sportsmanship Attitude Scales," *Research Quarterly,* 40:312-316, May, 1969.

40. Jones, Harold E., "Motor Performance and Growth," Berkeley, Cal.: University of California Press, 1949.

41. _____, "Physical Ability as a Factor in Social Adjustment in Adolescence," *Journal of Educational Research,* 4:287, 1946.

42. Kappes, Eveline E., "Inventory to Determine Attitudes of College Women Toward Physical Education and Student Services of the Physical Education Department," *Research Quarterly,* 25:429-438, December, 1954.

43. Kenyon, Gerald S., "A Conceptual Model for Characterizing Physical Activity," *Research Quarterly,* 39:96-105, 1968.

44. _____, "Six Scales for Assessing Attitude Toward Physical Activity," *Research Quarterly,* 39:566-74, October, 1968.

45. Keogh, Jack, "Extreme Attitudes Toward Physical Education," *Research Quarterly,* 34:27-33, 1963.

46. _____, "Analysis of General Attitudes Toward Physical Education," *Research Quarterly,* 33:239-248, May, 1962.

47. Kistler, J. W., "Attitudes Expressed About Behavior Demonstrated in Certain Specific Situations Occurring in Sports," in *60th Annual Proceedings, National College Physical Education Association, 1957, pp. 55-59.*

48. Kroll, Walter, "Sixteen Personality Factor Profiles of Collegiate Wrestlers," *Research Quarterly,* 38:49-57, 1967.

49. _____, and B. Robert Carlson, "Discriminant Function and Hierarchial Grouping Analysis of Karate Participants' Personality Profiles," *Research Quarterly,* 38:405-11, 1967.

50. Kroll, Walter, and Kay H. Peterson, "Personality Factor Profiles of Collegiate Football Teams," *Research Quarterly,* 36:533-40, 1965.

51. Kuhlen, Raymond G., and Beatrice J. Lee, "Personality Characteristics and Social Acceptability in Adolescence," *Journal of Educational Psychology,* 34:321, 1943.

52. Lakie, William L., "Expressed Attitudes of Various Groups of Athletes Toward Athletic Competition," *Research Quarterly,* 35:497-503, December, 1964.

53. Lawrence, Trudys, "Appraisal of Emotional Health at the Secondary School Level," *Research Quarterly,* 37:252-257, May, 1966.

54. Leyhe, Naomi L., "Attitudes of the Women Members of the American Association of Health, Physical Education, and Recreation Toward Competition in Sports for Girls and Women" (Microcarded dissertation, University of Iowa, 1955, p. 99).

55. McAfee, Robert A., "Sportsmanship Attitudes of Sixth, Seventh, and Eighth Grade Boys," *Research Quarterly,* 26:120, March, 1955.

56. McCloy, Charles H., "Character Building Through Physical Education," *Research Quarterly,* 1:41-61, October, 1930.

57. _____, and Ferene Hepp, "General Factors or Components of Character as Related to Physical Education," *Research Quarterly,* 28:269-78, October, 1957.

58. McCraw, L. N., and J. W. Tabert, "Sociometric Status and Athletic Ability of Junior High School Boys," *Research Quarterly,* 24:72-78, 1953.

59. McGee, Rosemary, "Comparison of Attitudes Toward Intensive Competition for High School Girls" (Microcarded dissertation, University of Iowa, June, 1954, pp. 18, 72).

60. McKenna, Helen M., "The Effects of Two Methods of Grouping in Physical Education Upon the Social Structure of the Group" (Unpublished master's thesis, University of California, 1948).

61. McPherson, B. D., and M. S. Yuhansz, "An Inventory for Assessing Men's Attitudes Toward Exercise and Physical Activity," *Research Quarterly,* 39:218-19, March, 1968.

62. Moyer, L. J., J. C. Mitchem, and M. M. Bell, "Women's Attitudes Toward Physical Education in the General Education Program of Northern Illinois University," *Research Quarterly,* 37:515-19, December, 1966.

63. Nelson, Dale O., "Leadership in Sports," *Research Quarterly,* 37:268-75, May, 1966.

64. Nelson, Jack K., and Barry L. Johnson, "Effects of Varied Techniques in Organizing Class Competition Upon Changes in Sociometric Status," *Research Quarterly,* 39:634-639, 1968.

65. O'Neel, F. W., "A Frequency Rating Scale for the Measurement of Character and Personality in High School Physical Education for Boys," *Research Quarterly,* 7:67-76, May, 1936.

66. Ondrus, Joseph, "A Sociometric Analysis of Group Structure and the Effect of Football Activities on Inter-personal Relationships" (Unpublished doctoral dissertation, New York University, 1953).

67. Peterson, James A., and Rainer Martens, "Success and Residential Affiliation as Determinants of Team Cohesiveness," *Research Quarterly,* 43:62-75, March, 1972.

68. Peterson, Sheri L., Jerome C. Weber, and William W. Trousdale, "Personality Traits of Women in Team Sports Versus Women in Individual Sports," *Research Quarterly,* 38:686-90, 1967.

69. Popp, James, "Case Studies of Sophomore High School Boys with High and Low Physical Fitness Indices" (Unpublished master's thesis, University of Oregon, 1959).

70. Rarick, G. Lawrence, "A Study of Twenty Third-Grade Children Exhibiting Extreme Levels of

Achievement on Tests of Motor Proficiency," *Research Quarterly,* 20:142-152, May, 1949.

71. Reaney, M. Jane, "The Correlation Between General Intelligence and Play Ability as Shown in Organized Group Games," *British Journal of Psychology,* 7:226-252, 1914.

72. Rice, Sidney, "Attitudes and Physical Education," *Journal of Health Physical Education Recreation,* 17:224, April, 1946.

73. Richardson, Charles E., "Thurstone Scale of Measuring Attitudes of College Students Toward Physical Fitness and Exercise," *Research Quarterly,* 31:638-43, December, 1960.

74. Richardson, Deane E., "Ethical Conduct in Sport Situations," *66th Annual Proceedings, National College Physical Education Association,* 1962, pp. 98-104.

75. Robinson, Virginia Ruth, "A Study of the Effects of Two Methods of Teaching Physical Education as Measured by a Sociometric Test" (Unpublished master's thesis, University of California, 1948).

76. Scott, Martha P., "Attitudes Toward Athletic Competition in the Elementary School," *Research Quarterly,* 24:352-361, October, 1953.

77. Signorella, Michael, "Social Adjustment and Athletic Participation" (Unpublished study, Purdue University, 1963).

78. Singer, Robert N., "Personality Differences Between and Within Baseball and Tennis Players," *Research Quarterly,* 40:582-88, 1969.

79. _____, "Athletic Participation: Cause or Result of Certain Personality Factors?" *Physical Educator,* 4:169-71, 1967.

80. Skubic, Elvera, "A Study in Acquaintanceship and Social Status in Physical Education Classes," *Research Quarterly,* 20:80-87, March, 1947.

81. Slusher, Howard, "Personality and Intelligence Characteristics of Selected High School Athletes and Nonathletes," *Research Quarterly,* 35:539-45, 1964.

82. Smith, Hope, and Marguerite A. Clifton, *Physical Education—Exploring Your Future,* Englewood Cliffs, N. J.: Prentice-Hall, 1962, pp. 77-78.

83. Sperling, A. P., "The Relationship Between Personality Adjustment and Achievement in Physical Education Activities," *Research Quarterly,* 13:351-363, October, 1942.

84. Stogdill, Ralph M., "Personal Factors Associated with Leadership: A Survey of Literature," *Journal of Psychology,* 25:35-71, 1948.

85. Thune, John B., "Personality of Weightlifters," *Research Quarterly,* 20:296-306, 1949.

86. Todd, Frances, "Sociometry in Physical Education," *Journal of Health Physical Education Recreation,* 24:23-24, May, 1953.

87. Trapp, William G., "A Study of Social Integration in a College Football Squad," in *56th Annual Proceedings,* College Physical Education Association, 1953.

88. Tryon, Caroline C., "Evaluation of Adolescent Personality by Adolescents," *Monograph of the Society for Research in Child Development,* Vol. 4, 1939.

89. Vincent, Marilyn F., "Attitudes of College Women Toward Physical Education and Their Relationship to Success in Physical Education," *Research Quarterly,* 38:130, March, 1967.

90. Walters, C. Etta, "A Sociometric Study of Motivated and Non-Motivated Bowling Groups," *Research Quarterly,* 26:107-112, March, 1955.

91. Wear, C. L., "Construction of Equivalent Forms of an Attitude Scale," *Research Quarterly,* 26:113-119, March, 1955.

92. _____, "The Evaluation of Attitudes Toward Physical Education as an Activity Course," *Research Quarterly,* 22:114-126, March, 1951.

93. Wells, Harold P., "Relationship Between Physical Fitness and Psychological Variables" (Unpublished doctoral dissertation, University of Illinois, 1958).

94. Wessel, Janet, and Richard Nelson, "Relationship Between Strength and Attitudes Toward Physical Education Activities Among College Women," *Research Quarterly,* 35:562-568, December, 1964.

95. Whilden, Peggy P., "Comparison of Two Methods of Teaching Beginning Basketball," *Research Quarterly,* 27:235-242, May, 1956.

96. Yarnell, C. Douglas, "Relationship of Physical Fitness to Selected Measures of Popularity," *Research Quarterly,* 37:287, May, 1966.

97. Zeleny, Leslie Day, "Status: Its Measurement and Control in Education," *Sociometry,* 4:193-204.

Chapter Twenty-one

The Measurement of Knowledge

The measurement of knowledge in physical education activity classes is just as important as knowledge measurement in other subject areas. When the physical educator elects not to secure a measure of knowledge, he has ignored one of the major objectives of our field and has failed to capitalize on the potential of such tests to further the learning process. Evaluation of the students' knowledge of rules, strategy, etiquette, and other pertinent information should be considered as an integral and vital part of every teaching unit.

The tools employed in the measurement of knowledge should be so designed that the teacher can easily determine what the students have learned in laboratory participation and from facts and materials presented within the unit. Knowledge tests consist of several types. The most common and practical type used in the classroom is the teacher-made test, which may be either objective or subjective in nature. The objective test calls for a brief response and, if properly constructed, has higher reliability and objectivity than the subjective or essay test, which usually calls for a long and detailed response.

A standardized test is merely one that has been subjected to rigorous steps and procedures in construction and usually is accompanied by norms. Most standardized tests are of the objective type consisting of true-false, matching, and multiple choice questions. Standardized tests have not had widespread use in physical education, at least not on the national level.

Uses of Knowledge Tests

Several ways in which knowledge tests in physical education classes may be utilized are listed as follows:

1. To determine the needs of the students as to what information should be imparted.
2. To evaluate student achievement and form the basis for determining grades at the end of an instructional unit.
3. To evaluate teaching effectiveness in that when a class (as a whole) fails to respond properly, some inadequacy on the part of the teacher may be noted.
4. To motivate students to learn the information deemed important by the teacher and perhaps stimulate the students to undertake more comprehensive study on the subject.
5. To further the learning process by providing a knowledge of the results. When immediate

_____ 1. The (1) event is conducted in a square. area approximately 40 by 40 feet on the floor.
_____ 2. The two American gymnastics events which are not contested
_____ 3. as part of the all-around competition are (2) and (3) .
_____ 4. (4) refers to assisting or helping someone during the performance of a stunt.
_____ 5. Strength is a term used to denote (5) being exerted against a resistance.

reports are provided, the desired responses are more apt to be learned than when the results are delayed or when the tests are not returned at all.

Practical Test Items for Knowledge Measurement

The most common types of test questions are the completion, multiple choice, matching, true-false, and the essay. Each of these methods is discussed briefly by presenting some sample questions and listing strong points and weak points of each.

Completion Items

These items require that the student supply a word or phrase in a blank to complete a sentence. Obviously, only key words or phrases should be asked for, since trivial information serves little instructional purpose.
Directions: Complete each sentence by writing in the correct answer in the blank to the extreme left.

Strong Points: (a) It reduces the problem of guessing. (b) Completion items can be used in a variety of ways to obtain the desired answers. (c) It requires intensive study on the part of the student in that he must recall and reproduce material rather than merely recognize it. (d) Completion items are relatively easy to prepare.

Weak Points: (a) Subjective judgment on the part of the teacher as to what specific items are most important may be a weakness. (b) It is easy to get different answers, each of which could be appropriate due to the wording of the statement. (c) There is a tendency to test on isolated facts in order to confine the answers to one word.

Multiple Choice Items

Questions of this type consist of an incomplete statement which is followed by several answers, one of which is the correct

Multiple Choice Samples:

_____ 1. Tonus is decreased by:
    a. Worry
    b. Exercise
    c. Lack of sleep
    d. Colds
    e. Inactivity

_____ 2. The normal college student needs:
    a. Light exercise
    b. Vigorous exercise
    c. No exercise
    d. Mainly team sports
    e. Infrequent exercise

_____ 3. One of the best measurements of physical fitness is through:
    a. Mental tests
    b. Blood tests
    c. Muscular strength tests
    d. Tests of agility
    e. Tests of balance

_____ 4. The inability of a muscle to contract as a result of continual contraction indicates:
    a. Nervous block
    b. Poor nutrition
    c. Malfunction of nerve impulse
    d. Destruction of end plate
    e. Fatigue

_____ 5. A person develops neuromuscular skill through:
    a. Occasional sports activity
    b. Studying films of movement
    c. Watching others perform
    d. Repeated practice of skills
    e. A corrective program of physical education

Matching Samples:

_____	1. Rectus abdominis	a. Flexion of neck
_____	2. Trapezius	b. Flexion of ankle
_____	3. Rhomboid	c. Trunk flexion
_____	4. Pectoralis major	d. Upward rotation of scapula
_____	5. Biceps	e. Downward rotation of scapula
_____	6. Triceps	f. Abduction of humerus
_____	7. Sternocleidomastoid	g. Flexion of forearm
_____	8. Biceps femoris	h. Extension of the hip
		i. Extension of forearm
		j. Abduction of femur

one. In some cases, the student may be directed to pick the only incorrect answer from among several correct responses or to pick the one best answer from among all correct responses.

Directions: Place the letter of the correct response for each statement on the line at the left.

Strong Points: (a) Multiple choice items can be applied to most types of material and information. (b) Such items are easy to score. (c) Such items can be used at practically all educational levels. (d) Guessing is discouraged if the questions are well constructed.

Weak Points: (a) Good multiple choice items are relatively difficult to prepare. (b) Too much emphasis is frequently placed on isolated facts, and it is difficult to avoid ambiguity when the tester tries to confine the choices to short statements.

Matching Items

A matching item usually consists of two columns of words or partial sentences, and the student is directed to correctly associate the responses of one column with those of the other. Letters by the responses in the right hand column are usually placed in blanks by the numbers along the left hand column.

Directions: Indicate in the space at the left by letter which muscle action is associated with each muscle.

Strong Points: (a) The matching items are usually quick and relatively easy to prepare. (b) Such items usually cover a maximum amount of material in a minimal amount of space. (c) It is easy to score.

Weak Points: (a) It is time-consuming on the part of students if the lists are lengthy. (b) It is limited in that it measures only recognition. (c) The choices should outnumber the questions, or else the students may be able to achieve the correct match through a process of elimination.

True-False Items

Questions of this type consist of statements which confront the student with two possible answers (either negative or positive).

Directions: Place a T in the blank before all true statements and an F before all false statements.

Strong Points: (a) It is possible to cover a wide range of topics in a short period of time. (b) It provides coverage of material which does not

True-False Samples:

_____	1. Walking in a handstand is considered as a weakness or fault in gymnastic competition.
_____	2. In performing a headstand, most of the weight should rest on top of the head.
_____	3. In performing a backward roll, the performer should place his hands on the mats so that his little fingers are next to his ears.
_____	4. Static balance is directly proportional to the area of the base on which the body is supported.
_____	5. A body will turn faster when the length of the radius of rotation about the center of gravity is increased.

lend itself to coverage by other test items. (c) It is objective and easy to score.

Weak Points: (a) It encourages guessing. (b) There is a tendency to test on isolated facts and to insert *trick* words, which tend to trap students who actually know the material. (c) The better students tend to read things into such statements and consequently may do worse than weaker students on true-false sections. (d) Students can develop a certain *knack* in taking true-false tests by identifying certain *keys* that are typical of this form of questions. For example, short sentences are more apt to be false and long sentences true, and questions containing words such as *never* and *always* are almost always false.

Essay Questions

Essay questions consist of statements which direct the student to discuss with some detail and organization the pertinent information related to a particular topic. They are often referred to as short-question-long-answer items. Such questions usually direct the student to summarize, contrast, compare, describe, or explain some subject.

Samples:
1. Summarize the contributions of early German gymnastic instructors to the development of the sport of gymnastics.
2. Compare the Swedish system of gymnastics with the German system.
3. Name four organizations which have contributed to the development of gymnastics in the U.S.A. and discuss the importance of each organization's contributions.
4. Identify the present Olympic gymnastics events and briefly summarize their description, characteristics, and values.
5. List and explain four scientific principles of balance.

Strong Points: (a) Essay questions are quickly constructed. (b) Essay tests require the learning of larger units of subject matter rather than isolated facts. (c) Essay items are effective in testing such skills as synthesizing pertinent information, organizing, and relating the facts and material that have been learned. (d) Guessing is held to a minimum in essay items. (e) Essay items allow for greater freedom of response and permit variety in expression.

Weak Points: (a) Essay tests have low objectivity and reliability. (b) Essay tests require considerable time to grade. (c) Bluffing and rambling are inherent dangers in essay tests. Also, students who write slowly or have difficulty organizing their answers are severely penalized.

Test Evaluation

Few physical educators take the time to analyze the results of a test to determine its effectiveness. In other words, we frequently fail to "test our tests." While the physical educator's time is limited and he could not undertake the elaborate methods utilized by test publishers in the establishment of standardized tests, he can and should find time to use a few simple techniques to determine if his test can, in fact, withstand a test.

Three important criteria to remember in test evaluation are usability, reliability, and validity. Usability can be determined as the test is being administered and scored, since it pertains to satisfactory completion time, ease of interpretation of directions, and ease of scoring. However, the determination of reliability and validity requires an analysis of test scores and the individual items of the test.

Reliability

There are several methods the teacher might use to determine whether test scores are accurate indications of the student's actual achievement. The *test-retest method* requires two administrations of the same test to the same group. The two sets of scores are then correlated to produce a reliability coefficient. This method may annoy students with written tests but is probably used more advantageously with physical performance tests. The *parallel forms method* involves the construction of two similar tests of the same subject. The two tests are then administered to the same group, and the scores are correlated to determine the reliability coefficient. Great skill is required to prepare two such tests which actually measure the same subject to the same degree.

The Kuder-Richardson Method (26) is one which requires only one administration of the test, and it utilizes the following formula:

$$r\,tt = \frac{n\sigma t^2 - M(n-M)}{\sigma t^2(n-1)}$$

$r\,tt$ = reliability of the test
n = number of items on test
M = mean of test scores
σt = standard deviation of test

To illustrate, we might assume that we have a test of fifty items, with a mean of 30 and a standard deviation of 6. Thus, we would substitute and compute the formula as follows:

$$r\,tt = \frac{[50 \times (6)^2] - [30(50-30)]}{(6)^2 (50-1)} = \frac{1800-600}{1764}$$

$$= \frac{1200}{1764}$$

$$= \frac{[50 \times 36] - [30 \times 20]}{36 \times 49} = .68$$

The coefficient of .68 would be considered low for a standardized test but typical of most teacher-made tests. Since the above formula tends to underestimate reliability, the above coefficient might be assumed to give some indication of the actual achievement of the students who took the test.

The Split-Halves Method utilizes a correlation between the correct odd and the correct even numbered items scored for each student. Thus, the resulting *r* is the reliability of only half of the length of the test.

However, the *Spearman-Brown Prophecy Formula* may be utilized to predict reliability for the entire test. The formula is presented below:

$$r\text{wt} = \frac{2r\text{ht}}{1 + r\text{ht}}$$

*r*wt = reliability of the whole test
*r*ht = reliability of half the test

If we computed an *r* of .60 on the split-half method, the formula would be as follows:

$$r\text{wt} = \frac{2 \times .60}{1 + .60} = \frac{1.2}{1.6} = .75$$

Thus, the Spearman-Brown Prophecy Formula predicts a correlation coefficient of .75 for the whole test.

Validity

As we learned earlier, validity concerns measuring what was intended to be measured. Perhaps the most important type of validity to be considered in an achievement test is that of *content validity.* Here the teacher's major concern is in relation to the test covering the material as he taught it. When the teacher has included questions that sample all major areas of a unit in the same proportion in which they were taught, content validity should be sufficiently high. The teacher may wish to classify each test item according to subject matter and objective to determine if the test has content

validity. Another method to determine validity is to correlate test scores with other measures of achievement on the same subject matter.

Item Analysis

A test may be both reliable and valid and yet still have room for improvement. Such improvement can be brought about by identifying individual items that do not function satisfactorily. The two criteria by which individual test items are judged are *discrimination power* and *difficulty level.*

Discrimination Power

To determine how valid an individual item is in relation to the entire test, one may take the top quarter of the high scorers and the bottom quarter of the low scorers and divide by the number of scorers to get an index of discrimination (ID).

$$\text{Example: ID} = \frac{\left(\begin{array}{c}\text{No. correct} \\ \text{in top group}\end{array}\right) - \left(\begin{array}{c}\text{No. correct} \\ \text{in bottom group}\end{array}\right)}{\text{No. in top and bottom group}}$$

$$\text{Thus, ID} = \frac{6-3}{16} = \frac{3}{16} = .19$$

From the example, we may conclude that the item discriminates positively and, therefore, agrees with the test. However, a negative discrimination index occurs when the bottom group scores more correct answers than the top group. When this happens, the item does not agree with the test and there is something about that item which causes the better students to see implications that were not intended. The top group is thus penalized for thinking too well.

Difficulty Level

This refers to the number of students who missed the item. Items scored correctly by all students are obviously too easy, and those missed by all students are too hard. Such test items should be discarded from the test. A quick and simple method of determining the difficulty level is to merely divide the number of correct responses by the number of students taking the test. Ideally, an item should have a difficulty level of about 50 percent. Those items falling below 10 percent or above 90 percent should be eliminated.

Sources for Physical Education Knowledge Tests

The following list of knowledge tests represents the majority of studies conducted for the purpose of constructing test items for use in physical education activity classes. Although a number of tests are now out of date, they may still be valuable in giving teachers ideas about new test items as well as serving as examples of procedures utilized in constructing the tests. The knowledge tests are presented in alphabetical order according to activities.

Archery

Ley, Katherine L., "Constructing Objective Test Items to Measure High School Levels of Achievement in Selected Physical Education Activities" (Microcarded doctoral dissertation, University of Iowa, 1960).

Snell, Catherine, "Physical Education Knowledge Tests," *Research Quarterly,* 6:83-86, October, 1935.

Badminton

Fox, Katherine, "Beginning Badminton Written Examinations," *Research Quarterly,* 24:135-146, May, 1953.

French, Esther, "The Construction of Knowledge Tests in Selected Professional Courses in Physical Education," *Research Quarterly,* 14:406-424, 1943.

Goll, Lillian M., "Construction of Badminton and Swimming Knowledge Tests for High School Girls" (Microcarded master's thesis, Illinois State University, 1956, pp. 65-75).

Hennis, Gail M., "Construction of Knowledge Tests in Selected Physical Education Activities for College Women," *Research Quarterly,* 27:301-309, October, 1956. (Also, see Physical Education Microcards.)

Hooks, Edgar W., Jr., "Hooks' Comprehensive Knowledge Test in Selected Physical Education Activities for College Men," *Research Quarterly,* 37:506, December, 1966.

Ley, Katherine L., "Constructing Objective Test Items to Measure High School Levels of Achievement in Selected Physical Education Activities" (Microcarded doctoral dissertation, University of Iowa, 1960).

Phillips, Marjorie, "Standardization of a Badminton Knowledge Test for College Women," *Research Quarterly,* 17:48-63, March, 1946.

Scott, Gladys M., "Achievement Examination in Badminton," *Research Quarterly,* 12:242-253, May, 1941.

Baseball

Goldberg, Isidor H., "The Development of Achievement Standards in Knowledge of Physical Education Activities" (Microcarded doctoral dissertation, New York University, 1953).

Hemphill, Fay, "Information Tests in Health and Physical Education for High School Boys," *Research Quarterly,* 3:82, December, 1932.

Rodgers, E. G., and Marjorie L. Heath, "An Experiment in the Use of Knowledge and Skill Tests in Playground Baseball," *Research Quarterly,* 2:128-130, December, 1931.

Snell, Catherine, "Physical Education Knowledge Tests," *Research Quarterly,* 7:87-91, May, 1936.

Basketball

Bliss, J. G. *Basketball,* Philadelphia: Lea and Febiger, 1929.

Fisher, Rosemary B., "Tests in Selected Physical Education Service Courses in a College" (Microcarded doctoral dissertation, State University of Iowa, 1950, pp. 158-181).

French, Esther, "The Construction of Knowledge Tests in Selected Professional Courses in Physical Education," *Research Quarterly,* 14:406-424, 1943.

Goldberg, Isidor H., "The Development of Achievement Standards in Knowledge of Physical Education Activities" (Microcarded doctoral dissertation, New York University, 1953).

Hemphill, Fay, "Information Tests in Health and Physical Education for High School Boys," *Research Quarterly,* 3:82, December, 1932.

Hennis, Gail M., "Construction of Knowledge Tests in Selected Physical Education Activities for College Women," *Research Quarterly,* 27:301-309, October, 1956. (Also, see Physical Education Microcards.)

Ley, Katherine L., "Constructing Objective Test Items to Measure High School Levels of Achievement in Selected Physical Education Activities" (Microcarded doctoral dissertation, University of Iowa, 1960).

Schwartz, Helen, "Knowledge and Achievement Tests in Girls' Basketball on the Senior High Level," *Research Quarterly,* 8:153-156, March, 1937.

Snell, Catherine, "Physical Education Knowledge Tests," *Research Quarterly,* 7:79-82, March, 1936.

Body Mechanics

French, Esther, "The Construction of Knowledge Tests in Selected Professional Courses in Physical Education," *Research Quarterly,* 14:406-424, 1943.

Bowling

Hennis, Gail M., "Construction of Knowledge Tests in Selected Physical Education Activities for College Women," *Research Quarterly,* 27:301-309, October, 1956.

Ley, Katherine L., "Constructing Objective Test Items to Measure High School Levels of Achievement in Selected Physical Education Activities" (Microcarded doctoral dissertation, University of Iowa, 1960).

Canoeing

French, Esther, "The Construction of Knowledge Tests in Selected Professional Courses in Physical Education," *Research Quarterly,* 14:406-424, 1943.

Dance and Rhythm

French, Esther, "The Construction of Knowledge Tests in Selected Professional Courses in Physical Education," *Research Quarterly,* 14:406-424, 1943.

Garcia, Mary Jane, *An Objective Knowledge Test of Aerobic Dance and Fitness,* Portland, Tx.: Brown and Littleman Company (P.O. Box 473), 1978.

Murry, Josephine K., "An Appreciation Test in Dance" (Unpublished master's thesis, University of California, 1943).

Stockard, Sara, "The Development and Evaluation of an Information Test in Beginning Modern Dance for Undergraduate College Students," *LAHPER Journal,* Fall Issue, 1972, p. 29.

Football

Goldberg, Isidor H., "The Development of Achievement Standards in Knowledge of Physical Education Activities" (Microcarded doctoral dissertation, New York University, 1953).

Hemphill, Fay, "Information Tests in Health and Physical Education for High School Boys," *Research Quarterly,* 3:82, December, 1932.

Fundamentals

Snell, Catherine, "Physical Education Knowledge Tests," *Research Quarterly,* 6:79-83, October, 1935.

Golf

French, Esther, "The Construction of Knowledge Tests in Selected Professional Courses in Physical Education," *Research Quarterly,* 14:406-424, 1943.

Ley, Katherine L., "Constructing Objective Test Items to Measure High School Levels of Achievement in Selected Physical Education Activities" (Microcarded doctoral dissertation, University of Iowa, 1960).

Snell, Catherine, "Physical Education Knowledge Tests," *Research Quarterly,* 7:79-80, May, 1936.

Waglow, I. F., and C. H. Rehling, "A Golf Knowledge Test," *Research Quarterly,* 24:463-470, December, 1953.

Gymnastics

Fisher, Rosemary B., "Tests in Selected Physical Education Service Courses in a College" (Microcarded doctoral dissertation, State University of Iowa, 1950, pp. 145-156).

French, Esther, "The Construction of Knowledge Tests in Selected Professional Courses in Physical Education," *Research Quarterly,* 14:406-424, 1943.

Gershon, Ernest, "Apparatus Gymnastics Knowledge Test for College Men in Professional Physical Education," *Research Quarterly,* 28:332, December, 1957.

Johnson, Barry L., *An Objective Knowledge Test of Gymnastics (Including Tumbling and Trampoline),* Portland, Tx.: Brown & Littleman Company (P.O. Box 473), 1977.

Nipper, John, "A Knowledge Test of Tumbling and Gymnastics" (Unpublished study, Northeast Louisiana University, 1966).

Handball

Phillips, Bernath E., *Fundamental Handball,* New York: A. S. Barnes and Company, 1937.

Hockey

Dietz, Dorthea, and Beryl Trech, "Hockey Knowledge Test for Girls," *Journal of Health Physical Education Recreation, 11:366, 1940.*

French, Esther, "The Construction of Knowledge Tests in Selected Professional Courses in Physical Education," *Research Quarterly,* 14:406-424, 1943.

Grisier, Gertrude J., "The Construction of an Objective Test of Knowledge and Interpretation of the Rules of Field Hockey for Women," *Research Quarterly Supplement,* 5:79-81, March, 1943.

Hennis, Gail M., "Construction of Knowledge Tests in Selected Physical Education Activities for College Women," *Research Quarterly,* 27:301-309, October, 1956. (Also, see Physical Education Microcards.)

Kelly, Ellen D., and Jane E. Brown, "The Construction of a Field Hockey Test for Women Physical Education Majors," *Research Quarterly,* 23:322-329, October, 1952.

Snell, Catherine, "Physical Education Knowledge Tests," *Research Quarterly,* 6:86-89, October, 1935.

Horseback Riding

Snell, Catherine, "Physical Education Knowledge Tests," *Research Quarterly,* 7:80-84, May, 1936.

Physical Fitness

Johnson, Barry L., and Mary Jane Garcia, *An Objective Knowledge Test of Conditioning, Fitness and Performance,* Portland, Tx.: Brown & Littleman Company (P.O. Box 473), 1977.

Stradtman, Alan D., and T. K. Cureton, "A Physical Fitness Knowledge Test for Secondary School Boys and Girls," *Research Quarterly,* 21:53-57, March, 1950.

Recreational Sports

Fisher, Rosemary B., "Tests in Selected Physical Education Service Courses in a College" (Microcarded doctoral dissertation, State University of Iowa, 1950, pp. 285-319).

French, Esther, "The Construction of Knowledge Tests in Selected Professional Courses in Physical Education," *Research Quarterly,* 14:406-424, 1943.

Soccer

Fisher, Rosemary B., "Tests in Selected Physical Education Service Courses in a College" (Microcarded doctoral dissertation, State University of Iowa, 1950, pp. 123-143).

French, Esther, "The Construction of Knowledge Tests in Selected Professional Courses in Physical Education," *Research Quarterly,* 14:406-424, 1943.

Heath, Marjorie L., and E. G. Rodgers, "A Study in the Use of Knowledge and Skill Tests in Soccer," *Research Quarterly,* 3:33-53, October, 1932.

Knighton, Marion, "Soccer Questions," *Journal of Health and Physical Education,* Vol. 1, October, 1930.

Ley, Katherine L., "Constructing Objective Test Items to Measure High School Levels of Achievement in Selected Physical Education Activities" (Microcarded doctoral dissertation, University of Iowa, 1960).

Snell, Catherine, "Physical Education Knowledge Tests," *Research Quarterly,* 7:76-79, March, 1936.

Softball

Fisher, Rosemary B., "Tests in Selected Physical Education Service Courses in a College" (Microcarded doctoral dissertation, State University of Iowa, 1950, pp. 254-270).

French, Esther, "The Construction of Knowledge Tests in Selected Professional Courses in Physical Education," *Research Quarterly,* 14:406-424, 1943.

Hennis, Gail M., "Construction of Knowledge Tests in Selected Physical Education Activities for College Women," *Research Quarterly,* 27:301-309, October, 1956. (Also, see Physical Education Microcards.)

Hooks, Edgar W., Jr., "Hooks' Comprehensive Knowledge Test in Selected Physical Education Activities for College Men," *Research Quarterly,* 37:506, December, 1966.

Ley, Katherine L., "Constructing Objective Test Items to Measure High School Levels of Achievement in Selected Physical Education Activities" (Microcarded doctoral dissertation, University of Iowa, 1960).

Waglow, I. F., and Foy Stephens, "A Softball Knowledge Test," *Research Quarterly,* 26:234-237, May, 1955.

Sportsmanship

Haskins, Mary J., "Problem-Solving Test of Sportsmanship," *Research Quarterly,* 31:601-605, December, 1960.

Swimming

Fisher, Rosemary B., "Tests in Selected Physical Education Service Courses in a College" (Microcarded doctoral dissertation, State University of Iowa, 1950, pp. 182-253).

French, Esther, "The Construction of Knowledge Tests in Selected Professional Courses in Physical Education," *Research Quarterly,* 14:406-424, 1943.

Goll, Lillian M., "Construction of Badminton and Swimming Knowledge Tests for High School Girls" (Microcarded master's thesis, Illinois State University, 1956).

Scott, M. Gladys, "Achievement Examinations for Elementary and Intermediate

Swimming Classes," *Research Quarterly,* 11:104-111, May, 1940.

Team-Game Activities

Rodgers, Elizabeth G., "The Standardization and Use of Objective Type Information Tests in Team Game Activities," *Research Quarterly,* 10:103, March, 1939.

Tennis

Broer, Marion R., and Donna M. Miller, "Achievement Tests for Beginning and Intermediate Tennis," *Research Quarterly,* 21:303-313, October, 1950.

Fisher, Rosemary B., "Tests in Selected Physical Education Service Courses in a College" (Microcarded doctoral dissertation, State University of Iowa, 1950, pp. 271-284).

French, Esther, "The Construction of Knowledge Tests in Selected Professional Courses in Physical Education," *Research Quarterly,* 14:406-424, 1943.

Hennis, Gail M., "Construction of Knowledge Tests in Selected Physical Education Activities for College Women," *Research Quarterly,* 27:301-309, October, 1956. (Also, see Physical Education Microcards.)

Hewitt, Jack E., "Hewitt's Comprehensive Tennis Knowledge Test," *Research Quarterly,* 35:149-154, May, 1964.

————, "Comprehensive Tennis Knowledge Test," *Research Quarterly,* 8:74-84, October, 1937.

Hooks, Edgar W., Jr., "Hooks' Comprehensive Knowledge Test in Selected Physical Education Activities for College Men," *Research Quarterly,* 37:506, December, 1966.

Miller, Wilma K., "Achievement Levels in Tennis Knowledge and Skill for Women Physical Education Major Students," *Research Quarterly,* 24:81-89, March, 1953.

Scott, M. Gladys, "Achievement Examination for Elementary and Intermediate Tennis Classes," *Research Quarterly,* 12:43-49, March, 1941.

Snell, Catherine, "Physical Education Knowledge Tests," *Research Quarterly,* 7:84-87, May, 1936.

Track and Field

French, Esther, "The Construction of Knowledge Tests in Selected Professional Courses in Physical Education," *Research Quarterly,* 14:406-424, 1943.

Volleyball

Fisher, Rosemary B., "Tests in Selected Physical Education Service Courses in a College" (Microcarded doctoral dissertation, State University of Iowa, 1950, pp. 82-122).

French, Esther, "The Construction of Knowledge Tests in Selected Professional Courses in Physical Education," *Research Quarterly,* 14:06-424, 1943.

Hennis, Gail M., "Construction of Knowledge Tests in Selected Physical Education Activities for College Women," *Research Quarterly,* 27:301-309, December, 1957.

Hooks, Edgar W., Jr., "Hooks' Comprehensive Knowledge Test in Selected Physical Education Activities for College Men," *Research Quarterly,* 37:506, December, 1966.

Langston, Dewey F., "Standardization of a Volleyball Knowledge Test for College Men Physical Education Majors," *Research Quarterly,* 26:60-66, March, 1955.

Ley, Katherine L., "Constructing Objective Test Items to Measure High School Levels of Achievement in Selected Physical Education Activities" (Microcarded doctoral dissertation, University of Iowa, 1960).

Snell, Catherine, "Physical Education Knowledge Tests," *Research Quarterly,* 7:73-76, March, 1936.

Problems and Limitations of Knowledge Measurement

1. Most standardized knowledge tests in physical education are not available on a commercial basis and consequently must be located from various sources and be prepared for distribution. There appears to be a definite need for the encouragement of commercial interest in physical education knowledge tests.

2. Standardized tests do not always fit the local situation. They may cover materials which are not covered in some schools due to limited time, equipment, facilities, or emphasis.

3. Knowledge tests require careful security measures to ensure that all students are exposed to the test at the same time. Students sometimes use ingenious methods to gain an unfair advantage in order to ensure success on knowledge tests. There is also the problem of students passing on information about the test from one class to another.

4. Norms for standardized knowledge tests are

of doubtful value since they are dependent upon such specific factors as age group, unit of instruction, length of unit, and content presented. Since these factors can vary so greatly, such norms are seldom applicable to many groups.

5. The standardized test frequently encourages the teacher to emphasize certain information while leaving out other information which is important but not covered in the standardized test. This practice is often referred to as *teaching for testing* with the obvious purpose of helping the students, and thus the teacher, look good on norm comparisons.

6. The construction of good tests is a much more difficult task than it might appear. The tests must be valid, and the teacher must continually ask himself whether the questions are fair and pertinent to the material covered in class.

7. The writing of good test questions requires skill in expression which, unfortunately, many physical educators lack.

8. The physical educator must guard against the temptation to make the questions too comprehensive and difficult in an unconscious attempt to prove that physical education is not a *snap* course.

Findings and Conclusions from Knowledge Measurement and Research

Numerous tests of knowledge in physical education activities have been available for years; however, test constructors have been quick to point out that such tests should only be used in situations where the distribution of factual information is in relatively close agreement with the specifications of the published test (21, 28). Many knowledge tests are presented in their entirety in professional publications and can serve as guides for constructing teacher-made tests (13, 14, 15, 17, 23).

A number of test constructors have established norms which may be used for comparative purposes when the test is used in its entirety (16, 20, 21, 24, 27, 30, 40). However, as previously pointed out, there are so many specific factors involved that norms are seldom applicable.

Concerning a possible relationship existing between knowledge about an activity and skill in the activity, Scott (38) noted that a direct relationship did not exist in tennis measurement. However, Hewitt (22) found a high relationship between knowledge in tennis and playing experience in tennis. The author has often noted that students who are highly skilled in an activity frequently take for granted their knowledge of the activity and do not do as well on the activity knowledge test as students who are less skilled in the activity.

In 1960 Ley (28) studied objective knowledge test items in selected physical education activities, and some of her comments might prove valuable to future test constructors. They are listed as follows:

1. Test constructors since 1940 have not used any particular method of determining the relevance level of individual items.

2. The knowledge tests studies contained too many factual items while neglecting items in the generalization, understanding, application, and interpretation categories.

3. Examinations by committee groups were not found to be superior to those by an individual in regard to topical content, relevance level, and the worth of the individual items.

4. Rules of play have dominated physical education knowledge tests, and it is doubtful that such a practice can be justified in many situations.

5. If accurate, pictures and diagrams are of value in developing test items.

6. Highly relevant items can be written for all topical areas found in physical education activity knowledge tests.

Ley (28) found physical education major students significantly higher than non-major students in only one out of six physical activity knowledge tests. If this finding is characteristic of the knowledge of physical education majors across the nation, then greater emphasis should be placed on a more thorough understanding of *what is what* in physical activities for majors.

Several investigators have researched the effect of knowledge on learning to perform skills in various activities or tasks. Operating on the hypothesis that exposing students to an understanding and application of mechanical principles will bring about greater improvement than instruction without reference to these principles, Mohr (31), Broer (7), Ruger (37), and Colville (11) found such knowledge to be beneficial.

Numerous investigators have used such

knowledge measures as grade point average, standard achievement test scores, and intelligence scores to determine the relationship between mental ability and physical ability. Most studies of such relationships have varied, with some reports indicating little or no relationship (3, 5, 8, 26, 40), while others indicated a low but positive relationship (12, 25, 29, 43). However, Clarke (9) has pointed out that most of the investigations which showed little or no relationship did not allow variances in the intelligence of the subjects. Along this line, the authors would like to stress the fact that one needs extremes in the variables concerned in order to obtain a high coefficient of correlation. If the sample is too homogeneous in the variables, such as is the case concerning most traits possessed by students in a typical class, it is simply mathematically unrealistic to expect high correlations even though a significant relationship could exist.

Through the years, various physical educators and researchers have held the belief that physical fitness improves the effectiveness of the individual's mental capabilities. Research which supports this contention is presented as follows:

1. Studying two groups of college men with nearly equal intelligence quotient averages, Rogers (36) found the scholarship in the physically stronger group to be considerably higher than that of the low strength group.
2. Terman (41) noted that symptoms of general weakness were reported 30 percent less frequently for gifted students than for non-gifted students.
3. Brace (6) has reported studies from England which revealed that only 2.35 percent of students who were above average in scholarship were below average in body build as compared to 39.7 percent of students with poor scholarship who were below average in body build.
4. A report from Massachusetts (35) revealed that the average Physical Fitness Index for 126 high school honor students attending Brookline public schools was 117, which is two points above the national third quartile score.
5. Studying one high group and one low group of children in motor proficiency, Rarick (34) found that the high motor group demonstrated better scholastic adjustment than the low group in reading, writing, and comprehension.

6. Two studies noted that male freshmen at large universities with low physical indexes were also low in scholastic accomplishment as compared to other students, in spite of the fact that these same low fitness students were above average in scholastic aptitude (10, 32).
7. Shaffer (39) found that as intelligence increased, failures on the Kraus-Weber Test decreased.
8. Popp (33) compared boys of low physical fitness with boys of high physical fitness and noted that eight out of twenty in the low fitness group failed to graduate from high school, whereas only two out of twenty in the high fitness group failed to graduate.
9. Clarke (9) found that subjects high in physical measures had a consistent and significant tendency to have higher means on knowledge measures than subjects low in physical measures. The groups were previously equated by intelligence scores.
10. Two studies indicated that physical fitness is an important factor in the improvement of mental tasks (18, 19).

References and Bibliography

1. Barrow, Harold M., and Rosemary McGee, *A Practical Approach to Measurement in Physical Education,* Philadelphia: Lea and Febiger, 1964, p. 358.
2. Berk, Robert, "Comparison of Performance of Subnormal, Normal, and Gifted Children on the Oseretsky Tests of Motor Ability" (Unpublished doctoral dissertation, Boston University, 1957).
3. Bond, M. H., "Rhythmic Perception and Gross Motor Performance," *Research Quarterly,* 30:259-265, October, 1959.
4. Brace, D. K., "Motor Learning of Feeble-Minded Girls," *Research Quarterly,* 19:269-275, December, 1948.
5. _____, "Studies in the Rate of Learning Gross Bodily Skills," *Research Quarterly,* 12:181-185, May, 1941.
6. _____, "Some Objective Evidence of the Value of Physical Education," *Journal of Health and Physical Education,* 4:36, April, 1933.
7. Broer, Marion, "Effectiveness of a General Basic Skills Curriculum for Junior High School Girls," *Research Quarterly,* 29:379-388, December, 1958.
8. Burley, L., and R. L. Anderson, "Relation of Jump and Reach Measures of Power to Intelligence Scores and Athletic Performance," *Research Quarterly,* 30:259-265, March, 1959.
9. Clarke, H. Harrison, and Boyd O. Jarman,

"Scholastic Achievement of Boys 9, 12, and 15 Years of Age as Related to Various Strength and Growth Measures," *Research Quarterly,* 32:155, May, 1961.

10. Coefield, John R., and Robert H. Collum, "A Case Study Report of Seventy-eight University Freshmen Men with Low Physical Fitness Indices" (Microcarded master's thesis, University of Oregon, 1955).

11. Colville, Frances, "The Learning of Motor Skills as Influenced by a Knowledge of General Principles of Mechanics" (Unpublished doctoral dissertation, University of Southern California, 1956).

12. Distefano, M. K., and others, "Motor Proficiency in Mental Defectives," *Percep. Mot. Skills,* 8:231-234, 1958.

13. Fisher, Rosemary B., "Tests in Selected Physical Education Service Courses in a College" (Microcarded dissertation, State University of Iowa, 1950, p. 72).

14. Fox, Katherine, "Beginning Badminton Written Examination," *Research Quarterly,* 24:135, May, 1953.

15. French, Esther, "The Construction of Knowledge Tests in Selected Professional Courses in Physical Education," *Research Quarterly,* 14:406-424, December, 1943.

16. Gershon, Ernest, "Apparatus Gymnastics Knowledge Test for College Men in Professional Physical Education," *Research Quarterly,* 28:332, December, 1957.

17. Goll, Lillian M., "Construction of Badminton and Swimming Knowledge Tests for High School Girls" (Microcarded master's thesis, Illinois State University, 1956, p. 54).

18. Gutin, Bernard, "Effect of Increase in Physical Fitness on Mental Ability Following Physical and Mental Stress," *Research Quarterly,* 37:211, May, 1966.

19. Hart, Marcia E., and Clayton T. Shay, "Relationship Between Physical Fitness and Academic Success," *Research Quarterly,* 35:445, October, 1964.

20. Hemphill, Fay, "Information Tests in Health and Physical Education for High School Boys," *Research Quarterly,* 3:82, December, 1932.

21. Hennis, Gail M., "Construction of Knowledge Tests in Selected Physical Education Activities for College Women," *Research Quarterly,* 27:301-309, October, 1956.

22. Hewitt, Jack E., "Hewitt's Comprehensive Tennis Knowledge Test," *Research Quarterly,* 35:147-155, May, 1964.

23. _____, "Comprehensive Tennis Knowledge Test," *Research Quarterly,* 8:74-84, October, 1937.

24. Hooks, Edgar W., Jr., "Hooks' Comprehensive Knowledge Test in Selected Physical Education Activities for College Men," *Research Quarterly,* 37:506, December, 1966.

25. Johnson, G. B., "Study of the Relationship that Exists Between Physical Skill as Measured, and the General Intelligence of College Students," *Research Quarterly,* 13:57-59, March, 1942.

26. Kuder, G. Frederic, and M. W. Richardson, "The Theory of the Estimation of Test Reliability," *Psychometrika,* September, 1937, pp. 151-160.

27. Langston, Dewey F., "Standardization of a Volleyball Knowledge Test for College Men Physical Education Majors," *Research Quarterly,* 26:60-66, March, 1955.

28. Ley, Katherine L., "Constructing Objective Test Items to Measure High School Levels of Achievement in Selected Physical Education Activities" (Microcarded dissertation, University of Iowa, 1960, p. 25).

29. McMillan, Betty Jo, "A Study to Determine the Relationship of Physical Fitness as Measured by the New York State Physical Fitness Test to the Academic Index of High School Girls" (Unpublished master's thesis, Springfield College, 1961).

30. Miller, Wilma K., "Achievement Levels in Tennis Knowledge and Skill for Women Physical Education Major Students," *Research Quarterly,* 24:18-89, March, 1953.

31. Mohr, Dorothy R., and Mildred E. Barrett, "Effect of Knowledge of Mechanical Principles in Learning to Perform Intermediate Swimming Skills," *Research Quarterly,* 33:574, December, 1962.

32. Page, C. Getty, "Case Studies of College Men with Low Physical Fitness Indices" (Unpublished master's thesis, Syracuse University, 1940).

33. Popp, James, "Case Studies of Sophomore High School Boys with High and Low Physical Fitness Indices" (Microcarded master's thesis, University of Oregon, 1959).

34. Rarick, Lawrence G., and Robert McKee, "A Study of Twenty Third-Grade Children Exhibiting Extreme Levels of Achievement on Tests of Motor Efficiency," *Research Quarterly,* 20:142, May, 1949.

35. *Report of the School Committee and Superintendent of Brookline, Massachusetts,* December 31, 1941.

36. Rogers, Frederick R., "The Scholarship of Athletes" (Unpublished master's thesis, Stanford University, 1922).

37. Ruger, Henry A., "The Psychology of Efficiency," *Archives of Psychology,* 2:85, 1910.

38. Scott, M. Gladys, "Achievement Examinations for Elementary and Intermediate Tennis Classes," *Research Quarterly,* 12:40-49, March, 1941.

39. Shaffer, G., "Interrelationship of Intelligence Quotient to Failure of Kraus-Weber Test," *Research Quarterly,* 30:75-86, March, 1959.

40. Start, K. R., "Relationship Between Intelligence and the Effect of Mental Practice on the Performance of a Motor Skill," *Research Quarterly*, 31:644-649, 1960.
41. Terman, Lewis M., ed., "Genetic Studies of Genius," in *Mental and Physical Traits of a Thousand Gifted Children,* Stanford, Cal.: Stanford University Press, 1926.
42. Waglow, I. F., and Foy Stephens, "A Softball Knowledge Test," *Research Quarterly,* 26:234-237, May, 1955.
43. Weber, John R., "Relationship of Physical Fitness to Success in College and to Personality," *Research Quarterly,* 24:471, December, 1954.

The evaluation of posture has been a problem for tests and measurements people for nearly a century. The problem has been attacked in a variety of ways using rating charts, posture screens, photographs, silhouettes, plumb lines, aluminum pointers, angle irons, and adhesive tape. Unfortunately, even the most sophisticated techniques of photographic analysis with body landmarks, angles, etc., have not met with a great deal of success. Primarily, this failure is because posture experts can not agree on what constitutes good posture. This is not meant as criticism; instead, it merely points up the fundamental complexity of the problem—what is good posture?

This text cannot presume to answer the question; it can only adopt a working concept from which to base our approach to measurement. It is generally recognized that posture involves mechanical considerations, such as the alignment of body segments, the strength and stress of the muscles and ligaments, and the effects of gravity on the body parts. It is also acknowledged that posture is of an aesthetic nature as well as being a reflection of the individual's total being, his self-image, his physical state, and his concept of himself in relation to his environment. Above all, it should be realized that posture, like all human characteristics, not only involves differences among individuals but also differences within the individual. Posture is not just the ability of the individual to stand in one position in front of a plumb line while someone examines him from various angles. The evaluation of an individual's posture should include the appraisal of his posture while walking, running, climbing, descending, sitting, and standing. Moreover, the appraisal should be in accordance with the individual's skeletal architecture and body build (21).

Utilization of Posture Tests

Primarily, posture tests are employed for (a) remedial work in an adaptive program or (b) as a means of providing information and motivation for the student in a planned program of posture improvement. Adaptive work requires a specialist. In analyzing a student's posture, a tester must be able to identify abnormalities and be able to determine whether or not improvements can be made by strengthening and stretching certain muscles. If the person is not well prepared in this area, there are no objec-

Chapter Twenty-Two

The Measurement of Posture

tive tests that will enable him to intelligently evaluate posture. If he is well qualified, it is doubtful that any objective measuring devices will give him any more information than his own eyes and hands (26). However, he may well want to utilize objective devices as teaching aids in attempting to motivate the student to strive for improvement.

In selecting posture tests, the physical education teacher should be guided primarily by the needs of the program, his own preparation and competency, and, of course, the cost and administrative feasibility of the test.

Measures of Posture (Rating Scales)

Iowa Posture Test*

This test is recommended for use in classes. Groups of ten students can be rated at a time. The posture ratings are subjective, but the examiner has specific criteria on which to evaluate the elements in posture while standing, walking, running, sitting, and stair climbing. This test represents a practical approach to the problem of assessing posture of the individual when he is moving and performing daily activities rather than just standing in a fixed position.

Validity and Reliability: No coefficients are given, although Moriarity (22) reported a reliability coefficient of .965 using dual but independent ratings.

Test Equipment and Floor Space: Ten chairs are arranged in a row about 2 feet apart. Open floor space is needed for the students to be able to walk ten or more steps away from the chair. Stairs may be constructed, or real ones utilized. The stairs should be sufficiently wide to accommodate two students at a time. The subjects should be dressed in swimsuits or leotards and should also be barefoot.

Foot Mechanics Test

Directions: The students take turns walking approximately ten steps forward and then back to their chairs. The examiner stands at the side and rates each subject on heel contact, weight transfer, and toe drive.

*Mimeographed form published by the Department of Physical Education for Women, University of Iowa. The test and scoring charts are also presented in Scott and French, *Measurement and Evaluation Physical Education* (25).

The examiner then stands in front of each subject, who walks first toward the examiner and then away as the examiner assesses foot alignment and the absence or presence of pronation.

Scoring: The suggested three-point scoring scale is primarily based on ratings of good, fair, and poor, which are given point values of three, two, and one, respectively. More specific criteria for making each rating are presented here, as provided by McCloy (21).

Criteria for foot mechanics test:
1. Heel-toe walking.
   a. Heel contacts the ground first.
   b. The weight is transferred through the outside of the foot and then diagonally across to the ball of the foot.
   c. Toes are used in gripping action.
   d. Spring in the walk.
   Scoring: Good = 3, fair = 2, poor = 1.
2. Absence of pronation.
   a. No bony bulge in front of and below the medial malleolus.
   b. No noted inward protrusion of the navicular.
   c. Heel cord is not noticeably turned outward.
   Scoring: No pronation = 3, some pronation = 2, marked pronation = 1.
3. Feet parallel.
   a. A slight angle of toeing out is considered good.
   b. Some degree of toeing in may be permissible but unattractive.
   Scoring: Normal = 3, moderate toeing out = 2, marked toeing out = 1.

Standing Position Test

Directions: The subjects stand with their left side toward the front of their chairs. The tester, viewing from the side, rates the alignment of the body segments and the weight distribution.

Criteria for correct alignment of body segments:
1. An axis approximating a straight line running through the head, neck, trunk and legs.
2. The head and neck are erect (although there may be some slight forward inclination).
3. Chest high, abdomen flat.
4. Slight roundness of the upper back and slight hollow of lower back (i.e., normal curves).
5. Over-all impression of ease and balance.
Scoring: Good alignment = 3, slight general deviation = 2, marked general deviation = 1.

Walking Test

Directions: The subjects walk around the row of ten chairs, keeping 5 or 6 feet from one another. The tester stands to the side and checks for body alignment, weight distribution, stiffness, and unnecessary movements while walking.

Criteria for walking test:

1. Alignment of body segments while walking. The rating is the same as for standing.
Scoring: Same as for walking—3, 2, and 1.
2. Weight distribution. The weight should be carried farther forward than in standing position, but only slightly. There should be no forward or backward deviation from the perpendicular.
Scoring: Good weight distribution=3, some deviation=2, marked deviation=1.

Sitting Test

Directions: The examiner stands at the side and rates each subject in the sitting position. The subject then is instructed to lean forward about 30 degrees and is rated in this position. After this rating the subject rises and walks forward a few steps. Body mechanics and carriage while rising from a sitting position are assessed during this movement. If desired, the tester could rate the subject's performance in sitting down as well.

Criteria for sitting test:

1. Sitting position.
   a. Upper trunk balanced over pelvis.
   b. Head erect, chest high, shoulders back (but not stiff).
   c. Abdomen controlled and normal upper-back curve.
   d. Hips should be well back, and back of chair utilized for support.
Scoring: Correct position=3, some deviation =2, marked deviation=1.
2. Rising from a sitting position.
   a. One foot slightly under the chair, the other foot slightly in advance. The trunk is inclined from the hips, and the arms are relaxed.
   b. The hips should be kept well under the body when rising, with no appreciable bending of the back or dropping of the head.
   c. The movement should be smooth and graceful with no stiffness.
Scoring: Good=3, fair=2, poor=1.

Stooping to Pick Up Light Object Test

Directions: A small object is placed on the floor a few feet in front of the subject. The subject is instructed to walk to the object, pick it up, and then return it to the floor. The examiner views the subject from the side.

Criteria for picking up light object test:

1. The subject should bend mainly at the knees and a slight bend from the hips.
2. The feet and hips are kept well under the body with one foot slightly ahead of the other.
3. Trunk forms a relatively straight line, but arms are relaxed and back controlled, avoiding a stiff appearance.
4. The object is picked up (and replaced) slightly ahead of the foot. The movement should be smooth with good balance maintained throughout.
Scoring: Good=3, fair=2, poor=1.

Ascending and Descending Stairs Test

Directions: Each subject ascends and descends eight or ten stairs. The examiner stands at the side and rates the subject's carriage for ascending and descending separately.

Criteria for ascending and descending stairs test:

1. Ascending.
   a. The weight should be only slightly forward, and the bend should be from the ankles, not the hips.
   b. The push-up is from the ankles and knees with no swinging of the hips.
Scoring: Good=3, fair=2, poor=1.
2. Descending.
   a. Weight is lowered in a controlled manner (not a relaxed drop).
   b. Movement is smooth with no bobbing.
Scoring: Good=3, fair=2, poor=1.

Additional Pointers: (a) If desired, the physical educator could include running, picking up and carrying heavy objects, jumping, etc. (b) The desired mechanics for each test may be explained, or they may not, depending upon whether the teacher wishes to evaluate the student's normal behavior or whether the teacher wishes to observe their performance after instruction. (c) The teacher may also wish to devise a system in which each subject is evaluated covertly, as, for example, while another student is performing or during a pause between tests.

Achievement Level	Percentile Rank	Posture Score
10	99	––
9	98	65
8	93	63
7	84	61
6	69	59
5	50	57
4	31	53-55
3	16	49-51
2	7	43-47
1	2	39-41
0	1	13-37

New York State Posture Rating Test (23)

Posture evaluation is included in the New York State Physical Fitness Test. This assessment involves thirteen areas of the body. The rating chart (Figure 22-1) shows three profiles: the correct position (5 points), a slight deviation (3 points), and a pronounced deviation (1 point) from the correct position for each of the thirteen areas. The examiner rates each area on the 5-3-1 basis, and the total point value is the student's score.

The testing area consists of a plumb line suspended over a line on which the subject stands which is 3 feet in front of a screen. Another line is drawn at a right angle to the first line and extends 10 feet farther back from the screen (a total of 13 feet). This is where the examiner is positioned in order to view the subject against the screen.

The subject is rated from two viewpoints. In one position the subject stands facing the screen, so that the plumb line bisects the back of his head, runs down the spine, and passes down between his legs and feet. Lateral deviations are assessed from this position.

The subject then turns to his left and stands sideward so that the plumb line passes in a line through the ear, shoulder, hip, knee, and ankle. The left lateral malleolus must be in line with the plumb bob. Anteroposterior posture is rated from this position.

The student's cumulative posture ratings from grades four through twelve are contained on the one chart. Reliability coefficients ranging from .93 to .98 are reported for girls and boys at different grade levels.

Norms for the ratings have been established for boys and girls grades 4 through 12 as shown above.

Theoretically, the regular assessment of posture, as an integral part of the student's overall fitness, should do much to make the students and teachers posture conscious. It could also make a significant contribution toward health appraisal in general and meeting individual needs by special programs and medical referrals.

Objective Posture Tests and Instruments

Brief mention is made here of some of the objective tests and instruments that have been devised in attempting to analyze and evaluate posture. Readers who desire more information and detailed descriptions of the tests are referred to the original sources. Considerable effort was expended during the thirties and forties in developing objective devices. Since then there has not been a great deal of work done in the way of invention.

Cureton-Gunby Conformateur (5)

Cureton was an early leader in the attempt to

POSTURE RATING CHART

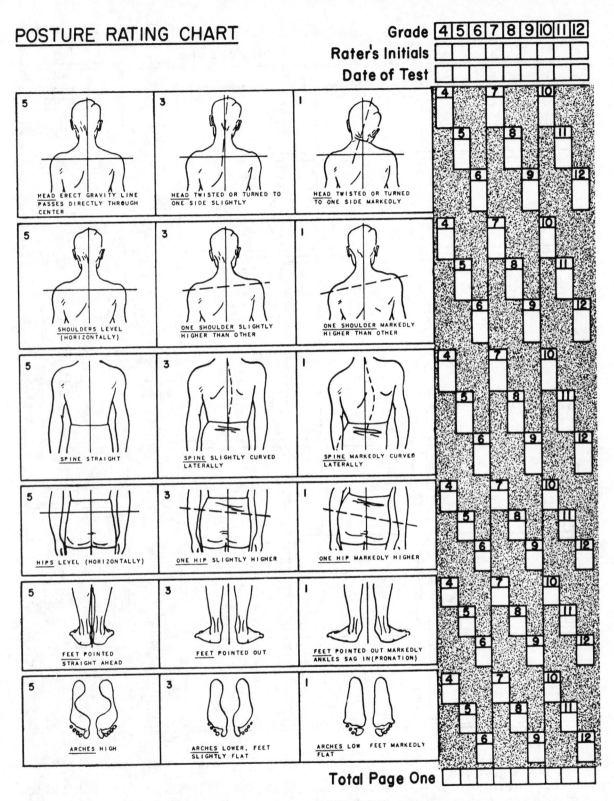

Figure 22-1. New York State Posture Rating Chart
Courtesy of the New York State Education Department.

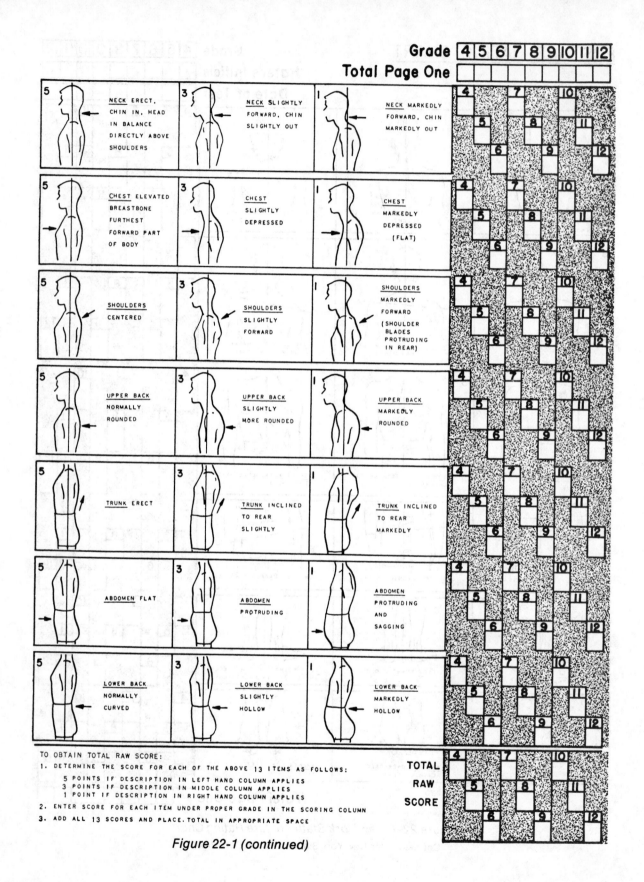

Figure 22-1 (continued)

develop objective, reliable instruments for measuring anteroposterior spinal curvature. Unsatisfied with the errors of exaggeration in using silhouettes, Cureton and Gunby devised the conformateur. This instrument utilizes metal rods which slide through holes placed in an upright. The subject stands with his back toward the upright, and the metal rods are pushed through the holes so that they make contact with the subject from his head down the entire length of the spine. The rods are locked in place, thus presenting an outline of the spinal curvature. Cureton recommends that it be used in conjunction with silhouettographs in order to facilitate interpretation and allow for a personal record for student motivation.

Woodruff Body Alignment Posture Test*

An inexpensive device for measuring body alignment was developed by Woodruff at the University of Oregon. By the use of a wooden frame (see Figure 22-3) containing nine strings

*Janet Woodruff, School of Health, Physical Education, and Recreation, University of Oregon, Eugene, Oregon. Described in H. Harrison Clarke, *Application of Measurement to Health and Physical Education,* 4th ed., Englewood Cliffs, N.J.: Prentice-Hall, 1967, pp. 123-124.

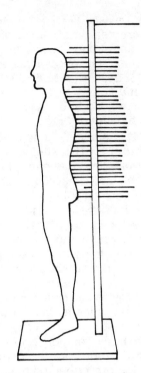

Figure 22-2. Cureton-Gunby Conformateur

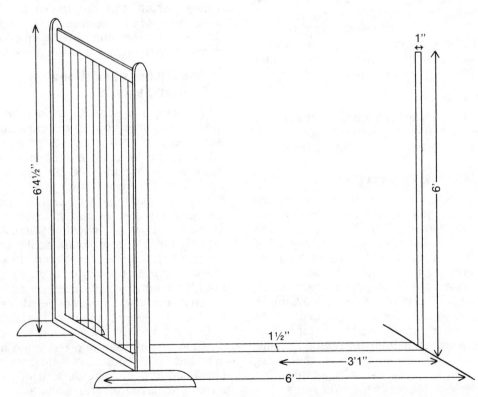

Figure 22-3. Woodruff Body Alignment Test

running lengthwise, ¾ of an inch apart, an objective score can be obtained of deviations in the alignment of body segments. The inventor believed this test represented a more reliable means of assessing body alignment than subjective ratings and, at the same time, was less time consuming and less expensive than most of the objective devices.

Directions: The subject stands between the wall and the frame. The subject's left side is toward the frame, and the left foot is placed at the 1½ inch line that is marked on the floor. The tester then directs the subject to adjust the foot position until the base line is directly under the instep. The tester stands 10 feet from the frame and, looking through the strings, aligns the center string with the 1 inch line drawn on the wall. The subject is instructed to stand in a *normal* position.

Scoring: This test is basically a plumb line test. The tester starts at the alignment of the ankle with the center string and proceeds upward, scoring each body segment's deviation from the one below it (not from the center line). In other words, the prescribed points at the ankle, knee, hip, shoulder, and ear are scored in terms of the number of strings each segment is found to deviate in either direction from the segment below it. A perfect score is twenty-five, and one point is subtracted for each deviation.

Norms: There are no published norms, although Clarke reported a mean of twenty, and a range of sixteen to twenty-five had been obtained for college women (3).

Spinograph (5)

This instrument utilizes a pointer that traces the student's spine and records the contour of the spine on a blackboard or poster board.

Wellesley Posture Test (17)

Utilizing aluminum markers taped on the subject's sternum and spine, a method of objective measurements from photographs was developed by MacEwan and Howe. The pointers were attached at the lower end of the sternum and on the spinous process of the seventh cervical and every other vertebra down to the sacrum. After photographing the subject, the tester could draw the actual position of the spine and the chest on the photograph from knowing the actual length of the pointers. In this way certain body parts such as the arms, breasts, back muscles, and projecting scapulae would not mask the true spinal cur-

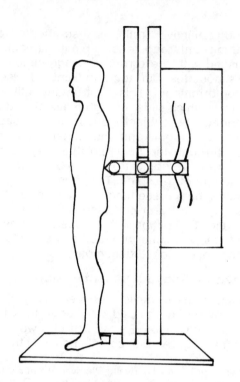

Figure 22-4. Spinograph

vature, which had heretofore been a noted weakness of silhouettes and photographs. Three measurements were taken and weighted to make up the posture grade of each subject.

The Wickens and Kiphuth Posture Test (28)

Wickens and Kiphuth developed a test by which the anteroposterior curvature of the spine could be measured objectively from photographs by using aluminum pointers and flesh pencil markings. Markings are made on the points of the body through which the plumb line should pass by a black flesh pencil, and five pointers are utilized to capture the true spinal curvature and chest position. After making tiny holes in the picture at the sites of the pointer attachments, at the flesh pencil markings, and at the most protuberant part of the abdomen, the picture is placed face down on an illuminated mimeoscope. Measurements are then drawn on the back of the picture.

Using a vernier caliper and protractor, the position of the head and neck, the amount of kyphosis and lordosis, and the positions of the chest, abdomen, shoulders, trunk, hips, and knees are measured and evaluated.

Massey Posture Test (20)

Massey developed a technique of assessing posture from silhouettes in which the following measurements are determined: (a) angle of the head and neck with the trunk; (b) trunk with the hips; (c) hips with thighs; and (d) thighs with legs. The angles are in degrees away from a straight line. The sum of the angles are converted to a letter grade.

Howland Alignometer (14)

The alignometer, designed by Howland, consists of two sliding pointers which are calibrated and attached to a vertical rod. These pointers are adjusted so as to fix the position of the center of the sternum and the superior border of the symphysis pubis. Howland determined from research that the structural balance of the trunk approximated the line of gravity when the upper trunk and tilt of the pelvis were in vertical alignment. Disalignment is noted on the alignometer by the difference in the readings of the two calibrated pointers. If the subject's alignment is balanced, the difference in readings will be zero.

Symmetrigraf

The Symmetrigraf is used for fast screening of front and side views. If posture of subject is within normal range, no further analysis is necessary. (See Figure 22-6.)

Skan-a-Graf

This instrument is used to record individualized posture measurements for future comparison to detect remedial progress, if any. It provides visual screening with the aid of an angle sight. (See Figure 22-7.)

Problems Associated with the Measurement of Posture

The problems and limitations of posture appraisal have been discussed at length in various meetings, in professional journals, and in books. While there is considerable disagreement about various aspects of posture measurement, there is consensus that posture is difficult to measure. Some of the problems of posture appraisal are listed below:

1. Probably first and foremost has been the inability of workers in this area to establish standards of posture that will take into account individual differences.
2. Individuals tend to assume an unnatural pose when they know they are being tested for posture.
3. Problems are sometimes encountered in retesting and scoring because of the difficulty of standing in exactly the same pose as before.
4. In terms of administration and analysis, the techniques for posture appraisal are generally quite time consuming, and some of the devices are expensive.
5. The use of photographs and silhouettes have in the past required considerable skill in lighting and lens adjustment, etc., in order to obtain clear and well-defined pictures. However, recent advances in photographic equipment, such as Polaroid cameras and equipment with automatic adjustments, have alleviated this problem considerably.
6. The subjective ratings of posture have generally been criticized for low reliability and objectivity.

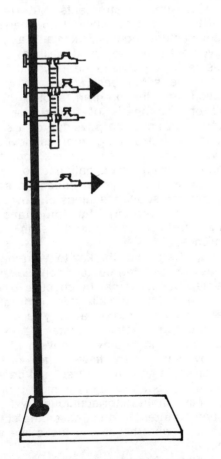

Figure 22-5. Howland Alignometer

Figure 22-6. Symmetrigraf
Courtesy of Reedco, Inc., Auburn, N.Y. 13021.

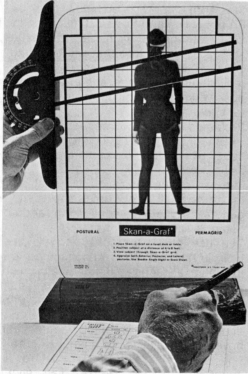

Figure 22-7. Skan-a-Graf
Courtesy of Reedco, Inc., Auburn, N.Y. 13021.

7. Because of the many variables involved, doubts have often been expressed concerning the accuracy of the measures. Even more basic have been the questions raised as to the real significance of the measures once they are obtained.

Despite the many problems associated with posture appraisal, there is much that a skilled and imaginative teacher can do to help students to become conscious of posture and to strive for improvement. To conclude that posture work is a waste of time because of the problems of measurement is just as indefensible as concluding that social adjustment is not important because it too does not lend itself readily to measurement.

The evidence, while contradictory, does tend to indicate that posture is related to certain physiological and emotional factors which make up the general health status of the individual. Clarke (3) suggests that perhaps many of the contradictory findings in the literature could be due to the lack of precision of the measuring instruments. Nevertheless, even if there were no relationship whatsoever between posture and physical health, a posture improvement program could well be justified for aesthetic purposes alone. Physical education has the same basic goals as general education, and the program should thus be based on the needs of the student. Not everyone can have the physique of a superb athlete or the looks of a glamorous movie star. However, everyone does have the opportunity and perhaps even the obligation to do the best with what he has. Physical education should profit from the subtle teachings of movies and television concerning the importance of posture and graceful carriage for good appearance.

Perhaps herein lies the key to the rather difficult task of fostering posture consciousness. For some students, it may be effective for them simply to be led to the realization that frequently persons who make a very attractive appearance are actually quite plain—their grace, poise, and beauty of movement completely overshadow any flaws in face or form. For other students a more direct and personal approach is needed. One of the most powerful and effective motivating techniques is the use of motion pictures. In most cases the student has no idea what he or she looks like while moving.

A modified version of *candid camera* was employed in a high school health class wherein motion pictures were secretly taken of each class member and then shown during class for analysis and discussion of posture. In each instance, the student was unaware of the picture taking. Some of the pictures were taken away from the school grounds. Needless to say, there was a great deal of interest in the project. There was no appreciable expense involved, as the camera was borrowed and the class members each contributed a small amount for film. While no drastic changes were brought about, the project was very effective in calling attention to posture, and considerable value was derived from the discussions. As a result of the unit, three class members began exercise programs in an attempt at re-education of posture habits, and two individuals began dieting.

The elementary grades are undoubtedly the most important in terms of being able to identify and then help to remedy faulty posture. This is where concentrated efforts should be made to install posture screening programs. Well-planned motivational devices should be employed to create favorable attitudes toward good posture and body mechanics, rather than relying on the typical nagging admonition to *sit up straight.*

In conclusion, the ratings and objective measuring devices used for posture evaluation have not met with a great deal of success insofar as being generally accepted by the profession. Despite the problems, however, it is felt that posture and body mechanics are important facets of physical education. Until better measuring tools are developed, the logical approach would seem to be to begin planned posture screening and improvement programs early in the elementary grades and to strive to diagnose and evaluate posture in relation to each individual's structure and capacity for improvement.

Findings and Conclusions from Posture Measurement and Research

In an early study Maple (19) reported some observations concerning the influence of chronological age on certain postural characteristics. Among the conclusions were that the head is not held completely erect until the age of six or seven; that the scapulae do not lie flat until after ten years of age; that the sacral angle increases markedly from three to six or seven; and that the infant is more erect than the child. In another early study Korb (16) found the comparograph, in which an outline of good posture was placed on the subject's picture, to be a valid, reliable, and inexpensive method for grading posture. Cureton and others (5) in 1935 concluded that objective measurement was more precise than subjective methods.

Flint (9) found no significant correlation between lordosis and strength of the abdominal muscles or the back extensor muscles, or between lordosis and hip or hip-trunk flexibility. The position of the center of gravity was not found to be affected by lordosis or pelvic inclinations. Flint and Diehl (10) had previously found trunk-strength balance, abdominal strength, and back extensor strength all to be significantly related to anteroposterior alignment. Hutchins (15) found supporting evidence to the above and concluded that the balance of strength between trunk-flexor and trunk-extensor muscles and other muscle groups was an important factor in anteroposterior alignment. She further reported that the results of her study provided evidence in support of the current posture training methods which involve specific strength and flexibility exercises. Anderson (2) found that over 90 percent of the high school subjects in her study had posture deviations. She concluded that photography could be effectively used in posture education and that posture education resulted in improvement in posture.

Coppock (4) reported that tightness of the pectoral muscles did not correlate significantly with round shoulders. Fox (11) concluded that faulty pelvic tilt was not associated with any appreciable weakness in the abdominal muscles, nor was swayback related to weak abdominal musculature. She did report that dysmenorrhea was more severe among women having swayback than among the control group. Swim (27) observed a definite pattern of body sway in females in different age groups from three to twenty-two years of age. Haynes found that body sway during 1 minute of erect standing had little influence on postural alignment (13).

DiGiovanna (8), in an early investigation, studied the relationship of athletic achievement and posture. The results, although not statistically treated, indicated a fairly definite relationship between the two variables. Davies (7), however, found little or no relationship between motor ability and judges' ratings of postural divergencies.

Several individuals have studied the

gravitational line of the body and have recommended specific points on the different segments of the body along which a plumb line should fall. Basically, the line passes through the lobe of the ear, the tip of the shoulder, the great trochanter of the hip, behind the knee cap, and in front of the external malleolus. There has been some disagreement concerning the exact location of these body sites. For example, Phelps, Kiphuth, and Goff (24) objected to the criterion that the mastoid bone be in line with the acromion process because of individual variations in the mobility of the shoulders. Minor differences have also been noted with regard to the point at which the gravitational line passes through the ankle. Fox and Young (12) concluded that the line of gravity lay anterior to the center of the ankle joint and near enough to the anterior border of the tibia to be considered on line with it.

Various investigators have attempted to relate posture to health and to certain physiological and emotional characteristics. In 1931 Alden and Top (1) found no relationship between posture and the factors of weight, vital capacity, and intelligence. Cyriax (6) stated that poor dorso-cervical posture which induces cardiac impairment may cause sudden heart failure, angina, and functional heart troubles. Moriarity and Irwin (22) reported a significant relationship between poor posture and certain physical and emotional factors, including self-consciousness, fidgeting, restlessness, timidity, fatigue, underweight, disease, heart defects, hearing problems, and asthma.

References and Bibliography

1. Alden, Florence D., and Hilda Top, "Experiment on the Relation of Posture to Weight, Vital Capacity and Intelligence," *Research Quarterly,* 2:38-41, October, 1931.
2. Anderson, Melba Kay, "An Investigation of the Need for Posture Education Among High School Girls and a Suggested Plan for Instruction to Meet These Needs" (Unpublished master's thesis, University of Texas, 1966).
3. Clarke, H. Harrison, *Application of Measurement to Health and Physical Education,* 4th ed., Englewood Cliffs, N.J.: Prentice-Hall, 1967, p. 79.
4. Coppock, Doris E., "Relationship of Tightness of Pectoral Muscles to Round Shoulders in College Women," *Research Quarterly,* 29: 146-153, May, 1958.
5. Cureton, Thomas, J. Stuart Wickens, and Haskell P. Elder, "Reliability and Objectivity of Springfield Postural Measurements," *Research Quarterly Supplement,* 6:81-92, May, 1935.
6. Cyriax, E., "The Relation of Dorso-Cervical Postural Deficiencies to Cardiac Disease, Especially from Middle Life Onwards," *Research Quarterly,* 7:74-79, December, 1936.
7. Davies, Evelyn A., "Relationship Between Selected Postural Divergencies and Motor Ability," *Research Quarterly,* 28:1-4, March, 1957.
8. DiGiavanna, Vincent G., "A Study of the Relation of Athletic Skills and Strengths to Those of Posture," *Research Quarterly,* 2:67-79, May, 1931.
9. Flint, M. Marilyn, "Lumbar Posture: A Study of Roentgenographic Measurement and the Influence of Flexibility and Strength," *Research Quarterly,* 34:15-20, March, 1963.
10. _____ , and Bobbie Diehl, "Influence of Abdominal Strength, Back Extensor Strength and Trunk Strength Balance upon Antero-Posterior Alignment of Elementary School Girls," *Research Quarterly,* 32:490-498, December, 1961.
11. Fox, Margaret G., "Relationship of Abdominal Strength to Selected Posture Faults," *Research Quarterly,* 22:141-144, May, 1951.
12. _____ , and Olive G. Young, "Placement of the Gravital Line in Antero-Posterior Standing Posture," *Research Quarterly,* 25:277-285, October, 1954.
13. Haynes, Betty Ann, "Postural Sway and Antero-Posterior Alignment During One Minute Erect Standing" (Unpublished master's thesis, Michigan State University, 1966).
14. Howland, Ivalclare Sprow, *Body Alignment in Fundamental Motor Skills,* New York: Exposition Press, 1953, p. 78.
15. Hutchins, Gloria Lee, "The Relationship of Selected Strength and Flexibility Variables to the Antero-Posterior Posture of College Women," *Research Quarterly,* 36:253-269, October, 1965.
16. Korb, Edward M., "A Method to Increase the Validity of Measuring Posture," *Research Quarterly,* 10:142-149, March, 1939.
17. MacEwan, Charlotte G., and Eugene C. Howe, "An Objective Method of Grading Posture," *Research Quarterly,* 3:144-147, October, 1932.
18. Malina, Robert M., and Francis E. Johnston, "Significance of Age, Sex, and Maturity Differences in Upper Arm Composition," *Research Quarterly,* 38:219-230, May, 1967.
19. Maple, Katherine N., "Chronological Variations in the Posture of Children Ages One to Seven and Ten to Thirteen," *Research Quarterly,* 1:30-33, March, 1930.
20. Massey, Wayne W., "A Critical Study of Objective Methods of Measuring Antero-Posterior

Posture with a Simplified Technique," *Research Quarterly,* 14:3-10, March, 1943.

21. McCloy, C. H., and Norma D. Young, *Tests and Measurements in Health and Physical Education,* 3rd ed., New York: Appleton-Century-Crofts, 1954, Chapter 21.

22. Moriarity, Mary J., and Leslie W. Irwin, "A Study of the Relationships of Certain Physical and Emotional Factors to Habitual Poor Posture Among School Children," *Research Quarterly,* 23:221-225, May, 1952.

23. *New York State Physical Fitness Test for Boys and Girls Grades 4-12,* Albany: New York State Education Department, 1966.

24. Phelps, W. W., R. J. H. Kiphuth, and C. W. Goff, *The Diagnosis and Treatment of Postural Defects,* 2nd ed., Springfield, Ill.: Charles C. Thomas, 1956, pp. 118-138.

25. Scott, M. Gladys, and Esther French, *Measurement and Evaluation in Physical Education,* Dubuque, Iowa: Wm. C. Brown Company, 1959, pp. 414-421.

26. Smithells, Philip A., and Peter E. Cameron, *Principles of Evaluation in Physical Education,* New York: Harper and Brothers, 1962, pp. 334-340.

27. Swim, Carol Lee, "A Comparative Study of Body Sway in the Antero-Posterior Plane with Reference to the External Malleolus in Females Ages 3 through 22" (Unpublished master's thesis, University of North Carolina, 1965).

28. Wickens, J. Stuart, and Oscar W. Kiphuth, "Body Mechanics Analysis of Yale University Freshmen," *Research Quarterly,* 8:38-44, December, 1937.

Appendix A

Practice Data—Isotonic and Isometric
Press Scores of 25 Junior High School Boys

Subject	Isotonic Scores	Isometric Scores
1	63	76
2	78	80
3	46	92
4	82	102
5	74	73
6	103	87
7	78	70
8	103	85
9	87	79
10	73	93
11	95	82
12	82	90
13	89	83
14	73	81
15	92	85
16	85	72
17	80	81
18	81	96
19	90	81
20	78	85
21	86	90
22	78	75
23	101	73
24	65	90
25	84	86

Appendix B
Steps for Computing Square Root

Computing Square Root

The easiest method of finding square root is to consult a table. In practically any school situation, the teacher has access to these tables through the mathematics or science teachers, the school library, etc. However, it is valuable and sometimes more expedient for the teacher to be able to compute square root himself. The following method is one that is often taught in schools:

We will find the square root of 698.4, i.e., $\sqrt{698.4}$

Step 1: Separate the number into two-digit units in each direction from the decimal. (We added zero in front of the 6 merely to demonstrate the fact that you move to the right *and* to the left from the decimal point.)

$$\sqrt{06'98'.40'}$$

Step 2: Determine the largest number that will square itself into the first pair of digits, 06. The largest square in 06 is 2×2, or 4. Therefore place 2 as the first digit of the square root. Then subtract 4 from 6 and bring down the next pair of digits, 98.

$$
\begin{array}{r}
2 \\
\sqrt{6'98'.40'} \\
4 \\
\hline
298
\end{array}
$$

Step 3: Double the partial square root, 2, and place the sum, 4, to the left of 298:

$$
\begin{array}{r}
2 \\
\sqrt{6'98'.40'} \\
4 \\
\hline
4298
\end{array}
$$

Determine the next digit of the square root by dividing 298 by 10×4, or 40: $298 \div 40 = 6$. Now place the 6 as the next digit of the square root and also add the number 6 to the 4 to make the divisor 46. Then multiply 46 by 6, subtract the product from 298, and bring down the next pair of digits. The remainder is now 2240.

Step 4: Double the partial square root, 26, and place the sum, 52, to the left of 2240:

```
           26.
      √6'98'.40'
         4
  46  |298
      |276
  52    2240
```

The third digit is now determined by multiplying 52×10 and dividing the resulting product, 520, into 2240, which equals 4. Place 4 to the right of the decimal as the third digit in the square root and also place 4 to the right of 52 to form the divisor 524. Multiply 524 by 4 and subtract the product, 2096, from 2240. Bring down the next pair of zeros to form the remainder of 14,400.

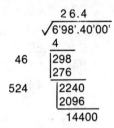

```
           26.4
      √6'98'.40'00'
         4
  46  |298
      |276
  524  |2240
       |2096
          14400
```

This process may be continued for as long as you wish to carry it out. The square root of this number carried out to two more places is shown below:

```
            2  6. 4  2  7
        √6'98'.40'00'00'
           4
  46     |298
         |276
  524     |2240
          |2096
  5282      |14400
            |10564
  52847       |383600
              |369929
                 13671
```

Appendix C

Table C-1
The F Distribution (Values of F .05)*

| | \multicolumn{13}{c}{Numerator Degrees of Freedom} |
	1	2	3	4	5	6	8	10	12	15	20	24	30
1	161	200	216	225	230	234	239	242	244	246	248	249	250
2	18.5	19.0	19.2	19.2	19.3	19.3	19.4	19.4	19.4	19.4	19.4	19.5	19.5
3	10.1	9.55	9.28	9.12	9.01	8.94	8.85	8.79	8.74	8.70	8.66	8.64	8.62
4	7.71	6.94	6.59	6.39	6.26	6.16	6.04	5.96	5.91	5.86	5.80	5.77	5.75
5	6.61	5.79	5.41	5.19	5.05	4.95	4.82	4.74	4.68	4.62	4.56	4.53	4.50
6	5.99	5.14	4.76	4.53	4.39	4.28	4.15	4.06	4.00	3.94	3.87	3.84	3.81
7	5.59	4.74	4.35	4.12	3.97	3.87	3.73	3.64	3.57	3.51	3.44	3.41	3.38
8	5.32	4.46	4.07	3.84	3.69	3.58	3.44	3.35	3.28	3.22	3.15	3.12	3.08
9	5.12	4.26	3.86	3.63	3.48	3.37	3.23	3.14	3.07	3.01	2.94	2.90	2.86
10	4.96	4.10	3.71	3.48	3.33	3.22	3.07	2.98	2.91	2.85	2.77	2.74	2.70
11	4.84	3.98	3.59	3.36	3.20	3.09	2.95	2.85	2.79	2.72	2.65	2.61	2.57
12	4.75	3.89	3.49	3.26	3.11	3.00	2.85	2.75	2.69	2.62	2.54	2.51	2.47
13	4.67	3.81	3.41	3.18	3.03	2.92	2.77	2.67	2.60	2.53	2.46	2.42	2.38
14	4.60	3.74	3.34	3.11	2.96	2.85	2.70	2.60	2.53	2.46	2.39	2.35	2.31
15	4.54	3.68	3.29	3.06	2.90	2.79	2.64	2.54	2.48	2.40	2.33	2.29	2.25
16	4.49	3.63	3.24	3.01	2.85	2.74	2.59	2.49	2.42	2.35	2.28	2.24	2.19
17	4.45	3.59	3.20	2.96	2.81	2.70	2.55	2.45	2.38	2.31	2.23	2.19	2.15
18	4.41	3.55	3.16	2.93	2.77	2.66	2.51	2.41	2.34	2.27	2.19	2.15	2.11
19	4.38	3.52	3.13	2.90	2.74	2.63	2.48	2.38	2.31	2.23	2.16	2.11	2.07
20	4.35	3.49	3.10	2.87	2.71	2.60	2.45	2.35	2.28	2.20	2.12	2.08	2.04
21	4.32	3.47	3.07	2.84	2.68	2.57	2.42	2.32	2.25	2.18	2.10	2.05	2.01
22	4.30	3.44	3.05	2.82	2.66	2.55	2.40	2.30	2.23	2.15	2.07	2.03	1.98
23	4.28	3.42	3.03	2.80	2.64	2.53	2.37	2.27	2.20	2.13	2.05	2.01	1.96
24	4.26	3.40	3.01	2.78	2.62	2.51	2.36	2.25	2.18	2.11	2.03	1.98	1.94
25	4.24	3.39	2.99	2.76	2.60	2.49	2.34	2.24	2.16	2.09	2.01	1.96	1.92
30	4.17	3.32	2.92	2.69	2.53	2.42	2.27	2.16	2.09	2.01	1.93	1.89	1.84
40	4.08	3.23	2.84	2.61	2.45	2.34	2.18	2.08	2.00	1.92	1.84	1.79	1.74
60	4.00	3.15	2.76	2.53	2.37	2.25	2.10	1.99	1.92	1.84	1.75	1.70	1.65
120	3.92	3.07	2.68	2.45	2.29	2.18	2.02	1.91	1.83	1.75	1.66	1.61	1.55
∞	3.84	3.00	2.60	2.37	2.21	2.10	1.94	1.83	1.75	1.67	1.57	1.52	1.46

(left margin label: Denominator Degrees of Freedom)

*Abridged from M. Merrington and C. M. Thompson, "Tables of Percentage Points of the Inverted Beta (F) Distribution," *Biometrika*, 33:73-88, 1943. By permission of the *Biometrika* Trustees.

Table C-2
The F Distribution (Values of F .01)*

	Numerator Degrees of Freedom												
	1	2	3	4	5	6	8	10	12	15	20	24	30
1	4050	5000	5400	5620	5760	5860	5980	6060	6110	6160	6210	6235	6260
2	98.5	99.0	99.2	99.2	99.3	99.3	99.4	99.4	99.4	99.4	99.4	99.5	99.5
3	34.1	30.8	29.5	28.7	28.2	27.9	27.5	27.3	27.1	26.9	26.7	26.6	26.5
4	21.2	18.0	16.7	16.0	15.5	15.2	14.8	14.5	14.4	14.2	14.0	13.9	13.8
5	16.3	13.3	12.1	11.4	11.0	10.7	10.3	10.1	9.89	9.72	9.55	9.47	9.38
6	13.7	10.9	9.78	9.15	8.75	8.47	8.10	7.87	7.72	7.56	7.40	7.31	7.23
7	12.2	9.55	8.45	7.85	7.46	7.19	6.84	6.62	6.47	6.31	6.16	6.07	5.99
8	11.3	8.65	7.59	7.01	6.63	6.37	6.03	5.81	5.67	5.52	5.36	5.28	5.20
9	10.6	8.02	6.99	6.42	6.06	5.80	5.47	5.26	5.11	4.96	4.81	4.73	4.65
10	10.0	7.56	6.55	5.99	5.64	5.39	5.06	4.85	4.71	4.56	4.41	4.33	4.25
11	9.65	7.21	6.22	5.67	5.32	5.07	4.74	4.54	4.40	4.25	4.10	4.02	3.94
12	9.33	6.93	5.95	5.41	5.06	4.82	4.50	4.30	4.16	4.01	3.86	3.78	3.70
13	9.07	6.70	5.74	5.21	4.86	4.62	4.30	4.10	3.96	3.82	3.66	3.59	3.51
14	8.86	6.51	5.56	5.04	4.69	4.46	4.14	3.94	3.80	3.66	3.51	3.43	3.35
15	8.68	6.36	5.42	4.89	4.56	4.32	4.00	3.80	3.67	3.52	3.37	3.29	3.21
16	8.53	6.23	5.29	4.77	4.44	4.20	3.89	3.69	3.55	3.41	3.26	3.18	3.10
17	8.40	6.11	5.18	4.67	4.34	4.10	3.79	3.59	3.46	3.31	3.16	3.08	3.00
18	8.29	6.01	5.09	4.58	4.25	4.01	3.71	3.51	3.37	3.23	3.08	3.00	2.92
19	8.18	5.93	5.01	4.50	4.17	3.94	3.63	3.43	3.30	3.15	3.00	2.92	2.84
20	8.10	5.85	4.94	4.43	4.10	3.87	3.56	3.37	3.23	3.09	2.94	2.86	2.78
21	8.02	5.78	4.87	4.37	4.04	3.81	3.51	3.31	3.17	3.03	2.88	2.80	2.72
22	7.95	5.72	4.82	4.31	3.99	3.76	3.45	3.26	3.12	2.98	2.83	2.75	2.67
23	7.88	5.66	4.76	4.26	3.94	3.71	3.41	3.21	3.07	2.93	2.78	2.70	2.62
24	7.82	5.61	4.72	4.22	3.90	3.67	3.36	3.17	3.03	2.89	2.74	2.66	2.58
25	7.77	5.57	4.68	4.18	3.86	3.63	3.32	3.13	2.99	2.85	2.70	2.62	2.54
30	7.56	5.39	4.51	4.02	3.70	3.47	3.17	2.98	2.84	2.70	2.55	2.47	2.39
40	7.31	5.18	4.31	3.83	3.51	3.29	2.99	2.80	2.66	2.52	2.37	2.29	2.20
60	7.08	4.98	4.13	3.65	3.34	3.12	2.82	2.63	2.50	2.35	2.20	2.12	2.03
120	6.85	4.79	3.95	3.48	3.17	2.96	2.66	2.47	2.34	2.19	2.03	1.95	1.86
∞	6.63	4.61	3.78	3.32	3.02	2.80	2.51	2.32	2.18	2.04	1.88	1.79	1.70

Left axis label: Denominator Degrees of Freedom

*Abridged from M. Merrington and C. M. Thompson, "Tables of Percentage Points of the Inverted Beta (F) Distribution," *Biometrika*, 33:73-88, 1943. By permission of the *Biometrika* Trustees.

Appendix D
t Tests for Small Samples

The t Test

In testing the null hypothesis for the difference between two sample means, the t test may be used to determine the significance of the difference. The t distribution is based on the concept that a normal distribution results when a large number of samples are drawn, but when samples are small the probability of rejecting a test hypothesis, usually the null hypothesis, decreases.

While it is beyond the scope of this book to provide a comprehensive explanation of the t distribution and hypothesis testing, we can perhaps convey the basic concept of the t distribution with a very simple example. If a teacher were to adopt a new method of teaching, he would want to be reasonably sure that that method was superior to his old method. Consequently, he would not be nearly as willing to change his method as a result of a study in which a difference favoring the new method was found when just a few subjects were used as when the same difference resulted when such a study involved large samples. It is thus common sense that the chances are much greater that a large sample will more closely approximate the population from which it is drawn than will a small sample. The t distribution is based on that premise. Therefore, in essence, the difference between sample means must be larger when samples are small than when they are large in order for that difference to be significant. The t values are shown in Table D-1. It should be pointed out that the values in the table are not the observed differences but rather the ratio between the observed difference and the reliability estimate (standard error) of the sample means in approximating the true means of their respective population(s).

It can be noted in the table that there are three columns. The column on the left is *Degrees of Freedom*. It refers to the size of the sample, or more specifically, $n-1$. As was mentioned before, the t values necessary for significance are larger when the degrees of freedom are small.

The other two columns are headed .05 and .01. These refer to the probability of rejecting the null hypothesis. The .05 level of probability means that the chances are only 5 out of 100 that a difference as large as was obtained could be attributed to chance error of sampling. At the .01 level, the chances of sampling error are only 1 in 100. Thus one could be more confi-

Table D-1
Table of t, for Determining Significance*

Degrees of Freedom	Probability .05	Probability .01	Degrees of Freedom	Probability .05	Probability .01
1	$t = 12.71$	$t = 63.66$	19	2.09	2.86
2	4.30	9.92	20	2.09	2.84
3	3.18	5.84	21	2.08	2.83
4	2.78	4.60	22	2.07	2.82
5	2.57	4.03	23	2.07	2.81
6	2.45	3.71	24	2.06	2.80
7	2.36	3.50	25	2.06	2.79
8	2.31	3.36	26	2.06	2.78
9	2.26	3.25	27	2.05	2.77
10	2.23	3.17	28	2.05	2.76
11	2.20	3.11	29	2.04	2.76
12	2.18	3.06	30	2.04	2.75
13	2.16	3.01	40	2.02	2.70
14	2.14	2.98	60	2.00	2.66
15	2.13	2.95	120	1.98	2.62
16	2.12	2.92	∞	1.96	2.58
17	2.11	2.90			
18	2.10	2.88			

*Entering the table of t with N-2 or 14 df, we find that our t of 4.64 is greater than the t of 2.14 at the .05 level of probability and also greater than the 2.98 needed for significance at the .01 level. Our t is therefore significant at the .01 level of probability, and we can reject the null hypothesis. Hence only 1 time out of 100 would we expect to get a difference as large as this due to chance or sampling error.

Table abridged from Table III of Ronald A. Fisher and Frank Yates, *Statistical Tables for Biological, Agricultural and Medical Research,* 6th ed., 1963, published by Oliver and Boyd, Edinburgh, and used by permission of the authors and publishers.

dent that the difference is real at the .01 level than at the .05; the t values needed at the .01 level are therefore greater than those needed for the .05 level. It should be mentioned that there are other probability levels that may be used, but the most common are the .05 and .01.

The t Test for the Significance of the Difference Between Means in Small Independent (Uncorrelated) Samples. There are many occasions where the investigator wishes to compare two groups that represent independent samples. A physical educator may want to compare running times of two groups who had trained by different methods, or perhaps com-

pare the physical fitness scores of students of whom one group had a required physical education program and another group had not, or possibly compare social adjustment inventory scores of boys against the scores of girls. In each comparison, the samples are drawn from independent populations, hence the means are considered to be uncorrelated means.

To illustrate the steps involved in a comparison of independent samples, let us suppose that in order to establish evidence of validity for a basketball skills test we constructed, we administered the test to two groups of players. One sample represented varsity players, the other sample intramural players. We will assume that our sampling procedures were sound.

Step 1: Compute the mean for each group. The observed difference between these two means is to be tested for significance.

Step 2: Establish a deviation (x) column by subtracting the mean from each score. For example, in group one, the mean is 9. Thus $10-9=1$, $17-9=8$, etc. This is done for each group.

Step 3: Square the deviation (x^2) and add each column (Σx^2).

Step 4: Compute the standard deviation. When the samples are small, it is better to pool

Table D-2
t Test for Small Independent Groups

Group I Varsity Basketball Players			Group II Intramural Basketball Players		
Scores	x_1	x_1^2	Scores	x_2	x_2^2
10	1	1	3	.5	.25
16	7	49	1	−1.5	2.25
5	−4	16	2	− .5	.25
6	−3	9	0	−2.5	6.25
12	3	9	4	1.5	2.25
8	−1	1	1	−1.5	2.25
9	0	0	5	2.5	6.25
6	−3	9	4	1.5	2.25
$\Sigma X = 72$		$\Sigma x_1^2 = 94$	$\Sigma X = 20$		$\Sigma x_2^2 = 22.00$

$$\overline{X}_1 = \frac{\Sigma X}{n} = \frac{72}{8} = 9 \qquad\qquad \overline{X}_2 = \frac{\Sigma X}{n} = \frac{20}{8} = 2.5$$

$$s = \sqrt{\frac{\Sigma x_1^2 + \Sigma x_2^2}{(n_1 - 1) + (n_2 - 1)}} \qquad s_D = (s)\sqrt{\frac{n_1 + n_2}{n_1 n_2}} \qquad t = \frac{\overline{X}_1 - \overline{X}_2}{s_D} \qquad df = n_1 - 1 + n_2 - 1$$

$$s = \sqrt{\frac{94 + 22}{(8-1) + (8-1)}} \qquad s_D = (2.88)\sqrt{\frac{8+8}{(8)\,(8)}} \qquad t = \frac{9 - 2.5}{1.4} \qquad df = (8-1) + (8-1)$$

$$s = \sqrt{\frac{116}{14}} \qquad s_D = (2.88)\sqrt{\frac{16}{64}} \qquad t = \frac{6.5}{1.4} \qquad df = 14$$

$$s = \sqrt{8.29} \qquad s_D = (2.88)\sqrt{.25} \qquad t = 4.64$$

$$s = 2.88 \qquad s_D = (2.88)\,(.5)$$

$$s_D = 1.4$$

the Σx^2 to compute a single standard deviation (s), which provides a better estimate of the population standard deviation. The formula is

$$s = \sqrt{\frac{\Sigma x_1^2 + \Sigma x_2^2}{(n_1 - 1) + (n_2 - 1)}}$$

Step 5: Compute the standard error of the difference between the two means by the formula

$$s_D = (s)\sqrt{\frac{n_1 + n_2}{n_1 n_2}}$$

Step 6: Compute the *t* ratio.

$$t = \frac{\overline{X}_1 - \overline{X}_2}{s_D}$$

Step 7: The number of degrees of freedom (*df*) is N-2 since we had eight subjects in each group and one *df* is lost in calculating each mean. Hence, $n_1 - 1 = 7 + n_2 - 1 = 7$, or 14 *df*.

Step 8: Refer to the table of *t* (Table D-1) with 14 *df* to determine significance. The results of the preceding steps are shown in Table D-2.

Table D-3
t Test for Correlated Means in Small Samples

Regular Endurance Test	Motivated Endurance Test	Difference	x	x^2
45	54	9	1	1
33	50	17	9	81
59	58	−1	−9	81
32	38	6	−2	4
30	42	12	4	16
27	35	8	0	0
29	38	9	1	1
59	66	7	−1	1
44	48	4	−4	16
40	49	9	1	1
		80		$\Sigma x^2 = 202$

Mean Difference $\overline{X}_D = \dfrac{\Sigma X_D}{N} = \dfrac{80}{10} = 8$

$s = \sqrt{\dfrac{\Sigma x^2}{N-1}}$ $s_D = \dfrac{S}{\sqrt{N}}$ $t = \dfrac{\overline{X}_D}{s_D}$ $df = N - 1$

$s = \sqrt{\dfrac{202}{10-1}}$ $s_D = \dfrac{4.74}{\sqrt{10}}$ $t = \dfrac{8}{1.5}$ $df = 10 - 1$

$s = \sqrt{22.44}$ $s_D = \dfrac{4.74}{3.16}$ $t = 5.33$ $df = 9$

$s = 4.74$ $s_D = 1.5$

The _t_ test for the Significance of the Difference Between Correlated Means in Small Samples. For illustrative purposes, let us assume that we have administered a muscular endurance test to ten students and then a week later we re-administer the same test to the same group except that we bring in a few spectators and play march music throughout the test period. Thus, we want to determine if there is a mean gain and, if so, is it significant? This is determined through the following steps as seen in Table D-3.

Step 1: List the scores for each group and establish a column of differences between the pairs of scores.

Step 2: Compute the mean difference.

Step 3: Establish a deviation (x) column for the group by subtracting the mean difference from each difference score.

Step 4: Square the deviations and determine the Σx^2.

Step 5: Determine the standard deviation of the differences by the formula

$$s = \sqrt{\frac{\Sigma x^2}{N-1}}$$

Step 6: Compute the standard error of the mean difference by the formula.

$$s_D = \frac{s}{\sqrt{N}}$$

Step 7: Substitute the proper values into the t ratio formula

$$t = \frac{\overline{X}_D}{s_D}$$

Step 8: Refer to the table of t (Table D-1) with N-1 df to determine significance.

Entering Table D-1 with 9 df, we find that our t of 5.33 is greater than the t needed for significance at the .01 level of probability (3.25). Therefore, it is concluded that the application of motivational techniques significantly improves endurance performance.

Two commonly used methods of expressing norms, the T-scale and percentiles, were discussed in Chapter 3, and methods of calculating each were described. There are other scales such as stanines, the sigma scale, the C-scale, the Hull scale, and Z-scores that are also used for the purpose of standardizing scores. The latter two scales, the Hull scale and Z-scores, are briefly discussed in this section.

The Hull Scale

The Hull scale is quite similar to the T-scale in that the mean is 50 and the scores extend from 0 to 100. The only difference between the two scales is that the Hull encompasses 3.5 standard deviations above and below the mean, whereas the T-scale includes 5 standard deviations on either side of the mean. Because of this difference you can expect students to obtain higher (and lower) scores on the Hull scale than on the T-scale since over 99 percent of the scores in a normal distribution lie between 3 standard deviations above and below the mean. As was discussed in Chapter 3, T-scores normally range from 20 to 80 since this represents a range of 3 standard deviations on either side of the mean. However, it was pointed out that the 2 standard deviation cushion above and below this range is advantageous in that it virtually precludes the possibility of encountering future scores that cannot be placed on the scale.

Calculations for the Hull scale are very similar to those followed in constructing the T-scale. Instead of taking one-tenth of the standard deviation to use as the constant to serially add and subtract from the mean as is done in the T-scale, the Hull scale is computed from the formula:

$$\text{Hull Scale Constant} = \frac{3.5 \, (\text{raw score} \; \text{standard deviation})}{50}$$

For example, the mean for a vertical jump test is 16 inches and the standard deviation is 7. Inserting the standard deviation in the formula, we have:

$$\frac{3.5(7)}{50} = .49$$

A Hull scale numbering from 0 to 100 is prepared, and the raw score mean is then placed next to 50. The constant value of .49 is added to raw scores above the mean of 16 and subtracted from values below the mean of 16 in order to determine the Hull scores, as follows:

Hull Score	Raw Score
•	•
•	•
•	•
55	18.45
54	17.96
53	17.47
52	16.98
51	16.49
50 (Raw score mean = Hull scale of 50)	16.00
49	15.51
48	15.02
47	14.53
46	14.04
45	13.55
•	•
•	•
•	•

Z-Scores

Z-scores are merely scores expressed in terms of standard deviations from the mean. The mean of Z-scores is zero; thus scores below the mean are expressed in negative values and scores above the mean in positive values. The formula for computing Z-scores is

$$Z\text{-Scores} = \frac{\text{Raw Score} - \text{Mean of Scores}}{\text{Standard Deviation}}$$

Using the previous example of vertical jump scores, we shall compute the Z-score for a jump of 14 inches:

$$Z = \frac{14 - 16}{7} = -.29$$

A jump of 23 inches would be a Z-score of 1.0; a jump of 26.5 inches would equal a Z of 1.5 and so on. Since Z-scores are usually small, involve decimals, and are expressed in both positive and negative values, they are not as frequently used as some of the other scales. However, a tester should understand the Z-score concept since *all of the other standard scales such as T-scores, Hull-Scale, etc., are related to the Z-score.* Specific scores on different tests may be readily and meaningfully compared by simply using Z-scores (assuming, of course, that the test distributions are similar).

The tester may also have occasion to use Z-scores to determine the percentage of scores above and below a particular score. A table of percentage parts of the total area under the normal probability curve must be consulted. The tester may wish to discover what percentile a particular raw score (converted to Z-score) represents or what percentage of the population lies between certain scores, or perhaps to determine the probability (odds) of a particular score occurring.

It is hoped that the reader will be stimulated to pursue the topic of probability and the normal curve and hence statistics in order to improve his or her teaching and to arrive at a fuller understanding of the measurement of human behavior.

Appendix F
Conversion Tables for English and Metric Systems of Measurement

Length

	inch	foot	yard	millimeter	centimeter	meter
1 inch	1.0	.083	.028	25.4	2.54	.0254
1 foot	12.0	1.0	.33	304.8	30.48	.3048
1 yard	36.0	3.0	1.0	914.4	91.44	.914
1 millimeter	.039	.003	.001	1.0	.1	.001
1 centimeter	.3937	.033	.011	10.0	1.0	.01
1 meter	39.37	3.28	1.09	1000.0	100.0	1.0

1 mile = 5280 feet
1 mile = 1760 yards
1 mile = 1609 meters
1 mile = 1.609 kilometers

1 kilometer = 1000 meters
1 kilometer = 3281.5 feet
1 kilometer = 1093.8 yards
1 kilometer = .6215 mile

Weight

	ounce	pound	gram	kilogram
1 ounce	1.0	.0625	28.0	.028
1 pound	16.0	1.0	448.0	.448
1 gram	.035	.0022	1.0	.001
1 kilogram	35.2	2.2	1000.0	1.0

1 ton = .907 metric ton
1 metric ton = 1.102 tons

Temperature

$32°$ Fahrenheit = $0°$ centigrade
$212°$ Fahrenheit = $100°$ centigrade
To change centigrade to Fahrenheit: $F° = \dfrac{9}{5} C° + 32$

To change Fahrenheit to centigrade: $C° = \dfrac{5}{9} (F° - 32)$

Capacity

	fl. oz.	liq. pt.	liq. qt.	cu. in.	cu. cm.	dl.	l.
1 U.S. fluid ounce	1.0	.0625	.0313	1.8047	29.574	.2957	.0296
1 U.S. liquid pint	16.0	1.0	.5	28.875	473.18	4.7317	.4732
1 U.S. liquid quart	32.0	2.0	1.0	57.75	946.35	9.4633	.9463
1 cubic inch	.554	.0346	.0173	1.0	16.387	.1639	.0164
1 cubic centimeter	(1 cubic centimeter = 1 milliliter)						
1 milliliter	.0338	.0021	.0011	.0610	1.0	.01	.001
1 deciliter	3.3815	.2113	.1057	6.103	100.0	1.0	.1
1 liter	33.815	2.1134	1.0567	61.025	1000.0	10.0	1.0

Area

1 square inch	=	6.4516	square centimeters
1 square foot	=	929.03	square centimeters
1 square foot	=	.092	square meter
1 square yard	=	.82	square meter
1 square centimeter	=	.155	square inch
1 square centimeter	=	.0011	square foot
1 square meter	=	10.764	square feet
1 square meter	=	1.196	square yards

Work Units

1 foot-pound	=	.13825	kilogram-meter
1 kilogram-meter	=	7.23	foot-pounds

Energy Units

1 kilocalorie	= 3086	foot-pounds
1 kilocalorie	= 426.4	kilogram-meters

(1 kilocalorie is the heat required to raise the temperature of 1 kilogram of water
1 degree centigrade. 1 kilocalorie = 1000 calories.)

Power Units (Work per Unit of Time)

	horsepower	watt	ft. lbs. min.	kg.m. min.	ft. lbs. sec.	kg. m. sec.
1 horsepower	1.0	746.0	33,000.0	4564.0	550.0	76.07
1 watt	.0013	1.0	44.236	6.118	.7373	.1019
1 foot-pound/min.	.00003	.0226	1.0	.1383	.0167	.0023
1 kilogram-meter/min.	.0002	.1634	7.23	1.0	.1205	.0167

I. Measuring Distance
   A. Yardsticks
   B. Rulers
   C. Tape measures (36 inches)
   D. Tape measures (for field marking)
   E. Panel mats (each panel is usually 1 foot)
II. Measuring Time
   A. Stopwatch
   B. Wristwatch with second hand
   C. Metronome
   D. Nelson reaction timer
III. Marking Material and Boundary Markers
   A. Masking tape
   B. Chalk
   C. Flags
   D. Chairs
   E. Boundary cones
   F. Rope or cord
IV. Special Equipment
   A. Mats
   B. Horizontal bar (or chinning bar)
   C. Parallel bars (or dipping bars)
   D. Barbells and dumbbells
   E. Benches
   F. Weight scale
   G. Stadiometer
   H. Springscale
   I. Climbing rope
   J. Medicine ball (6 pounds)
   K. Balance sticks (12 inches long, 1 inch high, 1 inch wide)
V. Special Materials
   A. Chains
   B. Cane poles
   C. Blindfold
   D. S-hooks
   E. Chain links

Appendix G
Sample Checklist of Physical Performance and Skills Testing Materials and Supplies

Appendix H
Elementary School Flexibility Norms

Table H-1
Modified Sit-and-Reach Test

Grades 3 and 4

Boys	Level	Girls
20½ - Above	Advanced	20½ - Above
19¼ - 20¼	Adv. Intermediate	19¼ - 20¼
17¼ - 19	Intermediate	17¼ - 19
16½ - 17	Adv. Beginner	16¼ - 17
Below - 16¼	Beginner	Below - 16

Based on 80 scores obtained by Gary Beveridge, Corpus Christi, Tx., 1977.

Table H-2
Bridge-up Test

Grades 3 and 4

Boys	Level	Girls
9 - Less	Advanced	8¼ - Less
11¾ - 9¼	Adv. Intermediate	9½ - 8½
15 - 12	Intermediate	12 - 9¾
19 - 15¼	Adv. Beginner	14¾ - 12¼
Higher - 19¼	Beginner	Higher - 15

Based on 144 scores obtained by Gary Beveridge and Janice Leal, Corpus Christi, Tx., 1977.

Table H-3
Front-to-Rear Splits Test

Grades 3 and 4

Boys	Level	Girls
6¾ - Lower	Advanced	½ - 0
8¼ - 7	Adv. Intermediate	2¼ - ¾
11 - 8½	Intermediate	7½ - 2½
13 - 11¼	Adv. Beginner	8¼ - 7¾
Higher - 13¼	Beginner	Higher - 8½

Based on 64 scores obtained by Felipe Garcia, Corpus Christi, Tx., 1977.

Table H-4
Side Splits Test

Grades 3 and 4

Boys	Level	Girls
7½ - 0	Advanced	1¾ - 0
8½ - 7¾	Adv. Intermediate	2½ - 2
10 - 8¾	Intermediate	6¼ - 2¾
11½ - 10¼	Adv. Beginner	9¼ - 6½
Above - 11¾	Beginner	Above - 9½

Based on 63 scores obtained by Steve Kurtz, Corpus Christi, Tx., 1977.

Table H-5
Shoulder-and-Wrist Elevation Test

Grades 3 and 4

Boys	Level	Girls
6½ - 0	Advanced	4¼ - 0
11¾ - 6¾	Adv. Intermediate	8 - 4½
15 - 12	Intermediate	14¼ - 8¼
16 - 15¼	Adv. Beginner	17½ - 14½
Above - 16¼	Beginner	Above - 17¾

Based on 67 scores obtained by Cherie Bushwar and Felipe Garcia, Corpus Christi, Tx., 1977.

Table H-6
Shoulder Rotation Test

Grades 3 and 4

Boys	Level	Girls
3¾ - 0	Advanced	1½ - 0
5¾ - 4	Adv. Intermediate	5 - 1¾
13 - 6	Intermediate	9¼ - 5¼
14¾ - 13¼	Adv. Beginner	14¾ - 9½
Higher - 15	Beginner	Higher - 15

Based on 67 scores obtained at St. Pius School, Corpus Christi, Tx., 1977.

Table H-7
Ankle Extension (Plantar Flexion) Test

Grades 3 and 4

Boys	Level	Girls
3/8 - Less	Advanced	1/4 - Less
5/8 - 1/2	Adv. Intermediate	1/2 - 3/8
1 - 3/4	Intermediate	1 1/4 - 5/8
2 1/8 - 1 1/8	Adv. Beginner	1 5/8 - 3/8
Above - 2 1/4	Beginner	Above - 1 3/4

Based on 66 scores obtained by Felipe Garcia, Corpus Christi, Tx., 1977.

Appendix I
Alternate Flexibility Tests without Flexomeasure

Sit-and-Reach Test*

Purpose: To develop hip and back flexion as well as extension of the hamstring muscles of the legs.

Sports Specificity: (1) Vaulting, diving, and trampoline skills. (2) Straight arm-straight leg press to handstand in gymnastics as well as other gymnastic skills.

Equipment: Yardstick and tape or the flexomeasure.

Directions: Line up the 15-inch mark of a yardstick with a line on the floor and tape the stick to the floor. Now, sit down and line up your heels with the near edge of the 15-inch mark and slide your seat back beyond the zero end of the yardstick. With knees locked and heels not more than 5 inches apart, stretch forward and touch the fingertips of both hands as many inches down the stick as possible.

Preliminary Training: Be sure to warm up thoroughly and concentrate on slow, steady stretching and holding motions.

Testing Procedure: Same as in the directions section except that a partner should stand and brace his toes against your heels as you stretch forward. This will keep your heels from slipping over the 15-inch mark. Also use two assistants to hold your knees in the locked position. Slowly stretch forward on each trial and hold for a count of two at the farthest point.

Scoring: The best of three trials measured to the nearest quarter of an inch is your test score.

Standing-Bending Reach Rating Test†

Directions: From a standing position, bend forward with knees locked and follow the applicable procedure in Table I-2.

Shoulder-and-Wrist Elevation Test††

Purpose: To develop shoulder and wrist flexion.

Sports Specificity: (1) Gymnastics (bars and

---

*Johnson, Barry L., and Mary Jane Garcia, *Fitness and Performance for Everyone,* Portland, Tx.: Brown and Littleman Books, 1977, p. 58.

†Presented by the author of the preconvention symposium, "The Assessment of Physical Fitness and Motor Performance," Little Rock, Arkansas, SDAAHPER Convention, 1978.

†† Modified from flexibility tests described by T. K. Cureton.

Table I-1
Sit-and-Reach Test

Men	Level	Women
23¾ - Above	Advanced	25¾ - Above
21¼ - 23½	Adv. Intermediate	22½ - 25½
18¾ - 21.0	Intermediate	20 - 22¼
17 - 18½	Adv. Beginner	18 - 19¾
0 - 16¾	Beginner	0 - 17¾

Table I-2
Standing-Bending Reach Rating Test

Males	Level	Females
Touch mid-joints of fingers to floor	Advanced	Touch palms of hands flat to floor
Touch fingertips to floor	Adv. Intermediate	Touch mid-joints of fingers to floor
Touch fingertips to top of toes	Intermediate	Touch fingertips to floor
Touch fingertips to top of insteps	Adv. Beginner	Touch fingertips to top of toes
Touch fingertips to midpoint between knees and ankles	Beginner	Touch fingertips to top of insteps

Table I-3
Shoulder-and-Wrist Elevation Test*

Men	Level	Women
6 - 0	Advanced	5½ - 0
8¼ - 6¼	Adv. Intermediate	7½ - 5¾
11½ - 8½	Intermediate	10¾ - 7¾
12½ - 11¾	Adv. Beginner	11¾ - 11
Above - 12¾	Beginner	Above - 12

floor exercise skills). (2) Butterfly stroke in swimming. (3) Wrestling.

Equipment: Ruler, yardstick, and adhesive tape or the flexomeasure.

Directions: (1) Assume a prone (facedown) position with your arms straight and about shoulders width apart. (2) Grasp the ruler or yardstick in each hand and raise it upward as high as possible while keeping your chin on the floor and the elbows straight.

Preliminary Training: Raise the stick as high as possible and have your partner grasp it at the center and slowly raise it to an even higher level (as your shoulders permit).

Testing Procedure: (1) Roll a couple of small strips of adhesive tape to one side of a ruler and assume a prone position so that your body is straight and your arms extended with fists pressing against the base of a smooth-surfaced wall. Now raise your arms (keeping chin against the mat) and stick the ruler (horizontally) as high up the wall as possible. The chin must remain in contact with the mat throughout the lift. (2) Take a yardstick and measure to the top center level of the ruler. (3) Repeat this for three trials and record the best score. (4) Measure your arm length from the acromion process (top of the arm at the joint) to the middle fingertip.

Scoring: Subtract your best of three lifts from arm length and record the remainder as your score.

$$
\begin{aligned}
\text{Example:} \quad \text{Arm length} &= 30 \\
\text{Arm lift} &= \underline{16} \\
\text{Score} &= 14
\end{aligned}
$$

The closer your arm lift gets to your arm length, the better your score. Thus, a score of zero would be perfect.

Bridge-up Test*

Purpose: To develop hyperextension of the spine.

Sports Specificity: (1) Balance beam and floor exercise routine in gymnastics. (2) Modern

*Johnson, Barry L., and Mary Jane Garcia, *Fitness and Performance for Everyone,* Portland, Tx.: Brown and Littleman Books, 1977, p. 60.

dance and ballet movements. (3) High jump event. (4) Butterfly event.

Equipment: Mat and tape.

Directions: Assume a supine (back-lying) position on the mat and tilt your head back as you push upward, arching your back while walking the hands and feet as close together as possible. This exercise may also be executed by leaning backward until contacting a wall and handwalking down the wall as far as possible.

Preliminary Training: (1) Practice the correct starting position and push upward without walking the hands and feet together. Be sure that the hands are turned so that the thumbs are next to the ears before you push your head and shoulders from the floor. (2) As your strength increases in lifting the body to the arch position, gradually move your feet and hands closer together over a period of several weeks of training.

Testing Procedure: (1) Place the toes of your feet against the base of a wall and mark your heel line. (2) Resume your (toes against wall) position, sit down, and bridge up, keeping feet flat on the floor and toes to the wall. (3) Walk your fingertips as far toward your heels as possible and have an assistant mark the farthest spot reached by the fingertips. You may take three trials. (4) Now, stretch out beside the mark pressing feet flat against wall, and match your fingertip mark to the nearest body part (shoulder blades, small of back, seat line, mid-thigh, knee joint).

Scoring: Compare the body part matched to Table I-4 for your level of performance. Or see Table I-5.

Table I-4
Bridge-up Test

Men	Level	Women
Fingertips to knee joint or farther	Advanced	Fingertips to mid-calf or farther
Fingertips to seat line or farther	Adv. Intermediate	Fingertips to knee
Fingertips to lumbar area (lower back)	Intermediate	Fingertips to seat line
Fingertips to scapula (shoulder blades)	Adv. Beginner	Fingertips to lumbar area
Fingertips to neck line	Beginner	Fingertips to scapula (shoulder blades)

Table I-5
Alternative Bridge-up Scores*

Based on the best of three measures between the heels and fingertips. Measure to nearest quarter of an inch.

Men	Level	Women
4¾ - 0	Advanced	3¾ - 0
12¾ - 5	Adv. Intermediate	10¾ - 4
29¾ - 13	Intermediate	24¾ - 11
37¾ - 30	Adv. Beginner	31¾ - 25
Above - 38	Beginner	Above - 32

*The authors are indebted to Carlos Macias and David Castillo of Corpus Christi State University for collection of flexibility data.

Trunk-and-Neck Extension Test*

Purpose: To develop ability to extend the trunk.
Sports Specificity: (1) Gymnastics (floor exercise, beam). (2) Butterfly stroke. (3) Wrestling.
Equipment: Yardstick, tape, and mats or the flexomeasure.
Directions: Assume a prone position (face down) on the mat and with your hands resting at the small of your back, raise your trunk upward as high as possible from the floor. You may wish to have a partner hold your hips down.
Preliminary Training: (1) Perform the same movement as described in the directions section but use the hands to push on the floor in raising the trunk as high as possible.
Testing Procedure: (1) Have your assistant get an estimate of your trunk and neck length measurement by taking the distance to the nearest quarter of an inch between the tip of your nose

and the seat of the chair you are sitting in. Your sitting position must be erect with the chin level during the measurement. (2) Tape a yardstick vertically to a wall, zero end touching the floor and lie face downward so that your nose tip is touching the stick. Now, with your hands resting at the small of your back and an assistant holding the hips down, raise upward, extending your trunk and neck and hold for a count of three. Take the reading at the highest point reached by the nose. The best lift of three trials is recorded as the trunk lift score.
Scoring: Subtract your best of three lifts from your estimated trunk and neck length score.

Example: Trunk and neck length = 32
Best trunk lift = 15
Score = 17

The closer your trunk lift gets to your estimated trunk and neck length the better your score. (See Table I-6.) Thus, a score of zero would be perfect.

*Modified from flexibility tests described by T. K. Cureton.

Table I-6
Trunk-and-Neck Extension Test

Men	Level	Women
3 - 0	Advanced	2 - 0
6 - 3¼	Adv. Intermediate	5¾ - 2¼
8 - 6¼	Intermediate	7¾ - 6
10 - 8¼	Adv. Beginner	9¾ - 8
Above - 10¼	Beginner	Above - 10

Ankle Extension (Plantar Flexion) Test*

Purpose: To measure ability to flex and extend the ankle.

Age Level: Ages 10 through college.

Sex: Satisfactory for both boys and girls.

Reliability: Has been reported as high as .73.

Validity: Face validity was accepted for this test.

Equipment and Materials: Materials needed are paper, long pencils, protractors, thumb-tacks, and several cardboard squares about 18 inches high and 18 inches wide. Several stations may be set up to save time during testing.

Directions: The performer sits on the floor with the back of the knee touching the floor. Keeping the heel stationary, he dorsi-flexes the foot as much as possible. The tester traces the outline of the foot (keeping the pencil horizontal) from just above the ankle to just beyond the big toe on a sheet of paper placed at the side of the foot. The performer then extends (plantar flexes) the foot as far as possible, and the outline is again traced on the same sheet of paper. The angle of each of the lines with the horizontal is measured with a protractor. (See Figure I-1.)

Scoring: The score is the measure taken from the protractor for each foot. An average score for the feet is then figured. (See Table I-7.)

*Cureton, T. K., "Flexibility as an Aspect of Physical Fitness," *Research Quarterly Supplement,* 12:388-389, May, 1941.

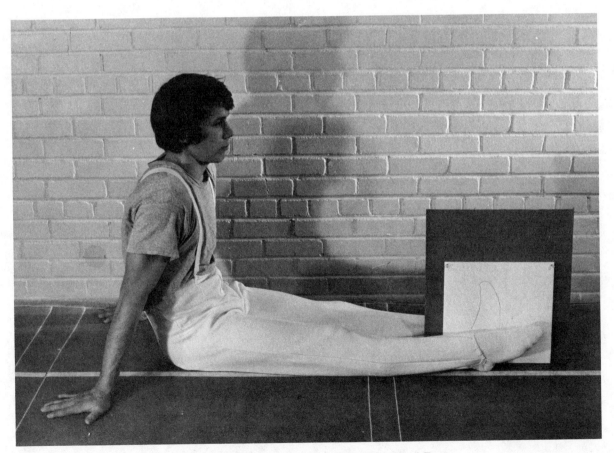

Figure I-1. Ankle Extension (Plantar Flexion) Test

Table I-7
Ankle Extension (Plantar Flexion) Test

Men	Level	Women
82 - Above	Advanced	84 - Above
67 - 81	Adv. Intermediate	71 - 83
39 - 66	Intermediate	50 - 70
24 - 38	Adv. Beginner	37 - 49
0 - 23	Beginner	0 - 36

Based on the scores of 100 male and 100 female students at Corpus Christi State University, Corpus Christi, Tx., 1977.

The Margaria Anaerobic Power Test *(5)*

Objective: To measure maximal anaerobic power.

Age and Sex: High school and college males and females. It can be given to elementary children with appropriate modification such as was done by Chaloupka (7).

Validity: The test has face validity in that it includes the components of mechanical power: work per unit of time. Margaria computed anaerobic power output in Kcal/kg/hr by the stair climb test and found results comparable to those of another method in which the measurements were taken with the subject running on a treadmill. Furthermore, in terms of construct validity, sprinters have been found to have higher scores than distance runners, and athletes higher scores than non-athletes.

Equipment and Materials: The test can be given in different ways, but in all of the methods a timer sensitive to .01 seconds is needed. An electric timer with switch mats to start and stop the timer at the desired steps is preferable. Although not advisable for research purposes, it is possible to obtain quite consistent results with a .01-second stopwatch. A staircase of preferably 12 to 16 stairs of normal incline is necessary, with steps measuring between 6 and 8 inches (15-20 cm). A weight scale is required since body weight is part of the calculations.

Directions: There are several versions of the test. For example, Margaria computed power by measuring the vertical component of the speed between the second and fourth seconds of the stair climb. It is usually measured, however, by allowing a short sprint on the floor and then timing the speed of climb between certain steps.

A short sprint of about 6 feet (2 meters) is recommended so that the subject can begin the stair climb at near maximal forward velocity. The timing should encompass about four to eight steps, i.e., somewhere between .5 and 1.0 seconds.

DeVries (2) described a testing situation utilizing a flight of stairs of at least 16 steps with the subject starting 6 feet in front of the first step and running up the stairs as fast as possible taking two steps at a time. The timing interval is between the fourth and twelfth steps. Kalamen (3) revised the Margaria test as follows: the subject starts 6 meters from the stairs and runs up the stairs 3 steps at a time; the

Appendix J

459

switch mats are located on the third and ninth steps. Kalamen found that this procedure produced maximum power scores. Chaloupka's adaptation for elementary school boys involves the timed vertical distance speed between the second and sixth steps (7).

We will describe the deVries test arrangement (Figure J-1) because it may be applicable to a more general population since it requires running up two steps at a time instead of three and necessitates only 6 feet of running space before the first step instead of about 20 as in the Kalamen version.

In the deVries test the subject is first weighed wearing the clothing and shoes he or she will run in. The weight is recorded to the nearest pound (or converted to kilograms by dividing by 2.2). The subject begins from a line 6 feet (or 2 meters) from the first step. The timer (with a stopwatch) is positioned so as to be able to observe the subject's foot when it strikes the fourth and the twelfth steps.

The subject is instructed to run up the stairs as fast as possible taking two steps at a time. The subject should continue *past* the twelfth step and not try to stop at that step.

Three trials are given. The timer starts the watch when the subject's foot strikes the fourth step and stops the watch when the subject's foot hits the twelfth step. The vertical height of each step is determined in inches (or mm) and multiplied by 8. For example, if each step is 7.5 inches, the total vertical distance the subject lifts his or her body weight is 7.5 inches × 8 steps = 60 inches, or 5 feet.

Scoring: The average of three trials to the nearest .01 seconds is used as the time score. The subject's body weight is multiplied by the total vertical distance and the product is divided by the average time in seconds:

$$Power = \frac{Work}{Time} = \frac{Body\ Weight \times Distance}{Seconds}$$

Example: A person weighing 140 pounds runs up the 8 steps (5 feet) in .8 seconds.

$$Power = \frac{140\ lbs. \times 5\ ft.}{.8\ sec.} = \frac{700\ ft.\text{-}lbs.}{.8}$$
$$= 875\ ft.\text{-}lbs./sec.$$

Same Example Expressed in Metric Units:
140 lbs. = 63.6 kg; 5 ft. = 1.5 m.

$$Power = \frac{63.6 \times 1.5}{.8} = \frac{95.4\ kilogram\text{-}meters\ (kgM)}{.8\ sec.}$$
$$= 119.25\ kgM/sec.$$

The power scores can be expressed in horsepower by dividing ft.-lbs./sec. by 550 and kgM/sec. by 76.07. In the above example, 875 ft.-lbs./sec. ÷ 550 = 1.59 hp.

Additional Pointers: (a) Mechanical work is expressed in foot-pounds or kilogram-meters. Therefore, the distance must be converted to feet or meters. If, for example, the step is 7.25 inches, and the number of steps is 6, the vertical distance in feet would be 7.25 in. × 6 = $\frac{43.5\ in.}{12}$ = 3.6 ft. Or the tester may first wish to multiply body weight times the distance in inches and divide the product by 12. For example, a 150-pound person × 7.25 in. × 6 = $\frac{6525}{12}$ = 543.75 ft.-lbs. In metric units, if the step measures 180 millimeters, this must be converted to meters. In this example, 180 millimeters is .18 meters (mm ÷ 1000) so 6 steps × .18 m = 1.08 m. Thus, a 150-pound person represents 68.2 kg × 1.08 m = 73.7 kg/m. (b) One of the advantages of the Margaria test is that it does not require skill or training. However, as with nearly any test item, familiarization is important. A couple practice trials are advisable. (c) The mechanical power output can be expressed in terms of energy consumption (Kcal/min/kg) if one uses an assumed work efficiency value of 25 percent.

Additional Findings Regarding the Margaria Test

Costill and others (1) correlated power of the legs as measured by the Margaria test with selected explosive leg strength tests. It was concluded that anaerobic power is related to dynamic leg strength and body weight.

Kalamen (3) modified the Margaria test to allow for greater maximal forward velocity before starting up the stairs and then running up the stairs three steps at a time, which resulted in greater power output.

Lawson (4) found significant correlations between 100-yard running performance and the Margaria-Kalamen Index, maximum oxygen deficit, and the cross-sectional area of fast twitch fibers of the vastus lateralis muscle.

References

1. Costill, David L., and others, "Relationship among Selected Tests of Explosive Leg Strength and Power," *Research Quarterly,* 39:785-787, October, 1968.

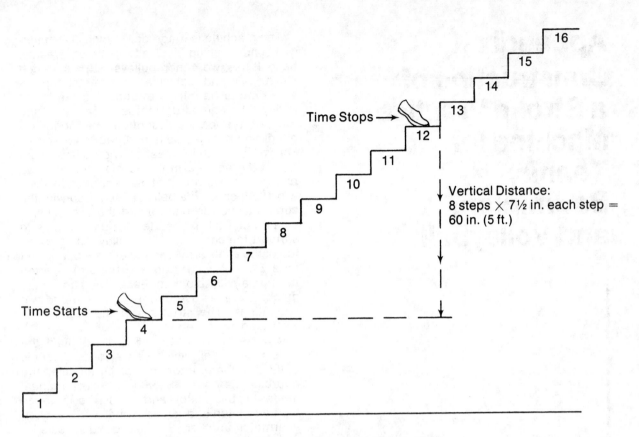

Figure J-1. Margaria Anaerobic Power Test

2. deVries, Herbert A., *Laboratory Experiments in Physiology of Exercise,* Dubuque, Iowa: Wm. C. Brown, 1971, pp. 101-104.
3. Kalamen, J., "Measurement of Maximum Muscular Power in Man" (Doctoral dissertation, The Ohio State University, Columbus, Ohio, 1968).
4. Lawson, David L., "Physiological Parameters Limiting Performance in Middle Distance and Sprint Running" (Doctoral dissertation, Kent State University, 1975).
5. Margaria, Rodolfo, Piero Aghemo, and Emilio Rovelli, "Measurement of Muscular Power (Anaerobic) in Man," *Journal of Applied Physiology,* 21:1662-1664, September, 1966.
6. Mathews, Donald K., and Edward L. Fox, *The Physiological Basis of Physical Education and Athletics,* 2nd ed., Philadelphia: W. B. Saunders Company, 1976.
7. _____, *Measurement in Physical Education,* 4th ed., Philadelphia: W. B. Saunders Company, 1973.

Appendix K
Construction of a Stroke Practice Machine for Tennis, Badminton, and Volleyball

The machine is made of 1½-inch O.D. thick-wall conduit tubing attached to a 24-square-inch base. It has two 4-inch pulleys with a 180-inch A-type belt and eight plastic or metal cups. A small metal handle is attached to the lower pulley. The angled upright is 13 feet from the top to the floor. As described, the model will handle both tennis balls and badminton birds. For volleyball, there must be two pulleys at the top of the angle arm of the machine and two pulleys at the lower point of the angle arm. Also, two 180-inch A-type belts are required with the cups attached in pairs along the two belts. A small metal tab is inserted inside the cups to support the carrying of the volleyball up to the top of the angle arm. The pulleys are supported by a 7½-inch shaft (top and bottom) inserted through a pillar block for each. The base of the machine makes use of one "T" fitting and two "L" fittings. The structure of the machine is illustrated in Figure K-1.

It costs approximately $55.00 to build the volleyball model, which can also drop tennis balls and badminton birds. Otherwise, the approximate cost is $35.00 to build a manual model for badminton and tennis. To motorize the badminton and tennis model with a Dayton gearmotor, another $35.00 is added in costs.

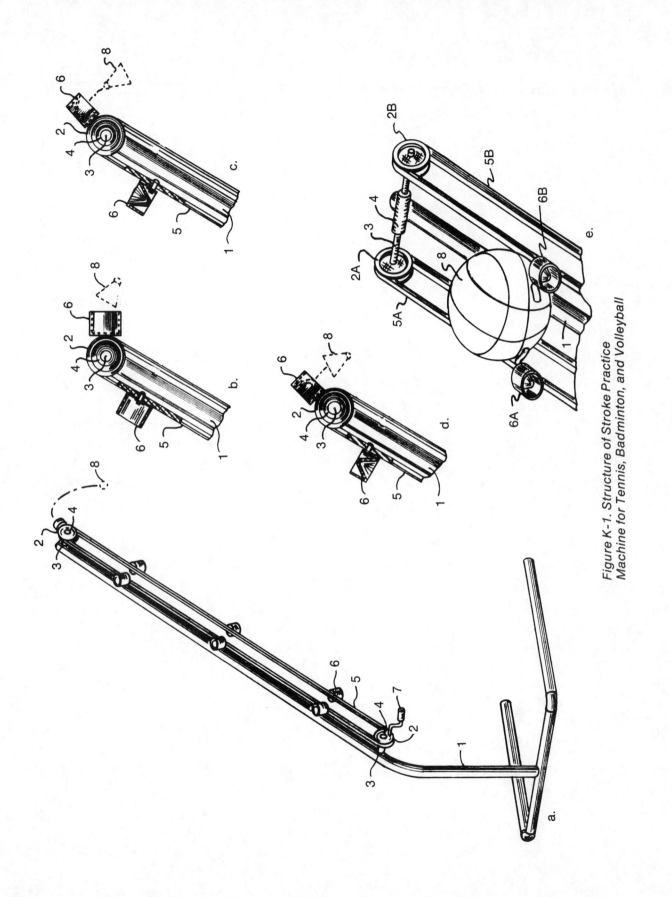

Figure K-1. Structure of Stroke Practice Machine for Tennis, Badminton, and Volleyball